CAN'T GET THERE FROM HERE

NEW ZEALAND RAILWAYS

SAFETY · COMFORT · ECONOMY

Your Railways for your Welfare

utu Station

mut Station, for The Overlander
r   vices. The Overlander travels daily
     Wellington. The Northerner travels
ii h   uckland and Wellington.

Daily Train rriv ls and   rtures

		Departs
therner	From Wellington to Auckland	4.24am
lander	From Auckland to Wellington	11.05am
ander	From Wellington to Auckland	5.04pm
erner	From Auckland to Wellington	11.12pm

 nes s own are approximate only. T e train may
     all booked passengers are on board. Passengers
vi   be at t   minutes before
me shown

okings
free on

     ervi   hased
     Visi   n Centres
     n a   sed on

CAN'T GET THERE FROM HERE

NEW ZEALAND PASSENGER RAIL
SINCE 1920

André Brett

Maps by Sam van der Weerden

OTAGO UNIVERSITY PRESS
Te Whare Tā o Te Wānanga o Ōtākou

CONTENTS

List of maps 7
Legend to maps 8
Abbreviations and usage 9
Foreword by Anthonie Tonnon 10

INTRODUCTION 13
   What trains are we talking about? 17
   Limited expresses, mixed trains and other members of the railway vocabulary 22
   Power, control and branding 24

CHAPTER 1. The network in 1920 26
   An emerging competitor 38

CHAPTER 2. 1920–1928: The regional railway falters 42
   1920–28: Grand visions realised incompletely 51
   1920–28: The end of the rural branch line 60
   1921: The first cuts 63
   1926–28: The buses are coming 66

CHAPTER 3. 1929–1934: A royal commission and its aftermath 70
   1929–30: Reconsidering rail's role 78
   1930: Tinkering at the edges 81
   1930–31: Outcomes of the royal commission 85
   1932: Whanganui loses suburban rail 92
   1931–33: Legislative protection, rural contraction 93
   1933: Something to celebrate 97

CHAPTER 4. 1935–1945: A network unified in the face of adversity 100
   1935–37: A modern railway for the capital 110
   1936–39: Wairoa gets its railway 115
   1936–40: Linking Canterbury and Marlborough 117
   1936–40: Regulation and contraction 119
   1940–45: Closing the gaps 123

CHAPTER 5. 1945–1954: The drift to road 128
   NZR and the post-war transition 137
   1945–50: Post-war contraction 138
   1951–54: The waterfront dispute and its consequences 146
   1951–54: More lost opportunities 151
   1946–54: A different purpose for rail 156

CHAPTER 6. 1955–1968: The Fiat fiasco 162

1955–58: Railcars and the Remutakas 171

1958–59: Finalising the railcar network 177

1956–66: 'An important principle of policy' in Invercargill 179

1955–60: Rural attrition 182

1967–68: Flawed Fiats and trimmed timetables 187

CHAPTER 7. 1970–1989: 'The emotive term "railcars"' – Cancellations in town and country 194

1970–76: Farewell to rural and miners' trains 203

1971–78: Railcar routes rot 208

1972–82: Suburban subtractions 217

1983–88: The final echoes of the developmental railway 229

1989: The platforms are quiet 235

CHAPTER 8. 1990–2020: The false dawn 236

1991: Revival? 245

1993–2000: Privatisation and the passenger train 246

2001–02: The regional passenger train's annus horribilis 251

The difficult 2000s 256

2003–20: Changing fortunes in Auckland 260

CHAPTER 9. Whither passenger rail in New Zealand? 268

How did we get here? 271

The network in 2020 272

What might the future hold? 274

The myths we must not tell ourselves 276

What will we need to revitalise passenger rail? 278

Upper North Island 281

Lower North Island 282

North Island Main Trunk 284

South Island 285

Hamilton 289

Tauranga 291

Napier–Hastings 292

Christchurch 294

Dunedin 295

Where else? 296

All aboard! 297

Notes 300

Appendices 335

Bibliography 341

Acknowledgements 351

Index 353

List of maps

26–33 Rail routes open to passengers at 1 January 1920

42–49 Rail routes open to passengers 1920–1928

52 Far North 1920

54 Eastern North Island 1920

54–55 East Coast Main Trunk and Mount Maunganui Branch 1920–1928

57 Upper South Island 1920

58–59 Stratford–Ōkahukura Line 1920–1933

62 Western Taranaki 1912

65 Oxford Branch and Eyreton Branch

65 Kurow Branch and Waitaki Dam Branch

70–77 Rail routes open to passengers 1929–1934

83 Network cuts of 1930

85 Westfield Deviation opens 1930

87 Projects suspended between 1929 and 1931

88–89 The Royal Commission September 1930

96 Tapanui Branch

100–07 Rail routes open to passengers 1935–1945

111 Wellington 1937

114 Proposed Paeroa shortcut

118 Main North Line options

123 Dargaville options 1941

126–27 Main North Line and Waiau Branch 1939–1945

128–35 Rail routes open to passengers 1946–1954

150 Sockburn–Styx Deviation proposed in late 1940s

157 Hutt Valley changes 1946–1955

158 Greater Wellington rail 1935

159 Greater Wellington rail 1955

161 Auckland Rail proposals 1946–1950

162–69 Rail routes open to passengers 1955–1968

174–75 Proposals for railcar routes 1950–1951

181 Invercargill passenger rail 1950–1966

184–85 Seaward Bush Branch and Catlins River Branch

186 Palmerston North railways at 1960

190 Northland services August 1967

194–201 Rail routes open to passengers 1970–1989

218 Christchurch passenger rail 1950–1976

222 Dunedin passenger rail 1970–1982

225 Auckland rapid transit

226–27 Auckland passenger rail 1973–1980

228 Wellington passenger rail 1973–1983

236–43 Rail routes open to passengers 1990–2020

248–49 Long-distance services 1991–2002

254 Dunedin railways network summer of 2019–2020

262 Auckland 2003–2024

286–87 Long-distance services (proposal)

289 Hamilton passenger rail (proposal)

291 Tauranga passenger rail (proposal)

293 Napier–Hastings passenger rail (proposal)

294 Christchurch passenger rail (proposal)

296 Dunedin passenger rail (proposal)

LEGEND TO MAPS

PASSENGER NETWORK PROGRESSION MAPS
at the beginning of each chapter

Main line open to passengers

Branch line open to passengers

Lincoln — minor station
BLENHEIM — major station
DUNEDIN — main-centre station

Line with a passenger services not operated by New Zealand Railways

(or successors, e.g. Tranz Rail, KiwiRail)

- *PRIV.* — private
- *PWD* — Public Works Department
- *WHB* — Westport Harbour Board
- *MCC* — Manawatū County Council
- *ŌHB* — Ōhai Railway Board
- *DR* — Dunedin Railways

Passenger services commenced

Passenger services ceased

Reefton — closed station

Holiday/seasonal services only

OTHER PASSENGER NETWORK PROGRESSION MAPS

Electrified or proposed electrification

If a station had a different name in the past:
Manor Park —— current name
Haywards —— old name

SCHEMATIC PASSENGER NETWORK MAPS

Heavy rail track

Street-running track*

Station

Interchange station

Line terminus

Connection with proposed long-distance rail*

Airport*

XYZ

*Only used in Chapter 9 proposal maps

Abbreviations and usage

AJHR: Appendices to the Journals of the House of Representatives

ANZ: Archives New Zealand Te Rua Mahara o te Kāwanatanga

ANZ-ARO, -CRO and -DRO refer to the Auckland, Christchurch and Dunedin regional offices

ARA: Auckland Regional Authority

ARTA: Auckland Regional Transport Authority

ATL: Alexander Turnbull Library, National Library of New Zealand

DTM: District Traffic Manager

MoW: Ministry of Works

NAC: National Airways Corporation

NZPD: New Zealand Parliamentary Debates (also known as Hansard)

NZR: New Zealand Railways (also known at various times as the New Zealand Government Railways; New Zealand Railways Department; New Zealand Railways Corporation; New Zealand Rail Limited)

ŌRB: Ōhai Railway Board

PWD: Public Works Department

Waka Kotahi NZTA: Waka Kotahi New Zealand Transport Agency

WCR: West Coast Railway (Australia)

MACRONS

The line above a vowel in te reo Māori indicates a long vowel and is a helpful guide to pronunciation. We use macrons consistently to aid the reader. We have, however, retained macron-less spellings in citations where researchers may require the exact formatting to locate archival documents.

ŌHAI RAILWAY BOARD

The board usually described itself as operating a private railway. Although separate from NZR, it was a partially elected local authority, the specifics of which were outlined in the Ohai Railway Board Act 23 Geo. V local no. 2 (1932) and subsequent acts of amendment. This book treats the ŌRB as public.

RAILWAY LINE NAMES

The **North Island Main Trunk** refers to the railway from Auckland to Wellington; the **South Island Main Trunk** is a collective term for the **Main North Line** (Christchurch–Picton) and the **Main South Line** (Lyttelton–Christchurch–Dunedin–Invercargill). The **East Coast Main Trunk** runs from Hamilton via Tauranga to Kawerau; before 1978 Tāneatua was the terminus and the line to Kawerau was considered a branch.

Secondary main lines generally take the name of terminal towns or the region served. Most branch lines were named after their terminus. Suburban routes in Auckland and Wellington have their own branding; for example, the Kāpiti Line in Wellington uses the North Island Main Trunk as far as Waikanae.

LOCOMOTIVE NUMBERS

Except for the RM class, locomotive classes with two/three letters were written until 1979 with the first letter capitalised and subsequent letters in superscript, e.g. A^B class. From 1979, the introduction of a new computerised system meant that all letters became normal capitals, e.g. the D^A class became DA. An individual locomotive is then identified with its road number, e.g. U^B 332.

Foreword

In Dunedin in the suburb of Green Island there is an underpass beneath the motorway. It's just a functional piece of 1960s concrete engineering, but if you grew up in Dunedin in the 1990s as I did, it stands out. Not only because its well-lit tunnel seems an unusually generous gesture to pedestrians, or because it links Green Island and Abbotsford in an odd spot, but because, near the Abbotsford side of the underpass, there is a locked gate. Behind that gate is a ramp that, unmistakably, must once have led to a passenger railway station.

I grew up near this underpass and its ghost station. I rode past its Green Island entrance hundreds of times on an Otago Road Services school bus. I drove over it in my 1983 Toyota Starlet – the vehicle that enabled my escape from Otago Road Services. But for three decades of my life I was unaware the station was there, and I was never told that children like myself took trains from that station to get to school, joining commuters from Mosgiel, Abbotsford and Caversham.

The idea that in my city – 1990s Dunedin, a place of infrequent diesel buses and low expectations – we had once spent the time, the money, the pure volume of concrete, on *public transport*, was astounding to me, particularly because of when that underpass went in. It wasn't a relic of the celebrated steam train or electric tram eras. The underpass had been built during a modernist, future-obsessed, *The*

Jetsons-watching era of motorway building. But even then New Zealanders had thought it natural to make room for railway passengers.

I left Dunedin in my early twenties, in large part due to those low expectations and infrequent buses. I moved to Auckland, because I wanted to be part of a city that was rediscovering what it was to be a city – one that was improving its bus frequency, electrifying its trains, delighting in walking, cycling and celebrating its areas of dense population. But I believed what we New Zealanders have told ourselves for thirty years: that only in big cities could urbanism and public transport work, and that most of New Zealand simply wasn't populated enough to do it well.

When I stumbled upon that gate in Green Island a few years ago, I knew at once that I'd left Dunedin on a lie. And as I travelled around other towns and cities in Aotearoa looking at their public transport, and in particular the rail services they used to have, I saw a public transport network beyond what I had thought possible. And yet it had existed and, most shockingly, some of it had survived into my lifetime: services like the *Southerner* and the *Bay Express* were still running around the time I sat my driver's licence.

The trouble was, information was so hard to find. New Zealand Rail was sold in the early 1990s, and the services it handed over to Tranz Rail were mostly shut in the first year or two of the millennium – just at the time that Google reached New Zealand. No wonder we New Zealanders have forgotten our former public transport system – the evidence simply isn't on the internet.

You can get glimpses in locally produced books, but for me there was always a problem. I wasn't looking for *what*: machines like locomotives or multiple units and the kind of power they used. My fascination with the railways was with *where* they used to run, *when*, and *how often* in the day or week. What I needed was timetables. And the only way to find timetables is to go into the ephemera collections at archives like the Hocken or the Alexander Turnbull Library.

What a marvel those archives are, and how humbling it is when you find that information exists – not just old information but material from the 1970s, 1990s, 2000s. But no matter how much you dig up, you always need more to get a fuller picture. New Zealand is a bigger society than we tell ourselves, and the project of remapping it through time seems endless.

Can't Get There from Here is a major feat that takes on this impassable gulf, and it has a wonder to show for it. It presents us with a twin viaduct – between the passenger railway system we had, the one we have now, and the system we could have. In André Brett we have a historian who has not only spent his life learning to tunnel through New Zealand's archives more efficiently than you or I can ever hope to do, but who can also explain the relationship between the where, the when, the how often and the what. How changes in machinery, in locomotion preference and in infrastructure and investment have influenced how we got here from there, and what we might learn from the results.

This book also gives instant clarity to mysteries I've been chasing for a number of years. Gone are the back-of-the-mind maps that combine a relative's memory, a brochure in a library, an out-of-date timetable nailed to a post and a page you found on the Wayback Machine. In their place we have a comprehensive vivid set of maps by Sam van der Weerden that would fit elegantly into any modern public transport system. Taking them in, you feel as if you could just jump on the railcar to Little River this afternoon.

Until this book, it was possible to write a shocking thinkpiece about New Zealand's public transport by simply stating things that existed. Great arguments about public transport have been held back because, as a society, we can no longer remember our baseline. New projects have been timid because we've forgotten the context. The new *Te Huia* service runs twice a day in each direction, which is a welcome breakthrough, but we've forgotten that as recently as 2001 there were five passenger trains a day between Hamilton and Auckland in each direction. Here is a work that will strengthen and futureproof our memory and inspire us to rebuild an even better public transport system.

Anthonie Tonnon
30 June 2021
Songwriter and musician,
performer of *Rail Land: A tour celebrating passenger rail in Aotearoa*

Introduction

A Matangi electric multiple unit from Wellington arrives at Pukerua Bay on 8 December 2018, bound for Waikanae. André Brett

The foreign traveller upon arrival at Auckland International Airport, the main hub for flights to New Zealand, might be surprised to find the terminal is not connected to the city by any form of rail transport. They might be even more surprised to learn that they cannot board a passenger train to one of the country's most famous attractions, Rotorua. Yet such a service once existed: at its peak in the 1930s the *Rotorua Limited* was one of the premier express trains to depart from Auckland's grand railway terminal on Beach Road.[1] But Rotorua is by no means New Zealand's only city – nor the largest – to have lost its passenger trains. The demise of rail passenger services during the past century has been a common fate for communities across the country.

At first glance, New Zealand's railway statistics do not suggest that a sharp decline in passenger train coverage. There is an extensive network of 4128 kilometres – a relatively modest contraction from the peak of 5689 kilometres in 1953, when legislation restricted the ability of road transport to compete with rail. Some of today's lines are mothballed, however, and passenger trains run on only a handful of the rest. Few services extend beyond Auckland and Wellington's suburbs: there are two regional commuter services to Wellington, the *Capital Connection* from Palmerston North and the *Wairarapa Connection* from Masterton, and the new *Te Huia* runs between Auckland and Hamilton. At the start of 2020, just one long-distance train, the *TranzAlpine* between Christchurch and Greymouth, operated daily year round. The *Northern Explorer* between Auckland and Wellington had an attenuated tri-weekly schedule, and the *Coastal Pacific* between Christchurch and Picton ran only from

spring to autumn. Dunedin Railways, founded to operate railway-enthusiast excursions, grew to provide comparable tourist services; its *Taieri Gorge Limited* to Pukerangi even exceeded the *TranzAlpine*'s frequency during peak seasons in the 2010s. But these are the only passenger services in the country. It is a stark contrast to 1953, when many railway lines accommodated passengers, and with 1920, when almost every line carried passengers as well as goods. For the first half of the twentieth century the railway represented the primary mode of long-distance travel in New Zealand, and until the late 1970s it provided significant mobility for travellers nationwide.

New Zealand is now dependent on cars and airlines. This is not sustainable. Shaun Hendy, a physicist at the University of Auckland and a frequent flyer, became so concerned about his carbon emissions that he did not set foot in an aeroplane during 2018. He chronicles his experiences and the relevant science in a short but significant book, *#NoFly: Walking the talk on climate change*.[2] Hendy concludes that, to have a sustainable future, New Zealand must move away from single-occupant cars and air travel. Passenger rail must be prominent in this modal shift: trains are not only one of the most energy-efficient forms of transport, but they also offer the sort of local service necessary to ensure New Zealand's regions are not left behind in any large transition.

Two councils, Canterbury and Nelson, declared a climate emergency on 16 May 2019, setting a precedent for numerous other local governments, and Parliament made a national declaration on 2 December 2020. Public transport, often defined by absence or inadequacy, was also an important issue at the October 2019 local elections and a year later at

Once a familiar sight throughout both islands – Fiat railcar RM 101 north of Paraparaumu, 26 May 1955.
ANZ AAVK 6390 B6105

the national election. If New Zealand is to take seriously Hendy's message and the declarations of climate emergency, it must ask why it allowed a vast passenger rail network to be lost – and use this knowledge to inform a more efficient and sustainable balance of transport modes in the future.

This book takes up Hendy's call for a modal shift by examining how the current imbalance between road and rail emerged. It identifies distinctive periods of network growth and – more commonly – shrinkage from 1920 to the present to reveal what the network once was and to suggest what it might become. To be clear, this is not a comprehensive history of the passenger train in New Zealand; it is an account of the passenger network's evolution. It describes the first or last regularly scheduled passenger service on every railway line to show why a region or town obtained a service and what decisions guided its demise. In some instances services were reduced to the extent that a meaningful timetable for most travellers ended years prior to the cessation of the last timetabled train. Take, for example, the Seaward Bush Branch east from Invercargill to Tokanui, where in 1951 passenger accommodation went from being offered daily to only weekly. This service, of little use to anyone but railway employees and their families, survived until 1960.[3]

Little-noticed decisions in the regions often presage big changes in cities, and this is abundantly true for rail. This book gives prominence to trains that might not feature elsewhere or may be passed over as trivial. Alice Kranenburg, a policy planner in local government, has observed that small towns are often perceived as unimportant and are 'typically neglected in political and academic discourses, even though they are a key part of the rural economy'.[4] In the story of New Zealand's passenger rail, these towns are significant. The demise of passenger services in lightly populated rural areas was a harbinger of cancellations of trains to larger service towns, then regional hubs and, finally, major cities. This means that some famous trains feature here only ephemerally, making way for trains whose significance has been overlooked. The *Silver Star* luxury overnight express between Wellington and Auckland neither expanded the geographic scope of the network when it began in 1971 nor contracted it upon cessation in 1979, since other passenger trains also plied the North Island Main Trunk. On the other hand, slow trains to villages such as Hakataramea in Canterbury, Ngāpara and Tokarahi in Otago, and Glenham in Southland take centre stage. They are unlikely to figure much in a general

history of the New Zealand passenger train, but their cessations inaugurated great change for the whole network.

Speaking broadly, passenger rail in New Zealand has withered for a century. World War I placed great strains on the railway – services were reduced and dining cars abolished – and the 1918 influenza pandemic delayed the post-war recovery. But network expansions were pushed ahead in the 1920s; Chapter 1 outlines the network at the start of the decade and Chapter 2 describes the railway projects, large and small, that extended its reach. This was the last phase of rural branch-line growth, and coincided with the first cancellations of passenger services on general-purpose railways.

Chapters 3 and 4 show how railway officials responded to the enormous upheavals of the Great Depression and World War II. Governments on both sides of the House worked to protect state investment in railways from private road competition; the Labour Party, upon taking power in 1935, also resumed construction of incomplete trunk routes. During this time, however, the New Zealand Railways Department – NZR – began to shift passengers from rail to its new Road Services buses, a move that had far-reaching consequences.

In the hard years following World War II, chronicled in Chapter 5, rural passenger trains became increasingly scarce. Interprovincial routes remained important, but a major investment in new rollingstock during the 1950s went awry. Chapters 6 and 7 describe these ill-fated trains and the failure to replace them. As a result, New Zealand's rail passenger network declined substantially. Between the late 1960s and the late 1980s many intercity routes disappeared, as did local passenger trains in rural areas and all commuter services in the South Island. Decision-makers scorned passenger rail and rejected opportunities to revitalise it.

Chapter 8 carries the story through the restructures of the 1990s, a decade that offered much for passenger rail but culminated in a further retreat in the early 2000s. The exception was Auckland, where a suburban rail revival contrasted with the situation throughout most of the country. Chapter 9 considers future directions for passenger rail in New Zealand and shows that trains can and should contribute significantly to mobility in and between cities and regions. As we tell the story of the passenger network case by case, new perspectives on the past century of New Zealand's railway history emerge to suggest how current needs and future challenges might be met.

The story of New Zealand's passenger network touches many lives, professionally and socially. New Zealand Railways was one of the country's largest employers for decades, and major depots and workshops sustained the economies of entire towns. New Zealand has many railway enthusiasts and appreciators – a more diverse group than it first seems. A cliché exists of old Pākehā men 'playing trains', but in reality, people from all walks of life take an interest: the retiree recording tutorials about how to make delicate model railways; the young woman who prefers to catch trains; the children at the marae who flock to watch a preserved steam locomotive pass on an adjacent railway. Not all people who take pleasure in trains – riding them, watching them, learning their history or imagining their future – identify as enthusiasts, but common threads of appreciation and interest unite them. For some, an interest in passenger rail is born of academic or professional concerns: historians,

geographers, urbanists and planners all seek to comprehend patterns, trends and policies. Pivotal moments – such as cancellations – afford a window into wider processes of modal change and system decline. Today's public-transport advocates and policymakers might have their eyes fixed on the future, but to shape that future they need to draw on lessons and ideas from the past.

Readers will find in these pages cause for regret *and* inspiration for action. The trend away from passenger rail might appear irreversible, but it is not. New Zealand is not locked into car dependency. Patterns and decisions about the purpose and role of rail transport have shaped the network's evolution, and it is very easy to imagine how it could have been – and still could be – different.

WHAT TRAINS ARE WE TALKING ABOUT?

This book focuses on the routine operation of timetabled passenger trains. If there was a public passenger service with a regular timetable, it appears here. This includes trains run predominantly for schoolchildren and miners. It was often possible for an enterprising traveller to hitch a ride in the guard's van of a goods train, but that is beyond this book's scope; so too are excursion and picnic trains, once popular means of transporting large social groups. For many years NZR also facilitated travel on isolated lines by manual and motorised jiggers (also known as trolleys or velocipedes), but a policy promulgated in 1911 made clear that such transport was only for emergencies or for workers who needed access to the railway corridor.[5] Therefore, jigger rides are not included, and neither are the 'rail carts'

– modified golf carts and similar vehicles – that local tourism companies obtained permission to run on disused railway lines in the 2010s.

Almost all passenger trains in New Zealand have been operated by NZR and its predecessors and successors: it is currently known as KiwiRail. Some were operated by other public authorities, most commonly the Public Works Department (PWD). A few have been run privately. There used to be a strict division of responsibility between the PWD, which constructed new railway lines, and NZR, which operated trains and maintained existing lines. This dated from 1878 when the railways gained a commissioner in each island who reported directly to the minister of public works. A general manager, answerable to said minister, controlled all railways from 1880. This lasted for over a century, punctuated by short periods of control by independent boards of commissioners in the 1890s, 1920s, 30s and 50s. Railway operations came under a dedicated minister of railways in 1895, and despite periodic suggestions that this minister should also oversee construction, the PWD retained its nation-building role. It was absorbed in 1948 into the Ministry of Works, which had been created in 1943 as a complementary body to oversee reconstruction after World War II.[6] Prior to 1920, over 70 percent of the PWD's annual construction expenditure went on railways. This hovered at 40–50 percent in the 1920s and 10–20 percent in the 1930s, after which it rarely exceeded 5 percent.[7] This reflects the fact that by 1920 most of the core network was in place, and also the way in which railway projects sank in importance as road competition became more significant.

Despite the separation of responsibilities between the PWD as builder and NZR as operator, the PWD often ran trains prior to handing over control of a line. These trains sometimes used temporary or incomplete alignments and consisted of old rollingstock, including goods wagons converted to carry passengers, so journeys were often slow and subject to change or cancellation at short notice. It is sometimes hard to obtain details of these services, especially as many PWD files were destroyed in the 1952 Hope Gibbons Building fire that catalysed the establishment of Archives New Zealand.

The NZR opening date of a line is usually taken as authoritative for this book, as this was the point when passenger trains began operating over a completed railway to a routine timetable. In general, if the PWD ran passenger trains briefly before NZR took possession, these are disregarded. PWD services that became well established do feature, however – for example, it operated trains along the Bay of Plenty coast for 15 years – as do NZR trains that ran over a line by agreement with the PWD prior to the formal handover. This book also encompasses the small number of passenger services operated on private railways or by other public authorities. These are limited to routine services akin to those on the national network.

Trams are not included here. Graham Stewart's *The End of the Penny Section* charts the rise and fall of urban passenger tramways admirably. Industrial and bush tramways were typically rough-and-ready lines for a specific owner, such as a sawmill; only a few provided regular passenger services. Paul Mahoney gives a good overview of this intriguing aspect of rail history in *The Era of the Bush Tram in New Zealand*.[8] A few tramways do not neatly fit any category, and one of these, the Sanson

B^B 618 at Glen Afton with a service for Huntly on the afternoon of 3 November 1965. Most passengers on this line were coalminers, along with a few schoolchildren and local residents.

J.M. Creber

Tramway of the Manawatū County Council, was effectively a railway and appears in Chapter 3.

In general, this book is not concerned with heritage railways, most of which provide pleasure rides over short sections of restored track. Some run on only a few days a year while others enjoy a large enough clientele to operate on most days. It is, however, increasingly hard to distinguish KiwiRail's long-distance subsidiary, Great Journeys of New Zealand, from some heritage railways, as these trains cater so heavily for tourists that they feature onboard commentary and open-air viewing carriages, not normally features of public transport. The largest heritage operator, Dunedin Railways, operated a schedule as frequent as anything offered by KiwiRail during the 2010s, and is therefore included.

Another notable heritage railway is the famous *Kingston Flyer* – originally a nickname given to the expresses that ran between Gore and Kingston until 1957. NZR revived the name in December 1971 for a steam-hauled tourist train from Lumsden to Kingston and, in subsequent years, different destinations. The last steam locomotives in revenue service finished their duties in October 1971, and the reborn *Flyer* was not intended to serve regular passengers, even if an enterprising local could have used it. Officials were unambiguous: the *Kingston Flyer* was a 'museum piece', a moving exhibit rather than public transportation.[9] It is, therefore, not included.

This book builds on an excellent corpus of literature about New Zealand's railway history: accounts of locomotives, lines, workshops

A contrast at Stillwater, 2 September 1967. At right is a Fiat railcar running from Ross to Christchurch. On the left is a much slower 'with-car goods' (passengers and goods) from Ōtira to Greymouth. J 1237 leads a train that includes D^S class diesel shunters to replace some of the West Coast's steam engines. Wilson Lythgoe

and railway folklore exist to suit all tastes. Neill Atkinson's *Trainland* is indispensable for anyone interested in what railways have meant to New Zealanders and how that meaning has changed over time. Geoffrey B. Churchman and Tony Hurst's *The Railways of New Zealand* and Robin Bromby's *Rails that Built a Nation* both summarise every railway line in New Zealand. David Leitch and Brian Scott describe the remnants of closed lines in *Exploring New Zealand's Ghost Railways*, contextualising each closure with useful brief histories – and although the most recent edition came out in 1998, railway archaeologists can happily still find many of the relics described. An earlier book by Leitch, *Railways of New Zealand* (1972), largely stands the test of time as an overview of the first century of railways in New Zealand; since its publication, numerous authors have

published their own national overviews. For those with a geographic bent, the slim *New Zealand Railway and Tramway Atlas* (the 'Quail Map' to aficionados) is a must, although the most recent edition, the fourth, was published in 1993, since when much has changed. More broadly, James Watson places railways in the context of all forms of transport in his expansive volume *Links*.[10]

The decline of passenger rail is often presented within descriptions of large macroeconomic trends that make contraction seem inexorable. Some authors have been reluctant to criticise NZR and its officials, but it is necessary to engage rigorously with the choices made – and options not taken – to understand how transport evolves. One short booklet, written against the backdrop of privatisation in the 1990s, uses political science

A handsome example of a railcar: RM 34 'Tainui' of the Standard class, looking resplendent in fresh paint at Woburn on 22 March 1951. J.F. Le Cren, ANZ AAVK 6390 B1205

theories to describe a culture of 'non-decisions' since the 1960s that deferred investment until it was too late for railway advocates to mobilise. The author attributes this to small-government, right-wing politicians and road transport lobbyists.[11] It is necessary to look further into the past, however: passenger rail's contraction had its roots in events as far back as the 1920s, and the question is not merely why it has declined, but why its growth stopped. Both sides of politics shaped outcomes that favoured road, as did NZR policies and decisions made without partisan motivations. Geographers have shown that planning assumptions since the 1950s have created 'path dependence': an institutionalised

inability to design, implement or even accept a need for public transport. They describe a cycle whereby planners provide only for cars, then attribute widespread car usage to dislike of other transport modes and continue making car-centric policy.[12] This has fostered the perception of the car as a necessity for personal transport.

New Zealand is fortunate in the quality of its published railway histories, but the archival record is yet to give up all its insights. This book serves a new and different purpose, and information that was irrelevant to past authors is of great significance here. The importance of archival research becomes clear after just a few hours in an Archives New Zealand reading room. NZR's vast files give insight not only into when services began and finished, but also into the reasoning of decision-makers. Annual reports of the ministers of railways and public works furnish official information and statistics. Historical newspapers recount railway openings and inaugural trains – often major events for a region – and debate alterations and cessations.

Historians, as the famed English philosopher R.G. Collingwood put it, do not simply describe the past; they ask questions of it. This book is no mere chronology or assortment of dates; it examines why changes occurred in the way they did.

LIMITED EXPRESSES, MIXED TRAINS AND OTHER MEMBERS OF THE RAILWAY VOCABULARY

Railways have a distinctive lexicon, and prominent terms in this book will be unfamiliar to some readers, especially younger ones and those not immersed in railway culture.

An 'express' is a fast train that skips some stops, and 'limited express' designated a faster service with even fewer stops. These were NZR's flagship trains. 'Railcars', self-propelled passenger carriages, replaced many locomotive-hauled expresses from the 1930s and also ran some suburban services; 'multiple units' are self-propelled trains that comprise two or more semi-permanently coupled carriages.

At the other end of the spectrum were the 'mixed trains' and the 'with-car goods' (sometimes 'goods with car'). Once common throughout New Zealand, the 'mixed' carried goods as well as passengers – it was timetabled with both in mind – and stopped often to shunt wagons in station yards and industrial sidings. The 'with-car goods' was timetabled for freight,

involved more shunting and had a passenger carriage appended for anyone who wanted to travel at the same time. A with-car goods had to run in case there were passengers; a regular 'goods train' could be cancelled if there was insufficient freight.

In the nineteenth century passengers and goods were both important sources of revenue, but in the final decades of with-car goods trains after World War II, passenger accommodation became an afterthought. Clientele on with-car goods trains during the 1970s comprised mainly the confused, the desperate, the enthusiast and the most local of travellers. Railfan accounts from this period suggest that a passenger could often enjoy undisturbed occupancy of a rickety worn-out carriage and might be invited into the guard's van for company and refreshments, or even into the locomotive cab.

Goods trains ran with a guard's van until 1987; today's long-distance passenger trains have luggage vans, the modern-day successor. Some guard's vans were dimly lit and quite uncomfortable. It was not uncommon for passengers – mainly men – to ride in the van of goods trains, especially in regions with poor roads. To do so, a traveller was supposed to sign an indemnity, but the practice was often more informal, especially on lines far from officialdom. Passengers sat wherever they could among the guard's equipment and the many items he handled – parcels, milk churns, egg crates, newspapers and all the paraphernalia of rural life.

Guidelines in 1908 instructed that women could ride only in a guard's van that was equipped with 'proper accommodation for passengers', such as an actual seat.[13] Later instructions removed the need for 'proper accommodation' but prohibited single women

W^F 404 hauls a short mixed train from Nelson near Glenhope, 19 May 1954. At the rear is the guard's van.
J.F. Le Cren, ANZ AAVK 6390 B4762

from riding with the guard. Policies varied about whether groups of women could travel in the guard's van without a male companion. Some women put their request to do so in writing, but even in cases of demonstrable need a lone woman was often denied permission: archival holdings attest to rejections but naturally but do not tell of women carried against regulations.[14] It is currently unclear whether this limitation to women's mobility was consistently enforced, or how significant its effects were when few travellers of either sex sought to travel by goods train in the first place. It is possible this varied greatly by time and location.

There are two types of timetable used on railways: public and working. Public timetables inform prospective travellers about what trains are available to carry passengers; at their simplest they state where trains go and when. More detailed versions indicate connections to other transport modes, give ticket prices, suggest daytrips, list luggage and refreshment services and other facilities available to passengers and so on. They are printed in many formats, such as posters, handbills, brochures and booklets. NZR during the 1930s produced thick pocket-sized books listing every passenger service, along with a large amount of advertising. As road and air competition intensified, the public timetable needed an eye-catching design, and by the 1970s this had become a larger and rather attractive annual publication with colour artwork.

Working timetables are quite different and, to the uninitiated, can be difficult to follow. They are distributed to staff for internal use and list every train – goods and passenger – with all information necessary for their operation. They also indicate facilities at stations – such things as crossing loops, signalling and traffic control and, back in the days of steam, whether coal and water were available for locomotives.

POWER, CONTROL AND BRANDING

Railways in New Zealand have, for most of their history, been built and operated by the state. From 1895 to 1996 a minister of railways – no woman ever held the portfolio – sat as a cabinet minister in the government. Between 1895 and 1982 he oversaw a Railways Department that was known as 'New Zealand (Government) Railways' or simply 'the Railways'. In 1982 Robert Muldoon's National government transformed the department into the New Zealand Railways Corporation, which its Labour successor then turned into a state-owned enterprise in 1986 before splitting it in 1990: the Railways Corporation retained the land beneath the track and New Zealand Rail Limited owned the track and trains. After returning to power, National privatised NZR Limited in 1993. Since 1996 railway policy has fallen within the responsibility of the minister of transport, a portfolio established in 1928, and the minister for state-owned enterprises, established in 1987.

The private consortium that purchased NZR Limited renamed it Tranz Rail in 1995, and progressively stripped assets in a manner both deleterious to the future of rail transport in New Zealand and repugnant to rational economic sensibilities. Australian firm Toll Holdings mounted a successful takeover bid in 2003, then sold the physical infrastructure back to Helen Clark's Labour government for $1 in 2004. It became the property of the Railways Corporation, which traded as Ontrack, and Toll paid an access fee for exclusive use. Toll and Ontrack, however, struggled to agree on this fee. New Zealand's ill-fated adventure in railway privatisation concluded on 1 July 2008 when the Clark government paid Toll $690m for its rail and ferry operations and re-nationalised them as KiwiRail. Ontrack merged with KiwiRail a few months later and its branding was retired in 2011, although the merger was partially unwound in 2012. Today, the division is like that of 1990–93, with New Zealand Railways Corporation possessing the land and KiwiRail owning the above-ground assets except some that regional councils own. The later chapters of this book delve into the breakup of NZR and its consequences for passengers.

In the corporatised and privatised atmosphere that has prevailed since the 1980s, passenger operations have acquired distinctive branding. NZR branded long-distance trains and its Road Services buses as InterCity from 1987 (InterCity Rail, after NZR sold Road Services in 1991), and commuter services in Auckland and Wellington were first Cityline and then CityRail. When NZR became Tranz Rail in 1995 these services were rebranded as Tranz Scenic and Tranz Metro respectively. The Tranz Scenic brand survived for 16 years, morphing into KiwiRail Scenic Journeys in 2011, followed by the Great Journeys of New Zealand in 2017 when combined with the Interislander ferries plying Cook Strait.

Suburban services have gone through an even greater confusion of branding. Tranz Metro did not bid to operate Auckland's trains when its contract with Auckland Regional Council expired in 2003; it ran Wellington's trains until 2016. At the time of writing, Auckland trains fall under the AT Metro brand of Auckland Transport, a council-controlled organisation that plans and funds rail and other regional transport; Wellington trains take the Metlink brand of the Greater Wellington Regional Council. Transdev, a private company based in France, operates services in both cities under contract, using rollingstock owned by the respective councils or leased from KiwiRail; in March 2022, Auckland One Rail, a joint venture of Singaporean and Australian rail companies, will commence an eight-year contract to operate Auckland's trains. It is a perfect muddle, one that would beget confusion even from the pen of the clearest author. Future readers, hopefully enjoying this book in a time without such frequent churning of brands, might find this a peculiar and wasteful quirk of the period.

The following pages show how NZR responded to a century of change in passenger transport. Maps illustrate where and how the network evolved from 1920 to today; the text explains why decisions to alter the network happened when they did, what passenger trains meant to communities, and why the pattern has been one of retreat. This reveals when NZR conceded defeat to road and air competition, when it fought on and when it succeeded.

Rail has always mattered to our communities and it still has an important place in New Zealand. The network at the dawn of the 2020s might be attenuated, but it represents a large investment in mobility that provides the basis for better, cleaner, more efficient transport in the future.

Upper North Island
Rail routes open to passengers at 1 January 1920

Ōpua
Kaikohe
Kawakawa
Ōtiria
Hikurangi
WHANGĀREI
Ōnerahi
Whatoro
Kaihū
DARGAVILLE
Ranganui
Wellsford
Tahekeroa
HELENSVILLE
Henderson
AUCKLAND
Onehunga
Ōtāhuhu
Papakura
Drury
Pukekohe
Mercer
Waikato R.
Pukemiro
Huntly
PRIV.
Glen Massey
Ngāruawā
HAMILTON
FRANKTON
Te Awamutu
Ōtorohanga

C^H 1

The network in 1920

Moutohorā

Ōtoko

Te Karaka

Makaraka

Ngātapa *PWD* GISBORNE

L. Waikaremoana

Wairoa R.

Mōhaka R.

Ngaruroro R.

NAPIER

HASTINGS

Waipawa

Waipukurau

Lower North Island
Rail routes open to passengers at 1 January 1920

Upper South Island
Rail routes open to passengers at 1 January 1920

Seddonville

Mōkihinui Mine

Ngākawau

Waimangaroa

WHB

Cape Foulwind

WESTPORT

Kawatiri / Buller

Īnangahua

Reefton

Ikamatua

Blackball

Rewanui

Ngahere

GREYMOUTH

Stillwater

L. Sumner

Kūmara Junction

Moana

Hokitika

Ōtira

Ross

Arthur's Pass

Craigieburn

Oxford West

L. Coleridge

Springfield

Sheffield

Rakaia R.

Whitecliffs

R

Methven

Ro

Springburn

Rakaia

Mount Somers

Hakatere / Ashburton R.

Rangitātā R.

ASHBURTO

Tinwald

Aoraki / Mt Cook

Hinds R.

Maukatua / Mt Sefton

L. Tekapo

NELSON

PICTON

Richmond

Belgrove

enhope

BLENHEIM

Wairau R.

Awatere R.

Ward

Wharanui

Waiou Toa / Clarence R.

Waiau Uwha R.

Hurunui R.

Waiau

Parnassus

Culverden

Waikari

Scargill

Waipara

Bennetts

Rangiora

Kaiapoi

Waimakariri R.

Darfield

CHRISTCHURCH

on

Lyttelton

Lincoln

Southbridge

Little River

L. Pūkak

L. Ōhau

Haast R.

Tititea / Mt Aspiring ▲

L. Wanaka

L. Hāwea

Pikirakatahi / Mt Earnslaw ▲

Wedderbu

CROMWELL
PWD

Ōmaka

Clyde

Alexandra

L. Wakatipu

L. Te Anau

Kingston

Athol

Waikaia

Edievale

Beaumont

Ōreti R.

Lumsden

Lawrence

Mossburn

Waikākā

Mataura R.

Tapanui

Mata-Au / Clutha R.

Dipton

Riversdale

Waiau R.

Waipahi

L. Manapōuri

Aparima R.

Wairio

L. Hauroko

Hedgehope

BALCLUTHA

Winton

GORE Clinton

L. Poteriteri

Tūātapere

Ōtautau

Edendale

Glenomaru

Wyndham

Ōwaka

Thornbury

Glenham

Orepuki

Riverton

Tahakopa

INVERCARGILL

Tokanui

Bluff

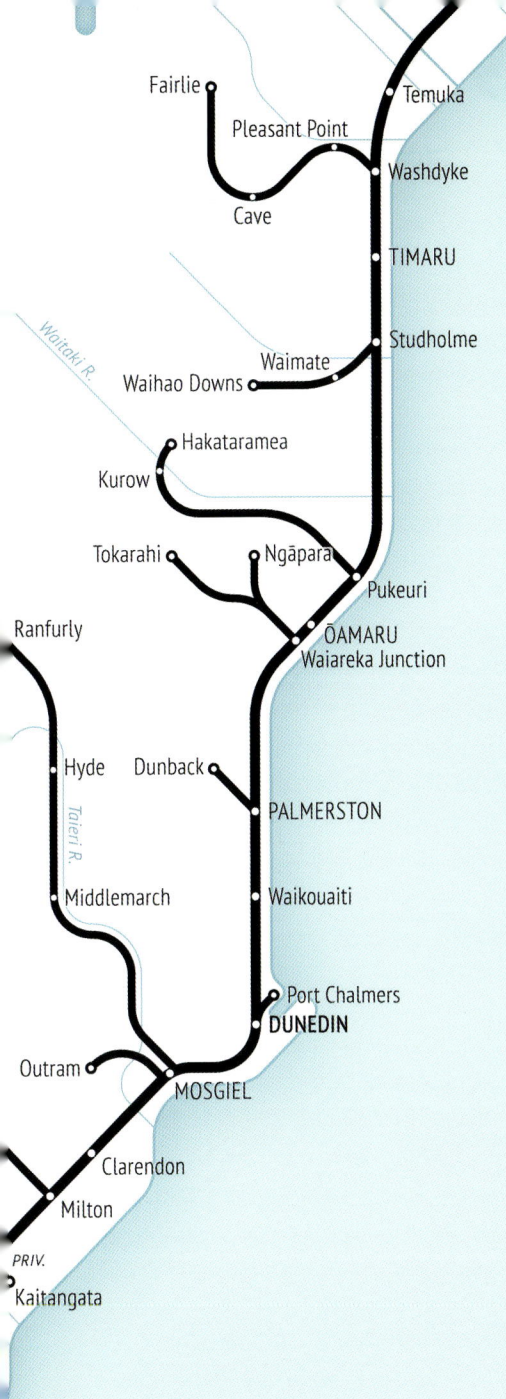

Fairlie
Pleasant Point
Temuka
Cave
Washdyke
TIMARU
Studholme
Waitaki R.
Waimate
Waihao Downs
Hakataramea
Kurow
Tokarahi
Ngāpara
Pukeuri
Ranfurly
ŌAMARU
Waiareka Junction
Hyde
Dunback
Taieri R.
PALMERSTON
Middlemarch
Waikouaiti
Port Chalmers
DUNEDIN
Outram
MOSGIEL
Clarendon
Milton
PRIV.
Kaitangata

Lower South Island
Rail routes open to passengers at 1 January 1920

Railways were New Zealand's dominant provider of land-based transport in 1920. The primitive nature of roads, the lack of navigable rivers and the speed of trains compared to other modes of transport meant that almost wherever a railway went, trains accommodated passengers. Only a handful of lines – spurs for industries such as sawmills and cargo ports – never carried passengers (see Table 1, page 40). By 1920 a few railways had already closed or lost their passenger services (see Table 2, page 41), but these lines were of little consequence. One such was the Taonui Branch in the Manawatū, which railway historians David Leitch and Brian Scott dismiss as an 'elongated siding' on which horses usually provided motive power.[1] A person could generally trust that if they saw railway tracks, there would be a passenger service.

New Zealand's railway network represents the linking of numerous isolated lines built to connect major towns with a port and the nearby hinterland. The first railway lines were authorised in the 1860s by the former provincial governments of New Zealand, quasi-federal institutions similar to the states and provinces that today make up Australia, Canada and the United States. The capacity of most provincial governments to finance or administer railways, however, fell far short of public expectations. In 1870 there were only 74 kilometres of railways open in New Zealand, mainly in Canterbury. Auckland Province abandoned construction of a railway to the Waikato, and Southland built an experimental wooden railway with poor-quality timber: the trains were too heavy for the flimsy kahikatea rails and the province went bankrupt.[2] Otago's provincial government discussed extensive railway plans but did not start construction of its first line, from Dunedin to Port Chalmers, until 1870. None of the other

six provinces got beyond talk, although there was lots of that.

Enter Julius Vogel, founder of the *Otago Daily Times* and once an enthusiastic advocate for Otago's provincial autonomy and even its independence. Vogel became treasurer in William Fox's central government in 1869 and his vision grew to encompass the entire country. In light of sustained provincial failures, Vogel planned a national railway network with construction funded by loans that only the central government had the creditworthiness to raise. To spread investment across New Zealand's dispersed population, and to bestow the benefits of railways on as many regions as possible, this Great Public Works Policy began with lines to serve local needs, which would progressively be knitted together into trunk routes. These were to be developmental railways, built not to make direct profits but to improve the value of land, expand and sustain the economy and provide mobility for everyday purposes. This rationale recognised that many social and economic activities required transport infrastructure, and the fact that New Zealand did not have the population or the financial capital for private railways to succeed. It was also a clear example of railways as a tool of colonisation, enabling Pākehā to settle more widely and densely throughout New Zealand.

Vogel presented his scheme to Parliament on 28 June 1870. Railways were one of the 'great wants of the Colony', he said, and to meet this he proposed an extensive network:

Auckland to Wanganui by Taupo, with connections to Napier and New Plymouth. Wanganui to Wellington. Nelson to Greymouth, and Hokitika, with connection to Westport. Picton to Amuri, Christchurch, Timaru, Oamaru, Waikouaiti,

Railway Station, Ashburton. N. Z.

A postcard from the 1910s depicting Ashburton station, for many years a busy intermediate stop between Christchurch and Dunedin on the Main South Line.

Collection of Lemuel Lyes

Dunedin, Tokomairiro, Molyneux, and Winton, with connections to Tuapeka, Clyde, Cromwell, Arrow, and Queenstown. These railways should be commenced from a number of different points, and be constructed as cheaply as possible – the works being continued as traffic demanded.[3]

His vision was never realised fully. Politicians with one eye on re-election secured the construction of branch lines within their electorates at the expense of trunk railways. Others, acting from provincial or personal self-interest, stripped away the measures to provide financial security for repaying loans. The abolition of the provinces in 1876, another initiative that owed much to Vogel, did not quash parochial approval of railway construction.[4]

Even when placed within the context of a developmental state, the priorities were often skewed. The government approved too many branch lines to lightly populated hinterlands ahead of interprovincial main trunks. The most egregious examples occurred in rural areas of

the South Island. In the early 1870s, for example, Canterbury Province appeased parochial demands in North Canterbury by building parallel branches inland from Kaiapoi and Rangiora that ran a mere 10 kilometres apart and met near Oxford. This needless duplication doomed both to unprofitability.[5] Two branches in Southland reached localities with similar names at about the same time: a branch to Waikākā, north of Gore, opened in 1908, a year before one further west to Waikaia. When Leitch and Scott depict the latter as running through a sparsely populated valley of 1700 people, they actually overstate matters: this was the population of the entire Waikaia Riding, some of whom had better access to the Kingston and Waimea Plains railways. Barely 330 people lived in Waikaia and its vicinity, and the railway ran on the opposite side of the valley to its largest settlement, 550-strong Wendon. Waikākā was even more lightly populated: 224 people lived in or near the branch's terminal hamlet.[6]

Some unprofitable routes had a large regional role, such as the Otago Central Railway. New

The junction station, once a common sight. This example is Rakaia, 29 March 1950. The nameboard reads 'Change here for Methven Branch'.

J.F. Le Cren, ANZ AAVK 6390 B57

extensions were built over decades in the belief the line would eventually pay, but although it crept through Ranfurly and Alexandra to reach Cromwell, it never made money.[7] At the risk of falling into the same trap (or offending my Cromwell-born grandmother), the line went a long way to end nowhere in particular. If proposals to build it to Queenstown, Wānaka, or through Haast Pass to the West Coast had succeeded, it might today be a jewel in the network's crown.

The last portion of the Main South Line between Christchurch, Dunedin and Invercargill opened in 1879, but the commitment of so much time and money to a patchwork of rural branches meant that other key routes were still incomplete in 1920. Some regions had isolated railways that still lacked a connection to the main network of their island. The need

to operate workshops for each isolated railway, and the occasional transfers of locomotives and rollingstock by sea, increased costs and impeded economies of scale.

In the North Island the main network linked Auckland and Wellington with the other major centres of the time. Two isolated sections existed in Northland: one, from the Bay of Islands to Whangārei, was creeping south to join both the main network and an isolated line that ran from Dargaville through the Kaihū Valley. Gisborne's railway northwards to Moutohorā was also isolated and would remain so for some time. It was envisaged as part of an East Coast Main Trunk running from Napier to Gisborne, across to Ōpōtiki and along the Bay of Plenty via Tauranga to meet an existing line in Waihī. In the end Gisborne was only ever connected to Napier; the difficult landscape north of Moutohorā thwarted construction towards the Bay of Plenty.

The South Island possessed five separate sections, the largest of which was the Hurunui–Bluff network. It ran from North Canterbury down the east coast to Southland with a thick network of branches heading inland. A connection with the West Coast was in sight as the Ōtira Tunnel through the Southern Alps neared completion. This would link Hurunui–Bluff with the Greymouth Section, which

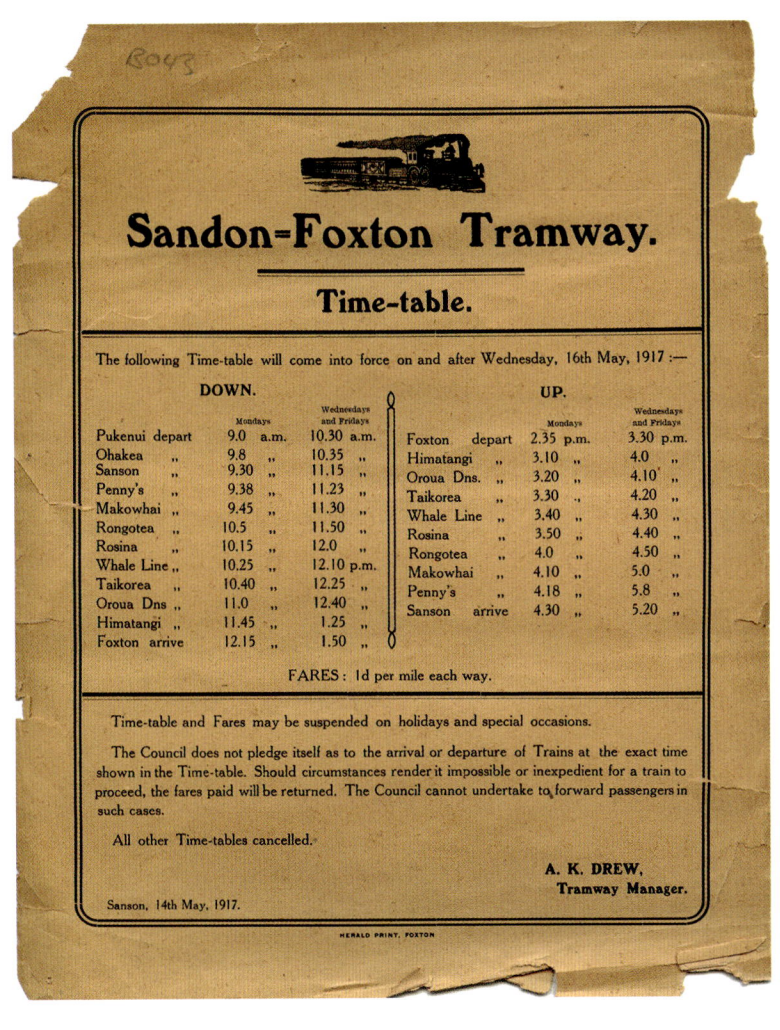

Sandon=Foxton Tramway.

Time-table.

The following Time-table will come into force on and after Wednesday, 16th May, 1917 :—

DOWN.				UP.		
	Mondays	Wednesdays and Fridays			Mondays	Wednesdays and Fridays
Pukenui depart	9.0 a.m.	10.30 a.m.		Foxton depart	2.35 p.m.	3.30 p.m.
Ohakea „	9.8 „	10.35 „		Himatangi „	3.10 „	4.0 „
Sanson „	9.30 „	11.15 „		Oroua Dns. „	3.20 „	4.10' „
Penny's „	9.38 „	11.23 „		Taikorea „	3.30 „	4.20 „
Makowhai „	9.45 „	11.30 „		Whale Line „	3.40 „	4.30 „
Rongotea „	10.5 „	11.50 „		Rosina „	3.50 „	4.40 „
Rosina „	10.15 „	12.0 „		Rongotea „	4.0 „	4.50 „
Whale Line „	10.25 „	12.10 p.m.		Makowhai „	4.10 „	5.0 „
Taikorea „	10.40 „	12.25 „		Penny's „	4.18 „	5.8 „
Oroua Dns „	11.0 „	12.40 „		Sanson arrive	4.30 „	5.20 „
Himatangi „	11.45 „	1.25 „				
Foxton arrive	12.15 „	1.50 „				

FARES : 1d per mile each way.

Time-table and Fares may be suspended on holidays and special occasions.

The Council does not pledge itself as to the arrival or departure of Trains at the exact time shown in the Time-table. Should circumstances render it impossible or inexpedient for a train to proceed, the fares paid will be returned. The Council cannot undertake to forward passengers in such cases.

All other Time-tables cancelled.

A. K. DREW,
Tramway Manager.

Sanson, 14th May, 1917.

HERALD PRINT, FOXTON.

A timetable for the Sanson Tramway, effective 16 May 1917. 'Sandon' is not an error: the town Sanson was founded on land known as the Sandon Block. Archives Central MDC 00060:1:1

Canterbury had stalled.

A few railways beyond NZR's control carried passengers on a regular basis. Three were private. Mining companies owned two: in South Otago, the Kaitangata Coal Company offered a service from Kaitangata to Stirling on the Main South Line near Balclutha; in the Waikato, Waipā Colleries ran passenger trains between Glen Massey and Ngāruawāhia on the North Island Main Trunk. The other private operation, the Castlecliff Railway Company, operated a suburban service between Whanganui and its coastal suburb, Castlecliff, although competition from municipal trams meant patronage was declining by 1920. Horse-racing clubs also built private lines to racecourses in Palmerston North, the Hutt Valley, Christchurch and Dunedin, although NZR operated the trains. Two were still carrying passengers in 1920, to Palmerston North's Awapuni Racecourse and Christchurch's Riccarton Racecourse, though trains only ran on race days. Awapuni lost its trains in 1939 and Riccarton's branch closed in 1954.[8]

fanned east to the Alps, south to Ross, and north to Īnangahua. Further up the West Coast was an isolated railway between Westport and Seddonville; grand ambitions for a line through the Buller Gorge to Īnangahua were as yet unrealised but came to pass eventually. Another railway was started in Nelson with the aim of reaching Īnangahua but never got there: in 1920 it terminated at Glenhope. The remaining isolated line was in Marlborough: it ran south from Picton through Blenheim as far as Wharanui, where work on a link to

Some public authorities separate to the Railways Department also ran passenger trains. The Manawatū County Council's Sanson Tramway, although legislatively a tramway, operated with railway rollingstock that NZR had owned previously, and the council had running rights on NZR's Foxton Branch for a mixed train between Sanson and Foxton. The Westport Harbour Board ran passenger services from Westport to Cape Foulwind, and the State Mines Department had railways to some coal mines but did not offer timetabled passenger services in 1920.

Easily the largest operator of passenger trains beyond NZR's purview was the Public Works Department. It ran four longstanding passenger services in 1920; all were in the North Island except for a service in Central Otago that began between Clyde and Cromwell in 1917. The PWD began running trains along the Bay of Plenty coastline in 1913; by 1920 these ran from Mount Maunganui through Te Puke to Matatā.[9] By the time the PWD handed control of this line to NZR eight years later, it was operating trains all the way from Tauranga to Tāneatua, a distance of some 95 kilometres. Further down the east coast the PWD had operated bi-weekly mixed trains since 1915 from Makaraka, near Gisborne, inland to Ngātapa. Like the railway between Gisborne and Moutohorā from which it branched, the Ngātapa line was envisaged as part of the East Coast Main Trunk from Hawke's Bay to the Bay of Plenty. Over in northern Taranaki, the PWD was busy constructing a railway through difficult terrain from Stratford to Ōkahukura, near Taumarunui on the North Island Main Trunk. Although work was ongoing at both ends, in 1920 trains operated from Stratford only: NZR provided them as far as Kōhuratahi, and the PWD onwards to

Tahora.[10] This bi-weekly service began in 1919; as construction pushed deeper into Taranaki's interior, the PWD ran services at both ends until handing over the complete line in 1933.

Across all of these sections, NZR and the assortment of smaller operators acted as general carriers of passengers and goods. Stations in cities and large towns were bustling places, the hubs of their communities. In New Zealand, as with countries globally, the railway and its stations reflected the social and economic development of a region.[11] In rural areas the railway was a crucial link with the outside world and a prominent manifestation – sometimes the only one – of the government and public services. At a time when everybody travelled by train, railway stations also fulfilled an important function as the settings in which to welcome dignitaries and famous visitors.[12] But shifting demographics and new technologies would affect railways profoundly.

AN EMERGING COMPETITOR

Road transport posed a challenge in 1920 – one that grew increasingly severe. Car ownership was becoming more achievable and, as the quality of rural roads improved, so too did the reach and flexibility of motor transport. NZR had seen off previous rivals, including steam traction engines on the South Island's east coast.[13] It competed with steamships for custom, especially from Auckland to Northland and Thames, and from Dunedin to Timaru, and usually won the contests.[14] Simon Ville, one of Australasia's leading economic historians, has shown that coastal shipping was strongest in areas without a railway, or where the railway was not yet connected to the trunk network.[15] Once rail linked a town to other regions, trains had the upper hand over seafaring vessels, which were slower and subject to the vagaries of weather and tides.

Commercial and private vehicles proved much harder to counter than coastal shipping: a rival mode that served communities inland could secure a greater proportion of the Railways' traffic. Service cars became popular in the 1920s. These large automobiles ran defined medium- and long-distance routes to a timetable, especially in country areas with small populations or with roads that were too rough for buses. Richard McVilly, NZR's general manager in 1923, lamented that 'motor-vehicles have practically free use of the highways [and this] has been to a great extent responsible for the growth of this form of competition'.[16]

After McVilly retired, a board of commissioners took over in early 1925. In its first report the board emphasised that steps had been taken to confine road transport to its 'proper sphere', 'namely, as feeders to the railways – where there is ample scope for the motors to afford a real service to the community'.[17] It also began identifying which branch lines were losing money, as past reports had given the revenue of each section as a whole rather than separating out the individual lines. The board's returns did not encompass all branches, but of those included most showed a loss on working; even more showed a loss when charged interest for the capital cost of construction. Some turned a small profit, or did once allocated a 'feeder value' for contributing to mainline revenue. Net losses were generally modest in 1926, and nine out of 32 showed a profit before interest; even with interest, individual losses rarely exceeded £5000. A decade later only seven out of 34 showed a profit before interest, and the net loss before interest had grown from £43,000 to almost £60,000. These losses were a small proportion of total revenue but they were expanding, consuming 0.57 percent in 1926 and nearly 1 percent in 1936.[18]

Transport licensing acts from 1931 to 1987 restricted road competition to varying degrees. Railways and roads were public investments; according to the prevailing logic of the period they should complement rather than duplicate each other. Competition was inefficient and wasteful, a pressing concern for politicians trying to rein in public expenditure. Yet in the same year that Parliament passed the first licensing act, and following a trickle of cancellations the previous decade, NZR made its first systematic cuts to services.

NZR might have gained protection against commercial road competitors but the private motorcar was no less a threat, and by the 1930s many rural dwellers owned or could access a car and used this in preference to the train. In the year to 31 March 1930, for example, the number of train tickets sold at Waitara, Taranaki, was 8964, less than half the 18,380 sold a decade earlier. The decline was less precipitous in more remote communities – in Whangamōmona, east of New Plymouth in rugged northern Taranaki, sales slipped from 15,939 to 11,559. But elsewhere the collapse in patronage was alarming: 30,578 people rode Gisborne's railway to Moutohorā in 1930 compared to 89,518 in 1920.[19] Railways had provided unprecedented mobility in the late nineteenth century, but the motorcar was now more convenient than walking what was often a long distance to the nearest station to wait for a once-daily train. By the 1950s, motorways were a symbol of the future and automobility was emblematic of personal autonomy. NZR had its work cut out, and it often struggled.

Table 1: Railway lines in New Zealand that never had a regular passenger service

JUNCTION (MAIN LINE)	TERMINAL	OPENED	CLOSED
Glenbrook (Waiuku Branch)	Mission Bush	1968	
In effect the Waiuku Branch closed at the same time as the opening of this line, which serves the Mission Bush steel mill. It uses the Paerātā–Glenbrook section of the Waiuku Branch.			
Hawkens Junction (East Coast Main Trunk)	Kawerau	1953	
Originally a branch of the East Coast Main Trunk (ECMT), which ran to Tāneatua, this has been considered the eastern end of the ECMT since 1978. The line from Hawkens Junction to Tāneatua is now a branch (mothballed since 2003).			
Kawerau (ECMT)	Murupara	1957	
Although considered a separate line, this is effectively an extension of the ECMT on which logs are conveyed to Kawerau.			
Awakeri (ECMT/Tāneatua Branch)	Whakatāne Board Mills	1939	2001
This private industrial branch served a timber mill on the west bank of the Whakatāne River, opposite Whakatāne township. Tranz Rail acquired it in 1999.			
Putāruru (Rotorua Branch)	Kinleith	1952	
Built on the formation of part of the Taupō Tōtara Timber Company's bush tramway.			
Waipuku (Marton–New Plymouth Line)	Lower slopes of Mt Taranaki	1908	1951
Known as the Mt Egmont Branch, this served a ballast quarry and trains ran when required.			
Taonui (Marton–New Plymouth Line)	Colyton	1879	1895
This branch was built to access a stand of timber and was usually worked by horses.			
Waimangaroa Junction (Seddonville Branch)	Conns Creek	1877	1967
At its terminus this branch met a steep rope-worked incline for wagons up to Denniston. The line had frequent coal trains. The public timetable advised passengers to ride in the guard's van.			
Blackball (Blackball Branch)	Roa	1909	1960
The State Mines Department operated this steep railway beyond Blackball to Roa. Passenger trains ran only for special excursions.[20]			
Rūnanga (Rewanui Branch)	Rapahoe	1923	
Although Rapahoe station had passenger facilities, requests for a regular passenger service were rejected. Excursions ran but the line was – and is – operated for the transport of coal.[21]			
Shag Point (Main South Line)	Mine near Shag Point boat harbour	1879	1934
This branch gave access to a coalmine. NZR ceased to shunt it in 1908, after which the mining company operated the line until 1934, when mine and line closed.[22]			
Inch Valley (Dunback Branch)	Mākareao	1900	1988
This industrial branch line existed solely to serve a limeworks.			
Green Island (Main South Line)	Walton Park	1874	1957
Industrial siding, shunt only. The first 580 metres were retained as a spur until 1980.			
Abbotsford (Main South Line)	Fernhill	1883	2002
Industrial siding, shunt only. Although formally closed in 2002, it had been disused for years; all rail use was banned in 1995 and most track had been lifted prior to closure.			

Table 2: Railway lines in New Zealand closed or freight only by 1920

JUNCTION (MAIN LINE)	TERMINAL	OPENED	CLOSED
Kumeū (North Auckland Line)	Riverhead	1875	1881
Pandora Point (Palmerston North–Gisborne Line)	Ahuriri	1874	
Taonui (Marton–New Plymouth Line)	Colyton	1879	1895
Beach (near Petone, Wairarapa Line)	Hutt Park	1885	1906
Lambton (Wairarapa Line)	Te Aro	1893	1917
Between Hillsborough and Heathcote (Lyttelton Line)	Ferrymead	1863	1868
Hillgrove (Main South Line)	Moeraki	1877	1879
Between Dunedin and Hillside (Main South Line)	St Kilda	1876	1938
Awarua (Bluff Branch)	Mokomoko	1866	1875

Kumeū (North Auckland Line) — Built as part of the Kaipara Railway from Riverhead to Helensville, this short section became redundant when the line from Auckland reached Kumeū. The remainder became part of today's North Auckland Line.

Pandora Point (Palmerston North–Gisborne Line) — Passenger services were withdrawn in 1908. This railway remains open for freight to the port of Napier.

Taonui (Marton–New Plymouth Line) — This branch was built to access a stand of timber and was usually worked by horses.

Beach (near Petone, Wairarapa Line) — Hutt Park Railway was a private line to serve Hutt Park Raceway. It fell into disuse for passenger traffic when the Wellington Racing Club moved its main activities to Trentham, though a portion survived as an industrial siding until 1982. Hutt Park Raceway was later accessed from the Gracefield Branch.

Lambton (Wairarapa Line) — An unsuccessful attempt to provide railway access to central Wellington: the smoke pollution was unpopular, and it could not compete with the municipal electric tramways. It ran from the former Lambton terminal, since replaced by the current Wellington Railway Station.

Between Hillsborough and Heathcote (Lyttelton Line) — New Zealand's first steam railway ran from Christchurch to Ferrymead. The final stretch to Ferrymead became redundant when the Lyttelton Tunnel opened in December 1867 and trains could run under the Port Hills; it closed to all traffic a few months later.

Hillgrove (Main South Line) — An ill-fated attempt to build a branch to Moeraki. The instability of the land and the eclipse of the port of Moeraki by other regional ports meant it survived for only two years.

Between Dunedin and Hillside (Main South Line) — The private Ocean Beach Railway first ran as a railway then provided passenger services with steam trams until 1882. Special trains to Forbury Park Raceway ran until 1904; renewal of the railway's agreement with the state in 1908 removed a clause permitting passenger conveyance. The only passengers carried after this date were troops in September 1914; goods services ran sporadically until 1938.[23]

Awarua (Bluff Branch) — Built to serve a jetty at Mokomoko that was superseded by the port at Bluff. This short spur carried little traffic in its lifetime.

Ōkaihau
Kaikohe
Ōpua
Kawakawa
Ōtiria
Hikurangi
Donnellys Crossing
Whatoro
Kaihū
Portland
Kirikōpuni
WHANGĀREI
Ōnerahi
Waiōtira
Waikiekie
Huarau
Maungatūroto
DARGAVILLE
Ranganui
Wellsford
Tahekeroa
HELENSVILLE
AUCKLAND
Henderson
Onehunga
Ōtāhuhu
Papakura
Drury
Pukekohe
Waiuku
Mercer
Pukemiro
Glen Afton
Huntly
Glen Massey
PRIV.
Ngāruawā
HAMILTON
FRANKTON
Te Awamutu
Ōtorohanga

Waikato R.

Ōkaihau–Kaikohe commenced 1923

Whangārei–Ōnerahi ceased 1927

Whangārei–Portland commenced 1920

Portland–Waikiekie commenced 1921 by PWD, handover to NZR 1925

Waikiekie–Huarau commenced 1922 by PWD, handover to NZR 1925

Huarau–Ranganui commenced 1920

Donnellys Crossing–Whatoro commenced 1923

Kirikōpuni–Waiōtira commenced 1928

Waiuku–Paerātā commenced 1922

Glen Afton–Pukemiro commenced 1924

Upper North Island
1920–1928

C^H 2

1920–1928
The regional railway falters

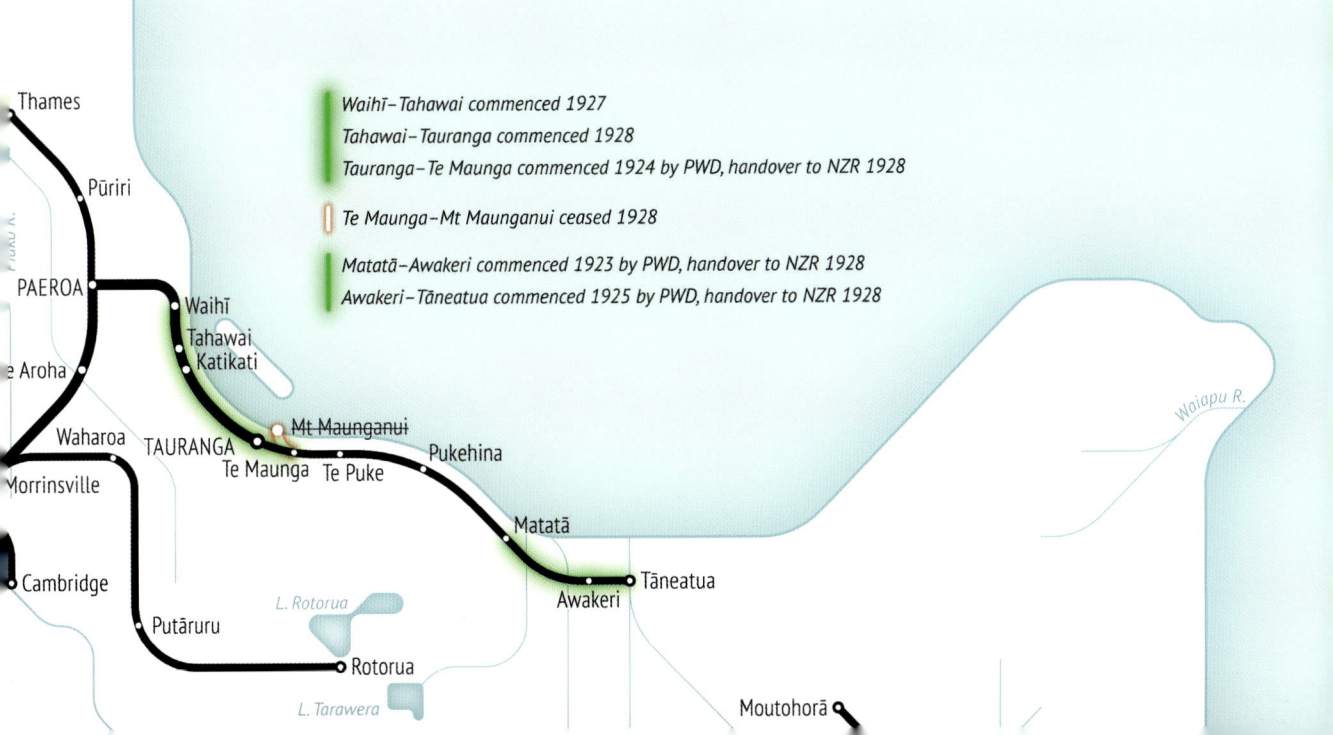

Waihī–Tahawai commenced 1927

Tahawai–Tauranga commenced 1928

Tauranga–Te Maunga commenced 1924 by PWD, handover to NZR 1928

Te Maunga–Mt Maunganui ceased 1928

Matatā–Awakeri commenced 1923 by PWD, handover to NZR 1928

Awakeri–Tāneatua commenced 1925 by PWD, handover to NZR 1928

Ōkahukura–Mātīere commenced 1922
Mātīere–Toi Toi commenced 1924
Toi Toi–Ōhura commenced 1926

Tāngarākau–Tahora commenced 1926
Tahora–Kōhuratahi handover PWD to NZR 1924

Ōpunake–Te Roti commenced 1926

Petone–Waterloo commenced 1927

44

Moutohorā

Ōtoko

Te Karaka

Makaraka

Ngātapa

GISBORNE

Ngātapa–Makaraka handover PWD to NZR 1924

L. Waikaremoana

Wairoa R.

Mōhaka R.

Eskdale

Eskdale–Napier commenced 1923

Ngaruroro R.

NAPIER

HASTINGS

Waipawa

Waipukurau

Lower North Island
1920–1928

Upper South Island
1920–1928

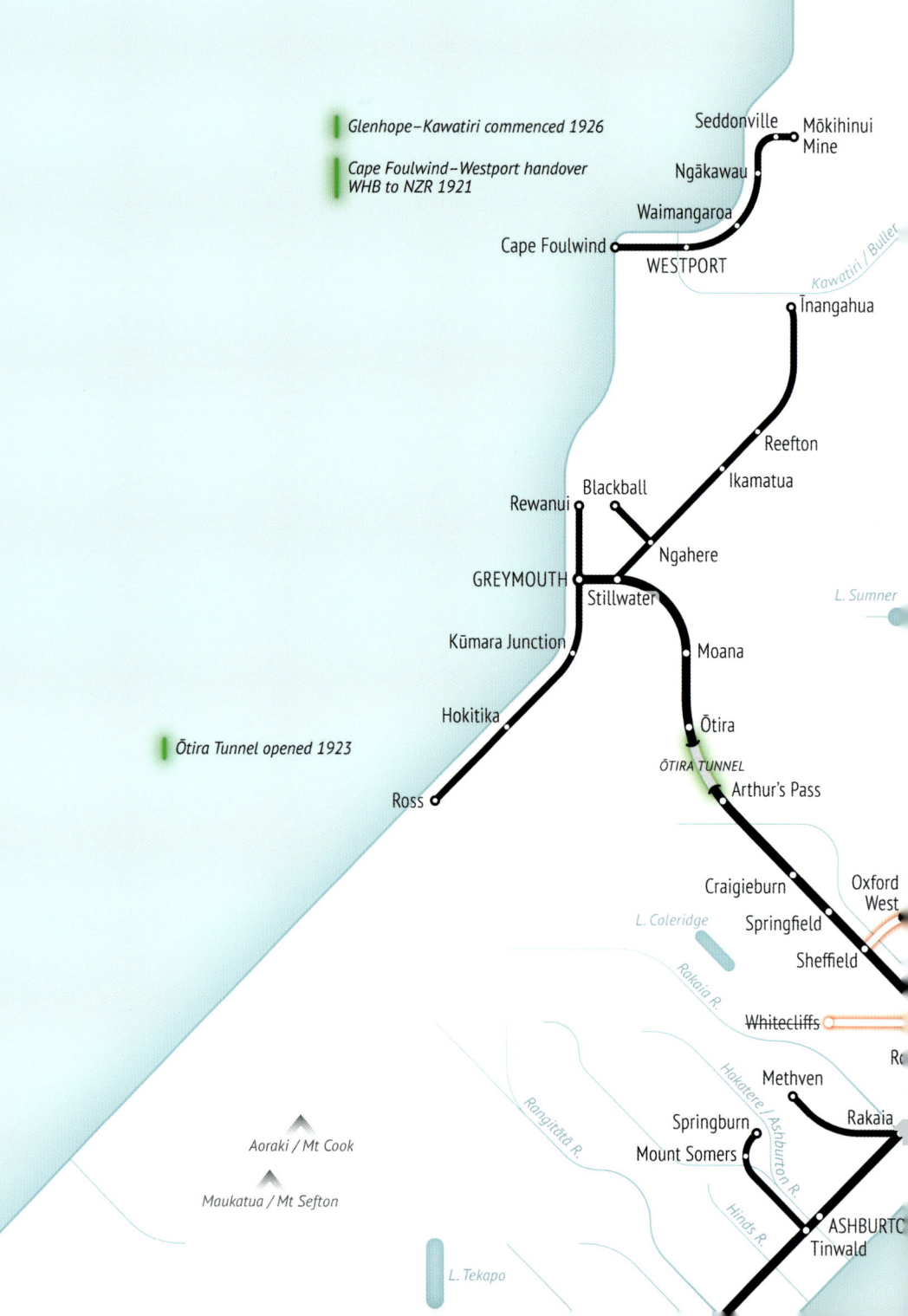

Glenhope–Kawatiri commenced 1926

Cape Foulwind–Westport handover
WHB to NZR 1921

Seddonville

Mōkihinui
Mine

Ngākawau

Waimangaroa

Cape Foulwind

WESTPORT

Kawatiri / Buller

Īnangahua

Reefton

Ikamatua

Blackball

Rewanui

Ngahere

GREYMOUTH

Stillwater

L. Sumner

Kūmara Junction

Moana

Hokitika

Ōtira

Ōtira Tunnel opened 1923

ŌTIRA TUNNEL

Arthur's Pass

Ross

Craigieburn

Oxford
West

L. Coleridge

Springfield

Rakaia R.

Sheffield

Whitecliffs

R

Methven

R

Hakatere / Ashburton R.

Springburn

Rakaia

Mount Somers

Rangitātā R.

Aoraki / Mt Cook

Maukatua / Mt Sefton

Hinds R.

ASHBURTON
Tinwald

L. Tekapo

Oxford West–Sheffield ceased 1921

Darfield–Whitecliffs ceased 1928

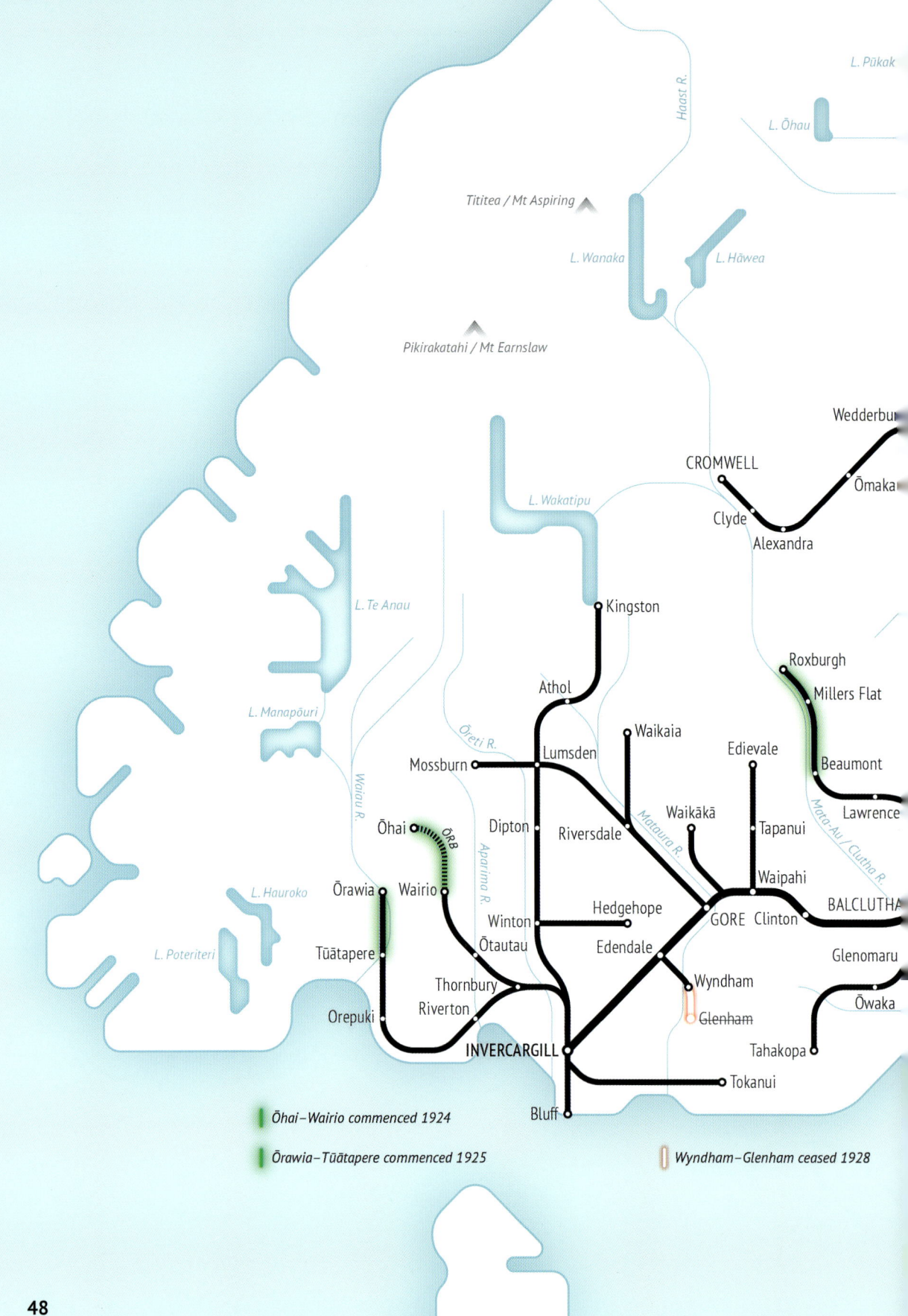

Ōhai–Wairio commenced 1924

Ōrawia–Tūātapere commenced 1925

Wyndham–Glenham ceased 1928

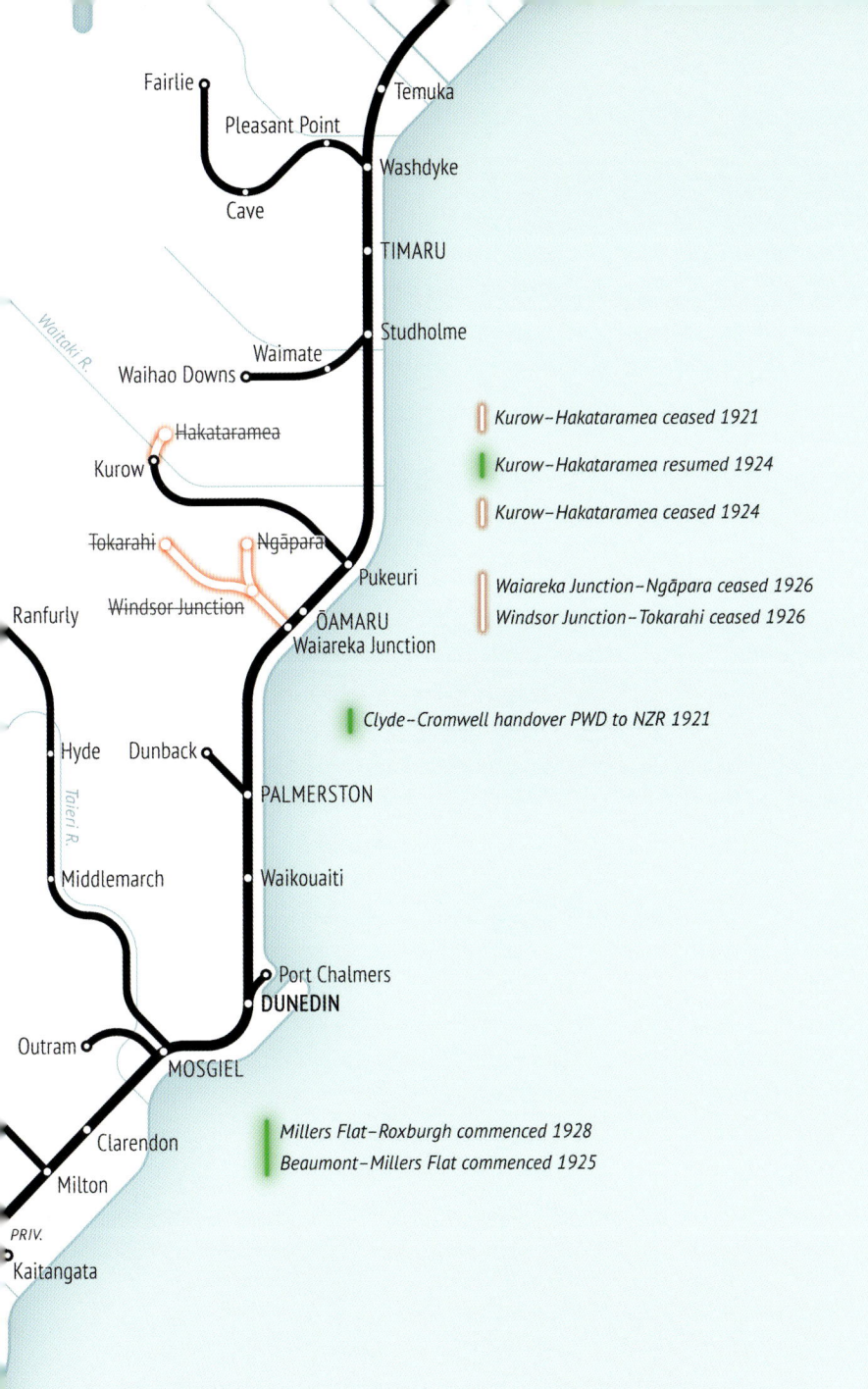

Fairlie

Pleasant Point

Cave

Temuka

Washdyke

TIMARU

Studholme

Waimate

Waihao Downs

Hakataramea

Kurow

Tokarahi

Ngāpara

Windsor Junction

Pukeuri

Ranfurly

ŌAMARU

Waiareka Junction

Hyde

Dunback

PALMERSTON

Middlemarch

Waikouaiti

Port Chalmers

DUNEDIN

Outram

MOSGIEL

Clarendon

Milton

PRIV.

Kaitangata

Kurow–Hakataramea ceased 1921

Kurow–Hakataramea resumed 1924

Kurow–Hakataramea ceased 1924

Waiareka Junction–Ngāpara ceased 1926
Windsor Junction–Tokarahi ceased 1926

Clyde–Cromwell handover PWD to NZR 1921

Millers Flat–Roxburgh commenced 1928
Beaumont–Millers Flat commenced 1925

Lower South Island
1920–1928

The *Otago Daily Times* on 9 December 1926 contained a remarkable announcement: bus services would replace passenger accommodation on trains in North Otago for travellers between Ōamaru and the settlements of Ngāpara and Tokarahi. Ōamaru sits on the Main South Line between Christchurch and Dunedin, and a branch railway once ran inland from Waiareka Junction, today on Ōamaru's western fringe. At the hamlet of Windsor this branch split to serve two termini: one line ran to Ngāpara and opened in 1877, and a fork to Tokarahi followed a decade later. Passengers were not plentiful in this lightly populated district – no town on either line had a population of even 500 – and the trains were slow: it took at least 70 minutes to travel between Ōamaru and Windsor, a distance of some 20 kilometres. Trains to Ngāpara needed only another 22 minutes to reach their destination, but those to Tokarahi spent an hour trundling along a circuitous route.[1]

Motorised road transport emerged as a serious competitor to rail in the 1920s, and passenger trains to small rural settlements struggled to survive. Few services were more vulnerable than those to Ngāpara and Tokarahi. NZR dabbled in operating buses – 'road motors' in the terminology of the day – from an early date: one introduced in 1907 from Culverden railway station to the spa town of Hanmer Springs in North Canterbury ran until 1917.[2] But the foray into road transport in North Otago was different: instead of allowing passengers to reach destinations beyond the railway network, buses actually *replaced* trains. Ngāpara and Tokarahi retained their goods trains, which now had more time to shunt on a looser schedule, but NZR acquired a local bus operator and began to convey passengers to Ōamaru by road.

NZR also acquired bus companies in Hawke's Bay in November 1926, which allowed it to run fewer local trains between Hastings and Napier, and during late 1927 and early 1928 it purchased all bus services between Wellington and the Hutt Valley.[3]

This was the dawn of the NZR Road Services, and it grew rapidly: the first bus manager was appointed on 30 May 1928. For some affected railways it was sunset: the line to Tokarahi closed to all traffic from 14 July 1930.[4] Freight trains endured to Ngāpara until 1959, but today there is no public transport – rail or road – to any communities on the former branches.

The retreat of rail from the countryside would have startled any reasonable observer in 1920. New Zealanders assumed the government would continue to authorise and construct rural branch lines, as successive ministries had since the 1870s, and they took it for granted that general-purpose railways accommodated passengers. A few lines had closed or had no passenger service, as described in Tables 1 and 2 on pages 40 and 41, but these examples were rooted in local circumstances and set no precedent. As New Zealand recovered from the effects of World War I and the 1918 influenza pandemic, politicians and senior officials at the PWD and NZR looked to push on with railway construction projects that had been delayed or deferred since 1914.

William Massey's Reform Party had governed since 1912, and when Gordon Coates became Minister of Public Works in April 1920, he brought to the position renewed energy and purpose. Coates was a rising star in Parliament and had served with distinction during World War I. He took the public works role from 80-year-old William Fraser, who had not pursued any clear national plan and was out of touch with technological advances.[5] Farmers and rural dwellers provided much of Reform's core support, and Coates prioritised railways for regions with poor transport. He handled multiple responsibilities well – his other titles included postmaster-general and minister of Native affairs – and in June 1923 he gained the railways portfolio in recognition of his interest in rail transport.

Massey died in May 1925, and Reform chose Coates as his successor. A year into the prime ministership Coates relinquished public works to his capable friend Kenneth Williams but retained railways – and, because of his fluent reo Māori, Native affairs – until Reform lost government at the end of 1928.[6] Under his stewardship, unfinished trunk routes crept closer to completion, though some did not take the shape originally planned for them.

Two visitors to New Zealand also influenced railway policy, albeit less than they might have hoped. Sam Fay and Vincent Raven, both senior British railwaymen, visited Australia in 1924 to lead a royal commission on railways in New South Wales. Coates invited them across the Tasman to do similar work in New Zealand. They obliged with a lengthy report compiled from personal observations and extensive inquiry. One of their most significant suggestions was to change how NZR was controlled. For most of its history, a general manager had answered directly to the minister of railways. The Fay–Raven report recommended that a board of management administer NZR, to provide greater independence from political instruction.[7] This new Railway Board came into being on 16 February 1925. It tempered, but did not extinguish, the expansionist spirit that had guided the network's size and scope.

Coates and NZR did not accept all of the Fay–Raven recommendations, however. The report advised against surrendering passenger services to road competition and proposed methods to regain lost patronage. Instead, the most marginal rural services began to disappear. Some reductions in service were necessary, but these created precedents that in subsequent decades would erode passenger rail, particularly with respect to road competition. Ngāpara and Tokarahi were but two of a handful of cancellations that signalled the beginning of the retreat of passenger rail in New Zealand.

1920–28: GRAND VISIONS REALISED INCOMPLETELY

Coates and the Reform government pursued a policy of regional rail expansion: they intended to finish projects that had been slowed or suspended because of labour and material shortages during the war, and they considered additions to the network. New lines fell into two categories: regional main lines whose construction had been forecast as early as 1870, and the last phase of general-purpose branch railways to lightly populated rural areas. Many lines in both categories were developmental, built not to meet immediate traffic needs but to expand Pākehā settlement and promote economic growth, including the absorption of local Māori industries into the national economy. Coates preferred to focus on the main lines, a factor that shaped some decisions to pursue or abandon projects, but when it was politically expedient he bent to parochial demands.[8]

Railway openings in Northland bookend this period neatly, although the original plans and the final results were quite different. The

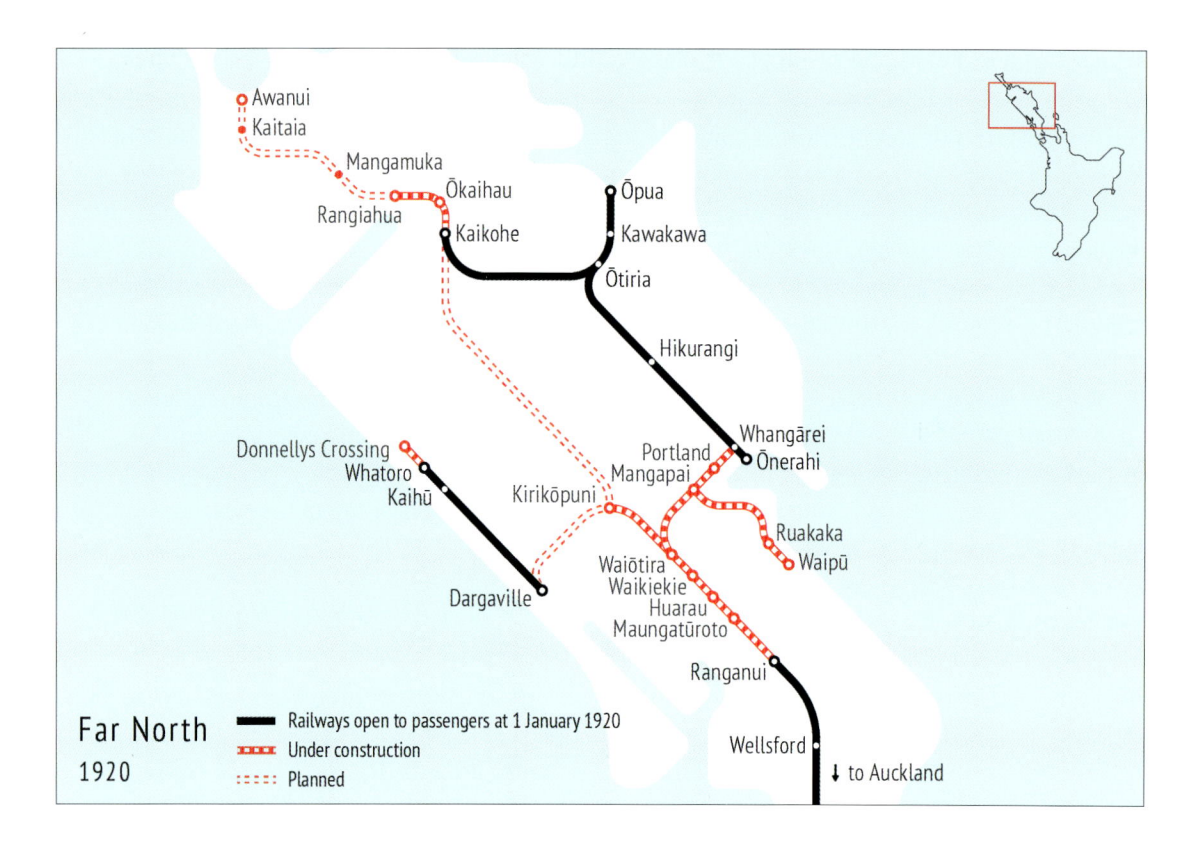

Far North 1920

━━━ Railways open to passengers at 1 January 1920
▪▪▪▪ Under construction
∷∷∷∷ Planned

North Island's first railway had opened in the Bay of Islands in 1868: a private wooden-railed tramway from Kawakawa to a nearby wharf, which the owners upgraded to a conventional railway in 1871 before selling it to the government five years later.

Construction of a line between Auckland and the Far North began from multiple points during the 1870s. This proceeded slowly and with poor co-ordination. The plan was to build the North Auckland Line (or North Auckland Main Trunk Railway) up the middle of the Northland Peninsula to the headwaters of the Hokianga Harbour, then either through or around the Maungataniwha Range to Kaitaia with a terminus in Awanui. Whangārei was to sit on a branch, with a sub-branch to Waipū; another branch would link Dargaville's isolated

Kaihū Valley Railway to the national network. But by 1920 a railway connected Whangārei with Kaikohe and the Bay of Islands, and work on the 'branch' from Waiōtira to Whangārei proceeded ahead of the 'main line'. In the end, the branch became the main.

NZR took over the first section of the so-called Whangārei Branch on 3 April 1920: it diverged from a railway to Ōnerahi, at the time the main port of Whangārei, and ran south to Portland. Two days earlier NZR had begun operating the newest section of the main line from Auckland, moving the railhead north from Ranganui to Huarau.[9] As the PWD worked to fill the gap between Huarau and Portland, it ran some passenger services itself. Trains began in early 1921, primarily for schoolchildren, between Waikiekie and Waiōtira, two settlements about as inland as it is possible to get in Northland.[10] One service a month continued to Portland so locals could visit Whangārei. Women and children rode wagons sheltered with tarpaulins while men sat in the open air, and passengers had to sign a waiver absolving the PWD of liability for injury or death. One aggrieved fellow, after enduring a 'blinding gale' in June, suggested that racehorses travelled in greater comfort.[11]

A passenger service between Auckland and Whangārei began in time for the holidays on 21 December 1922. Passengers had to switch between PWD and NZR trains, and until 19 February 1923 there was a gap of about 800 metres north of Huarau where motor vehicles shuttled passengers between trains and a five-horse team handled luggage and parcels.[12] From 1 September passengers enjoyed a single-seat ride as NZR began operating the whole journey. Huarau–Portland was, however, not yet a first-class line and the PWD had much to do, stabilising cuttings and embankments, finishing fences and yards and fixing damage caused by wet weather. NZR finally took ownership on 29 November 1925.[13]

Plans to extend the Kaikohe railway to Kaitaia faltered. Work proceeded slowly on the first stage to Ōkaihau during World War I, and in August 1918 the PWD began the next stage to Rangiahua, near the Hokianga Harbour. Trains began operating to Ōkaihau in October 1923 but that was as far as they got. A report in 1921 advised against an expensive crossing of the Maungataniwha Range to Kaitaia and favoured only a short extension past Rangiahua to Mangamuka as a hub for the Far North. Unstable soils beyond Ōkaihau made construction difficult and the PWD suspended work between 1921 and 1924, at which point

the completion of construction elsewhere in Northland freed up labourers and enabled work to continue.[14] The government was not yet ready to quash local ambition for a railway to the Hokianga, but it soon would be.

Construction continued on the original plan of a direct line north from Waiōtira to Kirikōpuni, but this project sank in importance once the 'branch' via Whangārei connected Auckland to Kaikohe. Officials anticipated that when the Kirikōpuni section opened, they would not push on to Kaikohe immediately but rather would use Kirikōpuni as a long-term terminus – it sat on the Wairoa River near its navigable limit, and multiple new roads converged on the settlement.[15] The eventual opening of a line to Kirikōpuni in May 1928, therefore, was hailed as another step in 'opening up the north'.[16] Kirikōpuni was home to just 35 people, but the railway facilities were significant and Prime Minister Coates officiated at the opening ceremony. The line ran around the hamlet in a balloon loop so trains could turn and have better access to a butter factory.[17] With this terminus established, attention turned to the branch to Dargaville and the line north of Ōkaihau. No plans were made in the 1920s to begin construction from Kirikōpuni to Kaikohe – and they never were.

Northland was not the only region with a grand vision taking shape haphazardly: the PWD was building an East Coast Main Trunk to connect railways at Waihī and Napier via Tauranga, Gisborne and Wairoa. At the start of the 1920s NZR operated an isolated section from Gisborne north to Moutohorā, while the PWD offered transport on two lines: a short one near Gisborne to Ngātapa and an increasingly large network east from Mount Maunganui. PWD trains ran to Ngātapa from 1915 in the

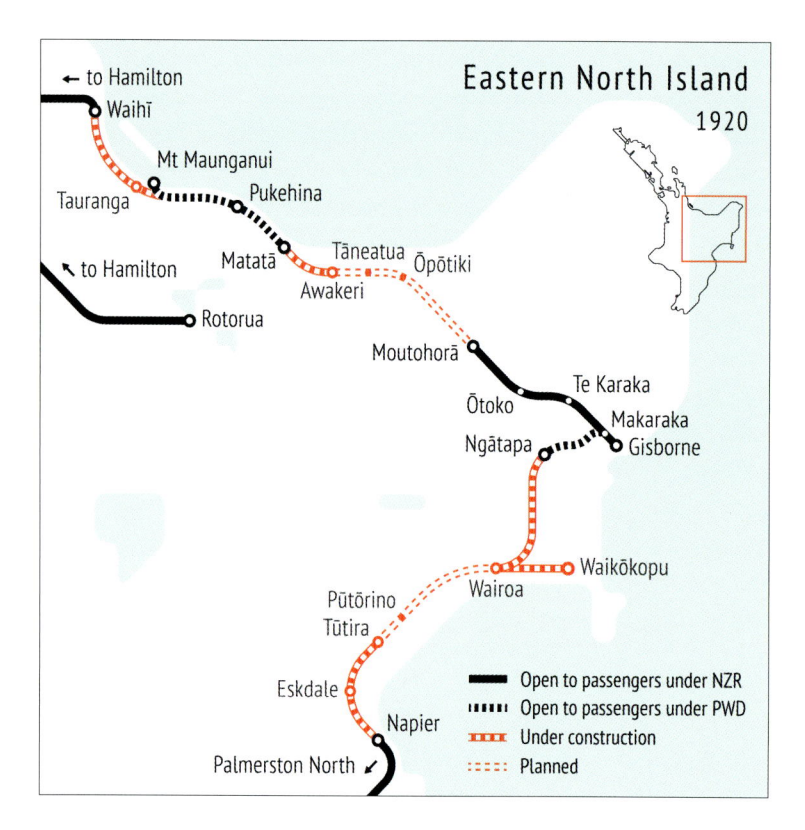

The PWD constructed a few kilometres of the line beyond Ngātapa before the inland route to Wairoa was abandoned; likewise, it performed some work north from Wairoa towards Frasertown. The Waikōkopu Branch eventually became part of the coastal main line.

expectation that this would be the first stage of the trunk line to Napier; without this purpose the line would never have been built, as the local population was tiny.[18] It came under NZR control in December 1924 and the Gisborne stationmaster-in-charge attested that the PWD 'only ran regular trains on Saturdays when they carried an average of about 20 passengers'. NZR tried to improve the local offering with three trains a week.[19] By this time, however, the PWD had serious doubts about the planned route via Ngātapa and construction stalled. Progress was little better at the Napier end. NZR began services to Eskdale in July 1923 but no further section northwards opened that decade.[20] For the time being, Gisborne remained New Zealand's most remote urban centre, dependent on coastal shipping.

Work on the East Coast Main Trunk was more rapid in the Bay of Plenty. From 1913 the PWD operated a regular service from Mount Maunganui wharf opposite Tauranga, initially to Te Puke and by 1919 as far as Matatā, and work progressed on bridging Tauranga Harbour. The section from Mount Maunganui to Te Maunga station, roughly where Baypark Stadium is

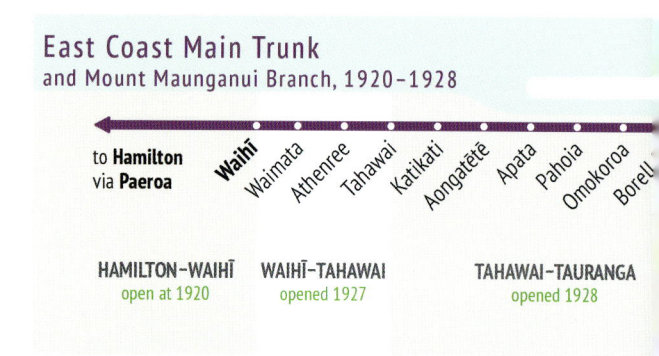

today, was always envisaged as a branch, and in March 1920 the first trains ran from Te Maunga to Matapihi at the eastern end of the harbour bridge.[21] It is unclear whether there was a regular passenger service to Matapihi before the bridge opened in June 1924, when trains began running from Tauranga to the eastern Bay of Plenty. The PWD maintained services with a fleet of 226 goods wagons and four passenger carriages.[22] From Matatā the line went inland to obtain an easier crossing of the Whakatāne River at Tāneatua. This demonstrates the intent to push on to Ōpōtiki and Gisborne but, as in the Far North, difficult geography stymied further plans. Trains began running to Tāneatua in September 1925 and a permanent station opened on 1 February 1926.[23] Northland had been fortunate that the 'branch' to Whangārei was built ahead of a proposed main line through the interior; the eastern Bay of Plenty could only rue that the main line did not enter the largest potential source of traffic, Whakatāne.

It was a momentous occasion for the region when NZR took control of the railway to Tauranga and Tāneatua. NZR trains first ran beyond Waihī through the Athenree Gorge to Tahawai in May 1927; with the joining of Tahawai to Tauranga the following March, NZR took responsibility for the Bay's coastal railway

after 15 years of PWD operation.[24] The *Auckland Star* celebrated the railway to Tauranga as a signal accomplishment for biracial relations. 'Maoris and Pakehas Unite' proclaimed the headline of an article that described the lavish opening ceremony and the 'fine community spirit which exists among the Maoris and Europeans who gathered in thousands from scores of miles around'. The author compared the event with 'the clash and chivalry of arms' in the Battle of Gate Pā of April 1864, memories of which were now 'mellowed by time and experience'.[25]

Biracial relations in Tauranga had a long way to go, however: in the following decade Māori women were excluded from some public toilets in the town.[26] And it would be many years before Pākehā began to acknowledge that railways, although conferring many benefits, also marginalised Māori communities throughout New Zealand. Rampant land acquisition, the purchases sometimes dubious and conducted with brazen disregard for prior agreements or promises about land and resource use, destroyed traditional lifeways. Expediency often trumped basic ethics: if railway construction required ballast, nearby stone was quarried even if Māori owners had not been informed, let alone given consent.[27] But even as iwi across

Mount Maunganui

Te Puna · Ōtūmoetai · **Tauranga** · Strand · Matapihi · **Te Maunga** · Kairua · Papamoa · **Te Puke** · Rangiuru · Paengaroa · Maniatutu · Pongakawa · Pukehina · Ōhinepanea · Ōtamarākau · Hauone · Pikowai · Matatā · Awakaponga · Otakiri · Edgecumbe · Awakeri · Whakatāne West · Pekatahi · **Tāneatua**

TAURANGA–TE MAUNGA
opened 1924 under PWD
handover to NZR 1928

MOUNT MAUNGANUI–TE MAUNGA
open at 1920 under PWD
regular passenger services
cancelled 1928

TE MAUNGA–MATATĀ
open at 1920 under PWD
handover to NZR 1928

MATATĀ–AWAKERI
opened 1923 under PWD
handover to NZR 1928

AWAKERI–TĀNEATUA
opened 1925 under PWD
handover to NZR 1928

New Zealand felt the sting of dispossession, many Māori believed that a local railway would bring economic gains and make travel easier. In 1928 the East Coast Main Trunk represented optimism and hope: it was a tool to bring people together and grow collective wealth.

The opening to Tauranga meant that passenger trains ran all the way from Auckland to Tāneatua. The PWD continued to operate the portion east of Tauranga until NZR's timetable commenced in June, a month before it took possession.[28] The PWD also retained the Mount Maunganui Branch and its passenger services ended; NZR excursions for Mount Maunganui terminated in Tauranga, where holidaymakers caught boats across the harbour. Complaints about this finally persuaded the minister of railways in May 1929 to let these trains run to the Mount.[29] Excursions continued through the 1930s but the line slid into disuse, and in 1942 the rails were lifted and relaid to a nearby Royal New Zealand Air Force base – now Tauranga Airport – and the station was demolished. One local lamented the failure of the town's elected officials to retain 'this most valuable asset'.[30] The line to the air force base became derelict after World War II, and when Mount Maunganui was chosen as the export harbour for forest products from Kawerau, a new line was built. This opened in March 1955 and came under NZR's control two years later.[31] No regular passenger service has ever used the current branch to the Mount.

Railway projects in the South Island also deviated from the original plans. The Otago Central Railway was pushing deeper into Otago's interior, and the PWD began carrying passengers on a temporary line from Clyde to Cromwell through Cromwell Gorge in late 1917 while it completed the permanent railway and Cromwell station. Travel was basic: until the

PWD added a proper carriage to its daily works train in January 1918, passengers sat on planks fitted to goods wagons. Construction difficulties delayed the handover to NZR until July 1921, and the first trains took 50 minutes through the rocky gorge – a far cry from today's 15-minute drive.[32]

Cromwell was not intended as the final terminus. Back in 1870 Vogel had envisioned a line through Kawarau Gorge to Arrowtown and Queenstown, and other plans provided for a railway to Wānaka, Hāwea, and even through the Haast Pass to Westland. Instead, a large rock at the far end of Cromwell station marked the end of the Otago Central Railway. Had railway officials and politicians possessed a crystal ball to foresee the value to tourism today of a line to Queenstown or the West Coast, they may have found a way around this obstacle.

Another proposal from Vogel's projected network of 1870 progressed during the 1920s. Nelson had a local horse-drawn railway as early as 1862, and the region sought connection with the rest of the island. The plan, which might now seem counterintuitive, was to link Nelson to Canterbury via the West Coast. During the provincial era of 1853–76, the border between Nelson and Canterbury provinces followed the Grey River, which flows to Greymouth on the West Coast. What we know today as Buller and the northern portion of the Grey District was 'Nelson South-West', more in touch with Nelson city and eastern Australia than with Canterbury. It made sense to build a line south from Nelson to Greymouth and then across to Canterbury. In 1886 the Midland Railway Company was formed to build this line, which would connect NZR's short, isolated railways in Nelson and Westland with the main network at Springfield in Canterbury. Misled by unrealistic cost estimates

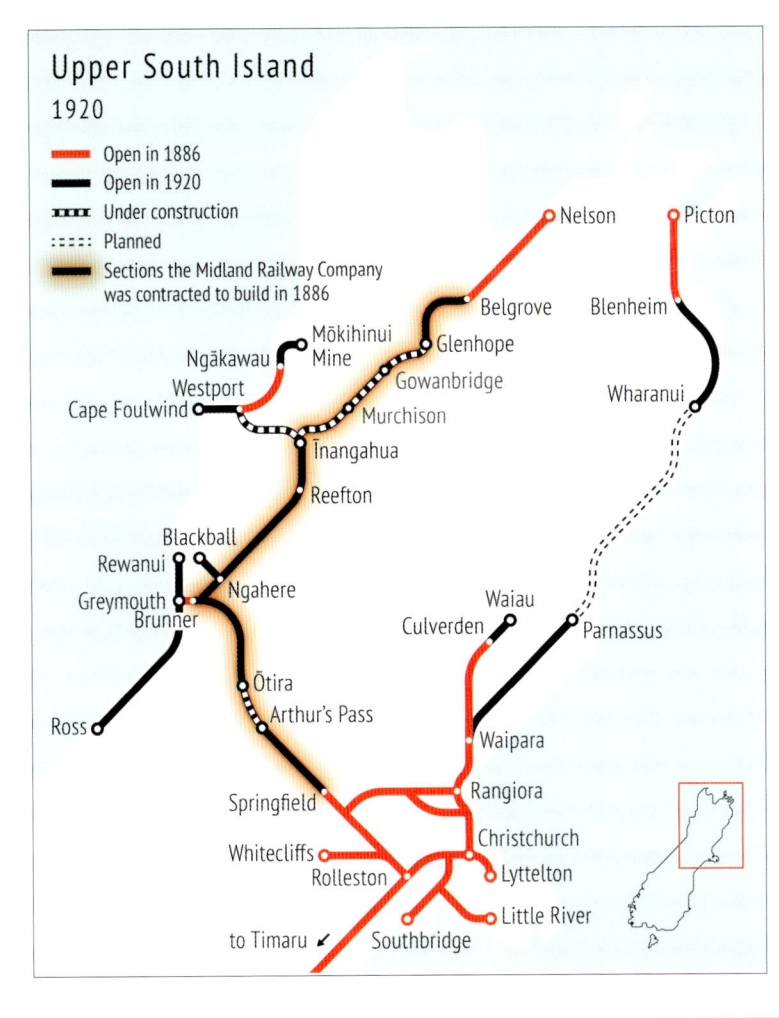

Upper South Island
1920

▬▬▬ Open in 1886
▬▬▬ Open in 1920
шшш Under construction
::::: Planned
▬▬▬ Sections the Midland Railway Company
was contracted to build in 1886

Nelson · Picton
Belgrove · Blenheim
Mōkihinui Mine · Glenhope
Ngākawau
Westport · Gowanbridge
Cape Foulwind · Murchison · Wharanui
Īnangahua
Reefton
Blackball
Rewanui
Greymouth · Ngahere · Waiau
Brunner · Culverden · Parnassus
Ōtira
Arthur's Pass · Waipara
Ross
Springfield · Rangiora
Whitecliffs · Christchurch
Rolleston · Lyttelton
to Timaru · Southbridge · Little River

from local railway advocates, the under-capitalised company struggled, and the government took possession in 1895.[33]

By 1920 the east–west link was almost complete save for the Ōtira Tunnel, a steep 8.5-kilometre passage under the Southern Alps from Arthur's Pass to Ōtira. This globally significant feat of engineering opened on 4 August 1923 and transformed the social and economic relationship between Canterbury and the West Coast. Once a slow and dangerous stagecoach ride, the trans-alpine journey could now be made in comfort in just a few hours. NZR operated the tunnel as an integral part of its system from the outset, although the

Above: The contract for the Midland Railway Company did not explicitly include a connection from Westport to Īnangahua but many people expected this would be built as a matter of course.

Right: Much too long for steam locomotives, the Ōtira Tunnel was New Zealand's first electrified railway. Pictured are two E⁰ class locomotives with a passenger train, soon after the tunnel opened. Tranz Rail removed electrification in 1997 and a large fan now extracts diesel locomotive fumes.

A.P. Godber, ATL APG-0324-1/2-G

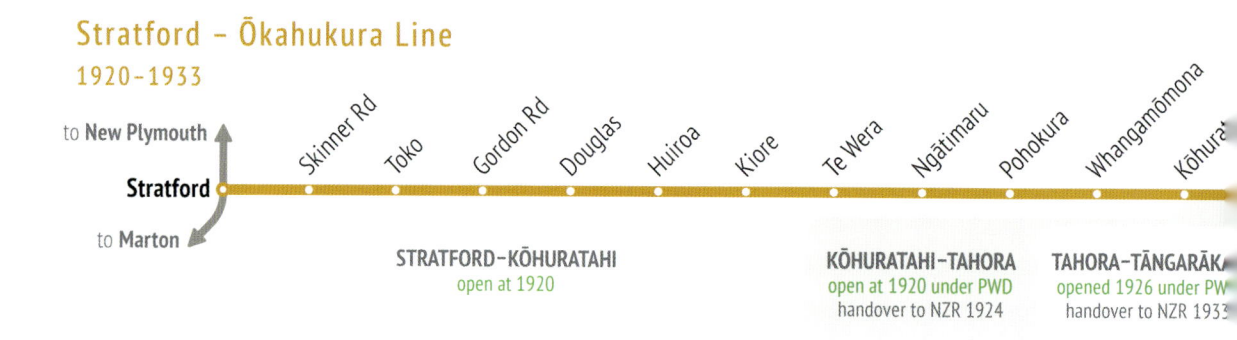

Stratford – Ōkahukura Line
1920–1933

to New Plymouth
Stratford
to Marton

Skinner Rd   Toko   Gordon Rd   Douglas   Huiroa   Kiore   Te Wera   Ngātimaru   Pohokura   Whangamōmona   Kōhura

STRATFORD–KŌHURATAHI
open at 1920

KŌHURATAHI–TAHORA
open at 1920 under PWD
handover to NZR 1924

TAHORA–TĀNGARĀKA
opened 1926 under PW
handover to NZR 193

PWD did not officially transfer ownership until May 1924.[34]

Meanwhile, work continued on the link from the West Coast to Nelson. At the southern end, trains from Greymouth ran through Reefton as far as Īnangahua in the Buller Gorge, the terminus since 1914. From the Nelson end, the railway scrambled from one valley to another to the village of Glenhope, and construction to an even smaller locality, Kawatiri, had been in hand since 1912. The line to Kawatiri finally opened in 1926 with the modest timetable of a with-car goods twice a week, an extension of a more frequent mixed service to Glenhope. Work continued towards Murchison and the Buller Gorge, and there was even discussion in 1929 about increasing the frequency of the Kawatiri train to thrice weekly and opening the next section of the line to Gowanbridge, some 6 kilometres south. These were heady days, when it appeared Nelson's railway might finally connect with the rest of the network.[35]

Some grand plans, at least, came to fruition in their intended form. In the North Island the PWD worked steadily throughout the 1920s to construct a railway from Stratford through the narrow river valleys of Taranaki's rugged interior, to connect with the North Island Main Trunk at Ōkahukura, near Taumarunui.

This would save people and goods travelling between Auckland and New Plymouth at least seven hours compared to the existing route via Marton, and would create a convenient bypass if the central part of the Main Trunk were ever blocked. Neither of these reasons, however, was enough to justify construction. In truth this railway had a strong developmental purpose: to increase Pākehā settlement of an isolated region and improve the rural economy. The PWD concentrated most effort on constructing the western section, so that in 1920 trains ran 68 kilometres from Stratford to Kōhuratahi under NZR control and another eight to Tahora under the PWD, while not a single kilometre was operational at the eastern end. This changed on 23 May 1922 with the inauguration of PWD services between Ōkahukura and Mātīere.

Lavish opening ceremonies indicate how important railways were to their communities, and indeed all the pomp of a typical NZR opening accompanied the first train to Mātīere, even though it was a PWD service. The train carried over 400 passengers to join delighted residents. Gordon Coates performed the ceremony in the company of two local members of Parliament, William Jennings and Robert Smith. Jennings told the crowd 'he had been battling for the line for 30 years, and it was the

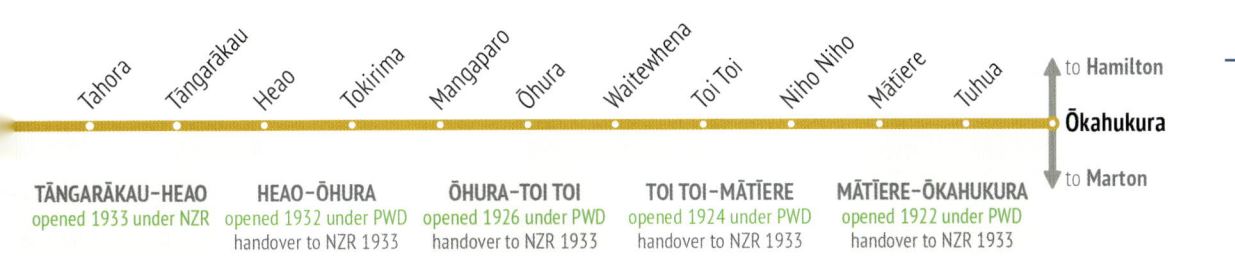

						to Hamilton
Tahora — Tāngarākau — Heao — Tokirima — Mangaparo — Ōhura — Waitewhena — Toi Toi — Niho Niho — Mātīere — Tuhua — **Ōkahukura** — to Marton

TĀNGARĀKAU–HEAO
opened 1933 under NZR

HEAO–ŌHURA
opened 1932 under PWD
handover to NZR 1933

ŌHURA–TOI TOI
opened 1926 under PWD
handover to NZR 1933

TOI TOI–MĀTĪERE
opened 1924 under PWD
handover to NZR 1933

MĀTĪERE–ŌKAHUKURA
opened 1922 under PWD
handover to NZR 1933

happiest day of his life to see it finished as far as Matiere at last'.[36] This may seem an excess of emotion, but for Jennings the occasion brought joy after the recent death of his wife and the loss of two sons in World War I – though his surviving children might have been a little put out to come second to a railway. Jennings did not live to see the full railway completed: he died the following February, aged 69.[37]

Had Jennings lived longer he would have appreciated the steady succession of openings. In June 1924 the PWD introduced a regular timetable for passengers beyond Mātīere to Toi Toi, a distance of 10 kilometres.[38] Ōhura, one of the main towns in the area, was another 7 kilometres away, and on December 1926 its first train burst through a ribbon in front of a crowd estimated to comprise most of the local population. At the controls of the locomotive was Kenneth Williams, the new Minister of Public Works. One resident proudly described the train's arrival as 'the most important event in the history of the district'.[39]

There was also progress at the western end of the line. NZR took over Kōhuratahi to Tahora in November 1924, ending five years of PWD mixed trains.[40] Tahora sat almost exactly halfway to Ōkahukura but some of the most difficult terrain, such as the Tāngarākau Gorge, remained

ahead. The PWD began operating a train from Tahora to its work camp at Tāngarākau twice weekly in April 1926 on what at first was a very rudimentary line; this was more permanent by 1928, and trains then ran thrice weekly.[41] The full route was finally opened in 1933. Unlike in other regions, the original vision had not wavered; it helped that there were no rival routes or branches to create distractions.

The Stratford–Ōkahukura Line was, at heart, a developmental railway from an era that was fading, and a project in the Hutt Valley suggested the future. The main line to the Wairarapa followed the western bank of the Hutt River, and in May 1927 a new line opened from Petone to Waterloo on the eastern side of the valley. It was built for four main reasons. First, NZR had outgrown its Petone workshops and had selected a new site at Gracefield. Second, the Coates government had endorsed construction of new suburbs in Lower Hutt with low-cost accommodation for workers, to alleviate a housing shortage in Wellington. The workshops would be one of the main employers; the new line would carry other residents to work in the city. Third, land in Gracefield and Seaview not used for the railway workshops was earmarked for industrial use, which required railway access. And finally, the new line was not simply intended to be a branch: NZR planned for it to become the main line to Upper Hutt, and increasing traffic would eventually necessitate duplication of the single-track Wairarapa Line. Railway engineers considered it easier to build a new line rather than duplicate the existing one, and more effective to locate it on the eastern side of the Hutt River among the growing suburbs.[42]

This marked a watershed. From Northland to Central Otago, Taranaki to Nelson, the justification for main lines had relied on a developmental rationale and a colonial-era drive to settle Pākehā as widely as possible. New railways, however, needed different justifications. They were no longer to be built ahead of economic activity with vague hopes that growth would follow; they were components of defined plans. It was not enough to simply fill gaps on a map.

1920–28: THE END OF THE RURAL BRANCH LINE

If the spirit of main-line expansion was dampened in the 1920s, that of branch-line expansion was extinguished fully. From the 1870s almost every main line had branches to nearby towns and districts. Even if these branches did not return direct profits, they were considered essential to the success of main lines, as small capillaries that in combination produced the traffic necessary for the whole network's survival. Passengers became familiar with guards calling out the junction stations where mixed trains waited for country passengers to disembark expresses and travel to their home town. The mixed trains were slow, but Crawford Somerset found this had its perks when he studied the community of Oxford in North Canterbury: the local mixed was a 'club

on wheels', a social space where rural residents met, did business, gossiped and relaxed.[43]

The Fay–Raven report accepted that in a country such as New Zealand that lacked a 'fully developed' network, working losses on branch lines were not only inevitable but acceptable – after all, the state earned greater taxation through, for example, the increased value of lineside properties.[44] The commissioners did not suggest any alteration of the network's scope. Rather, they believed road competition had made gains as a result of defects in management, timetabling and promotion.[45] On this topic, their report was out of date the moment it was written: proposals for new railways were stalling, and NZR had already begun contemplating new ways of operating.

This period was the start of the evolution of New Zealand's railways from a general carrier with many small customers to a bulk carrier, and two branches pointed to a future where a large industrial client justified new construction. Both carried mainly coal and the men who mined it. One, in the Waikato, ran west from Huntly: it opened as far as Pukemiro in December 1915 and Glen Afton in June 1924.[46]

The other, in western Southland, stands out as one of New Zealand's more unusual lines. It was neither built by the PWD nor operated by NZR but was the project of a single-purpose local authority: the Ōhai Railway Board (ŌRB). NZR had operated a branch to Wairio since 1882, and a handful of short-lived, poorly built private lines fanned from the terminus to local mines. To give a more satisfactory service, locals endorsed the formation of the ŌRB and empowered it to construct with higher standards. The board began a passenger service between Wairio and Ōhai in 1924 with a rudimentary and unreliable petrol railcar nicknamed 'the piecart', before acquiring a high-quality carriage manufactured in Invercargill in 1929.[47] Miners and schoolchildren were the main clientele, and travellers could connect at Wairio with NZR trains for Invercargill.

In a sign of the times, however, regular passenger trains did not run on a third coal railway opened in the early 1920s. Services began on the Rapahoe Branch north of Greymouth in 1923. Although the PWD outfitted the terminus with passenger facilities, NZR operated only coal trains.[48]

Most rural branches that opened in the 1920s were the last gasp of the old era and had been in the works for some years. A royal commission as far back as 1880 had endorsed a branch to Waiuku, on the southern reaches of Manukau Harbour, but the ease of waterborne travel to Auckland meant construction did not happen for decades.[49] Waiuku benefited from the success of its local MP, William Massey, who, soon after becoming prime minister in 1912, passed a bill authorising the railway. Still, the town's wait was not over. Even though goods trains began running as far as Patumāhoe in December 1917, passenger trains did not come to Waiuku until January 1922.[50] Similarly, in Northland, an isolated railway had been slowly extending up the Kaihū Valley from Dargaville since the 1880s and reached heavily timbered country at Donnellys Crossing in April 1923.[51] Future generations are fortunate no serious plans existed to push it further into the great kauri forest of Waipōua, or they might have been robbed of the singular privilege of standing in the presence of the giant kauri, Tāne Mahuta.

At the opposite end of the country, NZR began operating from Tūātapere to Ōrawia in November 1925, an extension that can only be described as optimistic. Tūātapere remained

the operational depot, so on the four days a week that trains ran from Ōrawia there were two services each way, despite low demand. The morning run from Ōrawia to Invercargill was formed by a train from Tūātapere to Ōrawia at 4.50am, and it is hard to imagine many people rode such an unsociably timed service.[52]

Perhaps the most remarkable of these Johnny-come-lately country railways, however, was that alongside the Clutha River Mata-Au to the stonefruit hub of Roxburgh. The first contracts for this railway had been let in 1873, when residents hoped it would become a main line to the Lakes District. It settled into a fairly satisfactory operation as a country branch from Milton to Lawrence, but local advocates sustained enough energy to persuade Parliament to keep authorising extensions. The PWD handed NZR a section from Beaumont to Millers Flat in December 1925, followed, at weary length, by the last stage to Roxburgh in April 1928.[53] This 95-kilometre line, the last general-purpose branch line opened in New Zealand, was built at an average pace of less than 2 kilometres per year, and at the time was the longest railway construction project in New Zealand, eclipsed only with the completion of the final section of the Main North Line from Christchurch to Picton in 1945.

The abbreviation of a construction project in Taranaki also showed that the writing was on the wall for branch lines. Railways across the plains south of Mt Taranaki had been a long time coming. A commission in 1912 proposed an extensive network comprising a coastal main line from New Plymouth around the mountain to Te Roti, near Eltham, plus two branches from Kāpuni: one to Manaia on the coast and another across the plains to Stratford. The PWD considered this excessive, and in 1914 confirmed

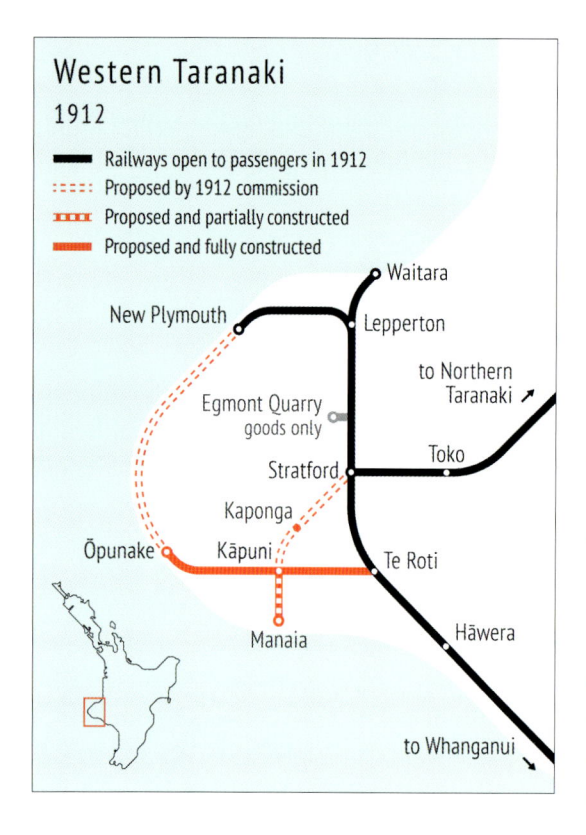

Western Taranaki

1912

━━━ Railways open to passengers in 1912
┄┄┄ Proposed by 1912 commission
▪▪▪▪ Proposed and partially constructed
▬▬▬ Proposed and fully constructed

Waitara
New Plymouth
Lepperton
to Northern Taranaki ↗
Egmont Quarry goods only
Stratford
Toko
Kaponga
Ōpunake   Kāpuni
Te Roti
Manaia
Hāwera
to Whanganui →

Built for nineteenth-century travel patterns, this was the North Island's last traditional country branch railway.

Ōpunake was fortunate to get its railway because projects elsewhere were cancelled entirely. Shortly after gaining power in 1912, Massey's government passed an act that authorised multiple railways, of which two were never built: an 18-kilometre line to Martinborough from Featherston on the Wairarapa Line, and a 34-kilometre line in Otago from Balclutha inland to Tuapeka Mouth.[58] Labour shortages during World War I delayed construction of both. A Clutha Valley Railway League pressed Tuapeka Mouth's case insistently, but officials turned against it: Richard McVilly, NZR's general manager, wrote in 1922 that the line had 'no justification'. The game was up in 1924 when the PWD's engineer-in-chief, Frederick William Furkert, concluded that it would be hopelessly unprofitable and recommended a road.[59] In the Wairarapa, a ceremony in Martinborough on 20 July 1914 accompanied the turning of the first sod, and a siding built during the war to serve Featherston's large military camp had the potential to become the start of the branch. But that was as far as things got: Martinborough residents disagreed about the route – some wanted it to run to Greytown instead of Featherston – and by 1925 even the town board conceded that private road operators met local needs.[60]

The debate about a railway to Waipū, a coastal farming community south of Whangārei, confirmed that the era of new rural passenger services was over. If the line from Waiōtira to Whangārei had been completed in the 1900s or 1910s instead of the 1920s, then the Waipū Branch might also have been built. Instead, work did not begin until March 1918, even though

its preference: a line west from Te Roti to Ōpunake, with a sub-branch to Manaia.[54] Even this did not come to pass. The PWD completed formation of the Manaia Branch but never laid rails into the town – only a short portion to a ballast pit ever became operational, between 1923 and 1926.[55] During June 1923 Coates met with Manaia businesspeople who indicated that they intended to continue to send local produce by road, thereby rendering the sub-branch uneconomic.[56] The government duly abandoned the project but pushed on with the Ōpunake line, and Coates – newly prime minister and with an election imminent – declared this open on 27 October 1925 even though the PWD had not finished work. Apart from special excursions, passenger trains did not operate until NZR took over the line on 12 July 1926.[57]

Parliament authorised construction in 1914. Most earthworks were complete in 1921 but Coates observed, 'Financial considerations may necessitate a modification of this programme.'[61] By 1923 it was moribund. 'Motor transport has almost effected a revolution,' proclaimed the *Northern Advocate*, a leading Northland newspaper, 'and experience has shown that branch railways are now unprofitable and inefficient.' Waipū had road connections to two stations on the North Auckland Line, and 'to go on with the railway is simply to fly in the face of all expert opinion.'[62] Locals met to consider a government offer of a bitumen road to follow the formation instead of a railway, and accepted it by the narrow margin of 144:123 – though supporters of a railway continued to press their claim into 1924.[63] Another edition of the *Northern Advocate* asserted, 'Branch railways for the most part are not held in favour nowadays.'[64]

The fact that no new general-purpose rural branch has since been approved anywhere in New Zealand suggests the *Advocate*'s editor was right. All subsequent lines have been trunk routes, or branches made to meet the specific needs of commuters, timber or steel.

1921: THE FIRST CUTS

It was one thing to abbreviate or cancel proposed railways, and quite another to call a halt to existing passenger services. Attrition began in 1921 at the obscure extremities of three modest South Island lines. Neither the officials at NZR who made these decisions, nor the locals aggrieved by them, realised that this was a harbinger of decades of cancellations.

One occurred at a windswept tip of the Buller region, the headland with one of New Zealand's most colourful placenames: Cape

ONE MORE PWD PASSENGER TRAIN?

One railway line that the PWD opened in the early 1920s does not appear to have had a regular passenger service. The PWD built an isolated railway east from Wairoa to a wharf at Waikōkopu, originally to be a branch of the Napier–Gisborne route but later incorporated into the main line. A limited goods service began in February 1923, and by 1925 the line regularly carried meat and other commodities.[65] The photo shows PWD officials giving Gordon Coates a tour of the line in April 1925. Locals anticipated a passenger service would commence soon after.[66] It appears, however, that the PWD never laid on an ordinary timetable for passengers; its annual reports refer only to goods services, and even the regularity of these slipped during the Depression.[67] Neither A.C. Bellamy nor Chris Wood, in their histories of the Napier–Gisborne railway, suggest the PWD operated regular passenger services.[68] Archival documents attest to occasional excursions, so clearly there was passenger rollingstock available,[69] but a passenger timetable did not begin until 1942, when NZR opened the entire Wairoa–Gisborne section.

Foulwind. The Westport Harbour Board began operating a railway in 1886 to Omau, at the cape, and extended it along exposed cliffs to Tauranga Bay in 1914. This extension was little used – in March 1920 only one train a week took passengers past Omau. The harbour board was nearly bankrupt, and legislation in 1920 transferred its operations to the Marine Department from 1 April 1921, with the exception of most of the railway. The Marine Department controlled the section from Omau to Tauranga Bay while NZR took over the rest. This meant passenger carriages stopped running past Omau. As the output of local industries slumped, NZR slashed the timetable on the rest of the line in September 1921. Trains ran on Saturdays only – but twice each way, echoing a harbour board practice that permitted cape residents to transact business in Westport and townspeople to visit the cape, a popular leisure destination.[70] When the wind was not foul, the locals boasted, it was the 'Scarborough of New Zealand' – a reference to the Yorkshire resort town.[71]

Westport's district traffic manager, P.L. Payne, identified a problem for Cape Foulwind trains that would soon affect railways throughout rural New Zealand. 'There is now a good motor road between Westport and Cape Foulwind,' he wrote. 'The distance is less than 8 miles [13km], a mere nothing for a motor, but a different thing when an engine has to be got in steam and three men provided to run a train.'[72] No train could run without a driver, fireman and guard, and steam locomotives do not start at the turn of a key – building a fire at the start of the day and cleaning at the end of duty are time-consuming. Payne could not justify a more frequent service when passengers were few and local goods output sometimes insufficient to

earn even £3 per train. In lightly populated areas with limited economic activity, road transport offered economies that no steam railway could match. If the line had been longer it might have tapped enough markets for a more regular service – people down the coast in Charleston had pressed for an extension – but a short line was vulnerable.

Two railways on the other side of the Southern Alps also illustrated this tendency and proved that cancellations were coming to more longstanding parts of the network. NZR had worked these two lines for almost 40 years. One was the farthest end of the Kurow Branch in North Otago; it crossed the Waitaki River to the South Canterbury locality of Hakataramea and had opened under private ownership in November 1881. NZR operated all trains and had acquired this line in 1885.[73] The 1.76-kilometre stub from Kurow across the Waitaki was a classic developmental railway, intended to open the Hakataramea Valley to closer settlement, but the area never boasted a large population.

The other was an extension of the Oxford Branch in North Canterbury which, when it opened in July 1884, established a link across the Waimakariri River to Sheffield on the Midland Line. It was part of a plan to construct a Canterbury Interior Main Line parallel with the Main South Line. The 1880 royal commission rubbished most of that idea but felt this portion could be useful.[74] It might have become an important shortcut from the West Coast to Marlborough and Wellington, had the necessary developments not been decades away: the Midland Line was not completed until 1923, the Main North Line followed even later in 1945, and it took until 1962 for NZR ferries to start plying Cook Strait.

Oxford Branch and Eyreton Branch

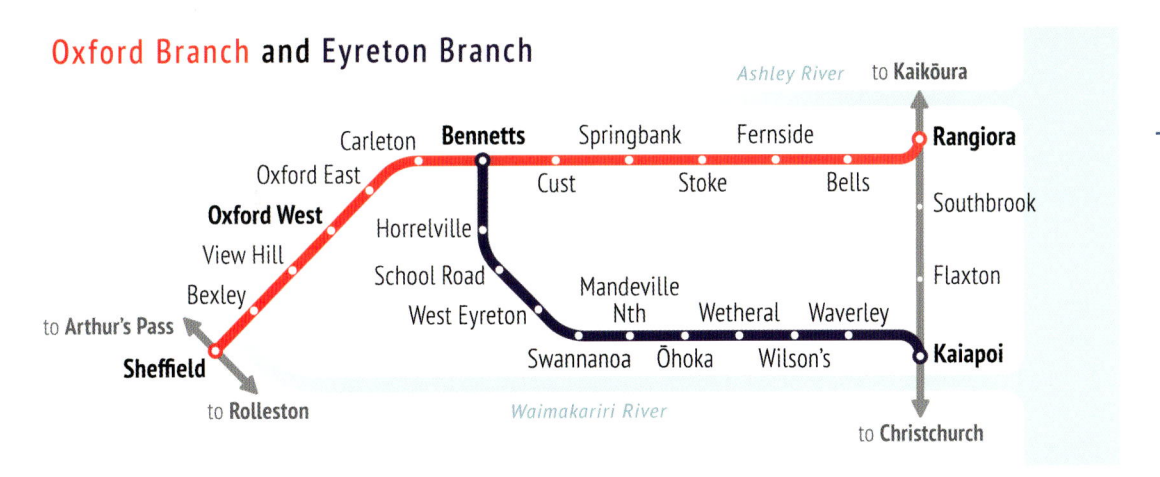

Neither line succeeded. Train services beyond Kurow had already been expendable: a temporary coal-saving timetable during a miners' strike in April 1917 suspended all trains to Hakataramea, prompting South Canterbury farmers to complain about the time lost travelling to Kurow to load freight.[75] In 1920 Hakataramea enjoyed a daily mixed to Ōamaru, but most of the loading came from Kurow and further down the line. In Canterbury, only two trains a week ran between Oxford West and Sheffield.[76] Both, therefore, fell victim when NZR introduced nationwide timetable modifications on 14 August 1921.[77] The changes in most places were reductions: trains ran less frequently, or specific services were suspended until summer. A weekly goods train from

Oxford West became the only service on the line to Sheffield, and it did not go all the way, leaving the grand Waimakariri bridge essentially unused, although the line remained available for excursion traffic. Farmers petitioned against the service reduction but focused on goods, and railway officials rejected their claims that a more frequent service would stimulate greater tonnages.[78] Further south, Hakataramea initially retained a twice-weekly mixed train in the August timetable, but traffic was minimal. The train from Ōamaru averaged three passengers to Hakataramea and none the other way. Hence, from 24 September 1921, Kurow–Hakataramea became goods only, shunted when required – that is, when at least five wagons of goods were in the offing.[79]

Kurow Branch and Waitaki Dam Branch

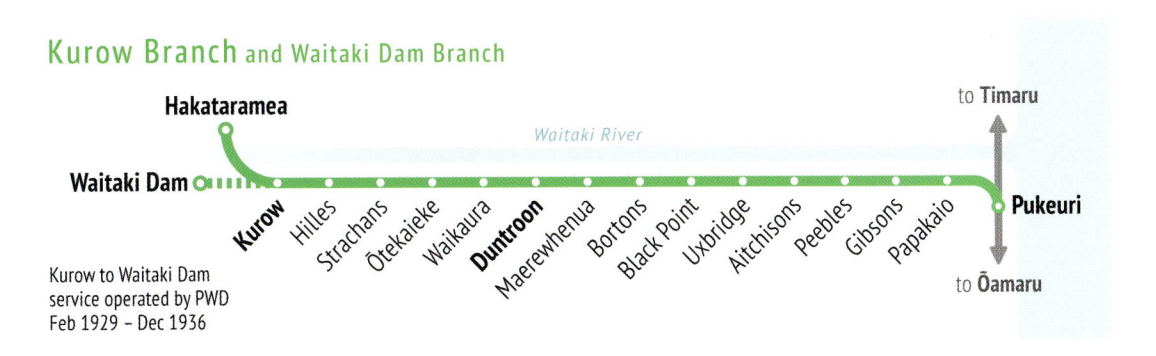

Kurow to Waitaki Dam service operated by PWD Feb 1929 – Dec 1936

Hakataramaea residents were quite unhappy, and their protests bore fruit: New Zealand's first resumption of a passenger service on a line where it had been cancelled. This, however, was almost an afterthought. Farmers wanted their regular goods trains back, and these ran mixed because it was easier – no need to remove the passenger carriage in Kurow. A three-month trial began on 13 May 1924 with trains every Tuesday and Friday morning and on Tuesday evening, the latter to facilitate travel between Hakataramea and the Ōamaru livestock market.[80] Gordon Coates found the trial's results 'most disappointing'. Goods loadings were poor and passengers almost non-existent: only one person ever rode the 6.50am mixed from Kurow to Hakataramea.[81] In fairness, this was a positioning move to form the 7.15am run to Ōamaru, but even the other trains rarely averaged more than one passenger a day from Hakataramea. The six people who boarded the morning train on Tuesday 22 July set a patronage record for the trial period – but the total absence of goods that morning means NZR did not recoup running costs.[82] It is odd that the trial ran through the winter months, the off-season for Hakataramea's main commodities of grain and livestock. H.P. West, the district traffic manager in Dunedin, recommended the trains cease at the end of the planned three months, but instead they ran for five months until Tuesday 14 October through what appears to be institutional inertia.[83] After that date the line beyond Kurow reverted to shunts when required until it closed entirely on 14 July 1930.[84] It shared the date of closure with the Oxford West–Sheffield line.

1926–28: THE BUSES ARE COMING

This chapter opened with buses replacing Ngāpara and Tokarahi mixed trains in 1926 and NZR making its first forays into suburban bus operation. The previous year, the Fay–Raven report had warned NZR against surrendering any market to road. It urged improvements in service quality, including the replacement of mixed trains with separate passenger and goods services. The commissioners found that passengers preferred rail to road if the offerings were of comparable quality, but many had switched to road because trains were slow and infrequent.[85] This finding has been replicated time and time again for a century.

One problem was that Fay and Raven found a department full of staff who believed they could not compete with road and did not see the point in trying. One was quoted as saying better train services were doomed because 'there are too many motor-cars'; others gave exorbitant – and incorrect – estimates for the cost of additional services. Staff who did desire improvements were 'disheartened by the absence of any determined attempt to meet the competition'.[86] The commission's findings did little to alter this; the same pessimistic talking points are repeated today as kernels of wisdom. The attitude of defeatism created its own reality.

Most rural services survived to the end of the 1920s but, from one end of the country to the other, NZR gave up passengers on the network's fringes. Not all of the services were viable – anticipated traffic had not materialised, or markets and demographics had changed – but some cancellations established precedents. One, the dismissive attitude to transporting schoolchildren, emerged in Whangārei. NZR had once sought school traffic, believing in the late 1890s that it would foster lifelong habits of railway travel. But the Education Department's subsidy did not always cover costs, and students were often unruly and fond of pranks and escapades – Neill Atkinson in *Trainland* gives one dramatic example of Te Puke High School boys in the 1920s who climbed over the roofs to the separate girls' carriage.[87] In Whangārei a railway ran to the port at Ōnerahi, but in 1927 most waterborne traffic, including steamships from Auckland, shifted to a new port closer to town. Schoolchildren were now the only regular travellers, and Ōnerahi lost both of its steam passenger services – ships and trains. From May 1927 the children rode buses to Whangārei.[88] The railway remained open for a few commodities still shipped from Ōnerahi, predominantly coal, but the old port could not compete and the last train ran in 1933. Admittedly the closure of this line was a sensible response to changing requirements, but officials do not appear to have considered retaining the school traffic – which, in coming decades, they abandoned on line after line.

Two rural passenger services disappeared in April 1928, each highlighting a trend in the rise of road transport. One, Glenham, exposed the effect private automobility had on all public transport; the other, Whitecliffs, revealed NZR's nascent preference for buses in rural areas and what passengers made of it.

Glenham is a small settlement in Southland, east of the Mataura River, that in 1890 became the terminal of a branch railway. The first section of the line opened in 1882 to link Wyndham, then easily the largest town in the area, with the Main South Line in Edendale across the Mataura. The extension from Wyndham to Glenham contained the second-most southern railway tunnel in New Zealand, one of the most southern in the world.[89] Passengers, however,

rode through it for fewer than four decades. Multiple trains shuttled between Edendale and Wyndham daily in 1927 but just one mixed continued to Glenham, and discussions were afoot to stop carrying passengers beyond Wyndham.[90]

This decision is an example of a justified cancellation: the railway had not induced population growth between Wyndham and Glenham, and since the emergence of the motorcar, average patronage had fallen to one passenger per train. Even a private road contractor did not consider Glenham profitable: he only served the area because of a contract to deliver evening newspapers from Invercargill. The Railway Board requested permission to cancel the passenger accommodation, remove depot facilities in Glenham, and operate a goods train three times a week; Coates approved this on 19 November 1927.[91] Local residents petitioned him to change his mind, but he did not.[92] Indeed, railway officials went further – the new timetable had only a twice-weekly goods service. Glenham trains carried passengers for the last time on Saturday 28 April 1928 and the line became officially goods only from the Monday.[93] Perhaps unsurprisingly, the token goods service did not last much longer. The line beyond Wyndham closed in July 1930.[94]

Although Glenham had no perceived demand for passenger services, either road or rail, similar alterations made in inland Canterbury were actually beneficial to the nascent NZR Road Services. R.S. Kent, the South Island's divisional superintendent, deliberated with national commercial manager Daniel Rodie about mixed trains between Christchurch and Springfield on the Midland Line. Their discussions included the branch from Darfield to Whitecliffs: it had a daily mixed plus a second service three days

WHEN A GOODS TRAIN IS NOT QUITE A GOODS TRAIN

Passenger rail to Whitecliffs had a curious afterlife. In 1930 a bus ran return from Darfield to Whitecliffs three days a week to provide a connection with Midland Line trains, but patronage averaged less than one person per trip. The bus ran to times not dissimilar to those of the goods train, so the bus timetable was amended to remove this service and, from September, passengers willing to sign an indemnity rode instead in the guard's van, on seating provided by Darfield's stationmaster.[95] This option was publicly advertised, though it appears the stationmaster did not need to do anything: trains between Whitecliffs and Darfield typically ran with a car-van, a carriage with a guard's compartment at one end and passenger seating at the other. These continued to Christchurch as mixed trains and provided local

connections for Christchurch–Greymouth expresses. In 1943 officials discussed redesignating the Darfield–Whitecliffs portion from 'goods' to 'with-car goods'.[96] They never did, though the 'goods' train averaged one passenger each journey.

Timetable revisions made the entire service from Christchurch to Whitecliffs goods only from 14 March 1949, and public notices emphasised that the train would no longer carry passengers.[97] Even this, however, was not the end of the matter: the district traffic manager advised his staff to continue using the car-van. In 1950 another official noted that while this provided 'an emergency service', passengers were 'a rarity'.[98] It appears the unofficial with-car goods did not truly disappear until September 1952, when NZR cancelled scheduled

services and shunted the branch as required.

Whitecliffs is an example of the fluidity and ad hoc nature of passenger provision in rural New Zealand. It was generally known that travellers – males at least – could sign an indemnity and travel in the guard's van on goods trains anywhere. What distinguished Whitecliffs was that the timetable advertised this option. Only a few examples of this exist. North of Westport in the 1920s, for instance, anyone wishing to ride the 2.7-kilometre branch from Waimangaroa to Conns Creek, at the foot of the fabled rope-operated Denniston Incline, was told: 'Goods Trains operate frequently … passengers may travel in guard's van'.[99] On an increasing number of branch lines, this soon became the only way to travel.

An example of one type of a car-van: A^F 106 in Dunedin, 1962. Juliet Rosalie Scoble collection, ATL PA1-q-839-48-1

a week. Patronage to Whitecliffs was slight: trains averaged between six and 12 ordinary ticketholders and five to seven schoolchildren during term time. The two men chose to replace these and some Midland Line mixed trains with bus services acquired from local companies.[100] NZR took over their operation from 16 April 1928, and Whitecliffs' goods-only timetable, like Glenham's, began on 30 April.[101] The operation of goods trains from Christchurch permitted further financial savings through the closure of the locomotive depot at Whitecliffs.

Not everyone was happy that buses had replaced trains in multiple regions. NZR issued a statement that this did not 'foreshadow a general policy of Government acquisition of road services', but officials and politicians were soon considering a national policy. The statement asserted that, as the private operators duplicated the railway service, combining both under government ownership was more economical.[102] The explanation did not soothe some Whitecliffs passengers, who were cynical of NZR's motives. They suspected that the real goal was to make more money while offering a lesser service. The Hororata Farmers' Union organised a meeting at which locals outlined grievances. Some wondered how mothers with prams would travel to town.[103] 'A Pioneer Resident' of Glentunnel wrote to the *Press* comparing NZR advertisements that encouraged travellers to use 'your own railways' with the new reality of being 'pack[ed] into the "buses" … at an increase of 2s [shillings] on train fare'.[104] Another scribe writing under the alias 'Disgusted' bemoaned that the passenger service 'has been taken away, without any consultation … Evidently the transport of pigs, potatoes, etc., is more

The advertisement that raised the ire of 'A Pioneer Resident' of Glentunnel in the *Press*, 13 April 1928, 15.

important to the railways than the transport of human beings.'[105] A year later one North Island newspaper, sneering in incredulity, suggested the Whitecliffs Branch was one of a handful of railways 'more than ready for the ceremony of turning the first sod of their destruction'. The author also found it ironic that buses to Ngāpara and Tokarahi departed from Ōamaru's railway station.[106] In years to come, passengers nationwide would wait at railway stations for buses rather than trains.

Ōkaihau
Ōpua
Kaikohe
Kawakawa
Ōtiria
Hikurangi
Donnellys Crossing
Portland
WHANGĀREI
Kaihū
Kirikōpuni
Tangowahine
PWD
Waiōtira

Kirikōpuni–Tangowahine commenced 1930

DARGAVILLE
Maungatūroto

Wellsford

Tahekeroa

HELENSVILLE

Auckland–Westfield commenced 1930

Henderson
AUCKLAND
Onehunga
Ōtāhuhu
Papakura
Drury
Pukekohe
Waiuku
Mercer
Waikato R.
Glen Afton
Huntly
PRIV.
Glen Massey
Ngāruaw...
HAMILTON
FRANKTON
Te Awamutu
Ōtorohanga

Upper North Island
1929–1934

C^H 3

1929–1934
A royal commission and its aftermath

Ōtorohanga

Te Kūiti

L. Tarawera

Waikato R.

Mangapēhi

L. Taupō

Ōhura–Heao commenced 1932 by PWD

Heao–Tāngarākau commenced 1933 by PWD

Ōkahukura–Tahora handover PWD to NZR 1933

Ōkahukura

Mātīere
Toi Toi
Ōhura
Heao
Tāngarākau
Tahora

Taumarunui

Waitara

Kōhuratahi

Raurimu

Mt Tongariro

NEW PLYMOUTH

Inglewood

Whangamōmona

National
Park

Mt Ngāuruhoe

Mt Ruapehu

Mt Taranaki

Toko

Raetihi

Ohakune

Tangiwai

Stratford

Waiōuru

Kāpuni

Te Roti

Taihape

Ōpunake

Hāwera

Waitōtara R.

Whanganui R.

Rangitīkei R.

Mangaweka

Pātea

Waitōtara

Kai Iwi

Hunterville

Waverley

Aramoho

WHANGANUI

Castlecliff   PRIV.

Marton

Ormondville

Dannevirke

Whanganui–Castlecliff ceased 1932

Feilding

Sanson

Woodville

Longburn–Foxton ceased 1932
Foxton–Sanson ceased 1932

PALMERSTON
NORTH

MCC

Pahīatua

Foxton

Shannon

Eketāhuna

Levin

Mauriceville

Ōtaki

Waikanae

MASTERTON

Paekākāriki

Carterton

Featherston

Greytown

L. Wairarapa

Johnsonville

Waterloo
Hutt Workshops

WELLINGTON

72

Moutohorā

Ōtoko — Te Karaka

Makaraka

Ngātapa — GISBORNE

Makaraka–Ngātapa ceased 1930

L. Waikaremoana

Wairoa R.

Mōhaka R.

Pūtōrino

Eskdale

Eskdale–Pūtōrino commenced 1930

Eskdale–Pūtōrino ceased 1931
Napier–Eskdale ceased 1930

Ngaruroro R.

NAPIER

HASTINGS

Waipawa

Waipukurau

Woburn–Hutt Workshops commenced 1929

Lower North Island
1929–1934

Upper South Island
1929–1934

Glenhope–Kawatiri ceased 1931

Seddonville–Mōkihinui Mine ceased 1932

Westport–Cape Foulwind ceased 1930

Seddonville Mōkihinui Mine

Ngākawau

Waimangaroa

Cape Foulwind WESTPORT

Kawatiri / Buller R.

Īnangahua

Reefton

Ikamatua

Rewanui Blackball

Ngahere

GREYMOUTH

Stillwater

L. Sumner

Kūmara Junction

Moana

Hokitika

Ōtira

ŌTIRA TUNNEL

Ross

Arthur's Pass

Craigieburn Oxford West

L. Coleridge Springfield

Rakaia R. Sheffield

Aoraki / Mt Cook

Rangitātā R.

Hakatere / Ashburton R.

Methven Ro

Springburn Rakaia

Maukatua / Mt Sefton

Mount Somers

Hinds R. ASHBURTON

L. Tekapo Tinwald

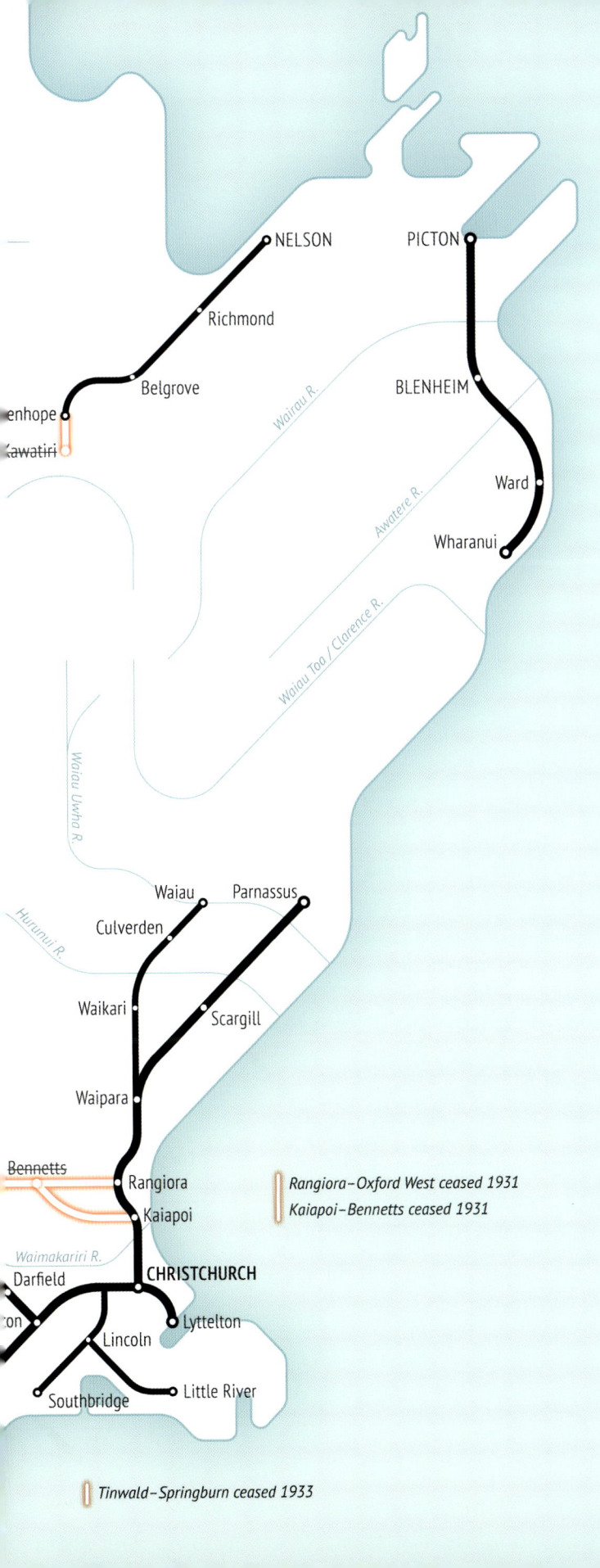

NELSON

PICTON

Richmond

Belgrove

BLENHEIM

enhope

Kawatiri

Wairau R.

Ward

Awatere R.

Wharanui

Waiau Toa / Clarence R.

Waiau Uwha R.

Waiau

Parnassus

Culverden

Hurunui R.

Waikari

Scargill

Waipara

Bennetts

Rangiora

Kaiapoi

Rangiora–Oxford West ceased 1931

Kaiapoi–Bennetts ceased 1931

Waimakariri R.

Darfield

CHRISTCHURCH

on

Lyttelton

Lincoln

Southbridge

Little River

Tinwald–Springburn ceased 1933

L. Pūkak

L. Ōhau

Haast R.

Tititea / Mt Aspiring

L. Wanaka

L. Hāwea

Pikirakatahi / Mt Earnslaw

Wedderbur

CROMWELL

Ōmaka

Clyde

Alexandra

L. Wakatipu

Kingston

Roxburgh

Millers Flat

Athol

L. Te Anau

Waikaia

Edievale

Beaumont

Mossburn

Ōreti R.

Lumsden

Waikākā

Tapanui

Lawrence

L. Manapōuri

Ōhai

ŌRB

Dipton

Riversdale

Mataura R.

Waipahi

Mata-Au / Clutha R.

Waiau R.

Ōrawia

Wairio

Hedgehope

BALCLUTHA

L. Hauroko

Aparima R.

Winton

Edendale

GORE

Clinton

Tūātapere

Ōtautau

Glenomaru

L. Poteriteri

Thornbury

Wyndham

Ōwaka

Orepuki

Riverton

Tahakopa

INVERCARGILL

Tokanui

Bluff

Fairlie
Temuka
Pleasant Point
Washdyke
Cave
TIMARU
Studholme
Waitaki R.
Waimate
Waihao Downs
Studholme–Waihao Downs ceased 1931
taki Dam
PWD
Kurow
Kurow–Waitaki Dam commenced 1929 by PWD
Pukeuri
Ranfurly
ŌAMARU
Palmerston–Dunback ceased 1930
Hyde
Dunback
Taieri R.
PALMERSTON
Middlemarch
Waikouaiti
Port Chalmers
DUNEDIN
Outram
MOSGIEL
Clarendon
Milton
PRIV.
Kaitangata

Tūātapere–Ōrawia ceased 1930

Winton–Hedgehope ceased 1931

Edendale–Wyndham ceased 1931

Waipahi–Edievale ceased 1933

McNab–Waikākā ceased 1931

Riversdale–Waikaia ceased 1931

Lower South Island
1929–1934

The railways of 1929 had new masters. The experiment with an independent Railway Board lasted only three years and concluded on 1 June 1928 when Herbert Harry Sterling became general manager. Like his predecessors before 1925 he answered directly to the minister of railways, and would serve under four in total: Gordon Coates for the final months of the Reform government in 1928, William Taverner to May 1930, Bill Veitch to September 1931 and finally George Forbes. The press of other commitments meant Sterling did not assume full duties until 1 December 1928; 10 days later, a new government took office.

Joseph Ward's new United Party defeated Coates and the Reform Party at elections in November but did not win a majority. United began the campaign as outsiders, and Ward – prime minister from 1906 to 1912 as a Liberal – startled his supporters when he promised to borrow £70 million to stimulate the economy, including £10 million for unfinished railways. One biographer explains that it will probably never be known whether Ward intended this promise or made a mistake, perhaps misreading his speech notes.[1] Nevertheless, United stuck to the pledge and surged in popularity, forming a government with Labour's support.

It is a truism that new occupants of senior positions embark on reviews and reforms, often needlessly, to stamp authority on an institution. In this instance, however, circumstances warranted large changes from Sterling and the revolving door of ministers to whom he answered. The rise of road transport could not be ignored. New Zealanders had registered a total of 217,357 motor vehicles to 30 June 1929, more than double the total of 1925.[2] Railways also represented the largest expenditure in the public works budget. Gross earnings still exceeded working expenses, but interest charges meant that NZR went from a £21,000 surplus in the year ended 31 March 1926 to a deficit of over £1.2 million in the year ended 31 March 1930. Malcolm McKinnon, in his account of the Great Depression in New Zealand, describes railways as the 'fly in the ointment' of the national accounts. McKinnon makes clear that the situation in New Zealand, even in early 1930, did not appear nearly as desperate as in Australia; Sterling, unless he had a crystal ball lurking under his desk, could not have foreseen the straitened conditions ahead.[3] The bare facts of the budget meant not only that trunk routes still under construction might go unfinished, but also that the existing passenger network might contract.

1929–30: RECONSIDERING RAIL'S ROLE

In January 1929 Sterling formed a committee of senior officials to examine each line, describe the effects of motor transport, and identify opportunities for more economical operation.[4] This proved timely as the onset of the Depression was prompting travellers to reconsider their need to travel.

In his first annual report as minister of railways in 1929, Taverner referred to the conundrum of whether the railways were to be run on a commercial or developmental basis, averring support for the latter when he condemned 'a tendency to regard the deficit as shown in the annual Statement as a "loss" … [for] the country has reaped very material indirect return from the existence of the railways'. The question, he felt, was about the appropriate size of the deficit.[5] Passenger numbers were almost in freefall. From a record of nearly 28.8m journeys in the year ended 31 March 1921, numbers slid modestly to 27.6m five years later and then plummeted: there were fewer than 22.8m journeys in the year ended 31 March 1931. Annual passenger revenue in the decade 1921–31 collapsed from over £2.65m to less than £1.8m. Season tickets showed an increase but sales of ordinary tickets halved – regular commuters were loyal to their railways but casual travellers were flocking to the road or were no longer in a position to travel.[6] Changes were necessary.

Taverner forecast in July 1929 that more services on short branches might need to be removed but not everyone took this seriously – either as a statement of policy or as sound electoral politics. The prevailing wisdom was that once a railway had been built it would continue in operation, since the greatest costs were in construction and had already been incurred. The editor of the *New Zealand Herald* suggested the prospect of wider cuts would 'arouse wide interest and not a little anxiety', especially in the South Island. He had spoken to an unnamed engineer who 'laughingly expounded the obvious':

You can't sell a cutting. You can't transport a tunnel to another place. You can't market an embankment. In a word, you can't sell the labour by which a line was created. You can't recover engineering costs. You can't offer the neighbouring farmer a bargain in sidings or in concrete laid in a stock loading yard. A railway is an asset only as a going concern. You might sell the land occupied by a line to the adjoining farmers, but they would not regard a disused permanent way as being of high agricultural value, elaborately drained though it be. The closing of a line is tantamount to scrapping it – and there is little value in scrap.[7]

The engineer, if brought into the twenty-first century, might be surprised to learn of the popularity of rail trails. But his comments capture the mindset of the late 1920s: a readiness to maintain all but the most hopelessly uneconomic railways as going concerns, for they were understood as serving the national good and their closure not reckoned to be a sound financial deal. This attitude would not hold sway for much longer among decision-makers.

Sterling reported outcomes of his internal review incrementally between April and June 1930, during which time Bill Veitch replaced Taverner as the responsible minister.[8] Notes made on the reports held at Archives New Zealand indicate that Veitch, a former engine driver and president of the Amalgamated Society of Railway Servants, read them closely. One urgent matter arose: the need to clarify government policy regarding the replacement of passenger trains with buses. In his report on a branch south of Dunedin from Mosgiel to Outram, Sterling noted that passenger numbers had slumped. Two mixed trains ran daily, plus a passenger train on Wednesdays and Fridays, but patronage was in single figures except for the morning mixed and its evening return, on which factory workers and schoolchildren travelled. All loadings were within the capacity of a bus. Sterling estimated that goods-only operation would save £900 a year on operating costs – but lose £500 in passenger revenue.

There were as yet no private buses running in opposition to the suburban trains between Dunedin and Mosgiel, but one operator had applied for a licence from the Dunedin City Council. To counter this, Sterling intended to acquire buses for NZR and prohibit competition by securing an exclusive licence to

Inside the new Hutt Workshops, 1929. A.P. Godber, ATL APG-1916-1/2-G

RURAL RAILWAYS OUT, INDUSTRIAL RAILWAYS IN

To external observers, there were few developments in 1929 to suggest that great changes were afoot: the only network modifications were the addition of two short new lines for industry. These, however, pointed towards the more focused role that railways would acquire in the coming decades.

NZR operated one of these lines, a short branch in the Hutt Valley from Woburn to its new Hutt Workshops at Gracefield. Specials for racegoers at the nearby Hutt Park Raceway ran on the line as early as 1927, but regular trains were not timetabled until after the workshops opened in 1929. With few other industries or residents yet located in the area, these ran specifically for NZR staff travelling to and from the workshops.

The PWD operated the other extension, a 6.5-kilometre line west of Kurow in North Otago, to expedite construction of the Waitaki hydroelectric dam. This 36m-high spill weir was the last dam built in New Zealand with pick and shovel rather than machinery, and a temporary town nearby housed construction workers and their families. NZR requested a passenger service between Kurow and the dam, then surprised the PWD by charging a fee to use its rollingstock, although the PWD succeeded in having this waived.[9] The first passenger services ran on 25 February 1929 and connected with trains to and from Ōamaru. Passengers were mostly schoolchildren and the carriages were old, but as dam construction progressed, NZR ran excursions from Dunedin, exhorting prospective travellers to view the 'stupendous works … the largest engineering scheme in the South Island'.[10] The line carried significant traffic until dam construction ended.

operate Dunedin–Mosgiel, with some services continuing to Outram.

His proposal raised bigger questions about how large a role NZR should take in road transport. Sterling viewed buses as the way of the future and wrote with the language of inevitability:

A very essential point is that we would be changing from a type of service that is becoming obsolete to a more modern type of service. Experience has shown that, in close proximity to cities, the rail cannot hold casual traffic against buses … We would commence the [NZR] bus service between Dunedin and Mosgiel with a minimum of plant for a beginning which we would develop as traffic warranted. As time went on, no doubt what has taken place in other suburban areas would take place in the Dunedin–Mosgiel area, namely that people would gradually transfer their patronage to the buses. When the traffic falls sufficiently we would be able to cut down the train services as has been done in the Hutt area … [If we do not get an exclusive licence, private] buses would obtain the more lucrative traffic while the unremunerative workers' traffic would be left with us.[11]

Veitch approached Cabinet for a policy decision. He knew he would soon need to make similar decisions elsewhere regarding whether NZR should abandon routes to private enterprise or run its own buses. Cabinet resolved that there were to be no new capital commitments for NZR Road Services until a newly constituted royal commission reported back.[12] The practical implication was to retain the status quo and only cancel railway passenger accommodation in extreme situations – in which case the traffic would, by necessity, fall to private enterprise.

1930: TINKERING AT THE EDGES

The first systematic reduction of services occurred in the second half of 1930 on the initiative of Sterling as general manager and Veitch as minister of railways. Before Sterling had even delivered all his internal findings, the government announced a royal commission on railways on 10 June 1930 to investigate railway finances and recommend cost-saving measures.[13] It was appointed six days later, the very day that Veitch asked Cabinet for its decision on NZR Road Services. The commissioners included former general manager Richard McVilly, under whom the first passenger cuts of the early 1920s occurred; he was the only railwayman on the team.

Before the royal commission had even completed its inquiry, Sterling and Veitch cut some of the most marginal trains. Their axe fell heavily on rural South Island branches but, like all cancellations made to date, this represented little more than a tinkering at the edges. One newspaper remarked that the changes did not 'represent an heroic cut'.[14] Some took effect on Monday 14 July; others followed in subsequent weeks. Main-line timetables were reduced, and goods-only railways between Sheffield–Oxford, Kurow–Hakataramea, Windsor–Tokarahi and Wyndham–Glenham all closed. Four branch lines lost passenger services: Waihemo Valley (Dunback) in North Otago, Cape Foulwind in Buller, Ngātapa near Gisborne and Ōrawia in western Southland, the last of which was originally planned to close to all traffic. Even if Cabinet had approved an expansion of Road Services, replacement with NZR buses was unlikely for most of these trains as they were short lines in lightly populated areas. NZR permitted some picnic excursions on the Cape

3

1929–1934

Foulwind line until early 1932, then handed control to the Marine Department, which operated it as required for harbour maintenance until 1940. Staff on the Waihemo Valley line received instructions to provide seating in the guard's van should any passengers seek transport, but this traffic was negligible.[15]

Five other lines with mixed trains were also suggested for total closure. Those to Eyreton and Mossburn were set to close on 23 August 1930, the same day as Ōrawia.[16] Closure of the last 5.5 kilometres of the Springburn Branch in Canterbury received Cabinet approval. The Greytown Branch in the Wairarapa and the last portion of the Tapanui Branch between Heriot and Edievale in West Otago were to close on an unspecified date, but survived thanks to further internal deliberations that found operational cost savings.[17] Most of these lines, if closed, would have required a bus replacement, whether by NZR or a private company.

The demise of passenger accommodation between Gisborne and Ngātapa is notable because the railway was built to be a main line. Planners now favoured connecting Gisborne to Wairoa with a coastal alignment, and the line inland to Ngātapa served a very sparse population. Had it traversed somewhere more densely settled or with greater economic output, the line might have been retained. Most freight in 1928 and 1929 came from the Repongaere quarry – ironically for roadmaking by the Gisborne Borough Council – and a daily mixed train averaged 20 passengers. All other traffic was slight, and working expenses were almost six times larger than revenue.[18] On 12 August 1930 Veitch concluded in a letter to local MP Kenneth Williams, 'there is no justification for running passenger trains on this Branch at all' – and passenger accommodation ceased on

1 September. The line remained available for excursion trains to popular picnic spots, but not for long.[19] The council had stopped using the quarry, and although local farmers succeeded in keeping the line open long enough to move their output for summer 1930–31, they could not persuade Veitch to retain it for future seasons. The Ngātapa Branch passed into history on 31 March 1931.[20]

Two themes emerge from these cuts. First, they sent a message nationwide that passenger accommodation was not a right; unremunerative services could no longer depend on developmental logic for their survival. The cuts of the 1920s had left little impression. Now, however, the *New Zealand Herald* concluded that the main effect of the reforms was 'that the idea of abandoning what is palpably hopeless business is introduced to the public mind'.[21]

The second theme is one of resistance. People were not ready to let their railways go, especially as they had often campaigned loudly for years to secure their construction. Farmers in particular appreciated the benefits of bulk rail transportation, but not everyone was sympathetic to their appeals. One resident of Wreys Bush in Southland decried the hypocrisy of 'the "cockeytoos" with their luggage climbing on to the buses. Yet these "Cockeys" are howling because their lime and manures will not now be carried by rail "free" as in years that go by.'[22] There was some truth to this: passengers and commodities that attracted high tariffs had drifted to road far more than those that were charged low tariffs or subsidised by the government.

Nonetheless, not all the appeals from rural communities fell on deaf ears. Local pressure ensured that passenger services on three

Network Cuts of 1930

Only lines operated by New Zealand Railways are shown here.

LINE STATUS

- 🔴 Passenger services cancelled
- 🟠 Goods-only line closed to all traffic
- 🟢 Closure proposed but deferred
- ⚪ No change

NELSON   PICTON

BLENHEIM

Glenhope
Kawatiri

Mōkihinui Mine

Wharanui

Cape Foulwind
WESTPORT

Īnangahua

Blackball
Rewanui
Ngahere
GREYMOUTH
Stillwater

Waiau   Parnassus

Ross

Waipara

Oxford West   Bennetts
Sheffield   Rangiora
Kaiapoi
CHRISTCHURCH

Methven   Rolleston
Springburn   Lyttelton
Mount Somers   Little River
Southbridge
ASHBURTON

Fairlie
Washdyke
TIMARU
Waihao Downs   Studholme

North Island

Moutohorā   Makaraka
Ngātapa   GISBORNE

Hakataramea
Kurow
Ngāpara–Ōamaru already goods only
Tokarahi   Ngāpara
Windsor   Pukeuri
ŌAMARU

CROMWELL

Dunback   PALMERSTON

Kingston   Port Chalmers
Roxburgh
Waikaia   DUNEDIN
Mossburn   Lumsden   Edievale   Outram
Heriot   MOSGIEL
Wairio   Milton
Ōrawia   GORE   BALCLUTHA
Tūātapere   Wyndham
Glenham   Tahakopa
INVERCARGILL   Tokanui
Bluff

MASTERTON
Woodside
Greytown
Waterloo
WELLINGTON

South Island

railways made it into 1931. Despite Cabinet approving the closure of the last portion of the Springburn Branch in Canterbury, assurances of future traffic won it a reprieve; similar assurances from Mossburn in Southland secured a year's trial and this railway actually ran until 1982, although the passenger service did not last past 1937.[23]

Most intriguing is the line in North Canterbury from Kaiapoi, on the Main North Line, through Eyreton to Bennetts on the Oxford Branch. Its service – a mixed train just four times a week from Bennetts to Kaiapoi and return – did not particularly foster patronage. The timetable in 1925 had offered evening passengers a connection to Oxford, but in the late 1920s the train from Kaiapoi arrived at Bennetts just *after* the Oxford-bound train departed.[24] The fact that the Eyreton and Oxford branches duplicated each other, never more than 10 kilometres apart, makes it unsurprising that NZR wished to consolidate operations on one line, but it wavered in its determination. The Christchurch *Press* on 8 July notified the public that all Eyreton trains would be suspended; on the 11th it reported that they would not be; and on 16 August it announced that the line would close entirely.[25] A few days later Veitch instructed another reversal: to maintain the existing timetable at least until the royal commission submitted its report.[26] This no doubt displeased Sterling who, the day before, had concluded a letter to Veitch with a forceful repudiation of Canterbury's traffic manager for suggesting that the line remain open with a twice-weekly service.[27]

In other regions, local resistance was sometimes enough to save a railway but not the passenger component of its timetable. Residents of western Southland around Ōrawia

rose up to defend their trains. The area was lightly populated and the railway had the lowest earnings per mile in the country – £81 compared to the national average of £2312, and a mixed that ran four times a week when the line opened in 1925 had already slipped to thrice-weekly in December 1929.[28] The locals made sufficient assurances of additional traffic that their campaign succeeded in part, but they were forced to accept the end of passenger services; come October 1930 there was only a twice-weekly goods train.[29] Senior officials had misgivings about prolonging the line's life, but Veitch emphasised to a sceptical Sterling that a 'promise of a year's grace must be fulfilled'.[30] As it happened, this railway survived until 1970, with a cement factory providing a good volume of traffic from 1956 to 1968.

It was not all doom and gloom for passenger services in 1930. Branch lines had begun wilting but main lines retained an air of national importance. Long-anticipated passenger services commenced on the Westfield Deviation of the North Island Main Trunk to coincide with the opening of Auckland's new central railway station on Beach Road in May. Expresses could now avoid the steeply graded route via Newmarket, which remained open for suburban trains and those bound for Northland. The deviation added much-needed capacity to Auckland's busy network: duplication of the Parnell tunnel north of Newmarket station in the 1910s had been insufficient to meet growth.[31] The new line required extensive reclamation in Hobson Bay for a causeway, and the men who dug the Purewa Tunnel encountered a 'weird and fantastic' environment. During construction, 'millions of glow-worms' and 'hanging bunches of fungus' inhabited the tunnel, and sparrows would 'chirp and flutter

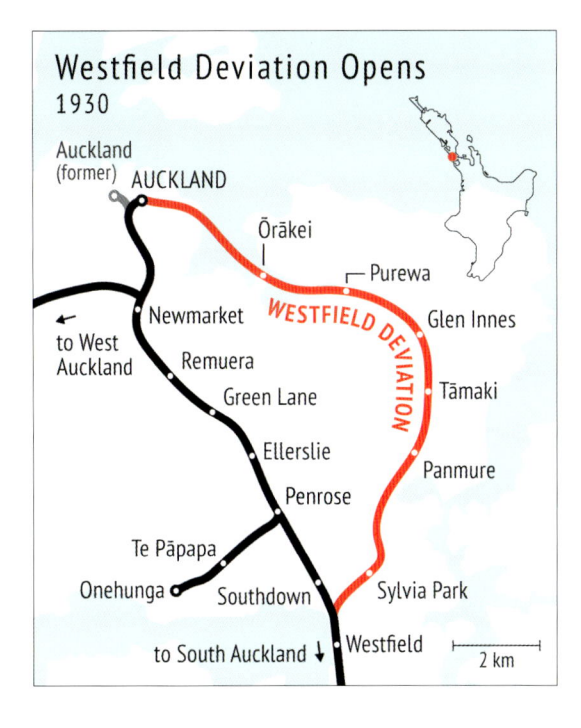

Westfield Deviation Opens
1930

around the working-face', unflustered by the tunnellers' explosions as they foraged for food scraps and pilfered from horse feedbags.[32]

In Hawke's Bay the next stage of the line north of Napier opened from Eskdale to Pūtōrino.[33] Despite doubts that an east coast railway would ever pay, the linking of Hawke's Bay to regions north represented an essential service. New Zealand's unstable geology would, however, soon imperil the line's future.

1930–31: OUTCOMES OF THE ROYAL COMMISSION

The royal commission had a broad remit to inquire into NZR's operations and management. It reported quickly, on 17 September 1930, and its findings were closer to what officials and politicians wanted to hear than Fay and Raven's report of six years earlier. The

commission provided justification – and became a convenient scapegoat – for unpopular decisions. Its recommendations of services to cancel would be some of the most consequential, a fact not lost on people who made written submissions or, in many cases, travelled far to attend hearings in the four main centres.

They were a diverse lot. Some were councillors or town clerks acting on behalf of municipal authorities. From Onehunga to Greytown, Tuapeka to Ōpōtiki, whether urban or rural, furnished with a railway or desirous of one, local bodies pressed their cases. Chambers of commerce and branches of the Farmers' Union sent representatives, as did Taieri Plains fruit growers, western Southland lime producers, the Dunedin Jockey Club, the Mount Cook Tourist Company of Timaru and the Federated Sawmillers' Association, to name just a few. In many districts the residents appointed someone to speak on their railway's behalf. Two men came forward on behalf of settlers between Wyndham and Glenham who had just lost their trains, and Hakataramea sent a Ratepayers' Association spokesperson to put the case for their closed line. People from across the nation impressed upon the commissioners their desire to retain local railways. Many of them, the commissioners concluded, 'did not in the past fully appreciate the facilities provided[;] now, with the possibility of abandonment, they expressed a keen desire to help the Department in every way'.[34] This became a familiar cry whenever railways were threatened, and one that in time has been viewed with increasing scepticism.

The commissioners reported that on rural branch lines 'to a large extent the passenger traffic has left the railways either for the service

The Ward and Forbes ministries responded to the Depression with what might today be called austerity by suspending almost every railway construction project indefinitely. These cuts occurred alongside the service reductions and cancellations that followed the royal commission. Expenditure on new railways plummeted from over £590,000 in the year ended 31 March 1931 to less than £100,000 the next year.[35] Some projects had already been attenuated, most notably the North Auckland Line beyond Ōkaihau. In 1929 Alfred Ransom, Ward's Minister of Public Works, suspended construction to Mangamuka, never mind Kaitaia – he deemed sufficient a terminus at Rangiahua, within shouting distance of Hokianga Harbour. He also cancelled a railway from Rotorua to Taupō; construction of the section to Reporoa had been underway.[36]

Ransom made a much more dramatic announcement just three days before Christmas 1930. The PWD had worked vigorously that year to join the southern end of Nelson's railway at Kawatiri with the main network at Īnangahua. Success was within sight: the line was basically complete between Kawatiri and Gowanbridge, construction to Murchison was in its final stages, and work had begun on the last section to Īnangahua. But as the workmen departed for their holidays they learned that the project was suspended.[37] It was the death blow for

Nelson's railway, and Nelsonians could only contemplate how close they had come to realising an ambition held since the 1860s. George Black, a local United MP, was so incensed that he voted against his party's straitened financial policy.[38] United expelled Black, but his stand secured him re-election as an independent in the 1931 election.

Ransom also drew the curtain on three other projects: Ōkaihau–Rangiahua and Kirikōpuni–Dargaville in Northland, both almost complete, and Waikōkopu–Gisborne.[39] The suspension of works in Northland left two railways in the hands of the PWD: one from Kirikōpuni to Tangowahine, halfway to Dargaville, and the 21-kilometre Rangiahua line. Construction to Dargaville had been progressing so well that a special passenger excursion reached Tangowahine on 18 November 1929, and officials had anticipated the full line would open during 1931 or 1932. Goods trains had begun serving Tangowahine in December 1929 and a regular passenger timetable had began in September 1930.[40]

Ransom's announcement left the PWD holding the bag. Kirikōpuni–Tangowahine was not absorbed into NZR's network for over a decade, and this obscure line became one of the PWD's longest-lived passenger services. It did not, however, run regular trains to Rangiahua, even though rails had been laid all the way to the terminus. It was a difficult,

unstable route, and Rangiahua station had not been constructed. The government employed local men during the 1930s to remove rails and other equipment for use elsewhere, and further leftovers were collected during World War II. State Highway 1 now uses some of the formation.[41]

A new Railways Board not only confirmed Ransom's decisions in September 1931; it also suspended construction of Westport–Īnangahua and the missing link on the South Island Main Trunk between Parnassus in Canterbury and Wharanui in Marlborough. The board claimed to be making decisions on commercial grounds, but its judgement was so persistently pessimistic as to be dubious. Most egregiously, it argued that 'there is no likelihood of the development of any substantial business' of coal from Buller to Lyttelton; it held a fatalistic belief that passengers could not be lured from existing road services to new rail ones; and it ridiculed the idea of rail ferries from Picton to Wellington as uncompetitive.[42]

Michael Joseph Savage's Labour government, elected in 1935, resumed most of these projects. Today, the *Coastal Pacific* is a famous passenger journey that uses the Parnassus–Wharanui route where the board had no appetite to compete with buses; coal from Buller to Lyttelton currently sustains the Midland Line; and the Interislander ferries have been a fixture of Cook Strait for decades.

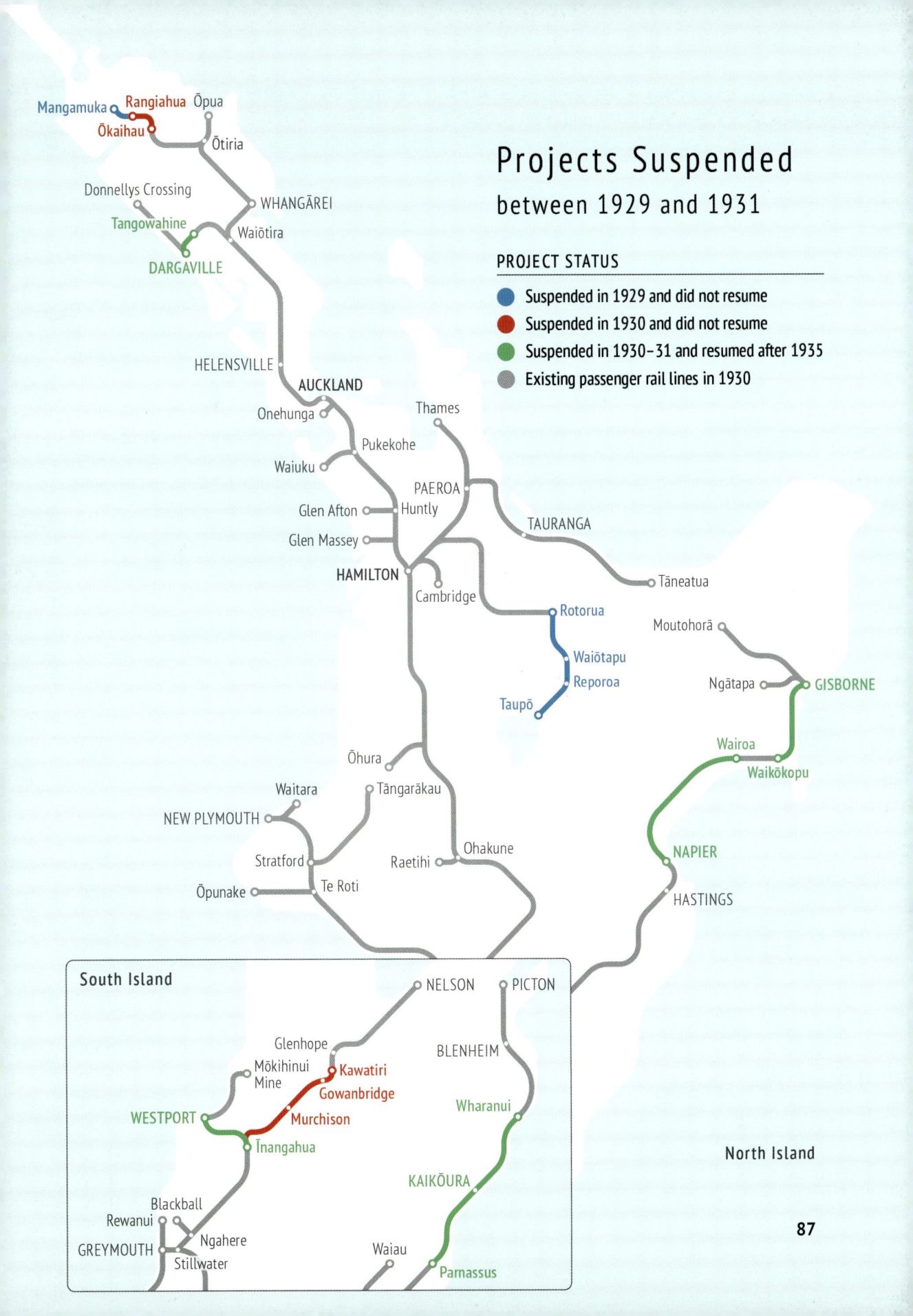

Projects Suspended
between 1929 and 1931

PROJECT STATUS

- 🔵 Suspended in 1929 and did not resume
- 🔴 Suspended in 1930 and did not resume
- 🟢 Suspended in 1930–31 and resumed after 1935
- ⚪ Existing passenger rail lines in 1930

Mangamuka · Rangiahua · Ōpua
Ōkaihau
Ōtiria
Donnellys Crossing
WHANGĀREI
Tangowahine · Waiōtira
DARGAVILLE
HELENSVILLE
AUCKLAND
Onehunga · Thames
Pukekohe
Waiuku · PAEROA
Glen Afton · Huntly
Glen Massey · TAURANGA
HAMILTON · Tāneatua
Cambridge
Rotorua · Moutohorā
Waiōtapu · Ngātapa · GISBORNE
Reporoa
Taupō · Wairoa
Waikōkopu
Ōhura
Waitara · Tāngarākau
NEW PLYMOUTH · NAPIER
Stratford · Raetihi · Ohakune · HASTINGS
Ōpunake · Te Roti

North Island

South Island

NELSON · PICTON
Glenhope · BLENHEIM
Mōkihinui Mine · Kawatiri
Gowanbridge
WESTPORT · Murchison · Wharanui
Īnangahua
KAIKŌURA
Blackball
Rewanui · Ngahere
GREYMOUTH · Stillwater · Waiau
Parnassus

87

The Royal Commission
September 1930

These maps show the 1930 royal commission's recommendations related to passenger services on New Zealand's railway network.

Recommendations were only made for NZR-operated lines, so non-NZR lines are not shown here.

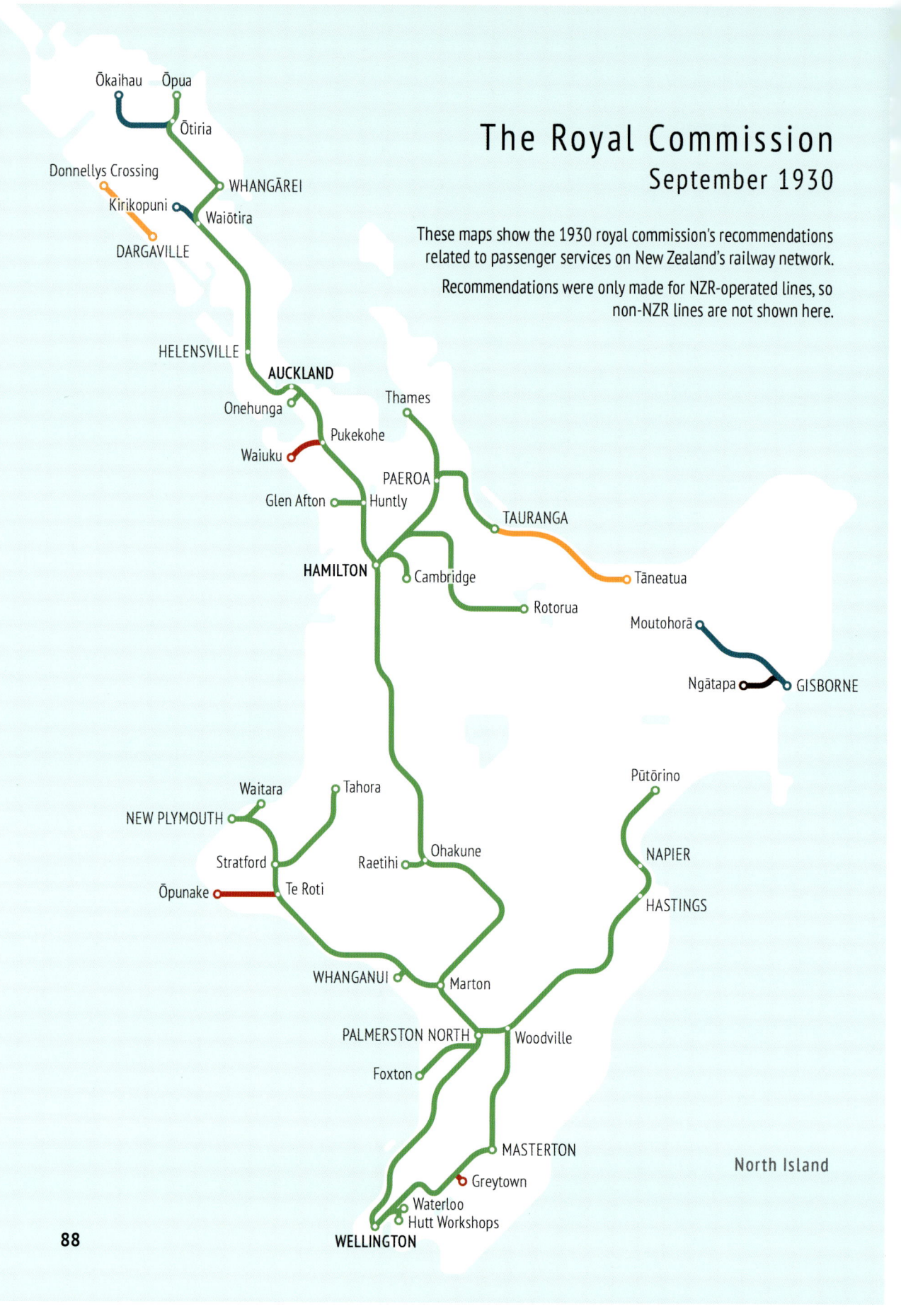

North Island

COMMISSION RECOMMENDATION

- ● Close entirely
- ● Close to passengers
- ● Reduce passenger services
- ● Keep under review
- ● No recommendation

NELSON
PICTON
BLENHEIM
Glenhope
Kawatiri
Wharanui
Mōkihinui Mine
WESTPORT
Īnangahua
Blackball
Rewanui
Ngahere
GREYMOUTH
Stillwater
Waiau
Parnassus
Ross
Waipara
Bennetts
Oxford West
Rangiora
Kaiapoi
CHRISTCHURCH
Rolleston
Lyttelton
Methven
Springburn
Little River
Mount Somers
Southbridge
ASHBURTON
Fairlie
Washdyke
TIMARU
Waimate
Studholme
Waihao Downs
Kurow
Pukeuri
CROMWELL
ŌAMARU
Dunback
PALMERSTON
Kingston
Roxburgh
Port Chalmers
Waikaia
DUNEDIN
Mossburn
Lumsden
Edievale
Outram
MOSGIEL
Waikākā
Lawrence
Ōrawia
Wairio
Milton
South Island
Tūātapere
Hedgehope
GORE
BALCLUTHA
INVERCARGILL
Wyndham
Tahakopa
Tokanui
Bluff

car or the private car'.[43] Unlike the Fay–Raven report, this one did not recommend concerted efforts to regain traffic beyond main centres and trunk lines: instead, it suggested cancellations. NZR did not always concur, and some passenger trains that the commissioners earmarked, such as those to Little River and Raetihi, survived for over two decades. Outram's passenger timetable, which had provoked the deliberation over bus policy, ironically survived; in late 1930 a senior official with updated statistics decided that lost passenger revenue would entirely negate the savings of going goods only, and proposed a pared-back timetable to reduce maintenance costs.[44] But the royal commission motivated a closer, sustained review of branch-line passenger offerings. The first cancellations made on its advice touched rural areas across the South Island. They became effective on Monday 9 February 1931, alongside significant reductions on other routes.

Waimate in South Canterbury was the largest town that the cancellations affected, and its situation revealed that NZR Road Services was now permitted to grow. This regional service centre of about 2300 people sat on a short branch of the Main South Line because engineers in the 1870s had opted to bypass it in favour of a more direct route to Otago. The branch had been extended through the Waimate Gorge as far as Waihao Downs, but this portion never saw heavy traffic. In 1930 four mixed trains shuttled most days between Waimate and the junction at Studholme; only one continued to Waihao Downs. From 9 February 1931, however, this was reduced to just one goods for the whole line.[45] The commissioners did not actually call for the end of passenger accommodation between Studholme and Waimate, only onwards to Waihao Downs; they

recommended that Waimate services 'be reviewed and reduced to a minimum'.[46] NZR, however, gained approval in late 1930 to replace trains with buses.[47] Waimate's proximity to the Main South Line made the loss of its passenger service less galling than it would have been for a more remote community, and buses began shuttling Waimate travellers to main-line trains on 9 February 1931. Road Services, able to access capital investment, would only continue to expand.

Oxford, with a population approaching 1000, also lost passenger rail services. Its corner of North Canterbury was particularly unfortunate, with mixed trains ending on two lines at once. Nobody was surprised at the demise of the mixed from Kaiapoi via Eyreton to Bennetts – it had only just clung to life in 1930. But the mixed from Rangiora to Oxford also ceased as its ridership had collapsed. Good flat roads meant buses ran faster than mixed trains, which at best averaged 18 passengers on arrival or departure at Rangiora, and just 10 at Kaiapoi. On both trains, schoolchildren made up about half the patronage, and the passenger carriages would be practically empty at Bennetts or Oxford. It did not help that the trains that were in direct competition with buses had the slowest timetables; quicker trains at other times indicated a better service was possible.[48] NZR also severed the link between the Eyreton and Oxford lines so that Eyreton's railway now terminated at Horrelville, the station before Bennetts. These changes, combined with the closure of two locomotive depots (Oxford and Bennetts), achieved considerable savings but greatly reduced transport facilities in the Oxford area.

Southland experienced the most cuts in February 1931. The mixed trains that took 70 minutes to trundle 25 kilometres between Waikākā and Gore became goods only, as did

3

1929–1934

One of the Model T Ford petrol railcars. Note the small brushes in front of the leading wheels to knock stones from the rails.

ANZ ABIN W3337 Box 256

those between Hedgehope and Winton.[49] On two other lines an experiment in replacing locomotive-hauled carriage trains with railcars came to an end. For years NZR had tried to find an efficient way to handle light passenger traffic on the web of rural branch railways that fanned throughout the region. Staff at Petone workshops in 1926 built two small railcars using a Ford Model T engine and transmission, with seating for a driver and 11 passengers. The diminutive vehicles were nicknamed teapots, coffeepots, piecarts and glasshouses. They ran from Edendale to Wyndham and from Riversdale to Waikaia, but were poorly balanced, rode roughly and overheated often.[50] They derailed in frosty weather or if rabbits scattered ballast onto the rails, and even the quaint addition of brushes in front of the wheels did not solve the problem entirely.[51] Officials conceded privately that better railcars would regain patronage – Wyndham services averaged

just three people per trip – but preferred to make the branches goods only to reduce railway operating costs.[52] In the space of a few short months, passenger services had ended on five of Southland's branch railways: first Ōrawia and then four more.

At the other end of the island the suspension of construction on the Nelson Section, referred to in the inset 'Pressing the pause button' (see page 86), induced a cancellation. The line between Glenhope and Kawatiri ran through rugged, sparsely populated country, and as Kawatiri was never meant to be a significant station the PWD did not erect the buildings and other facilities necessary for a permanent terminus. NZR continued to use Glenhope for transfers of passengers and consignments from points south. With construction suspended, the 7 kilometres from Glenhope to Kawatiri were superfluous, and instead of being the railhead of an interprovincial main line, it became an

91

unprofitable backblocks railway. How quickly things had changed: in December 1929 officials had contemplated authorising the Kawatiri with-car goods to continue south to Gowanbridge; from February 1931 all trains terminated at Glenhope and the extension to Gowanbridge was never used. NZR, moreover, accepted the commission's recommendation to cut trains beyond Belgrove (on the north side of Spooners Range) to Glenhope from daily to thrice weekly.[53]

1932: WHANGANUI LOSES SUBURBAN RAIL

Passenger cancellations until 1932 had been almost entirely in rural areas, but tramway competition had also affected railway passenger demand in urban centres. In Dunedin, electric trams had superseded the Ocean Beach Railway, which had an unsuccessful life from 1876 through to the cessation of occasional passenger trains for events at Tahuna Park in 1904. In Wellington one of NZR's lines had succumbed to tramway competition: from 1893 to 1917 an extension ran south from Lambton station, the NZR terminal before the construction of the current grand station, into Te Aro. Passenger traffic was its mainstay, but electric trams, which were faster and dropped people closer to workplaces and shops, reduced the need for trains from 212 a week in 1904 to 62 in 1916. A wartime coal-saving timetable in 1917 was the line's death sentence.[54]

In Whanganui, tramway competition brought a complete end to the city's suburban rail. This cancellation in 1932 is also distinctive because it occurred on the only private railway in the country to offer an urban commuter service at the time.[55] With a population of approximately 27,800, Whanganui was New Zealand's

fifth-largest city.[56] The Castlecliff Railway Company operated a line from the eponymous coastal suburb to Whanganui's central Taupō Quay station, itself on a branch from Aramoho on the main line between Palmerston North and New Plymouth. Opened in 1885, the Castlecliff Railway served the port and other local industries, and in its first decades it maintained a brisk trade in passengers. Eight trains ran daily in early 1910, with prams, bicycles, hampers and other luggage carried free of charge in the guard's van. Trains shuttled back and forth every 30–60 minutes bringing people to the seaside on public holidays, and late-night specials sometimes ran for Castlecliff residents to return from events in town.[57]

Whanganui's first electric tramway connected the city centre to Aramoho and the main-line railway station. When these municipal trams began in 1908, they worked together with the Castlecliff Railway to offer a cheap combined fare to Aramoho. Relations soon became competitive rather than cordial, however, when the trams were extended to Castlecliff in 1912 with a terminus right on the beach.[58] The railway's directors considered all options, from electrification to abandonment of services. In the 1916/17 financial year, six trains a day (seven on Saturdays) carried an average daily total of just 44 passengers, and from 1918 services were halved to three trains daily that ran at times to suit workmen. Even this failed to retain custom – no doubt a difficult sell when all trains, as an economy measure, now ran mixed. By 1929 passengers, usually four a day, rode in the guard's van, an unattractive proposition when compared to the trams; and in April 1932 this facility met its overdue demise.[59] Aramoho to Castlecliff is a natural corridor for public transport, but Whanganui's population was too

A fleet of Whanganui trams at Castlecliff carries people to a school picnic in 1914. Frank J. Denton, ATL 1/1-021549-G

small to support rival tram and train services. Moreover, as the Castlecliff Railway did not run through to Aramoho, it is little wonder that passengers connecting with main-line services chose trams instead. Had there been a single railway operator from Aramoho to Castlecliff things might have been different. The Castlecliff Railway continued as an industrial concern, absorbed into NZR's network in 1956.

Whanganui has the dubious distinction of being the first city in New Zealand to lose suburban passenger trains entirely; Invercargill, Christchurch and Dunedin would later follow suit, and Auckland came perilously close. Despite the closure of the Te Aro Line, Wellington is the only city in New Zealand where suburban trains have never experienced an existential threat.

1931–33: LEGISLATIVE PROTECTION, RURAL CONTRACTION

The Depression almost brought railway expansion to a complete stop, and the effects of the royal commission extended well beyond the reduced timetable of 9 February 1931. Internal deliberations within NZR combined with the commission's recommendations fostered new attitudes that underpinned cancellations for decades to come.

George Forbes became prime minister after Joseph Ward resigned in 1930 due to ill-health; he also held the railway portfolio for most of his term in the highest office, and his government accepted the commission's advice to re-establish an independent Railways Board. This comprised leading businessmen, who took control from 1 June 1931. Sterling joined the board as its chairman in December 1931, and Philip George Roussell, NZR's general superintendent of transportation, succeeded him as general manager. The board was expected to rein in expenditure, and one way to do this was to pare back marginal passenger services. When timetables were modified, it was almost exclusively by means of reduction or elimination. Between 1930 and 1937 new passenger services commenced on just one line.

One challenge the new board faced was what to do with the railway north of Napier after the devastating earthquake of 3 February 1931, which killed at least 256 people. Slips

A hand-coloured photograph of Hastings Street, Napier, immediately after the 3 February 1931 earthquake. Tram tracks are visible. Napier's trams never ran again.

Percy Caz Sorrell, donated by Mrs Knight, Collection of Hawke's Bay Museums Trust, Ruawharo Tā-ū-rangi, 70714

had crossed the line to Pūtōrino, bridges had collapsed and lengthy sections of track had subsided. It would be easy to write off this line as a victim of New Zealand's tectonic instability, but its demise was not monocausal. NZR initially decided to repair it, which in June 1931 looked achievable by year's end.[60] The under-construction line beyond Pūtōrino to Wairoa had sustained less damage, and at the time was within 12 months of completion: the only major works still in progress were two viaducts and a tunnel. The board and the government, however, were both now more prepared to abandon railways. As construction from Wairoa to Gisborne had been suspended the previous December, the board in September 1931 called time on the portion south of Wairoa too.[61] This meant it also abandoned repairs of the previously operational section. It saw little prospect of the line paying its way with Pūtōrino as a permanent terminus, especially not in such a depressed economy.[62] In general, senior officials in the early 1930s took an extremely

pessimistic view of traffic north of Napier.

For all the board's purported independence, it was subject to much the same political pressure as when the general manager had answered directly to the minister. One historian of the Gisborne line, Chris Wood, suggests that the Forbes ministry leaned on the board to make decisions, such as abandoning the Pūtōrino line, so that the blame for unpopular spending cuts and retrenchment did not fall on the government.[63] Whether this imputation is fair or not, the government still incurred great criticism, especially from locals who believed the board miscalculated and underestimated revenue. Later in the decade the Pūtōrino line would become a rare example of a route in New Zealand to regain a lost passenger service.

NZR did, however, gain important legislative protection in 1931. One reason the Pūtōrino line struggled was the failure of NZR's through-booking arrangements by rail and road to Gisborne. Private operators skimmed high-value traffic, leaving NZR with few passengers and unremunerative classes of goods. Commissioner of Transport James Hunter described the situation as chaotic. In rural areas:

unregulated competition held sway, with all its attendant evils of financial instability, duplicated services, unnecessary wear-and-tear on roads, irregular and unsatisfactory services, wasteful concentration of services on 'fat' routes, and avoidance of 'lean' or developmental routes.[64]

Motor transport regulations had increased during the 1920s, and the Forbes ministry now sought to co-ordinate and regulate all transport in a uniform manner. James Parr introduced the government's bill to the Legislative Council, the upper house of New Zealand's Parliament that was abolished in 1950. He commended it as putting 'on an entirely new basis the whole question of the regulation of land transport'.[65] The resultant Transport Licensing Act became law on 11 November 1931 and, with modifications, served for roughly 50 years. It created transport districts within which passenger services could only operate with an appropriate licence; licensing authorities would assess the public need for a service and could limit timetables, fares and vehicles. NZR had a large role, including the ability to give recommendations. Most importantly, it received preference when applying for a new route or extension of an existing one; road operators could no longer be licensed to operate routes that paralleled railway lines.[66]

Licensing extended to air routes from 1934, although aeroplanes did not yet present serious competition to trains and would not for a few decades. The most successful early aviation companies operated in rugged regions without railways or decent roads, and a multiple-stop

trunk route from Auckland to Dunedin did not begin until the Union Steam Ship Company launched Union Airways in January 1936. More significant from NZR's perspective – and, moreover, advantageous – was Union's inauguration of the Steamer Express in 1933, an upgrade on its ferry service between Lyttelton and Wellington, the primary route for travel between the North and South Islands.[67] Most ferry travellers caught NZR's Boat Train between Lyttelton and Christchurch. The Boat Train sometimes ran as an extension of the *South Island Limited*, the premier express to Dunedin and Invercargill.

The legislative preference for NZR applied to its Road Services as well as rail operations, so the Transport Licensing Act and follow-up legislation did not mean that passenger trains would necessarily continue on rural railways. One cancellation would have happened no matter what. Trains in Buller ran past Seddonville to a terminus called Mōkihinui Mine. The four mines near this station had slumped in the Depression, and the few trains that continued beyond Seddonville moved just 15 tons of coal and 72 passengers in the first half of 1932. New instructions provided for coal wagons to be shunted as required, and it is hard to imagine this occurred frequently. Passengers were last accommodated on 20 August 1932.[68]

A more substantive passenger service in the North Island, Foxton to Palmerston North, concluded on the same day. The commission had not actually recommended this and had noted, with a sense of history, that Foxton's railway was 'one of the oldest in New Zealand and at one time carried a heavy traffic'.[69] Sterling's internal report in 1930 remarked that passenger traffic was negligible and road competition stiff, but he too recommended no change.[70] The stationmaster at Foxton, one J. Martin, was therefore taken aback on 4 August 1932 when told that services on the line would be curtailed and operated from Palmerston North; all positions on the line would be made redundant except his own. He told a local newspaper the decision came 'as a shock to all concerned'.[71] But business at the port of Foxton was waning – it would cease to be a commercial port a decade later – and the *Levin Daily Chronicle* published telling figures of the fall in rail passenger traffic. Two trains ran daily between Foxton and Palmerston North, and in 1925 their passenger counts had ranged between 16 and 61; Saturday traffic was especially healthy. By 1932, however, they averaged a paltry four to eight passengers most days and around 20 on Saturdays.[72] Most of this slump occurred before 1930 so, if anything, it is surprising that cancellation did not happen sooner.

Operators of passenger services other than NZR and the PWD were becoming scarce, and the demise of the Foxton service also brought about the end of one passenger service beyond NZR's auspices. Manawatū County Council owned the Sanson Tramway, which ran north from Hīmatangi on the Foxton line to Sanson. It terminated opposite Bulls on the south bank of the Rangitīkei River, near the site of what became Ōhakea Air Force base. Although officially designated a tramway, it had a similar standard to NZR branch lines. The council used some ex-NZR locomotives and rollingstock, and a mixed train ran between Sanson and Foxton. From 1924 the popularity of cars on Manawatū's gentle plains meant the mixed ran just once weekly, ironically carrying roadmaking materials. Tragedy struck at 3am on 21 June 1925 when the goods shed at

Sanson caught fire with one of the tramway's passenger carriages and its guard's van inside. The shed was insured but not the rollingstock, and the council was forced to convert its second passenger carriage into a guard's van, which accommodated all passengers until 1932. It was hardly an attractive ride and the council was on the brink of ceasing to carry passengers when NZR made the decision easy: NZR cancelled its mixed to Foxton and the council halted its service, at the same time losing operating rights for goods between Hīmatangi and Foxton.[73]

One cancellation in West Otago during 1933 reveals that consultation as an artifice for decisions already taken is by no means a recent invention. NZR officials had, since 1930, considered closing the final Heriot–Edievale portion of the Tapanui Branch that ran north from Waipahi. In October 1933, rather than closing the line completely, they concluded that mixed trains should become goods only.[74] Their primary justification – falling passenger revenue from poor connections with main-line services at Waipahi – is somewhat perplexing

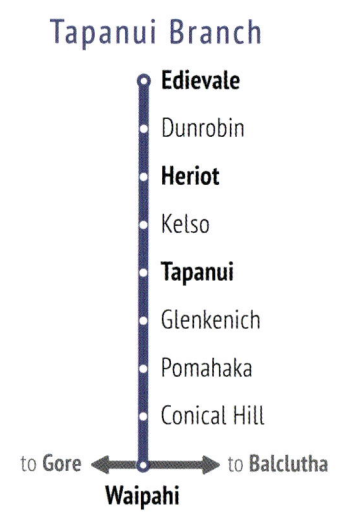

Tapanui Branch

- Edievale
- Dunrobin
- **Heriot**
- Kelso
- **Tapanui**
- Glenkenich
- Pomahaka
- Conical Hill

to **Gore** ←——→ to **Balclutha**

Waipahi

as it was within their power to rectify this. Bus services, however, were ascendant. Officials visited the area to 'consult' affected communities in November, but this appears to have been no more than a token gesture. People who wanted passenger rail services had little say; the visit was to ensure the new bus schedule received few complaints. Buses began on 18 December and the last mixed ran 12 days later.[75] Local newspapers waved the cancellation through and turned a blind eye to the contrived consultation. The slow train from Edievale and its poor connections motivated the *Tapanui Courier* to conclude that if 'reasonable roads are available mixed trains are anathema to the modern travelling public'.[76]

The Springburn Branch in Canterbury was similar to the Edievale line: its mixed trains were slow and NZR had considered closing the lightly used final leg from Mount Somers to Springburn. The royal commission, however, feared this might actually induce more road competition and recommended that NZR monitor the situation, while locals promised additional goods tonnages.[77] The line survived to Springburn until 1957 and as far as Mount Somers until 1968, but passenger facilities ceased from 9 January 1933.[78] Here, too, the local newspaper, the *Ashburton Guardian*, viewed the end of passenger accommodation as an inevitable part of the march of progress:

The alteration in the service, having been expected and fairly generally approved, is causing but little heart-burning, though some with more sentiment than logic declare it is going back 40 years. It is perhaps worth a moment's thought to consider the alteration of conditions since the opening of the line. Then the train replaced the bullock dray as the link with the outside world

… [now] to most residents the motor-car in its wonderful mobility has become the personal means of locomotion.[79]

It is true enough that railway passenger services could not have survived much longer on branches through rural districts where towns had just a few hundred residents. Some travellers felt aggrieved nonetheless, and not just people who perhaps liked the idea of local passenger trains more than they patronised them. NZR offered a £10 tourist fare that granted four weeks of train travel with very few restrictions. This, lamented the *Auckland Star* in July 1931, 'does not go as far in the South Island as formerly' on account of the various cancellations.[80] NZR's general manager in 1934 also attributed 'a great deal of the bus and service-car growth' to train timetables that did not provide 'a suitable one-day return trip to the nearest city or town' – something he and his officers could amend.[81] But it is hard to see how passenger rail to the likes of Dunback, Eyreton or most of the rural Southland destinations could have survived even if Parliament *had* restricted road competition more tightly. The 'wonderful mobility' of cars fulfilled needs that trains struggled to meet in lightly populated areas, especially those where residents lived at some remove from a station. That said, the people the *Ashburton Guardian* condemned for holding 'more sentiment than logic' were not entirely wrong to condemn the withdrawal of a public service. Great faith in automobility would soon lead to less justifiable cancellations.

1933: SOMETHING TO CELEBRATE

The Forbes government continued with two major railway projects during the Depression, the Tawa Flat Deviation and the

This photo, taken near Whangamōmona, gives some idea of Taranaki's rugged interior. A[B] 835 hauls an early-morning mixed train towards Stratford, November 1951.

J.F. Le Cren, ANZ AAVK 6390 B1706

Stratford–Ōkahukura Line, but only managed to finish the latter before losing the 1935 election. Construction of the Tawa Flat Deviation to provide a new route north from Wellington began in 1927 and would take a decade to complete. The Stratford–Ōkahukura Line had been under construction for three decades when the Depression hit, and was close to completion. It was lucky to escape the fate that befell the Nelson line. At the start of 1932 NZR operated the western section from Stratford to Tahora while the PWD provided trains onwards from Tahora to Tāngarākau, and, at the eastern end, between Ōhura and Ōkahukura on the Main Trunk.

The PWD extended passenger services deeper into Taranaki's interior during 1932. In May timetabled trains began running 18 kilometres past Ōhura to Tokirima and Heao.[82] A gap of only about 14 kilometres now separated the western and eastern railheads, but the country here was rough even by this region's standards and the PWD had to excavate six separate

tunnels. Nonetheless, by October it was possible, in a manner of speaking, to traverse the full route. Trains operated between Tahora and Heao for departmental purposes, sometimes stopping for locals. A Stratford newspaper found humour in this 'primitive' train of 'antiquated' carriages, which it said bore 'the same relation to the de luxe cars of the expresses as a wheelbarrow does to an eight-cylinder sedan motor car'.[83] NZR began running goods trains the length of the line in December 1932 but the PWD retained control, and as there was no timetabled passenger conveyance, travellers had to ride in the guard's van.[84] The PWD did, though, run relief trains from Tahora to Ōhura, after disastrous floods cut Ōhura off from Taumarunui in March 1933 and forced NZR to postpone plans to start running expresses in April.[85]

It was a momentous day when NZR took over the complete Stratford–Ōkahukura Line and initiated passenger expresses between Auckland and New Plymouth. NZR's timetable came into effect in September 1933. The first through-train left Auckland on 3 September at 7pm: three carriages attached to the Wellington-bound *Night Limited*, which were detached by another locomotive at Taumarunui and hauled to New Plymouth for a 6am arrival. Its opposite number reversed this procedure.[86]

The new service meant a lot to the residents of northern Taranaki, and many hoped the railway was a path to renewed wealth. In August 1932, when workers broke through the last tunnel, the mayor of Stratford had told a joyful crowd that they were 'getting through the depression and gloom': they had 'pierced the last obstacle, and would be able to see a vista of delight and prosperity in the near future'.[87] Now the *New Zealand Herald* attested that 'whole settlements turned out to see the first trains through'; the station platforms 'thronged with laughing and excited crowds' despite it being the middle of the night. The revellers of Whangamōmona appointed an impromptu mayor to give a speech to the first northbound train – a joyful frivolity that unwittingly foreshadowed the town proclaiming itself a republic and electing a president in 1989 as a protest against changed local council boundaries – and a gaggle of enthusiastic young men serenaded the train with a proud chorus of 'We Are the Boys from Whanga'.[88] It was a truly special occasion, the culmination of decades of advocacy, planning and onerous physical labour.

Taranaki had achieved its dream, construction workers were digging tunnels for Wellington's Tawa Flat Deviation, but elsewhere railway projects had stalled. Whether in Dargaville or Kaikōura, Nelson or Wairoa, people could only wonder if proposed lines would ever be completed. It is difficult to find a year in the first half of the twentieth century

The community took multiple opportunities to celebrate the completion of northern Taranaki's railway. Three thousand people attended this ceremony, at which Prime Minister Forbes drove the last spike. A regular passenger timetable was still 10 months away. Puke Ariki ARC2004-149

in which there was no change to the size of the New Zealand passenger rail network, so the fact that no alterations occurred during 1934 and 1935 reveals the difficult conditions. Finance for expansion was limited and further cuts were politically unpalatable. The Depression still cast a pall over the country, and after the 'Boys from Whanga' had greeted their first train, it would be six years until another town celebrated a new connection to the national railway network.

Ōkaihau
Kaikohe
Ōpua
Kawakawa
Ōtiria
Hikurangi
WHANGĀREI
Donnellys Crossing
Portland
Kirikōpuni
Kaihū
Tangowahine
Waiōtira
DARGAVILLE
Maungatūroto
Wellsford
Tahekeroa
HELENSVILLE
Henderson
AUCKLAND
Onehunga
Ōtāhuhu
Papakura
Drury
Pukekohe
Waiuku
Mercer
Waikato R.
Glen Afton
Huntly
Glen Massey
Ngāruaw...
HAMILTON
FRANKTON
Te Awamutu
Ōtorohanga

Kirikōpuni–Tangowahine handover PWD to NZR 1941
Tangowahine–Dargaville commenced 1941

Ngāruawāhia–Glen Massey handover to NZR 1935

Upper North Island
1935–1945

C^H4

1935–1945
A network unified in the face of adversity

Ōtorohanga

Te Kūiti

Mangapēhi

Ōkahukura

Ōhura

Tāngarākau

Taumarunui

Raurimu

Mt Tongariro

Mt Ngāuruhoe

Mt Ruapehu

Waitara

NEW PLYMOUTH

Inglewood

Whangamōmona

National Park

Mt Taranaki

Stratford

Toko

Raetihi

Ohakune

Tangiwai

Waiōuru

Taihape

Ōpunake

Kāpuni

Te Roti

Hāwera

Pātea

Waitōtara

Waverley

Kai Iwi

Aramoho

WHANGANUI

Mangaweka

Hunterville

Marton

Ormondville

Dannevirke

Feilding

PALMERSTON NORTH

Woodville

Pahīatua

Shannon

Eketāhuna

Levin

Mauriceville

Ōtaki

Waikanae

MASTERTON

Paekākāriki

Carterton

Featherston

Greytown

L. Wairarapa

Johnsonville

Waterloo

Hutt Workshops

WELLINGTON

Mōkau R.

Waikato R.

L. Taupō

L. Tarawera

Waitōtara R.

Whanganui R.

Rangitīkei R.

Tawa Flat Deviation opened 1937

Johnsonville–Tawa Flat ceased 1937

102

Moutohorā

Ōtoko   Te Karaka

GISBORNE

Gisborne–Moutohorā ceased 1945

L. Waikaremoana

Wairoa R.

Wairoa   Waikōkopu

Mōhaka R.

Pūtōrino

Napier–Wairoa commenced 1939

Wairoa–Gisborne commenced 1942

Eskdale

Ngaruroro R.

NAPIER

HASTINGS

Waipawa

Waipukurau

Lower North Island
1935–1945

Upper South Island
1935–1945

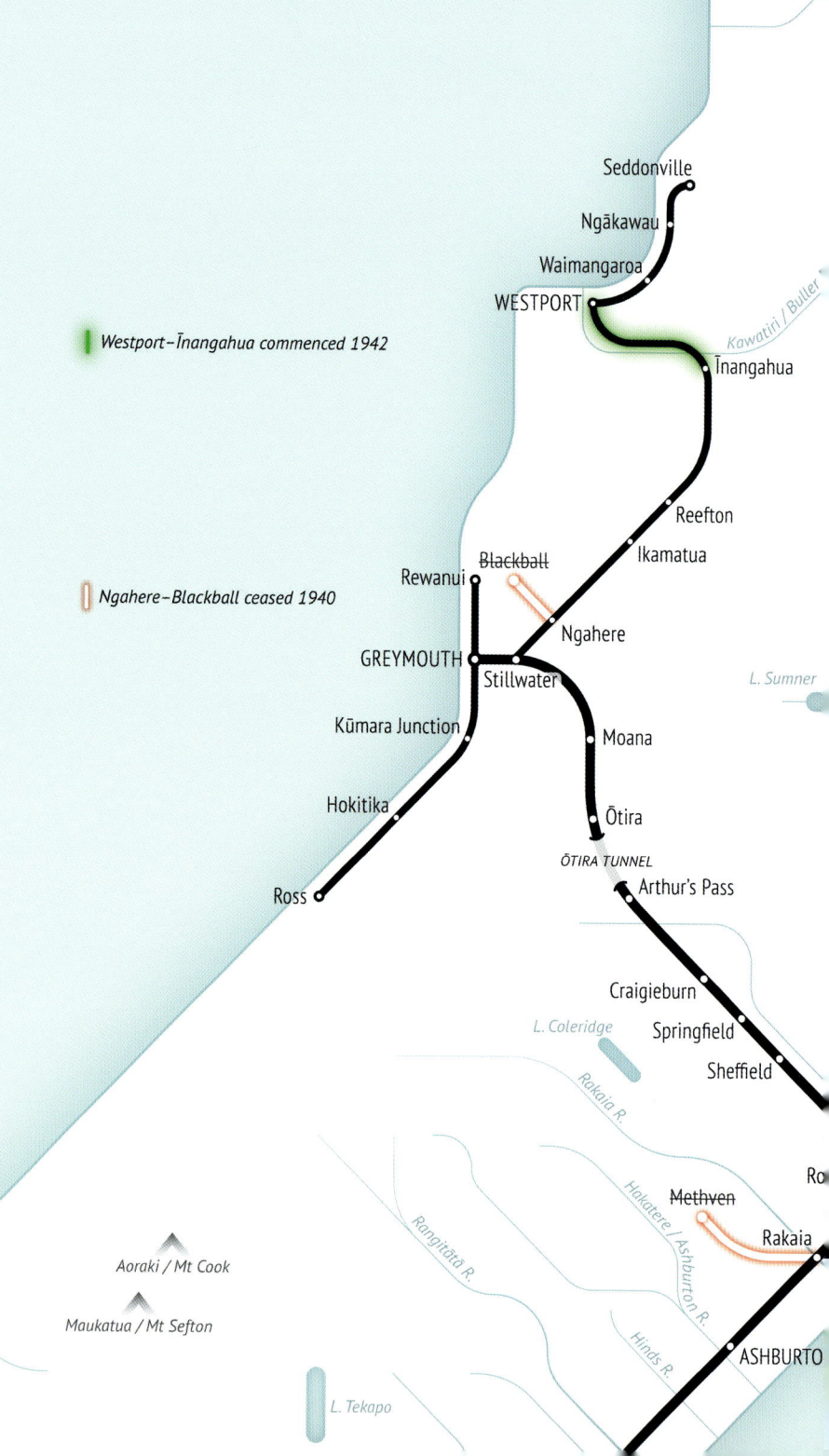

Seddonville

Ngākawau

Waimangaroa

WESTPORT

Kawatiri / Buller

Īnangahua

Westport–Īnangahua commenced 1942

Reefton

Ikamatua

Blackball

Rewanui

Ngahere

Ngahere–Blackball ceased 1940

GREYMOUTH

Stillwater

L. Sumner

Kūmara Junction

Moana

Hokitika

Ōtira

ŌTIRA TUNNEL

Ross

Arthur's Pass

Craigieburn

L. Coleridge

Springfield

Rakaia R.

Sheffield

Ro

Hokatere / Ashburton R.

Methven

Rangitātā R.

Rakaia

Aoraki / Mt Cook

Maukatua / Mt Sefton

Hinds R.

ASHBURTO

L. Tekapo

NELSON
PICTON
Richmond
Belgrove
enhope
BLENHEIM
Wairau R.
Ward
Awatere R.
Wharanui
Waiau Toa / Clarence R.
Clarence

Wharanui–Clarence commenced 1942
Clarence–Kaikōura commenced 1944
Kaikōura–Ōaro commenced 1945
Ōaro–Hundalee commenced 1943
Hundalee–Parnassus commenced 1939

KAIKŌURA
Waiau Uwha R.
Ōaro
Hundalee
Waiau
Parnassus
Culverden
Hurunui R.

Waiau–Waikari ceased 1939
Waikari–Waipara ceased 1940

Waikari
Scargill
Waipara
Rangiora
Kaiapoi
Waimakariri R.
Darfield
CHRISTCHURCH
on
Lyttelton
Lincoln
Southbridge
Little River

Rakaia–Methven ceased 1945

Gore–Lumsden ceased 1945, except during holiday periods

Lumsden–Kingston ceased 1937, except during holiday periods

Lumsden–Mossburn ceased 1937

Fairlie

Pleasant Point

Cave

Temuka

Washdyke

TIMARU

Studholme

Waitaki R.

...taki Dam

PWD

Kurow

 Kurow–Waitaki Dam ceased 1936

Pukeuri

ŌAMARU

Ranfurly

Hyde

Taieri R.

PALMERSTON

Middlemarch

Waikouaiti

Port Chalmers

DUNEDIN

Outram

MOSGIEL

Clarendon

Milton

Milton–Roxburgh ceased 1936

PRIV.

Kaitangata

Stirling–Kaitangata ceased 1937

Lower South Island
1935–1945

Train travel in New Zealand in 1935 was much the same as it had been for the past couple of decades despite changes to the network's size and reconsideration of the policies that guided its operation. A web of expresses linked cities and major regional towns, and hungry passengers crowded refreshment rooms at key stations along the way. Frankton Junction at Hamilton, Taumarunui on the Main Trunk Line, Woodville, Waipukurau, Ashburton and Ōamaru – the names entered traveller folklore. The bustling facilities served tens of thousands of pies, sandwiches and cups of tea a year and could satisfy an entire trainload of passengers in just a few minutes.[1]

Mixed trains ran to fewer towns than before but remained a regular part of the New Zealand transport experience. They were slow, but they got there. From Pukekohe to Waiuku, Paeroa to Thames, Rakaia to Methven or Balclutha to the Catlins, people could hop aboard a mixed train. In areas with poor roads, in particular, a mixed was still the best and sometimes the only option. Buses, service cars and private cars continued to skim away patronage, but NZR catered to all passengers: commuters, holidaymakers, day-trippers, businesspeople, backblocks residents, miners and more.

The distinctive and pungent smell of steam locomotion infused almost every journey, but changes to motive power were in the wind. Electric locomotives had worked the Ōtira Tunnel from its opening in August 1923; two years later NZR received a report on suburban electrification from respected British engineers Charles Merz and William McLellan, whose advice had guided the electrification of Melbourne's railways. They recommended NZR electrify Auckland and Wellington's suburban lines and Christchurch–Lyttelton.[2] Electric engines duly began hauling trains to Lyttelton from 1929, ending the smoke nuisance in the tunnel under the Port Hills, and electrification came to Wellington's suburban network from 1938 when the wires to Johnsonville became live, making the steep, twisting journey quicker for passengers and easier for railway workers.

The big innovation for intercity and regional journeys from the mid-1930s was the rise of the railcar. NZR hoped these self-propelled

Electric traction in Christchurch: E^C 9 hauls an early-morning Lyttelton suburban train through Linwood, 27 December 1963.
Weston Langford, no.103514

Opposite: The first day of electric traction in Wellington: a brand-new English Electric D^M/D multiple unit at Khandallah, 2 July 1938. It bears the original livery of royal-blue with a white band and grey roof. NZR repainted all units in Midland Red by 1949.
Wellington City Archives 00155-115

Above: The refreshment room at Paekākāriki, 1949. NZR did not operate dining cars between 1917 and 1970, and passengers queued to buy tea and sandwiches in refreshment rooms along the way.
ANZ AAVK 6390 B1241

vehicles could fill two niches – as cost-effective transport on lightly trafficked branches with insufficient demand for dedicated passenger trains, and as a cheaper option on main lines to the smaller regional cities. It monitored overseas innovations and experimented from 1906, but for three decades met with limited success. A popular battery-electric railcar operated services from Christchurch to Little River and Lyttelton from 1926 until its loss in a depot fire in 1934, but experiments with various petrol and steam-powered railcars failed. Some had unreliable technology, others were built poorly, rode roughly or could not handle New Zealand's steep grades and tight curvature. The Model T Ford railcars that attempted to save passenger traffic on quiet Southland branches in the late 1920s were, ironically, too diminutive for patronage elsewhere. From the mid-1930s, however, railcars became a viable option for main-line services.

The other transformation was in the shape of the network. A signal event for railway expansion occurred in 1935 when Michael Joseph Savage led the Labour Party into power. Labour had previously enabled United's minority government from 1928 to 1931; now it occupied the ministerial benches. The economy was regaining strength, and Labour hoped to stimulate a lasting and equitable return to prosperity. Some 65 years earlier Julius Vogel had inaugurated the national railway system, yet when Labour took office NZR was overseeing a network of seven disconnected parts – not to mention the PWD's lonely line between Wairoa and Waikōkopu. Bob Semple, the new Minister of Public Works, told Parliament in early 1936 that railways were 'the predominant factor in the country's transportation system, and the completion of the present isolated systems and

the linking-up of the various districts is … the proper and reasonable course'.[3]

In order to advance its railway policy, Savage's ministry obtained parliamentary consent to abolish the Railways Board and bring NZR back under ministerial control. General manager Philip Roussell had died unexpectedly in November 1932, and Garnet Hercules Mackley, a lifelong railwayman and talented administrator, replaced him. Mackley's ambitious programme to improve passenger rollingstock complemented Labour's expansion of the network. Dan Sullivan, who assumed the railways portfolio, undertook an extensive review in order to shape long-term planning in the public interest.[4] One outcome was the resumption of most suspended construction projects. The network began to grow again – and just in time: New Zealand was about to become embroiled in another global war, one that would place unprecedented strains on the nation, not least on its transport infrastructure.

1935–37: A MODERN RAILWAY FOR THE CAPITAL

When Labour entered government the PWD was constructing only one major railway project, the Tawa Flat Deviation. This had been authorised in 1924 and commenced in 1927, and was much needed to address a problem that beset railways into Wellington. An onerous 1-in-36 ruling grade on the North Island Main Trunk between Wellington and Johnsonville slowed trains and limited their loads.[5] The new route, double-tracked to accommodate traffic growth, had two tunnels and its steepest grade was 1-in-100 for southbound trains.

The deviation went hand-in-hand with construction of a new terminal to replace

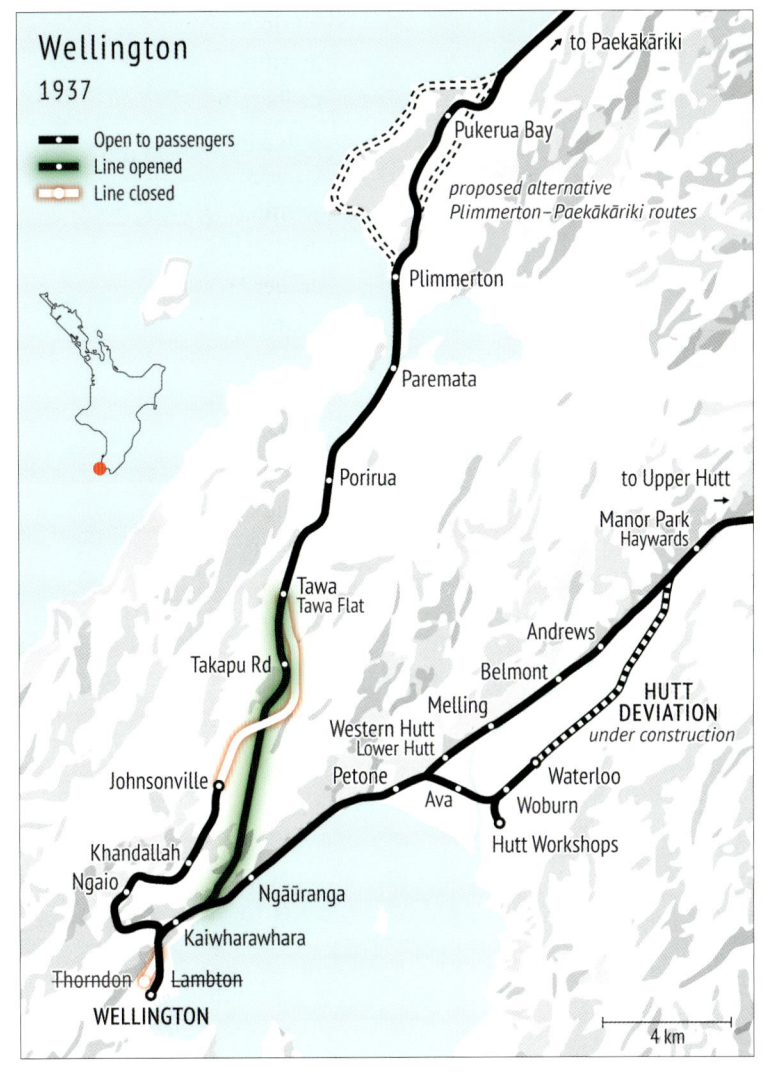

Wellington
1937

- ●──● Open to passengers
- ■──■ Line opened
- ▭──▭ Line closed

to Paekākāriki

Pukerua Bay

proposed alternative
Plimmerton–Paekākāriki routes

Plimmerton

Paremata

Porirua

to Upper Hutt

Manor Park
Haywards

Tawa
Tawa Flat

Andrews

Takapu Rd

Belmont

Melling

HUTT
DEVIATION
under construction

Western Hutt
Lower Hutt

Johnsonville

Petone

Waterloo

Ava

Woburn

Khandallah

Hutt Workshops

Ngaio

Ngāūranga

Kaiwharawhara

Thorndon   Lambton

WELLINGTON

4 km

to Longburn near Palmerston North in 1886, and competed with NZR's more circuitous Wairarapa route. NZR acquired the company in 1908 but the adjacent stations persisted for almost three decades more.

By the time the Tawa Flat Deviation was completed, the prime minister whose government had authorised it, William Massey, had been dead for over a decade. The deviation opened to goods trains in July 1935 but these ran only at night on a single track. The complete line and imposing new station opened to passengers on 19 June 1937 and immediately gave a fillip to passenger numbers.[6]

At the same time NZR severed the northern link between the old and new routes, closing the 6-kilometre section between Johnsonville and Tawa. This decision dated from 1929, when H.H. Sterling decided to retain most of the steep line through Wellington's northern suburbs because of substantial passenger traffic to the city, but not the portion beyond Johnsonville. Patronage in the late 1920s between Johnsonville and points north was minimal. Freight – mostly livestock – could be carried via Wellington, and the impressive Belmont Viaduct in Pāpārangi had high maintenance costs.[7] NZR received some complaints, mostly from farmers unhappy

Wellington's two cramped stations, Lambton and Thorndon. Lambton station sat at the foot of Mulgrave Street near the present station and served passengers for the Hutt and Wairarapa; passengers for Main Trunk trains had to go further up Thorndon Quay to Thorndon station. This was a consequence of NZR's earlier rivalry with the Wellington and Manawatū Railway Company, New Zealand's only successful private main-line railway, which built the line

OVERCOMING THE PUKERUA GRADE

The completion of the Tawa Flat Deviation left just one challenging section of railway between Wellington and Palmerston North. The photo above left shows the North Island Main Trunk sweeping through Pukerua Bay at the southern end of the Kāpiti Coast; the second shows a Matangi electric multiple unit above the Centennial Highway, near the bottom of the steep railway down to sea level at Paekākāriki. Ernest Haviland Hiley, upon his retirement as general manager of NZR in 1919, remarked that the Pukerua section was a weak point that 'could not remain any longer'.[8] If this line along an unstable hillside could be avoided, the entire railway between Wellington and Palmerston North would have no grade worse than 1-in-100. William Field, the Reform MP for Ōtaki and a passionate advocate for rail and road improvements, managed to have a Pukerua Deviation included in a Railways Authorization Act that year, but Coates and Massey claimed in 1920 that a labour shortage prohibited construction.[9] There the matter remained, despite the PWD engineer-in-chief F.W. Furkert using his annual report in 1924 to endorse a deviation at Pukerua Bay.[10]

In 1929, during his first year as NZR's general manager, Sterling asked senior officials to report on possible alternatives.[11] They considered two options, both expensive: a coastal route from Plimmerton around the rocky shore visible in the left-hand photo, and 'lowering' or 'flattening' the existing inland line with a new alignment, which included a 2.6-kilometre tunnel, to emerge near sea level below where the first photo was taken from. Coastal options had been considered before – including in the 1880s when the railway was first planned and in the 1919 Authorization Act – but these would have made the journey to Wellington longer and required extensive coastal reclamation works.

Sterling's officials rejected a deviation in favour of electrification, as electric locomotives would be able to haul trains south of Paekākāriki that weighed the same as the maximum permitted northwards for steam engines. This idea had history: the Wellington and Manawatū Railway Company had contemplated electrification as early as 1894. Bill Veitch, Minister of Railways, now believed electrification would postpone the need for a deviation 'indefinitely'.[12] Electric trains were duly introduced and ran to Paekākāriki from July 1940.

Left and above: André Brett, 8 December 2018

4

1935–1945

The straitened circumstances of the Depression certainly influenced decision-making – one Ōtaki resident claimed that Bob Semple told him a railway deviation alongside the Centennial Highway would have been built in the late 1930s if only the government had had the money.[13] But the miserly way in which subsequent governments have funded railways means that southbound trains still labour up the side of Paekākāriki Hill to Pukerua Bay. Proposals for a new alignment have persisted, including as part of wider plans to enhance links between the Porirua Basin and the Hutt, as discussed in Chapter 5. Recently, engineers have urged for a deviation at Pukerua Bay on the basis that the current route's geological instability limits Wellington's resilience to natural disasters.[14] The restrictions on train speed and capacity and the geological risks suggest that a deviation, though costly, is overdue. Historical plans from both NZR and the Ministry of Works contain worthwhile ideas that can be repurposed for future needs.

with the new arrangements for livestock. One resident worried that the line might be required as an alternative entry to Wellington, but received assurances that any blockage in the new tunnels could be 'speedily cleared'.[15]

Tawa Flat would have opened in 1937 no matter who formed the government, but Labour was able to claim subsequent openings for itself as it authorised the resumption of most projects that Forbes had abandoned in 1930–31. First up were Napier–Gisborne, Westport–Īnangahua and Parnassus–Wharanui.[16] Semple gave approval for work to recommence on the Dargaville Branch in 1937 then turned to the Bay of Plenty, where multiple routes competed for attention and funding. Inland residents, who aspired to a line from Tauranga to Rotorua and Taupō, or at least a resumption of the Ward government's line from Rotorua south to Reporoa, were disappointed, but those on the coast had cause to rejoice. In 1937 Semple authorised the Paeroa–Pōkeno line, a shortcut across the Hauraki Plains to slash journey times between Auckland and the Bay of Plenty, and the following year the government decided to continue the East Coast Main Trunk beyond Tāneatua through the Waimana Gorge to Ōpōtiki.[17] This would have left only the challenging ascent from Ōpōtiki to Moutohorā to link the Bay of Plenty and Gisborne.

But just as the Depression had stalled aspirations throughout New Zealand at the dawn of the 1930s, international circumstances would again intervene in domestic railway construction. The outbreak of World War II meant that Labour could not bring all of its railway policy to fruition.

THE MISSING LINK ACROSS THE HAURAKI PLAINS

One lesson of New Zealand's railway history is not to count chickens before they hatch. Few railways illustrate this more clearly than the proposed Paeroa–Pōkeno line. Anyone in 1938 would have been stunned to learn that all that came of this project is some abandoned formation, still visible today from State Highway 2.

Proposals for a railway across the Hauraki Plains emerged around 1906 and quickly became popular among residents of Paeroa, Thames and Waihī. Trains to Auckland via the 'horseshoe' through Morrinsville and Hamilton were tedious, and as work progressed on the East Coast Main Trunk towards Tauranga, the need for a shortcut from Auckland to the Bay of Plenty was apparent. This line would leave the North Island Main Trunk at the town of Pōkeno, between Pukekohe and Mercer, and cross easy country to meet the Thames and Waihī railways at their junction in Paeroa. Parliament authorised 10 kilometres at the Paeroa end in 1915 and the remaining 56 kilometres in 1918.[18] This simply permitted construction, however; it did not provide funds. Local residents waited. The East Coast Main Trunk reached Tauranga in 1928, but trains to Auckland had to trundle the long way by Hamilton. Residents waited some more. And waited. And waited.

When Labour entered office and revived suspended railway projects, it also turned attention to the Paeroa–Pōkeno line. Parliament in 1937 approved £75,000 of an estimated expenditure of just over £1 million (about $110 million in 2020 currency).[19] A large crowd gathered in Paeroa on 27 January 1938 to witness Bob Semple turn the first sod. One attendee recalled that Semple not only praised the project but also took the opportunity to condemn drunk drivers on

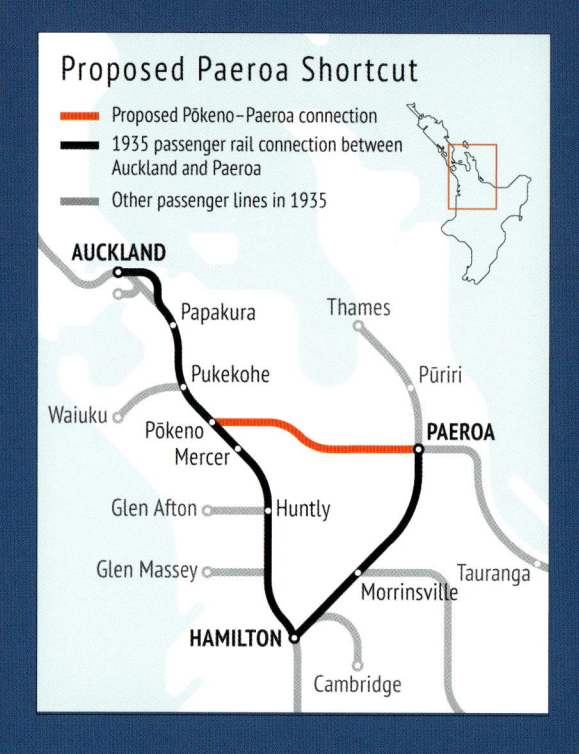

New Zealand's roads.[20] Labourers set to work making embankments and excavating cuttings.

By May 1940 the government had spent over £130,000, at which point Semple suspended the project for the duration of World War II.[21] Wartime required resources to be devoted to linking isolated towns to the railway network, not to creating shortcuts. Semple vowed the stoppage was temporary but it was not: a severe shortage of labour prohibited resumption after the war. In 1949 he told Parliament that the line 'should be completed as soon as the necessary man-power is available'.[22] But his time in government was over: Labour lost that year's election and Sidney Holland's National government had little appetite for the project, which lingered until 1962 when John McAlpine, Keith Holyoake's minister of railways, administered the final rites. McAlpine did not consider passenger traffic at all. He decided that growth at the port of Tauranga meant there was no need for a shortcut from the Bay of Plenty to the port of Auckland; rather, the Waikato and Rotorua needed better rail access to Tauranga. Federated Farmers and other National supporters favoured a tunnel under the Kaimai Range for this purpose. Cabinet accepted McAlpine's arguments and authorised disposal of the Paeroa–Pōkeno land and assets.[23] Construction of the 8879-metre Kaimai Tunnel, the longest in New Zealand, lasted from 1965 to 1978.

The Paeroa–Pōkeno line is one of the great 'what if?' questions of New Zealand railway history. If Labour had finished the project, would the Kaimai Tunnel have been built? Would passenger trains to the Bay of Plenty have been more competitive and longer-lasting? Would the port of Tauranga have grown more slowly?

The line still has its supporters – the New Zealand First party even included it in a 2014 policy for Railways of National Importance. As long as rail transport continues between Auckland and Tauranga, the question of this shortcut is likely to remain.

1936–39: WAIROA GETS ITS RAILWAY

Labour expected to open its first revived railway project, Napier to Wairoa, in 1937, but construction in rugged terrain and damage from floods slowed progress. Local residents had maintained that the closure of the Napier–Pūtōrino railway after the 1931 earthquake constituted a great injustice and a spectacular waste, and insisted that completion of the line to Wairoa was achievable. Only one major gap remained – the Mōhaka River crossing – and as the steel for the viaduct had already been procured, advocates suggested this 'giant gulch' could be bridged with modest expenditure.[24]

4

1935–1945

Wairarapa-class railcar RM 9 carries the official party over the Mōhaka Viaduct. Minister of Railways Dan Sullivan drove the railcar himself. W.B. Beattie, Auckland Libraries 1370-342-11

Once Labour gained power the PWD got to work quickly, and by October 1936 goods trains were again operating between Napier and Pūtōrino.[25] Opening of the whole Napier–Wairoa line to passengers seemed to be mere months away.

A new era of regional rail travel had arrived in the form of two types of railcar, and NZR decided to show one off with a daytrip to Wairoa on 30 June 1937 to celebrate the completion of the imposing Mōhaka Viaduct.[26] The new railcars, known as the Midland and Wairarapa classes, began running in 1936. In the South Island were the Midland railcars, a pair of small units built as much for delivering Christchurch newspapers to the West Coast as for carrying passengers. In the North Island, the Wairarapa class comprised seven railcars designed to run at speed over the Remutaka Incline. Both classes succeeded at their assigned tasks.[27] Wellington writer and editor O.N. Gillespie wrote effusively about the Wairarapa class:

Now vanishes that old bogey, the mixed train … Now enters the fairy; the new magic vehicle, the rail car. It can take care of all the human freight, leaving the drudgery of the carriage of goods to the everyday steam engine.[28]

Joyful locals travelled from miles around to witness this 'fairy' on its daytrip, but they had to wait some time for a regular timetable. The line beyond Pūtōrino was entirely unready for passengers: stations were not yet built, yards and fencing were incomplete, and some of the line's formation was temporary.[29] Special trains to horse races in February 1938 were to be the harbinger of timetabled services to start in June. Then on 25 April floods struck, destroying the Esk River bridge and washing out the line in

19 places between Eskdale and Pūtōrino.[30] The grand opening was on hold.

Wairoa had waited decades for a railway connection, and when regular services finally began on 1 July 1939 the town had extra reason to celebrate: the new timetable used the most modern rollingstock available. The Standard class of railcars were emerging from Hutt Workshops, each named for a waka hourua, the great canoes of Māori legend. Railcar technology was advancing rapidly, and the Standards offered greater passenger comfort and operational efficiency than the Midland and Wairarapa railcars. Class leader RM 30 'Aotea' starred in Wairoa's opening ceremony. Thousands of people filled the station, including 1650 travellers from Napier and Hastings who came by special carriage trains. The officials, including ministers Semple and Sullivan and general manager Mackley, arrived aboard 'Aotea'.[31]

Regular services began two days later. Railcars ran twice daily (except Sundays) between Wairoa and Napier, and on Saturdays an additional service ran through to Wellington, returning the next day. The timetables allowed 130 minutes for Napier–Wairoa, including stops.[32] This is testament to the quality of the new line and the railcars: eight decades later the solitary daily bus takes only 15–20 minutes less, and private cars are not much faster.

NZR took control of the line from Wairoa to Waikōkopu at the same time, but curiously did not timetable a passenger service. It operated excursions from Waikōkopu as early as the Christmas holidays of 1937, but traffic returns from Nūhaka – the largest town on the line, near the terminus – reveal no passengers for the first few months of NZR operation between July and November 1939.[33] The Gisborne Chamber

Standard railcar RM 34 'Tainui' in its original livery of silver with a green band, outside the Wairoa railcar servicing shed in 1939. A.N. Breckon, Auckland Libraries 1370-339-7

of Commerce petitioned NZR to extend the Wairoa railcar service to Nūhaka, which sat on the main road to Gisborne. Mackley responded that Wairoa had superior facilities for train and bus transfers; he believed that patronage beyond Wairoa would be limited and did not want the hassle of rearranging the timetable.[34] This was not the end of the matter, however: on 5 September 1940 the Kōpuawhara section of the Public Works Medical Association resolved to work with the Labour Party's local branch to obtain a passenger service to Waikōkopu. A report on 22 November that year, interestingly, describes the cancellation of a Saturday train, with the implication that local residents rode it.[35] But as it was, Wairoa enjoyed one of the finest services in the country, while people who lived further along the bend of the coast to the Māhia Peninsula could only look at their local railway, goods only for more than 15 years, and wonder when they might have passenger trains to call their own.

1936–40: LINKING CANTERBURY AND MARLBOROUGH

Down south another grand plan was taking shape in some of the most rugged terrain in New Zealand. After lengthy debate about coastal and inland options, ongoing since the 1870s, Canterbury and Marlborough's railways were finally inching closer to each other. People in Marlborough tended to favour a coastal alignment, but many leading Cantabrians preferred to go inland. A railway from Christchurch had reached Culverden in 1886, where it stalled for decades. Come 1935 two separate routes pointed north: the Culverden line, which had been extended to Waiau in 1919, and a coastal branch, which had grown in stages from Waipara to Parnassus between 1902 and 1914. The PWD had constructed some formation beyond both termini but little else had happened until Ward's United ministry decided to continue the line from Parnassus in 1929.[36] Although United suspended construction in 1931, its choice was definitive: when Labour ordered work to resume in July

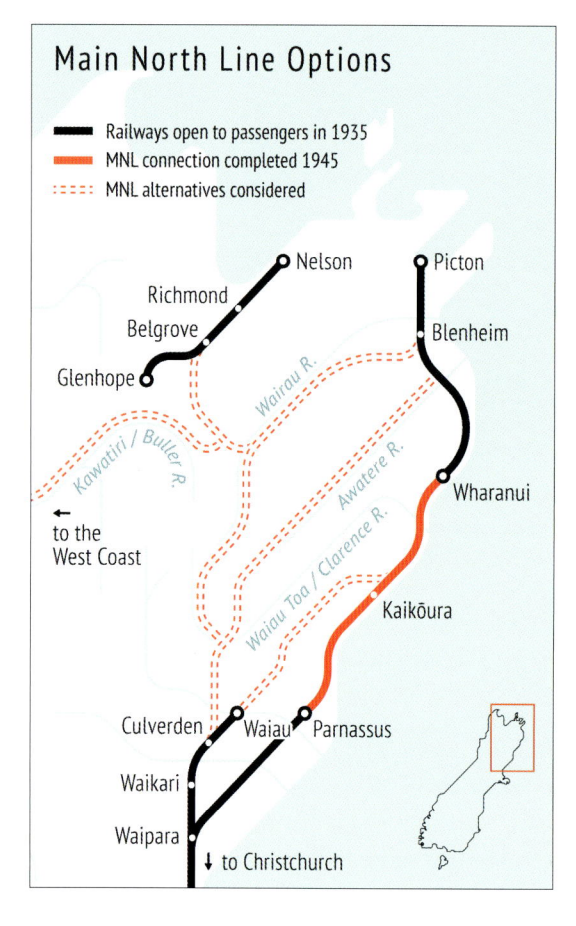

Main North Line Options

━━━ Railways open to passengers in 1935
━━━ MNL connection completed 1945
┄┄┄ MNL alternatives considered

Nelson
Richmond
Belgrove
Glenhope
Picton
Blenheim
Wharanui
Wairau R.
Awatere R.
Waiau Toa / Clorence R.
Kawatiri / Buller R.
← to the West Coast
Kaikōura
Culverden   Waiau   Parnassus
Waikari
Waipara
↓ to Christchurch

along a rocky precipitous coast it is necessary to provide in many places for extensive sea-walls ... this is a work of considerable magnitude.[38]

To make matters worse, a lot of past work had fallen into disrepair. All these reasons explain why just one new portion of the Main North Line opened before 1940: on 11 December 1939 NZR inaugurated passenger services to Hundalee, some 19 kilometres north of Parnassus.[39]

With the coastal route confirmed as the main line, the inland branch to Waiau declined. From the mid-1920s northbound expresses from Christchurch ran not to Culverden and Waiau but to Parnassus, where interprovincial travellers boarded buses and service cars to Marlborough.[40] Passenger numbers on the Waiau Branch fell further as people bound for Hanmer Springs and destinations beyond the Lewis Pass caught private buses from Christchurch rather than taking the train as far as Culverden. From 30 January 1939 passenger trains to Culverden and Waiau ceased; a modest service remained from Waipara through the Weka Pass to Waikari because the latter possessed a locomotive depot.[41] The cancellations came as part of a wider scheme to 'rationalise' services north of Christchurch, and the *North Canterbury Gazette* cited 'several authorities' (unnamed ones) who described the replacement of trains with buses as 'in line with progress' overseas.[42]

Railway histories often state that *all* passenger services ended on the Waiau Branch in 1939, overlooking the continuation of trains to Waikari. This is understandable: some NZR archival files overlook it too.[43] The surviving service was poorly patronised, and when NZR closed the Waikari locomotive depot and

1936, there was no doubt that it would take the coastal route. At the Marlborough end the isolated Picton–Blenheim railway crept as far south as Wharanui, where work stalled in August 1917.[37] Kaikōura, in the middle of this gap, was one of New Zealand's most isolated towns.

Sullivan tried to convey to Parliament some sense of how challenging the construction of the railway between Parnassus and Wharanui was:

> *... there are twenty tunnels to pierce of an aggregate length of some 3 miles [4.8km] ... a large number of bridges to construct of all sizes and types, some of them over very large and turbulent rivers ... owing to the location of the line*

transferred staff, the passenger trains ended. From 2 December 1940, all trains inland from Waipara carried goods only.[44]

1936–40: REGULATION AND CONTRACTION

The extension of trunk routes occurred alongside changes in transport regulations and the continued contraction of rural passenger services. In some cases these were intertwined.

The Savage government made a point of passing a Transport Licensing Amendment Act during its first year in power. The act gave NZR further protections: no licence would be granted for any service with 'substantially the same terminal points and route' as those operated by NZR, whether trains or Road Services buses.[45] A subsequent proclamation fixed 40 miles (64km) as the maximum distance over which a road service could compete with NZR. But this was not the advantage for rail that it might appear to be.

NZR's revenue was expected to cover its operating expenses, including the full cost of maintaining railway infrastructure plus the interest on capital. Road users faced nothing like this. The Main Highways Act of 1922 created a board to control the arterial roads that Kiwis have known since 1936 as state highways. Central and local governments funded the board evenly – this was later calculated on an ad hoc basis – and district road boards, borough councils and similar local authorities controlled other roads. Tolls, once charged in a number of regions, vanished with the Main Highways Act, and with them went any expectation that roads recover their costs. In the first half of the 1930s, all forms of motor taxation combined contributed less than a quarter of funds expended on roads – the rest came from other taxes, rates and loans.[46]

James Watson, in his history of New Zealand transport, emphasises this discrepancy: 'In reply to the statement "the railways don't pay", it was quite legitimate to ask whether the roads did.'[47] NZR's competitors did not need to maintain the infrastructure on which they depended, nor pay interest on its capital cost. NZR Road Services was also a beneficiary: while passenger trains were singled out for creating or exacerbating losses,

New Zealand's first Labour Cabinet, 1935. Dan Sullivan stands second from right; seated are Michael Joseph Savage (third from left) and Bob Semple (far right). ATL 1/2-055145-F

the buses ran on roads for which NZR was not responsible and which were not expected to generate financial returns. No wonder NZR officials looked favourably on Road Services.

The government permitted NZR to buy out competitors, and again this tended to favour road passenger operation over rail. Acquisitions were made in the belief that competition would be wasteful and drive the cost of transport up, not down, nationally. Sullivan boasted in 1940 that he had effected 'the almost complete cessation of competitive running on parallel routes', but this did not mean his acquisitions or transport legislation encouraged the operation of passenger trains.[48]

NZR buses began to replace trains in an increasing number of regions, and were often laid on to meet demand rather than being scheduled. The national timetable of November 1939 reveals this clearly. NZR operated buses along many similar routes to its own trains, including Auckland to Hamilton and Rotorua, Wellington to Whanganui, Hokitika to Greymouth and Christchurch to Dunedin.[49] To suggest these did not constitute competitive running because they did not run at the same time as trains was disingenuous.

One example of the government's policy bringing about the demise rather than revitalisation of passenger rail services occurred in northern Southland in 1937. Lumsden sat at the junction of two tourist runs that NZR dominated – Fiordland and Queenstown – and NZR vigorously promoted a range of holiday-season excursions and package tours from the early 1920s.[50] A typical journey began in Dunedin: holidaymakers caught the original *Kingston Flyer*, an express train via Gore and Lumsden to Kingston; at Lumsden they could connect with buses to Te Anau, and at Kingston

they could transfer to the NZR steamboats that plied Lake Wakatipu – one, the TSS *Earnslaw*, still sails today in private ownership. Passenger numbers were immense in summer and at Easter. Outside holiday periods, a train at Gore connected with Dunedin–Invercargill expresses and ran through to Kingston. A twice-weekly with-car goods also trundled west from Lumsden to Mossburn, halfway to Fiordland, but few locals and almost no tourists caught it – the buses on the adjacent road to Te Anau were more frequent.

Off-season patronage waned heavily during the 1930s, especially between Lumsden and Kingston, and NZR chose to replace trains in favour of bus offerings. Lumsden's passenger timetable was cut markedly on 4 October 1937.[51] NZR discarded the with-car goods to Mossburn, and passengers could now only ride north of Lumsden to Kingston during holiday seasons. An Invercargill–Queenstown bus replaced trains to Kingston for the rest of the year, and this connected in Lumsden with trains across the Waimea Plains to Gore.

Sullivan described the new timetable as a necessary reorganisation ahead of the introduction of railcars from Invercargill and Gore to Kingston.[52] This never happened; England's Vulcan Foundry delivered the railcars in question from 1940, but these never ran on Southland's branch lines. Instead, off-season passengers from Dunedin to Queenstown caught an Invercargill-bound mail train at 8.33am, disembarked at Gore for a 12.15pm guaranteed connection by rail to Lumsden, boarded a bus at Lumsden at 2.15pm and reached Queenstown at 5pm.[53] Travellers during holiday seasons fortunately did not have to deal with that. The timetable retained a 'runs as required' express all the way to Kingston where it connected with the

4

Dunedin railway station in the late 1930s, when it was an important terminal for suburban and intercity passengers and the starting place of countless holidays. Collection of Lemuel Lyes

lake ferries. In theory this could have operated daily, but in practice it ran only when demand was highest: for the first holiday season after regular trains ceased, the express ran from 18 December 1937 to 5 February 1938.[54] No other line retained runs-as-required passenger trains in its timetable after all routine services finished; elsewhere, if NZR put on holiday specials to relieve crowding on overwhelmed buses, the trains ran on special authority.

The government transport licensing system resulted in contraction of the passenger network on the West Coast, too, where NZR ran mixed trains from Blackball, a coalmining town and celebrated union hub, to Ngahere on the main line and sometimes to Greymouth. Schoolchildren aside, the needs of coal distribution constrained the timetable and made it unattractive to most passengers. At the same time, Isobel McGlashan operated a private bus between Greymouth and Blackball. Grey county councillor James Mulcare considered the local train and bus timetables inadequate

and the fares unaffordable; his own daughters and a niece were instead using the services of a local man, referred to in NZR files only as 'a man named Williams', who carried passengers in his private car from Blackball to Greymouth for a modest charge. McGlashan was frustrated by this unlicensed rival competing with her service, but in Mulcare's opinion it was 'up to the Government to provide suitable services … and that too much importance should not be given to the immediate financial results'. Superintendent of NZR Road Services F.K. Mackay was not impressed, saying: 'Mulcare desires us to provide a daily service for not more than twelve people at an uneconomical rate.'[55] The district traffic manager proposed to replace passenger trains on the branch with buses, and NZR negotiated with McGlashan to co-ordinate Grey Valley transport and put Williams off the road. McGlashan sold her licence to NZR, keeping for herself a short run between Greymouth and Cobden; from 4 November 1940 the branch became goods only.[56]

Only one other NZR service ended in the 1930s, and it was one for which local residents and some NZR officials had held high hopes. The Roxburgh Branch had been considered a potential route to Central Otago in the nineteenth century, and operated efficiently when it terminated in Lawrence, but the extension to Roxburgh was an expensive disappointment. With steep grades and sharp curves that limited speeds and loads, the full route never showed a profit.[57] By the time it reached its final terminus in 1928, road carriers were well established and many potential passengers owned a car. NZR tried numerous unsuccessful schemes to induce people to change their habits, including a train in 1930 that ran Roxburgh–Dunedin return on Thursdays, but this averaged only 5.3 passengers from Roxburgh.[58] Eight years after passenger facilities came to Roxburgh, and six years after the royal commission proposed to terminate them beyond Lawrence, the line became goods only in its entirety.[59] Passenger trains to Lawrence might have lasted longer if the railway had not been pushed through to Roxburgh, but on a long, unprofitable line they were vulnerable. The extension might also have been more successful if the government had funded the PWD to build it earlier and to better standards. NZR had put in a strong effort and shouldered less blame than elsewhere.

The few passenger offerings beyond NZR's network were also vanishing. Wilton Collieries owned a private railway in the Waikato that ran west from Ngāruawāhia to Glen Massey. In 1930 it had purchased the line from Waipā Collieries, the original owner, and from 1935 it contracted NZR to operate the trains. At that time, just four others sat outside NZR's control: the Ōhai Railway Board in western Southland, the Kaitangata Coal Company in South Otago and two PWD services, Kirikōpuni to Tangowahine in Northland and Kurow to the Waitaki Dam in North Otago.

The railway to the Waitaki Dam was never expected to outlive the construction scheme. The dam was declared complete in October 1934 and the temporary town that had sprung up beside it shrank as workers and their families moved away.[60] Passenger trains to Kurow for schoolchildren continued until December 1936 when, almost eight years after services began, the PWD returned the rollingstock to NZR; removal of the rails began in the new year.[61] The government continued to transform the Waitaki River and its Mackenzie Basin catchment with hydroelectric plants, artificial lakes and canals until the early 1980s, but the Waitaki Dam was the only one served by a railway. For the later

projects, NZR railed construction materials to Kurow from where they were transhipped to road.[62]

When Wilton Collieries handed over train operations to NZR, the Kaitangata Coal Company became the last private operator of daily passenger trains in New Zealand – at least until NZR passed out of public ownership in 1993. It carried passengers and coal between Kaitangata and Stirling, just outside Balclutha on the Main South Line. NZR operated the trains when the line opened in 1876, but before long the company acquired its own locomotive and rollingstock. In the 1930s it ran two trains daily, taking 20 minutes each way, to connect with NZR services in Stirling. Ridership was low: in October 1936 each train averaged four passengers, and this had slipped to three by May 1937.[63] Faced with the need to reduce staff hours to meet a new 40-hour-week award (its guard worked a gruelling 80–90-hour week), the company could see no way to maintain passenger accommodation without paying significant overtime, and the patronage hardly justified this. If the company did not cater for passengers it could schedule coal trains at more suitable times. NZR offered no objection – indeed, the change allowed more efficient main-line timetabling too – and a local bus operator took over the route from 17 July 1937.[64] Coal sustained the Kaitangata Line until 1970, six years shy of its centenary. The State Mines Department controlled the line for the last 12 years, and it was the longest-lived railway to exist outside the NZR network.

The demise of this passenger service left just two that NZR did not operate: those of the Ōhai Railway Board and the PWD – and with the missing link to Dargaville close to completion, the PWD would soon cease to run passenger trains too.

1940–45: CLOSING THE GAPS

World War II gave impetus to Labour's policy of completing trunk routes and missing links. As well as the immeasurable cost of the thousands of lives lost, the conflict crippled New Zealand's international production and trade. The government took over many private aircraft, leaving Union Airways and other companies flying a skeleton network, and petrol and rubber shortages restricted the use of buses, trucks and cars. For a few years railways resumed their dominance of land transport. Some trains were so overcrowded that passengers at night bedded down as best they could – even in the luggage racks – while soldiers sat on their kit in the aisles or vestibules.[65]

The gaps in the rail network needed to be filled more than ever, and the government, led by Peter Fraser after the death of Savage in March 1940, concentrated its resources on projects that were well advanced. Other projects fell by the way. The Paeroa–Pōkeno shortcut was no longer a priority, and Ōpōtiki's rail dreams were also over. Semple delivered the bad news there in person, saying it was 'simply out of the question during the war': money was short, materials difficult to obtain and workers were needed elsewhere. Tāneatua would remain the permanent railhead despite local protests. An 'up-to-date highway' to Ōpōtiki would, Semple felt, be 'of more value to the people of the district than the railway'.[66]

Work also ceased on some major deviations and improvements: a new terminal in Christchurch had to wait, and although the PWD had worked intermittently to bypass central Palmerston North (the Milson Deviation), trains would continue to steam through the town square for some years yet.

Work continued on four new lines, all of which connected isolated railway systems to the national network: Tangowahine–Dargaville, Waikōkopu–Gisborne, Hundalee–Wharanui and Westport–Īnangahua. The first gap to be closed was between Tangowahine and Dargaville, the main town of the northern Kaipara Harbour. The PWD operated a goods train to Dargaville on 30 April 1940, and from that date goods could be booked all the way from Donnellys Crossing to anywhere on the North Island network.[67] NZR took over operations from the PWD on 20 October 1941, running mixed trains from Waiōtira to Dargaville – although passengers initially had to change to buses at Tangowahine until a new timetable came into effect on 17 November 1941.[68] The PWD had run passenger trains throughout the country for well over half a century, but now its role of carrying the general public ended.

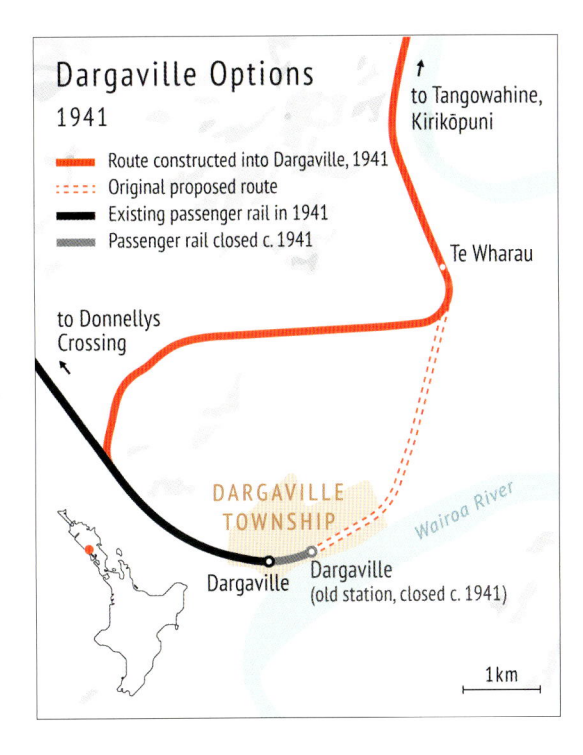

Dargaville Options
1941

— Route constructed into Dargaville, 1941
····· Original proposed route
— Existing passenger rail in 1941
— Passenger rail closed c. 1941

to Tangowahine, Kirikōpuni

Te Wharau

to Donnellys Crossing

DARGAVILLE TOWNSHIP

Wairoa River

Dargaville

Dargaville (old station, closed c. 1941)

1km

Although NZR operated trains to Dargaville from 1941, the PWD did not hand over control of the line until March 1943, as it was yet to complete the infrastructure. It was implementing a revised plan that reflected new ideas of how railways served communities. The original intention was to bring the line from Tangowahine into Dargaville alongside the Wairoa River, and it is extraordinary how close to completion this was when work was suspended in early 1931: earthworks were less than 3 kilometres from town, and ballast and track were not far behind.[69] Semple abandoned this, however, in favour of a circuitous route around the back of Dargaville to avoid multiple level crossings. It was, in his view, 'in keeping with modern trends in railway location, which are to keep railway-lines out of the more thickly populated and business areas'.[70] A new station on the town's western fringe replaced the cramped but centrally located terminus of the Donnellys Crossing line. The PWD also bypassed the balloon loop around Kirikōpuni as the butter factory it served had closed: this reduced the journey time by 10–30 minutes.[71] When this work was complete, NZR took over the whole line.

It is difficult to justify the slow completion of the Dargaville line, even in the context of the Depression. A few easy kilometres of track were all that was needed, and a complete line provided obvious efficiencies in joining the isolated Kaihū Valley Railway to the main network. Departmental estimates did not expect the line to be profitable, but these also forecast a loss from the Stratford–Ōkahukura Line in northern Taranaki, a route that filled a much larger gap through some of the roughest terrain traversed by rail in New Zealand. If that could be finished in straitened circumstances, so too

could the Dargaville line, especially as NZR wanted to eliminate the extra costs inherent in small isolated sections.

Dargavillians could feel aggrieved that passenger rail services came a decade late – and only ever as mixed trains. The report of 1936 that endorsed completing the line sanctioned a daily railcar all the way from Donnellys Crossing to connect with main-line expresses at Waiōtira. NZR, however, could not manufacture Standard railcars quickly enough, and as additional units purchased from the Vulcan Foundry in England were insufficient to meet all wants, the transportation superintendent in 1940 abandoned plans for a railcar.[72] After NZR took full control of the branch in 1943, it ran two mixed services daily. This still represented a good option for travel to Whangārei, but by now roads were sufficiently well developed that some Auckland-bound travellers preferred to catch a bus to Maungatūroto and board main-line trains there.[73] The circuitous railway and the station on the edge of town signalled NZR's intentions: it came to Dargaville to carry goods, not passengers.

The main line to Gisborne, on the other hand, was a priority for passengers as well as goods, and its completion in 1942 came not a moment too soon. Construction along the isolated, rugged coast between Waikōkopu and Gisborne was challenging and resulted in the loss of 25 lives, 22 of these during the small hours of 19 February 1938 when a flash flood demolished a construction camp at Kōpuawhara and caused damage at Boyd's Camp, closer to Gisborne. Fourteen people climbed onto the cookhouse roof to escape the torrent and survived. One elderly man tied himself to a hut with an electrical cable and held a young girl above the water for an hour. Not so lucky were 11 men who scrambled on top of a truck that the torrent then carried away, and the man who first raised the alarm by beating on doors and banging the cookhouse gong also died. The flood was New Zealand's deadliest during the twentieth century.[74] But neither this calamity nor the outbreak of war stopped construction; lesser hurdles in the past had seemed insuperable but now the project had an air of national importance. By December 1941 petrol and tyre shortages were severe and Gisborne was anxious for the railway to be finished.[75] At the time Semple was minister of railways – he had passed the works portfolio to Tim Armstrong in January 1941 but resumed it when Armstrong died in November 1942. Semple was probably relieved to announce in late August 1942 that trains to Gisborne would begin on 7 September.[76]

Gisborne residents turned out in droves to witness the inaugural service. Schoolchildren enjoyed a half-holiday and businesses closed as around ten thousand people enjoyed 'perfect spring weather' to cheer the first southbound train. The turnout, impressive in its own right, was even more astounding in light of the local population. An estimated 16,200 people lived in Gisborne, including 2300 in the greater urban area beyond the borough council's boundary.[77] If the attendance figure given by the *Auckland Star*'s correspondent is even moderately accurate, over 60 percent of the population attended the ceremony. Semple celebrated with them. He told the crowd that had the railway not been completed, as a result of the rubber shortage, 'Gisborne would probably have been cut off'.[78] Passenger rail, already so crucial to mobility in New Zealand, represented more than a link with the outside world during wartime: it was a lifeline.

Another essential passenger service began on the same day in Buller. Separate networks on the West Coast ran inland from the coal ports of Greymouth and Westport from the 1870s. As described in Chapter 2, the Ōtira Tunnel had linked Greymouth to the main South Island network in 1923. Almost 70 years after the first train chugged out of Westport, this town's isolation finally ended too. The people of Buller were so enthusiastic about their railway that they celebrated landmark occasions in 1941, 1942 and 1943. The PWD hosted the first at Slatey Creek in the Buller Gorge to drive a ceremonial last spike on 2 December 1941. Semple represented the government alongside the Minister of Labour, Paddy Webb, with whom he had much in common: both were former miners and trade union organisers born in Australia, migrants to the West Coast after being blacklisted across the Tasman – though now only Webb represented a West Coast constituency. Trains brought revellers from Reefton and Westport, one bearing a placard inscribed 'Travel by train, Seddonville to Bluff, 606 miles' (975km). J. Kelly, the oldest engineman in Buller, had the honour of driving his locomotive through a ceremonial tape.[79]

The PWD still had work to do before daily traffic could commence on the line. Occasional passenger services ran in early 1942 and a regular goods service was inaugurated during April.[80] Plummeting petrol and rubber supplies prompted Semple and Armstrong to reach an agreement for NZR to run trains on the Buller line before the PWD had handed over control and, as a result, on 7 September 1942 NZR began a twice-daily service between Westport and Greymouth, connecting with Christchurch expresses at Stillwater.[81] The service used new Vulcan railcars which were designed to run at speed on light track such as that between Stillwater and Reefton. NZR ordered 10 of these: one was lost to a German U-boat attack on the voyage to New Zealand, and the other nine entered service between 1940 and 1942.[82] The Vulcans spent their working lives in the South Island, while the six Standard railcars ran only in the North.

Semple could not join the people of Buller for their first railcar arrival but he returned in December 1943, exactly two years after the driving of the last spike. This time he and Webb were there to celebrate the official handover to NZR. The Westport Boys Band, fittingly, serenaded the two men on arrival with 'Waltzing Matilda'. The handover effected no changes for passengers, as trains continued to run as before, yet people crowded the platform to hear the mayor of Westport laud the railway as the most important public work ever built in Buller.[83] The large attendance suggests he was not exaggerating for his ministerial guests.

The one remaining gap, the Main North Line on the east coast between Hundalee in North Canterbury and Wharanui in Marlborough, was filled in stages from 1942 to 1945. A

30-kilometre stretch from Wharanui to the south bank of the Clarence River opened on 19 October. The task of reducing the gap between the northern and southern ends, Semple remarked, was 'the most essential job I know of at the moment for the saving of petrol and tyres'. It would reduce fuel consumption by 50,000 litres annually and avoid 160,000 kilometres of tyre wear.[84] Now only 74 kilometres separated the railheads. Service cars shuttled passengers between them, and Kaikōura, almost exactly in the middle, established itself as an important lunch stop.

Petrol and rubber shortages were so acute in early 1943 that NZR extended passenger services at the southern end from Hundalee to Ōaro as quickly as possible. Semple, ever the active participant in the network's growth, performed an opening ceremony at Ōaro on 12 April 1943, arriving from Christchurch in a railcar that then ran a short excursion for local children.[85] The ceremony was slightly ahead of time – the passenger timetable began on 17 May 1943. Interestingly, passenger trains began before goods ones, as Ōaro lacked facilities to replace Hundalee as a railhead for freight.[86]

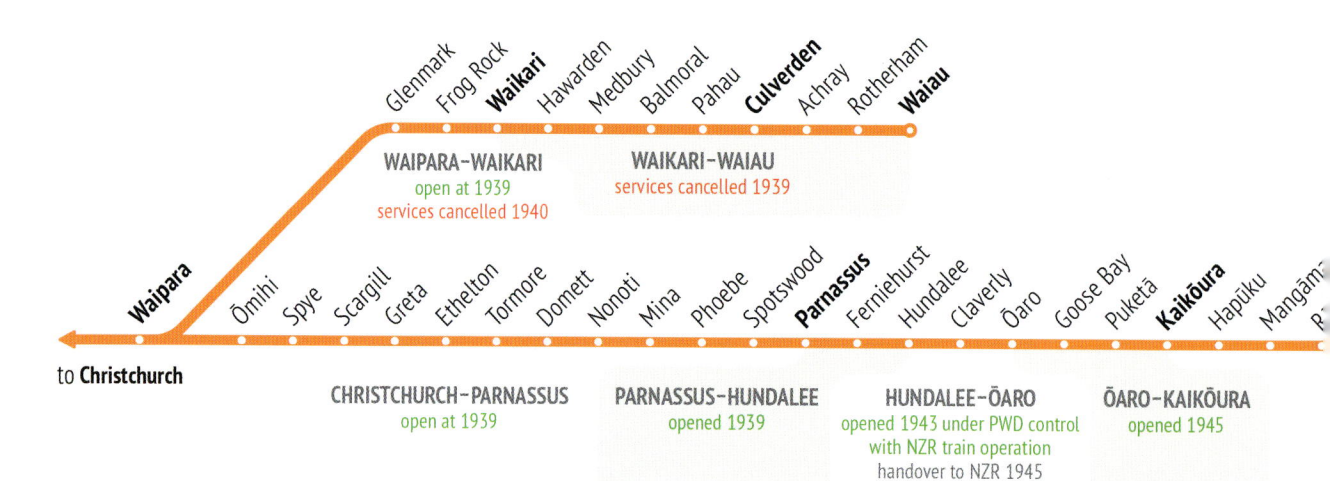

As in Buller, the PWD retained control of the line and did so until completion of the entire Main North Line in 1945, but at the northern end NZR took over a new section in 1944. Semple officiated at the opening ceremony of the railway from Clarence to Kaikōura on 11 March 1944. To cut the ribbon he rode in the cab of a locomotive, while local member of Parliament Edwin Meachen and NZR general manager James Sawers stood up front on its fender. Regular passenger services began the following week.[87] From 1941 to 1944 new passenger services were inaugurated every year without any counterbalancing cancellations, a streak that has not been replicated since.

The official opening of the railway from Ōaro to Kaikōura on 15 December 1945 marked the last completion of a general-purpose trunk railway in New Zealand.[88] After 80 years passengers could at last ride trains from Picton to Bluff. It is little wonder, then, that the arrival of a test train in Kaikōura three days earlier – an A^B locomotive with 69 wagons – occasioned much excitement.[89] On opening day, special trains from Christchurch and Blenheim helped swell the population of Kaikōura and over 3000 people gathered at the station. The county council hosted sporting events and distributed free ice cream and softdrinks to children.

Numerous politicians and officials addressed the crowd, with the leader of the opposition, the National Party's Sidney Holland, boldly – and, it transpired, inaccurately – suggesting the railway would arrest the drift of population to the North Island. But of course it was Bob Semple's day. The man who had directed so much effort to close New Zealand's missing links had seen the task through. The crowd, accompanied by the Blenheim Regimental Band, serenaded him with 'For He's a Jolly Good Fellow'.[90] At the ceremony Semple cast an eye to the future. World War II was over: 'We had to fight and live together or be enslaved together. We now have to develop New Zealand. We heard a lot about the new-born world during the war. Lip service is not enough.'[91]

The new railways were a key part of this world – but the rural branch-line passenger train was out of time. Before expresses even commenced between Christchurch and Picton, cancellations earlier in 1945 foreshadowed what was to come: the rail network would retreat in the countryside and shift from its common-carrier origins to more specialised bulk haulage.

Main North Line
and Waiau Branch, 1939–1945

...utara · Clarence · Parikawa · Kēkerengū · **Wharanui** · Mirza · Ward · Taimate · Hauwai · Lake Grassmere · Blind River · Seddon · Dashwood · Riverlands · **Blenheim** · Grovetown · Spring Creek · Tuamarina · Para · Koromiko · Mt Pleasant · Elevation · **Picton** · **Picton Wharf**

...IKŌURA–CLARENCE
opened 1944

CLARENCE–WHARANUI
opened 1942

WHARANUI–PICTON WHARF
open at 1939

Ōkaihau
Kaikohe
Ōpua
Kawakawa
Ōtiria
Hikurangi
WHANGĀREI
Donnellys Crossing
Portland
Kaihū
Kirikōpuni
Tangowahine
Waiōtira
DARGAVILLE
Maungatūroto
Wellsford
Tahekeroa
HELENSVILLE
AUCKLAND
Henderson
Ōtāhuhu
Onehunga
Papakura
Drury
Pukekohe

Paerātā–Waiuku ceased 1948

Waiuku
Mercer

Glen Afton
Huntly

Glen Massey
Ngāruawa

Ruakura–Cambridge ceased 1946

HAMILTON
FRANKTON
Te Awamutu
Ōtorohanga

Upper North Island
1946–1954

C^H 5

1945–1954
The drift to road

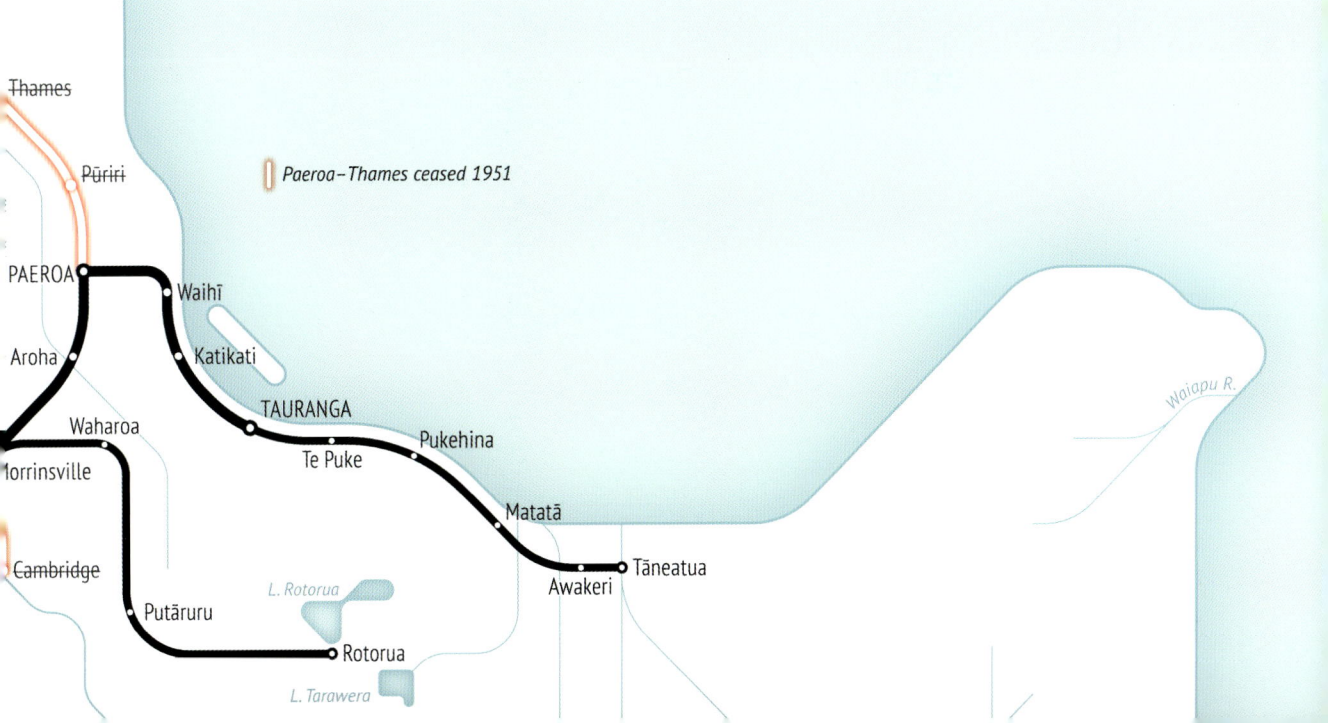

Thames

Paeroa–Thames ceased 1951

Pūriri

PAEROA

Waihī

Aroha

Katikati

Waharoa

TAURANGA

Morrinsville

Te Puke

Pukehina

Waiapu R.

Matatā

Cambridge

L. Rotorua

Awakeri

Tāneatua

Putāruru

Rotorua

L. Tarawera

Ōtorohanga

Te Kūiti

Mangapēhi

Ōkahukura

Ōhura

Taumarunui

Tāngarākau

Raurimu

National Park

Whangamōmona

Lepperton–Waitara ceased 1946

Waitara

NEW PLYMOUTH

Inglewood

Mt Tongariro

Mt Ngāuruhoe

Mt Ruapehu

Ohakune

Tangiwai

Raetihi

Waiōuru

Toko

Mt Taranaki

Stratford

Taihape

Kāpuni

Te Roti

Ōpunake

Hāwera

Mangaweka

Pātea

Ohakune–Raetihi ceased 1951

Waitōtara

Kai Iwi

Hunterville

Waverley

Aramoho

WHANGANUI

Ormondville

Marton

Dannevirke

Feilding

PALMERSTON NORTH

Woodville

Pahīatua

Shannon

Eketāhuna

Levin

Mauriceville

Ōtaki

Waikanae

MASTERTON

Paekākāriki

Carterton

Featherston

Greytown

Melling–Manor Park ceased 1954

Manor Park

L. Wairarapa

Manor Park–Taitā opened 1954

Melling

Taitā–Naenae opened 1947

Johnsonville

Taitā

Naenae–Waterloo opened 1946

Naenae

Waterloo

Hutt Workshops

WELLINGTON

Mōkau R.

Waikato R.

L. Tarawera

L. Taupō

Waitōtara R.

Whanganui R.

Rangitīkei R.

130

GISBORNE

L. Waikaremoana

Wairoa R.

Wairoa Waikōkopu

Mōhaka R.

Pūtōrino

Eskdale

Ngaruroro R.

NAPIER

HASTINGS

Waipawa

Waipukurau

Woodside–Greytown ceased 1953

Lower North Island
1946–1954

Upper South Island
1946–1954

Westport–Seddonville ceased 1946

Seddonville

Ngākawau

Waimangaroa

WESTPORT

Kawatiri / Buller

Īnangahua

Reefton

Ikamatua

Rewanui

Ngahere

GREYMOUTH

Stillwater

L. Sumner

Kūmara Junction

Moana

Hokitika

Ōtira

ŌTIRA TUNNEL

Ross

Arthur's Pass

Craigieburn

L. Coleridge

Springfield

Sheffield

Rakaia R.

Methven

Rangitātā R.

Hakatere / Ashburton R.

Rakaia

Aoraki / Mt Cook

Maukatua / Mt Sefton

Hinds R.

ASHBURTON

L. Tekapo

NELSON

PICTON

Nelson–Glenhope ceased 1954

Richmond

BLENHEIM

Belgrove

nhope

Wairau R.

Ward

Awatere R.

Wharanui

Clarence

Waiau Toa / Clarence R.

KAIKŌURA

Ōaro

Waiau Uwha R.

Hundalee

Parnassus

Hurunui R.

Scargill

Waipara

Rangiora

Kaiapoi

Waimakariri R.

Darfield

CHRISTCHURCH

n

Lyttelton

Lincoln

Hornby–Southbridge ceased 1951
Lincoln–Little River ceased 1951

Little River

Southbridge

Rakaia–Methven resumed 1948

L. Pūka[...]

L. Ōhau

Haast R.

Tititea / Mt Aspiring ▲

L. Wanaka

L. Hāwea

Pikirakatahi / Mt Earnslaw ▲

Wedderbu[...]

CROMWELL

Ōmaka[...]

Clyde

Alexandra

L. Wakatipu

Kingston

Holiday periods only

L. Te Anau

Athol

Lumsden

Ōreti R.

Mataura R.

Mata-Au / Clutha R.

L. Manapōuri

Dipton

Riversdale

Waipahi

BALCLUTHA

Wairau R.

Ōhai   ŌRB

Wairio

Aparima R.

Winton

GORE Clinton

Glenomaru

L. Hauroko

Ōtautau

Edendale

Ōwaka

L. Poteriteri

Tūātapere

Thornbury

Riverton

INVERCARGILL

Tahakopa

Orepuki

Tokanui

Bluff

Makawera–Tūātapere ceased 1954

Wairio–Thornbury ceased 1951

Wairio–Thornbury resumed 1952

Wairio–Thornbury ceased 1954

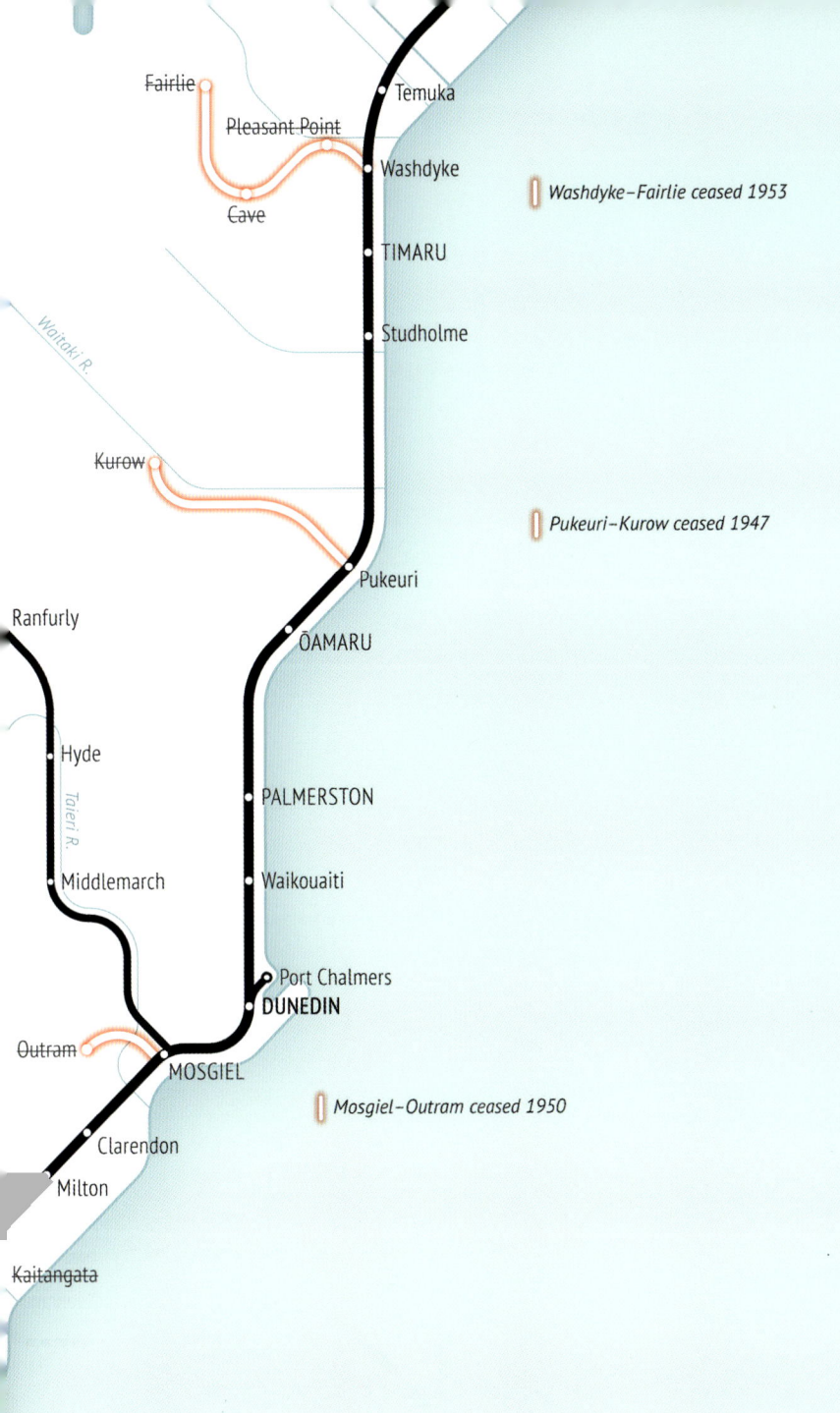

Fairlie

Pleasant Point

Temuka

Cave

Washdyke

Washdyke–Fairlie ceased 1953

TIMARU

Studholme

Woitoki R.

Kurow

Pukeuri–Kurow ceased 1947

Pukeuri

ŌAMARU

Ranfurly

Hyde

Taieri R.

PALMERSTON

Middlemarch

Waikouaiti

Port Chalmers

DUNEDIN

Outram

MOSGIEL

Mosgiel–Outram ceased 1950

Clarendon

Milton

Kaitangata

Lower South Island
1946–1954

Expresses between Gisborne and Wellington began in 1942 but passengers on the Moutohorā Branch were unhappy. Moutohorā trains did not connect with the expresses: the daily mixed, detained by shunting en route, arrived in Gisborne just 10 minutes after the southbound express departed. 'The whole passenger service in this district is bad,' lamented Bill Sullivan, MP for Bay of Plenty; 'A rail car is badly wanted for the passengers.'[1] No railcar was available, however, and NZR officials had already turned their minds to bus alternatives. Fifty or 60 people disembarked at Gisborne on a Friday, the region's market day, but fewer than 20 on other days.[2] Although initial proposals from NZR envisaged retaining the Friday trains, by August 1943 the district traffic manager in Wellington, who was exploring a regional reorganisation of bus operations, began to plan a bus timetable that could accommodate Friday's traffic.[3] The national rail passenger network had expanded in wartime, but this deliberation made it clear that there would be a further drift to road. Road Services had owned 58 vehicles in 1930 and steadily acquired more; the conditions of the late 1940s fostered further growth and by 1951 it ran 903 vehicles.[4] By the early 1950s NZR would be assessing its role in new ways.

NZR recorded its greatest-ever passenger numbers during World War II. New Zealanders made over 36.1 million train journeys during the 12 months to 31 March 1943, and over 38.6 million in the next 12 months.[5] For a national population of approximately 1.65 million – fewer than the estimated population of the Auckland region in 2020 – that meant each person took about 22 train trips per year. The previous peak had been in 1921–23, before the motorcar had fully taken hold, when New

Zealanders took roughly 19 trips per year, an annual total of over 28 million journeys. But the challenges of war and its enduring effects left NZR in a poor position and by 1952 rail patronage had dropped to pre-war levels.[6]

In World War II the unprecedented demand fell on a network lacking material resources and personnel – too few people were expected to do too much with too little. By the end of the war rollingstock was worn, the physical infrastructure was run down, staff were exhausted, and breakdowns and delays were common. Wartime strictures also contributed to multiple accidents, and timetables were slowed to reduce the risks.

Three Hutt Valley commuters died at Haywards on 8 November 1943 when their train derailed because of insufficient maintenance. Just a week earlier the Dunedin Supreme Court had followed the findings of a board of inquiry and sentenced an engine driver to three years' imprisonment for manslaughter after his Dunedin-bound train overturned near Hyde in Central Otago on 4 June 1943. Twenty-one people died at Hyde, making it the worst railway disaster in New Zealand at the time. The driver certainly bore some responsibility – he was speeding and had consumed some beer before his shift – but the board heard incomplete and inconsistent evidence and some of its findings have since been questioned.[7] Wartime pressures on working conditions and infrastructure had also played a part, but the driver was an easy scapegoat and blaming him meant NZR avoided confronting deeper challenges. Not so five years later: when a Picton to Christchurch express crashed at Seddon on 25 February 1948 killing six people, the driver's frank admission of culpability did not stop a Supreme Court jury finding the root cause to be NZR's inefficient

5

The memorial cairn to the Hyde disaster. It lists the 21 fatalities, including the author's great-great-grandfather, John Frater. John's wife Mary survived.

André Brett

administration and under-resourced operation.[8]

Pronounced coal shortages also made it impossible to operate a satisfactory service. During World War II insufficient labour and interrupted imports combined to deplete coal reserves, and a succession of coal-saving timetables with sharp reductions in services were rolled out from January 1944. The national network required approximately 13,000 tonnes of coal every week; in one week in April 1944 North Island locomotives consumed 6380 tonnes – but only 6266 tonnes were received into depot stockpiles.[9] Shortages persisted for years after the war, especially as Australian

supplies remained unavailable. Government policies to expand domestic coal output took time to implement, and NZR converted some locomotives to burn oil.[10] The crisis deepened during the 1951 waterfront dispute and continued to have a profound effect on passenger rail until the mid-1950s. It was impossible to run fast and frequent trains with a constrained fuel supply, and passengers began to choose other means of travel.

NZR AND THE POST-WAR TRANSITION

Peter Fraser's Labour government led a gradual transition from wartime restrictions to a peacetime economy. It sought to avoid inflation or the cycle of boom-and-bust that had occurred after World War I, and to reintegrate ex-service people into civilian life and employment. Labour also had to work within the limitations of an economy tied closely to that of Britain, whose recovery was necessarily protracted, and global trade networks that took years to regain stability. The rationing and shortages of essential materials persisted for years and the public became impatient.[11] Almost every corner of the community had pressing needs, and as well as investing in housing, the government injected large sums of money into hydroelectricity, irrigation, highways, railways and other public works.[12] Treasury began to emerge as an opponent of public works spending and warned that importing raw materials and competition for labour would restrict the supply of consumer goods and cause inflation. The government, however, was conscious of a serious infrastructure backlog.[13]

One of the largest passenger rail projects – indeed, the only one to serve new communities in the first decade after the war – occurred as part of suburban development in the Hutt Valley. There, rail was an essential component of the government's scheme to alleviate the housing crisis. In the regions, however, the post-war transition resulted in a contraction of rail passenger services. Bureaucrats considered mixed trains out of place in the modern world they were building: more buses and cars were available, supplies of petrol and tyres had improved, the government funded new roads handsomely. Road Services was operating in a better financial environment, so it is perhaps little wonder that NZR viewed it favourably. Pronounced delays in obtaining new railway rollingstock contrasted sharply with Road Services' growing fleet of modern buses, which ran routes covering nearly 10,000 kilometres in 1949.[14]

During this period there was increasing disagreement about railway policy and investment, both within NZR and between NZR and Treasury. The annual decline of a service's existing patronage was often seen as inevitable. But data is never neutral; the people who collect information shape its collation, presentation and use. Some of the figures used to justify cancellations or investment were unclear, and officials sometimes reached divergent conclusions about the same line or service depending on which stations passengers were counted at, on what days, and what operating costs and revenue were attributed to them. Most importantly, patronage and revenue were often taken in isolation rather than contextualised in light of past decisions and events. Rival interpretations of the same quantitative data became common, so it is perhaps more enlightening to investigate the underlying attitudes of decisionmakers.

The very question of paying interest on capital meant that the financial expectations placed on rail were different to those placed on road vehicles: bus services did not have to pay for asphalt or bridges, let alone tunnels. When NZR tallied operating losses on individual lines in its annual reports, it identified just the overall figure rather than the specific contribution of each form of traffic. Unpublished figures in archival files were often ad hoc too, and lacking methodological clarity. For mixed trains it can be hard to identify to what extent passengers created a loss. The usual argument was that if the train ran at times unsuited to passengers, it would earn greater goods revenue. As the coal shortages worsened, a passenger carriage began to be considered an extravagance that limited the goods a train could carry, even if only by a few tonnes.

1945–50: POST-WAR CONTRACTION

Moutohorā was a sign of things to come. Senior officials approved the replacement of trains with buses in late 1943, but deferred implementation because of the petrol and tyre shortages. Much to the indignation of local residents, the coal-saving timetable in 1944 meant even more inconvenience: the mixed train now ran thrice weekly instead of daily and as a result had to pause longer at stations to shunt.[15] On 30 May 1944 Bob Semple met with local representatives, who complained that the 'erratic' train, in trying to cater for both passengers and goods, meant travellers from Moutohorā had to ride for eight to 10 hours return in order to spend just three or four hours in Gisborne. When would the buses be running? Semple reminded them that coal shortages made train services erratic everywhere, and said he could not consider running a bus parallel to a railway. The residents 'would have to put up with the present inconvenience in the meantime'.[16] The estimated requirements for a bus show the severity of the situation: the service would require 22,000 litres of petrol and six heavy-duty tyres per year, and even this was too great a burden.[17]

One decision made the switch from rail to road inevitable. When NZR introduced the coal-saving timetable it transferred half of Moutohorā's staff to other locations. At some point over the summer a daily service had to resume to handle the goods on offer – but if this ran from Gisborne as a goods-only train rather than as a mixed from Moutohorā, it would only need the new, lower number of staff.[18] When summer arrived so did another problem: the mixed, timetabled with passengers in mind, ran at times unsuitable for cream producers. Since farmers now dispatched cream by road (to such an extent that their petrol and tyre usage exceeded that of a bus service), NZR obtained permission to operate all Moutohorā trains from Gisborne and cancelled passenger accommodation from 29 January 1945.[19]

Another cancellation later in 1945 appears almost inevitable with hindsight. The demise of passenger trains in 1937 between Lumsden and Kingston outside of holiday seasons had not affected the daily Gore–Lumsden mixed that ran across Southland's Waimea Plains. The topography presented no obstacles to road operation, so it seems remarkable that the mixed endured for another eight years – but, of course, shortages during World War II played a role. By August 1945 the superintendent of Road Services had sufficient vehicles and materials on hand to supersede the mixed, which stopped running on 17 September 1945.[20] This was not the end of passenger trains across the plains, however. The runs-as-required express from

Gore to Kingston remained in the working timetable for holiday seasons; in 1945–46 a daily train ran each way from 20 December to 7 January.[21] But Lumsden now had only one year-round passenger rail service: the daily mixed trains to Invercargill.

In the North Island bus services replaced two long-established passenger rail services in 1946. The first was Cambridge–Hamilton. Cambridge residents had for some years hoped that a railcar would replace slow mixed trains, one resident complaining that 'Taxpayers are paying for the upkeep of a service that cannot truthfully be called a service.'[22] Officials, however, took a dim view of potential passenger traffic on the Cambridge Branch and hoped private road operators would free them from carrying passengers by train. One wrote in 1943 that 'the Cambridge people had for some years patronised the road service … any move made at this juncture for improved services should, it is considered, be made by Messrs Buses Ltd' of Frankton.[23] It is little surprise, then, that NZR reduced the Cambridge service as part of its coal-saving timetable in 1944. Morning mixed trains carrying mainly schoolchildren now had to perform extensive shunting, and pupils often arrived late at school.[24] One businessman protested: Cambridge was not just 'a "back-water" town at the end of a line' where trains could arrive and depart at any old time: it deserved better service.[25] Local pride was at stake. The district traffic manager in Auckland, however, proposed to end passenger accommodation.[26] The change would allow each train to carry 50 additional tonnes of goods, and timetable revisions would effect annual savings, he estimated, of almost £2500.[27] A railcar might have been popular, but NZR never seriously considered the possibility of a commuter market to Hamilton – even with Department of Education subsidies, schoolchildren were an unwanted burden, and other passengers rarely averaged more than 10 per trip. So from 9 September 1946 the line became goods only and Buses Ltd provided transport from Cambridge.[28]

NZR also passed up an opportunity to revitalise passenger rail between New Plymouth and its original port, Waitara. This line, the first in Taranaki, opened on 14 October 1875 at a time when tensions were running high between Pākehā and Māori. Anyone interested in the history of New Zealand's railways must recognise that lines such as this were instrumental in confirming Pākehā control of land after hostilities in the 1860s gave way to an uneasy peace. On this line the now-unthinkable construction of a railway through a Māori urupā or burial ground proceeded, despite strong protests that culminated in the kidnapping of the contractor's seven-year-old daughter. (The culprit was never identified, and the 'girl' was found decades later living – contentedly, by her own account – in a Māori community near Whakatāne.[29]) Land purchases, confiscations and controversies, not least the shameful destruction of the Parihaka pacifist community, meant that by the 1940s Taranaki resembled a neat English patchwork of farms. Railways encouraged Pākehā economic growth and settlers prospered. Good roads were formed between major towns – on which ran buses. NZR acquired a local bus operator in December 1945 and, when a new timetable took effect on 29 April 1946, cancelled all passenger trains to Waitara. General manager James Sawers was pleased to report that this bus would run at a profit.[30]

While some residents were happy with the change, others saw the replacement of trains with buses as a cynical way to increase fares. A return train ticket from Waitara had been 2 shillings 1 penny (2/1d); the bus operator charged 3/6d, and NZR made no adjustment.[31] The Waitara Borough Council complained – not only about this fare but also that the buses were too small and that mothers could no longer travel with prams.[32] Controversy continued to rumble through local newspapers and at council meetings for some time. In the end, Semple was not willing to recommend the reinstatement of rail passenger facilities. Buses had come to stay.

They came to the West Coast also. The experience of passengers north of Westport is a good example of what happened in many places: people persistently requested better rail passenger services, not buses, but NZR officials were enamoured of new road technologies. One of the first trains through the Buller Gorge in 1941 had carried a placard proclaiming, 'Travel by train, Seddonville to Bluff, 606 miles' (975km), but within five years this was no longer possible. The northernmost portion of the route, some 45 kilometres from Westport to Seddonville, succumbed to buses in 1946. On the face of it this is surprising as the line had heavy passenger traffic: NZR's annual statistics, although incomplete, show 62,000 outbound journeys for the year ended 31 March 1945 – more than some lines with modern railcar services.[33] But demand was lopsided. Dedicated passenger trains ran on Saturdays when hundreds of coalminers flocked to Westport for entertainment. On all other days, according to a passenger count in July 1944, mixed trains averaged about 75 passengers on arrival and departure at Westport. Around 40 were ordinary ticketholders and the rest schoolchildren – most of whom travelled to stations on the first half of the line only. Typically, only 18 people went beyond the halfway point, Granity.[34] Residents complained regularly that the mixed trains were too slow and requested daily passenger trains but NZR rejected this as uneconomic. Sawers in August 1944 asked F.K. Mackay, the Road Services superintendent, to investigate bus options with the district traffic manager.[35] Wartime restrictions prohibited immediate action, and Mackay explained that there would be insufficient vehicles until completion of the Main North Line permitted redeployments.[36]

A new goods-only timetable for Westport–Seddonville was drawn up in May 1945 and approved in July but without a date for implementation.[37] The people of Buller grew impatient: 'It appears as if the proposed road transport service … is just a myth,' grumbled an anonymous scribe in the *Westport News* in February 1946; 'failure to keep this promise has not been appreciated by the people of this district'.[38] With evident relief, Semple informed local MP Paddy Webb at the end of September 1946 that the road service could commence, and from 14 October all passenger trains ceased north of Westport.[39] A railcar to Greymouth became Buller's only passenger rail offering.

The success of railcar technology did not halt the drift to road. In some regions NZR abandoned railcar plans, and viable rail services succumbed

to an institutional preference for buses. Two examples of this are the branches to Methven and Kurow. Both lines had a steady modest daily ridership and patronage held firm from the 1920s to the 1940s. Proposals to replace Methven's mixed trains with railcars were well advanced in 1936; a draft timetable provided for a twice-daily service to Rakaia, the interchange for Christchurch–Dunedin trains, but this was never implemented.[40]

Kurow, though, got one of the earliest railcars in 1926: an experimental steam contraption manufactured by Clayton Carriage and Wagon, England, which unfortunately turned out to be too small to accommodate demand on busy days.[41] A dedicated passenger train replaced the railcar in 1928, but Depression constraints soon forced traffic managers to offer only mixed trains. They contemplated a road replacement in 1936 when NZR acquired a bus service from Ōamaru to Lake Waitaki, but the people of North Otago preferred the train and the bus did poorly.[42] The national transportation superintendent reopened the topic of railcars to Kurow in 1940 when the new Vulcan units

The Clayton railcar on trial ahead of deployment to Kurow in 1926. In 1928 it went to Invercargill and ran until 1937, spending its final years rattling to and from Bluff.
A.P. Godber, ATL APG-0316-1/2-G

were about to enter service. Dunedin's traffic manager submitted a report seemingly in favour of railcars but in the end rejected the idea. His rationale likely found favour with his superiors: a Vulcan based at Kurow would only run return to Ōamaru a couple of times daily but would take away one railcar from longer, busier routes elsewhere.[43] The laudable proposal lapsed.

A few years later bus replacements entered the agenda for Methven. People clearly did not take kindly to such substitutions because Canterbury's district traffic manager in October 1944 told his stationmasters at Methven and Rakaia to be 'discreet' when making enquiries about shifting passengers to road. About 30 people per day travelled each way on the branch, and the traffic manager concluded they could go by bus. His correspondence emphasised the costs of goods transport and showed little interest in the preference of existing passengers or consideration of how to attract more. Once the war ended he got his wish: mixed trains to Methven ceased from 10 December 1945.[44]

At the same time the stationmaster at Duntroon, the most important intermediate station on the Kurow Branch, advocated replacing that line's mixed trains with buses.[45] The district traffic manager in Dunedin – a different man to the one who examined the railcar option – was receptive. A year later, with buses soon to become available, he drafted a goods-only timetable, and trains to Kurow ceased to carry passengers from 24 March 1947.[46] As late as November, NZR was still refunding passengers who had bought train tickets in Wellington where office staff were unaware that the service had ceased.[47]

Both Methven and Kurow suggest the larger pattern of missed opportunities. Had NZR moved a little faster with railcar technology in

the 1930s or been able to acquire more Vulcans, lines such as these could have had a quick and economical service superior to road. Instead, NZR replaced mixed and with-car goods trains with buses. On main lines this meant the end of local stopping trains that supplemented expresses; on branches it meant the demise of all passenger services.

Semple claimed buses gave 'general satisfaction' in place of mixed trains, but this was not accurate.[48] Local residents, especially pensioners, were unhappy with the Methven Road Services timetable, so from 8 June 1948 NZR attached a car-van to the goods train that ran return from Rakaia, which gave travellers a couple of hours in Methven over lunchtime. The service is a fine example of NZR providing the bare minimum: the car-van was old and had gas lamps, not electric lights; the timetable provided no meaningful connections at Rakaia; and travellers had to tolerate the needs of goods distribution.[49] As NZR made no attempt to encourage patronage, it is not surprising that few people used this service. NZR's counts reveal that the car-van usually ran empty in 1953, with the only regular passenger a pensioner who travelled to Methven weekly. However, broader operational requirements meant it was easier to keep running the train with a car-van than to make it goods only with a standard guard's van, so the service continued.[50]

Of course, not all cancellations were unjustified or reflected a defeatist attitude towards rural passenger trains. The solitary contraction to the passenger network in 1948 illustrates this well. Travellers had never flocked to trains on the Waiuku Branch at the southern tip of Manukau Harbour, and the royal commission of 1930 had recommended these passenger services be cancelled. But 18

An A class locomotive near Rakaia leads a with-car goods on the Methven Branch, 29 March 1950. The car-van is visible at the rear. J.F. Le Cren, ANZ AAVK 6390 B1

years later, with-car goods trains still trundled twice daily to connect with services on the North Island Main Trunk. Passenger numbers rarely exceeded single digits and were trending downwards – sometimes nobody boarded at all.[51] Road Services already ran buses between Waiuku and Auckland, and the national transportation superintendent was quite ready to accept the suggestion of his Auckland officials that passengers no longer be carried by rail. The carriage disappeared in July 1948, allowing two Main Trunk expresses to have their schedules slightly accelerated as they no longer had to stop at Paerātā for Waiuku connections.[52]

Waiuku was not the only passenger service that persisted after the 1930 royal commission had recommended cancellation. Another survivor, the Outram Branch, was especially remarkable. Its proximity to Dunedin had stimulated bus policy debate in the first place, and, on the face of it, road competition ought to have killed off passenger provision sooner. Yet it escaped numerous times. A report in 1944 recommended the entire line be closed, but officials let the matter rest until the end of war.[53] In 1945 Road Services acquired a

bus service between Dunedin and Berwick, southwest of Outram. F.K. Mackay attested that Outram residents complained to him about the train to Mosgiel taking 45 minutes to cover 14 kilometres. He therefore suggested that the mixed be replaced with a goods operated from Dunedin, and that the Dunedin–Berwick bus be routed via Outram. Dunedin's traffic manager, the unrelated W.M. Mackay, vetoed F.K.'s proposal as it would have actually increased operating costs; as long as the train continued to run from Outram, W.M. saw no justification for removing passenger facilities. To him, the question was whether to operate from Outram or close the branch entirely.[54] And so the passenger service remained, even as numbers slumped. In the year ended 31 March 1944, 4109 people rode the branch; in the year ended 31 March 1948, with restrictions on road transport easing, this halved to 2112.[55] In July 1949 a dozen workers at the Mosgiel Woollen Mills were practically the only passengers.[56]

Road Services again mooted a service via Outram, largely along the lines suggested in 1945, and this time it was not denied. Buses began on 6 February 1950, ostensibly on a

ELECTRIFICATION FAILS TO SPARK

Francis William Aickin's vision was never realised.

Aickin served with distinction in World War II, maintaining military railways in North Africa. In 1948 he took on the challenge of revitalising NZR as the general manager. The seemingly endless coal shortages proved to him the need for new motive power. Kip Farrington, a celebrated American sportswriter and rail enthusiast, wrote gushingly that NZR was:

> ... operated by a very attractive man and great railroader by the name of Frank Aickin ... He was all over the United States in 1950 studying this country's electrification. The New Zealand road is now electrifying the [North Island] main trunk ... there is no oil there and they simply do not want to bother with the labor problems connected with coal.[57]

What happened?

Frank Aickin as photographed for his passport in May 1949. ANZ AAVK 6390 B5046

Electrification was not a novel idea. During 1918 Evan Parry, the PWD's chief electrical engineer, urged electrification '[a]s soon as the limits of steam haulage have been reached on some critical section of the Main Trunk'. His colleague Lawrence Birks forecast a great future for electric motive power in Canterbury.[58] The Ōtira and Lyttelton tunnels were electrified in the 1920s, and Merz and McLellan's 1925 report endorsed suburban electrification in Auckland and Wellington, emphasising the lower cost of using hydroelectric power rather than coal. The lines out of the capital were progressively electrified from 1938.

In the post-war period it seemed electrification's time had come – it was a mature technology eminently suited to mainline railways in a country rich with hydroelectricity. Better still, the idea received bipartisan encouragement. The Fraser Labour government supported Aickin to study electrification overseas in 1949.[59] By the time he presented his report, Holland's National Party was in power, and considered his findings favourably. Aickin concluded that electrification was essential, writing: 'The railway problems of the future could largely be solved by the electrification of the North Island Main Trunk which is the transport life-line of the Dominion.'[60] Swedish experts Thorsten Thelander and R. Edenius visited New Zealand and submitted a follow-up report that confirmed Aickin's judgement, and in December 1950 the government endorsed electrification of Auckland to Frankton Junction in Hamilton as the first stage of the entire Main Trunk.[61] And that endorsement was as far as it got.

Aickin retired at the end of July 1951, even though he was only 57. He had found it difficult to work with some senior NZR officials and the Holland ministry. In his last annual report he left a warning:

I have given a great deal of study to the requirements of the future ... planning work for the electrification of the Auckland–Frankton Junction section of the North Island Main Trunk Line is well forward ... It is hardly necessary to mention the improved services that can be achieved. The Auckland–Frankton Junction electrification must be kept up to schedule, because ... electric locomotives have been considered as being in operation in 1955.[62]

His successor, Horace Lusty, ignored these words. He told a 1952 royal commission that Aickin had acted with 'undue haste' under an undefined 'influence from outside'. The commissioners found the conflict of opinion within NZR 'disturbing'.[63] Lusty postponed electrification and instead replaced steam locomotion with diesel.

Aickin lived to see Robert Muldoon's National government approve electrification of the central portion of the Main Trunk in December 1981 as part of its 'Think Big' programme of industrial projects. The first electric train ran between Palmerston North and Hamilton in 1988, six years after Aickin died, but even today the entire Main Trunk is yet to be electrified.

The cancellation of Aickin's scheme did not alter the passenger network at the time, but it had lasting effects. It is one of the great counterfactuals of New Zealand's railway history: if the Main Trunk had been electrified in the 1950s, Auckland would have had an electric suburban network six decades sooner. The wires might have been extended down major connecting routes – say, to Tauranga, Napier and through the Remutaka Tunnel. Would this have also given impetus to connect

Left to right: Thelander, Aickin and Edenius on the roof of Auckland railway station, 12 November 1950, looking across Beach Road to the intended portal of the Morningside Deviation tunnel. J.G. Duncan, ANZ AAVK 6390 B953

the South Island's two short electrified sections? What passenger services might have survived the cuts of the last 60 years if electric trains had rejuvenated the network from the 1950s? How much would it have helped NZR's finances and the environment if trains had run for decades on hydroelectricity rather than imported diesel?

New Zealand has been the poorer for rejecting Aickin's counsel.

three-month trial.[64] It was clear, though, that they were intended to be permanent. Road freight operators had cut deeply into railway income and the entire branch lasted not much longer. It closed on 4 December 1953.[65]

1951–54: THE WATERFRONT DISPUTE AND ITS CONSEQUENCES

Coal shortages persisted in the post-war years, and NZR was unable to restore services to pre-1944 levels. Meanwhile, other transport modes flourished. Labour legislated in 1945 to nationalise Union Airways and smaller airlines as the National Airways Corporation (NAC), which formally took over Union's licences on 1 April 1947. Air travel remained exclusive, but less so: NAC had a mandate to operate as a public utility and introduced flights to destinations such as Hamilton, Rotorua and Whangārei.[66] Cars proliferated and motorists enjoyed cheaper fuel.

NZR could not convert steam locomotives to burn oil quickly enough: between 1946 and 1952 it converted 75 locomotives of its fleet of hundreds and acquired 18 new oil-burners.[67] It still had to run a pared-back coal-saving timetable and struggled to assert itself against burgeoning air and road competition. The events of 1951 demanded even more service reductions and some 'suspended' trains never ran again.

After World War II, strikes occurred globally as governments struggled to manage post-war reconstruction. New Zealand lost fewer working days to strike action than many countries, such as Australia, France and the US, but 1949 set a domestic record for days lost.[68] That year, Sidney Holland led the National Party to victory over Labour. Most members of United and Reform combined their resources

as National in 1936, but the Savage and Fraser governments were so popular that the new party struggled to loosen Labour's hold on power. Holland, the leader since 1940, worked tirelessly to win the ministerial benches and then acted to consolidate National's position. When major industrial unrest began in early 1951 he took a tough stance towards militant trade unions, and almost every part of society felt the consequences. Railway travellers experienced sharp short-term effects; for some communities, these became permanent.

Waterfront workers on New Zealand's wharves refused overtime work in February 1951 as part of a pay dispute. In response, their employers locked them out. Some other unions went on strike in support of the 'wharfies', and so began New Zealand's longest and largest industrial dispute. Members of the Amalgamated Society of Railway Servants and the Railway Tradesmen's Association refused to handle goods unloaded by scab labour at the docks, but the wharfies' hopes of a national transport strike went unfulfilled.[69] In order to defeat the wharfies, Holland's government enacted emergency regulations that remain controversial – for example, it was illegal to give food to strikers or even to their children.

An obvious consequence of the dispute for NZR was the interruption to coal supplies, especially high-quality West Coast coal distributed to the North Island by coastal shipping. Domestic production slumped as miners walked out in support of wharfies, international imports could not be unloaded, unidentified saboteurs damaged a railway bridge near Huntly on the branch to the Glen Afton mines, and NZR, already short on coal, found itself almost without reserves.

A coal-saving timetable came into force

A^B 609 at the head of a train to Little River passes a maintenance worker on a jigger at Sockburn, 28 March 1950. A year later the coal-saving timetable ended this service. J.F. Le Cren, ANZ AAVK 6390 B31

in the North Island on 28 March 1951 and in the South Island on 12 April. NZR explicitly prioritised goods transport over passengers, and diverted staff and resources to keep freight moving. This pushed more travellers to other modes – NAC carried its millionth passenger during 1951, earlier than it expected.[70] Of the passenger trains that did run, timekeeping hardly presented NZR in a good light: in the 1951/52 financial year, 42 percent reached their destination five or more minutes late.[71] Regional expresses ran just twice a week. Branch-line trains were cut sharply, and six lines had passenger services suspended: Donnellys Crossing, Greytown, Little River, Southbridge, Thames and Wairio.

The dispute lasted for 151 days until the wharfies, worn down by one draconian measure after another, conceded defeat on 15 July. The North Island's suspended goods services were gradually restored over the next two months; the last to return, between Dargaville and Donnellys Crossing, did so in the guise of a mixed train from 10 September, so the Kaihū Valley retained its passenger facilities.[72] The other five branches with suspended passenger services were not so lucky.

Greytown regained some goods services on 16 August 1951 but NZR was in no hurry to restore the passenger timetable on this short branch. The local council made its displeasure clear, and a full weekday timetable containing two mixed trains began in January 1952.[73] But the branch's future was under threat: it existed only because the main line to Masterton bypassed Greytown in favour of an easier crossing of the Waiōhine River. The junction station, Woodside, was just 5 kilometres away and received more frequent services. Branch-line revenue of £478 in 1951 did not come close to covering operating costs of £6000. The waterfront dispute had affected these totals – all facilities had to be maintained even though no trains ran for over four months and no passengers were carried for most of the year – but Stan Goosman, National's first minister of railways, was correct to depict representations against closure as 'token resistance to the inevitable'.[74] The last trains ran on 24 December 1953, an inauspicious Christmas present to this

Wairarapa community.[75] Worthy of note is that passenger services endured until the branch's demise. Few other lines can claim such.

The so-called 'temporary' suspensions enabled officials to cancel services that they had not yet been able to discard. The opening of the East Coast Main Trunk to Tauranga in 1928 meant that Thames now sat at the end of just another rural branch line, which declined in importance. It endured poor timekeeping during the coal shortage: across three weeks in August 1946, for example, the morning mixed train arrived an hour late seven times out of 15. The situation improved little over the following year and officials agreed in principle to expand Road Services offerings – except there were no extra buses. Locals complained bitterly. One wondered if 'people [will] settle in Thames or even visit the town when such circumstances' – the attenuated train and bus timetables – 'make it more isolated than in the past'.

The Thames Branch provides an object lesson in how a poor service reduces patronage, which officials then use to justify cuts, which further reduce patronage, which then justifies further cuts or elimination. When the waterfront dispute ended the district traffic manager considered the resumption of passenger services unwarranted because patronage had been so low.[76] A working timetable at Archives New Zealand illustrates this graphically. It was printed after the mixed was suspended in March but before it was officially cancelled: the mixed is crossed out in red ink, then carefully dated 16 December 1951.[77]

Trains to Little River on Banks Peninsula, and Southbridge, south of Lake Ellesmere/ Te Waihora, were treated together. Both lines had dedicated passenger trains rather than mixed services.[78] These railways left the Main

South Line at Hornby, west of Christchurch, and ran together for 13 kilometres to Lincoln, where they split. Little River's line ran at a loss, but the Southbridge Branch made an operating profit until World War II.[79] NZR undertook a successful experiment to reduce costs and improve services to Little River with a battery-electric Edison railcar built in 1926. Passengers liked this quiet, comfortable vehicle, but Depression-era financial difficulties meant it was not replaced after it was destroyed in a depot fire in 1934, and the line reverted to steam-hauled carriage trains. A file note – unfortunately with unclear authorship – shows that by the mid-1940s NZR actively undermined passenger traffic on the branch and assumed that buses were a desirable replacement. Road Services instituted one from Little River to Christchurch via Greenpark, near Lincoln, at near-identical times to the trains, partly to stop a private operator gaining approval to operate to Greenpark and partly to divert passengers to road. It did not work: train fares were cheaper and the service satisfactory, so bus patronage was low. Even the Road Services superintendent in 1947 expressed doubt as to whether replacing trains would achieve the savings envisaged.[80]

When the coal-saving timetable suspended all passenger trains on both lines, Road Services took over the route to Little River and private operators provided a replacement service to Southbridge. The national transportation superintendent proposed restoring trains thrice weekly from January 1952 but this did not eventuate, and in July Canterbury's traffic manager concluded that as buses were now carrying all travellers, both lines should remain goods only – a short-sighted decision as both lines had established clientele.[81] Residents of more lightly populated areas had voted with

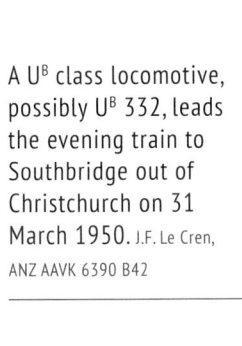

A U[B] class locomotive, possibly U[B] 332, leads the evening train to Southbridge out of Christchurch on 31 March 1950. J.F. Le Cren, ANZ AAVK 6390 B42

their feet – planted firmly on the pedals of motorcars – but those along the Southbridge and Little River lines liked the service their trains provided. NZR was simply not interested in running them or growing patronage, however, and the potential demonstrated by the Edison railcar went unrealised.

Confidence in buses as the cheaper passenger transport of the future conflicted with the needs of staff and communities such as Wairio in western Southland. The branch from Thornbury to Wairio connected with the Ōhai Railway Board's line and served important coalfields, but the local population was not large: Ōtautau, the biggest town, was home to just 737 people. Mixed trains carried a steady custom of 20–25 passengers, over half of them schoolchildren, but private buses had become well established, especially for trips to the nearest city, Invercargill. If passenger accommodation were removed, the train would only have to run when the Ōhai coalfields offered sufficient tonnage.[82] The Ōhai Railway Board continued to operate passenger trains north from Wairio, but the line south became goods only. In the absence of a passenger service, those children who attended a convent school in Riverton now had to complete their education in Ōtautau, but this did not trouble NZR. Bus operators with low overheads drove on roads made with public funds and took the best-paying passengers, leaving less remunerative traffic, such as schoolchildren, to rail.

NZR might have been more interested in passenger services if the demand that each line cover its costs had been accompanied by recognition that trains often carried passengers whom private operators did not want or served poorly. There was, however, one type of aggrieved railway passenger whose plight could inspire an official response. The Amalgamated Society of Railway Servants took up the cause of Wairio railwaymen in late 1951 because the demise of mixed trains had deprived them of one of the privileges of railway employment: concessionary travel. Most men on the line received minimal wages and claimed the bus fare to Invercargill was beyond their means.[83] NZR responded that the goods-only timetable was still a restricted one in the wake of the waterfront dispute; even if a passenger carriage were attached, trains ran

RAILWAY PROPOSALS OF THE LATE 1940s

Multiple railways, primarily for goods transport, complemented the plans for suburban railway investment in Auckland and Wellington. The lines considered in the late 1940s were, from north to south:

- An extensive suburban network for Auckland, of which no part was built, discussed in this chapter.
- Purchase of the Taupō Tōtara Timber Company's tramway from Putāruru to Mokai, northwest of Taupō, and its partial conversion into a railway. NZR began operating trains between Putāruru and Tokoroa in 1949, and followed with an extension in 1952 to a large new pulp and paper mill in Kinleith. Plans to extend the railway to Reporoa, between Taupō and Rotorua, never eventuated. This line has never had a regular passenger service.
- A branch of the East Coast Main Trunk from Edgecumbe to Kawerau and Murupara to carry timber from the Kaingaroa Forest to a pulp and paper mill in Kawerau and its products to Mount Maunganui for export. This line opened in stages between 1953 and 1957 and has never carried passengers. The Mount Maunganui Branch was rebuilt as part of this project and likewise has been goods only. The section from Hawkens Junction (near Edgecumbe) to Kawerau was re-designated as part of the East Coast Main Trunk in 1978, leaving the original line to Tāneatua a branch.
- A tunnel under the Remutaka Range to replace the Remutaka Incline, opened in 1955. This is discussed in Chapter 6.
- Extension of the Waterloo Branch in the Hutt Valley to become the main line, opened in 1946–54, discussed in this chapter.
- A railway from Haywards to Plimmerton to connect the Hutt Valley with the Porirua Basin and serve proposed new suburbs and industrial estates. The Ministry of Works contemplated this in various forms until the late 1970s, but it was never built.
- A loop line from Sockburn along Christchurch's western fringe and past the airport in Harewood to meet the Main North Line in Styx. This route would have served new industries and improved the flow of goods traffic to and from Christchurch, but was never built.

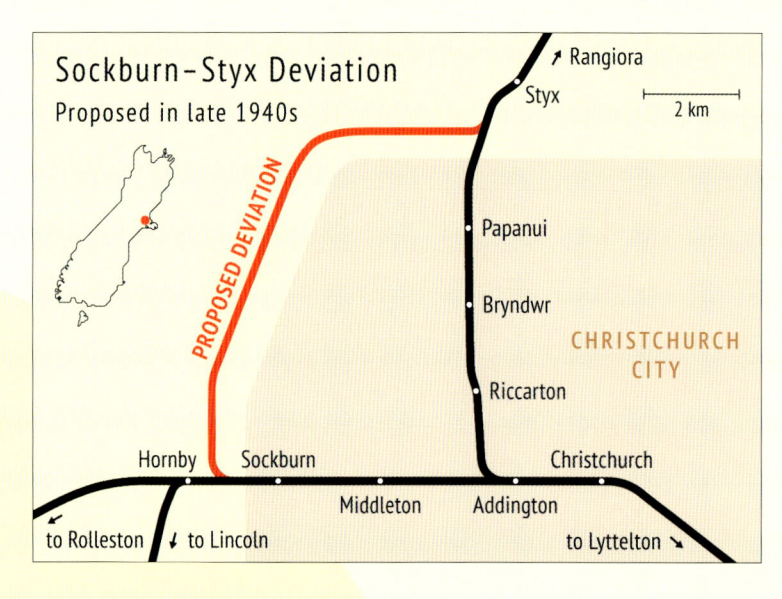

Sockburn–Styx Deviation
Proposed in late 1940s

Rangiora
Styx
2 km
Papanui
Bryndwr
CHRISTCHURCH CITY
Riccarton
PROPOSED DEVIATION
Hornby Sockburn Christchurch
Middleton Addington
to Rolleston to Lincoln to Lyttelton

at times that did not permit travellers to visit Invercargill and return on the same day.[84] But pressure paid off. Passenger accommodation resumed from 7 March 1952, albeit only every second Friday, railway payday. Travellers could spend just over three hours in Invercargill but to do so had to ride a slow with-car goods: three hours there and almost five to return.[85] Union representatives protested and the handful of passengers who rode the inbound train caught buses home instead.[86]

An unkind reading might suggest the bus fare was not beyond the men's means after all, but the counterpoint is that NZR had used the promise of discounted travel to attract employees to rural positions then removed the perk without providing either a bus concession, as some staff received elsewhere, or a wage supplement, known as an isolation allowance. A new timetable from the end of June gave more time in Invercargill and a quicker ride home but made no difference: not a single paying passenger occupied the carriage in July and rarely more than a couple thereafter.[87]

The demise of the Wairio passenger train was bound up with that to Riverton and Tūātapere: the two lines shared tracks as far as Thornbury. The coal-saving timetable in 1951 imposed severe cuts to Tūātapere, where mixed trains went from twice daily to twice weekly.[88] Residents endured the hardship at first, despite bad local roads, but in September 1951 the Riverton and District Progress League submitted protests, citing the case of hospital nurses who were forced to find alternative transport three days a week. The league pressed for a railcar, a service it felt would represent justice as 'this recent cut in what has always been a slow and tedious rail passenger service, has rendered an additional disservice to the District'.[89] NZR's

response was not at all satisfactory. An official informed the league that he would not even add a passenger carriage to goods trains. He claimed the extra weight would make it impossible to clear the backlog of goods amassed during the waterfront dispute without scheduling additional trains, something the coal shortage had rendered untenable.[90] This exaggerated the difficulty: it is hard to see how a car-van rather than a guard's van would have made such a difference. Instead of restoring the service NZR cut it further, and from June 1952 the Tūātapere mixed ran on Fridays only.[91] The measly timetable to Tūātapere and Wairio was obviously not meant to last, and even though trains in western Southland had stable patronage at the start of the 1950s, by 28 June 1954 NZR had discarded both offerings.[92]

By the early 1950s it was clear that NZR would continue to shift rural branch-line passengers onto Road Services buses even if there was obvious potential to improve train patronage. From loyal passengers in Canterbury to schoolchildren and nurses in Southland, NZR gave up regular clientele and induced people to use other modes of transport. They were hardly the actions of an organisation keen to drum up custom.

1951–54: MORE LOST OPPORTUNITIES

David Leitch and Bob Stott, authorities on New Zealand's railway history, write that NZR's management 'was still in the era of running trains rather than marketing transport services'.[93] They cite an example in which NZR deliberately fostered a road-based fertiliser industry in Hawke's Bay and the Wairarapa to avoid the hassle of timetabling and running fertiliser trains from Taranaki. A similar logic animated passenger policy: short on rollingstock and staff and keen to make operations as easy as possible for itself, NZR eroded its own foundations.

Holland's government called a royal commission into New Zealand's railways in 1952, which to some extent was meant to provide political cover for closing unprofitable goods-only branches in the South Island. The commissioners, nonetheless, championed passenger rail:

> *Although the bulk of the railways revenue actually comes from goods traffic, in the mind of the general public railways are associated with passenger trains and stations. Dissatisfied passengers can be the indirect means of losing goods traffic business. On the other hand, a high standard of passenger service can have far-reaching effects in other branches of the railways.*[94]

Passenger trains were, essentially, NZR's shop window. The more attractive and comprehensive they were, the better NZR could secure goods business and maintain voter support for government investment. The commissioners concluded their report by rejecting entirely 'the view held by many people that rail passenger traffic is dying and that the whole future of the railways lies in goods haulage'.[95] That this even needed to be said is telling.

Route cancellations immediately before and after the commission illustrate that attitudes against passenger rail were now ingrained within parts of NZR. A once-popular service in the central North Island, Raetihi to Ohakune, survived the coal-saving timetable but did not make it to the end of 1951. Raetihi was then the main town in the region, larger than Ohakune on the Main Trunk, and many people used the railway to visit relatives and friends in Raetihi's

district hospital. In 1946 a mixed train ran return daily from Ohakune – three times on Saturdays – and a private bus operator ran a brisk trade with five return trips daily.

Despite acknowledging that a railcar service would recover custom from road, head office rebuffed suggestions for this.[96] Under the coal-saving timetable Raetihi had dropped to a thrice-weekly passenger service from late March 1951. Passenger numbers had been in freefall since rejection of the railcar suggestion, with trains in September 1951 averaging fewer than two passengers. Somewhat laughably, the district traffic manager observed that the reduction to thrice-weekly services 'does not appear to have improved the average daily number' of passengers – as if it could have.[97] A service that might have been salvaged had been left to wither, and the trains were cancelled a couple of months later.[98]

A near-identical situation occurred two years later in Canterbury. Prior to the Depression a daily passenger train, fondly known as the 'Fairlie Flyer', ran between Fairlie and Timaru. Talk of a railcar did not amount to action, and locals in the late 1940s sarcastically renamed their daily mixed train, an interminably slow journey that in winter could be bitterly cold, as the 'Fairlie Depressed'.[99] In January 1951 the Saturday mixed was cancelled, leaving weekend passengers to rely on Road Services. It was a harbinger of things to come.[100] In 1953 NZR decided to close the Fairlie locomotive depot and operate trains from Timaru instead to save money, but since the predominant flow of passenger traffic was from rural towns to Timaru and return, this operational change spelled the end of mixed trains. Road Services expanded its timetable to include a new service between Timaru and Pleasant Point, as the bulk

TRAGEDY AT TANGIWAI

NZR experienced its darkest hour on Christmas Eve 1953. A lahar from Mt Ruapehu severely damaged a bridge and caused the engine and leading six carriages of the overnight express from Wellington to Auckland to plunge into the Whangaehu River at Tangiwai, near Waiōuru. This disaster remains one of New Zealand's worst, with 151 deaths (including two from the author's family). More lives might have been lost if not for driver Charlie Parker and fireman Lance Redman, who died at the controls as they tried to stop the train. The effects of railway accidents on those involved are incalculable; for NZR it was a harrowing reminder of the realities of operating in a geologically unstable country. The accident occurred as a result of poorly understood environmental forces, and a board of inquiry absolved NZR of culpability and motivated safety improvements.[101]

Top: Tangiwai, seen from beside the Whangaehu River railway bridge. The engine came to rest on the bank below this point, with carriages strewn downstream. The memorial site is visible beyond the bend in the river. **Bottom**: A tribute to the engine crew with a monument to all 151 victims behind. André Brett, 23 October 2018 (top) and 6 December 2019 (bottom)

Above: Railway staff at Nelson station, 19 May 1954. J.F. Le Cren, ANZ AAVK 6390 B4795

Left: Guard George Clent collects fares aboard an old carriage with longitudinal seating on the Nelson section, 19 May 1954. J.F. Le Cren, ANZ AAVK 6390 B4791 of railway passengers travelled between those two places, and the new method of operation began on 2 November 1953.[102] Because Fairlie was the railhead for the army's Balmoral Camp near Tekapo, NZR maintained the Fairlie Branch to a level suitable for passenger trains and could have done more to retain regular passenger traffic, but as a result of poor service provision and a willingness to shift people to Road Services, yet another line no longer enjoyed passenger rail.[103]

Lost opportunities were really starting to accumulate. Lois Voller has written an illuminating account of the demise of Nelson's railway. In 1947, as the Nelson Provincial Progress League sustained a 'Fill the Gap' campaign to have the line to the West Coast completed, a family new to the district complained about the poor condition of the carriages provided for Nelson schoolchildren on daily trains from Belgrove. They received enough support from other residents that Road Services introduced buses from the second term of 1948, which soon carried more ordinary passengers than schoolchildren. NZR cancelled the Belgrove trains, leaving just a with-car goods to Glenhope three times a week, the Friday timetable of which was framed for country residents to have a day in Nelson.[104] The 1952 royal commission found itself pulled in both directions. On the one hand, it acknowledged that Nelson had suffered decades of broken promises, and that the lack of a railway link to the rest of the island had compounded a sense of isolation and neglect. On the other, filling the gap would necessitate rebuilding the inadequately maintained line to Glenhope – at enormous cost.[105] And in the absence of an interprovincial railway, Nelson now possessed New Zealand's most efficient road freight

network: operators had taken advantage of transport licensing regulations and formed a confederation to rationalise their facilities and avoid competitive cost-cutting.[106] This made it even harder to justify saving the line to Glenhope, let alone extending it to the junction at Īnangahua. The commissioners declined to commit either way: closure was unpopular, extension too expensive.

Fred Potton, chief clerk at Nelson station, slammed the indifference and indecision that beset the line: 'No government has had the guts to close down the line nor … the guts to go on with it either.'[107] The Holland ministry soon found sufficient courage, although Goosman tried to have it both ways. He 'suspended' the railway after 12 June 1954, claiming to be ending an unprofitable service while not deviating from the government's policy of linking Nelson with the trunk system. But Goosman's background was in road construction and haulage, and his proposals for significant road investment in the Nelson region gave the game away.

Against all odds, the Nelson Provincial Progress League negotiated a stay of execution and trains resumed from 18 June 1954, but only for freight. Predictions of greater tonnages proved empty and NZR did not offer a passenger timetable during the line's dénouement. Voller describes one last passenger run on 31 August 1955, when a small band of locals took a farewell trip to Glenhope in a carriage attached to the regular goods train.[108]

The final closure, effective 3 September 1955, was not reversed despite protests that made international headlines. Schoolteacher Ruth Page led a group of women, including future Labour MP Sonja Davies, in a peaceful occupation of Kiwi station where they blocked demolition work. They sat on the tracks for a week, refusing to budge and even facing down a locomotive. The police finally arrested nine of them, and supporters quickly chipped in to pay their fines. The demolition crew got to work, and Nelson became New Zealand's first city to lose its railway.

1946–54: A DIFFERENT PURPOSE FOR RAIL

Construction projects sustained during wartime were now almost all complete. The last one finished, in 1947, was a major deviation at Turakina, east of Whanganui, to bypass 23 kilometres of steep, tightly curved track. Labour's programme for post-war development included multiple new railways, and these proved quite different to the general-purpose trunk routes and missing links of the early 1940s. The lines were for bulk transportation, whether of commuters or a specific commodity. Priorities for rail transport were clearly changing.

A pressing need for modernisation – especially for replacing steam locomotion – motivated the first National government to place NZR under an independent board in 1953. This was the third time NZR had been removed from political control since 1925, and again the experiment was brief. National abolished the board in 1957, finding it no longer politically advantageous, but by then the board's reforms were taking effect.[109]

Despite some suggestions to the contrary, the 1953 Tangiwai disaster did not dissuade potential riders significantly. Coal shortages, infrequent trains and poor on-time performance had already done that. The year 1952 was the nadir of the post-war decline in passenger journeys, which then trended slowly upwards for the rest of the decade as modernisation took place.[110]

Railways in the mid-1950s had a narrower role, one that downplayed passenger rail beyond the main trunks and Wellington and Auckland's urban areas. Wellington's network was transformed: it had evolved from steep steam railways into an electrified network of flatter modern lines. Proposals for Auckland were even grander, but the failure to open a single kilometre meant that its passenger rail followed a vastly different trajectory to Wellington's for the next 50 years.

A new railway in the Hutt Valley was central to the Fraser government's plans to relieve Wellington's severe housing shortage. Market gardens disappeared beneath state housing, commercial districts and new industries; swamps were drained; floodplains and tributaries of the Hutt River were built over, and Lower Hutt became a city.[111] The *Evening Post*'s fulsome praise in April 1945 was not exceptional: 'It will be a transformation more complete and more spectacular, and also more beautiful, than can be appreciated even from the great housing progress so far made.'[112]

The Waterloo Branch was built to main-line standards in the 1920s because planners anticipated it would become the route to the Wairarapa, and from 1944 the PWD began extending it through the new Hutt Valley suburbs. It was also to be electrified: NZR ordered another batch of the English Electric D^M/D class electric multiple units that already ran to Johnsonville and Paekākāriki, although initial services were steam hauled. The first stage, to Naenae, opened on 7 January 1946 with the double-tracked line still incomplete and temporary platforms at the stations; five trains took commuters to Wellington in the morning

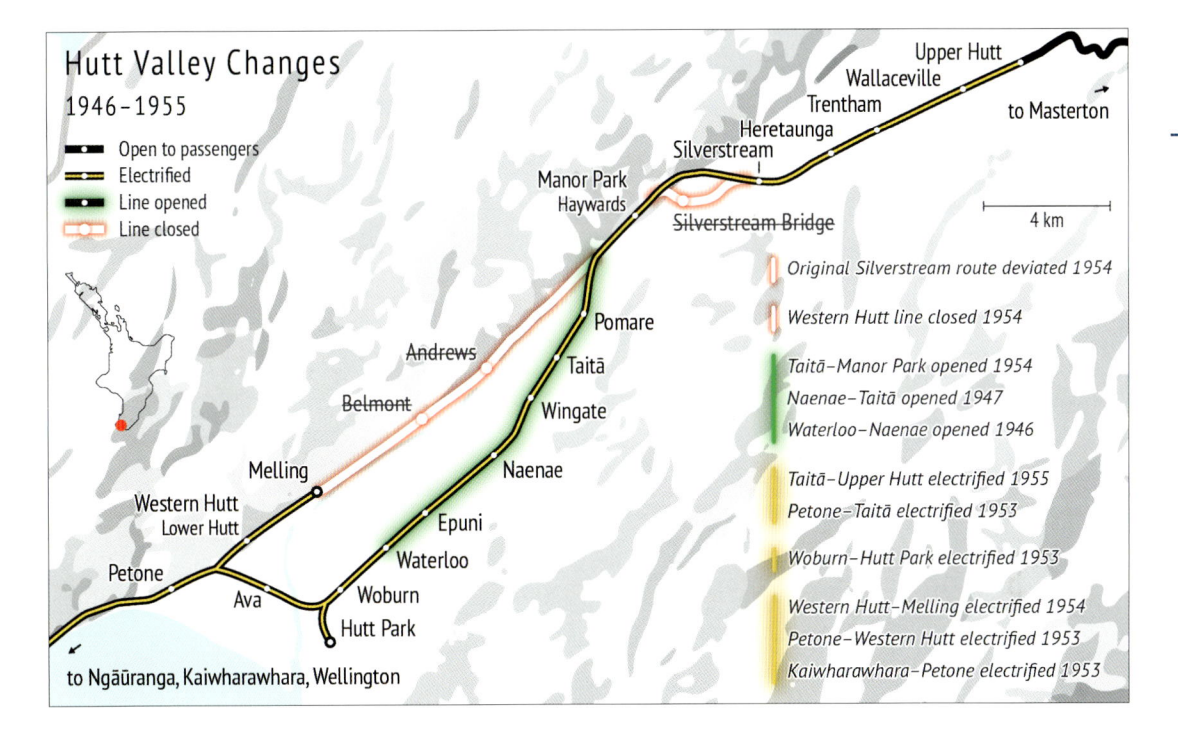

Hutt Valley Changes
1946–1955

- Open to passengers
- Electrified
- Line opened
- Line closed

Upper Hutt
Wallaceville
Trentham
Heretaunga
Silverstream
to Masterton

Silverstream Bridge
Manor Park
Haywards

4 km

Original Silverstream route deviated 1954

Western Hutt line closed 1954

Pomare
Andrews
Taitā
Belmont
Wingate
Melling
Naenae
Western Hutt
Lower Hutt
Epuni
Waterloo
Petone
Woburn
Ava
Hutt Park

to Ngāuranga, Kaiwharawhara, Wellington

Taitā–Manor Park opened 1954
Naenae–Taitā opened 1947
Waterloo–Naenae opened 1946

Taitā–Upper Hutt electrified 1955
Petone–Taitā electrified 1953

Woburn–Hutt Park electrified 1953

Western Hutt–Melling electrified 1954
Petone–Western Hutt electrified 1953
Kaiwharawhara–Petone electrified 1953

and back in the evening.[113] The line was quickly pushed on to Taitā on 14 April 1947, where the government established a large housing estate.[114] The modest length of the line from Waterloo to Taitā, 5 kilometres, should not obscure its significance for suburban growth in the Hutt Valley.

Work slowed beyond Taitā as the Ministry of Works (MoW) investigated multiple routes. This body, formed to oversee post-war reconstruction, had merged with the PWD. A bridge across the Hutt River between Pomare and Haywards (now Manor Park) finally connected with the railway to the Wairarapa on 1 March 1954, and the eastern route became the main line. The old western Hutt line closed that day between Melling and Haywards, and NZR retained the rest as a suburban branch: electric trains ran as far as Lower Hutt station (now

Western Hutt) from 23 November 1953, and to Melling on 1 March 1954.[115] Electric services had reached Taitā on 14 September 1953 and ran all the way to Upper Hutt from 24 July 1955. The branch to the Hutt Workshops was also electrified: first, in 1953, as far as the Hutt Park platform adjacent to the workshops for horseracing specials, and then – for goods only – to the Gracefield industrial terminal in 1964.[116]

The MoW also considered options for a railway from the Hutt Valley west to the Porirua basin. Planners anticipated large industrial and residential growth, including the transformation of Pāuatahanui from a small town to an urban centre of at least 45,000 people, and hoped the proposed railway would rectify the perceived problems in Wellington's commuting patterns: travel occurred mostly at peak times and in one direction, so that trains and roads alike

157

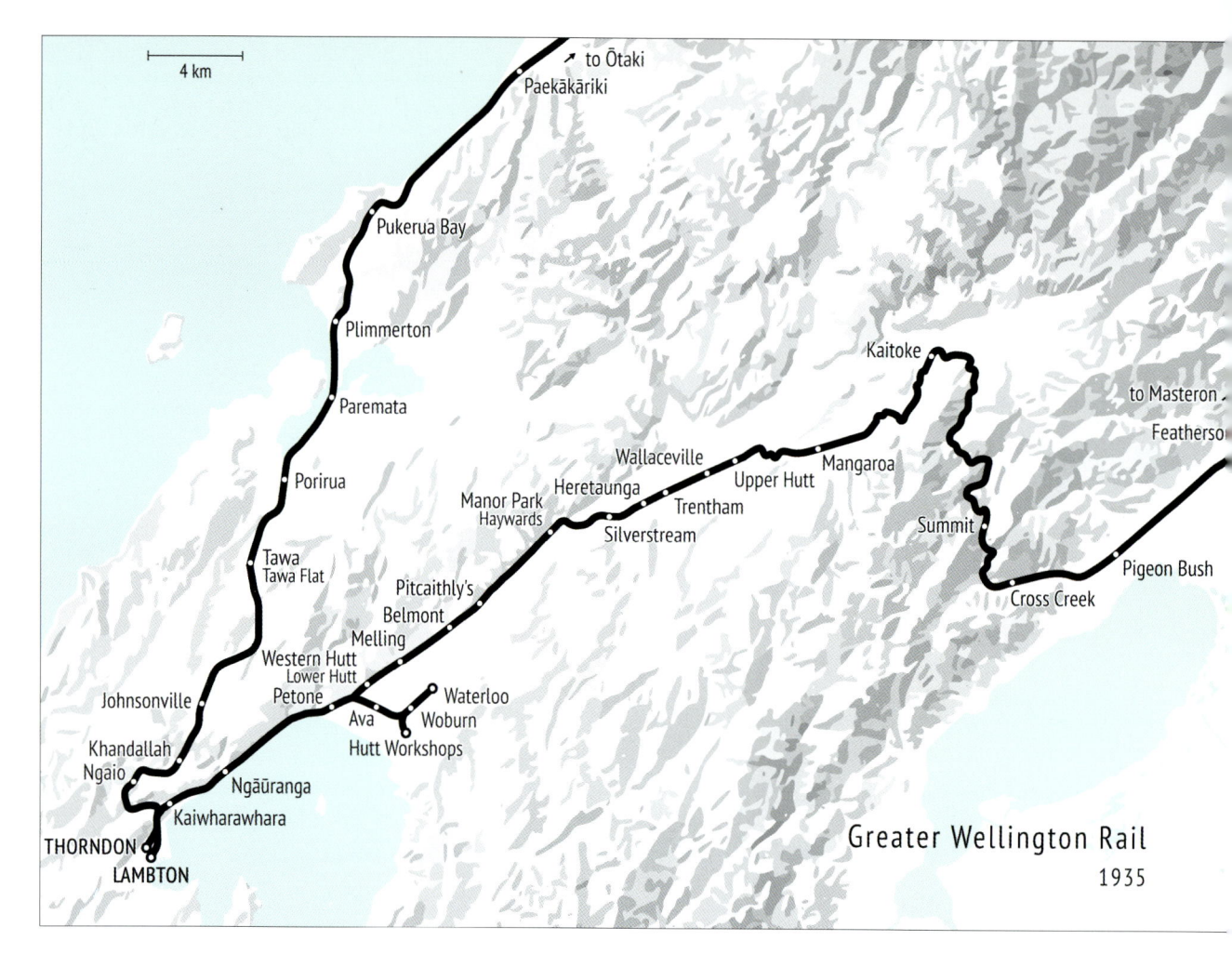

Greater Wellington Rail
1935

were under-used for the rest of the day.[117] This thinking was based on an increasingly common assumption that infrastructure is only used efficiently when near maximum capacity. The MoW abandoned these plans in the late 1970s because of changing economic conditions and increasing awareness of the environmental significance of Pāuatahanui Inlet. The only major upgrade was to straighten and double-track the Main Trunk from Porirua to Plimmerton between 1958 and 1961, with some reclamation of Porirua Harbour.[118]

The Hutt project of 1946–55 was the last major expansion of a suburban network anywhere in New Zealand until 1983, when electrification of the Kāpiti Line was extended from Paekākāriki to Paraparaumu. The Hutt also featured the last entirely new suburban railway alignment until Manukau in 2012.

Auckland was intended to be the beneficiary of even grander suburban railway growth. It was already a rail city, with three main corridors and an extensive tramway network, and 58 percent of motorised journeys were on public transport rather than in private cars.[119] The MoW proposed an extensive scheme in 1946, NZR made its own suggestions, and British civil engineers William Halcrow and J.P. Thomas endorsed an ambitious electrified network in 1950 (see map p. 161).[120] Halcrow's word carried weight: he was knighted in 1944 and served as president of the Institution of Civil Engineers.

The centrepiece of all proposals was the so-called Morningside Deviation, a tunnel

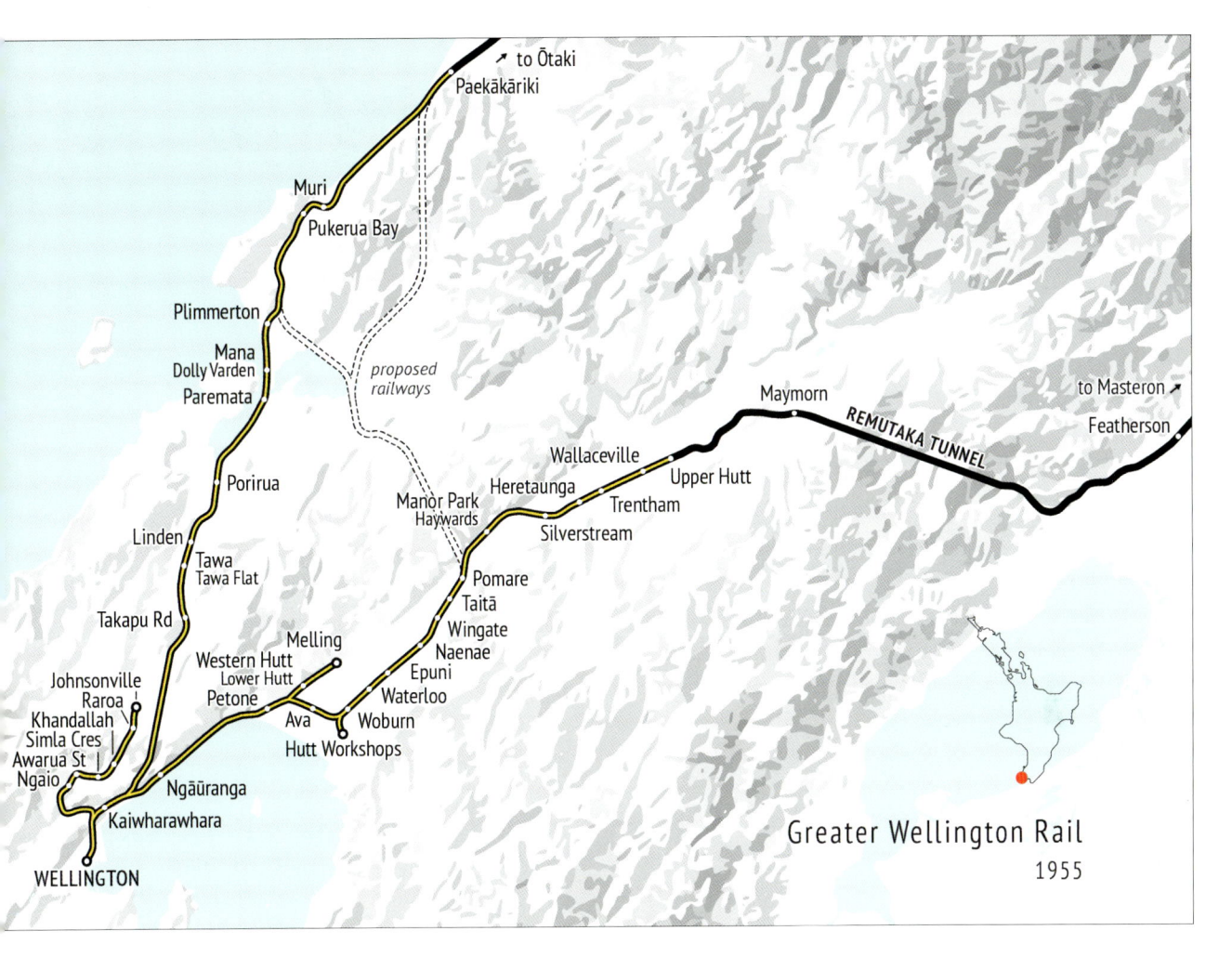

Greater Wellington Rail
1955

from Auckland's main station to Morningside with stations beneath the central business district, which had been planned in the 1920s to balance the Westfield Deviation. The Beach Road terminus was aligned with this in mind. The Avondale–Southdown Line was conceived primarily for goods trains from Northland to access a new yard at Westfield.

MoW surveyors also investigated a so-called 'Waterfront Railway' to Kumeū, which would access a proposed port at Pollen Island and release the Henderson line for suburban trains exclusively. This railway had prominent supporters. Arthur Morrish, a respected newspaper editor and community figure, promoted it as a combined road and rail project to create the 'finest marine road' in the Southern Hemisphere and slash time for express trains to Northland.[121] Graham Bush, however, judges this line as 'frankly wishful' in his history of Auckland's public transport, and without the port it probably was.[122] State Highway 16 realised at least some of Morrish's vision – and it suggests that political priorities changed.

The Halcrow–Thomas report should have been influential: the two internationally renowned engineers not only endorsed decades of local planning for railways but also provided an ambitious blueprint for the next 50 years. The immediate priorities, they argued, were electrification of the existing network and construction of the Morningside Deviation; the Avondale–Southdown Line could follow if needed. They outlined a network for the future, including the Waterfront Railway (though rejecting a connection from Avondale), a branch to Mount Roskill, and a line from Ōrākei across the Tāmaki Estuary to east Auckland and Papatoetoe. Halcrow and Thomas considered three options for a railway to the North Shore, rejecting as expensive and impractical an option to build the Auckland Harbour Bridge for rail as well as road. They suggested that congestion from the bridge would become severe enough within two decades that a separate railway crossing would be necessary, and they gave two tunnel options, preferring one between Devonport and Judges Bay. They also envisaged the retention of trams, which were powered by electricity where bus alternatives were not. Halcrow and Thomas stipulated that expenditure on roads must be restricted until the effects of the railway improvements were clear, as an efficient railway network would build on Auckland's strengths and reduce the need for new roads and parking buildings.

All of this fell on deaf ears. Auckland railway investment ostensibly had bipartisan support from Labour and National until 1954, but construction began on arterial roads and not on rail. In denial of an opportunity to capitalise on decades of public investment in rail and maximising the use of transport powered by locally generated electricity, a web of roads began to sprawl across Auckland. Official reports favouring motorways used visual tricks to influence readers' perceptions, such as images of glistening sun-drenched arterial roads from American engineering journals beside drab photographs of Auckland's existing infrastructure in the rain.[123] Politicians and public servants at both national and local level embraced American theories of modernisation

through motorways – what transport experts Paul Mees and Jago Dodson condemn as 'the American heresy'.[124] Indeed, Auckland's planners went further than much practice in the US. They imposed schemes derived from American experiences with dubious relevance for New Zealand, presented as value-free scientific expertise that Aucklanders simply had to accept.[125]

It is unclear whether many senior figures engaged critically with this vision of modernity, but Kenneth Cumberland, founding professor of geography at what is today the University of Auckland, provided academic clout to demote the Halcrow–Thomas report. He chaired a city council town planning committee and advocated that funds for railways be spent on motorways instead. Moreover, the Auckland Transport Board lent support to motorways as it had declined to purchase new trams, ripping out its allegedly inflexible tramways to make way for buses. Stan Goosman, who held most infrastructure portfolios in Sidney Holland's government, prevailed upon his colleagues to reject rail. For reasons unstated, he believed railways did not work in Wellington and surmised that they could not in Auckland either.[126] A masterplan in 1955 endorsed motorways over railways and shaped the congested, car-dependent city of the early twenty-first century.

NZR acquired land for the Avondale–Southdown Line, which KiwiRail still owns, and opened the Westfield goods yard in 1962, but the vision set out in the Halcrow–Thomas report went unrealised. Only now, with the City Rail Link currently under construction, will a project along the lines of the Morningside Deviation be completed.

The failure to open a single kilometre of

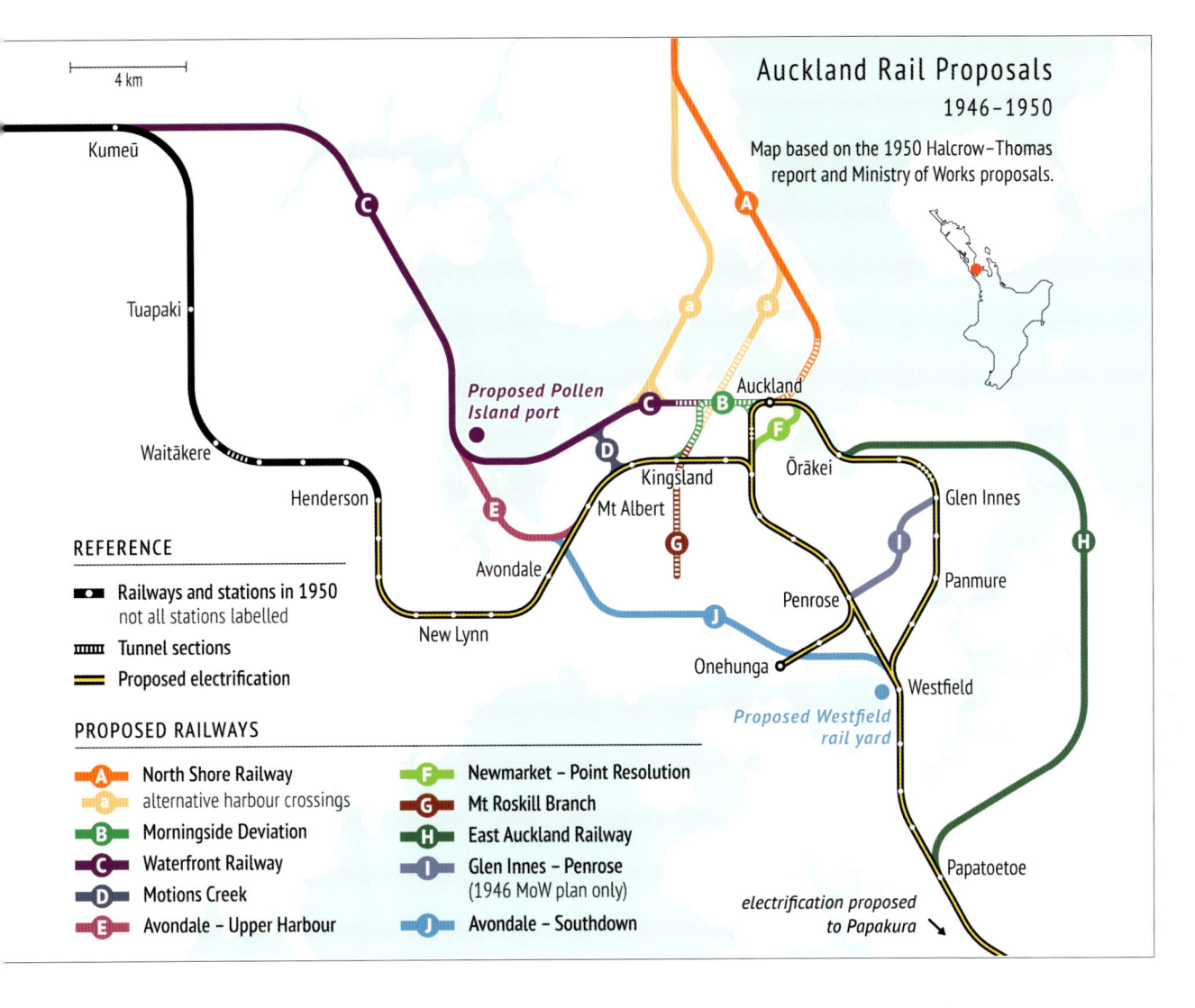

Auckland Rail Proposals
1946–1950

Map based on the 1950 Halcrow–Thomas report and Ministry of Works proposals.

REFERENCE

- Railways and stations in 1950 — not all stations labelled
- Tunnel sections
- Proposed electrification

PROPOSED RAILWAYS

- **A** North Shore Railway
- **a** alternative harbour crossings
- **B** Morningside Deviation
- **C** Waterfront Railway
- **D** Motions Creek
- **E** Avondale – Upper Harbour
- **F** Newmarket – Point Resolution
- **G** Mt Roskill Branch
- **H** East Auckland Railway
- **I** Glen Innes – Penrose (1946 MoW plan only)
- **J** Avondale – Southdown

Proposed Pollen Island port

Proposed Westfield rail yard

electrification proposed to Papakura

Stations: Kumeū, Tuapaki, Waitākere, Henderson, Auckland, Kingsland, Mt Albert, Avondale, New Lynn, Ōrākei, Glen Innes, Panmure, Penrose, Onehunga, Westfield, Papatoetoe

---

new passenger rail in Auckland in the decades immediately after World War II perhaps heralded the contraction of New Zealand's passenger network better than any closure could. Even in a city with large demands and sophisticated plans endorsed by local and international experts, the state had turned away from rail.

All of this presaged greater use of seemingly objective data to achieve desired outcomes in the coming decades – sometimes through uncritical assumptions that quantitative figures are, or can be, neutral, and sometimes through deliberate selection and presentation. But even before the government and city council repudiated rail publicly, Auckland's car-dependent future was sealed. At the opening of the first section of the Southern Motorway in 1953, *New Zealand Herald* photographer Graham Stewart suggested to Goosman that it should have been built with a centre reservation for a commuter railway or tramway. Goosman replied condescendingly, 'My boy, the future of Auckland is with the motorcar.'[127] Few comments could more accurately capture the attitude that prevailed upon New Zealand's transport planning for the rest of the century, with dire consequences for the passenger rail network.

Ōkaihau
Kaikohe
Ōpua
Kawakawa
Ōtiria
Hikurangi
WHANGĀREI
Donnellys Crossing
Kaihū
Portland
Kirikōpuni
Tangowahine
Waiōtira
DARGAVILLE
Maungatūroto

Waiōtira–Dargaville ceased 1967
Dargaville–Donnellys Crossing ceased 1959

Maungatūroto–Wellsford ceased 1967

Wellsford
Tahekeroa
HELENSVILLE
AUCKLAND
Henderson
Ōtāhuhu
Onehunga
Papakura
Drury
Pukekohe
Mercer
Waikato R.
Glen Afton
Huntly

Ngāruawāhia–Glen Massey ceased 1958

Glen Massey
Ngāruaw
HAMILTON

Frankton–Putāruru–Rotorua ceased 1968

FRANKTON

Putāruru–Rotorua resumed 1968

Te Awamutu

Ōtorohanga

Upper North Island
1955–1968

C^H 6

1955–1968
The Fiat fiasco

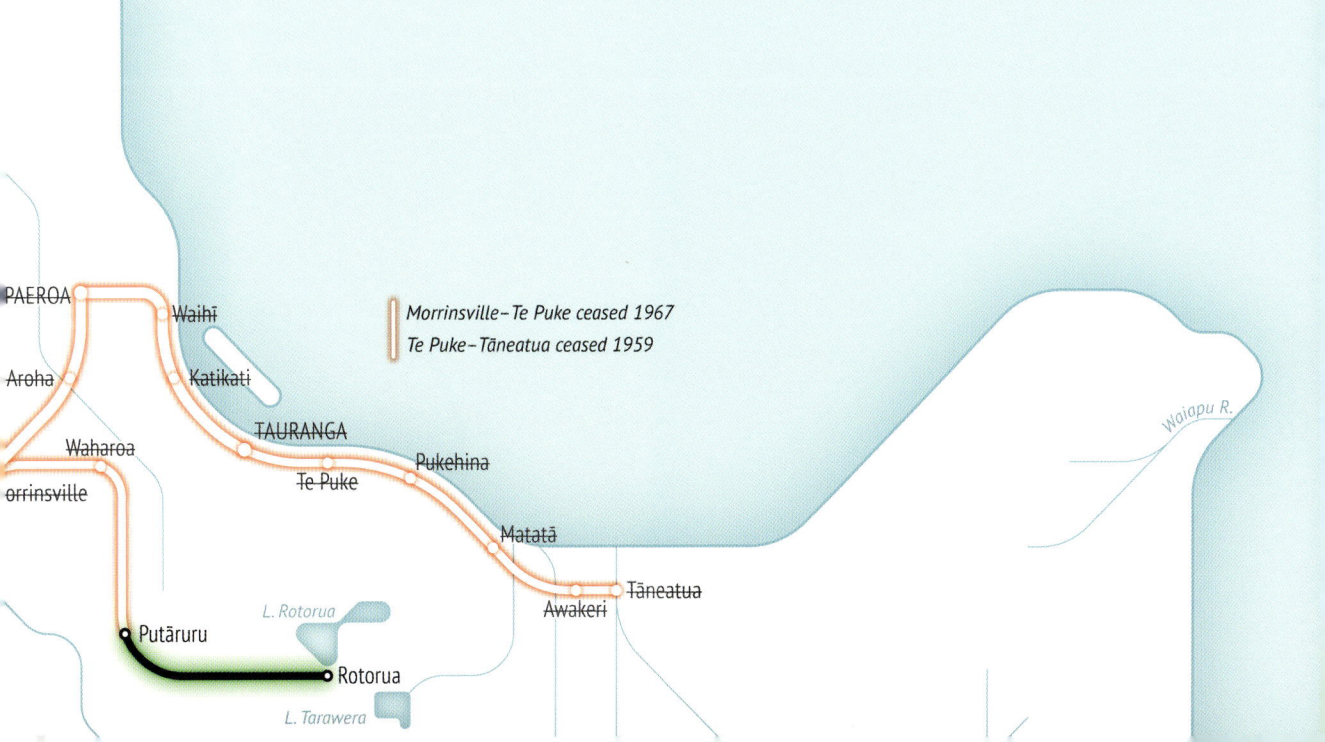

Morrinsville–Te Puke ceased 1967
Te Puke–Tāneatua ceased 1959

Ōtorohanga

Te Kūiti

Mangapēhi

Ōkahukura

Ōhura

Tāngarākau

Taumarunui

Raurimu

Mt Tongariro

Mt Ngāuruhoe

National Park

Mt Ruapehu

NEW PLYMOUTH

Inglewood

Whangamōmona

Toko

Mt Taranaki

Stratford

Ohakune

Tangiwai

Waiōuru

Kāpuni

Te Roti

Taihape

Ōpunake

Hāwera

Waitōtara R.

Whanganui R.

Rangitīkei R.

Mangaweka

Pātea

Te Roti–Ōpunake ceased 1955

Waitōtara

Kai Iwi

Hunterville

Waverley

Aramoho

WHANGANUI

Ormondville

Marton

Dannevirke

Aramoho–Whanganui ceased 1959

Feilding

PALMERSTON NORTH

Woodville

Pahīatua

Shannon

Eketāhuna

Levin

Mauriceville

Ōtaki

Waikanae

MASTERTON

Carterton

Paekākāriki

Featherston

Remutaka Tunnel opened 1955

L. Wairarapa

Melling

Upper Hutt

Remutaka Incline closed 1955

Johnsonville

Waterloo

Hutt Workshops

WELLINGTON

L. Tarawera

Waikato R.

L. Taupō

Mōkau R.

164

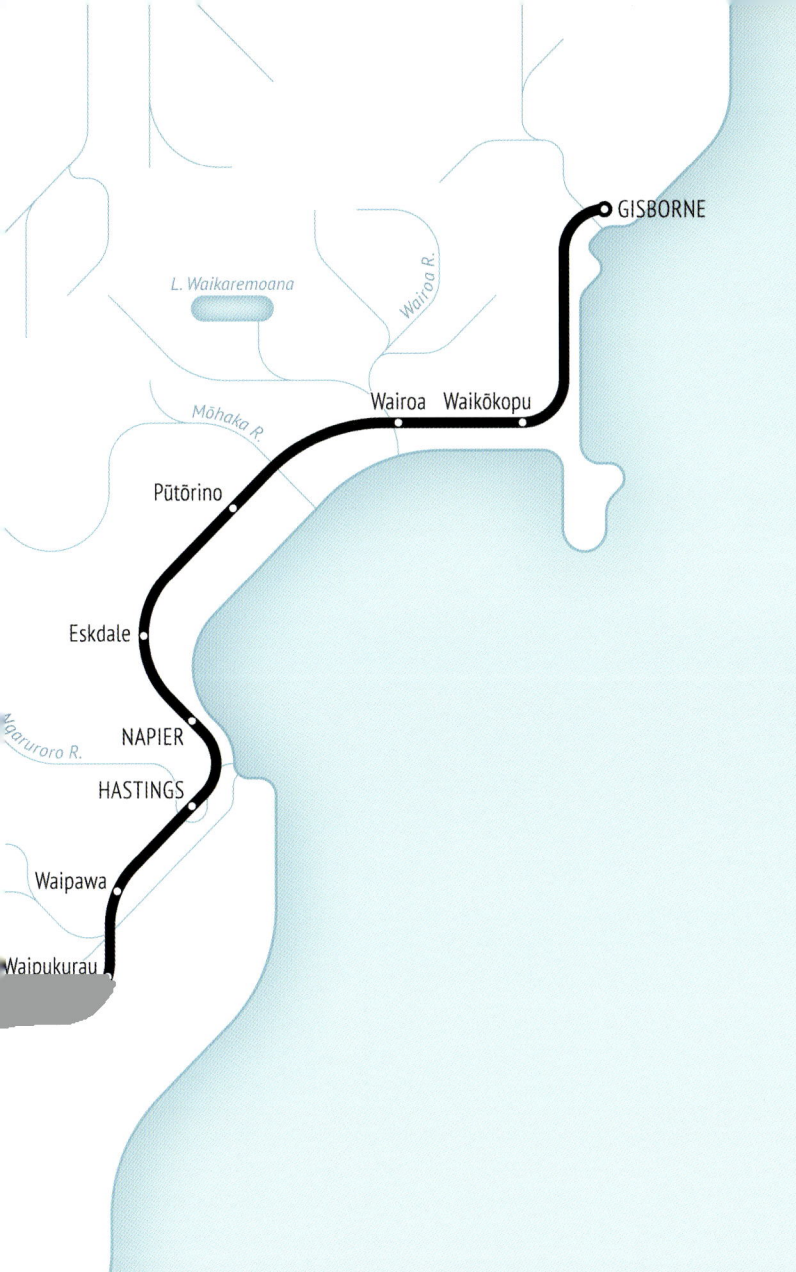

GISBORNE

L. Waikaremoana

Wairoa R.

Mōhaka R.

Wairoa Waikōkopu

Pūtōrino

Eskdale

Ngaruroro R.

NAPIER

HASTINGS

Waipawa

Waipukurau

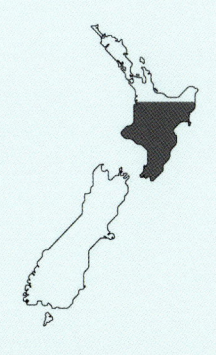

Lower North Island
1955–1968

Upper South Island
1955–1968

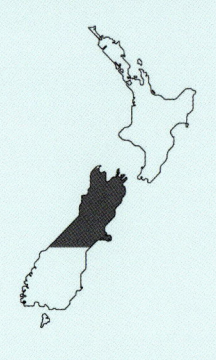

Stillwater–Westport ceased 1967

WESTPORT

Kawatiri / Buller

Īnangahua

Reefton

Ikamatua

Rewanui

Ngahere

GREYMOUTH

Stillwater

L. Sumner

Kūmara Junction

Moana

Hokitika

Ōtira

ŌTIRA TUNNEL

Ross

Arthur's Pass

Craigieburn

L. Coleridge

Springfield

Sheffield

Rakaia R.

Da

Hakatere / Ashburton R.

Methven

Rakaia

Rangitātā R.

Hinds R.

ASHBURTO

▲ *Aoraki / Mt Cook*

▲ *Maukatua / Mt Sefton*

L. Tekapo

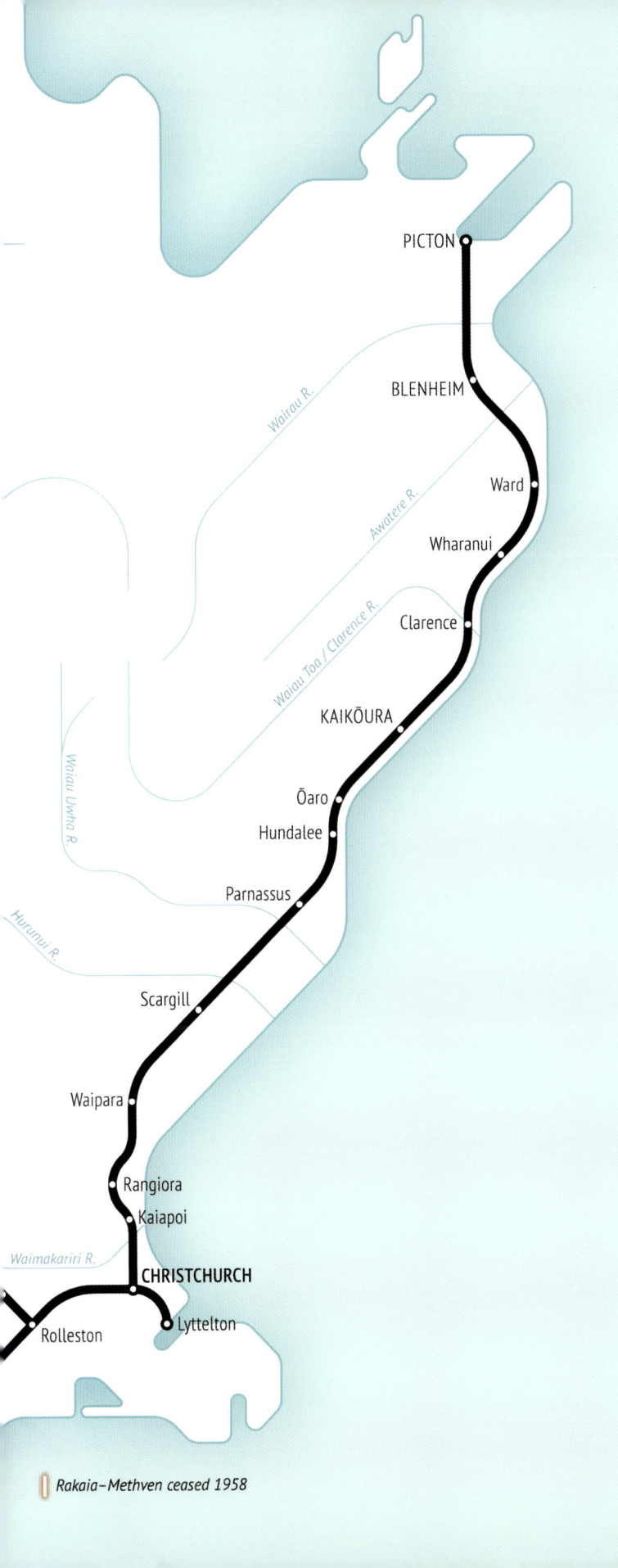

PICTON

BLENHEIM

Ward

Wharanui

Clarence

KAIKŌURA

Ōaro

Hundalee

Parnassus

Scargill

Waipara

Rangiora

Kaiapoi

CHRISTCHURCH

Lyttelton

Rolleston

Wairau R.

Awatere R.

Waiau Toa / Clarence R.

Waiau Uwha R.

Hurunui R.

Waimakariri R.

Rakaia–Methven ceased 1958

Lumsden–Kingston holiday trains ceased 1957

Gore–Lumsden holiday trains ceased 1957

Invercargill–Lumsden ceased 1956

Invercargill–Bluff ceased 1966

Invercargill–Tokanui ceased 1960

Temuka

Washdyke

TIMARU

Studholme

Waitaki R.

Pukeuri

ŌAMARU

Ranfurly

[] *Alexandra–Cromwell ceased 1958*

Hyde

Taieri R.

PALMERSTON

Middlemarch

Waikouaiti

Port Chalmers

[] *Port Chalmers terminus moved to Mussel Bay 1961*

DUNEDIN

MOSGIEL

Clarendon

Milton

[] *Balclutha–Tahakopa ceased 1958*

Lower South Island
1955-1968

By rights 1955 should stand out as a signal year in the history of New Zealand passenger rail. It was the year NZR introduced a type of railcar known by many names: 'articulateds', 'twinsets' or 'twin units' as they comprised two permanently attached carriages; 'Drewry' for their English manufacturer; and the self-explanatory '88-seater'. This book uses 'Fiat', for their Italian motors, as these became important. The reason this type of railcar has so many names is because NZR classified all railcars as RM, short for rail motor, which until the 1930s was a more common term than railcar. Other designations, therefore, have to be used to distinguish between types.

With 35 units, the Fiats formed the largest fleet of railcars. NZR had allowed some rural services to wither, but the Fiats represented a deliberate and concerted effort to rejuvenate passenger rail on main lines by replacing steam-hauled express trains that had operated only two or three times a week on many routes since 1951. Cheap to operate and able to maintain quicker timetables, the new railcars should have been a tonic.

Should have been.

Fiat class leader RM 100 about to depart Wellington on a trial to Napier, 14 March 1955.
J.F. Le Cren, ANZ AAVK 6390 B5983

1955–58: RAILCARS AND THE REMUTAKAS

One of NZR's headline achievements in 1955, a tunnel through the Remutaka Range, had been in the works for decades. (At the time the range was known as 'Rimutaka', a word without meaning in te reo Māori. The spelling was corrected in 2015.) NZR had wanted for decades to replace the onerous railway over the range. The steep climb from the Hutt Valley up the western slope to a station fittingly named Summit was within the capabilities of conventional locomotives, but the descent to the Wairarapa, the Remutaka Incline, required a system invented by English engineer John Barraclough Fell, whereby special locomotives and guard's vans gripped a raised centre rail for traction and braking.

The incline opened in 1878 after alternative routes to the Wairarapa, including a lengthy one around the coast, were rejected as even more difficult and expensive. It became the world's only long-term complete application of the Fell mountain railway system; other examples that lasted more than a few years, including two in New Zealand – the Rewanui and Roa inclines on the West Coast – used the centre rail for braking but not traction. Trains on the Remutaka Incline required up to five locomotives and travelled at little more than walking pace. Wairarapa railcars sped up passenger services from 1936, but the incline was a bottleneck.[1]

A tunnel under the Remutaka Range seemed impossible in the nineteenth century, but plans became serious after World War I. Gordon Coates called it a 'necessary work' in 1923, and a

6

1955–1968

A passenger train on the Remutaka Incline. The raised third rail is visible. Wairarapa Archive 17-152/2-4

comprehensive project of railway improvements envisaged construction commencing in the late 1920s.[2] It was not to be, and travellers grew agitated: one newspaper in 1937 condemned the incline as 'an eyesore and a danger … the greatest blot on Wairarapa progress', and expressed the hope that Bob Semple would include the tunnel in his expansive programme of railway construction.[3] Michael Joseph Savage announced the start of work in June 1938: the tunnel would cost £1 million and, as it would be too long for steam engines, he allocated an additional £215,000 to electrify the line from Upper Hutt to Featherston. 'The wonder to me,' Savage told a journalist, 'is that they ever tried to get over the hill at all with a railway.'[4] The incline remained in use for another 17 years, however.

Construction eventually began a decade after Savage had confirmed the project.[5] The finished tunnel was 8798 metres long, surpassing the Ōtira Tunnel as the longest in New Zealand by over 200 metres. Its completion in 1955 revolutionised travel to the Wairarapa but spelled the end of passenger services to the small communities along the old line. Almost the entire population of Cross Creek, a settlement at the base of the incline, rode the last train on 29 October 1955.[6]

The first official passenger train ran through the new tunnel on 3 November. Electrification, however, had stopped at Upper Hutt. The tunnel had been built with room for wires, but the arrival of diesel engines meant smoke was no longer such a nuisance. The Wairarapa railway line was the first in New Zealand to be fully dieselised.

Fiat railcars also entered operation in 1955. Protracted deliberations about railcars had resolved in favour of 25 articulated diesel-electric units in 1948, the year construction

began on the Remutaka Tunnel. But since the railcars were expected to arrive well ahead of the tunnel's completion, in 1949 the order was expanded to include 10 more, this time with diesel-mechanical transmission to handle the Remutaka Incline.[7] An existing contract obliged NZR to seek railcars initially from English Electric, but this company had difficulty designing something affordable with a sufficiently powerful but lightweight engine. The Drewry Car Company of Birmingham offered an attractive proposal for the diesel-mechanical railcars using lower-cost engines from Fiat, an Italian company that NZR's chief mechanical engineer Percy Roy Angus considered 'a first-class engineering concern'. Angus proposed to cancel the diesel-electric railcars and instead order 35 of the Fiat-powered model, 10 of which would be designed to operate over the Remutaka Incline. Frank Aickin approved this order on 12 January 1950.[8] The new railcars were to be shipped to New Zealand from early 1952.

NZR fell victim to delays mostly of its own making. Stan Goosman did not realise how right he was when he counselled in 1951 that 'delays in deliveries of rolling-stock and railway equipment generally seem to be inseparable from the trials of modern railroading'.[9] The first major hold-up came in November that year when NZR modified the design substantially. Completion of the Remutaka Tunnel was now close enough that the railcars would never have to operate over the incline, so NZR asked that they be built with lower floors and wider bodies to accommodate new general manager Horace Lusty's request for reclining seats.[10] The redesign spawned multiple delays: Drewry decided instead to prioritise an order for Nyasaland (today Malawi), and when the first two railcars were finally ready to be shipped to New Zealand

6

1955–1968

New and old railcars in Palmerston North, 14 March 1955. Above left is Fiat class leader RM 100; above right is Wairarapa railcar RM 7. Affectionately known as 'tin hares', the Wairarapa class ended their duties later that year when the Remutaka Tunnel opened. J.F. Le Cren, ANZ AAVK 6390 B5986 and B5987

a month-long strike on the London docks delayed their departure.[11] The first units finally landed in early 1955.

Officials considered numerous routes for railcar services, and transportation superintendent A.J. Ede had distributed proposals to his district traffic managers in November 1950.[12] In some areas Fiat railcars would replace locomotive-hauled expresses; elsewhere they would take over routes operated by older railcars that could then be reallocated, including to some lines served only by mixed trains. An extensive discussion followed, and traffic managers modified some suggestions. Canterbury's manager, for instance, rejected a daily service between Christchurch and Waipara and proposed four to Rangiora instead. He also suggested a thrice-weekly shuttle between Blenheim and Picton to connect with sailings of

Union Steam Ship's SS *Tamahine* to Wellington, and expressed the wish that railcars replace a daily steam-hauled Ashburton–Christchurch train.[13] Otago's manager modified Ede's timetable for the Otago Central Railway because communities between Ranfurly and Cromwell had been so vocal in demanding a railcar, and warned that 'unless we provide the daily service to Dunedin and back for the whole Branch, we are asking for it'.[14] The acting traffic manager for Southland was convinced that, with the introduction of railcar services throughout the region, 'much of our lost passenger traffic would be regained' from road, especially on the Bluff line.[15] It was a refreshing vote of confidence in rail's capacity to regain passengers.

NZR submitted its proposed allocation of railcars to the 1952 royal commission. The commissioners viewed it positively, but urged

Proposals for Railcar Routes
1950–1951

All routes discussed between November 1950 and February 1951.

The network shown is slightly larger than the most extensive proposals. Most proposed routes were complementary, but a few were mutually exclusive.

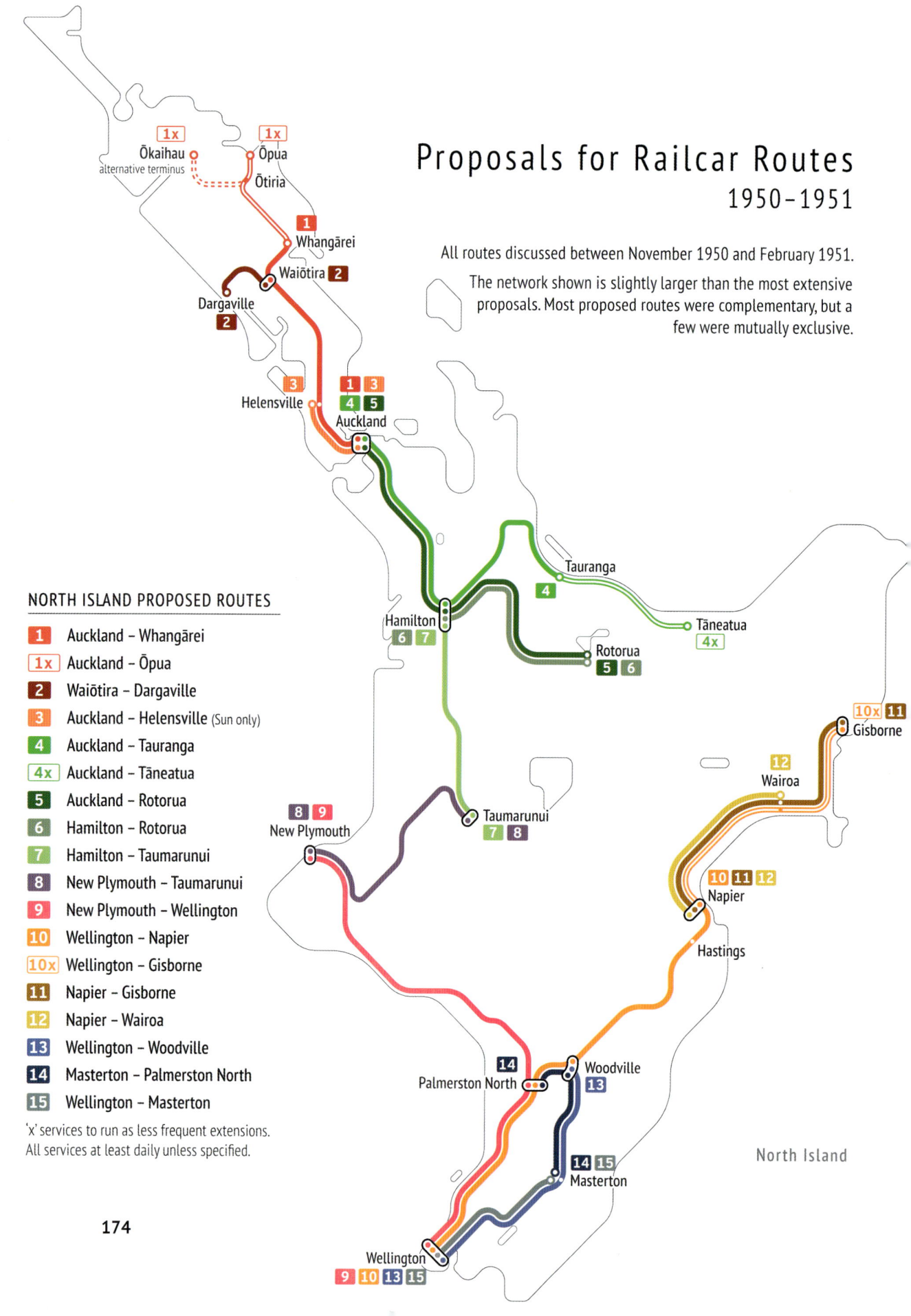

NORTH ISLAND PROPOSED ROUTES

- **1** Auckland – Whangārei
- **1x** Auckland – Ōpua
- **2** Waiōtira – Dargaville
- **3** Auckland – Helensville (Sun only)
- **4** Auckland – Tauranga
- **4x** Auckland – Tāneatua
- **5** Auckland – Rotorua
- **6** Hamilton – Rotorua
- **7** Hamilton – Taumarunui
- **8** New Plymouth – Taumarunui
- **9** New Plymouth – Wellington
- **10** Wellington – Napier
- **10x** Wellington – Gisborne
- **11** Napier – Gisborne
- **12** Napier – Wairoa
- **13** Wellington – Woodville
- **14** Masterton – Palmerston North
- **15** Wellington – Masterton

'x' services to run as less frequent extensions.
All services at least daily unless specified.

North Island

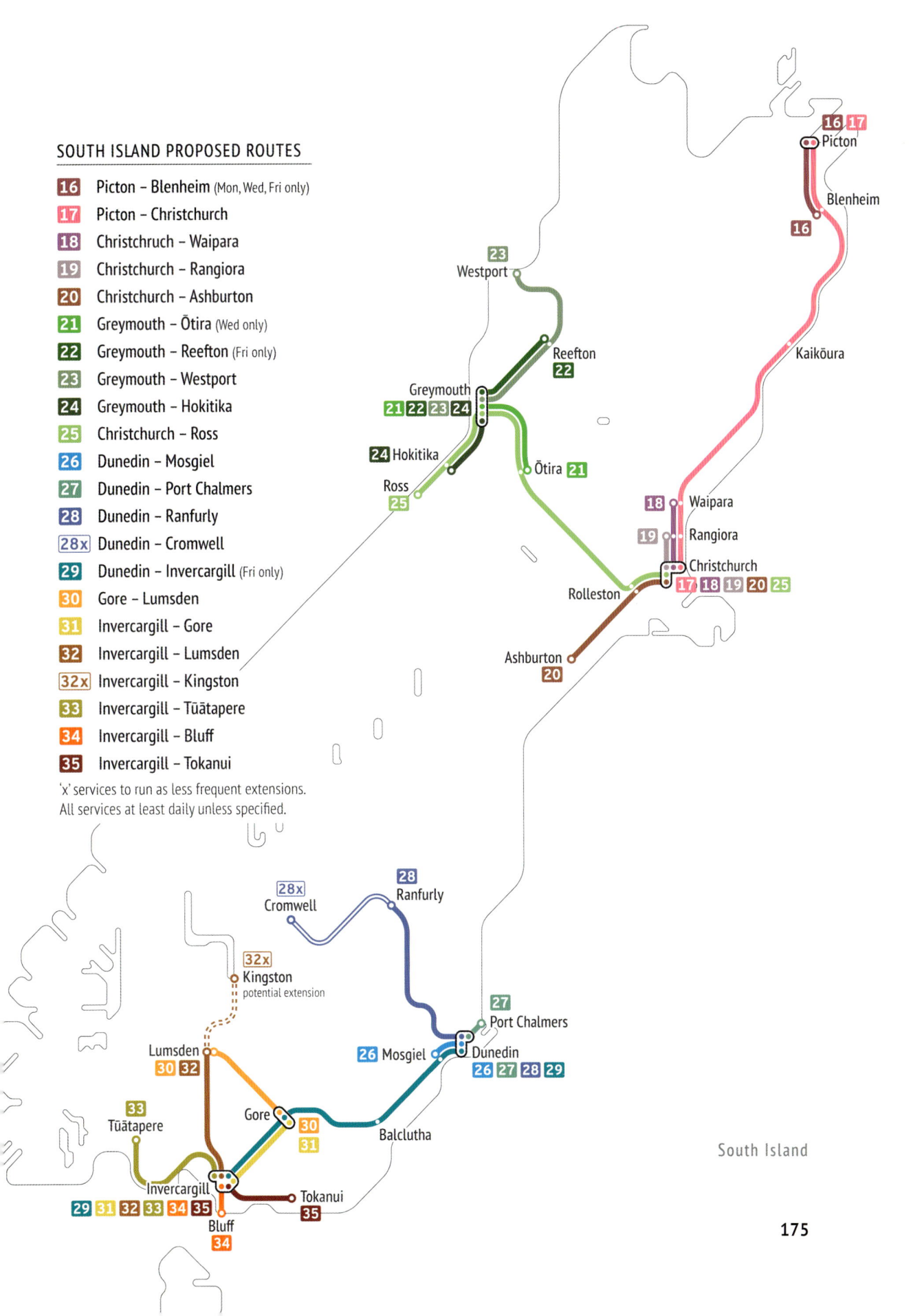

SOUTH ISLAND PROPOSED ROUTES

- **16** Picton – Blenheim (Mon, Wed, Fri only)
- **17** Picton – Christchurch
- **18** Christchruch – Waipara
- **19** Christchurch – Rangiora
- **20** Christchurch – Ashburton
- **21** Greymouth – Ōtira (Wed only)
- **22** Greymouth – Reefton (Fri only)
- **23** Greymouth – Westport
- **24** Greymouth – Hokitika
- **25** Christchurch – Ross
- **26** Dunedin – Mosgiel
- **27** Dunedin – Port Chalmers
- **28** Dunedin – Ranfurly
- **28x** Dunedin – Cromwell
- **29** Dunedin – Invercargill (Fri only)
- **30** Gore – Lumsden
- **31** Invercargill – Gore
- **32** Invercargill – Lumsden
- **32x** Invercargill – Kingston
- **33** Invercargill – Tūātapere
- **34** Invercargill – Bluff
- **35** Invercargill – Tokanui

'x' services to run as less frequent extensions.
All services at least daily unless specified.

South Island

that priority be given to daytime or evening services on the routes Auckland–Wellington and Christchurch–Dunedin–Invercargill to supplement the existing flagship limited expresses.[16] Railcars had originally been developed to provide a cost-effective and attractive service to rural areas, but the commission's suggestions crystallised a new purpose for them – as a modern offering between large cities.

Lusty endorsed an allocation of railcars in August 1954 ahead of their impending delivery. Any thought of a local Southland network was gone; in the North Island a brief reconsideration of the 1930s plan to run railcars to Dargaville had amounted to nothing; and railcars north of Whangārei were to terminate at Ōkaihau for connections to the Far North, not Ōpua for Bay of Islands holidaymakers. In the end, much of the railcar network replaced sluggish and rundown steam-hauled regional expresses.[17] Railcars were assigned to almost no lines that ran mixed trains only, and nowhere did they restore a service that had already been lost, despite lofty ambitions and two decades of hints to various communities. The Fiats improved regional travel but did not expand it; in fact, their protracted introduction eventually reduced the number of places served.

The first railcar landed in Wellington on 31 January 1955, and defects quickly became apparent. Metalwork had corroded in the toilets, the luggage and guard's compartments needed modification, and the driver's cab leaked in the rain.[18] To top it off, the Fiat motors overheated regularly. Although they were introduced in a blaze of publicity – 'as the means of providing a really first-class service' – the constant problems frustrated passengers and demoralised staff.[19] Daily breakdown statistics alarmed

Alan Gandell, Lusty's successor as general manager, who labelled the mechanical troubles 'disturbing'.[20] Drewry and Fiat conceded their workmanship was at fault on 1 June 1956 after NZR's chief mechanical engineer, Bob Black, compiled a list of flaws.[21]

Problems continued to arise. Drewry supplied replacement fans for cooling the motors but these were inadequate; carbon accumulated in the exhaust and sparked lineside fires; and crankcases began to break because they could not handle the engines' power. Black wrote a terse letter to Fiat's local representatives saying 'the position now is quite serious … Such defects should not be experienced.' He was more forthright with Gandell, telling him that 'the time has arrived for a show down' and insisting that senior representatives from Drewry and Fiat come to New Zealand to resolve the problems.[22] Black got his wish. Drewry and Fiat covered a substantial portion of the cost of bringing the railcars to an acceptable standard, albeit with the motors derated from 210 horsepower to 185, and six Fiat mechanics arrived from Italy in late 1957 to rebuild the engines.[23] The task took 12 months, but by October 1958 NZR could finally assume it had 35 railcars in good working order.

Despite all the problems, the Fiats were a hit and proved that existing patronage did not represent the entire market – rather, the moment a better service was offered, ridership improved. In the first year, almost everywhere the Fiats operated, patronage shot up 25–30 percent, and the Remutaka Tunnel underpinned remarkable growth of 115 percent in the Wairarapa.[24] They were not used on the onerous Auckland to Wellington run – the mechanical difficulties prevented that – but by November 1956 railcars had replaced or supplemented all other steam-hauled expresses except those to Rotorua and Tāneatua.

Before the Fiats were even delivered, NZR had contemplated ordering more railcars to meet their ambitious plans. The 1952 royal commission had calculated that an additional 41 were needed to replace all locomotive-hauled passenger trains and most mixed trains – or 47 without the Wairarapa railcars, which were nearly at the end of their working lives. In March 1954 Lusty had decided to trial the initial 35 before placing another order. By August that year, however, he emphasised that 15 more would be needed to operate even the minimum planned network. Once the Fiats landed, their poor reliability further highlighted the need for spare units. Cabinet approved an order for 15 more in September 1955, and senior officials debated whether these should seat 88 or a more modest 76, as they would run on secondary routes.[25] In June 1956 Bob Black raised doubts about placing any order; he had lost faith in the troublesome Fiats and questioned the merit of buying railcars for 'marginal' traffic. Black instead suggested buying up-to-date European diesel-electric multiple units for the North Island Main Trunk and Rotorua, so that the Fiats could be allocated elsewhere.[26]

The longer NZR took to decide, the pricier new railcars became. The original quote in 1949 had been for £46,000 each; this became £58,000–62,000 when they were delivered, and by September 1957 estimates for additional railcars ranged from £72,000 to £80,000.[27] Fiat hoped its generosity in funding repairs would elicit further orders, but it would be disappointed.[28] No order was ever placed, nor did NZR call for open tenders. Walter Nash led Labour to electoral victory in November 1957,

and his minister of railways, Mick Moohan, had little affection for the Fiats. He told Dargavillians in April 1959 that he would like 'many more' railcars but 'not the type that we now have'.[29]

There was a larger problem: Labour entered power to find a balance-of-payments crisis. It implemented import controls in January 1958 as prices tumbled on New Zealand's exports, and in June finance minister Arnold Nordmeyer's infamous 'Black Budget' attempted to salvage revenue through, among other measures, unpopular taxes on alcohol and tobacco.[30] NZR persuaded Cabinet to update the motors in the Vulcans, but new railcars fell off the agenda. The long-distance passenger network would struggle from the late 1960s as a result.

1958–59: FINALISING THE RAILCAR NETWORK

The unreliability of the Fiats and the failure to order more railcars had immediate effects on the passenger network's size. NZR could not introduce railcars as widely as it had intended, so it trimmed proposals and cancelled some trains in Central Otago, Southland, Whanganui and the Bay of Plenty. It was not always frank about the reasons for this. The railcars' defects were no secret, but NZR did not tell the full story publicly. It used the excuse of 'New Zealand conditions' to avoid the uncomfortable reality that it had bought a bad design. When shortening or cancelling services it blamed patronage rather than the need to reduce maintenance or the fact that it had too few railcars to fulfil its plans or meet public expectations.

The first service to be cut was in Central Otago, where the railway line had always had a conflicted identity – was it a main line through the interior, potentially even a route through Haast Pass to Westland, or a long branch serving rural communities? With no significant settlements for 64 kilometres from Wingatui through the Taieri Gorge to Middlemarch, the railway struggled to break even. Since 1921 a daily mixed had run from Cromwell to Dunedin, with passenger expresses in summer; improved loadings meant that the express ran year round from 1936 until the coal shortage in 1944 restricted it to thrice weekly.[31]

The effects of World War II scuttled plans to introduce Vulcan railcars to Central Otago, and although community groups secured a renewal of this commitment after the war, nothing happened. Indeed, worse than nothing: the coal-saving timetable of April 1951 took away the

An NZR Road Services Bedford bus in the Cromwell Gorge en route to Dunedin, February 1953.
J.G. Duncan, ANZ AAVK 6390 B3979

express except on holidays.[32] Passengers between Ranfurly and Cromwell now had only a thrice-weekly mixed.

As the Fiats spread throughout the network, NZR transferred Vulcan railcars from Canterbury to commence daily operation between Cromwell and Dunedin on 30 September 1956. The inauguration of a new railway service was still a major event, and a pipe band at Alexandra serenaded the first of these. Patronage from Clyde and Cromwell was not large, however. NZR was having difficulties with staffing and rostering, and both towns sat on Road Services routes from Dunedin via Roxburgh to Queenstown and Wānaka. From 11 May 1958 Alexandra became the end of the line for passengers, and the final 29 kilometres of the Otago Central Railway to Cromwell became goods only.[33] Making Alexandra the terminus was also an easy way to limit mileage for the railcars and reduce maintenance.

With the Fiats finally running satisfactorily some three years after entering service, senior officials in November 1958 confirmed new timetables to begin in February 1959.[34] Ironically, this move would contract the passenger network overall: the failure to order additional railcars meant the end of local services between Whanganui and Taranaki and all passenger trains to the eastern Bay of Plenty.

Since the 1920s NZR had operated a passenger train between New Plymouth and Whanganui to supplement expresses to Wellington. Notably, although main-line expresses stopped at suburban Aramoho, this passenger train ran to Whanganui's central station on Taupō Quay. Standard railcars usually operated this service in the 1950s, although Fiats were used occasionally.[35] Patronage during holiday periods was good but at other times it effectively halved. As a result, the district traffic manager proposed the train should operate only during holidays from 1958, using Road Services' local timetable as rationale.[36] Nothing happened and the train ran through 1958, and although critics in the press complained of poor advertising, NZR did try to promote it. One advertisement in major newspapers during October 1958 claimed that the service catered 'for true travel pleasure'.[37]

In the end, a timetable to suit travellers between Auckland and Taranaki took priority over local journeys. The railcars to Taupō Quay concluded on 7 February 1959 and the following week the reorganised timetable contained a weekend railcar between New Plymouth and Auckland instead.[38] This service was only made possible by the reallocation of a railcar from Whanganui. A with-car goods to Stratford operated from Taupō Quay for another three months, at which point the small custom on this train was diverted to a Road Services bus to Hāwera.

Residents of towns west of Whanganui were displeased as they now had to walk some distance to a bus stop, and officials agreed that the goods would continue to use a car-van on two days a week. Under the new timetable it ran between Palmerston North and New Plymouth, with the car-van put on at East Town and taken off at Waitōtara, so the Whanganui Branch remained goods only.[39] Taupō Quay station, once a destination for suburban services from Castlecliff and regional trains from New Plymouth, no longer exists.

The other change instituted in February 1959 finally brought railcars to the Bay of Plenty. The express trains to Rotorua and Tāneatua ran twice weekly and were in a bad state: the latter took at least an hour longer than a railcar.

Under the new timetable two daily Fiats ran together from Auckland to Morrinsville, where they diverged to their respective destinations. Additional services ran on Friday evenings so that Aucklanders could spend the weekend in the Bay of Plenty and Bay residents could do the same in Auckland.[40] The railcars were originally planned to run all the way to Tāneatua, but Black faced a maintenance backlog and requested that unprofitable mileage be reduced in the expectation of a commensurate reduction of repairs.[41] Te Puke became the terminus in the Bay instead. One aggrieved resident wrote to the *New Zealand Herald* 'to point out that the Bay of Plenty extends beyond Te Puke'.[42] Eastern Bay residents now had to take Road Services buses from Rotorua or Te Puke. Community organisations in Edgecumbe, Ōpōtiki, Tāneatua and Whakatāne protested, but Mick Moohan was unmoved.[43] Passenger trains have never again been timetabled to the eastern Bay of Plenty.

1956–66: 'AN IMPORTANT PRINCIPLE OF POLICY' IN INVERCARGILL

The November 1950 proposals for railcars in Southland made local officials optimistic about winning back riders, but the failure to implement these spelled the end of almost all of Invercargill's local passenger services by 1958.

In the killing season NZR ran dedicated workers' trains to the Southland Frozen Meat Company in Makarewa, on Invercargill's northern outskirts. These were first to go. The company already provided some road transport in the slack season, and it took on all transport responsibilities from 1952.[44]

At the start of the decade seven trains shuttled between Bluff and Invercargill every weekday, with an eighth on Friday nights.[45] These took between 43 and 60 minutes, and most were mixed. E.B. Baker, Invercargill's district traffic manager, rationalised Bluff's services in 1956 so that separate trains conveyed passengers and goods, but this was not the boon it seemed to be: the new timetable slashed passenger trains to only three a day, and they were almost as slow as the old mixed trains. Locals pushed for the proposed railcars but none were available. Baker rejected their appeals with the spurious claim that a railcar had to operate 23 of every 24 hours to be 'a payable unit' – a punishing schedule indeed.[46]

General manager Alan Gandell in 1958 claimed that patronage on the Bluff line had fallen to uneconomic levels on all services except the two used by schoolchildren.[47] This does not seem to stack up: NZR usually considered the break-even point for railcars to be around two-thirds capacity, and the 7am train to Invercargill and the 5.15pm to Bluff averaged 30 ordinary passengers – just shy of two-thirds of the 50-person capacity of a Vulcan railcar. The introduction of railcars would likely have had a tonic effect on patronage, as it had elsewhere, and would have been cheaper to operate than carriage trains. Gandell, however, calculated that elimination of the existing services would save £120 a week and hoped a bus company would fill the gap. By this point NZR was not even acquiring bus routes when it abandoned some services, and simply let other operators pick up the custom.

The locals were unimpressed. The Bluff Borough Council and the Southland Progress League registered stern opposition, while the Bluff Harbour Board and the Invercargill Chamber of Commerce expressed regret at the abandonment.[48] They were ignored.

The signalling infrastructure also imposed limitations: only one train was allowed on the track between Bluff and Invercargill at a time. Two trains could not cross at an intermediate location, nor could one follow another safely. Railway officials were simply not interested in maintaining the passenger service, and for the sake of easier timetabling of goods and to avoid any additional capital expenditure, NZR surrendered an entire suburban market. Apart from a term-time service for schoolchildren, passenger trains on the Bluff line ended on 29 September 1958.[49]

Roughly 220 pupils a day caught the train to Invercargill in 1966. Their hijinks and vandalism frustrated school and railway staff, worried parents and sometimes earned newspaper coverage even beyond Southland. The tabloid *NZ Truth* dubbed the train 'New Zealand's most notorious railway service', and recounted tales of schoolbooks burned in piles and a toilet seat thrown from a window at a school principal's car. By the mid-1960s the carriages required a serious overhaul.[50]

The timetable still clashed with goods shunting. Invercargill's traffic manager wanted to operate more trains for Bluff's port and industries, and he recommended cancelling the school trains rather than investing in signalling upgrades.[51] NZR opened discussions with the central Education Department and Southland Education Board in October 1966 about alternative transport for the children.

This highlighted larger issues. For years NZR had been dispensing with trains if many or all passengers were schoolchildren, since the discounted fares did not cover operating costs. Train travel, however, saved the Education Department money, as private bus companies charged higher rates. The department paid about

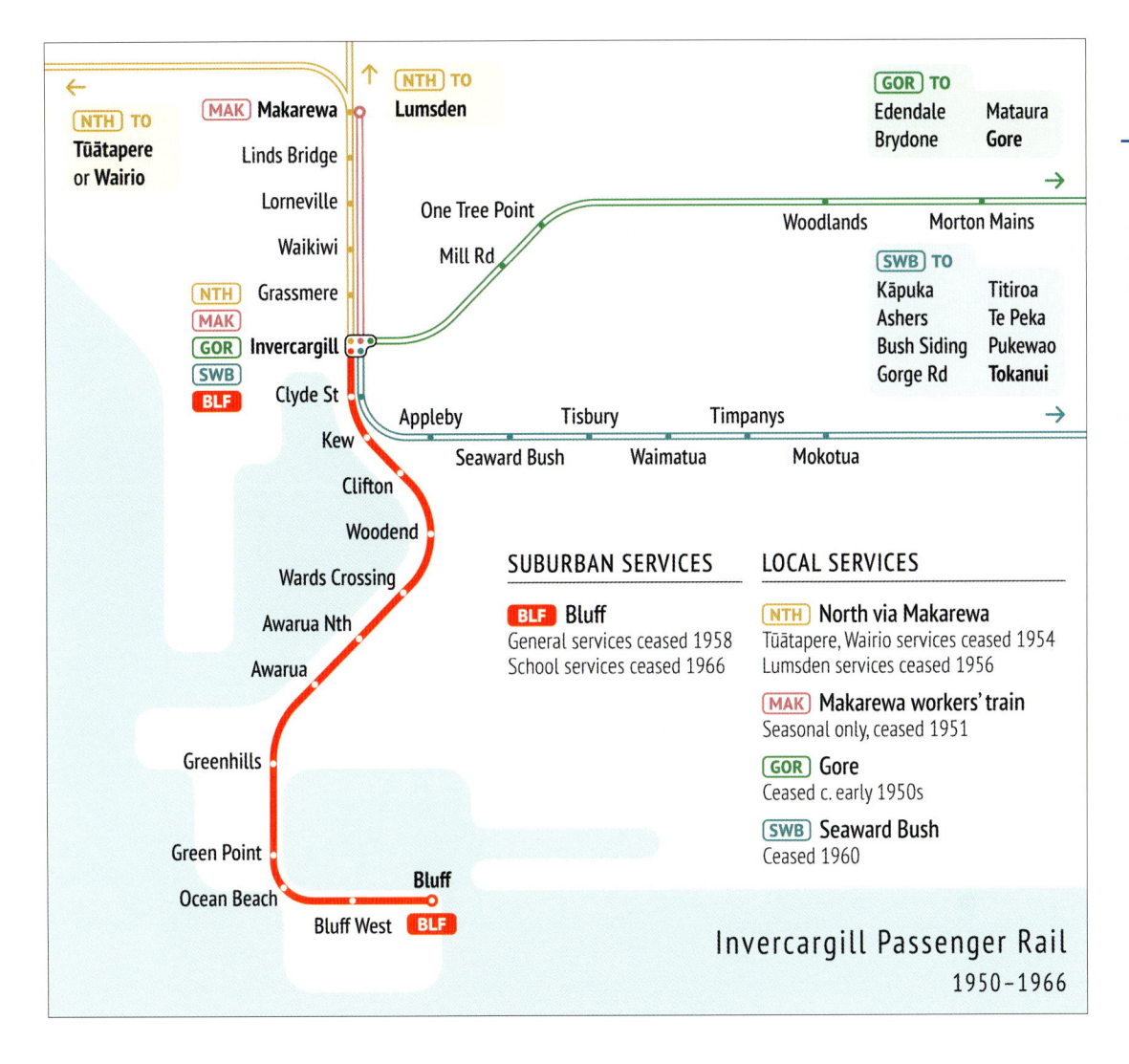

Invercargill Passenger Rail
1950–1966

£1000 of the Bluff school trains' annual expenses of £3500; buses would have cost around £8400. One representative protested to NZR that 'the existing passenger service provides a very satisfactory means of transporting the large number of children'.[52] Little wonder that he thought so. Another suggested that 'there is a national matter involved here … any saving of expenditure by one State Department increasing very considerably the expenditure of another State Department would not appear to be justified'.[53] In other words, NZR might save money, but overall government expenditure would rise. The only justification for cancelling the school trains would be if revenue from increased goods traffic exceeded the cost of hiring buses – and NZR pursued that argument. No evidence exists in railway or education archival files that either party requested or offered additional funds to cover operating costs, or if any case was made for capital investment to improve the line's capacity.

The last school trains between Bluff and Invercargill ran in early December 1966 for the final days of term but were not officially cancelled until early the next year – the origin of an often-repeated claim that they ran into 1967. Lengthy deliberations left education officials hanging, unsure how children would be transported when school resumed. 'In fact the matter has gone to the highest level of N.Z.R.,' one wrote on 11 January 1967, 'and it seems that an important principle of policy is involved.' He believed the Education Department was 'fighting a losing battle': 'rail services affecting export industries are being given top priority' in a 'far reaching plan to streamline transport'.[54] Trains of frozen meat were being given preference over children.

Ivan Thomas, who replaced Gandell as general manager during 1966, wrote to the Education Department on 17 January 1967 to confirm that NZR was cancelling the school trains. He did, though, offer to run them temporarily if the local board could not arrange a bus service in time for the start of term on 1 February 1967. Road Services declined to help as it had insufficient vehicles in Invercargill, but the board found a private operator that would take the children from the first day – and so NZR removed the trains from its timetable.[55] *NZ Truth* reported that the long-suffering railway staff were 'rumoured to be planning a monster celebration party' to mark the service's demise.[56]

Invercargill became the southernmost passenger station in New Zealand, a title it held for the next 35 years. There were occasional discussions about restoring commuter services, including conveying workers from Invercargill to the freezing works at Ocean Beach in 1981, but nothing came of these.[57]

1955–60: RURAL ATTRITION

Only a handful of rural branch railways remained open to passengers, and in most cases the service was rather paltry – be it a once-weekly train to Tokanui in eastern Southland or a car-van tacked onto a goods train between Rakaia and Methven. A senior official found many stations on the Methven Branch overgrown and decrepit when he visited in April 1958. He made an interesting proposal to run trains with car-vans from Ashburton to Methven and Mount Somers, but Mount Somers was already goods only and passenger provision to Methven ended later that year when Christchurch-based crews began operating the line.[58]

In the North Island NZR operated with-car goods trains for coalminers from Ngāruawāhia to Glen Massey on behalf of the State Mines Department, which in 1944 had taken over this unprofitable branch from Wilton Collieries. NZR rebuffed all offers to acquire it, especially as the mines were winding up. Regular services ended in May 1958.[59] Further north, the railway from Dargaville to Donnellys Crossing declined slowly as the Kaihū Valley forests were cut and turned over to farmland. Recommendations to reduce services or close the line accumulated from the late 1940s, with one report in 1956 concluding that it could 'never be an economic proposition'.[60] Mixed trains rattled through the valley until the line's dénouement on 13 July 1959.[61] On most closed railways in New Zealand, passengers ceased to be carried years before goods trains ended, but Donnellys Crossing and Glen Massey bucked the trend.

Another service that survived into the 1950s was the with-car goods between Ōpunake and Hāwera in southern Taranaki. The royal commission of 1930 observed that there was

BB 635 hauls the afternoon with-car goods – with no goods, only the car – to Glen Massey on 8 July 1957. It returned with coal and took miners home, although most had switched to road transport. This trestle was east of Glen Massey, before the Elgoods Road intersection. J.M. Creber

'practically no passenger traffic on this line' – trains averaged just three to seven passengers in the early 1930s – yet the service survived.[62] Attaching a passenger carriage on Ōpunake trains added little to operating costs and did not reduce the quantity of goods each train carried on such a flat line. The district traffic manager recognised this as a cheap source of goodwill and publicity, the cancellation of which 'would be resented and tend to reduce our connection with the settlers'.[63] These trains experienced little change until the 1950s, generally running daily but just three times a week in the depths of the Depression, and took two hours to get from Ōpunake to Hāwera, a distance that can be covered in a quarter of the time today. Roads in the area were good even before the railway opened, and by 1942 officials conceded the passenger market fully when they rejected a proposal to schedule trains to suit Hāwera market patrons and schoolchildren. NZR eventually cancelled passenger accommodation on 31 October 1955.[64] The Ōpunake Branch had

opened too late to become established in the travel patterns of southern Taranaki residents, and officials were probably right in their belief that they could not counter road. A greater effort would have been unremunerative.

Although some rural trains seemed to survive by dint of their very obscurity and cheapness, others served established markets, and NZR continued to neglect opportunities to sustain patronage. Few towns experienced a more dramatic decline in passenger rail transport than Lumsden. This important town in northern Southland had passenger trains to all four points of the compass until 1937 but, with the exception of holiday expresses to Kingston, the only service that survived after 1945 was the run to Invercargill. One mixed train plied this route daily and, on most days, demand justified a second – no wonder the route was considered for a railcar.[65] But the frequency of service tumbled: to thrice-weekly during the 1951 waterfront dispute and Fridays only from mid-1952. It endured to provide transport for railway employees but, as Lumsden's senior stationmaster observed, by May 1956 it had lost all appeal: 'To travel by these trains involves too long a day for the short time that is available to go shopping or visiting in Invercargill.' Passenger accommodation to Lumsden therefore ended that November.[66]

The holiday expresses to Kingston, which connected with NZR's ferries on Lake Wakatipu, were also on their last legs. NZR officials in the 1950s appreciated that winter sports were becoming increasingly popular in Queenstown but thought a rail-and-ferry service was unlikely to attract enough custom.[67] David Leitch and Brian Scott identify Easter 1956 as the last time passenger trains crossed the Waimea Plains in both directions on the same day; Easter of April 1957 was their final outing.[68] From that point on, all four railways into Lumsden were goods only. Road Services in Lumsden had acquired sufficient capacity to handle peak traffic and the runs-as-required expresses were cut from the working timetable in early 1959.[69]

The only subsequent passenger trains in northern Southland were enthusiast and heritage excursions, including the successful revival of the *Kingston Flyer*, which ran from Lumsden to Kingston during holiday seasons from November 1971 to February 1979. Railway

expert Robin Bromby records that it sometimes carried small consignments of freight when tonnages could not justify running that day's goods train to Kingston.[70] After floods damaged the line north of Lumsden the *Flyer* was confined to the section between Kingston and Fairlight, where it settled into the traditional operating patterns of a heritage railway. It is, admittedly, a fine distinction to draw between the Waimea Plains holiday expresses that ended in 1957 and the *Flyer* of the 1970s, but the former represented the last gasp of a regular passenger service, one for which the working timetable allowed year-round operation if needed; the latter was an attempt to capitalise on burgeoning nostalgia for heritage steam operations after its demise in revenue operation.

One of the last passenger trains on a rural branch – not a mixed train or a miners' train but a general-purpose carriage train – ran through settlements on the isolated coast south of Balclutha. The Catlins River Branch ran through the eastern (Otago) end of the Catlins region as far as Tahakopa, near the border with Southland. Tokanui, the terminus of the Seaward Bush Branch from Invercargill, is only about 35 kilometres away as the kererū flies, but no more than tentative plans were ever made to push a railway through the rugged country

Seaward Bush Branch and Catlins River Branch

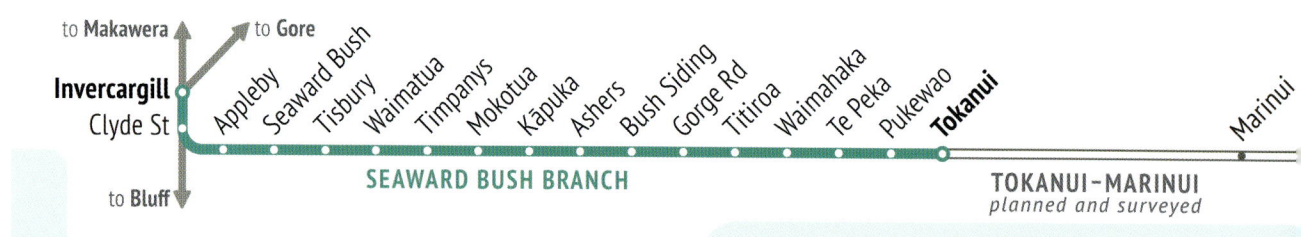

in between. Ōwaka was the main town on the Catlins River Branch, and notoriously poor local roads in the area meant trains were a lifeline. Nonetheless, NZR began planning to introduce buses in the late 1940s.[71] The daily rail service declined to the status of with-car goods in 1950, but Balclutha's market day still generated sufficient traffic that an extra passenger-only train ran on Tuesdays.[72] Service attrition was gradual: by 1956 the Tuesday passenger train only ran from Ōwaka instead of Tahakopa and the with-car goods operated just three times a week.[73] The death knell came on 1 December 1958, the last day on which Catlins River trains accommodated passengers.[74] The demand for a train on market day in the Catlins suggests that satisfactory patronage was there if NZR wanted to keep it on rail.

With-car goods trains to Tokanui did not last much longer. Services had declined from daily to twice weekly in April 1951, then to Tuesdays only in January 1952, and proposals for a railcar bandied about between 1950 and 1952 came to naught. The weekly with-car goods left Tokanui at 6am and reached Invercargill at 8.55am; the return train left at 4.15pm and arrived at Tokanui at 6.50pm – a long day for those who made the trip.[75] Economy measures eventually caught up with the line. Southland's traffic

manager proposed to save money by closing Tokanui's locomotive depot and operating the branch from Invercargill. This plan meant it would be impossible to travel to Invercargill and return in a day, so NZR stopped carrying passengers on the branch and the last with-car goods ran on Tuesday 26 April 1960.[76]

Remarkably, between this date and the end of the Bluff school trains in December 1966, the passenger network contracted by just 900 metres. In 1961 Dunedin's suburban trains on the Port Chalmers line were cut back from their original wharf-side terminus to Mussel Bay station, which NZR rebuilt and renamed Port Chalmers.[77] A number of branches that had closed to passengers some years earlier, however, perished entirely during the early 1960s.

Air travel continued to grow. NAC began flying Vickers Viscount turboprop aircraft from 1958, an improvement on older planes with piston engines, and a decade later came Boeing 737 jets.[78] Yet a 1960 survey of stationmaster reports suggested the turboprops had so far claimed few passengers from rail. Within the reports, though, was a hint of what was to come: while second-class passengers stuck with trains, those who could afford first-class railway tickets were prepared to spend even more money on flights.[79]

6

1955–1968

MARINUI–TAHAKOPA *planned* — Tahakopa · Campbell's Siding · Stuarts · Maclennan · Caberfeidh · Puketiro · Tawanui · Houipapa · Ratanui · **Ōwaka** · Parae · Hunts Rd · Glenomaru · Romahapa · Otanomomo · Finegand — CATLINS RIVER BRANCH — **Balclutha** · to Gore · to Dunedin

One of the more notable changes to the passenger network in the first half of the 1960s was the Milson Deviation in Palmerston North. The royal commission of 1952 had backed this on-again off-again plan, which had originated in the 1910s, because the railway through the central city was a notorious bottleneck with no room to expand.[80] As in Dargaville in the early 1940s, the station and yards were eventually moved to the edge of town in accordance with fashionable town-planning ideals. NZR relocated gradually: some goods trains began using the new line around the city's northern fringe in 1959, and passenger services began using the new station on Palmerston North's outskirts in 1963. Thousands of people crowded the city for final excursions through Te Marae o Hine/The Square in June 1964, although the western section from Longburn to the old yard remained in use for another year.[81]

One portion of the deviation was never completed. Known on its own as the Whakarongo Deviation, it would have removed the kink in the line to Napier as it travels through Kelvin Grove. The PWD constructed much of the formation but never finished the work, and NZR eventually gave up on the plan and released the land in 1983. Today, the curve at the northern end of McLeavey Drive follows the proposed railway route, as does the slanted southern boundary of Kelvin Grove Cemetery.

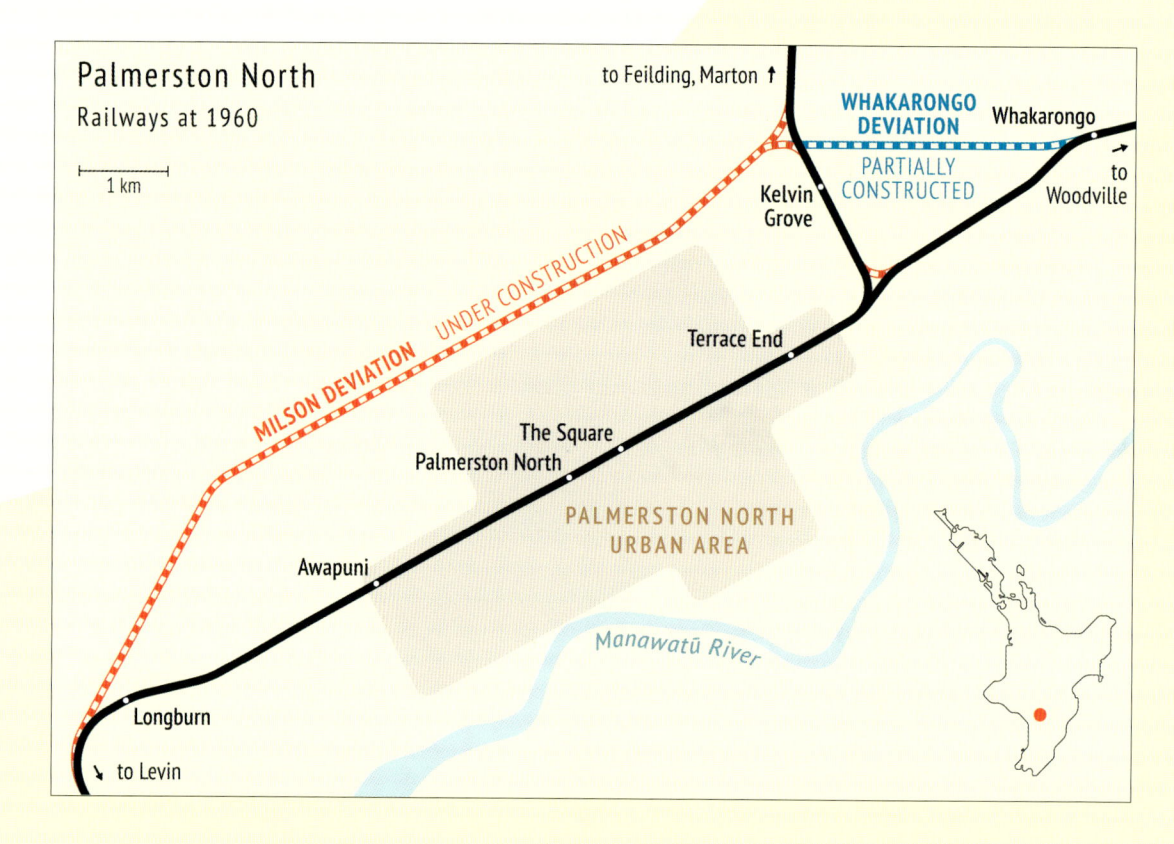

Palmerston North
Railways at 1960

1 km

to Feilding, Marton

WHAKARONGO DEVIATION
PARTIALLY CONSTRUCTED
Whakarongo

to Woodville

Kelvin Grove

MILSON DEVIATION UNDER CONSTRUCTION

Terrace End

The Square
Palmerston North

PALMERSTON NORTH URBAN AREA

Awapuni

Manawatū River

Longburn

to Levin

to Levin

6

A postcard from the 1920s depicts the busy station in the centre of Palmerston North.
Collection of Lemuel Lyes

A train steams through Te Marae o Hine/The Square in Palmerston North, 1930. Manawatū Heritage/Palmerston North City Library 2007N_Rm33_RAI_0680

Amid these advances the railway passenger network seemed settled, with core routes between major cities and towns, suburban trains in the four main centres and a few peripheral services, such as those for coal miners. Some timetables were reduced, and mixed and with-car goods trains were scarce, but there was little reason to believe the network would shrink rapidly. When the axe swung again, then, it came with little warning and cut deeply.

1967–68: FLAWED FIATS AND TRIMMED TIMETABLES

The defects in the Fiat railcars caused sweeping cancellations during 1967 and 1968. In 1965 Richard Harrison, MP for Hawke's Bay, queried Minister of Railways John McAlpine about the anticipated life of the railcars. NZR's chief mechanical engineer approved a hopelessly optimistic answer for McAlpine to present in Parliament: 15 years for the Vulcans and 25 for the Fiats. The minister's office revised this to be more guarded and McAlpine told Parliament that the railcars' lifespan would 'depend on the extent to which increasing repair and replacement costs and changing traffic trends make it uneconomic to continue overhauling them'.[82] In truth, only the railcar bodies had up to 25 years left in them; the Fiat engines would need to be replaced by 1970. Problems with them remained so commonplace that NZR sometimes flew in spare parts from Europe, and Auckland officials in March 1966 complained that the Fiats consumed over 50 percent of diesel maintenance staff hours – a much larger allocation than their proportion of the fleet justified.

NZR costed a plan for new engines at just over £1 million.[83] Although this required Cabinet approval, within the department senior officials behaved as if an international call for tenders were imminent. One letter in early November 1966 has an impatient-sounding 'still waiting authority' scrawled at the bottom.[84] When McAlpine approached Cabinet to gain approval, Treasury pounced. Until now it had not played a large role in railway policy: economic historian Brian Easton explains that before World War II its 'principal function was the administration of the government finances, and it was hardly equipped to provide economic advice'. A new generation of Treasury bureaucrats placed a premium on economic management and urged restraint on overseas expenditure.[85] Over £850,000 of the £1m price tag for the motors had to be met with foreign currency, exactly what they were trying to avoid, and they modelled long-term expenditure on the unreasonable assumption that new engines would be about as costly to maintain as the old ones, despite being more advanced and reliable. It did not help that the services operated by all railcars – the 35 Fiats, nine Vulcans and six Standards – lost a combined £250,000 per year.[86]

Treasury requested that NZR examine 'an economically acceptable form of long-distance passenger transport', by which it meant buses. The overriding consideration was cheapness; any possibility that other options might be better or more popular was not entertained. McAlpine replied that the engines needed replacement immediately; a detailed study would be useless if the government was 'not prepared to face up to the adverse public opinion' of cancelling railcars, a reaction that 'would be inevitable'.[87] Cabinet's works committee postponed a decision until January 1967, partly because of the divergent advice and partly to accommodate the 26 November 1966 election. The delay was not a good omen for the railcars.

Ivan Thomas, general manager after Gandell retired in 1966, hatched a plan over summer. Treasury was unlikely to approve new engines, but cancelling most long-distance passenger routes at once would provoke outrage. 'The reaction of the press, public and staff … would, I am afraid, be severely adverse … the effect on staff morale and recruitment could be very bad indeed'. He had a solution: to order 35 crankcases for £50,000 to maintain most services for another five years, 'the longer-term plan [being] to phase out the twinset cars with suitable public relations build up so that the change can be made with the least disturbance'. To further soothe public reaction, he proposed 'a passenger project such as new Main Trunk express trains'.[88]

Thomas was not the only new occupant of a senior railway post: McAlpine retired at the election and John Bowie 'Peter' Gordon took over the portfolio. He took Thomas's plan to Cabinet, where Treasury deemed it an acceptable compromise.[89] Gordon's memorandum explained that some services would have to be cancelled even before the new crankcases arrived, but as it transpired the overall programme of cancellations took longer than outlined in the schedule he gave to Cabinet.

In the spirit of Thomas's plan, NZR officials reached a cynical agreement in June. They did not want anything to militate against cancelling routes. If a railcar were to become unavailable – which was inevitable, as the full timetable left no railcar spare for breakdowns or other exigencies – it was not to be replaced by a carriage train. It did not matter if locomotives and carriages were obtainable: using them would imply to passengers that a service could keep operating with alternative rollingstock once railcars were withdrawn. Instead, if a railcar broke down it was to be replaced with a bus.[90] Perhaps it is not surprising that the district traffic manager who made this suggestion was that month promoted to the role of national transportation superintendent.

The first material outcome for passengers was that, between 3 April and 23 July 1967, railcars ceased to operate suburban services because frequent stopping was especially taxing on the engines. NZR reduced the Sunday timetable between Wellington and Masterton, cancelled the Sunday service between Dunedin and Palmerston, and removed railcars entirely from suburban runs between Auckland and Papakura, Christchurch and Rangiora, and Dunedin and Mosgiel.[91] All these lines retained some passenger trains but the schedules were thinner. The needs of schoolchildren were dismissed when writing the new timetables, and as a result many now found it difficult to attend their school of choice.[92]

Swingeing cuts began on 31 July 1967, when railcars ceased to run from Auckland to Whangārei and Ōkaihau. Construction of the Auckland Harbour Bridge had begun the same year the Fiats arrived. Early proposals to bridge

Waitematā Harbour had included a railway – the Sydney Harbour Bridge, constructed by the same company, had rail and tram lines – but the design chosen for Auckland had just four road lanes. It opened on 30 May 1959 to wild popularity: the millionth car crossed less than three months later.[93] Cars and buses now had a more direct route north than rail, which continued to take the long way round via Helensville. Robbed of their regional express function, railcars became more a means of local transport. Their demise was naturally controversial, and Parliament received a petition signed by 11,336 Northland residents demanding that railcars, or any suitable rail alternative, be retained: the railway represented a lifeline for many, especially those in isolated and poorer areas.[94] The department's mundane response was that people complained whether buses or trains were cut.[95]

The new timetable of August 1967 made paltry provision for travellers beyond Waitākere at the end of Auckland's suburban network. One daily passenger train ran Helensville–Auckland on weekdays, but the only accommodation provided for rail passengers further north was on slow with-car goods trains. These did not even encompass the whole Northland network. All passenger accommodation to Dargaville ended at the same time as the railcars.[96] Some of the with-car goods trains that operated from August 1967 ran just twice a week, and although it was possible to travel from Whangārei to Ōkaihau by changing from an Ōpua-bound train at Ōtiria, the reverse trip could not be done in a single day because the train from Ōkaihau arrived at Ōtiria after the Whangārei train had left.[97] In the gap between Maungatūroto and Wellsford, passengers were expected to rely on buses.

Northland's railcars ran at a loss of $54,000 per year, something critics suggested was the result of NZR competing with itself by running parallel road and rail services. Consolidation meant the buses now turned a profit. Ivan Thomas boasted that he had achieved this with minimal expense. In his view, 'Passenger *transport* was not curtailed in Northland by the railcar withdrawals. There was simply a *substitution* of one form of transport for another.'[98] The question of whether a railway should substitute trains with other forms of transport no longer entered into consideration. Road Services represented a major part of NZR's operations.

Faced with criticism, NZR became defensive. When R. Moses wrote a letter of complaint from Kaukapakapa, a town between Helensville and Wellsford, the general manager's office prepared a terse reply for Peter Gordon's signature. It is unclear if the minister's office edited it before sending, but the NZR ghost-writer claimed:

> At no stage have I [i.e. Gordon] stated that alternative transport would be provided for all … Some areas such as that between Helensville and Wellsford are sparsely populated and would not support daily road or rail services. However, carriages were attached to certain goods trains to make available a form of transport for people living in such areas.

As if to suggest Moses should be grateful for the mediocre service provided, the letter added what amounted to an indictment of government policy and planning trends that gave thought only to roads: 'I must point out that there are many areas throughout the country not served by public transport.'[99]

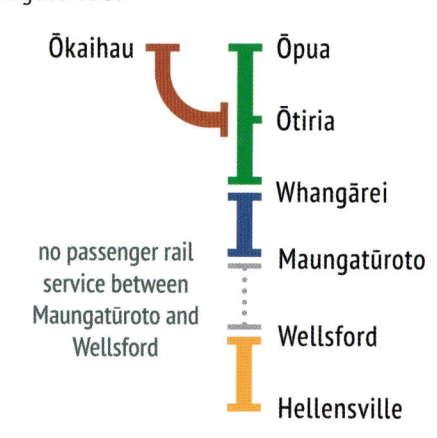

Northland Services
August 1967

Ōkaihau — Ōpua
Ōtiria
Whangārei
no passenger rail service between Maungatūroto and Wellsford — Maungatūroto
Wellsford
Hellensville

Efforts to regain a passenger service to Northland were in vain, although special expresses did run between Auckland and Whangārei during the holiday periods immediately after the railcars ended, at the request of the overwhelmed Road Services.[100] It was the last gasp.

The next cut, on 11 September 1967, eliminated two routes. One was Greymouth to Westport, and was part of a larger attenuation of services on the West Coast. Railcars operated local services from Greymouth to Hokitika, Ōtira and, on Friday evenings, Reefton. There was also a handful of mixed and with-car goods trains on various routes. These vanished alongside the Westport railcars.[101] A quarter of a century after Buller received its long-awaited interprovincial railway, all passenger trains in the region were gone. Passenger services on the West Coast now comprised only the Christchurch–Greymouth–Ross railcars and miners' trains to Rewanui.

The other route to go was Auckland to Te Puke, which spelled the end of all passenger trains to Tauranga and other coastal Bay of Plenty communities. The Bay of Plenty had

6

Vulcan railcar RM 52 stops at Raupo in the Grey Valley on its afternoon run from Westport to Greymouth, 2 September 1967. This service ended nine days later.
Wilson Lythgoe

railcars to Rotorua and Te Puke, and neither service was meant to last as long as it did: their cancellation was originally slated for June 1967.[102] This did not transpire, but stopgap reductions of capacity to reduce wear and tear meant the Te Puke service did not survive much longer.[103] NZR's surveys revealed that most railcars to Te Puke ran at about one-third capacity; only Friday evening and Sunday afternoon services had heavy loadings.[104]

Travellers voiced their anger in the local papers. One Auckland letter writer suggested that the characterisation of these routes as 'uneconomic' was an attempt to cover up railway policy blunders by the Holland and Holyoake governments; another asked if 'the Railways Department [was] more concerned with the profit on goods cartage than with passenger

needs?'[105] That question could only be answered in the affirmative.

Railcar mileage had fallen to about 64,000 kilometres per week, yet this was still too much for the deteriorating Fiats.[106] Two officials in February 1968 ventured that with so many route cancellations, any further cuts for mechanical reasons in the next five years would be unnecessary. Their superiors, however, fretted over rising maintenance costs and low patronage: most routes regularly slipped beneath the break-even mark of two-thirds full. A report in June indicated a number of reasons for this, including breakdowns, inadequate timetables and competing Road Services offerings, but its authors presented these to validate cancellations rather than to argue for better services with superior marketing.[107] They provided few details about how they had calculated costs or loadings and presented their data as objective measures of trends they could not influence – a common habit.

Decades of deprecation of passenger rail and strategies of providing the minimum possible service at the lowest cost predisposed negative interpretations and reactive rather than proactive conclusions. The authors of the June 1968 report suggested approaching private bus operators to take over some routes. All attention was on shedding passenger trains rather than improving them.

The recommendation that perhaps best betrays the anti-passenger stance was for the cancellation of Christchurch–Picton railcars. NZR had introduced wildly popular roll-on roll-off ferries between Wellington and Picton in 1962, and a private bus company provided the official connection to Christchurch for foot passengers because – astonishingly – the railcars ran at unsuitable times. The report suggested handing over the railcar patronage as well. This, the authors felt, would not pose a problem; after all, an overnight express goods (the 'cabbage train') would still have a carriage attached for anyone who insisted on travelling by rail. Regardless of the mechanical position, the report writers felt there was 'adequate justification for continuing the "phasing out" process'.[108]

It was unfortunate for rail travel that NZR's railcars were coming to the end of their working lives just as air travel was becoming mainstream. The June 1968 report suggested asking NAC to fly Christchurch–Hokitika so that railcars through the Ōtira Tunnel only needed to run once a day rather than twice. Fortunately the report was not implemented in full: NAC began flying Christchurch–Hokitika

in December 1968 but the railcars continued to run twice daily. Cabinet, though, endorsed two recommendations in September: to end local railcars between Napier and Gisborne from 7 October – the long-distance services between Gisborne and Wellington remained – and to cancel the entire passenger timetable to Rotorua from 12 November.[109]

The public could have been forgiven for thinking the Rotorua run was secure when Te Puke railcars disappeared: Aucklanders bound for coastal destinations were encouraged to take the train to Morrinsville or Rotorua and connect with buses. A junior member of staff in Auckland – he described himself as 'the boy' of the passenger enquiries room – proposed additional trains to Rotorua rather than fewer: a Saturday morning service, returning in the evening, struck him as a winner. His superiors rejected the idea, counselling him that NZR had to conserve railcar use.[110] It did not matter that engineers had found the railcars capable of managing a timetable that included Rotorua for a few more years; senior officials kept emphasising mechanical problems to justify cancellations. Peter Gordon spun this line to his Cabinet colleagues too, and boasted that the replacement buses to New Zealand's famed geothermal playground actually ran an hour faster.

The cancellations approved in September 1968 reduced Fiat operations by 8000 kilometres per week and saved $80,000 annually, mostly from the Gisborne curtailment.[111] That this was the result of under-investment in infrastructure, botched investment in rollingstock, conflicting objectives to serve local and long-distance travellers, a policy of running competing rather than complementary buses and a profound lack

Rotorua railway station became a 'travel centre', with a train platform on one side and bus bays on the other. This image, from 12 January 1964, shows the bus to Ōkere Falls, a service that complemented railway offerings. Weston Langford, no.103948

of forethought or imagination – all went unsaid or was ignored.

Rotorua had a curious postscript. Isolated communities in the Mamaku Ranges, which mainly comprised Māori kāinga and forestry camps, petitioned for some form of rail transport to enable them to shop in Putāruru.[112] Somewhat surprisingly, NZR acceded to their request. Barely a month after passenger trains ceased on the Rotorua Branch, they resumed on a portion of it. A morning goods ran from Rotorua to Putāruru on Tuesdays to Fridays, returning in the evening, and from 17 December 1968 it included a car-van rather than an ordinary guard's van. In the first three months, which were intended as a trial period, 51 passengers travelled in the direction of Putāruru and 30 the other way. This light patronage was nonetheless sufficient for NZR to retain the with-car goods permanently.[113] Between Hamilton and Putāruru the line remained goods only. One theme that emerges from recollections of with-car goods trains by railway workers and enthusiasts of the period is the distinct surprise people experienced when they found anyone else occupying the carriage. If any tourists noticed the car-van at Rotorua's railway station and were foolhardy enough to board it in the hope of reaching Hamilton or Auckland, they would have been sorely disappointed to find their journey ended in Putāruru.

Ōkaihau
Kaikohe
Ōpua
Kawakawa
Ōtiria
Hikurangi
WHANGĀREI
Portland
Waiōtira
Maungatūroto

Ōkaihau–Ōtiria ceased 1974
Ōpua–Whangārei ceased 1976
Whangārei–Maungatūroto ceased 197

Wellsford
Tahekeroa
HELENSVILLE
Waitākere
AUCKLAND
Henderson
Onehunga
Ōtāhuhu
Papakura
Drury
Pukekohe
Mercer

Wellsford–Helensville ceased 1975
Helensville–Waitākere ceased 1980

Penrose–Onehunga ceased 1973

Waikato R.

Glen Afton–Huntly ceased 1972

Glen Afton
Huntly
Ngāruav
FRANKTON
Te Awamutu
Ōtorohanga

Putāruru–Rotorua ceased 1971

Upper North Island
1970–1989

C^H 7

1970–1989
'The emotive term "railcars"' – Cancellations in town and country

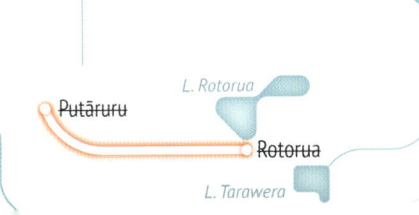

Ōtorohanga

Te Kūiti

Mangapēhi

L. Tarawera

Waikato R.

Mōkau R.

L. Taupō

Ōkahukura

New Plymouth–Stratford–Ōkahukura ceased 1983

Ōhura

Taumarunui

Tāngarākau

Raurimu

Mt Tongariro

NEW PLYMOUTH

Inglewood

Whangamōmona

National Park

Mt Ngāuruhoe

Mt Ruapehu

Mt Taranaki

Toko

Ohakune

Tangiwai

Stratford

Waiōuru

Te Roti

Taihape

Waitōtara R.

Whanganui R.

Hāwera

Rangitīkei R.

Pātea

Mangaweka

Waitōtara

Waverley

Kai Iwi

Aramoho

Hunterville

Stratford–Marton ceased 1977

Marton

Ormondville

Dannevirke

Feilding

PALMERSTON NORTH

Woodville

Pahīatua

Shannon

Eketāhuna

Levin

Ōtaki

Mauriceville

Waikanae

MASTERTON

Paekākāriki

Carterton

Featherston

L. Wairarapa

Melling

Upper Hutt

Johnsonville

Waterloo

Woburn–Hutt Workshops ceased 1982

Hutt Workshops

WELLINGTON

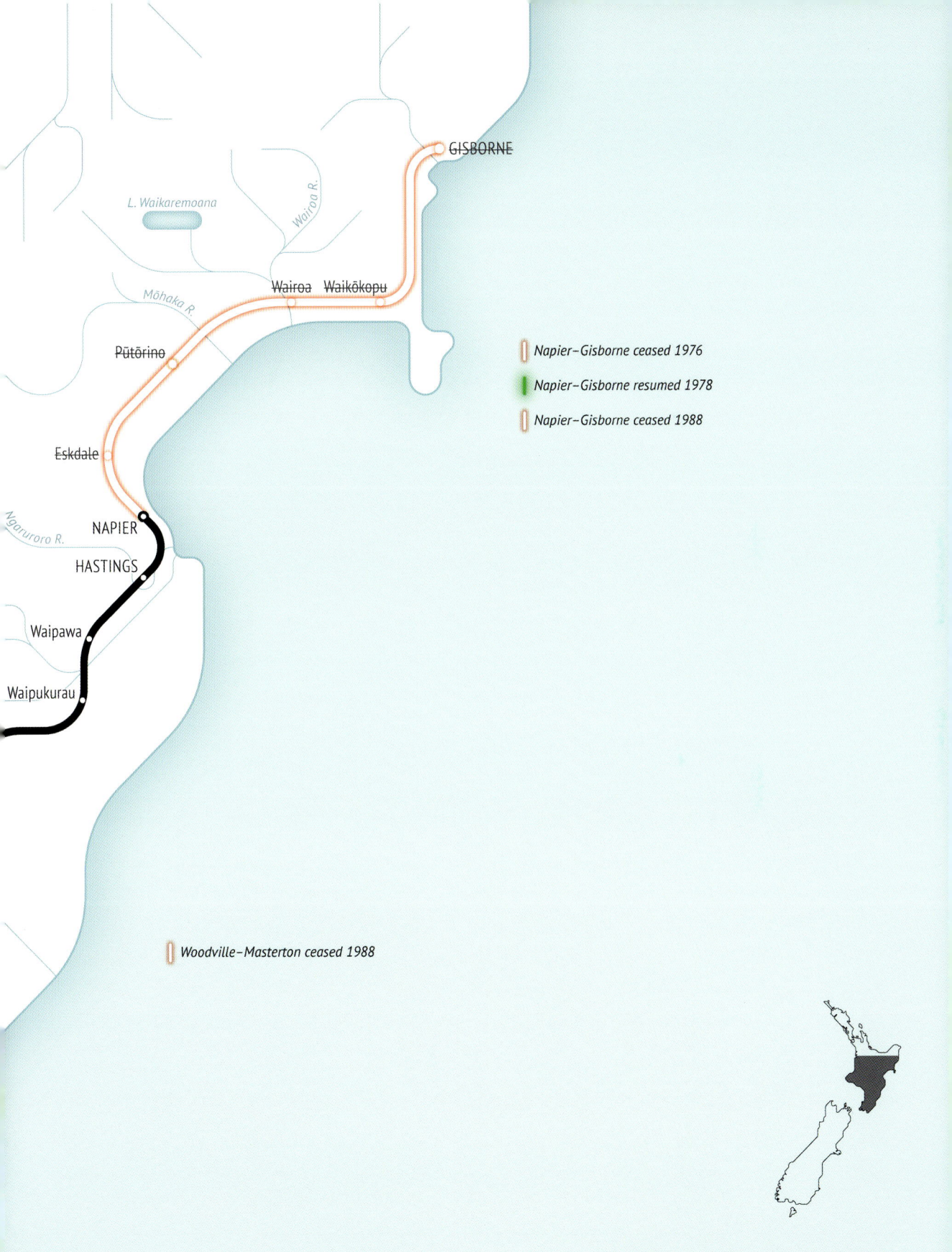

GISBORNE

L. Waikaremoana

Wairoa R.

Wairoa   Waikōkopu

Mōhaka R.

Pūtōrino

Eskdale

Ngaruroro R.

NAPIER

HASTINGS

Waipawa

Waipukurau

Napier–Gisborne ceased 1976

Napier–Gisborne resumed 1978

Napier–Gisborne ceased 1988

Woodville–Masterton ceased 1988

Lower North Island
1970–1989

Upper South Island
1970–1989

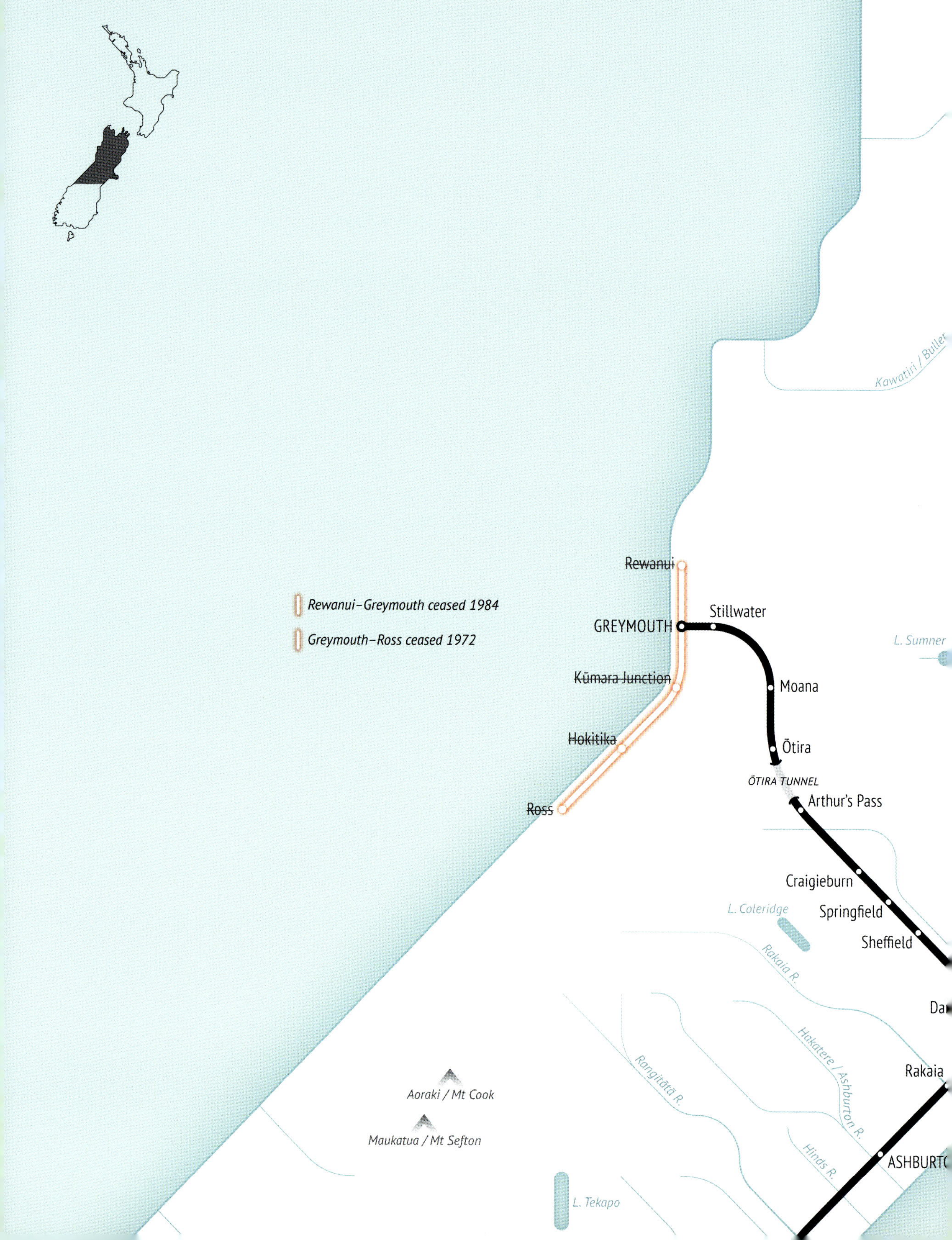

Rewanui–Greymouth ceased 1984

Greymouth–Ross ceased 1972

Rewanui

Stillwater

GREYMOUTH

L. Sumner

Moana

Kūmara Junction

Hokitika

Ōtira

ŌTIRA TUNNEL

Arthur's Pass

Ross

Craigieburn

L. Coleridge

Springfield

Sheffield

Da

Rakaia

Aoraki / Mt Cook

Maukatua / Mt Sefton

ASHBURTO

Kawatiri / Buller

Rakaia R.

Rangitātā R.

Hakatere / Ashburton R.

Hinds R.

L. Tekapo

PICTON

BLENHEIM

Ward

Wharanui

Clarence

KAIKŌURA

Ōaro

Hundalee

Parnassus

Scargill

Waipara

Rangiora

Kaiapoi

Waimakariri R.

CHRISTCHURCH

Rolleston

Lyttelton

Christchurch–Lyttelton ceased 1976

Wairau R.

Awatere R.

Waiau Toa / Clarence R.

Waiau Uwha R.

Hurunui R.

Ōhai–Wairio ceased 1975

Temuka

Washdyke

TIMARU

Studholme

Waitaki R.

Pukeuri

ŌAMARU

Ranfurly

Hyde

Taieri R.

PALMERSTON

Middlemarch

Waikouaiti

DR

Port Chalmers

DUNEDIN

MOSGIEL

Clarendon

Milton

Wingatui–Middlemarch–Alexandra ceased 1976

Wingatui–Middlemarch resumed 1987 by Dunedin Railways

Dunedin–Port Chalmers ceased 1979

Lower South Island
1970–1989

Confidence was low within NZR in the early 1970s, and journalists expressed concern for staff morale as annual losses mounted and services disappeared.[1] Some entire regions no longer had passenger rail. The cessation of many railcar services during 1967–68 meant that, apart from one service to New Plymouth, the only long-distance departures from Auckland were those bound for Wellington. Invercargill's suburban trains had ended, and Christchurch and Dunedin both had reduced timetables. NZR Road Services was ascendant; away from the North and South Island Main Trunks, it dominated passenger transport, and it also ran services that skimmed passengers from Main Trunk expresses.

Air travel was eating further into ridership. When NAC introduced the Vickers Viscount in 1958 it carried 500,000 passengers annually, less than a sixth of NZR's long-distance rail total of 3.2 million. But the Viscount and then the Boeing 737 transformed NAC. Long-distance figures approached parity in 1970: 1.44 million travelled with NAC and 1.85 million with NZR. Rail had price on its side – a flight between Wellington and Auckland cost nearly four times as much as the most expensive train fare – but inadequate timetables and declining service quality meant rail travellers were looking elsewhere.[2]

Capital investment in road outstripped all other modes: 1.17 million motor vehicles were registered at 31 March 1970, including 862,000 private cars and 29,000 motorcycles. The government's yearbook noted that car ownership outstripped population growth: in 1960 there were 4.7 people for every private car and 3.2 per motor vehicle; in 1970 this had tightened to 3.2 people per car and 2.4 per motor vehicle. The only countries with fewer people per vehicle

were Australia, Canada and the US.[3] NZR was in a bind: many people owned cars because railway services were inadequate, and railway services were inadequate because many people owned cars.

One potential source of increased patronage was tourism, which NZR had fostered in the early twentieth century but now seemed to be largely ignoring. The South Island Publicity Association and the Canterbury Progress League both drew attention to the tourism potential of the railway between Christchurch and Greymouth, suggesting that large scenic windows could be installed in carriages, but NZR representatives explained that this was not possible and they did not envisage purchasing new observation cars. It was not until the late 1980s that carriages on Greymouth trains were fitted with larger windows and became world famous as the *TranzAlpine*. At the start of the 1970s NZR did liaise with tourism associations, but in 1971 its main boast was the inauguration of the *Kingston Flyer* to 'provide a nostalgic link with steam traction' for 'the present-day automobile-oriented society'.[4] This fatalism did not suggest long-term confidence in passenger rail.

It was not just the passenger rail network that was contracting: local governments divested themselves of other transport modes, too. All urban tramways had been torn up by 1964, commuter ferries on Wellington and Dunedin's harbours had ceased, and the number of passenger vessels plying Auckland's Waitematā Harbour had plummeted. Reflecting a global pattern of rural railways struggling to compete as motor competitors enjoyed increasingly high-quality roads, some branch lines that were already closed to passengers now closed to all traffic.

There was much scope for reform of New Zealand's railways: the network had been built for nineteenth-century conditions and travel patterns, and it had been built cheaply. Modern freight-only lines, such as those to Kinleith and Murupara for forestry in the 1950s or a spur to the Waikato's new steelworks at Mission Bush in 1968, proved that rail had a future.

Overseas, especially in Europe and Japan, railways were experimenting with innovative technologies and better offerings. These ran far beyond headline high-speed rail achievements. NZR took some lessons on board to rejuvenate trunk services in both islands with better amenities, targeted marketing and new rollingstock. Bob Black, chief mechanical engineer from 1951 to 1964, was also inspired by the final flourishing of long-distance passenger rail in the United States, once a world leader in train travel. The comfortable stainless-steel carriages of American railway companies such as Santa Fe – and, closer to home, some Australian state railways – informed the design of the luxury overnight *Silver Star* between Auckland and Wellington, introduced after a long gestation in 1971. This rollingstock and the new daytime Silver Fern railcars were manufactured in Japan, where the railway industry was becoming a world-leading force.

Rather than echoing European and Japanese rejuvenation, however, the events of the 1970s resulted in New Zealand passenger rail entering a near-terminal decline akin to that in the US during the 1960s. Cancellations of rural and miners' trains, regional railcars and suburban networks were all substantial. By the 1980s there was little left to cancel, and New Zealand's remaining services appeared to have limited prospects.

1970–76: FAREWELL TO RURAL AND MINERS' TRAINS

After the severe cuts to services between January 1967 and November 1968, no routes were cancelled outright for almost three years. When next the axe fell, it struck a with-car goods rather than a route operated by Fiats. And whereas intercity routes struggled because of mechanically flawed railcars, local services for rural residents and workers were in trouble because their patronage had almost disappeared.

The first cancellation of the 1970s occurred on the line where NZR's failure to capture the passenger market was most telling: Rotorua. Ridership of the with-car goods between Putāruru and Rotorua was modest; an 18-week survey in 1970 counted 47 passengers on Putāruru-bound trains and just one every fortnight towards Rotorua. A change in operating patterns since 1968 had also made it less appealing for NZR to use a car-van on all four days, and in August 1970 it dropped the little-used passenger accommodation to Fridays only.[5] Another timetable revision the next year threatened to put paid to this entirely. Interestingly, in this case NZR consulted the local marae committee beforehand – it is hard to imagine officials of even a couple of decades earlier rousing themselves to do so. Although rangatira T.J. Amopiu managed to negotiate a month's grace for the community, the with-car goods between Rotorua and Putāruru ran for the last time on 25 June 1971.[6] Twenty years would pass before another timetabled passenger train served what is one of New Zealand's premier tourist destinations.

Three trains still ran for miners at remote coalmines: Huntly to Glen Afton in the Waikato, Wairio to Ōhai in Southland, and Greymouth to Rewanui on the West Coast. Rewanui's future

The Glen Afton Branch had its own platform at Huntly, separate from the island platform on the North Island Main Trunk. D^B 1001 awaits departure for Glen Afton on November 1971. Wilson Lythgoe

Below: D^B 1006 leads the afternoon passenger train from Glen Afton to Huntly past the tatty shelter at Pukemiro Junction in November 1971. Wilson Lythgoe

was secure so long as the large Liverpool Mine operated, as it had no road access. Glen Afton and Ōhai's trains were vulnerable: if mine bosses decided to lay on buses instead, they would be redundant.

Discussions about revising or cancelling the Glen Afton service involved mining officials and unions, a further indication that NZR was now prepared to engage interested parties rather than simply implementing unilateral cancellations. A railway ran west from Huntly to serve mines around Rotowaro, Pukemiro and the terminus; regular passengers included miners and a dozen schoolchildren. The average ridership of miners in the morning was over double that of the afternoon – about 110:50 – because

A morning miners' train from Wairio to Ōhai departs Nightcaps in March 1953. J.G. Duncan, ANZ AAVK 6390 B3896

many returned home by other means, such as carpooling.[7] The Mines Department subsidised the trains, paying a sum per worker who travelled, and was not keen to switch to buses as it would then have to pay per vehicle regardless of ridership.[8] Union representatives, on the other hand, supported the introduction of buses, which would be quicker.[9] The carriages were so decrepit that in March 1972 their leakiness prompted a hundred miners to refuse to travel in them until better accommodation was forthcoming.[10] NZR had wanted to cancel these trains since 1966 in a bid to save $8000 annually. As it was, the section beyond Rotowaro was on borrowed time – Glen Afton Collieries closed its underground mine in November 1971, and freight plummeted. The line held on until 1975, in part to remove scrap, but the passenger service ended sooner: on 24 June 1972 a local bus company took over.[11]

The Ōhai Railway Board's passenger service between Wairio and Ōhai – the only one left

beyond NZR's auspices – lasted three years longer. Multiple trains ran on weekdays in 1961, predominantly for miners and schoolchildren, plus one on Saturdays. A decade later this had slipped to one train on weekdays for miners, and buses carried those who worked weekends or odd shifts.[12] In November 1974 the ŌRB resolved to paint its carriages in a new midnight blue livery so they looked fresh when the board celebrated its fiftieth anniversary over Easter 1975.[13] But if this implied long-term operation of the passenger timetable, it was misleading. In June 1975 the traffic manager received authorisation to negotiate a bus replacement with the Mines Department. The negotiations concluded quickly, and buses replaced trains the following month.[14]

As a local statutory authority, the ŌRB had a close relationship with its community – which explains why it carried passengers for two decades longer than NZR did in western Southland. The board also had healthy finances and rebuffed NZR's regular takeover offers. Local government reforms in 1989, however, spelled the end for the ŌRB and most other single-purpose authorities, and established today's system of regional and territorial authorities. Southland District Council was not interested in operating the railway and passed it to NZR in 1990. The line survives as one of New Zealand's few remaining rural branch railways, but as calls grow for coal reserves to remain in the ground, its future is uncertain. At present it serves one mine near Nightcaps, but the last few kilometres into Ōhai have not been used since the early 2010s.[15]

At the same time that these miners' trains disappeared, so too did most with-car goods trains. These sluggish services ran through isolated regions where residents were often resigned to expecting little from the state and getting less. Records show that people were abandoning such tediously slow trains, preferring dirt roads to inadequate rail services. With-car goods trains remained in only three regions in 1975: the West Coast, Taranaki and Northland. Those for miners to Rewanui recalled the much larger network of local services on the West Coast that had augmented railcars until September 1967.[16] In Taranaki, a with-car goods ran Taumarunui to Stratford and return, complementing the railcar between New Plymouth and Taumarunui, but took six hours compared to the railcar's three. Passengers had under two hours to transact business in Stratford. It perished on 1 December 1975.[17] The railcar was a remarkable survivor and features further below.

Northland then was the last stronghold of rural with-car goods trains. Passenger carriages were coupled to a number of services, despite a recommendation that this practice cease at the same time as the railcars in 1967. Some settlements were far from any main road, and local Māori leaders made strong representations for passenger accommodation.[18] A review of services north of Whangārei in 1972 again recommended that NZR stop attaching passenger carriages to goods trains because, apart from occasional school parties, almost nobody rode the rails. The state of the two available carriages can be gathered from a comment that cancellation would permit one to be scrapped.[19] NZR deferred this, in no small part because of objection from Federated Farmers.

Folk musician Peter Cape often wrote about railways, and one of his popular songs celebrated the Ōtiria–Ōkaihau service in Northland. He sang of 'the smallest train you've seen', jokingly calling it an express and saying, 'the driver doesn't worry if he takes the journey slow'. He even stops for a swim in Lake Ōmapere.[20] Besides the fact that the lack of a connection to Whangārei discouraged all but the most local travellers, a shortage of suburban rollingstock in Auckland meant no replacement existed for the dilapidated carriage kept at Ōtiria.[21] If NZR had been serious about providing a service in Northland, a train between Kaikohe and Whangārei could have attracted patronage, but even the best-planned timetable would have required a subsidy. Instead, passenger accommodation disappeared on the Ōkaihau Branch from 26 January 1974.[22]

Northland's remaining with-car goods trains had peculiar schedules. The Wellsford–Helensville carriage ran Fridays only and gave passengers four hours in Helensville; Whangārei–Ōpua ran every weekday but with a turnaround time in Ōpua of 39 minutes, scarcely long enough to gaze upon the Bay

D[A] 1512 leads a with-car goods from Ōkaihau past Lake Ōmapere Road Crossing on 8 October 1973. The dilapidated state of carriages in Northland is clear. This carriage, built in 1934, formed part of the *New Plymouth Express* in its heyday. Wilson Lythgoe

of Islands; and Maungatūroto–Whangārei ran return Tuesday to Friday and allowed passengers to spend almost a full business day in Northland's largest centre.[23] These trains were not glamorous. A spokesperson for Federated Farmers decried the carriage used for the Ōpua service as unfit even for dogs, but feared that if NZR cancelled the offering, the community would never get passenger rail back.[24] He was right. NZR withdrew the carriage on 16 February 1976 as it was no longer safe to use. The train to Ōpua remained designated as a with-car goods, but passengers had to settle for limited seating installed in the guard's van, which the district traffic manager considered 'an unsatisfactory arrangement'.[25]

The Wellsford–Helensville with-car goods had already ceased on 30 March 1975; Maungatūroto–Whangārei followed on 15 September.[26] Formal cancellation of the car-less with-car goods from Whangārei to Ōpua was effective from 21 June 1976.[27] In terms of a

traditional mixed or with-car goods train that travelled slowly through the countryside and carried everything on offer, it was the last of its type in New Zealand. With-car goods trains for Rewanui coal and its miners continued until 1984.

A curious anomaly on the Main North Line between Christchurch and Picton highlights yet again how little NZR valued passenger accommodation. The concept of express goods trains was fairly new to New Zealand, and affixing a carriage to one was even more uncommon, but on this line a carriage ran attached to an overnight express goods. Nicknamed the 'cabbage train' for its role in distributing fresh produce, the express supplemented a railcar service which had such acute mechanical problems that, for most of the first half of 1976, a 'short' and 'unsatisfactory' carriage train ran instead.[28] NZR officials insisted the unheated carriages of this replacement train could not be used in winter, then withdrew the failing railcars as well, leaving the with-car express goods, briefly, as the only option from 8 June 1976.

Fortunately for Canterbury and Marlborough, bipartisan political consensus and pressure from the National Union of Railwaymen meant that passenger trains continued to be offered. The matter came down to the wire: on 3 June the union resolved to prevent NZR removing any carriages from the South Island as this would ensure the end of Picton trains. A few days later NZR accepted proposals for a new daytime train.

NZR treated the Picton trains as a service for North Canterbury and Marlborough communities rather than part of an inter-island travel network, but Labour's manifesto called for the co-ordination of ferry and rail timetables, and National's Edward Latter, MP for Marlborough, wanted the same.[29] It might seem extraordinary today that the railcars and Cook Strait ferries did not connect, but officials at the time were dismissive of the idea. Newmans successfully operated a bus that left Christchurch at 7am to meet the ferry, and one report in 1973 suggested that a train scheduled for this time would be 'too early to be attractive to prospective passengers'.[30] Conceding passengers to Newmans would allow more flexibility in scheduling goods trains.

The potential for increased patronage following the demise of Union Steam Ship's Steamer Express between Wellington and Lyttelton in mid-September 1976 figured surprisingly little in these deliberations. NZR had time up its sleeve if it only intended to substitute the Steamer Express, but staff at Addington Workshops hurried to renovate carriages so that a heated daytime train could replace the overnight with-car express goods

from 1 July.[31] This was acknowledgement that if NZR continued carrying passengers between Canterbury and Marlborough, the 'cabbage train' was insufficient. The new service also connected with the Cook Strait ferries. It is not flattering to NZR that ferry/train co-ordination required political pressure, and while some officials might not emerge well from this story, the skilled workshop staff do.

1971–78: RAILCAR ROUTES ROT

The cancellation of some railcar services in 1967–68 was a stopgap measure. Some were withdrawn, and the remaining engines were repaired and pronounced to have an estimated five more years of life.[32] This meant sacrificing some routes to maintain others, but it also bought time in which to order new rollingstock. However, almost no orders were placed.

Ivan Thomas got his wish: that NZR update trains on the main trunks of both islands to distract public attention from railcar withdrawals. In early 1968 NZR refurbished the most mechanically sound Fiat into the Blue Streak, an upmarket option for travellers between Hamilton and Auckland. Poor decisions about fares and timetables meant this service failed – most travellers took cheaper trains that followed the Blue Streak – and NZR abandoned a proposal for a similar offering between Palmerston North and Wellington. Once the Blue Streak was reallocated to the daylight Auckland–Wellington run later in 1968, however, it became so popular that two more Fiats were transformed into Blue Streaks to handle demand.

Their success enabled those within the NZR hierarchy who backed passenger rail to secure an order for three new railcars to operate the

Two coupled Blue Streak railcars pass Ōkahukura in early 1972 en route from Wellington to Auckland.
Wilson Lythgoe

route long term. Named Silver Ferns for their stainless-steel exterior, these units arrived from Japan in 1972 and released the Blue Streaks to improve the Wellington–New Plymouth service from 18 December.[33] The Silver Ferns' moniker echoed that of the *Silver Star*, a carriage train which, from its first run on 6 September 1971, substantially improved NZR's overnight service between Auckland and Wellington. It offered a level of luxury not seen on New Zealand rails either before or since.

Down south, the steam-hauled *South Island Limited* from Christchurch to Invercargill morphed into the diesel-hauled *Southerner* in December 1970, the first train since 1917 to have a dining car. Passengers no longer had extended stops at refreshment rooms; they could watch the scenery pass while enjoying porterhouse steak grilled to order, beef curry, ham or chicken rolls, freshly baked cakes, a range of alcohol and

Silver Fern railcar RM 3 emerging from a tunnel near Mangaweka on 16 December 1972, the third day of its tenure operating the Auckland–Wellington run.
J.M. Creber

Silver Fern railcar RM 3 working hard between Utiku and Mangaweka, 15 December 1972. NZR deviated this geologically unstable portion of the North Island Main Trunk in 1981. The line now runs on the eastern bank of the Rangitīkei River. J.M. Creber

an unspecified dessert, the '*Southerner* Speciale'.[34] Evening railcars and buses supplemented the *Southerner*.

Keith Holyoake's Cabinet approved 14 new diesel railcars on 26 October 1971, but Peter Gordon deferred placing an order pending advice from France about gas turbine propulsion. Jack Marshall became prime minister when Holyoake resigned in February 1972, and his moribund government made little progress with the matter. Once it became clear that gas turbines needed 'lengthy and expensive study', the government resolved to order the diesel railcars, but despite

soliciting interest from manufacturers it never called for tenders.[35] Norman Kirk led Labour to victory at the November 1972 election, and although his energetic Cabinet talked a fair bit about passenger trains, especially once the oil shock of 1973 suggested there was a future in rail as a fuel-efficient form of transport, tangible achievements were few. Moreover, a freeze that Labour imposed on railway fares and charges dented NZR's earning potential. Bill Rowling, prime minister after Kirk's untimely death in August 1974, led a government similarly short on action for rail. Colin McLachlan became minister of railways when Robert Muldoon took National back into power in November 1975, and in July 1976 he was blunt: the failure to order rollingstock meant that NZR had to cancel some regional trains.[36] All this indecision cost communities across the country dearly: while politicians debated and dithered, railcar services disappeared.

In November 1971 NZR reduced the North Island railcar timetable, a revision that set the tone for the rest of the decade. Wellington–Napier–Gisborne and Wairarapa trains became less frequent, and the Auckland–Taumarunui section of the Auckland–New Plymouth railcar was cancelled. An earlier plan in 1968 had proposed to delete the Taumarunui–New Plymouth portion of this line on account of low patronage, but the isolation of the area meant it survived and the Main Trunk portion ended instead.[37] The departure time was not amended, however, so the railcar left New Plymouth at 2.35am and returned from Taumarunui at 6.52am.[38] This schedule had been reasonable for travellers who wished to reach Auckland in the morning, but as a local service it was senseless. It connected with some buses in Taumarunui but not the Main Trunk expresses, and made shopping impossible. A newspaper company that had once subsidised the train for distribution now paid ordinary delivery rates. In December 1973 the timetable was finally amended.[39] The service now ran during the day, allowed passengers almost three hours in Taumarunui and connected with the Silver Ferns. It survived for another decade in one of New Zealand's most inaccessible regions, so remote that today it has the last unsealed section of the state highway network: SH43 in the Tāngarākau Gorge.

The next railcar cut eliminated the last passenger service south of Greymouth. A century earlier Hokitika had been one of New Zealand's largest centres, the capital of Westland Province. It was now a modest country town with a population of around 3500. Ross, further south, was the railhead for South Westland and home to a mere 429 people. Cabinet's interdepartmental committee on the West Coast rejected closure of all or part of the railway between Greymouth and Ross in September 1971, but it was too late for passengers.[40] NZR wanted to revise its West Coast offerings, both trains and buses. A report in May 1972 argued that patronage south of Greymouth was too limited, especially beyond Hokitika. Two railcars ran daily from Christchurch: one carried just 15–20 passengers between Hokitika and Ross, mostly schoolchildren, while the other averaged four. Buses could provide a comparable service.[41] Local complaints received little consideration, and when NZR officials visited council delegates, their purpose was not to consider counterarguments but to justify their decision. Railcars terminated at Greymouth from 9 October 1972.[42]

Fears that the whole service to Christchurch might be cancelled were baseless, however. The road through the Southern Alps, Arthur's Pass, was difficult and dangerous, and the comparative ease of the railway journey ensured that both daily railcars continued to run – though one Christchurch departure, at 1.50am, was more suited to newspaper distribution than passengers. As the railcars deteriorated, NZR did all it could to maintain this route.

Labour promised passenger rail investment before the 1972 election and, once in office, considered new rollingstock at length, but its failure to sign a contract spelled the end of many regional services.

NZR now had ample proof that improvements to the standard of service could reverse the decline of patronage. A new carriage train between Wellington and Napier, the *Endeavour*, had boosted patronage by 25 percent; the Blue Streaks had improved loadings between Wellington and New Plymouth by 60 percent; and the Silver Ferns underpinned a 121 percent increase in daytime travel on the North Island Main Trunk. Buoyed by these successes, in December 1973 NZR submitted optimistic plans for new carriages and railcars. The proposals did not extend to reviving cancelled routes and advised against trains to Rotorua and Whangārei, as patronage would come largely at the expense of Road Services, a rationale never applied in reverse.[43] It did, however, propose to purchase sufficient rollingstock to improve all routes operational in 1973: five railcars and 45 locomotive-hauled carriages, 18 guard's vans and three buffet cars.[44]

There was no unanimity within either NZR or the government, and opinions on the plans varied. The chief mechanical engineer considered passenger trains 'a drain on the Department's financial and manpower resources', and believed that attempts to boost patronage with better-quality trains would only make this worse: increased investment could only be justified if ridership grew beforehand.[45] Treasury opposed the plans vehemently, and so they bounced from one committee to another. Cabinet's sub-committee on transport in December 1974 recommended purchasing new rollingstock, especially as soaring oil prices made long-distance trains more economic, but Treasury insisted these plans did not 'stand up to quantitative analysis'.[46] Cabinet, reluctant to back NZR's confidence that new rollingstock would have a tonic effect on revenue or to enforce

Treasury's pessimistic outlook, did not rush the debate.

Otago was first to feel the effects of indecision. Dunedin's grand railway station was nowhere near as busy as it once had been, but in 1975 it still served trains to numerous destinations. The *Southerner* was a hit on the Christchurch–Invercargill route, but inadequate publicity meant the evening railcars were underutilised.[47] Railcars also ran to Alexandra and Palmerston – Vulcans, not Fiats, so their timetables had not been reduced – but these were now over 35 years old. Ron Bailey, Rowling's minister of railways, considered both routes his highest priority to re-equip, as they served communities away from main roads for whom buses were impractical. In September 1975 he recommended that Cabinet's committee on policy and priorities approve an order for three 50-seater railcars to be based in Dunedin, the estimated cost being $1.85 million of a larger $14.32 million plan to rejuvenate regional rail.[48] But although the committee noted international trends of passengers returning to rail following the 1973 oil shock, it deferred any decision.[49]

Treasury by this point was implacably hostile towards most passenger trains. Its contempt for the Palmerston service induced rhetoric that does not withstand even mild scrutiny, such as the idea that 'the children could be taken to school in chauffeur-driven Rolls Royces at less cost'.[50] Treasury also assumed that existing patronage represented the full market for rail travel and ignored the ridership increases that were occurring on refurbished trains. The dispute went unresolved before the election.

For Otago's railcars, 9 February 1976 was the decisive date. McLachlan and the rest of Muldoon's Cabinet accepted Treasury's pro-road representations and agreed to replace them with buses.[51] They received a flurry of letters in favour of the railcars from individuals, local councils, Ecology Action Otago and women's branches of Federated Farmers, and 57 Otago railway staff signed a petition calling for their retention. Although many made it clear they were not writing simply because of their attachment to one type of train, some observers still considered the protests to be based in nostalgia: people might love the railcars, but the machines were at the end of their working lives. Despite having pushed for the Picton ferry/train connection, MP Edward Latter referred to 'the emotive term "railcars"' as a 'trap'.[52] But as Joyce Herd of Ecology Action put it, 'we are advocating rail transport, not specifically railcars as at present utilised'.[53]

Their protests fell on deaf ears. Railcars in Otago and Southland ceased after 25 April 1976, ending all passenger services to Central Otago. Dunedin's suburban network and the *Southerner* became the only passenger trains south of Rolleston. It is worth noting that although Treasury did not want the railcars replaced, it saw potential for the Christchurch–Greymouth route to become a successful tourist attraction and encouraged NZR to plan accordingly.[54] On this point it proved entirely correct.

Another service, Napier to Gisborne, experienced a temporary lull in 1976. When NZR introduced the *Endeavour* on 6 November 1972, this freed some Fiats to operate a connecting service to Gisborne.[55] But with the railcars in a parlous state and no alternative rollingstock at hand, all services north of Napier ended on 30 May 1976. With-car goods trains between Gisborne and Wairoa had ceased by 1973, and private buses now provided the only public transport along the coast to Gisborne. Local councils

and residents protested vigorously. Many letters not only decried the poor roads and uncomfortable buses but also emphasised the expense of airfares from Gisborne. Bob Bell, MP for Gisborne, recognised that cancellation was probably 'inevitable' but demanded it be only temporary pending the arrival of new rollingstock. He submitted a petition signed by 5200 people to McLachlan's office; and when he led a deputation of reporters aboard one of the last services on 17 May 1976, a group of over 100 protesters met the train at sparsely populated Ōpoutama, near Waikōkopu, to plead for its retention.[56] One history of the Napier–Gisborne line suggests this popular opprobrium forced the government to rethink its decision. McLachlan, though, had emphasised to Cabinet that NZR intended to resume a daily service once carriages were available.[57]

The rollingstock to replace some railcars and restore Gisborne's service did not come from overseas, nor was it made new locally. Instead NZR, desperate to extract whatever value it could from the Fiats, explored the idea of converting 14 units into unpowered carriages. Tom Small, NZR general manager since 1972, in March 1976 instructed his chief mechanical engineer and chief traffic manager to confer and prepare plans, and a month later they confirmed that conversion was feasible.[58] The proposal went before Cabinet in September. Predictably, Treasury argued against most of the scheme and in favour of road options, but this time NZR submitted an effective rebuttal that emphasised the impracticality of Treasury's proposals. NZR had learned that trimming daily services to thrice weekly discouraged passengers further, while Treasury still assumed this met demand where it was.[59] Cabinet approved NZR's submission.

Proposed colour scheme for
Twin Set Railcar Conversion

A

The five paint schemes considered
for the Fiats that were converted to
unpowered carriages. NZR chose the
fourth, Resene Trendy Green.

ANZ ABJP 04/833/78

Proposed colour scheme for
Twin Set Railcar Conversion

B

Proposed colour scheme for
Twin Set Railcar Conversion

C

Proposed colour scheme for
Twin Set Railcar Conversion

D

Proposed colour scheme for
Twin Set Railcar Conversion

E

The carriages became known as 'grassgrubs' for their green-and-grey colour scheme. The Fiat railcars had been painted in Midland Red, NZR's longstanding livery, but railway author David Leitch, believing people associated Midland Red with poor service, urged in October 1976 that they be repainted as part of the conversion 'to look like new equipment rather than towed railcars'.[60] Leitch's letter was referred to the general manager, now Trevor Hayward. NZR considered five different paint schemes. Some senior officials wanted to stick with red, as did the Ministry of Transport, but Hayward insisted on the green and grey. Workshop staff renovated the units while travellers waited anxiously to learn whether their particular train would transform into a grassgrub or disappear entirely.

The first grassgrubs ran on 5 December 1977 between Christchurch and Picton. The decision to confine them to one route was particularly momentous: Hayward confirmed on 28 September 1976 that no train would replace the Blue Streaks between Wellington and New Plymouth, and McLachlan announced an end date of 30 July 1977. The *New Plymouth Express* had been the North Island's first long-distance express in 1886, and this train and its successor railcars had received premier rollingstock – in 1938 it was the first route allocated Standard railcars, followed by the Blue Streaks in 1972. The Standards were popular – 2000 people in Whanganui inspected the inaugural unit, and police in New Plymouth had to clear a path for passengers through the crowd that thronged the station for the first arrival.[61] Four decades later the people of the region still viewed railcars with affection despite the declining condition of the Blue Streaks. McLachlan insisted publicly that this deterioration was the sole reason they were withdrawn, but internal correspondence

suggests otherwise. Treasury was at pains to highlight low patronage, and McLachlan fell into their trap, noting that the railcars in 1976–77 were typically only half full on arrival or departure from Hāwera.[62] This was disingenuous: it depended entirely on where the count was taken, and Hāwera excluded all custom between Whanganui, Manawatū and Wellington. The railcars were usually at least two-thirds full in the middle of their run at Marton, despite such poor reliability that between January and May 1977 they experienced 61 delays and lost almost 45 hours of running time.[63]

Even with this level of service people in the area were reluctant to abandon rail, and the cancellation of the New Plymouth railcars aroused indignation. A Taranaki Rail Passenger Action Group promoted ideas for rail replacements of the Blue Streak, and local councils united to support the call for passenger trains. Hāwera Borough Council slammed McLachlan for 'considering economy rather than service to the people' and accused him of not providing information it had requested. Whanganui resident A.N. Fitch secured hundreds of signatures protesting against the cancellation and others wrote personally.[64] A Napier schoolteacher described the Road Services buses as 'execrable' and suggested that not to replace trains was 'short-sighted and arrogant':

> … *short-sighted in that it fails to appreciate the long-term economic benefits of using the rail facilities, not to mention the social benefits, and arrogant in that the Government and the Department are totally unsympathetic to the general travelling public.*[65]

One girl, worried that her grandmother, who experienced motion sickness on buses, would now be unable to visit her, wrote to Prime Minister Rob Muldoon: 'I don't want the Blue Streak to go away … will you keep it on please.'[66] A New Plymouth company contacted McLachlan with an offer to re-engine the railcars, but NZR's chief mechanical engineer dismissed its quotations and expressed doubt that the company would even be able to obtain spare parts for the existing engines.[67]

The environmental advantages of rail were yet to be appreciated widely, but voices were beginning to be raised on the subject. Tom Small, in his annual reports to Parliament as NZR's general manager, emphasised the environmental benefits that attended passenger trains and their capacity to reduce road congestion: 'No industry … can undertake any endeavour without considering its effects on the fuel crisis, the air we breathe, the water we drink, and the total surroundings in which we live.'[68] In 1973 the Kirk ministry designed 'environmental protection and enhancement procedures', official requirements for assessments of government proposals. Stephen Mills, then a University of Auckland law lecturer and today a Queen's Counsel, suggested in May 1977 that these procedures required an environmental impact assessment of the Blue Streak's cancellation. McLachlan flatly rejected this, claiming that a lack of rollingstock meant no adverse assessment would stop cancellation anyway.[69]

NZR officials and local MPs fronted well-attended public meetings during June 1977 but made it clear that no matter how loudly locals protested, the service would finish. R.W.D. Thompson, NZR's assistant general manager, unfairly pitted region against region by suggesting the New Plymouth train could only be restored at the expense of another.

David Thomson, MP for Stratford, told his constituents, '[T]hese railcars are going to die – no matter what happens.'[70] In the face of strong public objection, decision-makers fell back on fatalistic language. 'Facts just have to be faced,' wrote McLachlan, and 'the only alternative at this point is to replace the railcars with road coaches.'[71]

Whatever the truth of this claim – and it is undeniable that NZR in the 1970s had a passenger rollingstock crisis – the circumstances existed only because of indecision and bad choices made since the early 1950s. A year after the cancellation McLachlan reported to Cabinet that 'the bus service is not acceptable to many people'. Not only were opposition politicians promising to bring back trains, but 'our own man in New Plymouth [MP Tony Friedlander] is fighting me on this one'.[72] The trains never returned.

There was some good news in 1978: Gisborne regained its service in the form of grassgrubs. No small amount of credit belonged to Bob Bell, the National MP who worked hard to ensure that NZR used grassgrubs (unpowered Fiat carriages) to bring passenger trains back to his electorate. The Napier–Gisborne run resumed on 20 March 1978 and was popular.[73] Between May and August average daily ridership was 60 passengers, or 61 percent capacity – roughly the point at which NZR considered a service to break even. It compared to 58 percent capacity on Christchurch–Picton and 37 percent capacity on New Plymouth–Taumarunui.[74] And elsewhere, passengers had no trains to ride. Gisborne's success contrasted with the rest of the country. Basil Arthur, Labour MP for Timaru, told Parliament in June 1978 that 'the sad story of the railways will shortly be told'.[75] Although he was castigating Muldoon's government, as

Two trains of grassgrubs at Wairoa, c. 1980. The engine numbers indicate a major reform, the computerised Traffic Monitoring System, which required engines to be renumbered. DC 4231 is still prominently wearing its old number 1573.

A.T. Johnson, New Zealand Railway & Locomotive Society collection

minister of transport under Kirk and Rowling, he perhaps should have reserved some criticism for himself.

1972–82: SUBURBAN SUBTRACTIONS

The retreat of passenger rail occurred in urban centres of New Zealand too. After the demise of Invercargill–Bluff trains, suburban services ran in just Auckland, Christchurch, Dunedin and Wellington, and only Wellington reached the end of the 1980s with its suburban network in better shape than before. The capital enjoyed certain advantages: it had electric trains (a distinction shared only with Christchurch's Lyttelton line), favourable topography, and a main railway station located more centrally than those in Auckland or Christchurch. Perhaps valuable, too, is that Wellington's railway station is visible from Parliament: never discount the benefits of proximity to power.

Commuters on Auckland's Onehunga

Branch might have wished their line were more visible. Once celebrated as the North Island's first public railway, opened in 1873, a century later its passenger trains were moribund: four ran each weekday at a modest annual loss and, with one exception, passengers had to change to Southern Line trains at Penrose. Goods traffic was increasing and NZR had two options: to employ another shunting crew, which would enable it to move greater tonnages but incur greater costs, or cancel passenger trains.[76] NZR chose the latter. According to Auckland's district traffic manager, passenger services imposed on 'valuable time which could be utilised in shunting', and local officials in January 1973 were eager for cancellation.[77] The press of freight was such that Road Services buses replaced passenger trains between 18 and 22 December 1972, and again from 22 January 1973. The chief traffic manager was in no doubt: 'From an operational point of view it is quite clear we cannot continue to provide passenger train services on the branch.'[78] The Auckland Regional Authority declined to take over the service, so Road Services continued to run its buses. Although Friday 19 January 1973 remained the last day of passenger trains, they lingered on the working timetable for four years, suspended but not cancelled, until removed as part of changing the branch's status to an industrial line in 1977. By then passenger trains could not have been restored anyway: Auckland's suburban rollingstock was so run down that Onehunga's carriages had been repurposed and there were none to spare.[79]

Worse befell the South Island's main cities. Historically, Christchurch was a city of trams and bicycles, modes that gave way to buses and car ownership in the mid-twentieth century. Apart from the run to Lyttelton, rail had a more

Christchurch Passenger Rail
1950–1976

RNG Rangiora
Southbrook
Flaxton
Kaiapoi
Kāinga
Chaneys
Belfast
Styx
Papanui
Bryndwr
Riccarton

WAI TO
Waipara
Glasnevin
Greneys Road
Amberley
Grays Road
Balcairn
Sefton
Ashley

SPR TO
Springfield
Annat
Sheffield
Waddington
Racecourse Hill
Darfield
Kirwee
Aylesbury

ASH TO
Dunsandel
Bankside
Rakaia
Chertsey
Dromore
Fairfield
Ashburton

SUBURBAN SERVICES

RNG Rangiora ceased 1976
BUR Burnham ceased 1967
LTL Lyttelton ceased 1972
LWH Lyttelton Wharf ceased 1976

LOCAL SERVICES

WAI Waipara ceased c. 1960
SPR Springfield ceased 1968
STB Southbridge ceased 1951
LTR Little River ceased 1951
ASH Ashburton ceased 1958

Addington
Hornby Sockburn
Sandy Knolls   Islington
Templeton
Christchurch RNG BUR WAI ASH LTL LWH SPR STB LTR
Middleton
Linwood
Ōpawa
Woolston
Heathcote
Prebbleton
Ladbrooks
Lincoln
BUR Burnham
Rolleston
Norwood
Springston
Selwyn
Goulds Road
Greenpark
Ellesmere
Lake Road
Irwell
Doyleston
Leeston
Hills Road
Southbridge STB
Motukarara
Kaituna
Birdlings Flat
Little River
LTR
LTL Lyttelton   **LWH Lyttelton Wharf** connects with Wellington ferries

regional role. Daily trains from Little River and Southbridge ceased in 1951, followed by those from Ashburton in 1958 and Waipara a couple of years later. In November 1960 NZR opened a large new terminal at Christchurch railway station, located on Moorhouse Avenue on the southern fringe of the CBD. Its remoteness has been exaggerated – the walk to Cathedral Square took only 15 minutes – but it did not help the remaining trains to retain custom.

Christchurch's suburban ticketing zone extended as far as Rangiora and Burnham. A morning passenger train ran daily from the city to Burnham for soldiers at the army camp and workers in the industrial estates of Christchurch's western suburbs, returning in the evening. It ended in 1967, the year in which NZR also slashed Rangiora's daily trains from

A[B] 688 (right) hauls the evening train to Waipara out of Christchurch on 30 March 1950. At left is A[B] 689, awaiting departure to Ashburton.

J.F. Le Cren, ANZ AAVK 6390 B58

7

1970–1989

four to one. A mixed train from Springfield, the last of its kind in Canterbury, endured until 14 December 1968, serving suburban stations from Rolleston.[80] The run from the city to Lyttelton remained the backbone of the network; with over 20 daily services in the 1960s it was the most frequent passenger rail service in the South Island. In addition, the non-stop Boat Train from Christchurch ran onto Lyttelton wharf to meet the Steamer Express ferries to Wellington, often as an extension of main-line expresses that provided direct connections with Dunedin and Invercargill.[81]

Three events of the 1960s dealt blows to passenger rail to Lyttelton. The first was the inauguration of the Cook Strait ferry service. After years of officials dismissing the concept, NZR began operating the GMV *Aramoana* between Wellington and Picton in 1962. It was so popular that by 1974 the ferry fleet had been increased to four. This service, and the growing affordability of air travel, ate into the operating margins of Union Steam Ship's Wellington–Lyttelton service.

The second was the opening of the Lyttelton road tunnel, touted from the outset as an alternative to the railway. At the start of construction in 1956, MP for Lyttelton Harry Lake told Parliament that ferry passengers from Wellington would be able to catch taxis to Christchurch and forgo 'those wretched railway carriages down at Lyttelton'. He believed NZR would welcome not having to deal with this clientele anymore.[82] The 'wretched' carriages ran behind E[C] class electric locomotives that by the late 1960s were also near the end of their working lives. Now Christchurch Transport Board buses running to Lyttelton through the road tunnel competed with trains – ambitions to co-ordinate the two modes were never realised – and other travellers favoured private cars over the old, unheated train carriages. Enter the

J[A] 1253 prepares to depart Springfield in April 1967 with the morning mixed to Christchurch. At one time a passenger train, by 1935 it had become mixed. J.M. Creber

usual argument: current loadings could fit in a bus. Instead of improving the offerings, officials decided to cancel services.

The third factor to affect passenger rail was the removal of electric traction from the railway tunnel, originally installed to eliminate the smoke nuisance of steam engines. As NZR had now almost fully dieselised, this was no longer an issue, and electric traction ceased on 19 September 1970. Diesel trains had slower acceleration, a problem for suburban trains that stopped often, and were wanted for goods duties elsewhere.

One report in late 1971 examined sources of patronage between Christchurch and Lyttelton, but not with a view to retention or growth. The authors assumed that office workers who rode these trains did so only for want of a car. Casual journeys 'could probably have been made by bus' and such travellers 'would be little disrupted' by cancellation. The Education Department could

make other arrangements for schoolchildren and NZR staff could be accommodated elsewise.[83] It was the same old story as in the rest of the country: NZR was not interested in retaining the passenger market and, accordingly, the last suburban train to Lyttelton ran on 27 February 1972. The line did not become goods only immediately, as Boat Trains survived a few more years.

When the district accountant attempted to quantify savings from cancellations he found it impossible to evaluate some crucial categories precisely, including maintenance of track, locomotives and rollingstock. From what he could deduce, actual savings were only two-thirds of estimates.[84] And this did not account for new road costs that fell to taxpayers. It is remarkable that local councils rolled over and accepted the idea that buses would suffice. Trains took approximately 17 minutes to run from Christchurch to Lyttelton.[85] Today a private car can scarcely better this in the best traffic conditions, and the quickest peak-hour bus takes twice as long. Lyttelton residents should be offended that this exceptional method of commuting was allowed to end with so little objection.

At four or five a day, trains to Rangiora were never as frequent as those to Lyttelton, but they served commuters faithfully for decades. They had once been popular: in 1949 a new 6.55am departure from Rangiora introduced with just a car-van was rapidly expanded to five carriages. By July 1967, however, when Fiats stopped running suburban services, only one train remained: citybound in the morning, outbound in the evening.[86] NZR management in early 1976 had the impression that the only passengers were staff at Addington Workshops, which it learned was false the moment an industrial relations officer actually checked. Workshops staff also averred that more would catch the train if the offering were not so attenuated.[87] Although the officer claimed his investigation did not foreshadow discontinuance, the writing was on the wall. Average patronage was below 50, and a privately run bus replaced the train after 30 April 1976. Rangiora travellers now had to pay a 79c bus fare into the city, a significant increase on the 59c train fare.[88] McLachlan felt justified in calling the rail service 'a wasteful use of resources when a bus alternative is available … the decision to end it will release a much needed locomotive for more useful work'.[89] This 'useful work', according to local MP Derek Quigley, was freight haulage.[90] As with Bluff and Onehunga before, passengers were inconvenient. The Main North Line had not become freight only – the trains to Picton continued to run – but it was the end of suburban rail in Christchurch.

Interisland passengers flocked to Cook Strait ferries and NAC flights during the 1960s, and the Boat Trains – the last vestige of over a century of passenger travel in suburban Christchurch – outlived commuter services by under five months. The loss of 53 lives in the sinking of the TEV *Wahine* on 10 April 1968 dented Union Steam Ship's reputation, and with just one ship in service the Steamer Express now sailed four times a week, a far cry from the previous timetable of one ship each way daily. Not even the brand-new TEV *Rangatira* could save the route in 1972; it continued past July 1974 only because Kirk's government contracted Union to keep sailing. Muldoon's Cabinet, however, rejected requests for a greater subsidy and let the contract expire. The *Rangatira* sailed for the last time on 14 September 1976, and as a consequence passenger trains no longer ran to Lyttelton and New Zealand's oldest operational railway became goods only.[91] Christchurch's 16-year-old central station now only served trains to Picton, Invercargill and the West Coast, all with reduced timetables.

Dunedin's suburban network was the next to go, and already in 1976 there were ominous signs. McLachlan told Cabinet that decrepit rollingstock and daily patronage of about 1000 return trips meant buses were preferable.[92] It is unsurprising that these trains had limited ridership: besides the condition of the carriages, services were confined to peak hours only. In a sweeping reduction, in October 1968 NZR had cancelled off-peak weekday services and all Saturday trains, despite a ridership of 924,610 in the 1967/68 financial year.[93] Every Dunedinite, in other words, had averaged over eight suburban train journeys in the last year of a full timetable. Newspaper reports in September 1979, in which general administration officer

7

1970–1989

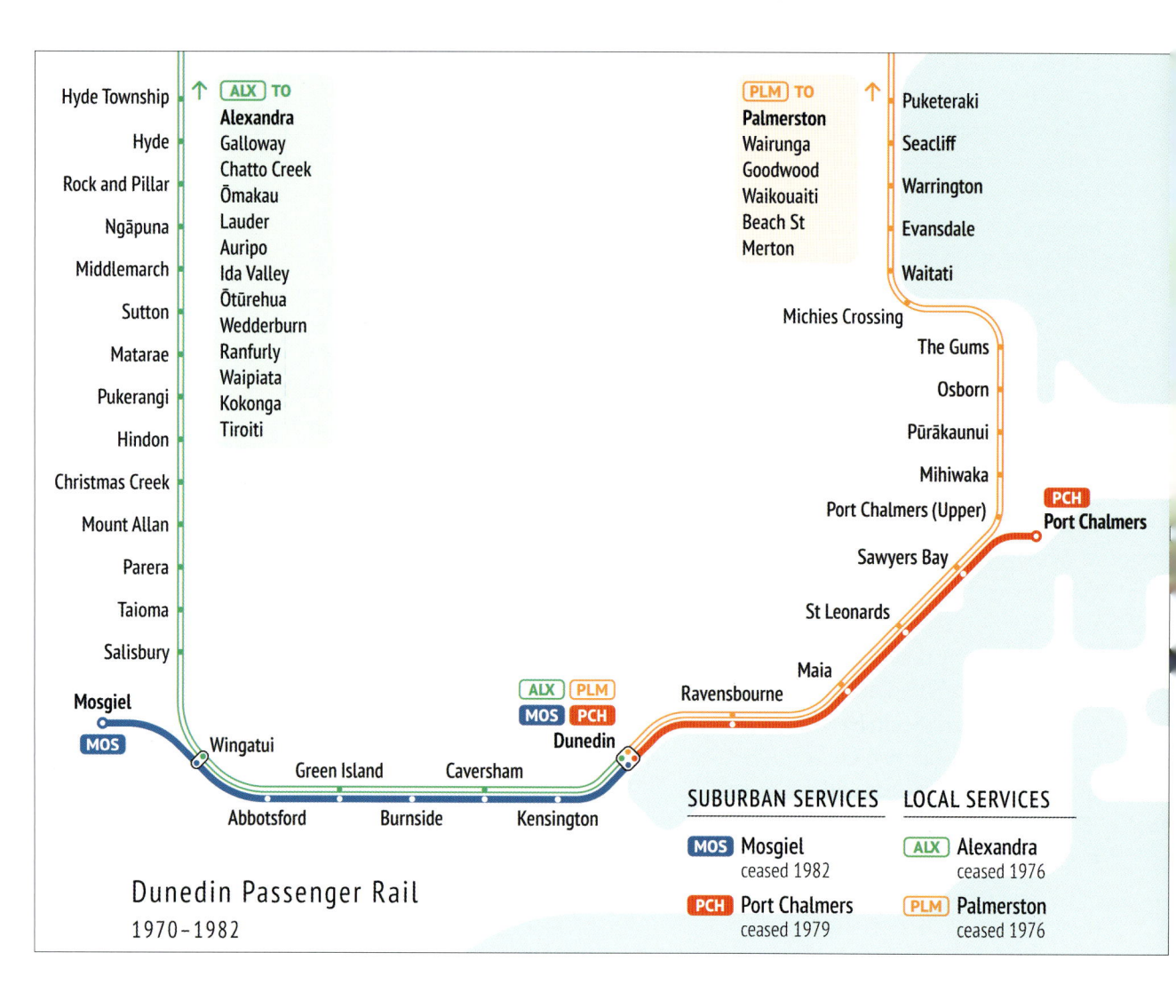

Dunedin Passenger Rail
1970–1982

Map labels:

Hyde Township, Hyde, Rock and Pillar, Ngāpuna, Middlemarch, Sutton, Matarae, Pukerangi, Hindon, Christmas Creek, Mount Allan, Parera, Taioma, Salisbury, **Mosgiel**, Wingatui, Green Island, Caversham, Abbotsford, Burnside, Kensington

ALX TO
Alexandra
Galloway
Chatto Creek
Ōmakau
Lauder
Auripo
Ida Valley
Ōtūrehua
Wedderburn
Ranfurly
Waipiata
Kokonga
Tiroiti

PLM TO
Palmerston
Wairunga
Goodwood
Waikouaiti
Beach St
Merton

Puketeraki, Seacliff, Warrington, Evansdale, Waitati, Michies Crossing, The Gums, Osborn, Pūrākaunui, Mihiwaka, Port Chalmers (Upper), **PCH Port Chalmers**, Sawyers Bay, St Leonards, Maia, Ravensbourne

ALX PLM
MOS PCH
Dunedin

MOS

SUBURBAN SERVICES

MOS **Mosgiel**
ceased 1982

PCH **Port Chalmers**
ceased 1979

LOCAL SERVICES

ALX **Alexandra**
ceased 1976

PLM **Palmerston**
ceased 1976

Euan McQueen emphasised that revenue covered only 28 percent of operating costs, warned travellers that the remaining services were in jeopardy.[94] One unhappy commuter from Mosgiel lamented, 'Trains are far more convenient than buses. They are faster and cheaper … You'd think they would be encouraging more people to use the trains and leave their cars at home.'[95] The comment could have come from almost anywhere in New Zealand in at least the past half-century.

Mosgiel trains survived 1979 albeit with the two evening services compressed into one, but Port Chalmers services did not. The short branch from Sawyers Bay to Port Chalmers had been part of Otago's first railway, but if usefulness was insufficient to save passenger trains, sentiment definitely could not. The decision in 1961 to rename Mussel Bay station Port Chalmers and terminate trains there had made them less convenient for waterfront workers. Later that decade the opening of what is today State Highway 88 alongside the railway replaced a circuitous route into Port Chalmers and dented patronage further. With the district traffic manager suggesting that the replacement buses would be 'more economic and equally effective', the last commuter services ran on 7 December 1979.[96] Since then, passenger trains to Port Chalmers have mainly been charters operated by Dunedin Railways for cruise ship tourists.

Mosgiel passengers expressed a strong preference for train travel in every survey and interview NZR conducted, and the local council was also in favour. No other form of transport offered such a fast journey between the city and Mosgiel, for only the railway slices under the Chain Hills. That passengers would favour rail despite riding in dilapidated 50-year-old carriages demonstrates the sincerity of their preference. A refurbished, frequent and well-marketed service would have secured more custom, but officials persisted with the belief that 'the transport needs of this area can best be served by the use of buses'.[97] They pointed to declining patronage – 781 daily passengers in 1982 compared with 1204 in 1978 – which is hardly surprising given the state of the rollingstock.

Dunedin's last suburban service ran on 3 December 1982, leaving the *Southerner* as the only passenger train operating south of Christchurch.[98] Much of the blame for this decline sits with the hostile attitudes held within Treasury and by some of the very officials who operated the railways. People who could see a future for passenger rail were too slow to counter these, and the failure to order new carriages during the 1970s was fatal. Without decent rollingstock, sufficient motive power or institutional backing from NZR, is it any

surprise that suburban trains perished in the South Island?

The North Island's suburban networks were also struggling. Throughout the 1970s officials bemoaned the state of rollingstock in Auckland, where revenue covered just 26 percent of operating costs: Wellington in comparison recovered 46 percent.[99] McLachlan told Cabinet in 1976 that many services in both cities were 'maintained only through the continued use of old pre-war rolling stock'; all components, he said, were in 'very poor shape'.[100]

The 1977 budget made provision for new rollingstock in Auckland and Wellington, and NZR called for tenders worldwide. Hungarian manufacturer Ganz-Mávag won the bid to build 44 EM/ET class electric multiple units for Wellington, which operated from 1982 to 2016. But after initially calling tenders for 50 carriages for Auckland's Southern Line to Papakura, the government decided instead to review Auckland's entire passenger transport requirements and cancelled the tender.[101]

Services to Helensville ended as part of a broad reduction of the suburban timetable on the Western Line. Since the 1960s, offerings beyond Waitākere had been gradually culled. In 1966, for instance, passenger accommodation on a Saturday with-car goods to Helensville was withdrawn. Many passengers on this service were trampers and day-walkers heading for the Waitākere Ranges, and NZR abandoned this clientele rather than encouraging its growth. The transportation superintendent wrote blithely, 'Most of them … would no doubt be able to arrange alternative transport'.[102] After railcars to Northland ended in July 1967, the only passenger service between Waitākere and Helensville was a solitary weekday return service. Trevor Hayward, NZR's general manager

One of the most famous public transport plans in New Zealand history is remembered as 'Robbie's Rapid Rail', a bold proposal from Auckland's longest-serving mayor, Dove-Myer Robinson, affectionately known throughout the country as Robbie.[103] One of his biographers describes him as a 'slight, bespectacled man whose tiny stature was offset by a booming voice and massive ego'.[104] Robinson carved out a national profile as a visionary who campaigned for a cleaner environment before green politics existed, and he created the Auckland Regional Authority (ARA) to achieve cohesive planning across the 32 different councils in and around Auckland. He once promoted motorway construction but later regarded this as his greatest political mistake. By the late 1960s he was convinced Auckland needed a rapid metro rail system, and the sooner the better, before motorways became hopelessly congested. After three years in the political wilderness, Robbie secured his return to the mayoralty in 1968 with a campaign that championed rapid rail. The map here depicts a potential network to be built in stages, based on a 1972 report.[105]

From the outset Robbie faced opposition from other local authorities and central government. Robert Muldoon, then Minister of Finance in Holyoake's Cabinet, was sceptical, and local councils made parochial demands that added to the cost, such as route diversions or stations within their boundaries, and complained that the project served central Auckland's needs at the expense of suburban hubs. Some mayors and councillors thought rail was dying, and politicians elsewhere disapproved of large expenditure for Auckland. Not even NZR was on board: it feared competition if the ARA built new lines and ran the trains, and did not want more passenger trains on its own tracks to impede the goods timetable. Vested interests, prejudices and personal animosity raised too many hurdles for one man to clear.

An inane dispute arose about the track gauge for rapid rail. Some insisted it should be 1435mm (international standard gauge), rather than New Zealand's 1067mm. This should never have been taken seriously: Australia's railway history demonstrates the mess that arises from multiple main-line gauges. Bob Stott, editor of *Rails* magazine, condemned the debate as 'illogical' because narrow-gauge metro systems operated successfully overseas.[106]

Robbie came close to success when Kirk's government approved an electrified underground city loop and major upgrades of the Southern Line to Papakura as a first stage in 1973.[107] This was to be a trial, with further stages to follow if it succeeded. Although the ARA accepted the scheme, Robbie considered it a pallid offering that did little to meet Auckland's future needs. Negotiations between the ARA and the government proceeded sluggishly, and in mid-1975 Labour effectively shelved plans ahead of the election. There would be no new lines or upgrades, just a managed decline of existing trains.

The whole saga reflects badly on the participants, including Robbie, who at times alienated potential allies with his domineering style and tactless public interventions – he reputedly told one critic, Tauranga mayor Bob Owens, to 'go jump in Tauranga Harbour'.[108] It also demonstrates how needlessly protracted debates can undermine important projects. It is an instructive case for the 2020s as rival bids for Auckland's proposed light rail network have stymied progress.

Auckland Passenger Rail
1973–1980

in 1979, indicated that passenger trains to Auckland's northwest were under threat.[109] A new timetable eliminated the Helensville train from 18 August 1980 and closed a handful of stations between Waitākere and Newmarket.[110] Waitākere was now Auckland's westernmost suburban station and remained so for most of the next 35 years, while the central terminal on Beach Road was New Zealand's northernmost passenger station, beating Waitākere by a fraction of latitude. The new Britomart station that replaced Beach Road in 2003 can claim to be a hair's breadth further north.

Further cancellations in the early 1980s

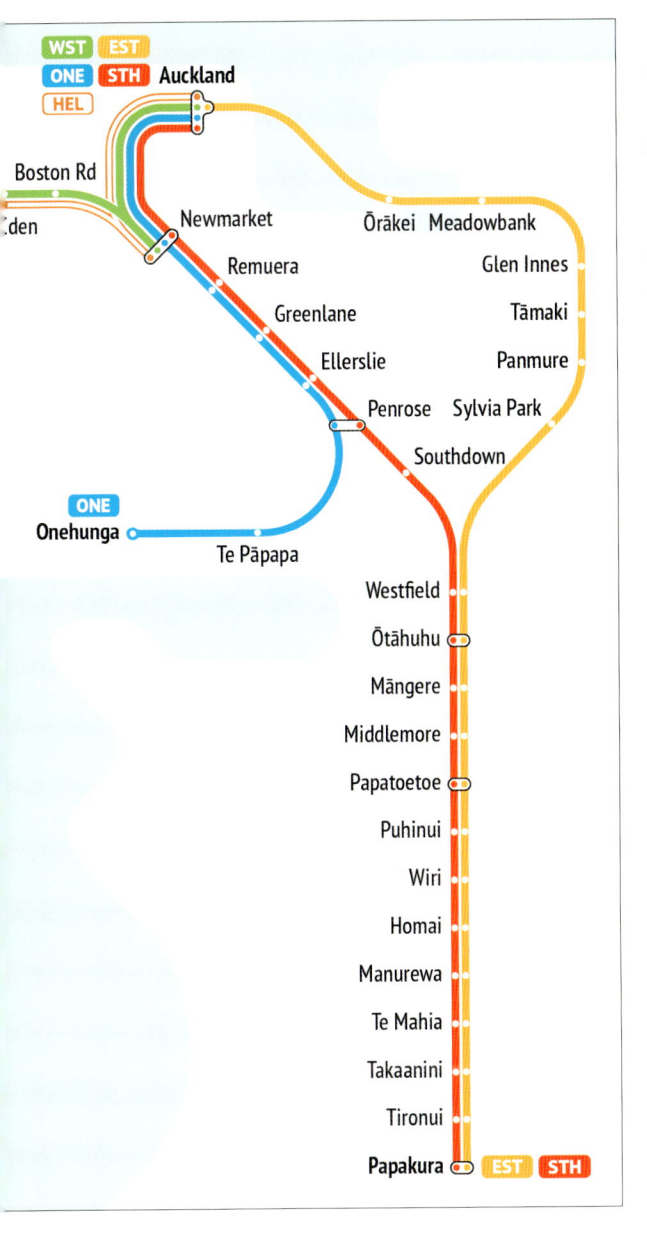

were few, in part because there was not much left to cancel. In 1982 Wellington's network became fractionally smaller when a daily train for workers at Hutt Workshops ended. A diesel locomotive propelled an electric multiple unit from Woburn along the Gracefield industrial line as far as the workshops. It ceased for the

7

1970–1989

1982 Christmas holidays as usual – and never returned.[111]

There was cause for celebration in 1983, however, as electric wires inched up the North Island Main Trunk from Paekākāriki to Paraparaumu. Commuter trains for the burgeoning Kāpiti Coast had been a long time coming. NZR had contemplated a Blue Streak-style railcar service from Levin or Palmerston North in 1967: 'The Paraparaumu people really want a workers' service,' wrote Ivan Thomas, 'and envisage about 900 people travelling to and from Wellington each day'. This was beyond the means of a railcar.[112] In lieu of extending the wires immediately, in 1973 NZR had modified a few electric multiple units so that diesel locomotives could pull them north of Paekākāriki, an 'interim' measure that lasted for a decade. Paraparaumu eventually became the northern terminus of Wellington's electrified network on 7 May 1983.[113] After years of mediocre service, the Kāpiti Coast received the full benefit of the new Ganz-Mávag units.

Up north the ARA released a 'short-term appraisal' of Auckland's suburban railways in May 1983, which in some ways demonstrated modest progress in assessing rail's value but failed to put two and two together. The report studied vehicle emissions, but only in terms of rail passengers switching to cars; it discussed the effects of doubling train patronage, but only to defer motorway upgrades.[114] The authors did not ask whether increased rail patronage would reduce emissions.

Worse, the report articulated how to run services into the ground. 'Many people enjoy the experience of riding trains,' the authors noted; if carriages were not overhauled, '[t]he gradual deterioration of service levels may cause people to shift to other modes of travel'.[115] The report

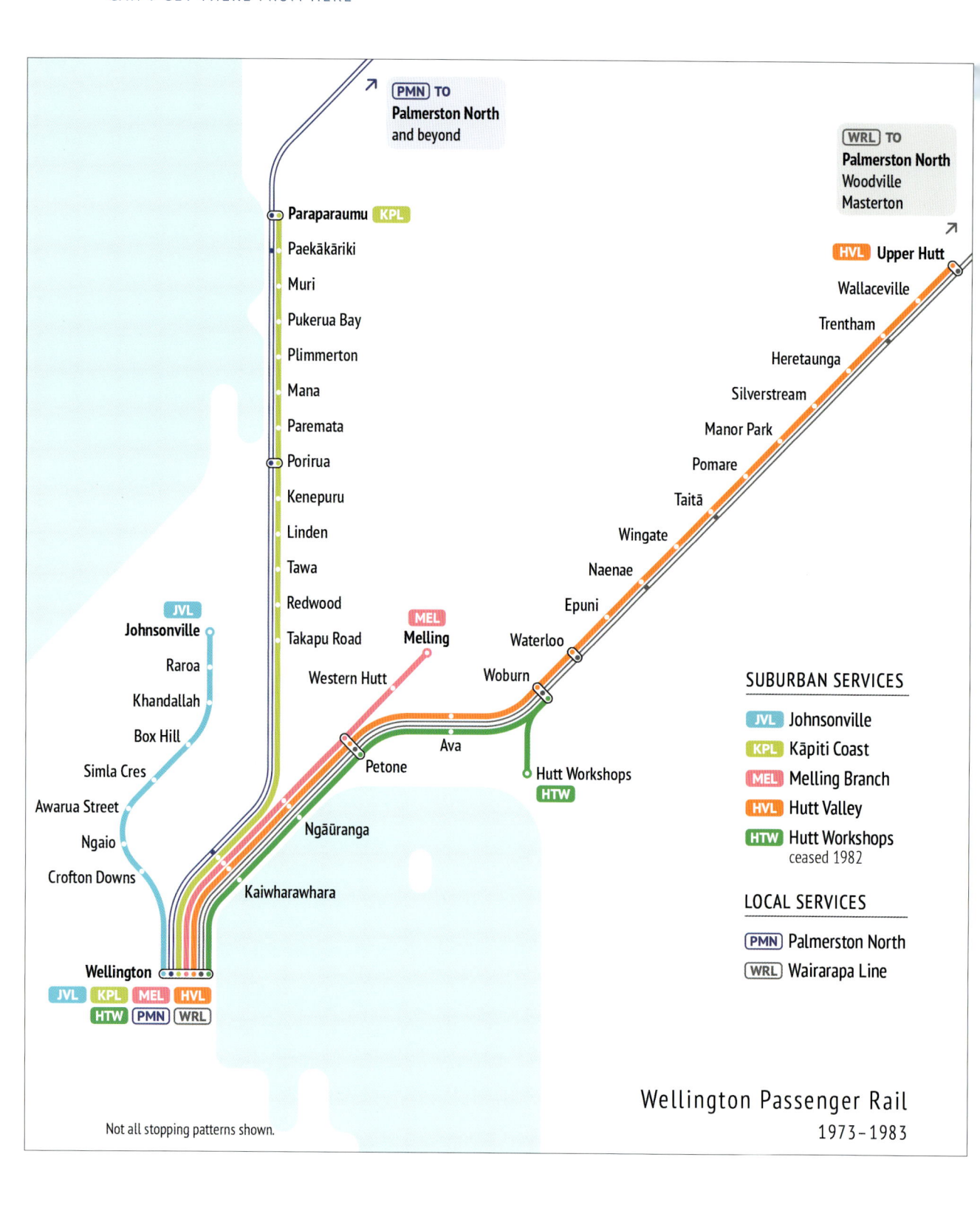

Wellington Passenger Rail
1973–1983

Not all stopping patterns shown.

SUBURBAN SERVICES

- JVL Johnsonville
- KPL Kāpiti Coast
- MEL Melling Branch
- HVL Hutt Valley
- HTW Hutt Workshops
  ceased 1982

LOCAL SERVICES

- PMN Palmerston North
- WRL Wairarapa Line

went on to endorse this cynicism: although it contemplated railway upgrades, light rail and bus rapid transit, it recommended only that overhauls be suspended at the end of the year and the situation be revisited in 1987.[116]

Few documents make clearer the lack of ambition for passenger rail. New Zealand could have had a good passenger network, but decisions made from the 1950s to the 1980s meant it did not.

1983–88: THE FINAL ECHOES OF THE DEVELOPMENTAL RAILWAY

The fate of New Zealand's finest passenger train, the *Silver Star*, was not a positive harbinger for the 1980s. The *Silver Star* had always complemented a slower, less luxurious overnight train between Wellington and Auckland, which became the *Northerner* in 1975. The refurbished carriages of the *Northerner* clearly appealed to budget-conscious passengers. In the year ended 31 March 1978, only two trains earned over $1 million: the *Silver Star* earned almost $1.4m and the *Northerner* just over $2m. The *Northerner* recouped most costs, but the *Silver Star* was in trouble: its operating loss, $1.57m, made up 36.5 percent of the entire $4.29m national loss. Moreover, although it was a 'prestige' service, tickets were more than $20 below cost per passenger, a much greater margin than 'social service' trains such as New Plymouth–Taumarunui, where tickets were nearly $5 below cost. Unsurprisingly, then, NZR cancelled the *Silver Star* in 1979.[117] If a premier train between the two largest cities could not survive, what fate awaited more marginal services?

Governments did not entirely abandon railways as a political tool. Muldoon's 'Think Big' scheme of public works included the long-awaited electrification of the North Island Main Trunk between Palmerston North and Hamilton. But Muldoon's government and, from 1984, its Labour successor led by David Lange, stepped back from railway management more than any previous administration. The ostensibly 'independent' railway boards of the past had been little more than scapegoats for unpopular policies, and were abolished when they became political impediments.[118] But the spirit of the 1980s was different. Muldoon's Cabinet approved NZR's transformation from a government department into a corporation during 1982, and the last vestiges of limitations on road competition ended in 1983. Popular economic beliefs – that competition produced the greatest efficiencies, financial profits would deliver social gains, and the cheapest service was the best – gave the now corporatised NZR wide latitude to reform itself as it faced the challenges of economic deregulation.

In a 1985 restructure, NZR split into three core business divisions: the Passenger Business Group held rail and road passenger services; Railfreight encompassed goods and workshops; and Interislander (initially SeaRail) controlled the Cook Strait ferries. The Passenger Business Group developed three brands: Cityline for suburban services, InterCity for long distance and Speedlink for parcels. From 1986 NZR was a state-owned enterprise, tasked with turning a profit.

The legacy of the colonial developmental railway lingered in the rhetoric of regional trains being a 'social service' that attracted public subsidies. The NZ Railways Corporation, however, had little appetite for passenger rail. It commissioned American consultants Booz Allen Hamilton to report on all aspects of its operations. Their analysis of passenger services

7

1970–1989

concluded that abolishing all long-distance passenger trains would save the most money – a fatuous conclusion – but recognised that the broader political context required that some be retained. The report anticipated that an NZR plan to refurbish the *Silver Star* rollingstock for daytime Auckland–Wellington services would come to fruition, which would allow the Silver Ferns to be redeployed on Christchurch–Dunedin and Christchurch–Picton routes, and recommended withdrawing all other long-distance passenger trains.[119] This galvanised a Labour 'Save Rail' campaign, but after Lange led the party to victory in 1984 his government went on to implement much of the report. The passenger recommendations were not followed directly, but the general tenor spelled the end for the developmental railway.

If regional services were to survive, they needed new justifications. Tourism was one. NZR was becoming more proactive about luring sightseers to rail, which enabled the Christchurch–Greymouth train to become the world-famous *TranzAlpine* from 22 November 1987, rather than devolving into Booz Allen Hamilton's proposed 'luxury bus'. Christchurch–Picton trains were refurbished next and became the *Coastal Pacific* on 25 September 1988, and from 11 December 1989 the *Bay Express* rejuvenated the Napier route after the *Endeavour* became associated with delays and a mishmash of rundown carriages. But the 1980s reveal a corporation that was yet to appreciate the potential of some of its assets, and Booz Allen Hamilton simply endorsed NZR's moves away from regional passenger operation.

New Plymouth's remaining passenger train was the first to disappear, before Booz Allen Hamilton had even written its report. It might surprise twenty-first-century readers to know that local trains in northern Taranaki outlived expresses to Wellington, but in those days the towns along the Stratford–Ōkahukura Line were more populous than they are now. The service survived numerous proposed cancellations and reductions in the late 1970s; instead, the decrepit railcars had been transformed into locomotive-hauled grassgrubs.[120] In December 1982, with the local roads somewhat improved, the minister announced that trains would be withdrawn early in the following year. Perhaps NZR missed a trick: it scheduled the last train for 21 January 1983, but so many people booked a final ride through what is one of New Zealand's most striking regions that additional carriages were transferred from Wellington and an extra excursion ran the following day.[121] After KiwiRail mothballed the line in 2009, Forgotten World Adventures converted golf buggies to run on rails and established these 'rail carts' as a profitable tourist attraction. Once again, the state had given up revenue from a public asset – this time not to a road competitor but to a private operator with permission to use the line.

Another train with tourism potential ran from Greymouth to Rewanui, in an isolated valley of the Paparoa Range. This line was so steep and had such tight curvature that a Fell centre rail had assisted braking in the steam era. Rewanui's passenger service, now the only one in the South Island that did not call at Christchurch, ran simply because of the isolation of the mines it served.

In 1929 NZR's own *Railways Magazine* had waxed lyrical about the splendid scenery, saying 'here Nature wears her finest robes', and in the early 1980s NZR ran sightseeing trips to Rewanui during the Christmas holidays.[122] These performed so poorly in the wet summer

A rail cart at Mātīere on the Stratford–Ōkahukura Line, 24 October 2018.

André Brett

of 1982–83 that only the intervention of local Labour MP Kerry Burke ensured that they ran the next year, when better weather saw passenger numbers treble to roughly 130 per train. This was still insufficient to cover half the operating costs, let alone maintenance.[123] Aware that the Liverpool Mine, the main client, was almost exhausted, NZR gradually let the line deteriorate, and it was decrepit in February 1984 when the Ministry of Energy confirmed the mine's closure for 30 September.[124] NZR estimated that $3m of upgrades would be necessary to maintain operations, and at that price was unwilling to keep the line open year round for tourism.

Burke convened a meeting of local government representatives, miners, unions, railway staff and motel operators in Greymouth during April that appointed a committee to consider options, including the purchase or lease of the line by a local consortium.[125] NZR's

chief civil engineer, quite rightly, highlighted the challenges of operating a railway in such mountainous terrain. Maintenance and operation required advanced skills, and the only option NZR would countenance was to have locals, through their council or another body, pay for reconstruction and then contract NZR to operate trains.[126] This was reasonable. But NZR went further. The railway had again been popular during the May 1984 school holidays and officials anticipated pressure to operate excursions at Christmas too – something they were not prepared to do.[127] The district engineer put his foot down: no passenger trains would run after 30 September, even though the line had to remain open until 31 March 1985 for salvage trains to remove mining equipment.[128] The area sales manager agreed, writing, 'Provided several months' notice is given, I can see no reason why the Corporation will not be able to "stick to its guns".'[129] It succeeded. The final services on 30 September were also the last with-car goods trains in New Zealand.

The trip to Rewanui had become a popular holiday activity despite limited promotion and patched-up carriages; it could have become a premier attraction in the Grey District, providing a glimpse of mining heritage and a departure point for trampers. By the late 1980s the tourism potential of the Christchurch–Greymouth line was proven: the *TranzAlpine* was so popular that carriages were appropriated from the *Southerner* to carry weekend crowds.[130] Many of these travellers and other visitors to the West Coast would have readily journeyed into the Paparoa Range. As the glaciers continue to retreat, the West Coast could use an attraction such as the Rewanui railway. It was not to be, and the organisation that did not value what it possessed let the opportunity go.

Some operators were more alert to the potential of tourism. The Otago Excursion Train Trust, formed in 1978, owned a number of ex-NZR carriages and ran excursions from Dunedin to destinations in Central Otago and elsewhere. As demand swelled during the 1980s, the trust inaugurated a regular service through the Taieri Gorge. On 21 February 1987, almost 13 years after the last Vulcan railcar ran along the Otago Central Railway, the *Taieri Gorge Limited* began daily operation, initially without winter services but later becoming year round. Like many heritage activities it relied on volunteer labour, which would have been unacceptable for NZR to do. The trust's operations, however, were distinct from normal enthusiast railways, both in scope and in its efforts to attract greater ridership by complementing its heritage fleet with new carriages that had large windows and air conditioning, and using main-line diesel

locomotives rather than steam engines. It also began employing staff.

When NZR closed the Otago Central Railway in 1990, Dunedin City Council purchased the line as far as Middlemarch. In late 1995 the trust and the council became joint shareholders of a new company, Taieri Gorge Railway Limited, later branded Dunedin Railways, and by 2017 the payroll had grown to 28 full- and 27 part-time employees. The trust owned 28 percent and the council's Dunedin City Holdings Limited owned 72 percent until April 2020, at which point the trust sold its shareholding to the council when services were mothballed during the Covid-19 pandemic. The *Taieri Gorge Limited* not only served sightseers but also provided transport for cyclists and walkers to access the Otago Central Rail Trail, which follows the old formation from Middlemarch to Clyde.[131]

Only two more NZR services ceased in the 1980s, those to Gisborne and the northern Wairarapa, and with them ended the era of the developmental railway. Unprofitable and unloved, the trains between Napier and Gisborne were vulnerable. They received minimal investment after reinstatement in 1978, and in 1981 were so neglected that 17 engine drivers and guards complained. The cleaning staff, they alleged, were doing such a poor job that some passengers had told guards they would 'never travel on these trains again because of the disgusting state of the cars'. It had become 'a big talking point' locally and crew members had even 'been slung off at by members of the public at social gatherings, clubs and hotels … many of us are now embarrassed to be seen working on the passenger trains'.[132]

Later that year NZR combined the *Endeavour* between Wellington and Napier

W^W 679 hauls a miners' train through the magnificent landscape near Rewanui on 3 January 1964. Note the Fell centre rail used for braking until 1966, when four steam engines were fitted with more powerful brakes. Diesels took over in 1969.

Weston Langford, no. 103735

with the unnamed connection to Gisborne as a through service. The section north of Napier was considered a social subsidy to East Coast communities. In 1986 the government revised its social subsidy payments to NZR, providing a block grant rather than 100 percent funding for specific trains. This created a shortfall of $10.1m for passenger rail.[133] Gisborne's train soldiered on for a couple of years in this difficult funding environment, but met an abrupt end when Cyclone Bola damaged the line severely in March 1988. All trains ceased north of Napier while Lange's government considered options, including closure of the line past Wairoa.[134] The line was ultimately repaired, but at the official reopening in October Minister of Railways Richard Prebble indicated that passenger trains would not resume. The *Gisborne Herald*, already pushing a campaign to reverse cuts to local air services, responded angrily, saying, 'Slashing the passenger service would do enormous damage to our communications with the outside world.'[135] Labour MP for Gisborne Allan Wallbank discussed the topic with Prebble at the reopening, and reported to his constituents that a revived service might be possible if the community made a proposal that was attractive to NZR.[136] They did not succeed, and the line beyond Napier has been goods only ever since.

The train from Palmerston North through the northern Wairarapa to Masterton and Wellington concluded less dramatically. Local roads had been improved and travellers between Palmerston North and Wellington had quicker options via the coast, so this train's market was a modest clientele between the Wairarapa and Manawatū. It did not help that the station for Pahīatua, the largest town in the northern Wairarapa, was 2 kilometres from the town centre. Treasury had wanted to cut trains north

of Masterton as early as 1976 during the demise of the Fiats; at the same time it had also proposed to offer a Masterton–Wellington service only once daily – with no explanation as to why this would be adequate when the Remutaka Tunnel made rail travel preferable to road.[137] Trains continued serving the northern Wairarapa for more than a decade, but NZR gradually whittled down the timetable. Weekend and evening trains ceased first, followed by the weekday train, which ran north of Masterton for the last time on 29 July 1988. NZR retained the Masterton–Wellington leg, offering three weekday services between the Wairarapa's main town and the capital.[138]

During this period, NZR lacked support at the highest levels of politics. Muldoon's government had merged NAC with international carrier Air New Zealand in 1978 – not without controversy – and competition between air and rail became more intense during the 1980s.[139] A Silver Fern railcar took just under 12 hours to run Auckland–Wellington; an Air New Zealand flight on a Boeing 737 took an hour. Minister of Railways Richard Prebble made the unhelpful claim that a plane 'can do 12 trips in the same time as it takes the railcar to do one'.[140] This was obvious hyperbole. No single commercial airliner has ever flown Auckland–Wellington return six times in 12 hours. The only person who could believe it is one who has never been to an airport to witness the lengthy taxiing, refuelling, safety checks, catering, cleaning and transfer of people and luggage. Prebble's exaggerated rhetoric also ignored all the intermediate journeys for which trains catered and planes could not. As minister of railways, he ought to have been attuned to the Silver Fern's ability to link cities and towns the length of the island. With friends like him, NZR did not need enemies.

1989: THE PLATFORMS ARE QUIET

Dismissing community support for passenger rail as mere emotional attachment became a bad habit that ultimately wasted a valuable resource. When a Lyttelton resident wrote to NZR in favour of passenger trains in 1972, the district traffic manager responded by contrasting the writer's 'sentimental references' with 'economics, [which] now feature as a most important factor'.[141] The argument recurred frequently over the next two decades. Whether in Alexandra, Pahīatua or Stratford, people had to 'face facts'. This shifted the blame: cancellations became the community's fault for supporting rail poorly rather than NZR's fault for unsatisfactory service provision or the government's for under-investment. Public goodwill and enthusiasm could well have been tapped to revive flagging services. Instead, as one popular travel guide told visitors in 1985, NZR's main aim appeared to be 'to dissuade people from using trains'.[142]

New Zealand at the end of the 1980s had an attenuated passenger rail network. Expresses still ran the length of the North and South Island Main Trunks, but only three other trains operated beyond greater Wellington and Auckland: the Wellington–Napier *Bay Express*, Wellington–Masterton, and the Christchurch–Greymouth *TranzAlpine*. Suburban trains in Christchurch and Dunedin were gone, mixed and with-car goods trains were a thing of the past, and country residents could no longer depend on trains to visit service towns. The corporatisation of NZR had spelled the end for what few rural trains remained. Almost every major passenger rail decision taken from the 1950s had negative implications. Within NZR, some officials ignored available opportunities or treated passenger traffic as a nuisance. Politicians failed to invest in rail until it was too late, then used specious language of inevitability to justify cancellations.

Unfortunately, NZR was sometimes its own worst enemy: its quality of service could be poor, and many travellers never returned. Physicist Shaun Hendy wondered what he might experience when he quit his frequent-flyer habits for the 2018 calendar year and opted instead to travel the country by rail and bus. He recalled how, in the 1980s, 'trains got you places, but seldom on time and sometimes not the places you expected'.[143] It was hard to maintain a good service with obsolete rollingstock and low morale, predictable outcomes of decades of under-investment. Ganz-Mávag electric units had revitalised Wellington's commuter network, but NZR's discussions with Ganz-Mávag representatives about purchasing railbuses for Auckland – lightweight railcars with bus-like design attributes or components – did not culminate in an order.[144] Instead, a fixation on motorway expansion induced commuters to abandon mediocre trains. The ARA followed its 1983 recommendations with a study in August 1988 that suggested replacing suburban trains with guided busways like the O-Bahn in Adelaide, South Australia.[145] There was little reason in 1989 to believe that passenger rail had a future in New Zealand beyond Wellington.

7

1970–1989

HELENSVILLE

Helensville–Waitākere resumed 2008

Helensville–Waitākere ceased 2009
Waitākere–Swanson ceased 2015

Extenstion to new Britomart station opened 2003
City Rail Link (Britomart–Mount Eden) to open 2024

Penrose–Onehunga resumed 2010

Wiri–Manukau commenced 2010

Waitākere
Swanson
Henderson
AUCKLAND (Britomart)
Onehunga
Ōtāhuhu
Manukau
Papakura
Drury
Pukekohe
Mercer
Waikato R.
Huntly
Ngāruawāhia
HAMILTON
FRANKTON
Te Awamutu
Ōtorohanga

Upper North Island
1990–2020

C^H 8

1990–2020
The false dawn

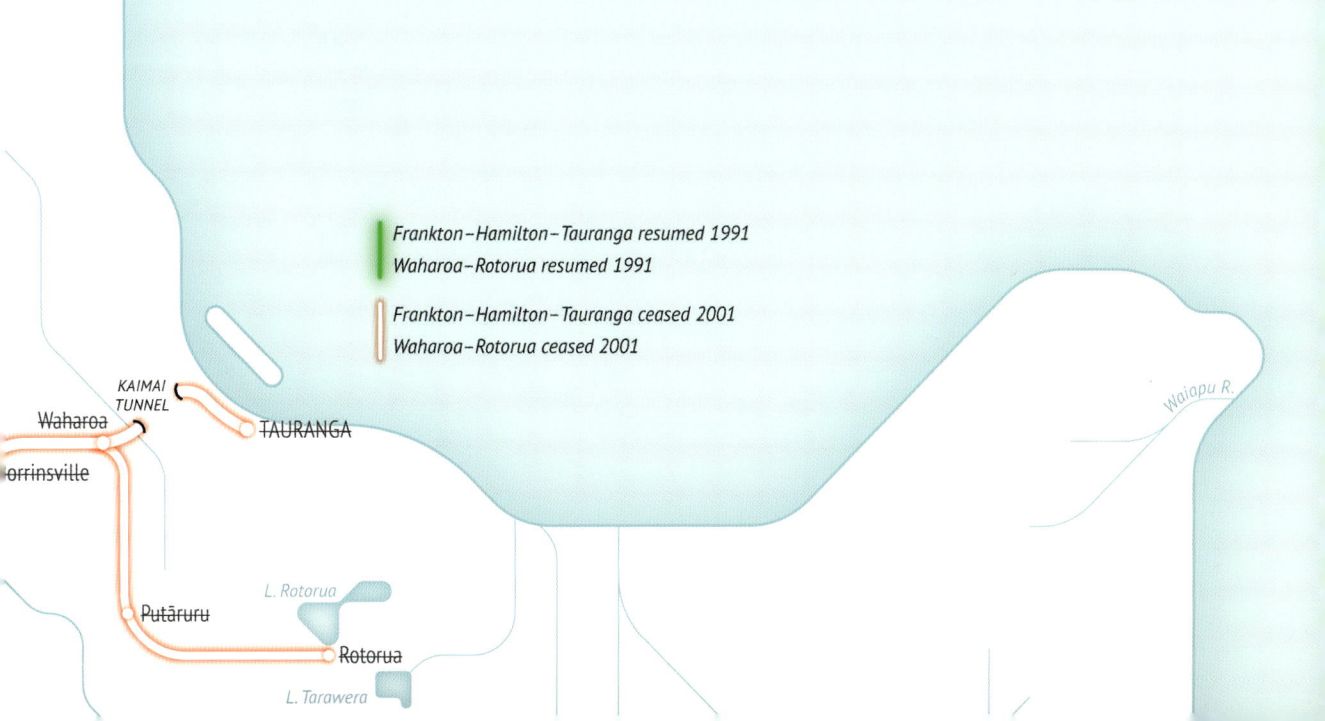

	Frankton–Hamilton–Tauranga resumed 1991
	Waharoa–Rotorua resumed 1991
	Frankton–Hamilton–Tauranga ceased 2001
	Waharoa–Rotorua ceased 2001

Waiapu R.

KAIMAI
TUNNEL

Waharoa

TAURANGA

Morrinsville

L. Rotorua

Putāruru

Rotorua

L. Tarawera

Ōtorohanga

Te Kūiti

L. Tarawera

Waikato R.

Mōkau R.

L. Taupō

Taumarunui

▲ *Mt Tongariro*

▲ *Mt Ngāuruhoe*

National Park

▲ *Mt Ruapehu*

Ohakune

Waiōuru

Mt Taranaki ▲

Taihape

Rangitīkei R.

Waitōtara R.

Whanganui R.

Marton

~~Ormondville~~

~~Dannevirke~~

Feilding

Woodville

PALMERSTON NORTH

~~Woodville~~

Shannon

Levin

Ōtaki

Waikanae

○ MASTERTON

Paekākāriki

Carterton

Featherston

L. Wairarapa

Melling

Johnsonville

Upper Hutt

Waterloo

WELLINGTON

238

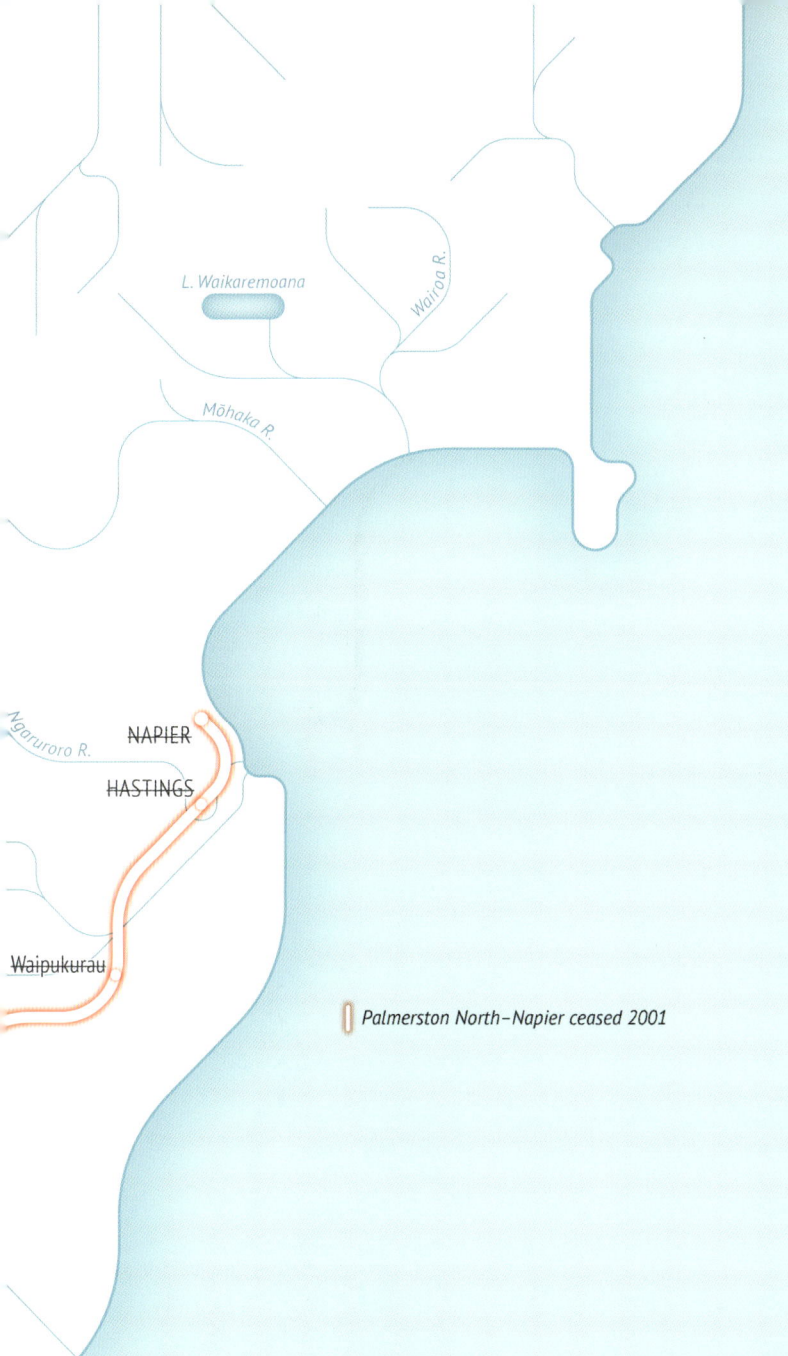

L. Waikaremoana

Wairoa R.

Mōhaka R.

Ngaruroro R.

NAPIER

HASTINGS

Waipukurau

Palmerston North–Napier ceased 2001

Lower North Island
1990–2020

Upper South Island
1990–2020

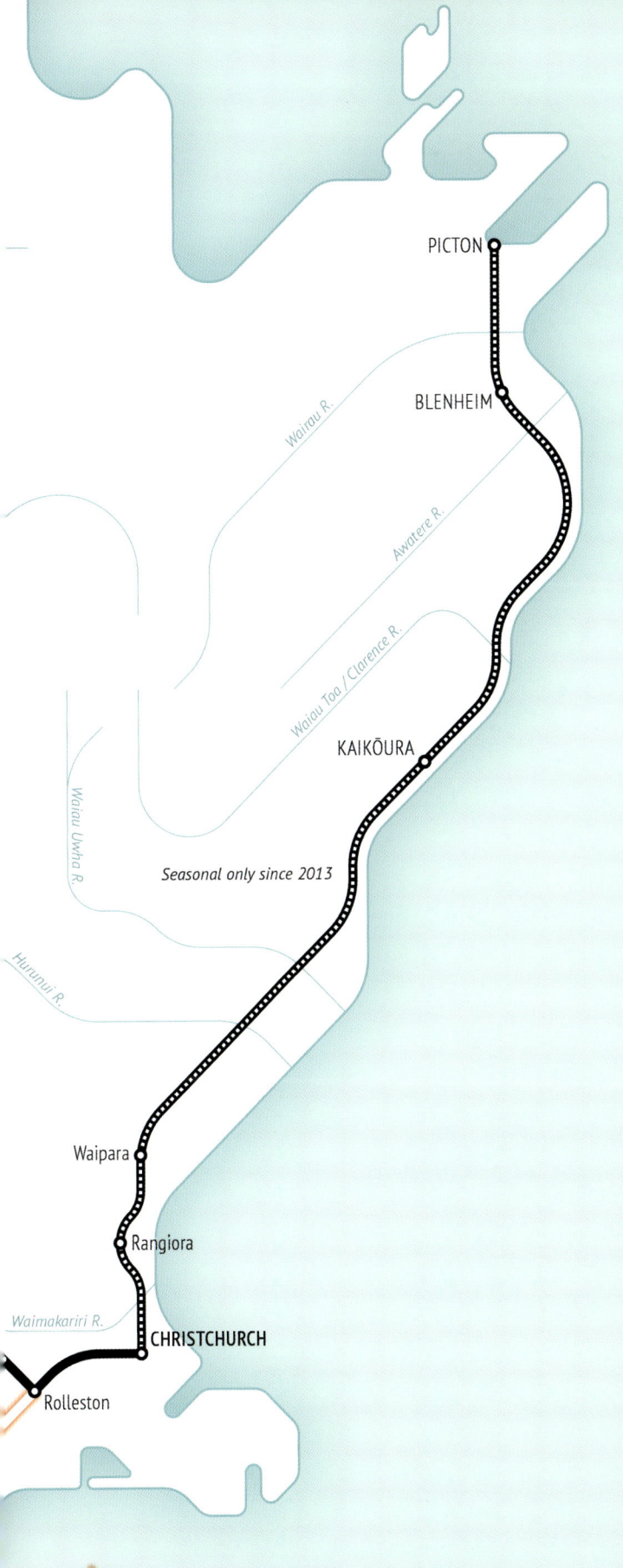

PICTON

Wairau R.

BLENHEIM

Awatere R.

Waiau Toa / Clarence R.

KAIKŌURA

Waiau Uwha R.

Seasonal only since 2013

Hurunui R.

Waipara

Rangiora

Waimakariri R.

CHRISTCHURCH

Rolleston

Rolleston–Invercargill ceased 2002

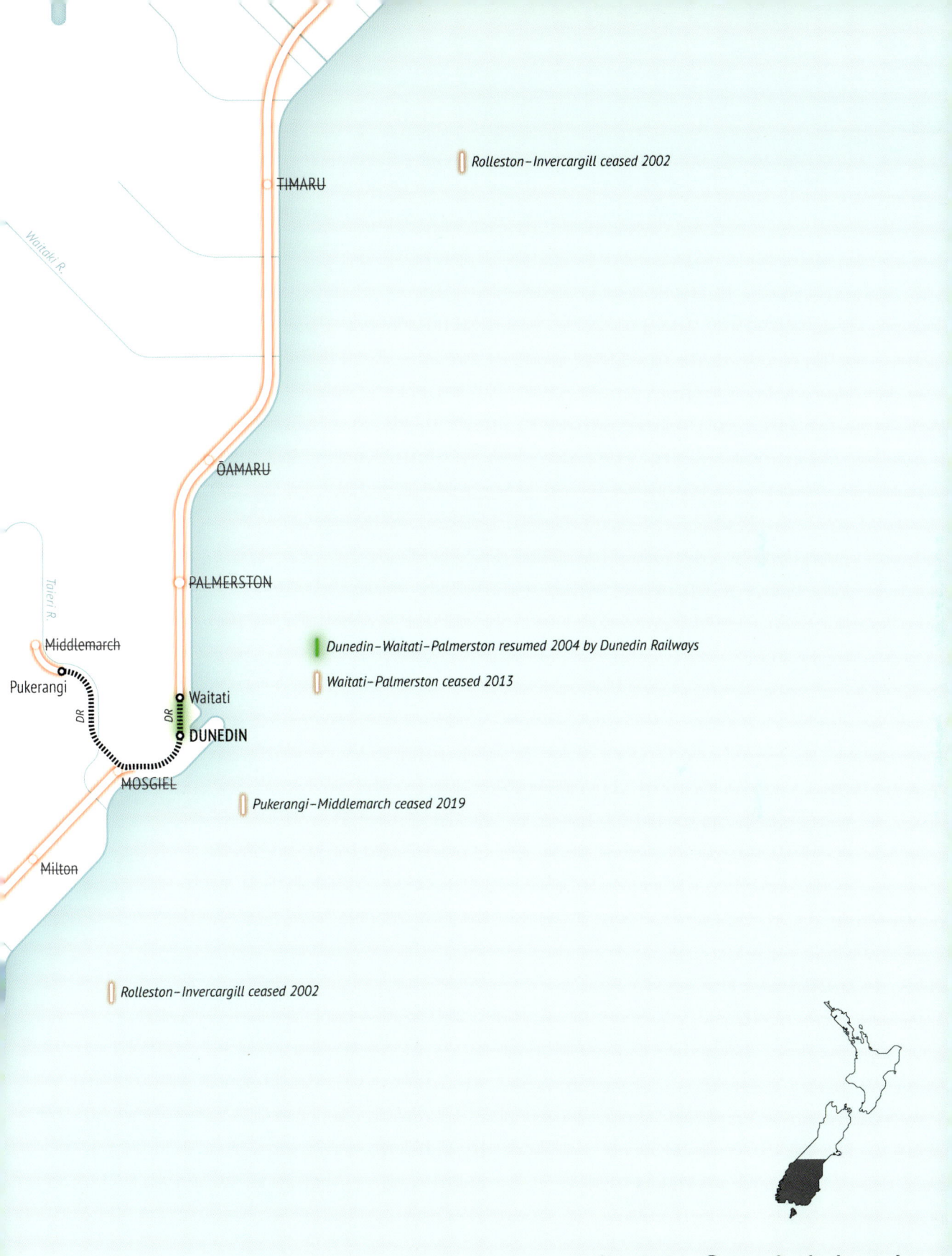

Rolleston–Invercargill ceased 2002

TIMARU

Waitaki R.

ŌAMARU

Taieri R.

PALMERSTON

Dunedin–Waitati–Palmerston resumed 2004 by Dunedin Railways

Waitati–Palmerston ceased 2013

Middlemarch

Pukerangi

DR

Waitati

DR

DUNEDIN

MOSGIEL

Pukerangi–Middlemarch ceased 2019

Milton

Rolleston–Invercargill ceased 2002

Lower South Island
1990-2020

In 1990, in town and country, road transport defined mobility for New Zealanders. It was costly. Auckland, Christchurch and Wellington in the early 1990s each spent 14–15.5 percent of their gross regional product on direct costs for all passenger transport, public and private – a very high proportion internationally: the US average was 12.5 percent. Much of this expenditure was on private vehicles and associated infrastructure. Compact European cities spent less, but so did other places: Toronto, a more suitable analogue, spent 7.4 percent. In general, researchers found that cities with stronger public transit networks, especially rail, spent a lower proportion of their wealth on transport.[1] But the costs of car dependency sometimes seemed abstract, and often were ascertained only in hindsight.

The winds of neoliberalism had blown across New Zealand, as they did in many advanced economies. Governments on both sides of politics were committed to the idea that New Zealand's railways had to be run on narrow business lines to be efficient. Not only did NZR have to cover capital and operating costs far beyond those of its competitors, but more than a century of state investment in rail infrastructure now had virtually no protection. Both Labour and National baulked at applying commercial principles to the road network, which received substantial public funding for maintenance and upgrades. Transit New Zealand, a precursor to today's Waka Kotahi New Zealand Transport Agency (NZTA), had multi-modal responsibilities but focused on road investment and guided funds away from other transport, reflecting its origins as the National Roads Board.[2]

Deregulation was not a good-news story for every road hauler as it sparked fierce competition among providers as well as with rail. To older generations, this was a wasteful and inefficient use of facilities that ought to be co-ordinated. Now, the market was seen as selecting 'winners', despite the funding disparity for physical infrastructure. Rural branch lines were frequent losers: like passenger rail, the goods network contracted.

The effects were personal and profound for many New Zealanders. NZR employed over 20,800 people in March 1982; nine years later staff numbers had dropped to 5900. The contraction was well in excess of the 1500–2000 job losses that Muldoon's government had anticipated when it approved deregulation.[3] 'Railway towns' had to find new identities and industries in the 1990s – or simply shrank.

Riven with internal disagreements, David Lange's Labour government imploded during its second term. Lange quit the leadership in August 1989, setting off a revolving door of prime ministers. Before losing power, however, Labour separated New Zealand Rail Limited from the New Zealand Railways Corporation. NZR Ltd possessed the track and owned and operated trains; the corporation retained the land beneath the track.[4] The move was made partly to protect the railway corridor and also with an eye to Treaty of Waitangi claims, as the Court of Appeal's landmark 1987 decision in *New Zealand Maori Council v. Attorney-General* prevented state-owned enterprises from disposing of land to which Māori had claim.

Jim Bolger led National to victory in the October 1990 election and became the fourth prime minister in under 15 months. His government was set on privatisation. First to go was the Speedlink parcels service, which NZR sold to New Zealand Post in March 1991. Then, in July, a consortium of bus companies acquired the buses and InterCity brand, ending 65 years of Road Services.[5] Cityline became CityRail; Auckland Regional Council, successor of the ARA, acquired Auckland's suburban trains in May 1991 and contracted NZR to operate them to 1993. This was soon revised to 2003.[6] Wellington's trains remained under the aegis of CityRail.

Finally, it was NZR Limited's turn to go on the market. The move was part of a wider trend: governments throughout Australasia were privatising railways, and New Zealand had sold numerous other state assets including Air New Zealand, the Bank of New Zealand, the National Film Unit and phone provider Telecom. A consortium of domestic and international investors led by merchant bankers Fay, Richwhite and Co. along with US railway Wisconsin Central purchased NZR Ltd in 1993, and two years later renamed it Tranz Rail. Now it was time to find out whether private enterprise could deliver passenger services superior to those of a public railway.

1991: REVIVAL?

NZR no longer provided a service; it sold a product: travel. The end of Road Services made that a greater challenge. Since the 1920s NZR had shifted passengers nationwide from rail to road; the sale of InterCity buses meant it now had to win those passengers back.

The success of the *TranzAlpine* and other reinvigorated offerings in the late 1980s led to further refurbishment of rollingstock. Despite longstanding plans for their reuse, this did not include the *Silver Star* carriages, which were deemed too costly to rebuild because of the presence of asbestos. NZR sold these in 1990 to a buyer who renovated them for the *Eastern*

and Oriental Express between Singapore and Bangkok, a role they still serve today.

Some of NZR's existing routes gained improved services. One of these, the *Capital Connection*, initially the *CityRail Express*, began between Palmerston North and Wellington in April 1991. Rather than reviving the Wairarapa route that had ended in 1988, the *Capital Connection* passed through rapidly growing towns in Horowhenua and the Kāpiti Coast and was timetabled to suit city workers. (CityRail did not forget the Wairarapa: it rebranded Masterton trains as the *Wairarapa Connection* from 31 May 1993.) Most significantly, on 2 December 1991 NZR replaced the daytime Silver Fern railcars between Wellington and Auckland with a carriage train, the *Overlander*.[7] This allowed the railcars to be redeployed and the network to expand.

NZR now set its sights on tourist travel. It established two new Silver Fern routes from Auckland: the *Geyserland Express* to Rotorua and the *Kaimai Express* to Tauranga, which was booming as a city, port and holiday destination. Communities in the Bay of Plenty had clamoured for passenger trains ever since the cancellations of 1967–68.[8] Their efforts paid off: the twice-daily *Geyserland Express* began on 9 December 1991, followed by the once-daily *Kaimai Express* on the 10th. The *Kaimai Express* was the first new service since 1955 to use a railway line never before employed for passenger trains: instead of the circuitous trip to Tauranga through the Karangahake and Athenree gorges, it now passed through the 8879m tunnel under the Kaimai Range and took under three and a half hours. There was talk of extending the *Kaimai Express* to Mount Maunganui, but this did not happen because the branch to the Mount had no passenger facilities.[9]

Silver Fern railcar RM 30 with a Tauranga-bound *Kaimai Express* at Matamata, 5 January 1992.

Christine Johnson, New Zealand Railway & Locomotive Society collection

Right: A service comprising two ADK/ADB diesel multiple units at Ōtāhuhu on 20 March 2014. This class was the older of the two acquired from Perth. New electric wires are visible; in September that year, electric trains displaced the ADK/ADB class entirely.

Simon Mathew

There was a hitch in Rotorua. NZR in 1988 had decided to relocate the railway station and yard from the centre of town to Koutu, in Rotorua's northern suburbs. Koutu was closer to the industries that goods trains served, and the move had released for sale valuable land in the heart of Rotorua. The old yard was dismantled during 1989, and in July 1990 the minister of railways gave permission to lift the remaining 2.4 kilometres of track that ran into the centre of the city.[10] This short-sighted decision meant the *Geyserland Express* had to terminate at a nondescript platform in the suburbs. NZR announced in September 1995 that it would build a new passenger terminus in the city close to the old station's location, but this never came to pass.[11]

The future of passenger rail looked bright when it passed into private hands. For the first time since the New Plymouth run ended in 1971, long-distance trains were now departing Auckland for destinations other than Wellington. Travel times compared well with road, and the onboard experience surpassed anything a bus could provide. New Zealand's regional trains had formerly been pitched to local communities, shoppers, businessmen (the gendered term is intentional: NZR marketed to business*men*) and families travelling during school holidays. Now the trains were named expresses and targeted as much at tourists as anyone else. As the 1990s wore on, this tourist market would supersede all others.

1993–2000: PRIVATISATION AND THE PASSENGER TRAIN

The extent of the passenger rail network remained unchanged for the rest of the 1990s despite the turbulence surrounding ownership of the trains. Even the Auckland suburban network survived the decade. Initially its prospects did not look promising: from patronage of almost 4 million in 1960, Aucklanders took just over 1 million journeys per year in the early 1990s. Enter Raymond Siddalls, the manager of CityRail Auckland, who restructured operations so that the 120 daily services returned a profit, and cannily negotiated a cheap purchase of 19 diesel multiple units from Perth. Western

Australia's capital had electrified its suburban network and no longer needed diesel trains, some of which had been built in 1982–85 and were relatively new. Even the older units, from 1967–68, were a major improvement on Auckland's carriages, which dated from 1936. The units arrived in 1993 and within a decade patronage had more than doubled.[12] A new central terminus, Britomart, opened in 2003 after a protracted urban planning debate, in which relocation of the railway station was not controversial but almost every related issue was. Siddalls played a role in Britomart's success, too, and deserves much credit for the fact that Auckland's suburban network has endured. For once, foresight and sound choices replaced inertia, bad decisions and a lack of imagination. To take a phrase from Graham Bush, a sharp observer of Auckland's history, the 1990s represented a transition from survival to revival for the city's public transport.[13]

This revival did not spread to the rest of the network, however. Tranz Rail's financial performance declined significantly after its listing on the New Zealand Stock Exchange and New York's NASDAQ in 1995. Philip Laird, inaugural national chair of the Railway Technical Society of Australasia, observed that although Tranz Rail initially grew freight traffic, it neither met maintenance demands nor monetised the wider environmental and social benefits of rail. A fixation on the most profitable revenue sources undermined others that contributed to the overall health of the network.[14] A similar pattern emerged with passenger traffic.

Long-distance Services
1991–2002

These maps depict the long-distance network between the service upgrades of 1991 and cancellations of 2001–2002.

Not all stations are shown.

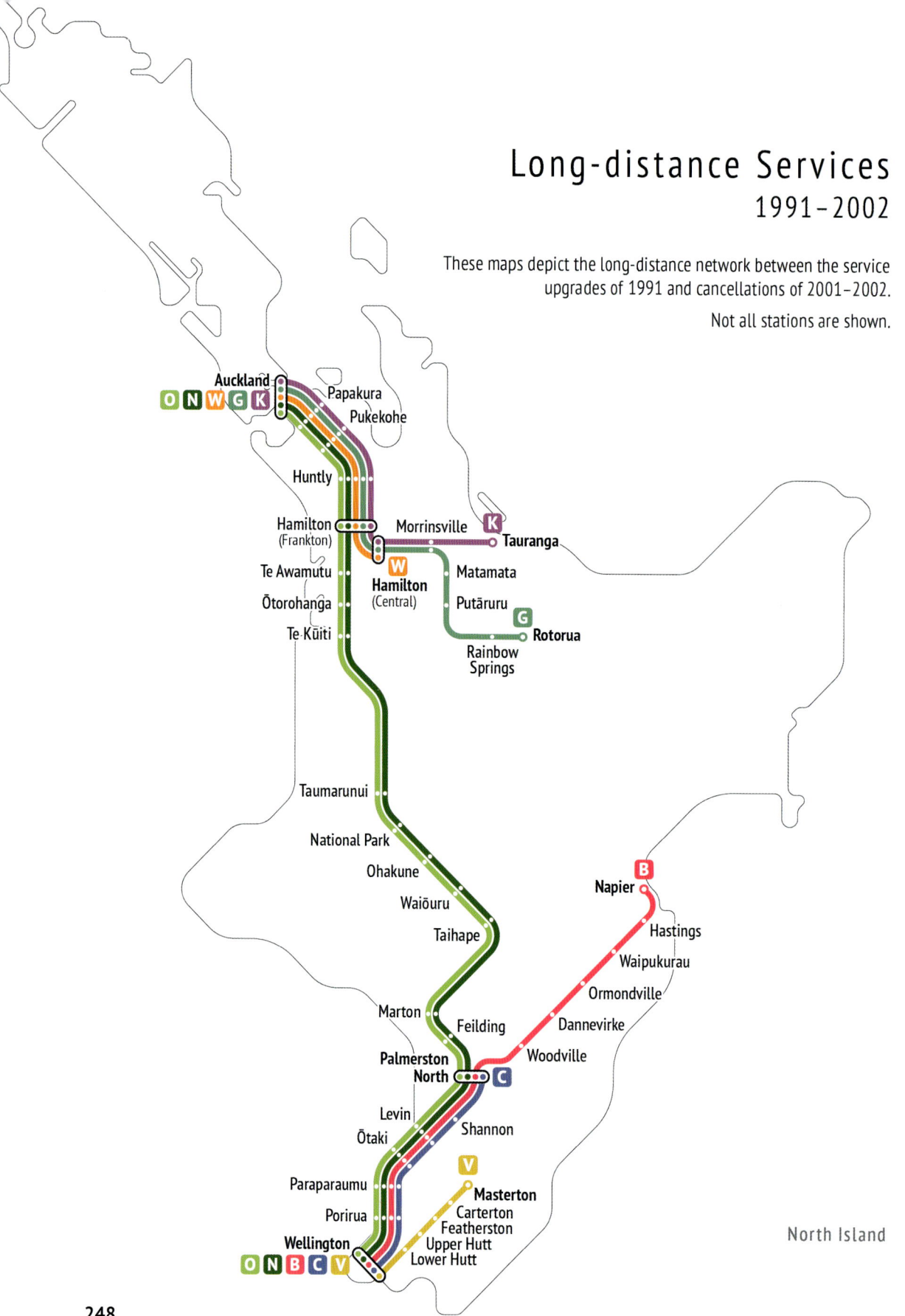

North Island

NORTH ISLAND SERVICES

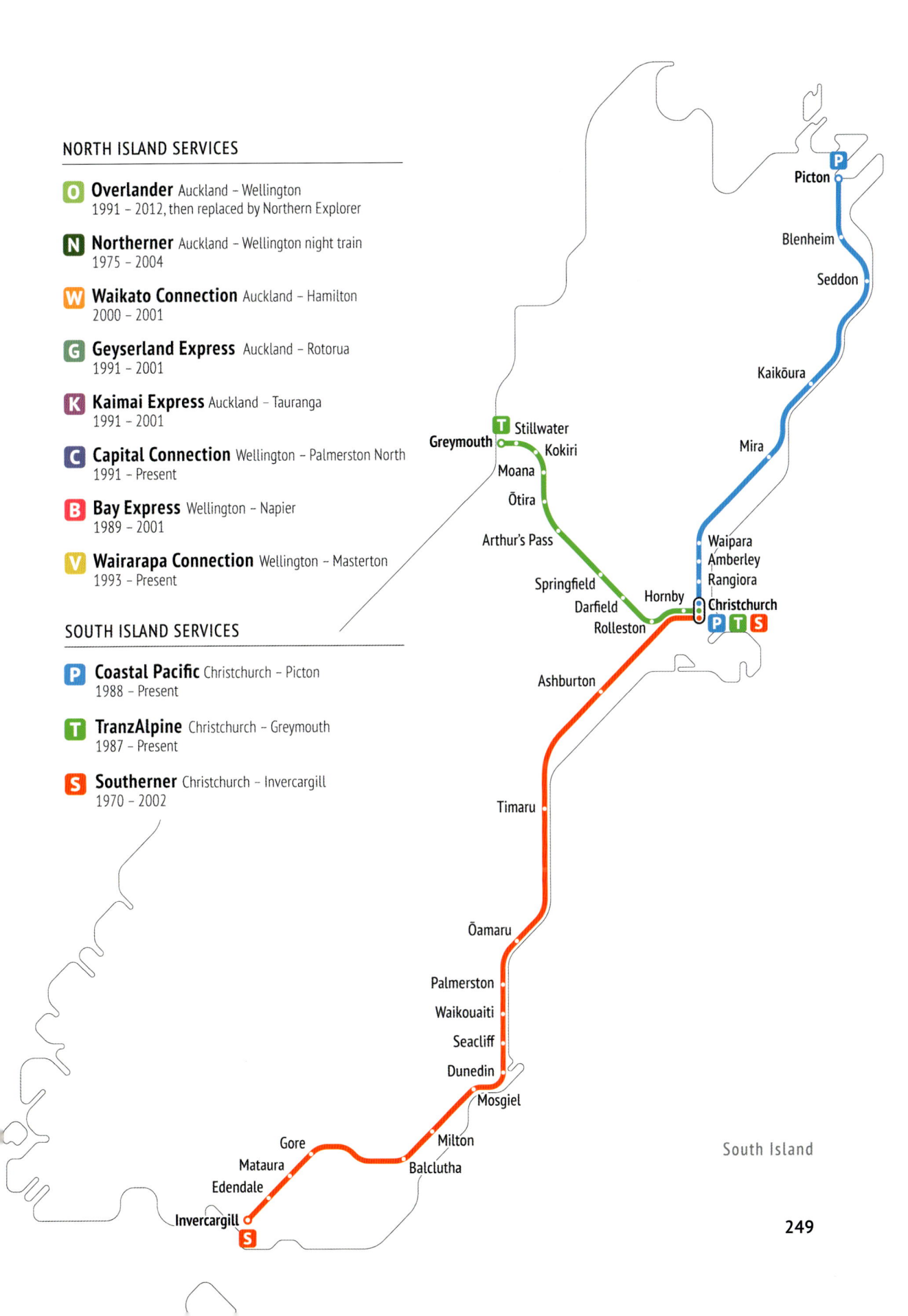

O **Overlander** Auckland – Wellington
1991 – 2012, then replaced by Northern Explorer

N **Northerner** Auckland – Wellington night train
1975 – 2004

W **Waikato Connection** Auckland – Hamilton
2000 – 2001

G **Geyserland Express** Auckland – Rotorua
1991 – 2001

K **Kaimai Express** Auckland – Tauranga
1991 – 2001

C **Capital Connection** Wellington – Palmerston North
1991 – Present

B **Bay Express** Wellington – Napier
1989 – 2001

V **Wairarapa Connection** Wellington – Masterton
1993 – Present

SOUTH ISLAND SERVICES

P **Coastal Pacific** Christchurch – Picton
1988 – Present

T **TranzAlpine** Christchurch – Greymouth
1987 – Present

S **Southerner** Christchurch – Invercargill
1970 – 2002

South Island

Rail travel suffered serious reputational damage from high-profile accidents in the first years of privatisation. On 25 August 1993 a truck collided with the *Southerner* in Rolleston, resulting in the deaths of three passengers.[15] Then, on 2 July 1994, six-year-old Morgan Jones fell from a gangway between two carriages of the *Coastal Pacific* when a handrail became dislodged. Jones was blinded and lost his right leg below the knee; his family's campaign for compensation captured national attention and culminated in an out-of-court settlement.[16] Tranz Rail also experienced at least 22 accidents from 1993 to 2000 that killed or seriously injured staff. Public outcry prompted a ministerial inquiry that found the company's safety standards and regulatory framework unsatisfactory.[17] The tragedies reflected poorly on the railway and its new owners, and Tranz Rail was singularly inept at restoring its image.

Long-distance trains struggled with custom, and one reason for this was the increasingly single-minded focus on the tourism market. Tranz Rail had successes: its Great Train Escapes – 74 holiday packages that combined train travel, accommodation and attractions – won the New Zealand Tourism Board's Supreme Award in July 1997.[18] But it was not the lasting solution for passenger rail that it appeared to be. The success of the *TranzAlpine* in scooping the tourism market seemed to suggest that *any* service could be a strong earner if it cornered this lucrative revenue stream. The train's name had inspired that of Tranz Rail, and the rebranding of the long-distance passenger division as Tranz Scenic further articulated the emphasis on tourism. But rail travel in New Zealand had many markets, some of which were surrendered without a fight, and Tranz Rail effectively pitted its own train journeys against

each other in the competition for leisure travel.

By the end of the 1990s Tranz Rail had become notorious for asset-stripping. It was in a strong financial position when privatised, but rather than buying new rollingstock or other assets it used debt to fund the shareholding of its original investors, who made a quick and mainly tax-free profit of $370m.[19] Much of the track was little better than in the 1930s. Indeed, some trains were now slower than in previous decades despite making fewer stops. Although tourists are not always time sensitive and consider a scenic journey part of the experience, the same cannot be said for business travellers, who value speed and punctuality. Rising fares put families off, the gradual elimination of stops deterred local travellers, and timetables targeted at tourists were often unsuitable for commuters or shoppers.

The fact that rail passenger numbers declined at the end of the 1990s despite the parlous state of the two major domestic airlines is a damning indictment of Tranz Rail. In April 2001 Ansett New Zealand went into liquidation, and later that year Helen Clark's Labour government renationalised a near-bankrupt Air New Zealand after the airline's foray into the Australian domestic market created a large operating loss.[20] If Tranz Rail had committed to upgrading routes and timetables, if it had provided a service that appealed to a wider clientele, and if it had marketed its products effectively and fostered a positive public image, long-distance passenger rail might have entered the new millennium in good health. Instead, Tranz Rail was so notorious that it won the inaugural Roger Award for the worst transnational corporation in New Zealand. In the first six years of the award, during which it enjoyed considerable media coverage, Tranz Rail won three times – in 1997,

2000 and 2002 – and was a finalist or runner-up in the other three. After that the organisers deemed the corporation ineligible for further awards and 'shunted' it into a 'Hall of Shame' in order to 'let somebody else have a go'.[21]

2001–02: THE REGIONAL PASSENGER TRAIN'S ANNUS HORRIBILIS

Efforts to revitalise and rebrand New Zealand's long-distance passenger trains largely came to nothing. Poor marketing, asset-stripping, aging rollingstock and a failure to upgrade infrastructure meant that trains that ought to have been viable were not. Tranz Scenic made one last effort to regain a market when it commenced the *Waikato Connection* between Hamilton and Auckland on 26 June 2000, but by this point the organisation was already undergoing a two-year restructure that would see it sell the passenger operations.[22] In the second half of 2000 passenger revenue was $63.9m, up $5.6m on the same period in 1999, but Tranz Rail's overall revenue showed a $6.7m loss compared to a net profit of $21m in 1999.[23] Making no apologies for this or other reductions in services, the company chose to focus on bulk freight and shifted most non-containerised commodities to road. Passenger trains were a soft target: passengers were not part of the company's 'core business', so they had to go.[24] Helen Clark led Labour to victory at the polls in 1999, by which point many of the party members who had been most enthusiastic about privatisation had left, but the new government did not intervene in Tranz Rail's activities during its first term.

Tranz Rail offered its long-distance trains for sale in October 2000 with tenders to close on 9 March 2001.[25] The package included the intercity commuter trains *Capital Connection* and *Waikato Connection* but not their *Wairarapa Connection* sibling, which ran entirely within Greater Wellington Regional Council's boundaries under the auspices of Tranz Metro, not Tranz Scenic. Australian company West Coast Railway (WCR) bid for the *Capital Connection*, the *Coastal Pacific*, the *Northerner*, the *Overlander* and the *TranzAlpine*.

No tenders had been received for the others by late June 2001.[26] It is astonishing that the railcar services from Auckland to Rotorua and Tauranga were not considered attractive. Even if the focus on tourists had come at the expense of other clientele, both routes ought to have been viable: they took scarcely any longer than buses, and comfort typically beats time sensitivity for leisure travellers. But Tranz Scenic had marketed the railcars so poorly that they had become unprofitable. It had reined in costs by reducing the *Geyserland Express* from twice to once daily in April 1995; Fridays and Sundays retained two services until November 1996. As in the past, the reduced frequency discouraged passengers: between 1996 and 2000 average patronage fell 24 percent to 33 passengers per trip on railcars that could carry 96. Over the same period the *Kaimai Express* lost 19.5 percent of its patronage, carrying on average just 30 people per trip. The infant *Waikato Connection* depended on a dozen regulars, one of whom noted, 'There's just been no marketing at all.' In the spirit of Tranz Rail's general disregard for passengers, managing director Michael Beard suggested the *Northerner* as an alternative. Considering this left Hamilton at 4.54am, it was a laughable proposition for commuters.[27]

Managing director of WCR Don Gibson indicated a willingness to negotiate with central and local governments about subsidies and

The former Koutu station platform on Rotorua's northern fringe, 13 December 2019. The station once had modest facilities including a waiting room. The billboard advertises a tourism venture, RailCruising, which uses the line between Mamaku and Tarukenga in the hills behind Rotorua. André Brett

other support to operate the services for which it had not lodged a bid.[28] For the *Bay Express*, which of all the services to be cut showed the smallest loss, chances of survival appeared good. During a meeting with government representatives on 28 June 2001, WCR agreed that an annual subsidy of $200,000–300,000 for three years would be sufficient.[29] Napier mayor Alan Dick co-ordinated efforts to save the *Bay Express*. Locomotive driver Alan Brabender raised an obvious avenue to improve patronage: to reinstate the buses that before privatisation had connected with the train in Napier for destinations north.[30] Other proposals suggested building on the popularity of Hawke's Bay's vineyards by luring wine connoisseurs to the train, and included re-routing it via the Wairarapa and extending it to Gisborne to link these three East Coast wine regions.[31]

Gibson and his colleague Gary McDonald,

chair of WCR, rode the *Bay Express* in July and met with interested parties in Napier. Afterwards Gibson told the *Dominion* he was 'quite optimistic' that the company might acquire it.[32] But at the start of August, when WCR presented a business plan to save the train, the company requested an annual subsidy of $1m, which surprised and disappointed government representatives.[33] Hawke's Bay Regional Council chair Ross Bramwell sheeted the blame to Tranz Rail, accusing them of demanding too high a rental from WCR.[34] His council declined to contribute funds, and Manawatū–Whanganui Regional Council and Horowhenua District Council did likewise.[35] Dick made last-ditch attempts to save the train but his efforts were in vain. Palmerston North city councillors discussed his representations and, like their Hawke's Bay counterparts, passed the blame to Tranz Rail.[36]

The *Geyserland Express* and *Kaimai Express* were in a more parlous position, requiring annual subsidies above $1m.[37] This was a challenge for the relevant local authorities; one subsidy alone was a steep call on their finances, and most were liable to support both trains. By late August it was clear that neither service would be saved. The Silver Fern railcars were ostensibly wanted for more profitable routes, so despite representations by eight affected local bodies, there would be no rollingstock to continue the *Geyserland Express*, *Kaimai Express* or *Waikato Connection*. South Waikato's mayor, Gordon Blake, described himself as 'bloody gutted' by the outcome.[38] The railcars ended up running as Auckland suburban services to Pukekohe, then charters for KiwiRail and Dunedin Railways. The Pahīatua Railcar Society purchased them for preservation in September 2020.

All of the affected North Island services were originally scheduled to cease on 30 September 2001. Tranz Rail, in perhaps the blandest possible expression of generosity, extended this to 7 October, the end of the school holidays.[39] After a decade of passenger services, railways east of Hamilton reverted to being goods only. The Palmerston North–Napier railway also became goods only, ending over a century of passenger trains. A crowd in Napier farewelled the last *Bay Express*, and passengers were quick to follow their elected representatives in blaming Tranz Rail.[40] The *Wairarapa Connection* became – and remains – the only passenger train to travel east of the mountain ranges that run from Wellington up the east coast. Thanks to the Remutaka Tunnel, trains are quicker and more convenient than the notoriously treacherous Remutaka Hill Road, which is often closed in bad weather.

The *Southerner* survived into 2002. It was not included in the October 2001 cull because talks in the South Island were more promising than those in the north. Some councils were prepared to contribute to the $500,000–600,000 annual subsidy that WCR requested.[41] Jim Anderton, Minister of Economic Development, committed $140,000 of central government funds to maintain the service for four months beyond October, and $30,000 for a feasibility study.[42] These efforts came to naught. The study suggested the *Southerner* could be viable, even profitable in the longer term, if annual patronage could be increased from 50,000 to 90,000. Media coverage – which likely provided better publicity than Tranz Rail ever had – drove a short surge in bookings, but this fell back quickly.[43] Anderton pointed out to local representatives that three times as many people hired a car to travel to Invercargill as rode the *Southerner*.[44] Of course, part of the reason for this was that the train ran infrequently and on a line urgently in need of upgrades. But in truth, the appetite to fund appealing passenger trains was simply not there; once again, buses were flagged as the alternative.

The *Southerner* ended on 10 February 2002 and affected communities felt the loss keenly. Mayor of Invercargill Tim Shadbolt had fought diligently to save the service, and described the loss as 'a bit like attending the funeral of an old friend'.[45] On the final run from Christchurch to Invercargill he led singalongs of 'Auld Lang Syne' and 'Morningtown Ride'. The train ran an hour late because large crowds turned out to bid it farewell. Supporters sought autographs from staff, children were given tours of the locomotive cab, and in true Southland style a highland piper joined the crowd that welcomed the train into Invercargill.[46] Green Party co-leader Rod Donald, who also rode the last train, spoke

The South Island railway network south of Rolleston was goods only after the end of the *Southerner*, with one important exception: the *Taieri Gorge Limited* between Dunedin and Middlemarch.[47] Taieri Gorge Railway was going from strength to strength in the early 2000s and operated a regular timetable through the gorge to Pukerangi. The train continued to Middlemarch once or twice a week, although some years not in winter. Travellers bound for Queenstown could take the train to Pukerangi for a bus connection, and frequent charters collected passengers from cruise ships docked at Port Chalmers.

One popular summer excursion nicknamed the *Seasider* ran north from Dunedin to Palmerston. From September to March 2004–05, Taieri Gorge Railway incorporated the *Seasider* into its timetable alongside the *Taieri Gorge Limited* and

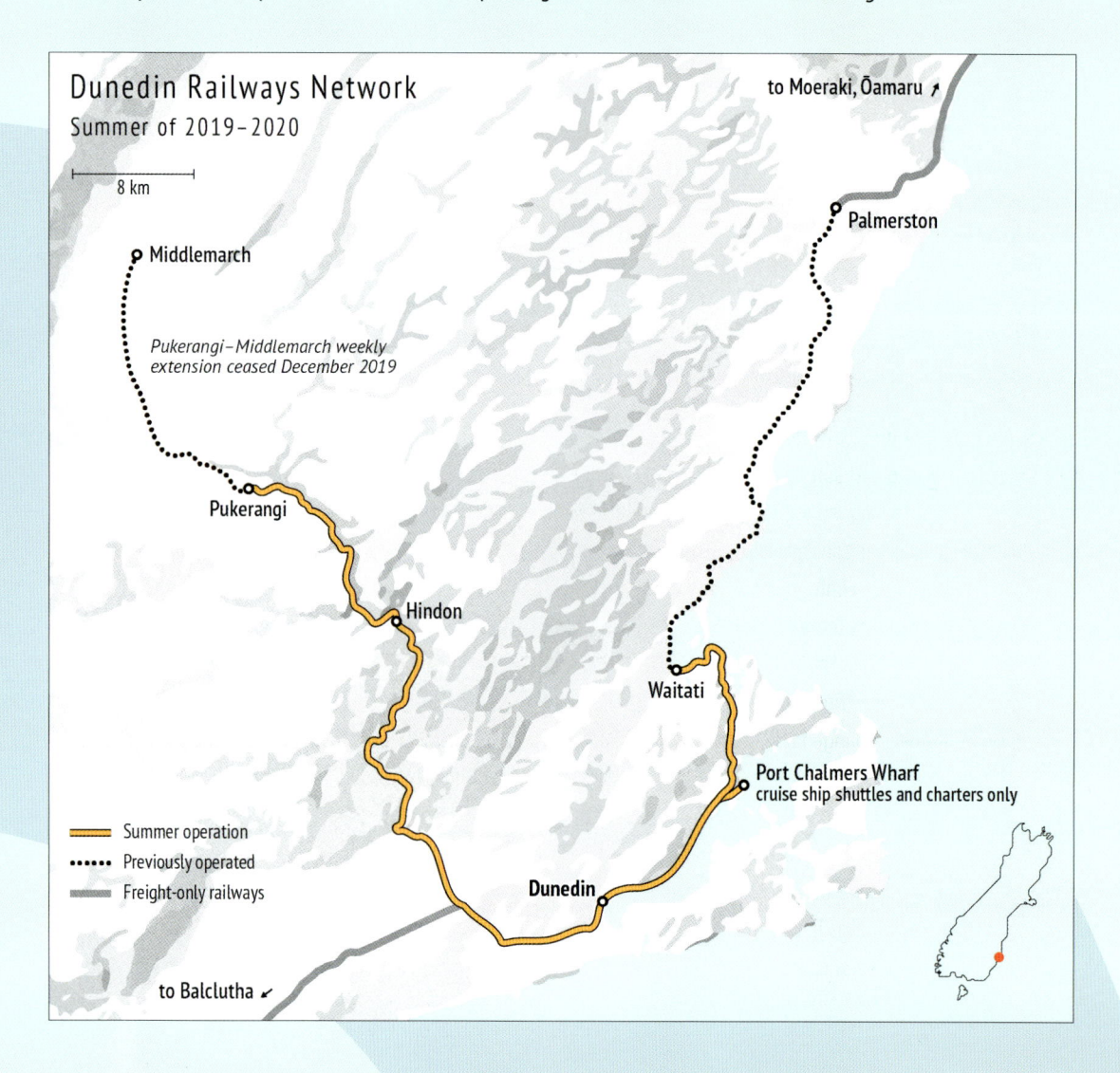

Dunedin Railways Network
Summer of 2019–2020

8 km

to Moeraki, Ōamaru

Palmerston

Middlemarch

Pukerangi–Middlemarch weekly extension ceased December 2019

Pukerangi

Hindon

Waitati

Port Chalmers Wharf
cruise ship shuttles and charters only

— Summer operation
····· Previously operated
— Freight-only railways

Dunedin

to Balclutha

D^J 1210 rests at Middlemarch before returning the *Taieri Gorge Limited* to Dunedin, 16 September 2018.
André Brett

operated it regularly on Wednesdays. It continued in subsequent summers and by 2009–10 demand justified a twice-weekly service; this continued once-weekly through the winter in 2012. Taieri Gorge Railway leased Silver Fern railcar RM 24 in the years 2012–19 primarily to run the *Seasider*.

Taieri Gorge Railway changed its name to Dunedin Railways in October 2014 to reflect its association with Dunedin and the fact that it operated more than one route.[48] Over 60,000 passengers rode its offerings in the 2006–07 financial year; a decade later this had grown to over 87,000. Timetables fluctuated to meet peak demand and to suit the requirements of tour groups and cruise ship schedules.

In 2013 the *Seasider* run was shortened to terminate in Waitati instead of Palmerston to accommodate the time constraints of cruise ship passengers. It became so popular that in some summers it ran three times on selected days. During 2015 Dunedin Railways also trialled a service to Ōamaru that ran monthly in winter and weekly in summer. The aim was to attract enough point-to-point tourists as well as railway enthusiasts and sightseers to build long-term demand, but this did not transpire. As well, the rollingstock was needed to cater for the lucrative cruise ship market. For the same reason, Dunedin Railways cancelled its weekly trains to Middlemarch at the end of December 2019. The future of the 19km of track from Pukerangi to Middlemarch was uncertain.[49]

Unfortunately, Dunedin Railways' reliance on cruise ship visitors proved disastrous when the Covid-19 pandemic hit. International tourism

cont'd overleaf

cont'd from page 255.

halted and cruise ships were suddenly infamous vectors for the virus. Trains ceased running in March 2020 and the Dunedin City Council mothballed Dunedin Railways from 20 April, with 51 jobs lost. The Rail and Maritime Transport Union proposed using the trains to revive Mosgiel and Port Chalmers suburban services, and former Alliance Party co-leader Victor Billot promoted a 'Keep Dunedin Rail Rolling' campaign. From 27 December 2020 to 28 March 2021 the trains returned for a 'summer of trains not planes': on Sundays the *Seasider* ran to Waitati and the newly christened *Inlander* went as far as Hindon in the gorge.

Dunedin Railways turned a profit for 10 of the past 13 years but faces a high bill for deferred maintenance.[50] In a near-unanimous vote on 13 April 2021, Dunedin City Council confirmed it would retain Dunedin Railways, with Mayor Aaron Hawkins emphasising that there was no desire to close or sell it. At the time of writing (May 2021) it is unclear what the services will be in the long term.

Our map depicts the Dunedin network for the summer 2019–20 season before the pandemic, when the two main routes were the *Seasider* to Waitati and the *Taieri Gorge Limited* to Pukerangi. Trains also ran regularly to Port Chalmers to collect cruise ship passengers dockside, and occasional excursions travelled to the Moeraki Boulders, Ōamaru and elsewhere.

to journalists and condemned both Bolger's National government for selling NZR and Clark's Labour government for not supporting southern railway services while stumping up for Auckland rail and Air New Zealand.

There have been regular calls to revive the *Southerner*. One company went so far as to charter rollingstock from Tranz Scenic to operate holiday services in July 2002, but lacked the marketing resources to drum up sufficient bookings to make the exercise viable.[51] For now, Otago and Southland lack rail transport to other regions.

THE DIFFICULT 2000s

Tranz Rail and WCR, under a $33m deal, each owned half of Tranz Scenic as a stand-alone subsidiary from December 2001, although Tranz Rail was not active in management.[52] In 2003 Tranz Scenic contemplated weekend services to Rotorua, but this venture depended on the Clark government buying a 35-percent stake in Tranz Rail and investing $44m to save the company from insolvency.[53] When this did not occur, the proposal lapsed. Instead, the government permitted Australian firm Toll Holdings to acquire a majority of Tranz Rail shares. Toll sold the physical infrastructure back to the Crown for $1 in 2004, and in the same year bought out WCR's half of Tranz Scenic. Toll retained exclusive use of the network subject to access fees – $38m in its first year – and a 'use it or lose it' clause that permitted other operators to step in if train services fell below specified minimums. The latter proved crucial to saving passenger rail between Auckland and Wellington after Toll cancelled the overnight *Northerner* and proposed the same for its daylight counterpart, the *Overlander*.

The demise of the *Northerner* in 2004 concluded almost a century of overnight trains between Auckland and Wellington. The nightly limited expresses along the great artery between New Zealand's largest city and the capital had loomed large in national life from the start of the first overnight timetable in February 1909, and for most of the twentieth century they were NZR's premier offering in the North Island. These fabled trains were innovative and essential, dirty and uncomfortable and everything in between. Peter Cape celebrated them in his well-known song 'Taumarunui on the Main Trunk Line', which narrates the story of an engine driver's unrequited love for a woman who works in the refreshment rooms at Taumarunui station. The rooms closed in 1975 after feeding passengers for almost 70 years, during which time a number of romances between 'refresh girls' and railwaymen culminated more happily than in Cape's song.[54]

The night trains, in their various guises, were interwoven in the lives of generations of New Zealanders. They enabled many joyful reunions; occasionally, they encountered great tragedy. As mentioned in Chapter 5, Tangiwai in the central North Island is fixed in the national consciousness after a lahar caused a bridge over the Whangaehu River to collapse beneath an express on Christmas Eve 1953, killing 151 people.[55] The author's grandfather, Ted Brett, was one of just two survivors from the second carriage, which, he recalled, was full of travellers excited about holidays and reunions. Like countless thousands of passengers over the years, they were passing time by reading, playing cards, knitting or trying to sleep.

Ted's carriage that fateful night was quiet, which was not always the case on the express. There are many tales of people who imbibed

so much alcohol that they missed their stop or bothered their companions. Young men, bored, exuberant or both, sometimes took risks to enliven the journey. Dunedin musician Shayne Carter in his autobiography recounts the traumatic fate in 1985 of DoubleHappys bandmate Wayne Elsey. The two friends snuck out a carriage door of the *Northerner* for a lark. There they hung from the handrails, 'laughing as the wind shook us around, while the countryside stood further out, black, lightened by fog. There was the comforting chug of the train … an explosion and a thump … Wayne was gone.'[56]

By the 2000s the *Northerner* seemed an anachronism: there had been no other night trains in New Zealand since the *Silver Star*'s demise, and Tranz Scenic's focus on tourists meant it had little interest in a train that ran when darkness obscured the view. The *Northerner* ran for the last time on 12 November 2004. Euan McQueen, chair of the Rail Heritage Trust and formerly NZR's assistant general manager, suggested this was 'a significant event but … not one to be too nostalgic about'.[57] Not everyone agreed, and many felt the cancellation keenly. As the last service rattled through Taumarunui in the small hours of the morning, Len Goodwin, who drove the *Northerner* often between 1960 and 1990, came to the station to pay his respects in his old NZR uniform and cap. Few of the 125 passengers were awake to see him walking the platform, waving a signal lamp and calling 'Taumarunui on the Main Trunk Line, for the last time'.[58]

The daytime *Overlander* came as close as possible to following the *Northerner* into oblivion without actually doing so. If it had perished, the entire line from Palmerston North to Pukekohe would have lacked a passenger

EF 30232 with the *Overlander* at Palmerston North, 27 November 2011. André Brett

service. Toll approached the government in 2006 for a $1.75m annual subsidy and a $500,000 capital injection, but Finance Minister Michael Cullen rejected this with the well-worn justification that alternative transport existed. Citing average passenger figures of 90 per trip, Toll announced in July that the train would end on 30 September. Resistance to cancellation grew swiftly. Hakan Svensson, chair of the National Park Village Business Association, responded that numbers in summer would swell to 300 and accused Toll, like Tranz Rail before it, of doing little to promote the service.[59] In Hamilton, 80-year-old Mary Russell-Bethune collected 500 signatures in a week; when she delivered them to the railway station she found two other petitions had also done the rounds. Popular opinion was that the train had been poorly promoted and maintained.[60] The Green Party ran a nationwide petition and pressured the government to save the train; local councils also banded together, with Auckland Regional Council chair Mike Lee taking a leading role. In late August the government was reportedly having 'second thoughts'.[61] On 14 September 2006 the Greens delivered their petition with roughly 16,000 signatures to Parliament; additions the following week swelled this to 23,495. The energetic Russell-Bethune also continued collecting signatures in Hamilton, although 1840 of 3600 would be ruled invalid on procedural grounds as she had resorted to blank paper after running out of official forms.[62]

The matter came down to the wire. Rumours circulated that Cabinet might fund a six-month extension but Acting Finance Minister Trevor Mallard could see 'no prospect' for the *Overlander*: communities on the line were 'well served by buses'. The use-it-or-lose-it provision reared its head: if Toll did not operate a route at least three times a week it lost its right of monopoly, and a Wellington-based consortium,

A southbound *Northern Explorer* near Waiōuru, 13 October 2014. Note the open-air observation car behind locomotive DFB 7173, a welcome inclusion for sightseers and photographers and an example of how these trains cater largely to tourists. Simon Mathew

the Manning Group, indicated it would introduce a luxury tourist train if the *Overlander* ceased.[63] Two days before the last *Overlander* was to run, Toll announced it would retain the service daily from December to Easter and three days a week at other times.[64] Many supporters of the *Overlander* had condemned Toll's Australian owners as out of touch, but now Toll could play the saviour. Sydney tabloid the *Daily Telegraph*, not usually inclined to report New Zealand railway news, was quick to trumpet: 'Aussies Save Kiwi Train'.[65]

Passenger figures suggest the government was short sighted in condemning the *Overlander*. The train enjoyed good promotion in the late 2000s and patronage grew 25.5 percent in the 11 months to May 2009, followed by another 24 percent in the 2010 financial year, the best of any long-distance service.[66] Greens MP Sue Kedgley, who campaigned strongly for the *Overlander*, observed, 'It's phenomenal … when you consider that only a few years ago the policymakers were arguing that there was no growth in rail.'[67]

The *Overlander* was replaced with the *Northern Explorer* in 2012, the year that Tranz Scenic became KiwiRail Scenic Journeys (later Great Journeys of New Zealand to encompass the Interislander). The *Northern Explorer* was targeted explicitly at tourists and had new carriages, higher fares and fewer stops, and operated thrice weekly all year. The rebranded service began on 25 June 2012 and passengers liked the carriages, but it lacked name recognition. It carried about 2000 people per month in July and August 2012, compared to 5810 and 3028 in the same months of 2011.[68] The old name had perhaps been discarded needlessly, but the *Northern Explorer*'s patronage grew 71 percent between 2013 and 2018, slightly exceeding that of the *Overlander* despite the lower frequency of trains.[69] The next step will be to regain a daily service.

2003–20: CHANGING FORTUNES IN AUCKLAND

There have been few changes to the scope of New Zealand's passenger network since the reductions of 2001–02. In February 2011 Wellington's electric suburban trains began operating to Waikanae, one town further up the Kāpiti Coast from Paraparaumu. For Waikanae commuters this was a major improvement on the once-daily diesel-hauled *Capital Connection*. At the same time, Greater Wellington Regional Council refreshed the fleet of electric multiple units with new rollingstock known as Matangi ('wind'), manufactured in South Korea by a consortium of Hyundai Rotem and Mitsui. Formally the FP/FT class, the first batch of 48 allowed the last English Electric units to be withdrawn in June 2012 after six decades of service. A second batch of 35 replaced the Ganz-Mávag units by the end of May 2016.

In the South Island, besides the changing contours of Dunedin Railways' offerings, the only alterations were temporary cessations of the *Coastal Pacific* as a result of damage to lines. Following the 22 February 2011 Canterbury earthquake, the *Coastal Pacific* was halted until 15 August 2011; the 14 November 2016 Kaikōura earthquake put it out of action again until 1 December 2018. KiwiRail chief executive Peter Reidy found 'our most experienced people … shocked at the scale of the job they faced' after the magnitude 7.8 Kaikōura quake. Railway historian Rob Merrifield, a civil engineer by training, describes it as 'the largest scale single catastrophe in terms of damage that has befallen

New Zealand's railway network'. KiwiRail had to completely rebuild portions of the Main North Line.[70]

The identities of suburban train owners and operators followed a convoluted path in this period. French public transport company Connex tendered successfully to operate Auckland's suburban trains when Tranz Metro declined to seek another contract, and took over in 2004. Connex later rebranded as Veolia and then Transdev, its current name. In the same year, the Auckland Regional Transport Authority (ARTA) came into existence. ARTA evolved into Auckland Transport in November 2010 when the various councils of Auckland merged to form a 'supercity'. Greater Wellington Regional Council acquired Wellington's suburban trains from KiwiRail in 2011, and Transdev tendered successfully to operate them under the council's Metlink brand from 2016. Graham Bush has published an instructive overview of Auckland public transit up to the electrification of the network, and the recent events – changing brands, council authorities, tenders, controversies and confusions – await their own historian.[71]

The removal of Auckland's station to Beach Road in 1930 might have been successful if the Morningside Deviation had been constructed and the network electrified. It might even have been wise – a spacious long-distance terminal linked to a busy commuter network. But, as it was, ridership was hampered until the station was relocated more centrally. Britomart's opening ushered in an unprecedented passenger rail boom for Auckland, and patronage accumulated rapidly on all three suburban lines. To meet demand, Auckland Regional Council imported seven SX class carriages from Queensland Rail in 2003 and refurbished 104 former British Rail

An SA/SD set at Britomart, 21 March 2014, showing the SD driver's cab. A locomotive, usually from the DC or DFT classes, provided power at the other end. Simon Mathew

Mark 2 carriages into SA/SD sets between 2004 and 2009. The SD carriages had a driver's cab so the train could be driven from either end, not just from the locomotive. Approximately 8 million rail journeys were made in the 2009 calendar year, effectively double those of 2005.[72] Annual patronage passed 10 million in 2011 and 20 million in 2016, vindicating everyone who had advocated for better suburban rail. The success of extending Southern Line services further down the North Island Main Trunk is illustrative: four trains a day began operating beyond Papakura to Pukekohe in 2003; by 2011, the timetable had 20. Auckland also obtained approval for electrification; ARTA commissioned technical studies in 2005 and contracts for the infrastructure and rollingstock were signed in 2010–11.[73]

Not every expansion was successful. Population growth had been predicted for some time in Auckland's west, and in 1998 Rodney District Council anticipated that trains would be restored to Helensville within two years.[74] Neither the population boom nor the resumption of passenger trains occurred, but calls for a passenger service beyond Waitākere did not abate. Chair of the Auckland Regional Council Mike Lee championed the cause and in June 2007 backed the provision of $450,000 to rebuild stations and operate a trial. Joel Cayford, head of the regional transport committee, accused Lee of 'pork-barrel politics', as the funds were added to ARTA's annual capital grant at short notice and with limited detail a few months before an election. Representatives from more densely populated areas with chronically

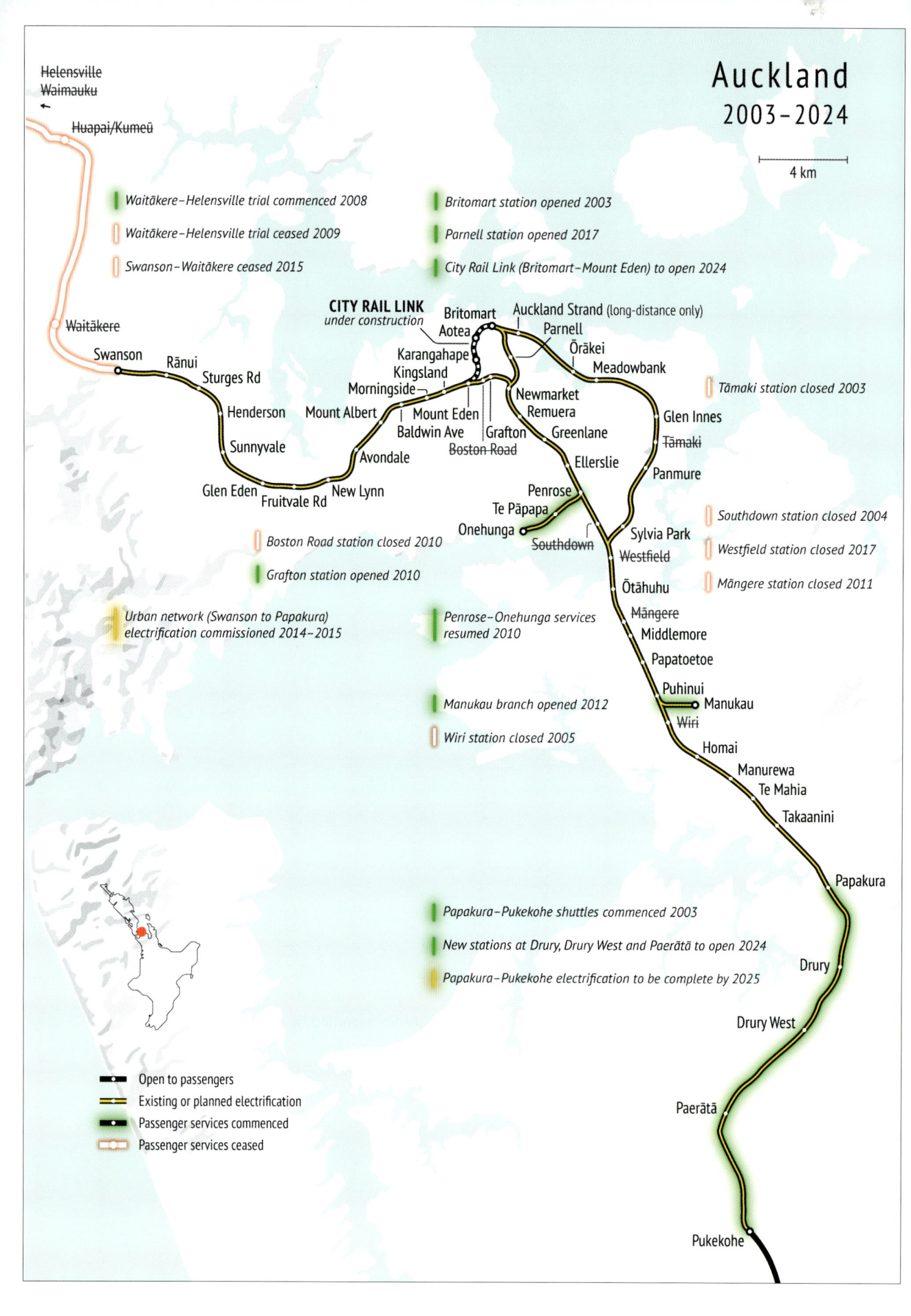

Auckland
2003–2024

4 km

Helensville
Waimauku

Huapai/Kumeū

Waitākere–Helensville trial commenced 2008
Waitākere–Helensville trial ceased 2009
Swanson–Waitākere ceased 2015

Britomart station opened 2003
Parnell station opened 2017
City Rail Link (Britomart–Mount Eden) to open 2024

Waitākere

Swanson
Rānui
Sturges Rd
Henderson
Sunnyvale
Glen Eden
Fruitvale Rd
New Lynn
Avondale
Mount Albert
Morningside
Mount Eden
Baldwin Ave
Boston Road

CITY RAIL LINK
under construction
Britomart
Aotea
Karangahape
Kingsland
Grafton

Auckland Strand (long-distance only)
Parnell
Ōrākei
Meadowbank
Newmarket
Remuera
Greenlane
Ellerslie
Penrose
Te Pāpapa
Onehunga
Southdown

Glen Innes
Tāmaki
Panmure

Tāmaki station closed 2003

Southdown station closed 2004
Westfield station closed 2017
Māngere station closed 2011

Sylvia Park
Westfield
Ōtāhuhu
Māngere
Middlemore
Papatoetoe
Puhinui
Manukau
Wiri
Homai
Manurewa
Te Mahia
Takaanini
Papakura
Drury
Drury West
Paerātā
Pukekohe

Boston Road station closed 2010
Grafton station opened 2010

Urban network (Swanson to Papakura)
electrification commissioned 2014–2015

Penrose–Onehunga services
resumed 2010

Manukau branch opened 2012
Wiri station closed 2005

Papakura–Pukekohe shuttles commenced 2003
New stations at Drury, Drury West and Paerātā to open 2024
Papakura–Pukekohe electrification to be complete by 2025

Open to passengers
Existing or planned electrification
Passenger services commenced
Passenger services ceased

DBR 1199 and 1254 operate a train of SX carriages in push-pull style across Hobson Bay on 21 March 2014. These unpopular carriages were nicknamed 'concrete mixers' for their ride quality. Electric trains replaced them not long after this photo was taken. Simon Mathew

bad public transport resented the cost. The proposal passed council by the narrow margin of 5:3, with Cayford one of two abstentions.[75]

As well as investment in three stations, Ontrack upgraded the North Auckland Line between Helensville and Waitākere to eliminate longstanding speed restrictions. This occurred in conjunction with extensive double-tracking work on the suburban Western Line. Costs ballooned from the outset, as new safety specifications required platforms to be made of concrete, not timber.[76]

On 14 July 2008 the Helensville service began a 12-month trial. Like its predecessor in 1980, it ran weekdays only. The threshold for permanent reinstatement was 40 passengers daily, but population growth in the area stalled and patronage averaged just 35 in June 2009. The train continued, however, while ARTA reviewed its future.[77] On 10 November 2009, although patronage had crept up to 43, the regional council announced that Helensville's train would end on 24 December, but considered retaining services as far as Huapai or Waimauku. Mike Lee blamed the poor condition

of the infrastructure for the failure to attract more passengers.[78] The fact that patronage now exceeded the minimum requirement set in 2008 went without mention, though cost blowouts suggest the goalposts had shifted. Lee did not wish the investment in stations at Huapai and Waimauku to go to waste and hoped their train service, running at least twice daily, would be reinstated by March 2010.[79] This did not happen, and Waitākere, after 17 months, resumed its role as the westernmost station on the Auckland suburban network.

Supporters of passenger rail to Helensville were aggrieved. The train did not stable overnight in Helensville, and Christine Rose of the Public Transport Users Association pointed out that the empty positioning runs – which had effectively no market even if they had been promoted to passengers – were sometimes included in the average passenger counts (including the figures quoted earlier).[80] This deflated the average; although the runs must be considered in operating costs, they do not belong in calculations of patronage. Among ongoing efforts to restore the service to

An AM class electric multiple unit resting between services at Onehunga on a pleasant afternoon in December 2017. André Brett

Huapai and Waimauku, the Public Transport Users Association and the North West District Business Association co-operated on a 'Trains to Huapai' campaign.[81]

The next two passenger services to be introduced, to Onehunga and Manukau, were more successful. The former began in 2010, some 37 years after the last timetabled passenger trains on the branch from Penrose, and was the result of many people's protracted efforts. Lee had advocated for this after observing the rundown state of the branch in the early 2000s: goods shunts were infrequent and the tonnages much lower than those busy days in 1973 that had forced the end of passenger trains. Lee emailed Cameron Pitches of Auckland advocacy group Campaign for Better Transport in 2002 to discuss 're-activating' the line, and

suggested there was 'great possibility in a Harbour to Harbour service Queen St [in central Auckland] to Queen St [in Onehunga]'.[82] Pitches agreed, but not everyone was convinced: sceptics suggested that patronage would be insufficient for the project to be worthwhile. The unannounced trial of an additional morning train on the Western Line in 2004 proved timely: this service between New Lynn and Britomart did not appear in timetables but quickly secured an average loading of 200. Lee used this to rebut the doubters.[83] His point was reasonable, for the growth of Auckland's rail patronage in the past decade had consistently exceeded expectations. Despite political and bureaucratic insistence that they were wedded to cars, Aucklanders continued to express support for greater public transport spending; at the 2004 local elections in a so-called 'freeway revolt' voters ousted pro-roads members of the city and regional councils in favour of public transport advocates.[84]

Campaign for Better Transport expanded its efforts in 2005: Onehunga resident Garth Houltham managed a team of volunteers who secured over 8000 signatures in support of re-activating the line. The proposal had strong local support, including from the Onehunga Business Association, and Better Transport presented its petition to the regional council in May 2006. Although ARTA managed Auckland's public transport, reopening the line was Ontrack's responsibility, so Lee forwarded the petition to Parliament's transport and industrial relations committee. In a stroke of good fortune, Labour MP Mark Gosche chaired the committee. His electorate, Maungakiekie, contained the branch, and he took a personal interest in its revitalisation. ARTA and Ontrack viewed the line as a low priority, but in the end Ontrack's acting CEO, William Peet, recommended a change in policy. On 13 March 2007 Finance Minister Michael Cullen and Transport Minister Annette King announced funding to resurrect the line.[85]

The Onehunga service was meant to resume in 2009 but took longer than anticipated. Rumours swirled in April and May 2009 that Ontrack lacked funds to restore the line through to Queen Street, now renamed the Onehunga Mall, and trains would have to terminate 300 metres short of central Onehunga.[86] Fortunately, the line was restored to the mall, but the project fell behind schedule. KiwiRail eventually confirmed an opening date of 19 September.[87] One last farce remained: the 55-metre platform would be too short for new trains after electrification. A Wellington newspaper chortled about 'dysfunctionalism at its Auckland best', while the ever-quotable Lee demanded to know, 'Why should Onehunga of all the stations of Auckland be made into a Lilliput station?'[88]

Test trains began in August 2010, and the opening ceremony on 18 September 2010, attended by Steven Joyce, Minister of Transport in John Key's new National government, demonstrated that inauguration of a new passenger service still retained some of its lustre, even if railways were no longer the vast state institution of the 1940s. Having waited so long for the line's restoration, Amanda Kinzett, general manager of the Onehunga Business Association, described experiencing 'a bit of a rush' when tests began.[89]

Approximately 1200 passengers were riding the line daily by June 2011, outpacing predictions.[90] Lee, Houltham, Pitches and their fellow advocates had proven sceptics wrong. Anyone suggesting in 2004 that the Onehunga Line would be the first electrified railway in Auckland would have been considered delusional, but after the troublesome short platform was extended, in April 2014 it claimed that very title.

The next expansion of the Auckland suburban network was even more momentous. The 2.5-kilometre branch from Puhinui to Manukau was the first new passenger railway built in Auckland since the Westfield Deviation opened in 1930 (Britomart notwithstanding), and the first to a new destination anywhere in New Zealand since the completion of the eastern Hutt Valley main line in 1954. Construction began in June 2009. KiwiRail, Manukau City Council and ARTA all contributed to the $90m project, with KiwiRail providing the lion's share, $50m, and Manukau furnishing $33m for a rail and bus hub at the terminus.[91] When total costs grew to $98m, ARTA covered the difference. During the planning stage in 2008, Manukau's council chose not to fund the railway through to the Southmall shopping centre, now Westfield Manukau City. The line instead stops 800 metres short, and in 2014 a new campus of Manukau Institute of Technology opened above the terminus.[92]

The Manukau Branch was meant to open in July 2011, but Auckland Transport and KiwiRail professed to be 'too busy' preparing the network for the Rugby World Cup and for electrification. On 4 April 2012 Mayor of Auckland Len Brown finally drove a train through a ceremonial ribbon to open Manukau station.[93] Timetabled passenger trains began on 15 April 2012 and steadily gained in popularity, despite attempts to portray patronage as poor before the line had an opportunity to establish itself. Three Auckland city councillors counted just 30 people boarding six outbound trains between 6am and 8am on Monday 28 May – but did not count incoming passengers, as if the railway's only purpose was to funnel people to central Auckland rather than bring them to destinations in Manukau.[94] Auckland Transport's statistics for June 2012 claimed daily patronage of 500–600, roughly equivalent to the early months of the Onehunga Line. Importantly, this report noted that more passengers travelled *to* Manukau rather than *from* it towards Auckland.[95] Manukau became the terminus for all Eastern Line services in December 2014 and by the end of the 2010s was one of Auckland's busiest stations.

The most recent alteration to the scope of Auckland's suburban network was the shortening of the Western Line from its longstanding terminus at Waitākere to Swanson. Indicative of the remarkable railway revival, Auckland Transport commissioned new electric units during 2014 and 2015, but these came at the cost of trains to Waitākere. The 4-kilometre line between Swanson and Waitākere includes a 274-metre tunnel so narrow that expensive works would be necessary to fit electric wires. Auckland Transport considered diesel train shuttles to connect with electric services at Swanson, but on 30 May 2013 it confirmed its preference for buses: they would be cheaper, travel times were similar, and patronage beyond Swanson was limited.[96] The bus substitution occurred on 20 July 2015 when the Western Line electrification came into use.[97] Since that date the entire Auckland suburban network has

been electric, except for a diesel shuttle between Papakura and Pukekohe. KiwiRail began preparatory work to electrify that final section in late 2020.

Like cancellations everywhere, the ending of services to Waitākere was contentious. Some local politicians and public transport advocates condemned it, especially as it reduced the likelihood of restoring services to Huapai.[98] The Public Transport Users Association supported a protest in June 2015 in which a procession dressed in black – including a Grim Reaper – carried a cardboard coffin aboard a train from Waitākere to Britomart and staged a funeral service outside the offices of Auckland Transport.[99] Their stance was not universal, however. One leading public transport advocate, Matt Lowrie, endorsed Auckland Transport's decision. Swanson–Waitākere did not experience the boom in patronage that had occurred across the rest of the network and Lowrie considered a captive diesel shuttle excessive for the 114 people who travelled this stretch on an average weekday.[100] As it was, some Waitākere residents drove to Swanson because many trains terminated there already.

This has not quelled requests for a restored service. The 'Trains to Huapai' campaign was prominent in the 2017 local body elections. It proposed the use of diesel trains displaced by electrification to operate 14 daily shuttles from Swanson to Huapai between 6am and 8pm. At the time of writing, some of these trains sit unused in Taumarunui. Recent regulation changes will require trains to have up-to-date fire suppression systems to operate through Waitākere Tunnel, and Auckland Transport cited this as an impediment to resuming services.[101] Phil Goff, Mayor of Auckland since 2016, was reportedly 'still ho-hum' about trains to Huapai

8

1990–2020

The existing lines in Auckland have been upgraded, including a new station at Parnell. An ADL/ADC diesel multiple unit passes the future site of the station in March 2014, three years before the station opened. Since 2015 these units have only run between Papakura and Pukekohe. Simon Mathew

in January 2020. The National Party released a transport policy ahead of the 2020 election that included funds for a diesel shuttle and foreshadowed future electrification. Others advocate light rail along State Highway 16 to Kumeū. This features in the 2018–28 Auckland Transport Alignment Project. but as a lower priority than light rail to Māngere.[102]

At present, the resumption of passenger rail services beyond Swanson is unlikely in the short term. Locals may be unhappy to know that the cessation of Waitākere's commuter trains did not rate a mention in Auckland Transport's annual report.[103] Unfortunately this is not unusual – the cancellations chronicled in this book routinely went without mention in the relevant annual reports. Officialdom has trumpeted the extension of passenger services but rarely drawn attention to their contraction.

Abandoned and run-down railway infrastructure dots the New Zealand landscape. Pictured in April 2010, the Waiōtira station on the North Auckland Line once had tracks on both sides of the platform and a building; a goods shed served a larger yard. André Brett

C^H 9

Whither passenger rail in New Zealand?

New Zealanders hoped the first few days of 2020 would be a sunny, comfortable end to the holiday season. Instead, from one end of the country to the other, the sky turned an eerie orange as smoke from catastrophic bushfires in Australia crossed 2000 kilometres of ocean. People shared photos on social media with captions that assured viewers they were not using sepia-toned filters. The particles in the air dusted the South Island's glaciers, transforming their appearance into a caramel-coloured wonderland misplaced within the apocalypse – a coating sure to exacerbate the already alarming rate of glacial retreat.

In 2007 Australia's federal, state and territorial governments had commissioned Ross Garnaut, a professor of economics at the Australian National University in Canberra, to report on the effects of climate change. His final report in September 2008 made for sobering reading. In it he noted that 'fire seasons will start earlier, end slightly later, and generally be more intense. This effect increases over time, but should be directly observable by 2020.'[1] His words were startlingly prescient, and New Zealanders gaped and gasped at the proof that Garnaut was right.

The effects of climate change are diverse, variable and uneven, so our response must be broad. New Zealand aspires for its greenhouse gas emissions to be carbon neutral by 2050, a goal that Parliament enshrined in law in November 2019 with only one dissenting vote out of 120. Now, how do we achieve this?

One path to a better and more sustainable future is transport policy. Rail must feature prominently: the low friction of steel wheels on steel rails means that trains are the most energy-efficient way to move people and goods, far outperforming rubber tyres on asphalt.

Best of all are electric trains, which can draw power from hydroelectricity, wind, solar and other renewable sources, and do so at scale: Melbourne's tramway system, the world's largest, has been entirely solar powered since July 2019.[2] In the UK, booming patronage between London and Glasgow has not only seen rail's market share surge to almost a third of all travellers, but also slashed carbon emissions on the route by a sixth as more people opt for trains instead of air travel.[3] Railways and tramways are essential for mobility in a carbon-neutral world, and unlike so many inheritances of the Industrial Revolution that are as yet poorly adapted for change, innovations since the early twentieth century mean that trains are ready for a decarbonised future. The sooner we act to expand the railway network, the better our future will be.

Rail has a large role to play for both goods and passengers. Great environmental gains can be made by removing trucks from the roads, and KiwiRail must be a common carrier, more agile and accountable than NZR ever was. The distribution of goods is where railways obtain much of their revenue, so network upgrades and expansion should support existing and new sources of freight. Most people's direct experience with rail, however, will be as a form of personal transport. The attitude that passengers are an impediment to goods traffic must be left in the past. If rail can be positioned as an attractive alternative to the private car, this will represent real action on climate change, persuade travellers that the transition is beneficial as well as necessary, and foster a sense of individual and community accomplishment in working towards climate goals. Rail is a public good that must become a public desire.

This chapter reflects on the state of the

current rail network and suggests possibilities for the future. We will never again have the networks of the past, and in any case must develop one that suits future requirements. It will not come cheaply, but our future will be poorer if New Zealand continues to depend too heavily on roads. Of course, rail upgrades alone will not fix our problems, but they are an essential part of the solution.

HOW DID WE GET HERE?

Poor administration and policymaking have left New Zealand with an attenuated railway passenger network unfit for the twenty-first century. The country possesses only the scraps of a 1930s network; if New Zealand's state highways recalled travel patterns and technology from the 1970s, let alone the 1930s, it would be a national scandal.

Back at the dawn of the twentieth century our steam locomotives were pacesetters, but New Zealand has not kept up with global innovations in rail technology and now lags far behind many countries. The Fay–Raven commission of 1925 advised that rural services would not stay competitive or useful if they remained as slow mixed trains, but NZR took little action. This became a trend, and the setbacks of the Depression and World War II further compounded the drift away from passenger trains.

Numerous factors have contributed to shrink the network to what it is today. One of the earliest was the rise of NZR Road Services. It was not an inherently bad idea: road transport was sufficiently advanced by the mid-1920s that buses made sense, both as extensions to NZR's offerings to areas without railways, and to replace mixed trains on branch lines with

A Blue Streak railcar between Puketutu and Kopaki, south of Te Kūiti on the North Island Main Trunk, on 20 July 1972. J.M. Creber

small population catchments. Passengers did not demand that buses replace trains, but to some senior officials buses became symbolic of modernity; to others they were a quick way to cut costs or simplify timetables. Officials routinely assumed these substitutions would not deter passengers, but one source of patronage after another drifted away.

NZR rarely sought to retain or grow custom, interpreting its role as simply carrying those who came to it. When train ridership declined, instead of improving its offerings, NZR typically reduced services to meet the supposed lower demand. Naturally this resulted in a vicious cycle of further decline.

NZR also became a victim of political and economic demands it could not meet. While many valid criticisms may be made of the service NZR did or did not provide, the expectation to turn a profit while meeting network construction and maintenance costs – of the sort that no road competitor had to meet – has had serious and enduring consequences for rail.

Other wounds were self-inflicted. Attitudes that prioritised goods over passengers did NZR no favours. Passenger trains were NZR's shop window, the first impression most people had of the railway. Treating passenger services as an inconvenience made it harder to build a popular constituency and make the case for investment. To claim that the transport of goods was more lucrative was counter-productive – people do not like to be told that their personal transportation matters less than shifting a trainload of coal or a few wagons of merchandise, regardless of how it might appear on a balance sheet. This bumbling argument comes from the 'our hospitals would run smoothly if only there were no patients' school of public relations. Ultimately, placing goods above passengers meant many services were cancelled before their time, 'temporary' substitutions became permanent cessations, and opportunities were neglected or avoided. Not all routes would have survived to the present if they had continued running past the year of their cancellation, but many ended when local demand and preference for rail still existed. Had they endured longer, the effects of constructing and maintaining more rollingstock would have helped some services to survive.

The Fiat fiasco captures neatly the failings at all levels. NZR ordered too few railcars, and contributed to construction delays by repeatedly changing its mind. The manufacturer delivered a substandard vehicle, and politicians failed to take action once the need for replacements became clear. When Muldoon's Cabinet rejected a package to save regional services in 1976, Labour and National had already had an entire decade in which to act. Successive governments had considered detailed proposals. The 1973 oil shock should have pushed Kirk's Cabinet into action, but the decision kept being deferred as MPs found themselves torn between NZR's requests, Treasury's exaggerated arguments against rail and their own political calculations. The fact that passenger numbers rose significantly during the early years of Fiat operation confirmed that New Zealanders were still keen to travel by rail if there were *any* improvements. So, too, did the increased patronage on key routes in the late 1960s and early 1970s, when NZR introduced the Blue Streak and Silver Fern railcars and inaugurated trains such as the *Southerner* and the *Endeavour*. These won back travellers even as more people than ever could afford air travel.

But such initiatives were limited and fleeting. Bad rollingstock, inadequate timetables, poor attitudes and ever-contracting services kept pushing people into cars. It is shocking just how few efforts have been made to retain custom, let alone increase it, since 1955. Across generations, many railway officials and politicians have wanted as little as possible to do with passenger rail.

THE NETWORK IN 2020

New Zealand's passenger rail network at the start of 2020 was much smaller than that of 2000, and paled in comparison to 1960. The mileage covered by all trains, suburban and long distance, was just under 1500 kilometres, including 82.5 kilometres used by Dunedin Railways. Only about a third of the railway lines in New Zealand possessed any sort of passenger train, and most

9

of these were tourist services that were too infrequent or expensive for regular travellers.

The last time New Zealand's passenger network was this short was in 1877, when only 1150 kilometres existed at the end of the 1876/77 financial year. Then, construction was progressing so fast that a year later the network was almost 1700km long, and every open railway accommodated passengers.[4] The alterations to the scope of the Auckland network in the 2010s – the addition of the Onehunga and Manukau branches and the cessation of Swanson to Waitākere – meant a net gain of about 1.8km. Dunedin Railways shed 37.6km when it abbreviated the *Seasider* from Palmerston to Waitati in 2013 and another 18.8km at the end of the decade when it stopped running regularly to Middlemarch. The total national change during the 2010s then, a loss of 54.6km, was the smallest variation in the extent of the passenger rail network of any decade in New Zealand's railway history.

Auckland's network will expand in the coming decade. The City Rail Link will fulfil plans that began with the Morningside Deviation proposal of the 1920s: a 3.5km tunnel under the central city between Britomart and Mount Eden. The decision to electrify Auckland's suburban network made this project possible, and it is under construction with opening planned for 2024. The length may appear modest, but the improvements in urban accessibility and railway capacity are massive and will further transform passenger rail in Auckland.

The Covid-19 pandemic temporarily halted long-distance passenger trains from 23 March 2020 and exposed the perils of KiwiRail's fixation on tourism to the exclusion of other markets. For a time, most of KiwiRail's trains

were deemed non-essential.[5] The *TranzAlpine* was back in action in July, followed by the *Coastal Pacific* and the *Northern Explorer* in October, but in the years to come they will need to attract a larger proportion of the national transport mix to thrive.

The pandemic dealt a serious blow to Dunedin Railways. It was already facing a $10m bill for track maintenance in Taieri Gorge, and its heritage trains are costly to operate. International visitors made up roughly 80 percent of patronage; with borders closed, naturally the primary revenue stream has dried up.[6] The city council has committed to retaining Dunedin Railways, and while the journeys it operates in the future may differ to those before the global pandemic, it has become one of Otago's major attractions and should remain so.

Another long-distance train was under construction at Dunedin's Hillside Workshops, where a private company has had former Auckland suburban carriages refurbished for a proposed Auckland-to-Invercargill luxury service to be called the *Antipodean Explorer*. This did not launch before the pandemic struck, and at the time of writing its prospects are unknown. Hillside will, however, continue to maintain KiwiRail locomotives and assemble wagons, with the Ardern government's May 2021 Budget confirming $85m for revamped facilities.[7]

Covid-19's effects extended to a commuter service not yet begun, delaying the reintroduction of trains between Hamilton and Auckland. This service, *Te Huia*, was to begin on 3 August 2020 but finally began on 6 April 2021.[8] It has not expanded the length of the passenger network, but the twice-daily timetable is a significant improvement on the tri-weekly *Northern Explorer* and enables Waikato residents to commute to Auckland

Hamilton station in Frankton, the junction of the East Coast and North Island main trunks (left and right respectively), 24 March 2014. Only the *Overlander/Northern Explorer* stopped here between 2004 and 2021. It is now the origin station for *Te Huia*.
Simon Mathew

by rail. Moreover, this is not the Blue Streak of 1968 or the *Waikato Connection* of 2000–01: the trial is to last five years to give patronage time to develop. *Te Huia* departs from the station in Frankton – the underground Hamilton Central station will remain unused for now – and also calls at a new transport hub at Rotokauri, adjacent to New Zealand's largest shopping centre, The Base. KiwiRail has refurbished former Auckland suburban carriages into trainsets with a buffet and wifi. There are hurdles to overcome: *Te Huia* must initially terminate at Papakura because of capacity constraints further north and because diesel locomotives can no longer operate into Britomart. This transfer to suburban trains means that Frankton to Britomart takes 2.5 hours, but a morning journey on the congested southern motorway is a tedious two hours, during which drivers cannot work, read or rest. Current investments to improve Auckland's suburban network should ameliorate these problems and facilitate a more frequent timetable.

WHAT MIGHT THE FUTURE HOLD?

It is risky to make predictions, and authors can sometimes appear goofy with hindsight. As well, the Covid-19 pandemic is teaching the global community about the wide reach of unpredictable events. On 6 May 2021 Minister of Transport Michael Wood released a New Zealand Rail Plan, which offers the most positive government vision for railways since the 1940s. It provides a framework for investment rather than promising specific projects or funds.[9] The following sections discuss possibilities for a future in which passenger rail is at the forefront of urban and regional planning. In them, Sam van der Weerden's maps and my text seek to debunk myths, outline important principles, and suggest new services across New Zealand. Rather than detailed, costed plans, these are historically informed conversation starters which recognise that rail transport serves many beneficial purposes. The reality of New Zealand's attenuated railway network is that we first have

9

The three electric multiple unit classes to operate in Wellington, seen on 22 November 2011. From right: a new Matangi FP/FT class unit; two sidings of English Electric DM/D class units, including 'Phoenix' in Midland Red; three sidings of Ganz-Mávag EM/ET class units. André Brett

to outline a long-term vision, identify needs and choose priorities before specific options can be chosen and costed. Our suggestions sketch the contours of what is plausible – not high-speed trains under Cook Strait, which belong to science fiction, but realistic schemes for different parts of the country. Some will require significant investment, and as proposals become firmer there will be tough choices to make; others provide modest local transport for everyday mobility. They need not be taken separately; as intercity expresses, regional trains and urban networks grow they will become strands of a larger steel web.

Our focus is on rail, but rail does not exist in isolation. Our communities will be more accessible and sustainable with integrated systems of buses, trams/light rail and pedestrian and cycling infrastructure, and roads will be freer for those needing to drive. We present these ideas to encourage serious consideration of passenger rail nationwide.

At the moment, rail's future is secure only in Wellington and Auckland, where modern electrified services carry millions of passengers annually. But what about the rest of the country: the fast-growing cities like Christchurch or Tauranga, the satellite towns like Ashburton or Morrinsville that want to thrive on their own terms, the small towns like Reefton or Waipara that are often overlooked? Regional inequality is significant, and it is increasing. Economist Shamubeel Eaqub warns that there is no easy solution to these inequalities, and suggests national policies need to be attuned to regional variation.[10]

One way to reduce inequality and improve prosperity is to improve mobility so that people have fewer barriers to opportunities. A recent book, *Heartland Strong: How rural New Zealand can change and thrive* (2019), presents the outcomes of over a decade of research into regional communities.[11] Its editors argue that people outside of large cities are not passive victims of depopulation and job losses but a resilient and diverse group who have options. Residents and policymakers alike can harness the resources and positive attributes of rural life to reshape their futures. Rural residents often have transport problems: inadequate facilities create challenges even for people who live close to cities. Interviewees in Taumarunui highlighted the negative social and economic effects of KiwiRail trains ceasing to stop in the town. One chapter reflects on how future agricultural and digital technologies will affect rural communities. It is also worth considering the role of railway technology in reviving and enhancing connectivity and mobility. The allure of modern attempts to 'disrupt' economies and lifestyles can overlook proven, mature technologies such as rail.

The problem is that few people today can recall the time when there was a good railway network in New Zealand, when trains went everywhere and rail's finest services were the pinnacle of transport technology. Millennials and those younger have known only a country in which rail is practically confined to two cities. Generation X experienced the last gasp of regional trains, and baby boomers grew up with a decaying network – some of them completing the dismantling that their parents' generation began. New Zealanders old enough to recall life during World War II experienced the peak years of rail patronage – but on overcrowded and rundown trains that kept society moving through extreme privations. Only the very

elderly know what it was like for train travel in this country to be desirable and forward thinking.

No wonder, then, that New Zealanders are so wedded to their cars and unable to imagine that rail might replace car travel, and likely assume that even if it does it won't be as good as car ownership. Even if they have enjoyed good-quality rail networks overseas, many believe that it cannot be done here. It *can* be done here. It was done here once, and it should be done again. As transport expert Philip Laird puts it, the challenge is 'to make the train services so good that people want to use them'.[12] This requires leadership that knows the value of rail and backs its potential. If the second half of the twentieth century teaches us anything about mobility, it is that imbalanced transport planning and a fixation on one mode of travel to the exclusion of others is foolish and unsustainable.

THE MYTHS WE MUST NOT TELL OURSELVES

It is necessary to debunk some myths about passenger rail in New Zealand.

First, our national narrow track gauge of 1067mm is not the restriction it might seem. The main limitations to speed are steep grades, tight curves and a small loading gauge (the maximum width of rollingstock to not hit lineside structures). Wider track gauges offer improved stability at very high speeds, but the prohibitive cost of earthworks for new lines to achieve speeds above 200km/h means that this is not a serious option for New Zealand. Speeds of 160–200km/h, however, are attainable with upgrades to existing lines, at least through flatter regions like the Canterbury Plains. A New Zealand locomotive once held the world speed record for narrow gauge – the Wellington and Manawatū Railway Company's No. 10 reached 103.6km/h on 20 July 1892 between Levin and Shannon. It is not unreasonable to imagine that the world's first narrow-gauge trains timetabled to reach 200km/h in regular service could run between, say, Timaru and Christchurch. Tilting technology, mechanisms that enable increased speed around curves on regular tracks, can improve timing through more rugged terrain. Queensland's Tilt Trains operate at 160km/h on the same track gauge as New Zealand, and one holds the Australian rail speed record of 210km/h. Implementing tilt trains will require upgrades and deviations because of maintenance backlogs, but these will benefit goods trains as well.

Second, the different forms of electrification are not an impediment. Auckland's suburban network and Hamilton–Palmerston North use 25kV AC and need to be linked promptly. Wellington's system is 1700V DC, boosted from 1500V after the Matangi units replaced older rollingstock, and some people have spent too long claiming this is an obstacle to electrifying the whole Main Trunk. Trains that operate on multiple electric systems are commonplace overseas.

This relates to another motive power issue: it will not be a problem to acquire trains that can draw electricity from overhead wires where possible and use other power, such as diesel-electric or battery storage, where overhead systems are not in place. As with tilt trains, the technology for bimodal multiple units and locomotives is mature. They operate in European countries and will soon be in use in New South Wales. Numerous railways are also considering partial electrification: battery trains that recharge from overhead wires strung along

short sections en route, such as at stations. New Zealand has many options.

Another common objection to rail investment is that New Zealand has a small, dispersed population. The argument is applied to suburban and long-distance services alike: cities are too sprawling, regions are not populous enough. These shibboleths might sound like nuggets of wisdom, but they are empty without evidence, as is the 2019 Bay of Plenty Regional Council report which claims that no Australasian city with a population below 400,000 has a 'rail service'.[13] To give just five examples in Australia: Newcastle and Wollongong have their own suburban lines as well as commuter trains to Sydney, and Victoria's passenger network has fast, frequent trains to Ballarat, Bendigo and Geelong. It is also unclear why this claim is restricted to Australasia when many small cities worldwide have effective public transport.

The Bay of Plenty report also emphasises a need for urban density, a common proxy for the likelihood of success. Recent research suggests this is misleading: physicists Vincent Verbavatz and Marc Barthelemy have shown that ease of access to public transport increases ridership more than heightened population density – increasing density alone is not a solution.[14] Verbavatz and Barthelemy studied access to rapid transit in large cities, but their findings are scalable and relevant to more modest proposals for New Zealand.

There is ample proof that New Zealand's demography and topography do not preclude good passenger rail. It is not uncommon for New Zealanders to return from Europe or East Asia, enthusiastic for the railway technology they encountered there to be introduced here, only to be told that other countries make for

The El 18 class of electric engines are a mainstay of Norway's intercity trains. They also work the Flåm Line, which, like New Zealand's *TranzAlpine*, bounced back from near-cancellation to become a major tourist attraction. Here, El 18.2255 leads a train out of Flåm on 1 May 2017. André Brett

unsuitable comparisons. This can be true, but one country is eminently suited to comparison: Norway. It has similar, and indeed more difficult, topography; its population is less than half a million greater than New Zealand's; and its land area, likewise, is only modestly larger (especially when counting only Norway proper, not Svalbard or other possessions). Its largest city, Oslo, has roughly half Auckland's population; second-place Bergen is smaller than Christchurch or Wellington; Stavanger and Trondheim are comparable in size to Hamilton or Tauranga; and no other city has more than 100,000 people.

Norway's railway network is remarkably similar in length to New Zealand's, and also had an investment backlog in the 1980s.[15] Today, Norwegians enjoy regular trains between all the major cities. In early 2020 Oslo had seven departures daily to Stavanger, four to Bergen and four to Trondheim, from where two daily connections ran to Bodø. Many more suburban and regional services exist, and almost none

depend on tourism. All this, despite the fact that Norway's only high-speed railway links Oslo with its airport; none of the main intercity trips take under 6.5 hours and Trondheim–Bodø is approximately 10 hours. Inadequate roads or air services cannot explain the superior railway timetable: Norwegian roads are better than New Zealand's and intercity flights are frequent. Like New Zealand, Norway generates much hydroelectric power; unlike New Zealand, however, Norway has electrified many of its railways and is transitioning all non-electrified lines to zero-emission operation with battery trains.[16] If Norway can operate a good long-distance railway network despite great obstacles, so can New Zealand.

WHAT WILL WE NEED TO REVITALISE PASSENGER RAIL?

There are many good ways to revive passenger rail; some are quick fixes and others require serious effort. First, we must take advantage of existing assets and exploit economies of scale to minimise costs. Rail corridors run through the centre of many New Zealand cities and towns. A dedicated right-of-way, the efficiency of steel wheels on steel rails and the ability to handle heavy patronage effectively provide natural advantages. In many places the railways could become trunks of local multimodal networks that use buses, ferries, cycleways, trams and other technologies, with well-designed interchanes, integrated timetables and free transfers.[17] Rollingstock need not be designed anew for each city or region as long as common design principles are followed, and new, simple stations, perhaps built to standard plans as they were a century ago, will be required.

Standard designs and modal integration only do so much to reduce costs, however. Climate change, regional inequality, energy inefficiency and social isolation cannot be met with half-hearted trials using clapped-out equipment on inadequate tracks. Serious investment is necessary and will need sources of funding both traditional and new. Large works require some measure of borrowing to complement farebox revenue, rates and taxes, and tax incentives should support public transport rather than car ownership and road use. Harking all the way back to Vogel, the state can develop land along railway corridors – including in partnership with the private sector – and fund better transport through improved land values.

Nick Lovett, a former Christchurch city transport planner, highlights a persistent fallacy: that funds raised from roads should be spent on more roads. Congestion and pollution charges – which can take various forms – should be used to improve the entire transport system, not just roads.[18] Cost/benefit analyses in New Zealand in recent decades have consistently favoured

road and more often than not undervalued or overlooked the benefits of rail.[19] Waka Kotahi NZTA, which is responsible for land transport, is historically a road agency, and its priorities and funding allocations continue to reflect this. To secure a sustainable future, a greater proportion of investment from its National Land Transport Fund must support rail and other public transport. Previous researchers have described car dependence as an 'economic drain': it entails large direct expenditure and imposes many indirect, external and opportunity costs through factors such as dispersed land use (sprawl), pollution and accidents. A more balanced multimodal system will reduce transport expenditure as a proportion of national wealth.[20]

Our cities and regions are what we make them. Visionary policies and large investment are possible when people know that the outcomes will improve their communities. In the 1950s and 1960s New Zealand underwent a radical transition from multimodal transport to car dependency; we can undo this mistake. For rail to play its role, bottlenecks such as steep grades, tight curves and circuitous routes must be deviated, single lines duplicated, and track upgraded for faster and more frequent trains with commensurate signalling and safeworking improvements. When KiwiRail says that goods timetables preclude passenger trains, this is justification for upgrades rather than inaction.

Easy access is paramount to maximise the use of new services. Stations require good signage and wayfinding so passengers can locate destinations and connect with other transport modes, and ticketing and online route planning must be accessible. At the time of writing, a national ticketing system is being planned to supersede over 15 different regional systems;

known as Project NEXT, this will be invaluable if implemented well.

Fares also need to be considered thoughtfully. Tourists will remain a significant source of revenue, but tickets must be affordable for other passengers. The current branding of long-distance trains suggests the reason for high fares: these are the Great Journeys of New Zealand, a once-in-a-lifetime experience. We need affordable 'Everyday Rapid Journeys' of New Zealand.

Aotearoa should heed lessons from overseas. In the first stages of reintroducing passenger rail, it is important not to be distracted by unproven technologies. It is not worth risking potential failures, delays and cost overruns when off-the-shelf options exist that require few modifications to suit New Zealand's track and loading gauges. One overseas technology that could prove especially beneficial is the tram-train, a vehicle that operates on both traditional

railway lines and urban streets, bridging the gap between the accessibility and flexibility of on-street running and the advantages of higher train speeds and existing rail corridors. The 'Karlsruhe model' of tram-train is named for a German city that began operating tram-based technology on heavy rail as well as city streets in 1992. Some cities invert this – such as Zwickau in Germany, where fairly conventional diesel trains (sometimes dubbed train-trams rather than tram-trains) run on city streets. Regardless of the exact rollingstock, this technology can link existing railways to destinations that would otherwise be expensive or impractical to reach.

To revive passenger rail in New Zealand requires non-partisan political will. Economists and industry figures lament that funding promises from central and local authorities often did not materialise in the 2010s and planning between successive governments had little continuity.[21] Transport historically has fallen

The Karlsruhe model in action at Bad Rappenau, Germany. On the Elsenztalbahn, express trains run between main stations, while stopping services switch to tram tracks at Neckarsulm to enter central Heilbronn. Heavy rail electric multiple unit 8442 602 (left) exchanges passengers with AVG tram-train no. 962 on 10 July 2020. Moritz Krähe

9

into the left/right divide: parties on the left are pro-rail, those on the right are pro-road. This is unhelpful. Debates about details – sources of finance, ownership structures, fares – are to be expected. But the fact that an advanced economy requires good multimodal transport – for its environmental benefits, economic efficiencies, accessibility and choice – is not a question of ideology. In the 2020 election most parties placed greater emphasis on rail than has been typical in recent decades. The Greens released an ambitious and realistic national plan to revive rail; across the political divide, National proposed to extend Auckland's Western Line to Huapai, to examine commuter rail between Dunedin and Mosgiel, and to implement various projects to improve network capacity. For a party often criticised for over-emphasising motorways, this was a notable development.

Planners and politicians need to engage with their communities. Philip Laird and Peter Newman, both with wide experience in transport policymaking, warned in 2001 that New Zealand does not have 'decision-making systems that are open to public discourse and which can more fully reflect social values'.[22] Two decades later, much of the substance of this charge remains true. In particular, stuttering engagement with Māori has to become a genuine Treaty partnership so that service, benefits, costs and outcomes are informed by te ao Māori as well as Pākehā concepts. All people must be empowered to share their needs and wants with the assurance that these will be taken seriously.

The future has no room for the condescension of the 1983 Auckland report that noted traveller preferences for rail but recommended that services be run down to persuade them to take other modes. Policy

decisions since the 1950s have turned a choice of ground transport modes into no real choice at all – those who can, drive. Beyond Auckland and Wellington, there is not an uneven playing field; there is *no* field, just roads.

It is time to rectify historical imbalances and bring *all* transport to a high standard. New Zealand's leaders should be able to agree that rail is a public good that transcends partisan disagreement in broad terms, even as its specifics require scrutiny and debate. Long-term railway planning will bring substantial benefits to the country.

UPPER NORTH ISLAND

Auckland, Hamilton and Tauranga form the points of a so-called 'Golden Triangle' that takes in their surrounding regions. This triangle is home to about half of New Zealand's population; it is growing rapidly and experiencing significant economic change. After decades of neglect, the Golden Triangle's railways now enjoy considerable advantages. KiwiRail is boosting goods capacity, and commuter rail is central to Auckland's transport planning. The region benefits from well-organised advocates such as Greater Auckland, whose Regional Rapid Rail plan provides a concise and achievable blueprint for high-quality transport between the major centres that will also stimulate growth in intermediate towns. It introduces, in stages, a fast and frequent service using tilt trains, electrification and, potentially, major deviations around bottlenecks.

Our map builds on Greater Auckland's Regional Rapid Rail to the Waikato and Bay of Plenty. There are further possibilities, such as extending Tauranga services to the eastern Bay of Plenty. We concur with Greater Auckland in reviving the mothballed line from Putāruru to Rotorua, which will play to KiwiRail's strengths in the tourism market; it could be complemented with a service on the existing goods-only line from Putāruru to Tokoroa. For example, limited expresses could operate Auckland–Hamilton–Putāruru–Rotorua, with Hamilton–Putāruru–Tokoroa trains providing a feeder service for smaller towns.

Many Northlanders are passionate advocates for rail too. Although local politicians promote major projects to redress decades of under-investment, these usually emphasise goods traffic, such as a new branch to Marsden Point to support its growth as an export harbour, fixing aged track and narrow tunnels, and regaining forestry tonnages that go by road because of rundown railway facilities. The issues with Northland rail are complex, and while the short-term emphasis must necessarily be on goods, passenger trains should be a longer-term aspiration. The big challenge is the North Auckland Line's circuitous route via Helensville. A direct route through the North Shore would be expensive, possibly prohibitively so, and a long way off even if it were viable. There is a realistic option, though: a scenic train akin to KiwiRail's current offerings, running from Auckland to Whangārei and the Bay of Islands. This could at first operate during peak seasons only, to build demand.

Greater Auckland researcher Harriet Gale's 2017 back-of-the-envelope calculations suggest that passenger and goods upgrades combined would cost about $500 million – much less than expressways, which cost billions and do nothing to reduce carbon emissions. In the time since Gale published her estimates, Jacinda Ardern's Labour government has committed $200 million to rail in Northland. KiwiRail

is reopening the mothballed northernmost section to Ōtiria; bridges, curves and tunnels are being upgraded; and the Marsden Point Branch is inching closer to reality.[23] The Bay of Islands Vintage Railway, which currently runs between Kawakawa and Taumarere, is restoring its line to the waterside in Ōpua. KiwiRail would need to reach an agreement for a Bay of Islands passenger train to share this route; in return, it could permit the Vintage Railway to run heritage services between Ōpua and Whangārei as an attractive activity for holidaymakers.

LOWER NORTH ISLAND

The *Capital Connection* and *Wairarapa Connection* provide a basis to improve passenger rail in the lower North Island. The need for better passenger rail is clear to many local representatives – Kāpiti Coast councillor Gwynn Compton, for example, is promoting a plan for rapid, regular electric trains between Wellington and Palmerston North by 2050.[24] Our three-stage plan encompasses the lower North Island.

Stage one requires bimodal trains that can operate on Wellington's 1700V DC electrified network and on battery or diesel power beyond the wires. These will enable a frequent service between Palmerston North and Wellington. Two services a day can operate further. One should start at Marton, so that residents of Marton and Feilding can travel to Wellington with the same ease as those of Palmerston North. The other should operate from Wellington to Napier return, with the option of additional evening services on Fridays and weekends. The latter is a historically popular service that can succeed again.

DFB 7158 leads a *Wairarapa Connection* out of Wellington on 8 December 2018. Also visible is shunting locomotive DSC 2515, which pulled the train from the yard to the platform. André Brett

Stage two is bolder and involves electrification between Palmerston North and Waikanae. Trains from Wellington to Waikanae (and possibly as far as Ōtaki) need only be basic suburban units; beyond there, travel times mean that additional facilities, such as toilets and a buffet, are necessary for passenger comfort. This creates an appropriate division for the electrification systems: suburban units will only need to be built for 1700V DC, while trains travelling to Manawatū will have dual voltage technology for the 25kV AC already in use at Palmerston North.

Electrification provides a basis for more services from Marton and Palmerston North, while the bimodal trains will have two uses. One will be to increase the frequency of the Hawke's Bay timetable. The other will be to serve Whanganui on a schedule that builds connections with the Manawatū region as well as Wellington. Railway stations in most towns are located centrally, but Palmerston North will require seamless bus connections to Te Marae o Hine/The Square, Massey University and other destinations. It is also worth considering additional stations in Palmerston North to serve the airport and nearby suburbs.

Stage three goes even further – literally. As well as increasing the frequency of trains between Wellington, Palmerston North, Napier and Whanganui, it involves three new long-distance services and two infrastructure upgrades.

First, the services. Wellington–New Plymouth trains were cancelled in 1977 for want of railcars rather than poor patronage. Bimodal trains will revive this route, and can be complemented by a morning local service from Hāwera or even Whanganui that arrives in New Plymouth for the start of the workday and returns in the evening.

Another service to reintroduce is to Gisborne. At present, the line north of Wairoa is mothballed; by the time stage three is ready to begin, the needs of goods traffic should have brought about its reopening. A feasibility study in 2019 endorsed reviving the railway for goods. Although it focused on tourism rather than local or regional journeys, it identified tourism and heritage operators interested in regular or occasional passenger services.[25] The revival of the lower North Island's passenger network could create broader possibilities. The parlous state of East Coast roads and the superb scenery will make this an attractive proposition, although it might not sustain daily or year-round operation at first.

The third long-distance suggestion is for at least one daily Wellington–Napier train to run via the Wairarapa. This could be introduced in stages two or three, and will enhance regional connectivity and reduce demands on the Main Trunk. A premium 'Winelander' offering to connect vineyards in the Wairarapa, Hawke's Bay and Gisborne is worth exploring. This concept received community and industry support in 2001 during the campaign to save the *Bay Express*, but time was against its proponents. Since then these wine regions have grown in popularity and quality.

The proposed infrastructure upgrades for stage three include realising longstanding plans for a deviation to avoid the steep single-track climb south of Paekākāriki to Pukerua Bay. This will improve travel times and provide capacity for frequent and rapid regional rail to coexist with goods and commuters. The deviation could take a number of forms, such as a tunnel between Paekākāriki and Plimmerton, or a new line linking the Kāpiti Coast and the Hutt Valley. Commuter units to Waikanae will continue to serve communities along the existing route while regional services and goods trains take advantage of the new deviation. The other upgrade is to harness electrification's benefits for passenger and goods trains alike from Palmerston North to Napier and New Plymouth. New Zealand must maximise its clean energy resources to power a rail revival.

NORTH ISLAND MAIN TRUNK

The regional networks proposed for the upper and lower North Island will permit faster timetables for longer-distance trains too. When thinking of intercity trains, many New Zealanders immediately picture the trunk between Auckland and Wellington. As an environmentally friendly alternative to flying and driving, the *Northern Explorer*, which operates three times a week, is useful only to tourists. At the moment the journey takes almost 11 hours, yet as far back as 1938, special trains completed the run in under 10.[26] If the time can be reduced to seven hours at an average speed of just below 100km/h, or five hours at an average speed of 135km/h, it will provide an attractive service. The most time-sensitive travellers may still favour air travel, but this faster service will provide a competitive offering between the North Island's three largest cities, facilitate regional journeys that air travel cannot, and do so in a way that is quicker, safer and has greater capacity than buses. Hamilton to Levin, Taihape to Auckland, Te Awamutu to Paraparaumu – the connections are many. A daily *Northern Explorer*, renamed to avoid colonial connotations, is a good short-term goal.

New tilting rollingstock will enable better timings through the central North Island, so any order of tilting trainsets for regional networks should include units for the Main Trunk. Local councils have been increasingly assertive in seeking better Main Trunk passenger services, with Thomas Nash of Greater Wellington Regional Council one of those leading the charge for a night option. Overnight trains are resurgent overseas, and such an offering would not even require a fast timetable: an 8–9pm departure from one end that reaches the other at 6–7am would be ample. Transdev, Auckland and Wellington's suburban operator, has expressed interest in offering this if KiwiRail does not, although track access and timetabling would be complex.[27] Sleeper rollingstock will need to be bespoke, either as dedicated carriages or daytime accommodation that converts to beds. A long-term goal of generating demand to restore the old frequency of three trains daily between Wellington and Auckland – one daytime, one afternoon/evening and one overnight – is not unreasonable.

We have not included proposals for the Auckland and Wellington urban areas for two reasons. First, these cities have complex public transport networks and well-organised advocates, and prospective improvements require more detailed analysis than a chapter such as this can provide. Second, many initiatives are likely to be tramways – light rail – rather than railways, and so fall beyond this book's scope. We support the reintroduction of trams to both cities. A great counterfactual is

what might have happened if Wellington had converted the Johnsonville Branch for the use of its superb Fiducia trams in the 1930s. The core of its tram network, dismantled in 1964, may well have survived.

SOUTH ISLAND

KiwiRail at present operates only the *TranzAlpine* and the *Coastal Pacific* in the South Island, leaving much of the network without a passenger service. The *TranzAlpine* is one of the world's most celebrated trains and, until Covid-19 struck, it ran daily all year. The *Coastal Pacific* ceased year-round operation in 2013 and ran instead from September to April; Jacinda Ardern announced investment in November 2018 to restore a year-round timetable and provide additional rollingstock.[28] The main problem with both trains is that fares have risen beyond the means of many local travellers.

Extending the *TranzAlpine* to Hokitika is worthy of consideration. After all, tourists heading south to the glaciers already join buses in Greymouth and travel parallel to the Hokitika railway. Westland Mayor Bruce Smith proposed in 2017 that the district council rebuild the station in Hokitika to enable this extension.[29] Another option is to introduce a train from Hokitika to Westport that would showcase the beauty of the Buller Gorge and Grey Valley and enhance transport between the Coast's most populous towns. KiwiRail commissioned a feasibility study for this in July 2018 but, crucially, the terms of reference framed it as a tourist train. The consultants therefore assumed that patronage would be identical whether the southern terminus were in Hokitika or Greymouth, and that locals would ride the train just once or twice a year. The study concluded

9

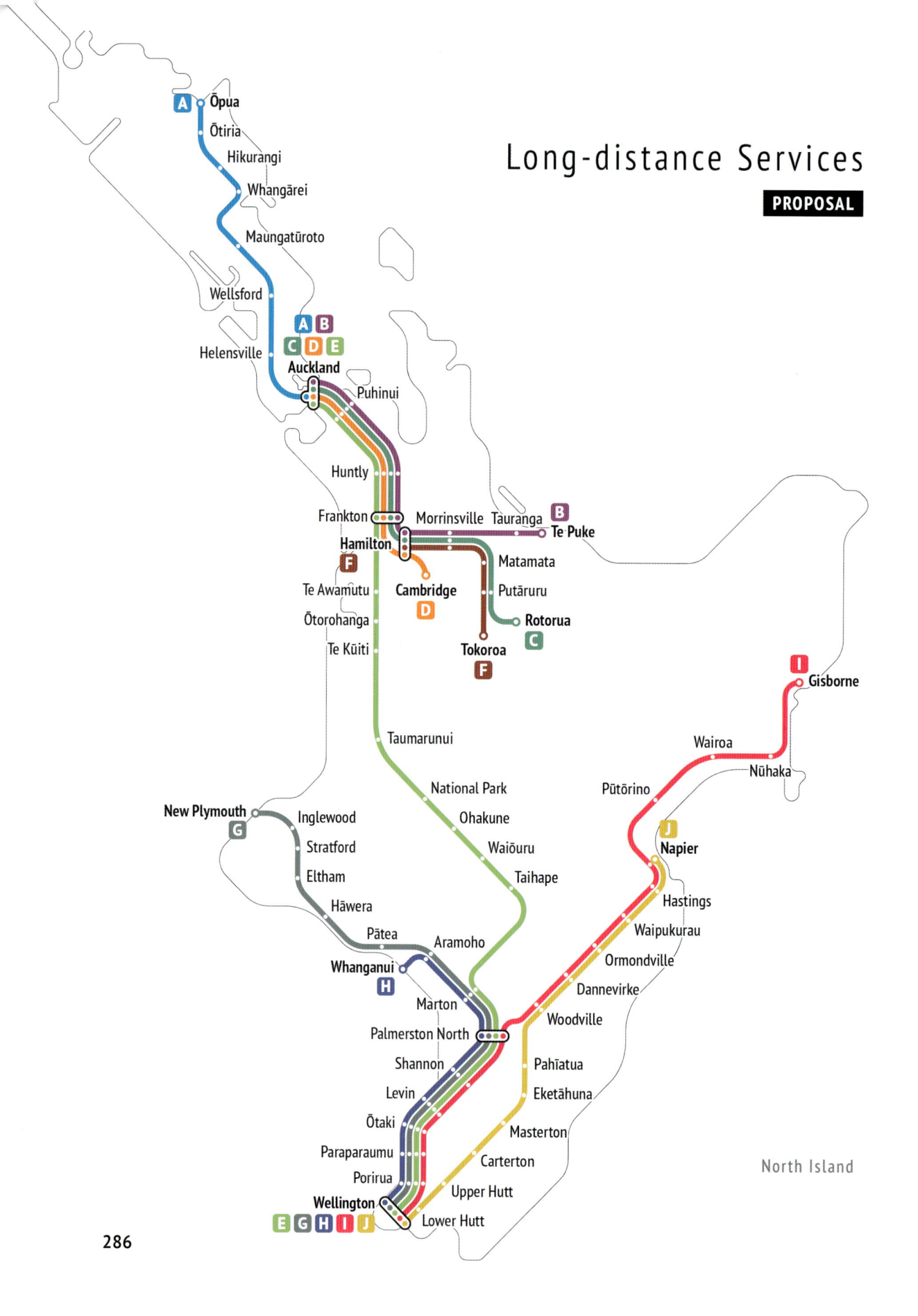

Long-distance Services

PROPOSAL

Ōpua
Ōtiria
Hikurangi
Whangārei
Maungatūroto
Wellsford
Helensville
Auckland
Puhinui
Huntly
Frankton
Morrinsville   Tauranga
Te Puke
Hamilton
Matamata
Te Awamutu
Putāruru
Cambridge
Ōtorohanga
Rotorua
Te Kūiti
Tokoroa
Gisborne
Taumarunui
Wairoa
National Park
Nūhaka
Ohakune
Pūtōrino
New Plymouth
Inglewood
Waiōuru
Napier
Stratford
Taihape
Eltham
Hastings
Hāwera
Waipukurau
Pātea
Aramoho
Ormondville
Whanganui
Dannevirke
Marton
Woodville
Palmerston North
Pahīatua
Shannon
Eketāhuna
Levin
Ōtaki
Masterton
Paraparaumu
Carterton
Porirua
Upper Hutt
Wellington
Lower Hutt

North Island

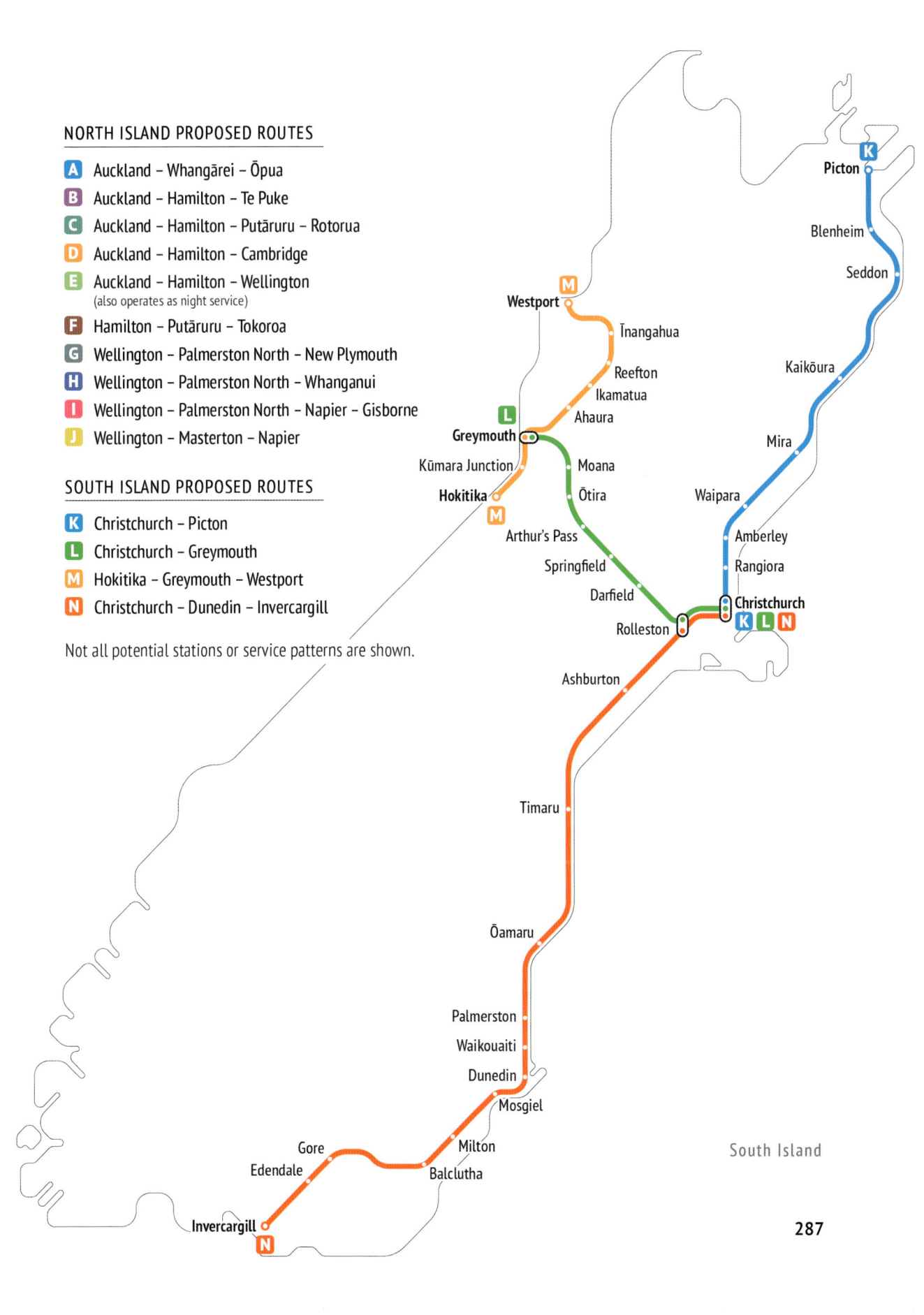

NORTH ISLAND PROPOSED ROUTES

A Auckland – Whangārei – Ōpua

B Auckland – Hamilton – Te Puke

C Auckland – Hamilton – Putāruru – Rotorua

D Auckland – Hamilton – Cambridge

E Auckland – Hamilton – Wellington
(also operates as night service)

F Hamilton – Putāruru – Tokoroa

G Wellington – Palmerston North – New Plymouth

H Wellington – Palmerston North – Whanganui

I Wellington – Palmerston North – Napier – Gisborne

J Wellington – Masterton – Napier

SOUTH ISLAND PROPOSED ROUTES

K Christchurch – Picton

L Christchurch – Greymouth

M Hokitika – Greymouth – Westport

N Christchurch – Dunedin – Invercargill

Not all potential stations or service patterns are shown.

M Westport

Īnangahua

Reefton

Ikamatua

Ahaura

L Greymouth

Kūmara Junction

Moana

Hokitika

Ōtira

M

Arthur's Pass

Springfield

Darfield

Rolleston

Ashburton

Timaru

Ōamaru

Palmerston

Waikouaiti

Dunedin

Mosgiel

Gore

Milton

Edendale

Balclutha

Invercargill

N

K Picton

Blenheim

Seddon

Kaikōura

Mira

Waipara

Amberley

Rangiora

Christchurch

K **L** **N**

South Island

such a train was unlikely to be commercially viable.[30] It did not consider any role rail could have in local transport, such as arrangements with businesses to get workers out of cars and commuting by train. As the West Coast shifts away from extractive industries, rail needs to serve locals as well as visitors. Len Richardson, in a recent book about the Coast's history and its historians, suggests the region has received 'scant respect' in recent decades, being expected to respond passively to change rather than participate in it.[31] Mobility is not only for visiting or leaving; it is a way of staying, of accessing the fullness of community life, and attentiveness to these needs will build a more participatory future.

On the other side of the Alps, the Main South Line offers considerable potential. Between Christchurch and Ōamaru it has an ideal alignment for higher-speed trains.[32] As a first stage, reintroduction of the *Southerner* with new tilting stock will provide a high-quality service to regions with a combined population of 850,000. Most cities and towns in the east retain central railway stations that require refurbishment rather than reconstruction, so the first stage will mainly involve deferred maintenance and modest track upgrades. Two trains each way daily from Christchurch to Invercargill – possibly just one south of Dunedin – will offer a competitive service. The old *Southerner* offered a faster trip from Christchurch to Timaru and Ōamaru than is possible by car today, and this revival will aim for an average speed north of Ōamaru of 100–110km/h rather than the 75–80km/h average of the 1990s.[33]

Further stages will upgrade infrastructure and add rollingstock for faster speeds and additional services. Grade separation from road is desirable but trains can use protected level crossings up

to 160km/h; speeds of 200km/h are possible before dedicated high-speed lines are necessary. The timetable will not only offer a swift intercity journey but also facilitate commuting such as Ashburton to Christchurch, Balclutha to Dunedin, or Gore to Invercargill. Local trains can complement expresses: for example, north of Timaru, a morning express from Dunedin could stop only at Ashburton and Rolleston, with a second train serving intermediate stations.

The staged implementation of a revived *Southerner* would also allow two major infrastructural projects to be constructed progressively. One is electrification. It is now a century since engineers first mooted electrifying the South Island's railways to take advantage of hydro power, an initiative that today will reduce dependence on imported fuel and facilitate cleaner, more efficient trains. It will be expensive, but could occur in conjunction with electrifying the Christchurch and Dunedin suburban networks as described below. Rail might be a potential consumer of spare electricity production capacity at Manapōuri when the Tīwai Point aluminium smelter closes.

The other challenge is the notoriously slow railway between Dunedin and Palmerston. The *Southerner* lost its time advantage over road thanks to this tortuous coastal route. As early as 1888 the PWD considered four possible deviations; the Savage Labour government examined the possibility of a tunnel from Sawyers Bay to Waitati in the late 1930s but the scheme fell by the wayside during World War II.[34] A tunnel would save much time for goods and passengers alike, with the old route retained for Dunedin Railways' *Seasider* sightseeing train. This scheme is necessarily bold, but it will maximise railway's advantages and provide cleaner, quicker transport than road.

HAMILTON

Hamilton is a prominent node in Greater Auckland's Regional Rapid Rail scheme, and it is worth considering the city's suburban rail potential as well. Hamilton's population, and that of surrounding towns, is growing faster than the national average and is likely to continue doing so. Waikato Regional Council's transport plan for 2018–28 envisages a mass transit network 'to enable unobstructed movement of mass transit vehicles, whatever those vehicles might be'. It suggests these will first be buses, with the potential for light rail or 'emerging technologies' in the future.[35] Future Proof, a partnership between central government, Waikato local government bodies, iwi and Waka Kotahi NZTA, in February 2019 published 'Hei Awarua ki te Oranga: Corridor of

9

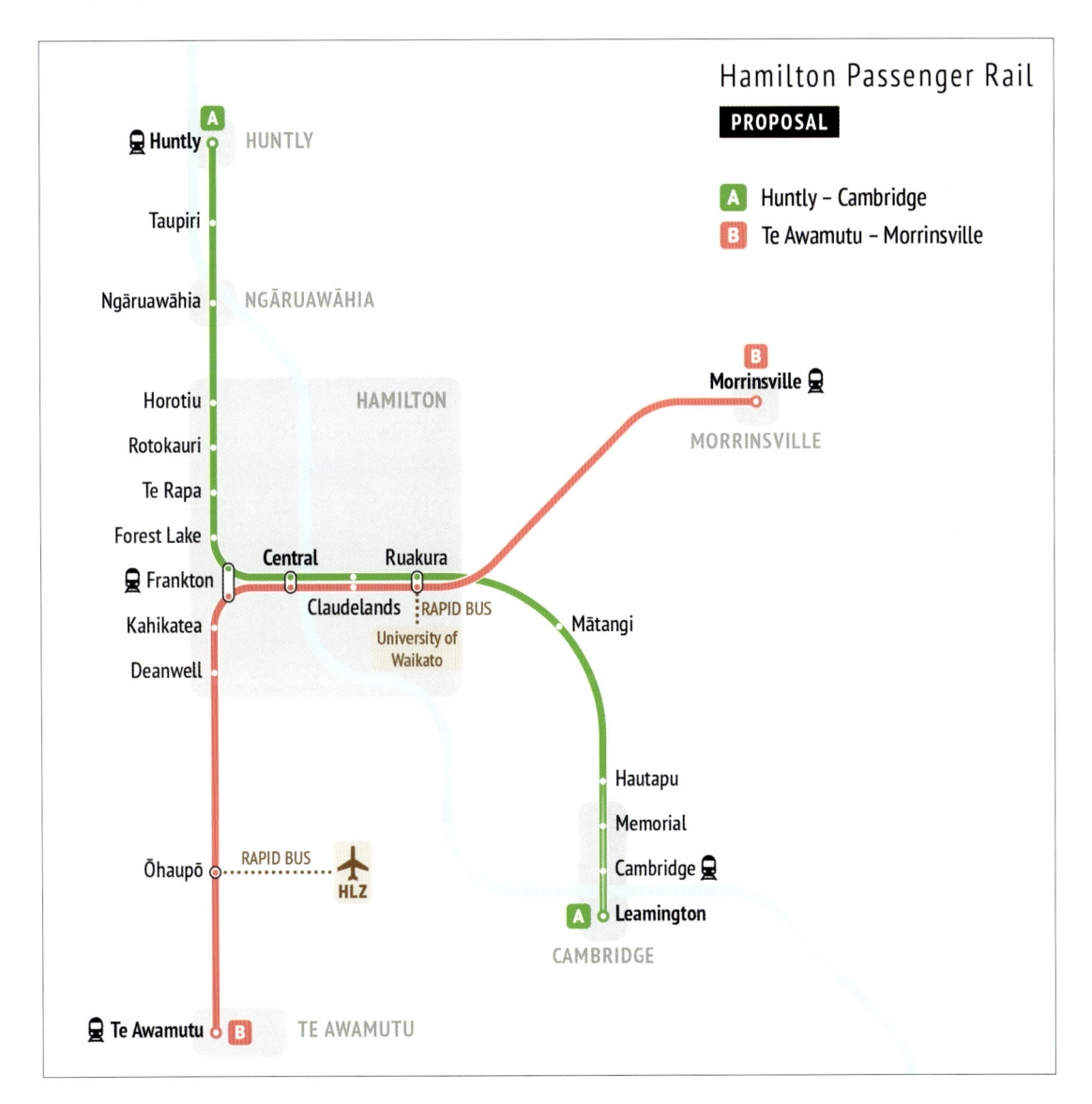

289

Te Awamutu station in December 2019. The nameboard remains and the shelter shed was repainted during the 2010s, even though passenger trains do not stop here. We propose that this station be rejuvenated to serve both long-distance trains and a local Waikato network. André Brett

Te Awamutu, is concerned about car dependency in new subdivisions and wants to shift the focus from cars to people.[37] Our formulation presents two suburban lines. Some new stations will be required, including in Hamilton's suburbs and Morrinsville, while others, such as Te Awamutu station, will need cosmetic repairs.

Wellbeing', a plan for the Hamilton to Auckland corridor. It describes a metro rail service from Huntly through Hamilton to Cambridge as the trunk of a mass transit network, with a railway spur to Hamilton Airport.[36]

Hamilton needs public transport fit for purpose. Future Proof offers some of the bold vision necessary, and more is possible. Best of all, much of the infrastructure is already in place: the East Coast Main Trunk runs directly through the city via a disused underground central station, and railways run to major outlying towns and pass near traffic generators, such as shopping centres and stadiums.

Covid-19 has prompted Waikato's politicians to urgently consider local commuter trains as an economic stimulus. Hamilton city councillor Dave Macpherson outlined his ambition to have the first services operational within two years – a vision made possible by the extant infrastructure. Waikato Regional Council has also indicated support for these ideas and anticipates modest capital costs, and Waipā District Council, which takes in Cambridge and

Two large infrastructural issues must be addressed. The first is the capacity of the existing railways through Hamilton. Suburban trains might well obstruct goods trains on one of the busiest parts of the freight network, and here, if anywhere, the old anti-passenger attitudes are likely to emerge. The line under the city and over the Waikato River is a single track and will be expensive to duplicate. But as freight volumes in the Golden Triangle keep growing, expansion will benefit all traffic.

The other challenge is to restore rail into Cambridge. The branch line from Ruakura currently terminates at a dairy factory in Hautapu. Most of the old railway corridor survives as the wide median of Victoria Street and a conventional railway could be restored into town, but light rail is worth considering so that it can continue across the Waikato River into Leamington. This would require tram-trains, enabling other light rail options in Hamilton. The

290

University of Waikato, notably, is too far from the railway to be easily walkable.

Future Proof's proposal of an airport branch is possibly a step too far, as the airport is not currently one of New Zealand's 10 busiest. Light rail or a high-frequency bus may be better options.

TAURANGA

Tauranga is a natural option for commuter rail. It might not seem so: it has no passenger trains and has never possessed a commuter network. But Tauranga's population is growing rapidly. In 1996 the city had fewer than 78,000 people; some 25 years later it has over 150,000. Its population swells during holidays, and existing railway lines pass important destinations. The East Coast Main Trunk runs through the central

9

city and alongside Baypark Stadium; the Mount Maunganui Branch is near the Bay Oval, Bayfair shopping centre and Tauranga Airport. Why are cricket audiences and cruise ship passengers not already coming and going by train?

The core of the network would operate around the harbour from Tauranga to Mount Maunganui. At the western end it would run through coastal suburbs to Ōmokoroa; at the eastern end to Te Puke. A new station at the junction of the East Coast Main Trunk and the Mount Maunganui Branch, adjacent to Baypark Stadium, would serve large events and facilitate transfers between Mount Maunganui, Tauranga and Te Puke. The capacity of the existing lines can be improved as service frequency increases. Tram-trains into central Mount Maunganui are worth considering rather than a terminus in the rail yards. All of this is achievable.

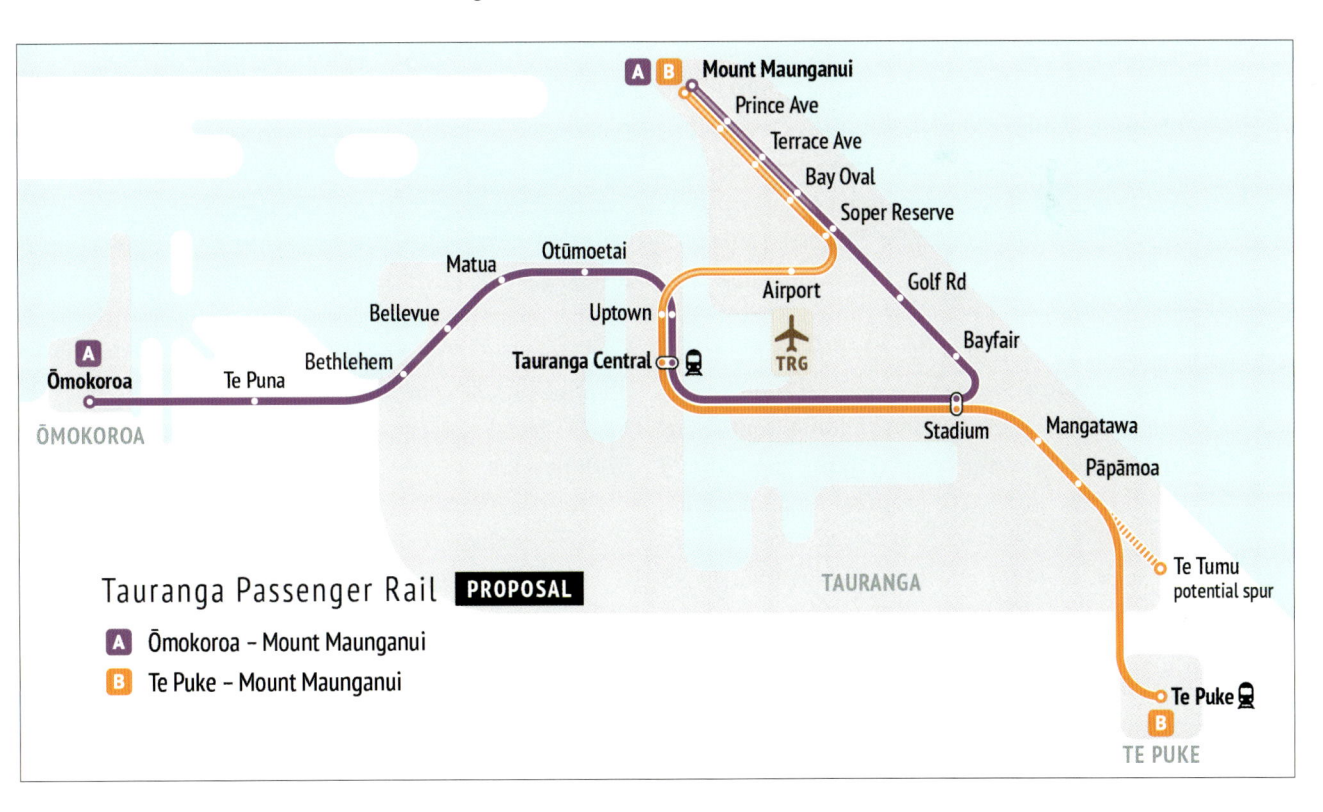

The Bay of Plenty Regional Council included passenger trains in long-term planning as far back as a 2007 regional rail strategy. A more recent plan used inaccurate assumptions about necessary population size and density to downplay passenger rail, but still endorsed studying rail as a solution to road congestion. Tauranga is New Zealand's most car-dependent city: in 2017, 97 percent of trips were taken in private vehicles.[38]

A second stage could address the absence of a direct railway from central Tauranga to Mount Maunganui. This problem has bedevilled planners for decades. The road bridge that carries Te Awanui Drive over Tauranga Harbour was debated in Parliament from the early 1970s and opened in 1988, and a second bridge was added in 2009. NZR worked unsuccessfully with the National Roads Board to include a railway on the first bridge, and further investigations of a railway bridge in the late 1990s also led nowhere, although it remained in the 2007 regional rail strategy. The main issues are that a low bridge will impede maritime activity while a high bridge requires steep grades or sharp curves.[39] Planners in the past conceived a new bridge as a freight shortcut that would allow the original alignment to be abandoned. Suburban rail provides an opportunity to approach this seemingly intractable problem from another angle, including the option of adding tram-trains to the existing bridges and retaining goods on the current railway. The proposal might remain untenable, but it warrants renewed investigation.

What about the eastern Bay of Plenty? More is the pity that no railway ever ran into Whakatāne. The only town of significant size with a railway is Kawerau, and the line there terminates at a yard on the town's industrial fringe rather than entering the town. It is

unlikely that a service is possible in the short term. Tram-trains could provide a cost-effective means of accessing central Kawerau and Whakatāne, and rapid population growth throughout the Bay of Plenty suggests that corridors should be reserved so that some form of passenger rail can serve these towns in the longer term.

Another area that requires futureproofing is Te Tumu, a planned suburban development east of Tauranga between Pāpāmoa Beach and the mouth of the Kaituna River. Protecting land for a spur from the main line to Te Tumu will aid efforts to reduce car dependency in coastal suburbs.

NAPIER–HASTINGS

The main line from Palmerston North runs through the centre of Hastings and Napier with a branch to the port at Ahuriri, which is now a trendy suburb. The two cities are small – Napier is home to approximately 66,000 people and Hastings 49,000 – but the railway is located so conveniently that it makes an excellent spine for local transport. Hawke's Bay can harness this for future benefit, with new stops that allow passengers to access significant destinations and connect with buses to Taradale, Havelock North and elsewhere. Trains could also operate directly into the port to collect cruise ship visitors to spare central Napier's streets from being overrun with buses.

A second northern terminus might be possible: some services could continue to Bay View or even Eskdale instead of Ahuriri. The population in this area is small, but Hawke's Bay Airport is beside the railway, and although it is not busy enough to justify trains on its own, local travellers plus co-ordination with airlines could make a service viable. A rail service could also partner with local vineyards to allow tourists to visit cellar doors.

At the other end of the proposed route, some trains could continue beyond Hastings to Waipukurau. Mayor of Central Hawke's Bay Alex Walker reported in March 2019 that 'a good number of residents' had approached her about commuter trains. Alan Dick, chair of Hawke's Bay Regional Council's transport

Right: The railway in Hastings is centrally located. DFT 7199 and DC 4185 rumble past the Hastings clock tower with a Napier-bound goods train on 10 October 2014. Simon Mathew

Napier–Hastings Passenger Rail

PROPOSAL

A1 Waipukurau – Ahuriri
A2 Waipukurau – Bay View

- Eskdale — weekend excursions
- Bay View **A2**
- Airport NPE
- Westshore
- Wharf — cruise ship extension
- **A1** Ahuriri
- Napier
- Pandora
- Napier South
- NAPIER
- Te Awa
- Awatoto
- Clive
- Whakatū
- Mayfair
- Hastings
- Raureka
- HASTINGS
- Ōtāne
- Waipawa
- WAIPAWA
- Waipukurau
- WAIPUKURAU
- **A1** **A2**

committee and the man who tried hard to save the *Bay Express*, suggested a bus might suit Central Hawke's Bay better, but that all options were worth considering.[40] Hawke's Bay would do well to put its railway to good use.

CHRISTCHURCH

Depending on which figures you use and where you draw urban boundaries, Christchurch is now New Zealand's second-largest city, ahead of Wellington, and its projected growth is faster than that of the national capital. It appears that Christchurch could sprawl in almost any direction, but transport and housing policy blogger Brendon Harre points out that a range of factors – the airport noise zone, floodplains and liquefaction risk areas – mean it will likely grow from its current 'small apple' shape into a 'fat banana' stretching from Rangiora to Rolleston.[41] James Dann, a perceptive writer on issues facing Christchurch, emphasises the undesirability of some aspects of this banana-shaped growth, such as the loss of farmland to suburban sprawl. Former industrial sites closer to the city, he writes, should be transformed into residential areas.[42] The two visions are compatible and, best of all, much growth can occur near rail corridors. At the moment, the communities emerging and consolidating along the banana depend on motorways and other roads. This is no way to expand a city.

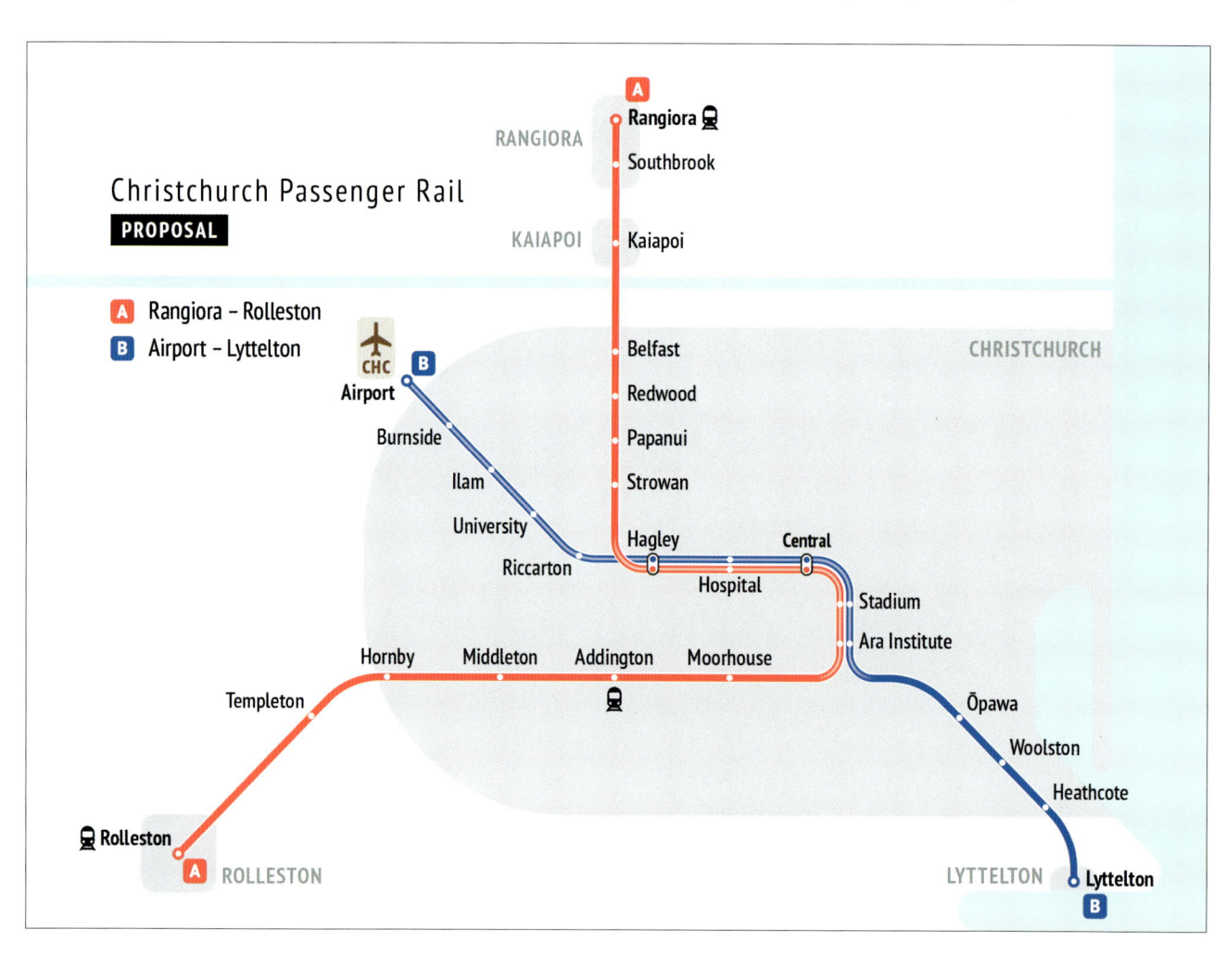

Rail must be part of Christchurch's future if it is to grow sustainably. Many proposals have been made in the past decade, but unfortunately during the city's rebuild following the 22 February 2011 earthquake John Key's government squandered the opportunity to introduce light rail and reinstate passenger trains. A common objection to commuter rail in Christchurch is the lack of a central station, a factor that has scuttled proposals for which Environment Canterbury has commissioned reports. Nonetheless, one of these reports, from 2010, was in favour of a staged implementation of tram-trains to a new central terminus. Environment Canterbury is currently identifying rapid transit corridors, without committing to specific modes.[43]

The tram-train suggestion is worth developing, and Christchurch will benefit from multimodal transport that exploits the existing rail corridors, implements light rail for trunk routes and uses buses for other journeys. The heavy rail lines are convenient to suburbs and towns as far north as Rangiora and southwest to Rolleston; a light rail line into the central city will bring passengers close to major destinations and enable efficient through-routing. Our map suggests one way that this could occur. It obviates the need for an expensive new railway terminus, although the existing Addington station will probably need upgrading or relocating to accommodate the revived *Southerner*.

Historically, Christchurch's main rail commuter corridor went to Lyttelton via the tunnel. The city's changing shape means this line will not regain its status as the core of the network, but it can form part of another tram-train route: from Lyttelton, this will follow the light rail loop through the city and continue past the University of Canterbury to the airport.

Space is available to resolve most capacity issues on the existing corridors with double-tracking or passing loops. The Lyttelton Tunnel is a potential bottleneck – although it accommodated over 20 suburban trains a day until 1972 in addition to numerous goods services. It may be worth devising a modern version of the Sockburn–Styx Deviation proposal (see page 150) to divert goods from the central city. Ideally, additional light rail routes can, and should, extend from the city loop to serve existing suburbs and support new residential development, but these are beyond our scope. Electrification is important to this scheme, to restore what should never have been removed from the Lyttelton Tunnel and provide a start for electrifying the Main South Line.

DUNEDIN

Although a small city, Dunedin has one of the best cases for commuter rail. The railway between Port Chalmers and Mosgiel follows important commuting corridors and runs past Forsyth Barr Stadium and close to the University of Otago, and the Dunedin railway station is centrally located. Proposals to revive suburban trains are frequent – city councillor Jim O'Malley, for example, has steadfastly championed a service between Dunedin and Mosgiel to reduce congestion on the Southern Motorway, which deposits 35,000 cars onto city streets daily.[44] The mothballing of Dunedin Railways during the Covid-19 pandemic inspired detailed proposals for commuter trains, and it is time now to turn talk into action. At peak hour, the Mosgiel train timetable of the 1960s was quicker than cars today and the Port Chalmers timetable was on a par; modern trains

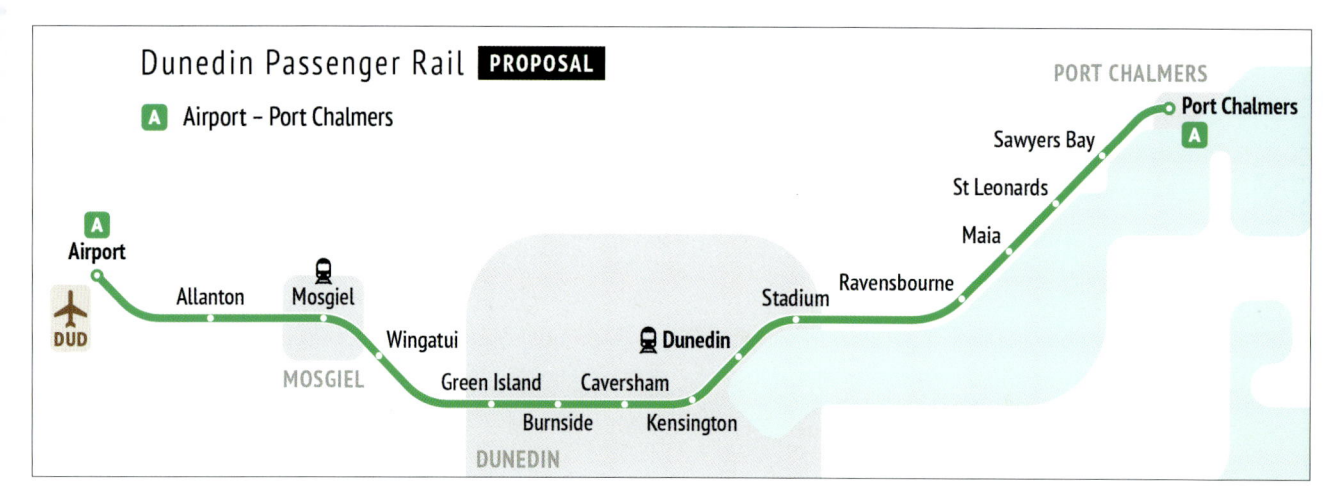

Dunedin Passenger Rail PROPOSAL

A Airport – Port Chalmers

will be even faster. The railway can form a spine for the city bus network and integrate with recently introduced harbour ferries.

The main problem is infrastructure loss: NZR reduced the Main South Line from two tracks to one during the mid-1980s, and most suburban stations are long gone. KiwiRail is unlikely to agree to a commuter service unless some double track is rebuilt, as it will otherwise disrupt goods trains. But duplication will have benefits: at present, residents around Port Chalmers endure many trucks on the local road; a second track will allow more goods trains to shuttle between the harbour and a proposed 'inland port' at Milburn as well as enabling commuter trains. It is important that duplication does not disrupt the cycle path that follows the railway, however, as this is also vital for reducing car dependency.

Another topic worthy of consideration is a connection with Dunedin Airport, which is located at some remove in rural Mōmona, near Mosgiel. There is currently no public transport into the city, and visitors face an expensive taxi fare or a shared shuttle with no defined schedule or route. The Main South Line runs near the airport but at some distance and on the wrong side of the runway from the terminal. Projected passenger numbers alone probably do not warrant a spur to the terminal, but if adjacent land were used as a depot for suburban trains a rail link would be more realistic. This would also add Allanton to the network and avoid the need to install sidings at Mosgiel to service trains or to park them between runs. The key is for the airport link to be one among multiple justifications for the service.

WHERE ELSE?

If New Zealand achieves a modal shift to rail, it will catalyse investment and additional services might become possible. Some, such as local trains around Invercargill or long-distance expresses between Auckland and New Plymouth, would use existing tracks. Others would require new construction. There are many longstanding projected railways that are desirable but costly and difficult to build: beyond the main centres, a new line can usually only be justified by significant goods tonnages alongside passenger traffic. Taupō railway proposals spring eternal; if one eventuates it will likely serve forestry, which would dictate the alignment,

The masterpiece of architect George Troup: Dunedin railway station, built in 1906, looking resplendent on 15 September 2018. André Brett

possibly to the detriment of passenger timings. For some tourist destinations, such as Queenstown and Fiordland, the difficult terrain makes rail eye-wateringly expensive. Likewise, a large hill separates Wainuiōmata from Lower Hutt and a commuter railway tunnel would require concurrent suburban intensification.

In any instance where lines currently used for heritage or rail cart operations are reintegrated into the railway network, the costs to restore services will be lower by dint of years of maintenance by volunteer societies or small businesses. Shared operation with or compensation of the existing users must be available. Heritage railways serve Waiuku, south of Auckland, and Waitara, east of New Plymouth; if the local populations continue to

grow, negotiations for preserved and commuter trains to coexist should not be out of the question.

ALL ABOARD!

The history of New Zealand's passenger network may seem discouraging but should not be taken that way. New Zealanders have persisted with their trains despite poor rollingstock, dismissive officials and politicians, and narrowly framed economic arguments. Popular services have often taken authorities by surprise. It is time we replaced 'will it return a direct financial profit?' with 'will the community benefit?'

The state funds many activities and institutions with no expectation of profit, simply because their existence enriches people's lives and improves our country. All we ask is that funds are spent wisely and effectively. This rationale used to apply to rail. Michael Joseph Savage put it well in 1938:

There is more to be done than to make figures to show whether the railways are paying or not. You have to take into consideration the areas to be tapped and the development of the country through which the railway passes … Instead of that, people bought and sold land and they got rich; and it was almost painted on the clouds that the railways were not paying.[45]

Australian economic historian Mac Boot explains that 'railways have difficulty capturing enough of the benefits they create in the form of revenue', and this is why governments throughout Australasia constructed and operated them.[46] If KiwiRail is to deliver the full benefits of rail transport, it must be empowered and funded appropriately.

Technology and travel patterns changed substantially between 1920 and 2020, but there was nothing inexorable in the way the railway network's size and use changed. Cabinet deliberations and stationmaster suggestions alike shaped the network, and some seemingly minor choices and decisions had wide-ranging effects. Between 1920 and 1945, NZR transitioned from a common carrier with a developmental aegis into a trunk network operating between regions and major centres. Much of this was a sensible response to automotive transport. Cars and trucks met the needs of sparsely populated rural areas better than slow, infrequent mixed trains, while urban and trunk railways maximised rail's best qualities: commuter trains, main-line expresses and regional railcars complemented

each other and loomed large in daily life.

Harder to justify are the decisions made about NZR Road Services. Instead of extending services beyond the rail network, buses often replaced still-viable rural trains and duplicated main-line offerings. Understandably, many riders saw these substitutions as an excuse to charge more for a lesser service. Likewise, post-war city planners overstated the domestic benefits of the motorway, turning away from rail just when it was most needed to handle swelling urban populations. With many suburban trains rundown or cancelled, New Zealand cities by the 1980s were congested and offered residents fewer transport choices.

Parliament legislated to protect state investment in rail during the 1930s, but as the twentieth century progressed regulation and funding decisions favoured road transport more and more. Competing demands for NZR to both be profitable and provide social services became invidious. Neoliberal governments expected rail to deliver returns on investment without asking the same of roads, and privatisation left a sorry legacy of abandoned services and asset-stripping. Sometimes, rail has been so constrained that it was unable to respond well to changes.

Too many decisions were for short-term gain or to ease workloads rather than to provide a quality service that would endure or meet emerging needs. Egregious examples include the cancellation of passenger trains so that goods timetabling required less effort. Air travel between major cities became increasingly popular and affordable from the 1960s, but there are countless journeys unsuited to flying where rail had a large regional role. NZR and Tranz Scenic abdicated this role, but it is one that KiwiRail can fill again.

9

People with ambition for rail have long been told that their goals are unrealistic, rather than being empowered to achieve them. Too often since the 1940s the vision for rail has been narrow, and the Covid-19 pandemic exposed the risks of a laser focus on tourism for long-distance patronage. Yet rail has had many markets, and most were surrendered with little fight or discarded willingly. Generations of New Zealanders have embraced even modest improvements in their passenger trains with open arms and are less wedded to sitting in traffic jams than stereotypes suggest. Passengers flocked to the Fiat railcars despite the mechanical difficulties, and second-hand equipment was enough to spark Auckland's recent suburban railway revival, with patronage skyrocketing from barely a million to over 20 million in under 25 years.

The first draft of this chapter was written as Australian bushfires spilled smoke across New Zealand; it was revised as the country locked down to stop the initial spread of Covid-19. The pandemic's effects will echo globally for years to come and may yet create a rupture in our society and economy rather than a brief pause of routines. Government stimulus in the form of ongoing investment will be necessary to reinvigorate the economy and will define the New Zealand of the future.

Transport is a crucial component of this. Will our communities become more vibrant and accessible? Will travellers attain modal choice? Will the country transition to a more sustainable future? Central and local governments need to work together, much as Vogel intended before vested interests compromised key components of his sweeping plan for a national railway network in 1870. Local authorities provide important knowledge of daily needs and wants, which central government can slot into larger national visions. It is essential that this involves meaningful bicultural partnerships. The possibilities outlined in this chapter are the sorts of projects to stimulate and invigorate post-pandemic New Zealand.

Transport is what we make it. Car dependency is reversible, not inevitable. There are decades of bad decisions and under-investment to overcome, decades of local insights and international innovations to enact. If we are to accommodate the changing global climate, New Zealanders – politicians, planners, voters, travellers, all – must make changes quickly. A larger, accessible, efficient and above all up-to-date passenger rail network will improve national resilience and make our cities and towns better places.

Rail has been allowed to wither, despite its potential, and must not be allowed to expire beyond Auckland and Wellington. Who wants congested cities? Rail has the capacity to move large volumes of people in a way road does not. Who wants opportunities in rural areas to go wanting for lack of mobility? Rail is an important part of reviving regions and empowering communities. It may not cater for every journey, nor could it, but it can cater for many more than it does now. Rail provides mobility not only for those with the physical or financial means to access it, as cars and air travel do: rail is mobility for everyone. The passenger network must grow again, so that in future we *can* get there from here.

Notes

INTRODUCTION

1. J.D. Mahoney, *Kings of the Iron Road: Steam passenger trains of New Zealand* (Palmerston North: Dunmore Press, 1982), 42.

2. Shaun Hendy, *#NoFly: Walking the talk on climate change* (Wellington: Bridget Williams Books, 2019).

3. David Leitch and Brian Scott, *Exploring New Zealand's Ghost Railways*, rev. edn (Wellington: Grantham House, 1998 [1995]), 125.

4. Alice Kranenburg, 'Down on Main Street: The depopulation of the Central North Island', in Paul Spoonley (ed.), *Rebooting the Regions: Why low or zero growth needn't mean the end of prosperity* (Auckland: Massey University Press, 2016), 111.

5. Circular memoranda from Thomas Ronayne, general manager, of 11 and 23 March 1911 and 20 March 1912, ANZ-DRO DABM 11/290 (trolleying passengers on isolated lines). This practice endured into the 1960s when miners who worked atypical shifts were carried by motorised jigger on the Rewanui Branch: C. Clark, chief civil engineer, to Alan Gandell, general manager, 22 July 1963, ANZ-CRO CAHV 11/658 part 2 (trolleying passengers on isolated lines).

6. Rosslyn J. Noonan, *By Design: A brief history of the Public Works Department* (Wellington: A.R. Shearer, 1975), 37–38, 177–96, 263.

7. Ibid., 295.

8. Graham Stewart, *The End of the Penny Section: When trams ruled the streets of New Zealand*, rev. edn (Wellington: Grantham House, 1993 [1973]); Paul Mahoney, *The Era of the Bush Tram in New Zealand* (Wellington: IPL Books, 1998).

9. J.M.K. Hill, Cabinet paper no. 710 (1970), 17 July 1970, ANZ AAFD CAB 183/6/2 part 1 (railways – passenger services – termination of services).

10. Neill Atkinson, *Trainland: How railways made New Zealand* (Auckland: Random House, 2007); Robin Bromby, *Rails that Built a Nation: An encyclopedia of New Zealand railways* (Wellington: Grantham House, 2003); Geoffrey B. Churchman and Tony Hurst, *The Railways of New Zealand: A journey through history* (Auckland: HarperCollins, 1990); David Leitch, *Railways of New Zealand* (Auckland: Leonard Fullerton, 1972); Leitch and Scott, *Exploring New Zealand's Ghost Railways*; James Watson, *Links: A history of transport and New Zealand society* (Wellington: G.P. Publications, 1996); J.R. Yonge, *New Zealand Railway and Tramway Atlas*, 4th edn (Exeter: Quail Map Company, 1993 [1965]). Note that Bromby recently published *New Zealand Railways: Their life and times* (Sydney: Highgate Publishing, 2014), in some respects an updated *Rails that Built a Nation*.

11. Robert Miles, *The End of the New Zealand Passenger Train* (Timaru: the author, 1995).

12. Michael Gunder, 'Auckland's motorway system: A New Zealand genealogy of imposed automotive progress, 1946–66', *Urban Policy and Research* 20:2 (2002), 129–40; Christopher E. Harris, 'Slow train coming: The New Zealand state changes its mind about Auckland transit, 1949–56', *Urban Policy and Research* 23:1 (2005), 37–55; Muhammad Imran and Jane Pearce, 'Discursive barriers to sustainable transport in New Zealand cities', *Urban Policy and Research* 33:4 (2015), 392–415; Paul Mees and Jago Dodson, 'Backtracking Auckland:

Bureaucratic rationality and public preferences in transport planning', *Urban Research Program Issues Paper 5* (2006).

13. New Zealand Government Railways, *Appendix to the Working Time-Tables*, effective 1 August 1908, Hocken Collections Uare Taoka a Hākena MS-3070.

14. See the communication in ANZ ADQD 1903/111/1 parts 1–3 (passengers travelling by goods trains). David Leitch, in *Steam, Steel and Splendour* (Auckland: HarperCollins, 1994), 12–13, narrates one example from Southland in the late 1960s of women carried against regulations in a locomotive cab.

CHAPTER 1

THE NETWORK IN 1920

1. David Leitch and Brian Scott, *Exploring New Zealand's Ghost Railways*, rev. edn (Wellington: Grantham House, 1998 [1995]), 33.

2. For more on Southland's wooden railway, see André Brett, 'Wooden rails and gold: Southland and the demise of the provinces', in *Rushing for Gold: Nineteenth century trans-Tasman society, mining, and enterprise*, Lloyd Carpenter and Lyndon Fraser (eds) (Dunedin: Otago University Press, 2016), 253–70. For a broader account of provincial governments and public works, see André Brett, *Acknowledge No Frontier: The creation and demise of New Zealand's provinces, 1853–76* (Dunedin: Otago University Press, 2016), especially Chapters 6, 10 and 12. An older and still valuable political history of the provinces is W.P. Morrell, *The Provincial System in New Zealand, 1852–76*, rev. edn (Christchurch: Whitcombe and Tombs, 1964 [1932]).

3. This text is a composite of *New Zealand Parliamentary Debates* (*NZPD*) vol. 7 (1870), 108, and the government's press summary in *Evening Post*, 29 June 1870, 2. The final sentence does not appear in the *NZPD* (the sentiment is expressed less clearly), while the network description in the press contains mistakes, e.g. 'Milton' for 'Winton'.

4. The definitive account of Vogel's life is Raewyn Dalziel, *Julius Vogel: Business politician* (Auckland: Auckland University Press, 1986). Articles on specific aspects of the Great Public Works Policy, parochial politics, provincial abolition and Vogel's role therein include André Brett, 'Dreaming on a railway track: Public works and the demise of New Zealand's provinces', *Journal of Transport History* 36:1 (2015), 77–96; André Brett, 'A sudden fancy for tree-planting? Forest conservation and the demise of New Zealand's provinces', *Environment and History* 23 (2017), 123–45; J.A. Dowie, 'Business politicians in action: The New Zealand railway boom of the 1870s', *Business Archives and History* 5:1 (1965), 32–56; G.J. Rosanowski, 'The West Coast railways and New Zealand politics, 1878–1888', *New Zealand Journal of History* 4:1 (1970), 34–53; Graeme Wynn, 'Conservation and society in late nineteenth-century New Zealand', *New Zealand Journal of History* 11:2 (1977), 124–36; and Graeme Wynn, 'Pioneers, politicians and the conservation of forests in early New Zealand', *Journal of Historical Geography* 5:2 (1979), 171–88.

5. Robin Bromby, *Rails that Built a Nation: An encyclopedia of New Zealand railways* (Wellington: Grantham House, 2003), 83; W.A. Pierre, *Canterbury Provincial Railways: Genesis of the N.Z.R. system* (Wellington: New Zealand Railway and Locomotive Society, 1964), 63–66.

6. Leitch and Scott, *Exploring New Zealand's Ghost Railways*, 114; population figures from *Census of New Zealand 1906*, table 27.

7. David Leitch, *Railways of New Zealand* (Auckland: Leonard Fullerton, 1972), 86–88.

8. Bromby, *Rails that Built a Nation*, 121–22.

9. *Appendices to the Journals of the House of Representatives* (*AJHR*) 1920 D-1, viii.

10. Ibid., ix.

11. Jeffrey Richards and John M. MacKenzie, *The Railway Station: A social history* (Oxford: Oxford University

Press, 1986), 87. See also J.D. Mahoney, *Down at the Station: New Zealand railway stations remembered* (Palmerston North: Dunmore Press, 1995).

12. Neill Atkinson, *Trainland: How railways made New Zealand* (Auckland: Random House, 2007), 165.

13. This is recounted in ANZ DAFV 23/603 part 1 (motor competition – wool traffic, Kurow to Dunedin).

14. See ANZ ADQD 1900/2881 part 1 (passenger steamer competition – Auckland northwards) and ADQD 1922/400/5 part 1 (steamer competition – Auckland/Thames Valley).

15. Simon Ville, 'The coastal trade of New Zealand prior to World War One', *New Zealand Journal of History* 27:1 (1993), 75–89.

16. *AJHR* 1923 D-2, xiv.

17. *AJHR* 1925 D-2, xxvii.

18. Ibid., xxxvi, *AJHR* 1926 D-2, 14 and 27, and *AJHR* D-2 1936, 12 and 24. The returns encompass 'developmental' branches and isolated sections, but the criteria are not stated and some absences are hard to explain in light of other inclusions. Branches that do not appear include Ahuriri, Onehunga, Raetihi, Rotorua and Thames in the north, and Blackball, Kingston, Rewanui, Seddonville and Tūātapere in the south.

19. *AJHR* D-2 1920, 15–18 and *AJHR* 1930 D-2, 25–28.

20. G.H. McLean, acting DTM Christchurch, to Garnet Hercules Mackley, general manager, 26 January 1940, ANZ ADQD 1908/1357/5 part 2 (Greymouth–Blackball train services).

21. See letters in ANZ ABJP 08/1357/17 part 1 (Rapahoe Branch trains), e.g. R.W. McVilly, general manager, circular memorandum, 11 September 1923; and R.S. Kent, divisional superintendent South Island, to P.G. Roussell, acting general superintendent of transportation, 28 March 1927. Useful letters are also in ANZ-CRO CAHV 1929/975/3 (Rapahoe, opening of line between Rapahoe and Runanga).

22. Documents in ANZ ADQD 1916/2334 part 2 (Shag Point railway line) show that only coal wagons were used on this line.

23. J.A. Dangerfield, *Dunedin's Matchbox Railway: The Dunedin, Peninsula and Ocean Beach Railway Company and other suburban transport ventures* (Wellington: New Zealand Railway and Locomotive Society, 1986), Chapter 5 and pages 96–100.

CHAPTER 2

1920–1928: THE REGIONAL RAILWAY FALTERS

1. Working timetable effective 15 November 1925, ANZ-DRO DAFV D454 20155 Box 10/d (New Zealand Railways – Working Timetable).

2. *AJHR* 1908 D-2, vii; *AJHR* 1918 D-2, xvii.

3. A.C. Bellamy, *New Zealand Railways Road Services* (Dunedin: Southern Press, 1981), 9–10, 60; Geoffrey B. Churchman and Tony Hurst, *The Railways of New Zealand: A journey through history* (Auckland: Harper Collins, 1990), 83–85; Laurence Evans, *The Commuter, the Car and Metropolitan Wellington* (Wellington: Victoria University of Wellington, 1972), 38–39.

4. Train advice no. 746, 8 July 1930, 6, in ANZ-DRO DAFV D454 20155 Box 12/a.

5. Rosslyn Noonan, *By Design: A brief history of the Public Works Department* (Wellington: A.R. Shearer, 1975), 100.

6. Michael Bassett, *Coates of Kaipara* (Auckland: Auckland University Press, 1995).

7. *AJHR* 1925 D-2a, 66.

8. Bassett, *Coates of Kaipara*, 64–66.

9. McVilly, circular to stationmasters, 19 May 1920, ANZ-ARO BAEI 10003/155/a 7985 (extension of North Auckland Railway).

10. *Northern Advocate*, 18 February 1921, 1 and 5 March 1921, 2; the PWD operated special passenger excursions all the way from Waikiekie to Oakleigh, near Portland, in late 1920. See for example *Northern Advocate*, 26 October 1920, 2.

11. *Northern Advocate*, 8 June 1921, 4.

12. *New Zealand Herald*, 5 January 1923 and 16 February 1923, 6; *AJHR* 1923 D-1, 31; *AJHR* 1924 D-1, 36.

13. *New Zealand Herald*, 26 November 1923, 11, and 25 November 1925, 10.

14. *AJHR* 1919 D-1, v; *AJHR* 1921 D-1, v, and D-4, 7; *AJHR* 1925 D-1, 36. Note that construction continued in some capacity on Kaikohe–Ōkaihau throughout World War I except for January to September 1916, contra claims it ceased for much longer (e.g. David Leitch and Brian Scott, *Exploring New Zealand's Ghost Railways*, rev. edn (Wellington: Grantham House, 1998 [1995]), 9). See *AJHR* 1916 D-1, 19, and *AJHR* 1917 D-1, 20.

15. *AJHR* 1921 D-1, v; *AJHR* 1924 D-1, iv.

16. *Evening Post*, 16 May 1928, 14.

17. *NZPD* 1929 vol. 281, 632; NZR Publicity and Advertising Office, 'Kirikopuni balloon loop', ANZ AAVK PUB 1/5 part 2 (construction and history of: North Auckland railways).

18. *AJHR* 1916 D-1, v.

19. *Poverty Bay Herald*, 13 December 1924, 7; F. Truman, stationmaster-in-charge Gisborne, to McVilly, 22 October 1924, Truman to McVilly, 22 October 1924, and McVilly to Truman, 12 December 1924, ANZ AAEB 16/5896/2 (timetable Gisborne–Ngatapa Branch).

20. *New Zealand Herald*, 21 July 1923, 8.

21. *Bay of Plenty Times*, 29 March 1920, 2.

22. *AJHR* 1924 D-1, 37; *AJHR* 1925 D-1, 41.

23. *AJHR* 1926 D-1, 41.

24. *Waihi Telegraph*, 5 May 1927, 2; *AJHR* 1927 D-1, 40.

25. *Auckland Star*, 29 March 1928, 10–11.

26. *Bay of Plenty Times*, 27 August 1936, 3. My thanks to Scott Hamilton for bringing this to my attention.

27. For more, see Waitangi Tribunal, 'Te Mana Whatu Ahuru: Report on Te Rohe Pōtae Claims' (Wai 898, 2018), especially Chapter 9.

28. *Auckland Star*, 18 April 1928, 8; *New Zealand Herald*, 12 June 1928, 8.

29. *Bay of Plenty Times*, 17 May 1929, 2.

30. *Bay of Plenty Times*, 10 March 1945, 2.

31. J.R. Yonge, *New Zealand Railway and Tramway Atlas*, 4th edn (Exeter: Quail Map Company, 1993 [1965]), 6.

32. J.A. Dangerfield and G.W. Emerson, *Over the Garden Wall: Story of the Otago Central Railway*, 3rd edn (Dunedin: Otago Railway and Locomotive Society, 1995 [1962]), 34, 41; *Dunstan Times*, 11 July 1921, 4; *Otago Daily Times*, 5 July 1921, 7.

33. For close analysis, see John Rosanowski, 'Politics and railways: The Midland Line, 1887–1918', in Philip Ross May (ed.), *Miners and Militants: Politics in Westland, 1865–1918* (Christchurch: Whitcoulls, 1975), 80–100.

34. *Press*, 23 May 1924, 8; Press, 28 May 1924, 11.

35. New Zealand Government Railways Timetable, no. 352 (effective 13 August 1928), 102–03; F.C. Cullen, Nelson stationmaster-in-charge, to P.G. Roussell, general superintendent of transportation, 18 December 1929, ANZ ADQD 1916/2624/1 part 3 (timetable–Nelson Section). See also Lois Voller, *Rails to Nowhere: The history of the Nelson railway* (Nelson: Nikau Press, 1991), Chapter 11.

36. *New Zealand Herald*, 24 May 1922, 8.

37. *Stratford Evening Post*, 7 February 1923, 5.

38. *AJHR* 1924 D-1, 39; *AJHR* 1925 D-1, 43; Yonge, *New Zealand Railway and Tramway Atlas*, 11.

39. *New Zealand Herald*, 20 December 1926, 16.

40. *Stratford Evening Post*, 18 November 1924, 1.

41. *AJHR* 1926 D-1, 44; *AJHR* 1928 D-1, 44.

42. David P. Millar, *Once Upon a Village: A history of Lower Hutt, 1819–1965* (Wellington: New Zealand University Press, 1972), 140–42.

43. H.C.D. Somerset, *Littledene: Patterns of Change* (Wellington: New Zealand Council for Educational Research, 1974 [1938]), 149. See Neill Atkinson, *Trainland: How railways made New Zealand* (Auckland: Random House, 2007), 66–67, for more discussion of Somerset and the social context of mixed trains.

44. *AJHR* 1925 D-2a, 12.

45. Ibid., 15.

46. *New Zealand Herald*, 13 June 1924, 1.

47. Jill Adams and Norma Nisbet, *East of the Twinlaws: Centennial history of the Wairio school and district* (Invercargill: Craigs Printing, 1981), 184–85; G.W. Emerson, J.A. Dangerfield and A.C. Bellamy, *Coalfields Enterprise: Private railways of the Ohai District, Southland*, 2nd edn (Dunedin: New Zealand Railway and Locomotive Society – Otago Branch, 1975 [1964]), 21.

48. See discussion in ANZ ABJP 08/1357/17 part 1 (Rapahoe Branch Trains).

49. *AJHR* 1880 E-3, vii.

50. *Pukekohe and Waiuku Times*, 7 December 1917, 1; *Pukekohe and Waiuku Times*, 12 March 1918, 2; *New Zealand Herald*, 30 June 1921, 4; *Pukekohe and Waiuku Times*, 10 January 1922, 4.

51. *AJHR* 1924 D-2, xxii; *New Zealand Herald*, 11 April 1923, 9 (supplement).

52. Working timetable effective 15 November 1925, ANZ-DRO DAFV D454 20155 Box 10/d, 76-79.

53. *Mt Benger Mail*, 23 December 1925, 3; *Evening Star* (Dunedin), 19 April 1928, 9.

54. *AJHR* 1912 D-1, vii and D-8, 4; *AJHR* 1914 D-1, vii.

55. Leitch and Scott, *Exploring New Zealand's Ghost Railways*, 25.

56. *Hawera and Normanby Star*, 8 September 1923, 6.

57. *AJHR* 1926 D-1, 45; *Opunake Times*, 9 July 1926, 3.

58. Railways Authorization Act 3 Geo. V no. 45 (1912) authorised Waiōtira–Whangārei, Paerātā–Waiuku, Te Roti–Ōpunake, Featherston–Martinborough, Culverden–Waiau, Balclutha–Tuapeka Mouth, and part of the East Coast Main Trunk west of Gisborne between Makaraka and Hangaroa. The Martinborough and Tuapeka Mouth branches never happened, and Makaraka–Hangaroa was abandoned beyond Ngātapa in favour of a coastal route; the rest were built.

59. *AJHR* 1924 D-1, 63–65.

60. See communication in ANZ ADQD 1914/2419, part 1 (proposed Martinborough railway).

61. *AJHR* 1915 D-1, iv; *AJHR* 1919 D-1, v; *AJHR* 1921 D-1, vii.

62. *Northern Advocate*, 24 September 1923, 4.

63. *New Zealand Herald*, 9 November 1923, 8, and 25 March 1924, 9; *AJHR* 1924 D-1, 36.

64. *Northern Advocate*, 9 November 1923, 4.

65. *AJHR* 1923 D-1, iii, 35; *AJHR* 1926 D-1, 43.

66. *Poverty Bay Herald*, 4 March 1925, 2; *AJHR* 1925 D-1, xxviii.

67. *AJHR* 1938 D-1, 29.

68. A.C. Bellamy, *The Napier–Gisborne Railway: The story of its construction and development* (Napier: New Zealand Railway and Locomotive Society–Hawke's Bay Branch, 1969), 7; A.C. Bellamy, *Private Railways in Hawke's Bay*, rev. edn (Wellington: New Zealand Railway and Locomotive Society, 1984 [1962]), 18–19; Chris Wood, *Steaming to the Sunrise: A history of railways in the Gisborne region* (Wellington: IPL Books, 1996), 80.

69. See letters in ANZ ABKU W3748 Box 35 PW 19/13 (Waikokopu Branch Railway – Railway Passenger Fares – Goods Rates).

70. P.L. Payne, DTM Westport, to McVilly, 15 April, 26 August and 8 September 1921; McVilly to Payne, 14 September 1921; Westport stationmaster-in-charge to McVilly, 26 April 1923; Eugene Casey, general manager, to Irwin Faris, 7 May 1940, with attachment 'Cape Foulwind Railway: History of the line'; all in ANZ ADQD 1915/2884/3 (timetable Cape Foulwind line). See also A.C. Bellamy, 'The Cape Foulwind Railway', printed across multiple issues of the *New Zealand Railway Observer*, 1951–52. For the harbour board, see Westport Harbour Act 11 Geo. V no. 33 (1920) and *Evening Post*, 9 August 1920, 8, and 30 September 1920, 10. Note also that sawmillers Bowater & Bryan ran a motorised trolley from Westport to Omau for their workers from January 1920 until it broke down in April 1921. The Westport Harbour Board's practice on Saturdays had been to run three trains daily, which NZR found uneconomic.

71. *Grey River Argus*, 8 January 1920, 4.

72. Payne to Hugh Buxton, chief traffic manager, 22 September 1921, ANZ ADQD 1915/2884/3.

73. *AJHR* 1885 D-5b, 6–8.

74. *AJHR* 1880 E-3, xiii, 21–22.

75. J. Reader to John Anstey, MP for Waitaki, 6 May 1917, ANZ ADQD 1917/4975/2 (train service between Kurow and Hakataramea Point).

76. Working timetable effective 5 December 1920, ANZ-DRO DAFV D454 20155 Box 9/b, 10 and 22–23.

77. *Press*, 4 August 1921, 6.

78. *Press*, 7 December 1923, 11.

79. Buxton to McVilly, 12 July 1921, including unsigned handwritten note; Buxton to McVilly, 10 September 1921; Buxton to W. Bowles, DTM Dunedin, 17 September 1921; Bowles to Buxton, 21 September 1921; Buxton to McVilly, 12 June 1923; all in ANZ ADQD 1917/4975/2.

80. Memoramdum for McVilly, 26 February 1924; H.P. West, DTM Dunedin, to McVilly, 22 March 1924; McVilly to West, 22 April 1924; train advice no. 527, 9 May 1924; all in ANZ ADQD 1917/4975/2.

81. Gordon Coates, Minister of Railways, to John Bitchener, MP for Waitaki, 16 October 1924, ANZ ADQD 1917/4975/2.

82. Return of traffic between Kurow and Hakatamarea, period ending 16 August 1924, ANZ ADQD 1917/4975/2. See also the other four-weekly returns on file covering the trial period.

83. West to McVilly, 28 July 1924; Coates to Bitchener, 7 November 1924; both in ANZ ADQD 1917/4975/2.

84. E.g. working timetable effective 15 November 1925, ANZ-DRO DAFV D454 20155 Box 10/d, 36–37; working timetable effective 8 December 1929, ANZ-DRO DAFV D454 20155 Box 11/e, 46–49. For closure, see train advice no. 746, 8 July 1930, 6 in ANZ-DRO DAFV D454 20155 Box 12/a.

85. *AJHR* 1925 D-2a, 55–57.

86. Ibid., 55.

87. Atkinson, *Trainland*, 82.

88. *Northern Advocate*, 30 April 1927, 4, and 2 May 1927, 4.

89. Leitch and Scott, *Exploring New Zealand's Ghost Railways*, 115.

90. Timetable for the New Zealand Government Railways, no. 349 (effective 4 December 1927), 137.

91. Frederick James Jones, chairman of the Railway Board, to Coates, 9 November 1927, and Coates to Jones, 19 November 1927, ANZ ADQD 1917/4652/1 part 3 (Glenham Branch line).

92. A.P. McLeod for Coates, to G.J. Anderson, Minister of Labour, 29 February 1928 (petition also on file), ANZ ADQD 1917/4652/1 part 3.

93. R.S. Kent, divisional superintendent South Island, to P.G. Roussell, general superintendent of transportation, 16 and 26 March 1928; Roussell to chief accountant, 15 June 1928; both in ANZ ADQD 1917/4652/1 part 3.

94. New Zealand Government Railways Timetable, no. 352 (effective 13 August 1928), 145; working timetable effective 10 August 1930, ANZ-DRO DAFV D454 20155 Box 12/a, 82.

95. J. Carnahan, bus manager, to Roussell, 23 May 1930, in ANZ ADQD 1913/3255 part 1; amendment effective 28 September 1930 to working timetable effective 10 August 1930, ANZ-DRO DAFV D454 20155 Box 12/a.

96. F.G. Clark, DTM Christchurch, to stationmasters of Christchurch, Coalgate and Darfield, 7 October 1943; F.S. Gray, stationmaster Christchurch, to Clark, 8 October 1943; S.G.A. Gaylor, stationmaster Darfield, to Clark, 14 October 1943, all in ANZ-CRO CAHV 1925/282/13.

97. Passenger counts, March and April 1948; W.A. Breach, DTM Christchurch, memorandum 1949/37; *Christchurch Star-Sun*, 11 March 1949, all in ANZ-CRO CAHV 1925/282/15 (train service, Whitecliffs Branch).

98. Breach to affected stationmasters, 10 March 1949, ANZ-CRO CAHV 1925/282/15; commercial agent Christchurch to commercial manager Wellington, 16 August 1950, ANZ ADQD 1913/3255.

99. Westport Section timetable effective 12 May 1924, ANZ ADQD 1902/1559 part 2 (train services Westport Seddonville section). Similar statements appear into the 1930s. A short line also operated from Westport to Te Kuha at the mouth of the lower Buller Gorge, with the timetable informing prospective travellers that 'Trains run only when specially arranged with the Stationmaster-in-Charge'.

100. G.T. Wilson, 'Motor Competition, Springfield–Christchurch 44 Miles', 26 October 1927, and acting DTM Christchurch to Kent, 9 February 1928, both in ANZ-CRO CAHV 1925/282/13 (train services, Whitecliffs Branch); Kent and Daniel Rodie to Railways Board, 5 March 1928, ANZ ADQD 1916/2333 part 2 (Springfield Branch train service).

101. *Press*, 13 April 1928, 15; Kent and Rodie to Railways Board, 14 April 1928, ANZ ADQD 1916/2333 part 2; Kent to Roussell, 20 April 1928, ANZ ADQD 1913/3255 part 1 (timetable – Whitecliff Branch).

102. *Press*, 13 April 1928, 8.

103. Frank Pawson, NZR business agent, to Kent, 18 April 1928, ANZ-CRO CAHV 1925/282/13.

104. *Press*, 20 April 1928, 11.

105. *Press*, 24 April 1928, 10.

106. *New Zealand Herald*, 20 July 1929, 9.

CHAPTER 3

1929–1934: A ROYAL COMMISSION AND ITS AFTERMATH

1. Michael Bassett, 'Ward, Joseph George', Dictionary of New Zealand Biography: http://web.archive.orgweb/20200306015509/https://teara.govt.nz/en/biographies/2w9/ward-joseph-george

2. *New Zealand Official Yearbook* 1930, section 15.

3. Malcolm McKinnon, *The Broken Decade: Prosperity, depression and recovery in New Zealand, 1928–39* (Dunedin: Otago University Press, 2016), 56–58; *AJHR* 1930 D-2, v.

4. H.H. Sterling, general manager, to P.G. Roussell, general superintendent of transportation, 26 January 1929, ANZ ADQD 1915/4135/8 part 1 (review of branch lines).

5. *AJHR* 1929 D-2, ii.

6. *AJHR* 1931 D-2, xv.

7. *New Zealand Herald*, 20 July 1929, 9.

8. B.R. Sword, DTM Dunedin, to stationmaster Kurow, 25 September 1928; R.S. Kent, divisional superintendent South Island, to Sword, 7 February 1929; NZR circular memo no. 1929/47, 5 March 1929; Sword to Kent, 13 March 1929; all in Hocken Collections Uare Taoka o Hākena MS-3088/008 (Papers relating to Kurow Branch Railway and Clayton Railcar).

9. Sterling to Veitch, 13 June 1930, plus 'Dunedin Mosgiel & Outram Branch' report,

ANZ ADQD 1903/3964 part 1 (Outram Branch).

10. *Otago Daily Times*, 2 February 1931, 9.

11. These extensive documents are in ANZ ADQD 1915/4135/8 part 1.

12. Veitch to Cabinet, 16 June 1930, and decision of Cabinet, 18 June 1930, ANZ ADQD 1903/3964 part 1.

13. *New Zealand Herald*, 10 June 1930, 13.

14. *New Zealand Herald*, 3 July 1930, 10.

15. Roussell to Kent, 25 June 1930, ANZ ADQD 1915/4135/8 part 1; Sword to Kent, 6 August 1930, ANZ-DRO DAFM 30/446/12 (economy proposals – Dunback Branch trains).

16. Roussell to Kent, 9 August 1930, ANZ ADQD 1915/4135/8 part 1.

17. *New Zealand Herald*, 9 October 1930, 13; Sterling to Veitch, 11 November 1930, ANZ ADQD 1915/4135/8 part 1.

18. *AJHR* 1930 D-4, 59.

19. Veitch to Kenneth Williams, MP for Bay of Plenty, 12 August 1930; Roussell to A.H. Northover, stationmaster-in-charge Gisborne, 21 August 1930; Northover to Roussell, 26 August 1930; Roussell to Northover, 4 September 1930; all in ANZ AAEB 16/5892/2 (timetable Gisborne–Ngatapa Branch).

20. Sterling to Veitch, 8 January 1931 (mistyped as 1930); Veitch to Williams, 14 January 1931; C. Blackburn to Veitch and George Forbes, prime minister, 22 January 1931;

Roussell to Northover, 27 January 1931; all in ANZ AAEB 16/5892/2 part 1.

21. *New Zealand Herald*, 3 July 1930, 10.

22. *Southland Times*, 17 July 1930, ANZ ADQD 1915/4135/8 part 1. 'Cockeytoo' is an old Australian pejorative idiom used to describe a small-scale farmer. It was used in New Zealand too, and farmers here are still referred to as 'cockies'.

23. Sterling to Veitch, 11 November 1930, ANZ ADQD 1915/4135/8 part 1.

24. Working timetable effective 15 November 1925, ANZ-DRO DAFV D454 20155 Box 10/d, 19–22; working timetable effective 8 December 1929, ANZ-DRO DAFV D454 20155 Box 11/e, 20–23.

25. *Press*, 8 July 1930, 10; *Press*, 11 July 1930, 10; *Press*, 16 August 1930, 25.

26. Veitch to Sterling, 19 August 1930, ANZ ADQD 1903/1866 part 1 (Eyreton Branch train service).

27. Sterling to Veitch, 18 August 1930, ANZ ADQD 1903/1866 part 1.

28. *AJHR* 1930 D-4, 58.

29. *Otautau Standard*, 30 September 1930, 2; working timetable effective 10 August 1930 and amendment effective 6 October 1930, ANZ-DRO DAFV D454 20155 Box 12/a, 90–91b.

30. Veitch to Sterling, 17 November 1930, ANZ ADQD 1915/4135/8 part 1.

31. *AJHR* 1930 D-2, ix.

32. *New Zealand Herald*, 1 July 1927, 12.

33. *AJHR* 1930 D-2, ix.

34. *AJHR* 1930 D-4, 45.

35. *AJHR* 1932 D-1, ii.

36. *AJHR* 1929 D-1, ii.

37. *Nelson Evening Mail*, 22 December 1930, 7.

38. *Evening Post*, 21 March 1931, 10; New Zealand Government Railways Timetable, no. 352 (effective 13 August 1928), 102–03, and no. 362 (effective 8 February 1931), 104–05.

39. *Nelson Evening Mail*, 22 December 1930, 7.

40. 'The commerce train', *New Zealand Railways Magazine* 4:9 (January 1930), 13; *Evening Post*, 22 August 1930, 10; *AJHR* 1931 D-1, xiv; report on Waiōtira–Kirikōpuni, ANZ ADQD 1915/4135/8 part 1.

41. My thanks to Bevan Shortridge for sharing his great-uncle Ernie Cook's reminiscences about the construction and removal of the Rangiahua railway line. These now feature in Jenny Couchman, *Okaihau: Our people, our places* (Kerikeri: the author, 2018).

42. *AJHR* 1931 D-3.

43. Ibid.

44. Roussell to Duncan, outdoor transportation assistant, 9 December 1930, ANZ ADQD 1903/3964 part 1.

45. *AJHR* 1930 D-4, 60; working timetable effective 10 August 1930 and amendment effective 9 February 1931, ANZ-DRO DAFV D454 20155 Box 12/a, 45.

46. *AJHR* 1930 D-4, 53.

47. Sterling to Veitch, 11 November 1930, ANZ ADQD 1915/4135/8 part 1.

48. Report on Christchurch–Parnassus, Christchurch–Waiau, Rangiora–Sheffield and Eyreton–Bennetts, ANZ ADQD 1915/4135/8 part 1. This report has some odd claims about timing. It outlines a timetable where mixed trains took between 90 minutes and 2 hours 25 minutes to run from Oxford West to Rangiora. It then claims that mixed trains were uncompetitive because buses took 2 hours while the trains took 2 hours 40 minutes. The loss of traffic to road is undeniable, but it is unclear if relative speeds were exclusively to blame.

49. Report on the Hedgehope Branch, ANZ ADQD 1915/4135/8 part 1.

50. Kent to Sterling, 25 September 1928; Gilbert S. Lynde, chief mechanical engineer, to Sterling, 17 October 1928; both in ANZ ADQD 1904/833/15 part 1 (Ford rail motor cars).

51. Lynde to the Railway Board, 18 October 1926; Kent to the Railway Board, 13 October 1927; and associated letters in ANZ ADQD 1904/833/15 part 1.

52. Roussell to Sterling, 29 October 1928, ANZ ADQD 1904/833/15 part 1; working timetable effective 10 August 1930 and amendment effective 9 February 1931, ANZ-DRO DAFV D454 20155 Box 12/a, 82.

53. F.C. Cullen, Nelson stationmaster-in-charge, to Roussell, 18 December 1929,

ANZ ADQD 1916/2624/1 part 3; New Zealand Government Railways Timetable, no. 362 (effective 8 February 1931), 104–05.

54. Robin Bromby, *New Zealand Railways: Their life and times* (Sydney: Highgate Publishing, 2014), 190–91; David Leitch and Brian Scott, *Exploring New Zealand's Ghost Railways*, rev. edn (Wellington: Grantham House, 1998 [1995]), 45; Geoffrey B. Churchman and Tony Hurst, *The Railways of New Zealand: A journey through history* (Auckland: HarperCollins, 1990), 168.

55. The Castlecliff Railway was the only private railway in the country to offer an urban commuter service between 1908 – when the government bought the Wellington and Manawatū Railway Company, which ran suburban trains in Wellington's northern suburbs – and the privatisation of NZR in 1993.

56. *New Zealand Official Year-Book 1933*, section IV. Dunedin was fourth-largest with 87,400.

57. Laraine Sole, *Castlecliff: The community on the coast* (Whanganui: the author, 2008), 166, 175. For special trains, see ads in e.g. *Wanganui Herald*, 10 October 1910, 3, and 24 December 1915, 2; and *Wanganui Chronicle*, 21 January 1910, 8, and 24 December 1913, 7.

58. Graham Stewart, *The End of the Penny Section: When trams ruled the streets of New Zealand*, rev. edn (Wellington: Grantham House, 1993

[1973]), 103–05.

59. Sole, *Castlecliff*, 177–78.

60. *Evening Post*, 16 May 1931, 14; *Poverty Bay Herald*, 30 June 1931, 8.

61. *Poverty Bay Herald*, 11 September 1931, 5.

62. *AJHR* 1932 D-2, vi-vii.

63. Chris Wood, *Steaming to the Sunrise: A history of railways in the Gisborne region* (Wellington: IPL Books, 1996), 86.

64. *AJHR* 1932 H-40, 11.

65. *NZPD* vol. 230 (7 November 1931), 864.

66. Transport Licensing Act 22 Geo V no. 38 (1931), clause 27.

67. Peter Aimer, *Wings of the Nation: A history of the New Zealand National Airways Corporation 1947–78* (Takapuna: The Bush Press, 2000), 18–19; Richard Waugh with Peter Layne and Graeme McConnell, *NAC: The illustrated history of the National Airways Corporation 1947–1978* (Invercargill: Kynaston Charitable Trust in conjunction with Craig Printing, 2007), 9–11. For more on Union Steam Ship, primarily its ascent in the colonial period, see Gavin McLean, *The Southern Octopus: The rise of a shipping empire* (Wellington: New Zealand Ship and Maritime Society, 1990).

68. J. Barnett, acting stationmaster-in-charge Westport, to J.C. Schneider, traffic superintendent, 27 July 1932; Schneider to P.G. Roussell, general manager, 5 August 1932; Barnett to

Schneider, 12 August 1932; all in ANZ ADQD 1902/1559 part 3 (train services Westport Seddonville section).

69. *AJHR* 1930 D-4, 49.

70. Report on the Foxton Branch, ANZ ADQD 1915/4135/8 part 1.

71. *Levin Daily Chronicle*, 5 August 1932, 3.

72. *Levin Daily Chronicle*, 17 August 1932, 3.

73. K.R. Cassells, *The Sanson Tramway* (Wellington: New Zealand Railway and Locomotive Society, 1962), 48–55.

74. Report to G.H. Mackley, general manager, 31 October 1933, ANZ ADQD 1917/4650/1 part 3 (Tapanui Branch Line [Waipahi to Edievale]).

75. *Otago Daily Times*, 28 November 1933, 13; *Otago Daily Times*, 9 December 1933, 13; Mackley to Tapanui Borough Council town clerk, 21 November 1933, ANZ ADQD 1917/4650/1 part 3; train advice no. 945, J.A. Lindsay, DTM Invercargill, 22 December 1933, ANZ-CRO CAHV 1933/348 (cancellation of rail passenger service on Tapanui Branch).

76. *Tapanui Courier*, 19 December 1933, ANZ ADQD 1917/4650/1 part 3.

77. *AJHR* 1930 D-4, 52; *AJHR* 1931 D-2, xxix.

78. G.H. Mackley, acting general manager, to Edward S. Brittenden, DTM Christchurch, 4 January 1933, ANZ ADQD 1917/1704 part 2 (Mount Somers Branch Line).

79. *Ashburton Guardian*, 9 January 1933, in ANZ ADQD 1917/1704 part 2.

80. *Auckland Star*, 2 July 1931, 9.

81. Mackley to Railway Board, 21 June 1934, ANZ ADQD 1920/1685/12 part 2 (road passengers services).

82. *AJHR* 1932 D-1, 28.

83. *Stratford Evening Post*, 7 November 1932, 3.

84. *New Zealand Herald*, 6 December 1932, 8; *New Zealand Herald*, 9 December 1932, 12.

85. The temporary PWD service between Ōhura and Tahora ran from 24 March 1933 until mid-May. This permitted Ōhura residents to visit Stratford in lieu of Taumarunui, but it was no day trip – eastbound travellers had to stay overnight in Whangamōmona. *Auckland Star*, 24 March 1933, 3; *Stratford Evening Post*, 25 March 1933, 4; *Hāwera Star*, 13 May 1933, 9.

86. *New Zealand Herald*, 4 September 1933, 10.

87. *Stratford Evening Post*, 3 August 1932, 5.

88. *New Zealand Herald*, 6 September 1933, 12. This was likely based on 'We Are the Boys from Old Florida'.

CHAPTER 4

1935–45: A NETWORK UNIFIED IN THE FACE OF ADVERSITY

1. Neill Atkinson, *Trainland: How railways made New Zealand* (Auckland: Random House, 2007), 173.

2. Merz and McLellan also investigated electrification for Christchurch–Rangiora and Dunedin's suburban network but considered it unnecessary. *AJHR* 1926 D-2, appendix B.

3. *AJHR* 1936 D-1, xcii.

4. *AJHR* 1939 D-2, ii.

5. A ruling grade is the steepest climb on a section of railway. It 'rules' in the sense that it dictates the maximum load of a train between two points, even if the rest of the route is much gentler.

6. *AJHR* 1938 D-2, ii-iv.

7. H.H. Sterling, general manager, to W.B. Taverner, Minister of Railways, 9 January 1929, ANZ ADQD 1909/3714/1 part 2 (Wellington–Paekakariki Deviation).

8. *Evening Post*, 2 June 1919, 6.

9. Railways Authorization Act 10 Geo. V no.34 (1919); *Otaki Mail*, 25 August 1920, 3.

10. *AJHR* 1924 D-2a, 17.

11. Sterling to F.C. Widdop, chief engineer, 29 October 1929, ANZ ADQD 1909/3714/1 part 2.

12. Reports of 4 and 25 March 1930, ANZ ADQD 1909/3714/1 part 2; *AJHR* 1931 D-2, iv; Rodger Redward, *Railway Electrification in New Zealand: An illustrated survey* (Wellington: Southern Press, 1974).

13. *Dominion*, 30 July 1955, in ANZ AAEB 09/3714/1 part 3.

14. Pathmanathan Brabhaharan, 'Let's get Wellington moving: Resilience of recommended programme of investment', WSP Opus report GER 2018-65 for the New Zealand Transport Agency, 5 September 2018: https://web.archive.org/web/20200111045339/https://lgwm.nz/assets/Documents/Technical-Documents/Resilience/19-Resilience-of-the-recommended-programme-WSP-Opus.pdf

15. James Sawers, acting general manager, to F.T. O'Neill, 3 January 1941, ANZ AAEB 09/3714/1 part 3 (proposed Wellington–Paekakariki Deviation).

16. *AJHR* 1936 D-1, xvii.

17. *AJHR* 1938 D-1, xvi–xviii; *Ōpōtiki News*, 9 May 1938, 2.

18. Railways Authorization Act 6 Geo. V no. 46 (1915); Finance (No. 2) Act 9 Geo. V no. 4 (1918), sec. 35.

19. Appropriation Act 1 Geo. VI no. 22 (1937), fifth schedule.

20. C.W. Malcolm, 'The railway that never was', *Ohinemuri Regional History Journal* 26 (1982): https://web.archive.org/web/20200111143638/http://www.ohinemuri.org.nz/journals/54-journal-26-november-1982/1055-the-railway-that-never-was

21. *AJHR* 1940 D-1, xii; *Auckland Star*, 16 May 1940, 7

22. *AJHR* 1949 D-1, 27.

23. Cabinet paper no. 290 (1962), 12 April 1962, ANZ AAFD CAB 183/6/2 (railways – passenger services – termination of services).

24. *Poverty Bay Herald*, 25 February 1932, 10.

25. *New Zealand Herald*, 31 October 1936, 14.

26. At 95 metres the viaduct was the fourth-highest in the world at the time and it remains the highest in Australasia. Geoffrey Thornton, *Bridging the Gap: Early bridges in New Zealand 1830–1939* (Auckland: Reed, 2001), 60–61.

27. *AJHR* 1938 D-2, xxvii.

28. O.N. Gillespie, 'The rail-car "Maahunui": Successful trial runs', *New Zealand Railways Magazine* 11:4 (July 1936), 15.

29. *Press*, 1 July 1937, 12; *Auckland Star*, 11 August 1937, 3; *New Zealand Herald*, 25 August 1937, 15.

30. *AJHR* 1938 D-1, xvii; *New Zealand Herald*, 8 February 1938, 8; *Northern Advocate*, 2 September 1938, 10.

31. *Evening Post*, 1 July 1937, 10.

32. *Evening Post*, 24 June 1939, 7.

33. *Evening Post*, 28 December 1937, 5; *Gisborne Herald*, 23 November 1939, 7.

34. *Gisborne Herald*, 21 February 1940, 5. See also the letter from 'Progress' urging the Gisborne Chamber of Commerce to take up the cause of railcars to Nūhaka in *Gisborne Herald*, 15 August 1939, 16.

35. *Gisborne Herald*, 7 September 1940, 5; 22 November 1940, 8.

36. *AJHR* 1929 D-1, iii.

37. Rob Merrifield, *Beyond Dashwood: A history of the railway in Marlborough* (Wellington: New Zealand Railway and Locomotive Society, 1990), 35–38.

38. *AJHR* 1937 D-1, xv.

39. *Press*, 6 December 1939, 11.

40. J.D. Mahoney, *Kings of the Iron Road: Steam passenger trains of New Zealand* (Palmerston North: Dunmore Press, 1982), 105.

41. *Press*, 28 January 1939, 16.

42. *North Canterbury Gazette*, 2 February 1939, 6.

43. See e.g. 'Co-ordination of road and rail passenger services: North Canterbury and Lindis Pass', F.K. Mackay, 27 January 1939, ANZ-CRO CAHV 25/282/4 (registered file – Train services Christchurch–Waiau).

44. *Press*, 27 November 1940, 11; J.S. Douglas, stationmaster Waikari, to G.H. McLean, DTM Christchurch, 8 November 1941, ANZ-CRO CAHV 25/282/4.

45. Transport Licensing Amendment Act 1 Edw. VIII no. 9 (1936), clause 15.

46. *AJHR* 1936 H-40, 11–13.

47. James Watson, *Links: A history of transport and New Zealand society* (Wellington: GP Publications, 1996), 185.

48. *AJHR* 1940 D-2, 4.

49. Timetable for the New Zealand Government Railways, no. 386, effective 5 November 1939.

50. Margaret McClure, *The Wonder Country: Making New Zealand tourism* (Auckland: Auckland University Press, 2004), 98–99.

51. *Otago Daily Times*, 24 September 1937, 10.

52. *Press*, 24 September 1937, 8.

53. *Evening Star*, 25 September 1937, 17.

54. *Lake Wakatip Mail*, 14 December 1937, 4.

55. F.K. Mackay, Road Services superintendent, to A.L. Smith, transportation superintendent, 24 April 1940, ANZ ADQD 1908/1357/5 part 2 (Greymouth–Blackball train services).

56. G.H. McLean, DTM Christchurch, to Smith, 27 July 1940; Smith to McLean, 24 October 1940; McLean's circular memoranda 1940/202 (30 October 1940) and 1940/210 (12 November 1940); all in ANZ ADQD 1908/1357/5 part 2.

57. David Leitch and Brian Scott, *Exploring New Zealand's Ghost Railways*, rev. edn (Wellington: Grantham House, 1998 [1995]), 100.

58. Report on the Roxburgh Branch, ANZ ADQD 1915/4135/8 part 1.

59. W.J. Cowan, *Rails to Roxburgh: The story of a provincial railway* (Dunedin: Molyneux Press, 2010), 110.

60. G.G. Natusch, *Waitaki Dammed: And the origins of Social Security* (Dunedin: Otago Heritage Books, 1984), 31, 49.

61. The PWD originally anticipated school trains might run during the first term of 1937. H.L. Gibson, DTM Dunedin, to stationmaster Kurow, 11 May 1937, and attached research notes by Jim Dangerfield, Hocken Collections Uare Taoka o Hākena, MS-3088/008.

62. Geoffrey B. Churchman and Tony Hurst, *The Railways of New Zealand: A journey through history* (Auckland: Harper Collins, 1990),

205; Catherine Knight, *New Zealand's Rivers: An environmental history* (Christchurch: Canterbury University Press, 2016), 133–35.

63. Gibson to G.T. Wilson, transportation superintendent, 3 June 1937, ANZ-DRO DAFV D455/30/i 00/540 (Kaitangata Coal Company's Private Line – Passenger Service).

64. J.H. Hay to Gibson, 1 June 1937; Mackley to Gibson, 29 June 1937; and Hay to Gibson, 5 July 1937, all in ANZ-DRO DAFV D455/30/i/ 00/540.

65. Eve Ebbett, *When the Boys Were Away: New Zealand women in World War II* (Wellington: Reed, 1984), 116–17; Richard Waugh with Peter Layne and Graeme McConnell, *NAC: The illustrated history of the National Airways Corporation 1947–1978* (Invercargill: Kynaston Charitable Trust in conjunction with Craig Printing, 2007), 12.

66. *Bay of Plenty Times*, 9 August 1940, 5. Local councillors and business leaders sought construction of the line to Gisborne into the post-war years. See for example *Opotiki News*, 31 August 1943, 2; 22 September 1944, 2; 8 April 1947, 2.

67. *New Zealand Herald*, 1 May 1940, 8.

68. Memo by Eugene Casey, general manager, 14 October 1941, and G.S. Reid, DTM Auckland, circular memorandum no. 1941/128,

14 November 1941. Strictly, these were with-car goods trains, one upgraded to a mixed in May 1943: A.L. Smith to Reid, 4 May 1943. All sources in ANZ ADQD 1916/913/8 part 1 (timetable – Kirikōpuni Branch).

69. *Auckland Star*, 7 January 1931, 3; *AJHR* 1931 D-1, xiv.

70. *AJHR* 1938 D-1, xvi.

71. *Northern Advocate*, 21 April 1942, 5; Reid to Smith, 28 April 1943, ANZ ADQD 1916/913/8 part 1; NZR Publicity and Advertising Office, 'Kirikopuni balloon loop', ANZ AAVK PUB 1/5 part 2 (construction and history of: North Auckland railways).

72. Mackley to Dan Sullivan, Minister of Railways, 19 August 1936; Smith to Reid, 8 July 1940; ANZ ADQD 1916/913/8 part 1.

73. *Northern Advocate*, 28 November 1942, 4.

74. Gillian Ward, *Tragedy and Heroism at Kopuawhara* (Gisborne: the author, 2019).

75. *Gisborne Herald*, 17 December 1941, 2, and 18 December 1941, 6.

76. *Auckland Star*, 25 August 1942, 4.

77. *New Zealand Official Year-Book 1943*, section 4.

78. *Auckland Star*, 7 September 1942, 4.

79. *Evening Post*, 3 December 1941, 13.

80. *Press*, 1 April 1942, 4.

81. *Press*, 14 August 1942, 4; *Otago Daily Times*, 8 September 1942, 2.

82. N.J. Cooper, *Vulcan Railcars in New Zealand* (Wellington: New Zealand Railway and Locomotive Society, 1981), 5.

83. *Press*, 4 December 1942, 4.

84. *Press*, 6 October 1942, 6, and 19 October 1942, 6; *Northern Advocate*, 14 October 1942, 2.

85. *Press*, 13 April 1943, 4.

86. *Press*, 11 May 1943, 2, and 22 May 1943, 4.

87. *Evening Post*, 13 March 1944, 4; *Press*, 14 March 1944, 6.

88. *AJHR* 1946 D-2, 7. Regular services began two days later.

89. *Press*, 14 December 1945, 8.

90. *Press*, 17 December 1945, 4.

91. Ibid.

CHAPTER 5

1945–54: THE DRIFT TO ROAD

1. Bill Sullivan to Bob Semple, 27 September 1943, ANZ ABJP 16/5896/1 part 5 (passenger timetable–Gisborne to Moutohora).

2. F.K. Mackay, Road Services superintendent, to Eugene Casey, general manager, and Friday rail counts attached to A.T. Parks, DTM Wellington, to A.L. Smith, transportation superintendent, 5 August 1943, both in ANZ ABJP 16/5896/1 part 5.

3. Parks to Smith, 5 August 1943, and related letters from subsequent months in ANZ ABJP 16/5896/1 part 5.

4. A.C. Bellamy, *New Zealand Railways Road Services* (Dunedin: Southern Press, 1981), 16.

5. G.T. Bloomfield, *New Zealand: A handbook of historical*

statistics (Boston: G.K. Hall, 1984), 241.

6. Neill Atkinson, *Trainland: How railways made New Zealand* (Auckland: Random House, 2007), 132.

7. *Otago Daily Times*, 2 November 1943, 2; Greg Mason, *An Accident in Waiting? The Hyde rail disaster 1943* (Kingston: E.E. Coleman, 2011); André Brett, 'Clues among the wreckage', *Otago Daily Times*, 1 June 2013, 47.

8. Geoff Conly and Graham Stewart, *New Zealand Tragedies on the Track: Tangiwai and other railway accidents*, rev. edn (Wellington: Grantham House, 1991 [1986]), 105–13.

9. *Press*, 20 April 1944, 6.

10. *AJHR* 1946 B-6, 32.

11. Jim McAloon, *Judgements of All Kinds: Economic policy-making in New Zealand 1945–1984* (Wellington: Victoria University Press, 2013), Chapter 3.

12. *AJHR* 1946 B-6, 28–29.

13. McAloon, *Judgements of All Kinds*, 59.

14. Bellamy, *New Zealand Railways Road Services*, 15.

15. Semple to Mr Harnett, chairman of the Gisborne Labour Representation Committee, 12 July 1944, ANZ ABJP 16/5896/1 part 5.

16. Semple to James Sawers, general manager, 14 June 1944, ANZ ABJP 16/5896/1 part 5.

17. Jim O'Brien to Semple, 9 August 1944, ANZ ABJP 16/5896/1 part 5.

18. Semple to O'Brien, 22 August 1944, ANZ ABJP 16/5896/1 part 5.

19. Sawers to G.L. Laurenson, commissioner of transport, 19 December 1944, and Alan Tolmie Hawken, transportation superintendent, to F.S. Gray, DTM Wellington, 18 January 1945, both in ANZ ABJP W4103 16/5896/1 part 5.

20. F.K. Mackay, Road Services superintendent, to Hawken, 1 August 1945, ANZ ADQD 1902/1559 part 4 (train services Westport Seddonville section); *Lake Wakatip Mail*, 13 September 1945, 2.

21. *Lake Wakatip Mail*, 13 December 1945, 2.

22. *Waikato Independent*, 22 February 1943, in ANZ ADQD 1902/329 part 2 (Cambridge Branch train service).

23. G.S. Reid, DTM Auckland, to Smith, 5 April 1943, ANZ ADQD 1902/329 part 2.

24. *Waikato Times*, 21 June and 30 June 1945, ANZ ADQD 1902/329 part 2.

25. *Waikato Independent*, 13 November 1944, ANZ ADQD 1902/329 part 2.

26. F. Gembitsky, DTM Auckland, to Sawers, 17 August 1945, ANZ ADQD 1902/329 part 2.

27. File note (signature unclear) dated 7 May 1946 and Gembitsky to C.G. Browett, transportation superintendent, 27 June 1946, ANZ ADQD 1902/329 part 2.

28. Sawers to Gembitsky, 19 August 1946, ANZ ADQD 1902/329 part 2.

29. A.B. Scanlan, *Taranaki's First Railway* (New Plymouth: the author, 1977).

30. Road Services circular no. 5, 18 April 1946, and Sawers to Semple, 30 April 1946, both in ANZ AAEB 03/381/1 part 2 (Waitara Branch passenger services).

31. Letter to the editor from 'Traveller', *Taranaki Herald*, 10 May 1946, in ANZ AAEB 03/381/1 part 2.

32. Waitara town clerk to Semple, 20 May 1946, ANZ AAEB 03/381/1 part 2.

33. *AJHR* 1945 D-2, 17. The returns of passenger and goods traffic from 'each station' in the annual reports do not, in fact, report all or even most stations. The selected stations on the Seddonville Branch are Waimangaroa and Granity. The table gives no indication of whether these figures encompass the 10 other stations on the line and, if so, which stations appear in which totals. They also do not distinguish the sale of train and bus tickets, mostly moot for Buller in 1945 but a serious hindrance to analysis for other lines.

34. F.G. Clark, DTM Christchurch, to Hawken, 2 August 1944, ANZ ADQD 1902/1559 part 4 (train services Westport Seddonville section).

35. Sawers to Mackay, 24 August 1944, ANZ ADQD 1902/1559 part 4.

36. Mackay to Sawers, 8 September 1944, ANZ ADQD 1902/1559 part 4.

37. NZR originally hoped these would commence by December 1945 but come

September it ceased to offer an estimate. Hawken to Clark, 11 July 1945, Mackay to Hawken, 1 August 1945; Semple to Webb, 27 September 1945; all in ANZ ADQD 1902/1559 part 4.

38. *Westport News*, 9 February 1946, in ANZ ADQD 1902/1559 part 4.

39. Semple to Webb, 30 September 1946, ANZ ADQD 1902/1559 part 4.

40. See contents of ANZ-CRO CAHV CH21/39/d 1925/282/17 (railcars, Methven Branch).

41. Operational figures for the Clayton railcar are in ANZ ADQD 1904/833/17 parts 3–4 (rail motor statistics).

42. The only change resulting from these deliberations was the elimination of first-class accommodation to Kurow in 1938. H.L. Gibson, DTM Dunedin, to Business Agent Dunedin, 25 August 1936, count of passengers on no. 272 Oamaru–Kurow train between 27/04/1936 and 24/07/1936, and A. Clark, DTM Dunedin, to G.T. Wilson, transportation superintendent, 5 September 1938, all in ANZ-DRO DAFV 30/446/8 (economy proposals – Kurow Branch train services).

43. A.L. Smith, transport superintendent, to R.J.A. Stirling, DTM Dunedin, 22 July 1940, and Stirling to Smith, 10 October 1940, both in ANZ-DRO DAFV 30/446/8.

44. F.G. Clark, DTM Christchurch, to W.W. Hannah, stationmaster Methven, and I.N. Barkle, stationmaster Rakaia, 25 October 1944; Clark to Hawken, 22 November 1944; memorandum no. 1945/156, 29 November 1945, all in ANZ-CRO CAHV CH21/39/e 1925/282/17 part 1 (train services, Methven Branch).

45. Stationmaster Duntroon to W.M. Mackay, DTM Dunedin, 16 November 1945, ANZ-DRO DAFV 30/446/8.

46. C.G. Browett, transportation superintendent, to W.M. Mackay, 21 November 1946; T. Johnston, DTM Dunedin, to Locomotive Engineer Dunedin, 6 March 1947; circular memorandum no. 1947/35, 13 March 1947; all in ANZ-DRO DAFV 30/446/8.

47. Johnston to R.S. Dawson, DTM Wellington, 13 November 1947, ANZ-DRO DAFV 30/446/8.

48. *AJHR* 1949 D-2, 4 and 9.

49. A.J. Ede, transportation superintendent, to W.A. Breach, DTM Christchurch, 11 May 1948; Stationmaster Christchurch to Breach, 20 May 1948; DTM's Office special notice, 2 June 1948; Breach to Ede, 3 August 1948; all in ANZ-CRO CAHV CH21/39/e 1925/282/17 part 1.

50. E.F. Parr, DTM Christchurch to A. Evans, transportation superintendent, 18 November 1953, ANZ AAEB 04/3962/1 part 4 (Rakaia–Methven service).

51. DTM Auckland and District Mechanical Engineer Auckland to A.J. Ede, transportation superintendent, 15 June 1948, and attached traffic figures, ANZ ADQD 1917/4540/1 (timetable – Waiuku Branch).

52. Ede to R. Boswell, DTM Auckland, 1 July 1948, ANZ ADQD 1917/4540/1.

53. S.G. Howie, DTM Dunedin, to Ede, 27 October 1948, ANZ AAEB 03/3964 part 2 (Outram Branch).

54. F.K. Mackay, Road Services superintendent, to Hawken, 1 February 1945; W.M. Mackay, DTM Dunedin, to Hawken, 2 March 1945, ANZ AAEB 03/3964 part 2.

55. Howie to Ede, 27 October 1948, ANZ AAEB 03/3964 part 2.

56. Road Services manager and train running officer to Frank Aickin, general manager, 3 July 1949, ANZ AAEB 03/3964 part 2.

57. S. Kip Farrington Jr, *Railroading Around the World* (New York: Castle Books, 1955), 151.

58. L. Birks, 'Economic and scientific developments resulting from the Lake Coleridge hydro-electric power-supply', *New Zealand Journal of Science and Technology* 1:1 (1918), 23; E. Parry, 'The electrification of railways in New Zealand', *New Zealand Journal of Science and Technology* 1:6 (1918), 323.

59. *AJHR* 1949 D-2, 4.

60. *AJHR* 1950 D-2, 15.

61. *AJHR* 1951 D-2, 2.

62. Ibid., 17.

63. *AJHR* 1952 D-3, 23–24.

64. Aickin to Howie, 4 January 1950; Howie to Aickin, 13 April 1950; both in ANZ AAEB 03/3964 part 2.

65. Memorandum no. 86, general manager's office, 25 November 1953, ANZ AAEB 03/3964 part 2.

66. Richard Waugh with Peter Layne and Graeme McConnell, *NAC: The illustrated history of the National Airways Corporation 1947–1978* (Invercargill: Kynaston Charitable Trust in conjunction with Craig Printing, 2007), 13–20.

67. NZR converted 75 locomotives to burn oil instead of coal between 1946 and 1950: all 30 of the K class, all 33 in-service K^A, and 12 of 40 J (reclassified J^B). A further 18 locomotives were built new as oil-burners: the last two K^A locomotives, delivered in 1950, and 16 of 51 J^A locomotives, delivered in 1952. For more on these locomotives, see Sean Millar, *The NZR Steam Locomotive* (Wellington: New Zealand Railway and Locomotive Society, 2011).

68. Michael Bassett, *Confrontation '51: The 1951 waterfront dispute* (Wellington: Reed, 1972), 10–13.

69. Ibid., 104.

70. Waugh, *NAC*, 55.

71. *AJHR* 1952 D-2, 14.

72. Curtailment of train services 1951, memo dated 10 October 1951, ANZ ADQD 500/3/11 part 3 (transport co-ordination: World War II and after – coal saving timetable – 1940 – S.I.).

73. J.G. Whetton, DTM Wellington, to stationmaster Featherston, 13 November 1951; memorandum no. 1952/2, DTM Wellington's office, 10 January 1952; both in ANZ ADRM 00/700/7/5 (Greytown Branch services).

74. Stan Goosman, Minister of Railways, to Foss Shanahan, secretary of the Cabinet, 22 October 1953, ANZ AAFD CAB 183/7/1 part 1 (railways termination of services – general).

75. A. Evans, transportation superintendent, to DTM Wellington, 30 November 1953, ANZ ADRM 00/700/7/5.

76. F. Gembitsky, DTM Auckland, to C.G. Browett, transportation superintendent, 11 September 1946; Road Services superintendent to Sawers, 20 March 1947; R. Boswell, DTM Auckland to A.J. Ede, transportation superintendent, 18 December 1947; *Thames Star*, 1 November 1948; DTM Auckland to transportation superintendent, 26 October 1951 and 17 April 1952; all in ANZ ADQD 1905/3261 part 4 (Thames Branch timetable).

77. ANZ ABIN W3337 Box 189 (working timetable – North Island main line and branches 1951–52), 78.

78. Acting DTM Christchurch to Ede, 26 July 1949, ANZ ADQD 1914/4756/1 part 8.

79. *AJHR* 1952 D-3, 55.

80. Road Services superintendent to Sawers, 28 July 1947, and file note, 11 November 1947, ANZ ADQD 1914/4756/1 part 8 (Little River Branch train service).

81. D.A. Clarke, transportation superintendent, to DTM Christchurch, 8 October 1951, ANZ-CRO CAHV 1925/282/10 part 2 (train service, Christchurch–Little River); J.J. Anderson, DTM Christchurch, to transportation superintendent, 25 July 1952, ANZ ADQD 1914/4756/1 part 8. Strictly, Clarke proposed restoring the original timetable from 17 December 1951 for the holiday period, falling to thrice weekly from 12 January 1952.

82. DTM Invercargill to Ede, 29 June 1951; Ede to DTM Invercargill, 20 July 1951; Goosman to Tom Macdonald, MP for Wallace, 6 August 1951, all in ANZ AAEB 16/3642 part 3 (Wairio Branch Line).

83. Wairio ASRS members to ASRS Invercargill branch secretary, 2 October 1951; W.A. Wright, ASRS assistant secretary, to K.G. Reid, assistant staff superintendent, 12 December 1951; both in ANZ AAEB 16/3642 part 3.

84. Clarke to Wright, 11 January 1952, ANZ AAEB 16/3642 part 3.

85. W.H. Preston, DTM Invercargill, to Clarke, 20 February 1952; Clarke to Preston, 4 March 1952; both in ANZ AAEB 16/3642 part 3.

86. Preston to Clarke, 31 March 1952, ANZ AAEB 16/3642 part 3.

87. J.F. Ericson, DTM Invercargill, to transportation

superintendent, 13 June 1952; J. Kelleher, acting transportation superintendent to Ericson, 30 June 1952; and Ericson's four-weekly statements of passenger traffic; all in ANZ AAEB 16/3642 part 3.

88. List of South Island trains that will run under coal saving timetable from 12 April 1951, ANZ ADQD 500/3/11 part 3.

89. M.M. Fossey, secretary of the Riverton and District Progress League, to DTM Invercargill, 15 September 1951, ANZ AAEB 16/6018 part 5 (train services Tuatapere Branch).

90. Acting DTM Invercargill to Fossey, 25 September 1951, ANZ AAEB 16/6018 part 5.

91. Ericson to Transportation Superintendent, 13 June 1952, ANZ AAEB 16/6018 part 5.

92. J.R. Yonge, *New Zealand Railway and Tramway Atlas*, 4th edn (Exeter: Quail Map Company, 1993 [1965]), 31.

93. David Leitch and Bob Stott, *New Zealand Railways: The first 125 years* (Auckland: Heinemann Reed, 1988), 100.

94. *AJHR* 1952 D-3, 15.

95. Ibid.

96. Sawers to V.E. Wilson of Raetihi, 5 January 1946, ANZ ADQD 1918/1998/1 part 2 (Raetihi Branch timetable).

97. A.E. List, DTM Whanganui, to Horace Lusty, general manager, 11 October 1951, ANZ ADQD 1918/1998/1 part 2.

98. Clarke to List, 5 November 1951, ANZ ADQD 1918/1998/1 part 2.

99. *Timaru Herald*, 12 April 1947 in ANZ AAEB 16/2222/1 part 4 (Fairlie Branch train services).

100. Ede to DTM Dunedin, 4 January 1951, ANZ AAEB 16/2222/1 part 4.

101. New Zealand Railways, *Tangiwai Railway Disaster: Report of the board of inquiry* (Wellington: Government Printer, 1954), 21–24.

102. Goosman to Clyde Carr, MP for Timaru, and David Kidd, MP for Waimate, 29 October 1953, ANZ AAEB 16/2222/1 part 4.

103. E.F. Parr, DTM Christchurch, to transportation superintendent, 3 November 1954, ANZ AAEB 16/2222/1 part 4.

104. Lois Voller, *Rails to Nowhere: The history of the Nelson railway* (Nelson: Nikau Press, 1991), 151.

105. *AJHR* 1952 D-3, 62.

106. Eric Pawson and Tony Hoare, 'Regional isolation, railways and politics: Nelson, New Zealand', *Journal of Transport History* 10:1 (1989), 22–40.

107. Potton cited in Voller, *Rails to Nowhere*, 158.

108. Voller, *Rails to Nowhere*, 159–76.

109. S. Orr, *New Zealand Railway Corporations: A short history of previous experiences with New Zealand Railways as a corporation* (Wellington: Ministry of Transport Economic Division, 1981), 19–23.

110. Bloomfield, Historical Statistics, 242; *AJHR* 1953 D-2, 18.

111. David P. Millar, *Once Upon a Village: A history of Lower Hutt, 1819–1965* (Wellington: New Zealand University Press, 1972), Chapter 12.

112. *Evening Post*, 12 April 1945, 6.

113. *Hutt News*, 19 December 1945, 5; *AJHR* 1946 D-2, 7.

114. *AJHR* 1947 D-2, 12.

115. *AJHR* 1954 D-2, 18.

116. Robin Bromby, *Rails that Built a Nation: An encyclopaedia of New Zealand railways* (Wellington: Grantham House, 2003), 70.

117. Laurence Evans, *The Commuter, the Car and Metropolitan Wellington* (Wellington: Victoria University of Wellington, 1972), 45–51. Plans and discussion can be found in ANZ AAEB 09/3714/1 parts 3–4 and AAEB 28/800 (rail link – Haywards to Plimmerton).

118. *NZR Staff Bulletin* 10:5 (1961), 66.

119. Paul Mees and Jago Dodson, 'The American heresy: Half a century of transport planning in Auckland', in Peter Holland, Fiona Stevenson and Alexander Wearing (eds), 2001, *Geography – A Spatial Odyssey: Proceedings of the third joint conference of the New Zealand Geographical Society and the Institute of Australian Geographers* (Dunedin: New Zealand Geographical Society, 2002), 279.

120. Halcrow-Thomas Report on Auckland's Transport Problems, ACC 275, Box 346, Record 50-299, Auckland Council Archives (copy courtesy of Chris Harris); and e.g. *AJHR* 1946 D-3, appendix B; *AJHR* 1948 D-1, 33.

121. *New Zealand Herald*, 2 February 1943, 5.

122. Graham Bush, *From Survival to Revival: Auckland's public transport since 1860* (Wellington: Grantham House, 2014), 158.

123. Mees and Dodson, 'American heresy'. This point does not appear in print, which was an edited version of a paper distributed electronically. It is on page six of the copy available at https://web.archive.org/web/20200417052119/https://www.cs.auckland.ac.nz/~cthombor/Pubs/AKtransportMees.rtf

124. Ibid., 281. See also Christopher E. Harris, 'Slow train coming: The New Zealand state changes its mind about Auckland transit, 1949–56', *Urban Policy and Research* 23:1 (2005), 37–55.

125. Michael Gunder, 'Auckland's motorway system: A New Zealand genealogy of imposed automotive progress, 1946–66', *Urban Policy and Research* 20:2 (2002), 130.

126. Goosman quoted in Bush, *Survival to Revival*, 164.

127. Graham Stewart, *Auckland Before the Harbour Bridge* (Wellington: Grantham House, 2002), 140.

CHAPTER 6

1955–68: THE FIAT FIASCO

1. The definitive account is W.N. Cameron, *A Line of Railway: The railway conquest of the Rimutakas* (Wellington: New Zealand Railway and Locomotive Society, 1976).

2. *AJHR* 1923 D-1, iv; *AJHR* 1924 D-2a, 8–9.

3. *Wairarapa Daily Times*, 12 October 1937, 4.

4. *Evening Post*, 10 and 11 June 1938, 10.

5. *AJHR* 1948 D-1, 11–12.

6. Cameron, *A Line of Railway*, Chapter 14.

7. Frank Aickin to Bob Semple, 10 August 1948; Aickin to Semple, 20 April 1949; both in ANZ ADQD 1904/833/60 part 2 (purchase of railcars).

8. P.R. Angus, chief mechanical engineer to Aickin, 4 January 1950; Aickin to Angus, 12 January 1950; both in ANZ ADQD 1904/833/60 part 2.

9. *AJHR* 1951 D-1, 2.

10. R.F. Black, chief mechanical engineer, to H.C. Lusty, general manager, 28 November 1951, ANZ ADQD 1904/833/60 part 2.

11. Black to Lusty, 5 November 1954, ANZ ADQD 1904/833/60 part 3; Pacific Maritime Association, 'The London Dock Strike October 1954', special research report, 22 November 1954: https://web.archive.org/web/20200129041807/https://digitalassets.lib.berkeley.edu/irle/ucb/text/lb000219.pdf

12. A.J. Ede to district traffic managers, 10 November 1950, ANZ ADQD 1904/833/60 part 2. Intriguingly, Ede also suggested refurbishing the Wairarapa railcars for use in northern Taranaki. The previous year, Aickin considered them so worn out that they would have to be retired once the Remutaka Tunnel opened, and this is what happened.

13. W.A. Breach, DTM Christchurch, to Ede, 23 November 1950, ANZ ADQD 1904/833/60 part 2.

14. S.G. Howie, DTM Dunedin, to Ede, 27 November 1950, ANZ ADQD 1904/833/60 part 2.

15. C.T. Phillips, acting district traffic manager Invercargill, to Ede, 31 January 1950, ANZ ADQD 1904/833/60 part 2.

16. *AJHR* 1952 D-3, 14–15.

17. Lusty to Railways Commission, 24 August 1954, ANZ ADQD 1904/833/60 part 3.

18. Gandell to Black, 21 June 1955; 'Twin car sets: delivery of 35 railcars ordered to V.R. 7776', unsigned file note c. January 1956; both in ANZ ADQD 1904/833/60 part 3; Black to advisory engineer, c/o New Zealand high commissioner, 23 March 1955, ANZ ADQD 34/280A part 8 (twinset railcars).

19. DTM Wellington to Gandell, 18 January 1956, ANZ ADQD 1904/833/60 part 3.

20. Gandell to Black, 16 January 1956, ANZ ADQD 1904/833/60 part 3.

21. Black to John McAlpine, Minister of Railways, 10 August 1956, ANZ AAEB 04/833/60 part 4 (purchase of railcars).

22. Black to Richardson, McCabe & Co., 7 March 1957, and Black to Gandell, 8 March 1975, both in ANZ AAEB 04/833/60 part 4; see also

acting DTM Christchurch to Black, 11 February 1957, ANZ ADQD 34/280A part 17.

23. Notes on verbal agreement, signed by Gandell, William Jefferson Wakley (for Drewry), and Franco Prosio (for Fiat), 28 June 1957, ANZ AAEB 04/833/60 part 4; Gandell to chief cashier, Reserve Bank, 1 December 1958, ANZ AAEB 04/833/60 part 5.

24. Note for McAlpine, 16 August 1956; 'Railcar services', figures to 9 February 1957; both in ANZ AAEB 04/833/60 part 4.

25. *AJHR* 1952 D-3, 14; Lusty to Railways Commission, 5 March 1954 and 24 August 1954, and secretary of the Cabinet to McAlpine, 14 September 1955, all in ANZ ADQD 1904/833/60 part 3.

26. Black to Gandell, 21 June 1956, ANZ AAEB 04/833/60 part 4; see also Black to Gandell, 3 September 1957, ANZ AAEB 04/833/60 part 5. Black appears to have been inspired in 1956 by an early design for the Swiss RAm class/Dutch DE4 class that Werkspoor and SIG constructed for the Trans Europe Express. His proposals in 1957 reveal an influence from the first generation of British Rail diesel multiple units.

27. Gandell to McAlpine, 22 March 1957, ANZ AAEB 04/833/60 part 4; '88-seater railcars', file note dated 11 September 1957, ANZ AAEB 04/833/60 part 5.

28. Prosio to Gandell, 12 August 1957, ANZ AAEB 04/833/60 part 5.

29. *Northland Times*, 3 April 1959, ANZ AAEB 04/833/60 part 5.

30. Jim McAloon, *Judgements of All Kinds: Economic policy-making in New Zealand 1945–1984* (Wellington: Victoria University Press, 2013), 105–07.

31. J.A. Dangerfield and G.W. Emerson, *Over the Garden Wall: Story of the Otago Central Railway*, 3rd edn, (Dunedin: Otago Railway and Locomotive Society, 1995 [1962]), 42–43.

32. List of South Island trains that will run under coal-saving timetable from 12 April 1951, ANZ ADQD 500/3/11 part 3.

33. Dangerfield and Emerson, *Over the Garden Wall*, 43–49.

34. 'Twin set cars', note of 3 November 1958, signature unclear; ministerial statement, 21 November 1958; both in ANZ AAEB 04/833/60 part 5.

35. Departmental communications assumed operation with Standard railcars. Photographs from the final days of the service, however, show that Fiats were also used: Tony Hurst, *Farewell to Steam: Four decades of change on New Zealand railways* (Auckland: HarperCollins, 1995), 74–75.

36. Murray to DTM Whanganui, 27 September 1957; DTM Whanganui to Murray, 14 November 1957; Murray to Gandell, 30 December 1957; all in ANZ AAEB 16/1795/10 part 2 (fast passenger trains numbers 524 and 525 ['Flier'] Wanganui–New Plymouth).

37. A.T. Fussell, publicity and advertising manager, to Murray, 3 October 1958, and attachment; *Wanganui Chronicle*, 17 February 1959; both in ANZ AAEB 16/1795/10 part 2.

38. File note, 3 November 1958, ANZ AAEB 1904/833/60 part 5; Murray to DTM Whanganui, 11 December 1958, ANZ AAEB 16/1795/1 part 5 (train services Wanganui–New Plymouth–Marton–Palmerston North).

39. Acting DTM Whanganui to transportation superintendent, 16 April 1959; DTM Whanganui to transportation superintendent, 7 October 1959; both in ANZ AAEB 16/1795/1 part 5.

40. *Bay of Plenty Times*, 6 February 1959, in ANZ AAVK PUB 7/6, part 1 (railcar services – Auckland southwards).

41. Black to Gandell, 15 April 1958, ANZ AAEB 04/833/60 part 5.

42. Horace of Bay of Plenty, *New Zealand Herald*, 17 February 1959, in ANZ AAVK PUB 7/6, part 1.

43. *Bay of Plenty Beacon*, 23 March 1959, in ANZ AAVK PUB 7/6, part 1.

44. DTM Invercargill to Ede, 6 July 1951, ANZ AAEB 16/5002/1 part 3 (Invercargill–Kingston train services).

45. New Zealand Railways Timetable no. 1 (effective 22 May 1950), 20.

46. *Southland Times*, 15 June 1956, and McAlpine to Ralph Hanan, 5 July 1956, both in ANZ ABJP 04/3785/1 part 4

(train service Invercargill–Bluff); amendment to the working timetable (14 April 1957), 97, ANZ ABIN W3337 Box 193 (working timetable – South Island main line and branches 1957).

47. Gandell to Mick Moohan, Minister of Railways, 12 August 1958, ANZ ABJP 04/3785/1 part 4.

48. Alan Alsweiler, secretary of the Southland Progress League, to Moohan, 8 August 1958; Southland Times, 16 August 1958; DTM Dunedin to F.R. Murray, transportation superintendent, 29 August 1958; all in ANZ ABJP 04/3785/1 part 4.

49. Murray to DTM Dunedin, 11 September 1958, ANZ ABJP 04/3785/1 part 4.

50. Precis of transport of schoolchildren, no date (c. late 1966), assistant transportation superintendent, ANZ ABJP 04/3785/1 part 5 (train service Invercargill–Bluff); NZ Truth, 31 January 1967, in ANZ-CRO CAAA CH45 box 155/a 33/10 part 2 (primary education–school transport Southland–Invercargill schools). A number of contemporary accounts and reminiscences are collected in Alex C. Glennie, The Invercargill–Bluff Railway and Bluff School Train (Invercargill: SBHS Old Boys Association, 2018), 126–45.

51. A.K. Neilson, DTM Dunedin, to J.T.P. Jones, transportation superintendent, 16 November 1966, ANZ ABJP 04/3785/1 part 5.

52. M. O'Byrne for the acting director-general of education to Ivan Thomas, general manager, 9 November 1966, ANZ ABJP 04/3785/1 part 5.

53. Christchurch to Head Office, 7 November 1966, ANZ-CRO CAAA CH45 box 155/a 33/10 part 2.

54. O'Byrne, telegrams no. 9 and 21 of 11 January 1967, ANZ-CRO CAAA CH45 box 155/a 33/10 part 2.

55. Thomas to the director-general of education, 17 January 1967; transport officer, Southland Education Board to stationmaster Invercargill, 27 January 1967; Neilson to Jones, 3 February 1967; all in ANZ ABJP 04/3785/1 part 5. J.F. Churstain, note for file, 27 January 1967, ANZ-CRO CAAA CH45 box 155/a 33/10 part 2. For term dates, see Southlandian, 1966 and 1967; I also thank Lynley Dear (archivist, Southland Boys' High School) and Barbara Clark (archivist, Southland Girls' High School) for their assistance with clarifying the dates.

56. NZ Truth, 31 January 1967.

57. See discussion in ANZ ABJP 04/3785/1 part 5, starting with N.J. Wilson, project manager of the Ocean Beach Freezing Company, to area traffic manager Invercargill, 16 February 1981.

58. File note by assistant transportation superintendent, 10 April 1958 and Murray to W.K. Thorn, acting DTM Christchurch, 15 August 1958, both in ANZ AAEB 04/3962/1 part 4 (Rakaia–Methven service). After the Rakaia locomotive depot closed on 14 September 1957, trains for Methven ran out of the Ashburton depot. They used an express goods van Ashburton–Rakaia and then switched to a car-van for Rakaia–Methven. DTM Christchurch to F.R. Murray, transportation superintendent, 5 November 1957, and Murray to DTM Christchurch, 12 November 1957; both in ANZ AAEB 04/3962/1 part 4

59. A. Evans, transportation superintendent, to Auckland DTM, 10 March 1954, ANZ ADQD 1911/1130/1, part 4 (Waipa Valley and collieries); A.W. Egan, DTM Auckland, to F.R. Murray, transportation superintendent, 15 May 1958, ANZ ADQD 1911/1130/1, part 5.

60. Report to Alan Gandell, general manager, 1 February 1956, ANZ ADQD 081/100/30 part 2 (Dargaville–Donnellys Crossing).

61. Gandell to chief accountant, 8 April 1959, ANZ ADQD 081/100/30 part 2.

62. AJHR 1930 D-4, 48;

63. H.C. Couch, DTM Whanganui, to J.C. Schneider, traffic superintendent, 6 May 1932, ANZ AAEB 25/985 part 1 (NZ Railway: General file – Opunake Branch).

64. A.J. Pritchard, DTM Wanganui, to A.L. Smith, transportation superintendent, 10 March 1942, ANZ AAEB 25/985 part 1; J.R. Yonge, New

Zealand Railway and Tramway Atlas, 4th edn (Exeter: Quail Map Company, 1993), 10. The decision to end passenger services does not appear to have survived in the Ōpunake files held by Archives New Zealand, which discuss only goods traffic during the mid-1950s.

65. *New Zealand Railways Timetable* no. 1 (effective 22 May 1950), 19.

66. List of South Island trains that will run under coal-saving timetable from 12 April 1951, ANZ ADQD 500/3/11 part 3; senior stationmaster Lumsden to E.B. Baker, traffic manager Invercargill, 17 May 1956 and D.M. Hoult, DTM Dunedin, to Baker, 22 November 1956, both in ANZ-DRO DAFV 20/358 (Invercargill–Lumsden–Kingston Train Services).

67. Phillips to road services manager, 6 March 1951, ANZ-DRO DAFV 20/358.

68. David Leitch and Brian Scott, *Exploring New Zealand's Ghost Railways*, rev. edn (Wellington: Grantham House, 1998 [1995]), 111–12.

69. A.E. Haigh, acting DTM Dunedin, to transportation superintendent, 23 March 1959, ANZ AAEB 16/6018 part 5.

70. Robin Bromby, *Rails That Built a Nation: An encyclopaedia of New Zealand railways* (Wellington: Grantham House, 2003), 102.

71. S.G. Howie, DTM Dunedin, to Aickin, 15 December 1949,

ANZ AAEB 03/3964 part 2 (Outram Branch).

72. Amendment effective 10 October 1950 in the working timetable effective 17 November 1946, ANZ-DRO DAFV D454 20155 Box 14/d, 89.

73. See e.g. acting DTM Dunedin to transportation superintendent, 25 October 1951, ANZ ADQD 500/3/11 part 3; working timetable effective 15 March 1954, ANZ-DRO DAFV D454 20155 Box 15/d, 89; working timetable effective 12 August 1956, ANZ-DRO DAFV D454 20155 Box 15/e, 89.

74. A.R. Tyrrell, *Catlins Rail: The story of the Catlins River Branch Railway 1879–1971*, 4th printing (Ōwaka: Catlins Historical Society, 2005 [1996]), 51

75. Working timetable effective 7 June 1959, ANZ ABIN W3337 Box 193, 101.

76. DTM Invercargill to transportation superintendent, 19 March 1960; review of Seaward Bush Branch Line, 29 April 1960; both in ANZ AAEB 04/3006/1 part 3.

77. See plans and correspondence in ANZ-DRO DAFV 13/331 (improvements at Mussel Bay – new station built and named Port Chalmers) and DABO D544 box 10/e (contract for erection of new station building Mussel Bay – contract no. 1466).

78. James Watson, *Links: A history of transport and New Zealand society* (Wellington: GP Publications, 1996), 238.

79. C.J. Millin, DTM Christchurch, to transportation superintendent, 23 May 1960, ANZ-CRO CAHV 14/1289 part 1 (passenger traffic general).

80. *AJHR* 1952 D-3, 27. See also *NZR Bulletin* 13:2 (1964), 24–28.

81. Tim White, 'The day the trains stopped coming through The Square in Palmerston North', *Manawatu Standard*, 3 June 2016: https://web.archive.org/web/20200212015118/https://www.stuff.co.nz/manawatu-standard/lifestyle/80700933/memory-lane-the-day-trains-stopped-coming-through-the-square-in-palmerston-north

82. *NZPD* vol. 343, 1353–54 (15 July 1965); draft cleared by H.Z. Purchase, 9 July 1965, ANZ AAEB 04/833/60 part 5 (purchase of railcars).

83. S.G. Muir, DTM Auckland, to J.T.P. Jones, transportation superintendent, 18 March 1966, ANZ AAEB 04/833/60 part 5; Purchase to chief accountant, 7 July 1966, and Ivan Thomas, general manager, to Peter Gordon, Minister of Railways, 13 December 1966, both in ANZ AAEB 04/833/60 part 6.

84. N.A. McGerty, comptroller of stores, to L.M. Johnston, chief mechanical engineer, 4 November 1966, ADQD 34/280A part 39 (twinset railcars).

85. Brian Easton, *Not in Narrow Seas: The economic history of Aotearoa New Zealand* (Wellington: Victoria

University Press, 2020), 255; Malcolm McKinnon, *Treasury: The New Zealand Treasury, 1840–2000* (Auckland: Auckland University Press, 2003), 239–44.

86. Background notes for government members from Peter Gordon, 22 November 1968, ANZ AAVK PUB 7/3 part 2 (railcars – services and timetables – general).

87. Ross Carroll, secretary to the Treasury, to Harry Lake, Minister of Finance, 7 November 1966, ANZ AEEB 04/833/60 part 6; McAlpine to Cabinet works committee, W(66)317, 25 November 1966, ANZ AAFD CAB 183/4/2 (railways – equipment – locomotives etc).

88. Thomas to Gordon, 9 January 1967, ANZ AEEB 04/833/60 part 6.

89. Gordon to Cabinet, 18 January 1967 (CP [67]55) and A.R. Perry, secretary of the Cabinet, to Gordon, 1 February 1967 (CM 67/2/26); both in ANZ AAFD CAB 183/4/2.

90. G.A.E. Weston, DTM Wellington, to Jones, 13 June 1967; Jones to all DTMs and chief mechanical engineer, 20 June 1967, ANZ AEEB 04/833/60 part 6.

91. G.A.E. Weston, transportation superintendent, to T.M. Small, 15 August 1968, ANZ AAVK PUB 7/3 part 2.

92. Jones to Thomas, 25 May 1967, ANZ AEEB 04/833/60 part 6.

93. Graham Stewart, *Auckland Before the Harbour Bridge* (Wellington: Grantham House, 2002), 154–60.

94. J.F. Johnson and 11,335 others, petition no. 60/1967, ANZ AAEB 04/833/23 part 6 (railcar services Auckland District).

95. Chief administration officer to Mr Geddes, 20 February 1968, ANZ AAEB 04/833/23 part 6.

96. Weston to DTM Auckland, 10 July 1967, ANZ AAEB 11/1511/1 part 2 (carriage accommodation and conditions of same on Auckland northwards line); 'Railways at Dargaville' (c. October 1967), 4, ANZ AAVK PUB 1/5 part 2 (Construction and history of: North Auckland railways). Some sources suggest the Dargaville mixed ended on 31 March 1967, but they ran until the end of the railcars.

97. *New Zealand Railways Timetables* (new series), nos 13 (10 July 1967), 14 (1 July 1968), and 16 (1 December 1970).

98. Thomas to Gordon, 28 January 1972, AAJM 4/833/23 part 7 (railcar services: Auckland District). Emphasis original.

99. Gordon to R. Moses, 20 October 1967 (draft), ANZ AAEB 04/833/23 part 6.

100. Weston to chief administration officer, 27 February 1968, ANZ AAEB 04/833/23 part 6.

101. Gordon to Cabinet, 20 August 1968, ANZ AAFD CAB 183/4/2.

102. Schedule B, Gordon to Cabinet, 18 November 1967, ANZ AAFD CAB 183/4/2.

103. DTM Auckland, circular memorandum no. 1967/53, 30 June 1967, ANZ AAVK PUB 7/6, part 1.

104. Thomas to Gordon, 11 August 1967; Thomas, press statement, 17 August 1967; both in ANZ AAVK PUB 7/6, part 1.

105. R.P. Thomson, *Auckland Star*, 12 August 1967, and Mrs F. Watson, *Auckland Star*, 19 August 1967, both in ANZ AAVK PUB 7/6, part 1.

106. Background notes for government members from Gordon, 22 November 1968, ANZ AAVK PUB 7/3 part 2.

107. Inspecting engineer (diesel and mechanical) and projects officer (transportation superintendent's office) to Thomas, 9 February 1968; Weston and F.K. Froggatt, chief accountant, to Thomas, 13 June 1968; both in ANZ AEEB 04/833/60 part 6. It is unclear how Weston and Froggatt arrived at their calculation of passenger loadings, as taking the average from certain intermediate stations over others could alter the figures significantly. Without more detail, it is difficult to say if they were fair.

108. Weston and Froggatt to Thomas, 13 June 1968, ANZ AEEB 04/833/60 part 6.

109. Perry to Gordon (appendix), 3 September 1967, ANZ AAFD CAB 183/6/2 part 1; schedule B, Gordon to Cabinet, 18 November 1967, ANZ AAFD CAB 183/4/2.

110. Thomas to T.D. Beale, 13 December 1968, ANZ AAJM 12/640 part 11 (Rotorua Branch – timetable).

111. Background notes for government members from Gordon, 22 November 1968, ANZ AAVK PUB 7/3 part 2.

112. Letters and petitions dated 5, 6 and 12 November 1968, ANZ AAEB 06/161 (carriage accommodation Rotorua Line). T.J. Amopiu to Paraone Reweti, MP for Eastern Māori, is a rare example of a letter in te reo Māori in the NZR files.

113. Weston to Thomas, 21 May 1970, ANZ AAJM 12/640 part 11.

CHAPTER 7

1970–89: 'THE EMOTIVE TERM "RAILCARS"' – CANCELLATIONS IN TOWN AND COUNTRY

1. *Rails* 2:10 (May 1973), 2.

2. *New Zealand Official Year-Book 1971*, section 11, parts B and D; Neill Atkinson, *Trainland: How railways made New Zealand* (Auckland: Random House, 2007), 134–35.

3. *New Zealand Official Year-Book 1971*, section 11, part C.

4. *AJHR* 1971 D-2, 18.

5. G.A.E. Weston, transportation superintendent, to Ivan Thomas, general manager, 21 May 1970, ANZ AAJM 12/640 part 11 (Rotorua Branch – timetable); Weston to DTM Auckland, 24 July 1970, ANZ AAEB 06/161 (carriage accommodation Rotorua Line).

6. Traffic manager Frankton to Weston, 10 May 1971, ANZ AAJM 12/640 part 11; H.I. Leonard, acting transportation superintendent, to DTM Auckland, 14 June 1971, ANZ AAJM 12/640 part 11.

7. G.A.E. Weston, chief traffic manager, to T.M. Small, general manager, 1 March 1972, ANZ ABJP 15/2130/1 part 8 (train service – Huntly to Rotowaro); cf. *New Zealand Railways Timetable* no. 13 (new series), effective 10 July 1967, 14.

8. Commercial agent Hamilton to R.W.D. Thompson, DTM Auckland, 17 November 1971, ANZ ABJP 15/2130/1 part 8.

9. Thompson to Weston, 6 December 1971; director, finance and accounts, to Weston, 18 February 1972; both in ANZ ABJP 15/2130/1 part 8.

10. Weston to Small, 10 March 1972, ANZ ABJP 15/2130/1 part 8.

11. Small to land officer, 9 June 1972; Weston to DTM Auckland, 23 June 1972; both in ANZ ABJP 15/2130/1 part 8.

12. District engineer Dunedin to chief civil engineer and transportation superintendent, 31 October 1961, and L.C. Brown, DTM Dunedin, to Weston, 9 February 1971; both in ANZ-DRO DABM 09/336 part 2 (Ohai Railway Board private line).

13. Minutes of Board meeting, 26 November 1974, and traffic manager's report to board meeting, 23 January 1975, Southland District Council Archives (SDCA).

14. Minutes of ŌRB meetings, 26 June and 22 July 1975, SDCA. This paragraph also draws on the files held in ORB01585 Box 53, SDCA.

15. *New Zealand Railway Observer* 78:5 (no. 364, 2020/21), 91–101.

16. Memorandum no. 1967/70, DTM Christchurch, 22 August 1967, and train advice no. 4680, DTM Christchurch, 27 November 1967, both in ANZ-CRO CAHV 25/282/23, part 3 (train services Hokitika–Ross).

17. *New Zealand Railway Observer* 32:4 (no. 144, 1975/76), 166.

18. G.A.E. Weston to deputy general manager, 22 March 1968, ANZ AAJM 16/913/1 part 12 (Auckland–Whangarei Training: Auckland–Whangarei–Opua Express Trains).

19. 'Review of NZR Operations North of Whangarei', June 1972, 53–54, ANZ AAEB 16/1544/1 part 8 (train services – Whangarei northwards).

20. Peter Cape, 'The Okaihau Express', in *An Ordinary Joker: The life and songs of Peter Cape* (Wellington: Steele Roberts, 2001).

21. Report of DTM Auckland, district engineer Auckland, and commercial agent Auckland, 22 August 1973, ANZ AAEB 16/1544/1 part 8.

22. Updated text of 'Otiria–Okaihau Railway', originally written 25 February 1964, attached to T.A. McGavin, publicity and advertising manager, to Ross Miller, 31 January 1974, ANZ AAVK

PUB 1/5 (construction and history of: North Auckland Railways).

23. *New Zealand Railways Timetable* no. 18 (14 December 1972), 14.

24. *Northern Advocate*, 25 March 1976, ANZ AAEB 16/1544/1 part 8.

25. M.C. Hudson, DTM Auckland, to R.W.D. Thompson, chief traffic manager, 20 May 1976, ANZ AAEB 16/1544/1 part 8.

26. *New Zealand Railway Observer* 32:1 (no. 141, 1975), 36–37, and 32:4 (no. 144, 1975/76), 168.

27. Small to Thompson, 10 June 1976; Thompson to Hudson, 11 June 1976, ANZ AAEB 16/1544/1 part 8; *New Zealand Railway Observer* 33:1 (no. 145, 1976), 37.

28. *New Zealand Railway Observer* 33:2 (no. 146, 1976), 79.

29. Ibid.; chief traffic manager to DTM Christchurch, 30 October 1973, ANZ-CRO CAHV 25/952/1 part 8 (railcars general); G.S. Roscoe, DTM Christchurch, to chief traffic manager, 4 June 1976, ANZ-CRO CAHV 25/2852/56 part 8 (North Line train services).

30. Christchurch district mechanical engineer and district traffic manager, 'Vulcan Railcars on Main North Line', 8 August 1973, ANZ-CRO CAHV 25/952/1 part 8. The district engineer submitted a dissenting report that argued for a connecting service.

31. Special notice, DTM Christchurch, 29 June 1976,

ANZ-CRO CAHV 25/282/56 part 8.

32. Inspecting engineer (diesel and mechanical) and projects officer (transportation superintendent's office) to Thomas, 15 August 1967, ANZ AEEB 04/833/60 part 6.

33. *Rails* 2:6 (January 1973), 13.

34. Southerner menu and liquor service, November 1971, Hocken Collections Uare Taoka o Hākena E210 Box 1012A (Ephemera–New Zealand Railways–Timetables and Menus).

35. Small to chief mechanical engineer, 8 May 1972, ANZ AAJM 72/282 (railcars for provincial services).

36. *NZPD* vol. 403, 14 July 1976, 538.

37. Joint report of 16 August 1968, ANZ AEEB 04/833/60 part 6.

38. NZR press release, 20 August 1971; circular memorandum no. 1971/63, 30 August 1971; both in ANZ AAVK PUB 7/3 part 2 (railcars – services and timetables – general).

39. *Rails* 3:6 (January 1974), 15.

40. Memorandum of J.S. Engel, chairman of the interdepartmental committee on the West Coast, 23 August 1971, AAFD CAB 183/6/2 (railways – passenger services – termination of services).

41. 'Economies in operations on the West Coast', 10 May 1972, ANZ-CRO CAHV 25/282/14 part 5 (train services Christchurch–Greymouth–Ross).

42. A.D. Campbell, DTM Christchurch, to Weston, 12 June 1972, and memorandum

no. 1972/25, Campbell, 20 September 1972, both in ANZ-CRO CAHV 25/282/14 part 5.

43. Small, 'New passenger services' memorandum, 27 July 1973, AAEB 09/5300/24 part 1 (review and planning of new provincial passenger trains 1973).

44. Tom McGuigan, Minister of Railways, to caucus transport committee, 24 December 1973, ANZ AAFD CAB 183/6/1 (railways – passenger services).

45. H.E. McLenaghin, chief mechanical engineer, to Small, 17 May 1973, AAEB 09/5300/24 part 1.

46. Minutes of the Cabinet sub-committee on transport, 20 December 1974, and secretary to the Treasury to Bob Tizard, Minister of Finance, 17 January 1975, both in ANZ AAFD CAB 183/6/1.

47. *Rails* 2:7 (February 1973), 2.

48. Ron Bailey to the Cabinet committee on policy and procedures, 18 September 1975, ANZ AAFD CAB 183/6/1.

49. Minutes of the Cabinet committee on policy and procedures, 1 October 1975, ANZ AAFD CAB 183/6/1.

50. S.A. McLeod, assistant secretary to the Treasury, to Tizard, 12 September 1975, ANZ AAFD CAB 183/6/1.

51. P.G. Millen, secretary of the Cabinet, to Colin McLachlan, Minister of Railways, 10 February 1976, ANZ AAFD CAB 183/6/1.

52. *NZPD* vol. 404, 28 July 1976, 1082.

53. Joyce Herd, president of Ecology Action Otago, to Venn Young, Minister for the Environment, 8 April 1976, ANZ AAEB 04/833/32 part 3 (railcars Otago Central). Other petitions and letters of advocacy are in this file.

54. Secretary to the treasury to the minister of finance, 16 September 1976, ANZ ABJP 04/833/78 part 1 (conversion of railcars to loco-hauled trains).

55. *Manawatu Evening Standard*, 4 November 1972, 15.

56. *NZPD* vol. 403, 7 July 1976, 349; Bob Bell to McLachlan, 19 May 1976, AAEB 23/551/1 part 13 (NZ Railway: Endeavour Passenger Service – Wellington–Napier).

57. McLachlan to Cabinet, no clear date (c. September 1976), ANZ AAFD CAB 183/6/1; Chris Wood, *Steaming to the Sunrise: A history of railways in the Gisborne region* (Wellington: IPL Books, 1996), 94.

58. Small to K.M. Fredric, chief mechanical engineer, 29 March 1976; Fredric and R.W.D. Thompson, chief traffic manager, to Small, 23 April 1976; both in ANZ ABJP 04/833/78 part 1.

59. 'Railway passenger services', Small, 23 September 1976, ANZ ABJP 04/833/78 part 1.

60. David Leitch to E.L. Teal, passenger manager, 4 October 1976, ANZ ABJP 04/833/78 part 1. This file also contains the internal debate about paint schemes; for the final decision,

see Hayward to CME, 14 June 1977.

61. *NZR Bulletin* 13:2 (1964), 22.

62. McLachlan to Tony Friedlander, MP for New Plymouth, c. 15 June 1977, AAEB 04/833/50 part 12 (railcar service Wellington–New Plymouth).

63. Handwritten passenger counts for January 1976 to July 1977, ANZ AAEB 04/833/50 part 12; 'Provincial railcars: Background to the Blue Streak withdrawal', June 1977, ABIN W3337 Box 36 (miscellaneous reports – provincial railcars).

64. 'Provincial railcars', ABIN W3337 Box 36; route proposals c. July 1976, ANZ ABJP 04/833/78 part 1. The petition is in AAEB 04/833/50 part 12; see part 11 for council letters such as Hāwera Borough Council town clerk to McLachlan, 19 May 1977.

65. Aidan Benefield to McLachlan, 3 June 1977, AAEB 04/833/50 part 12.

66. Juliet Roborgh to Robert Muldoon, 21 June 1977, AAEB 04/833/50 part 12.

67. H.W. Reinhart to McLachlan, 7 June 1977; chief mechanical engineer to R.W.D. Thompson, assistant general manager, 13 June 1977, AAEB 04/833/50 part 12.

68. *AJHR* 1974 F-7, 18. See also *AJHR* 1973 F-7, 18, and *AJHR* 1975 F-7, 16.

69. S.J. Mills to McLachlan, 31 May 1977, and McLachlan to Mills, 15 June 1977, AAEB 04/833/50 part 11. For more on the origin and function

of the procedures, see Anne C. Murray, 'Environmental assessment: The evolution of policy and practice in New Zealand' (MSc thesis, University of Canterbury, 1990), Chapter 4.

70. *Evening Post*, 18 June 1977, AAEB 04/833/50 part 12.

71. McLachlan to A.N. Fitch, 11 July 1977, AAEB 04/833/50 part 12.

72. McLachlan to Cabinet, no clear date (c. July 1976), ANZ AAFD CAB 183/6/1. Friedlander, ironically, later became a leading road lobbyist.

73. *NZPD* vol. 414, 20 October 1977, 3834; *NZPD* vol. 417, 24 May 1978, 241.

74. *NZPD* vol. 421, 27 September 1978, 3885.

75. *NZPD* vol. 417, 2 June 1978, 591.

76. Thompson to Small, 28 August 1972, ANZ AAEB 16/2134 part 3 (Auckland–Onehunga train services).

77. Weston to Thompson, 29 September 1972; Thompson to Weston, 11 January 1973; handwritten notes by multiple officers to Weston, 12–16 January 1973; all in ANZ AAEB 16/2134 part 3.

78. Weston to Small, 2 February 1973; Weston to Road Services director, 7 March 1973; ANZ ABJP 15/2130/1 part 8.

79. 'Penrose and Onehunga Branch', project report of 25 February 1976; chief traffic manager and chief engineer to Trevor Hayward, general manager, 11 August 1977;

both in ANZ ABJP 15/2130/1 part 8.

80. Leslie Dew, *The Country Commuter: The regional railway network of Christchurch* (Christchurch: Christchurch Transport Board, 1988), 32, 39–40.

81. Most service changes can be tracked through the *New Zealand Railways Timetable* nos 1–12 (1950 to 1967); see also the Timetable of Christchurch Suburban Train Services, effective 5 August 1962, Hocken Collections Uare Taoka o Hākena, E210 Box 1012A. For more on the Lyttelton Tunnel's construction – but little on the demise of the passenger trains – see David Welch, *Port to Plains: Over and under the Port Hills, the Story of the Lyttelton railway tunnel* (Invercargill: Craigs Design and Print, 2017).

82. *NZPD* 1956 vol. 310, 1,920.

83. 'Report on suburban train services Christchurch–Lyttelton', c. October 1971, CAHV 25/282/3 part 10 (Christchurch–Lyttelton train services).

84. 'Christchurch–Lyttelton rail passenger services', file note, 9 March 1977, ANZ AAVK PUB 13/6 part 2 (suburban train service – Christchurch); district accountant's report, 29 June 1972, CAHV 25/282/3 part 11 (Christchurch–Lyttelton train services).

85. This was true even under a diesel timetable, with poorer acceleration than electric trains: *Timetable of Christchurch Suburban Train Services*, effective 15 February 1971, Hocken Collections Uare Taoka o Hākena, E210 box 1012A. For council reaction, see K.D. Stills, Heathcote County Council clerk, to Gordon, 26 January 1972, ANZ ABJP 16/1546/1 part 7 (suburban train service – Christchurch–Lyttelton).

86. *New Zealand Railway Observer* 33:1 (no. 145, autumn 1976), 35.

87. Industrial relations officer, note of 30 March 1976, ANZ AAVK PUB 13/6 part 2.

88. *Press*, 1 May 1976, in ANZ AAVK PUB 13/6 part 2.

89. McLachlan, ministerial press release, 3 May 1976, ANZ AAVK PUB 13/6 part 2.

90. *Press*, 7 June 1976, in ANZ AAVK PUB 13/6 part 2.

91. 'Christchurch–Lyttelton rail passenger services', file note, 9 March 1977, ANZ AAVK PUB 13/6 part 2; New Zealand Maritime Museum, 'The turbo electric vehicle Rangatira of 1971', *New Zealand Maritime Record*: https://web.archive.org/web/20200825075345/http://www.nzmaritime.co.nz/r4.htm; note that at the time the death toll from the wreck of the TEV *Wahine* was given as 51. The toll has been revised to recognise two victims who died later from injuries received in the disaster.

92. McLachlan to Cabinet, undated (c. September 1976), ANZ AAFD CAB 183/6/1.

93. *Otago Daily Times*, 8 October 1968, in ANZ AAVK PUB 13/7 (suburban train services – Dunedin district).

94. *Evening Post*, 4 September 1979, in ANZ AAVK PUB 13/7.

95. Mr B. Smail in *Otago Daily Times*, 6 September 1979, in ANZ AAVK PUB 13/7.

96. *Otago Daily Times*, 21 November 1979, in ANZ AAVK PUB 13/7.

97. *Otago Daily Times*, 24 August 1982; H.G. Purdy, acting general manager, memorandum to senior officials, 27 September 1982; both in ANZ AAVK PUB 13/7.

98. *Otago Daily Times*, 29 September 1982 and 4 December 1982, both in ANZ AAVK PUB 13/7.

99. T.M. Hayward, *Time for Change* (Wellington: New Zealand Railways, 1979), 5.

100. McLachlan to Cabinet, no clear date (c. September 1976), ANZ AAFD CAB 183/6/1.

101. *AJHR* 1978 F-7, 14; *AJHR* 1979 F-7, 4.

102. J.T.P. Jones, transportation superintendent, to Ivan Thomas, general manager, 29 November 1966, ANZ AAJM 16/913/1 part 12 (Auckland–Whangarei training: Auckland–Whangarei–Opua express trains).

103. This box inset draws on John Edgar, *Urban Legend: Sir Dove-Myer Robinson* (Auckland: Hodder Moa, 2012), Chapters 18–21, and Graham Bush, *From Survival to Revival: Auckland's public transport since 1860* (Wellington: Grantham House, 2014), Chapter 8.

104. John Edgar, 'Robinson, Dove-Myer', *Dictionary of New Zealand Biography*: https://web.archive.org/web/20200311050456/https://teara.govt.nz/en/biographies/5r19/robinson-dove-myer

105. Rapid Transit Steering Committee, 'Report of the steering committee set up to investigate the recommendations of the working party which reported 30th May 1969' (Auckland: The Committee, 1972).

106. *Rails* 2:6 (January 1973), 2.

107. *Rails* 3:3 (October 1973), 21.

108. Edgar, *Urban Legend*, 232.

109. Hayward, *Time for Change*, 5; timetable effective 17 August 1980, ANZ ABIN W3337 Box 192 (working timetable – North Island main line and branches 1980), 11 and 14.

110. *Rails* (September 1980), 14.

111. *New Zealand Railway Observer* 40:1 (no. 173, 1983), 32.

112. Ivan Thomas, note of 26 February 1967 (typed as 1966), ANZ AEEB 04/833/60 part 6 (purchase of railcars).

113. *Rails* 3:2 (September 1973), 7 and 3:6 (January 1974), 14–15; *New Zealand Railway Observer* 40:1 (no. 173, Autumn 1983), 32; *AJHR* 1983 F-7, 9.

114. Transport Planning Department, 'The future of Auckland suburban rail services: A short-term appraisal' (Auckland: Auckland Regional Authority, 1983), 31–34.

115. Ibid., 31.

116. Ibid., 4.

117. Report in ANZ ABIN W3337 Box 209 (New Zealand railways country passenger services); see also Hayward, *Time for Change*, 6.

118. A Ministry of Transport report emphasised this point ahead of corporatisation: S. Orr, *New Zealand Railway Corporations: A short history of previous experiences with New Zealand Railways as a corporation* (Wellington: Ministry of Transport Economic Division, 1981), 24–25.

119. Booz Allen Hamilton, *Comprehensive Review of Operations and Strategic Options Evaluation*, 8 November 1983 (Wellington: New Zealand Railways Corporation), V-7.

120. 'Schedule of railcar withdrawals' annexed to minutes of Cabinet transport committee, 8 March 1976, and secretary of the Cabinet to minister of railways, 21 June 1977, CM 77/22/17, both in ANZ AAFD CAB 183/6/1.

121. *New Zealand Railway Observer* 40:1 (no. 173, autumn 1983), 34.

122. T.W. Fletcher, 'From Greymouth to Rewanui: A trip through one of New Zealand's coal-mining districts', *New Zealand Railways Magazine* 4:5 (September 1929), 30–31.

123. *Greymouth Evening Star*, 20 January 1984, and senior operating officer Greymouth to passenger manager Wellington, 30 January 1984, both in ANZ ABJP 08/1357/4 part 6 (train service Greymouth–Rewanui).

124. W.H. Cunliffe for the Deputy Secretary of Energy (Mines) to H.G. Purdy, general manager, 28 February 1984, ANZ ABJP 08/1357/4 part 6.

125. Minutes of meeting concerning the future of the Rewanui line, 16 April 1984, ANZ ABJP 08/1357/4 part 6.

126. W.I. Jones, chief civil engineer, to Purdy, 15 May 1984, ANZ ABJP 08/1357/4 part 6.

127. *Greymouth Evening Star*, 12 May 1984, in ANZ ABJP 08/1357/4 part 6.

128. R.J. Taylor, DTM Christchurch, to chief traffic manager, 11 May 1984, ANZ ABJP 08/1357/4 part 6.

129. Area sales manager Christchurch to commercial manager, 20 June 1984, ANZ ABJP 08/1357/4 part 6.

130. *New Zealand Railway Observer* 45:3 (no. 195, spring 1988), 123.

131. Information in this paragraph sourced from Grant Craig (operations manager, Dunedin Railways), personal communication and slides archived at: https://web.archive.org/web/20200318182703/https://www.rtsa.com.au/wp-content/uploads/files/Dunedin%20Railways%20and%20FRONZ%20powerpoint.pdf; Tony Hurst, *The Otago Central Railway: A tribute*, 5th edn (Wellington: Transpress, 2008 [1990]); *Rails* 25:3 (October 1993), 70; archived Taieri Gorge Railway/Dunedin Railways websites, e.g. 'Our Story': https://web.archive.org/web/20141105234741/

http://www.taieri.co.nz/our-story and 'Our Company': https://web.archive.org/web/20190120160958/https://www.dunedinrailways.co.nz/about/our-company

132. Petition to Hayward, 13 February 1981, ANZ AAJM 23/551/8 part 2 (rail passenger service: Napier–Gisborne [AC cars]).

133. Passenger Business Group planning section, 'Long distance passenger rail survival plan: Implementation', 17 February 1987, ANZ AAJM 09/5300/24 part 13 (review and planning: new provincial passenger trains).

134. Zvi Harmor, private secretary for Minister of Railways Richard Prebble, to Keith Strode-Penny of Seatoun, 12 April 1988, in ANZ AAJM 23/551/1 part 19 (rail passenger service: Wellington–Gisborne).

135. *Gisborne Herald*, 6 October 1988, 2; *New Zealand Railway Observer* 45:3 (no. 195, spring 1988), 124.

136. *Gisborne Herald*, 13 October 1988, 1.

137. Secretary to the Treasury to the Minister of Finance, 16 September 1976, ANZ ABJP 04/833/78 part 1.

138. *New Zealand Railway Observer* 45:3 (no. 195, spring 1988), 123.

139. For more on this merger see Peter Aimer, *Wings of the Nation: A history of the New Zealand National Airways Corporation 1947–78* (Takapuna: The Bush Press,

2000), Chapters 11–12.

140. Quoted in James Watson, *Links: A history of transport and New Zealand society* (Wellington: GP Publications, 1996), 246.

141. DTM Christchurch to W.T. Bradley, 25 February 1972, ANZ-CRO CAHV 25/282/3 part 10.

142. Excerpt from Tony Wheeler, *New Zealand: A travel survival kit* in ANZ AAJM 09/5300/24 part 13. B.G. Franklyn, NZR corporate affairs manager, wrote to publishers Lonely Planet on 22 January 1987 to condemn these remarks as 'unsavoury, boarding [sic] even upon libel'.

143. Shaun Hendy: *#NoFly: Walking the talk on climate change* (Wellington: Bridget Williams Books, 2019), 19.

144. R.J. Middleton, Passenger Business Group manager, to Ferenc Tordai, Ganz-Mávag sales director for railway rollingstock, 20 February 1987, ANZ AAJM 09/5300/24 part 13.

145. *New Zealand Railway Observer* 45:3 (no. 195, 1988), 123.

CHAPTER 8

1990–2020: THE FALSE DAWN

1. Peter Newman, Mark Bachels and Jeffrey Kenworthy, 'How We Compare: Patterns and trends in Australian and New Zealand cities', in Philip Laird, Peter Newman, Mark Bachels and Jeffrey Kenworthy, *Back on Track: Rethinking transport policy in Australia and New*

Zealand (Sydney: UNSW Press, 2001), 62–65.

2. Jago Dodson and Paul Mees, 'Realistic Sustainability? Urban transport planning in Wellington, New Zealand', *New Zealand Geographer* 59:2 (2003), 30–31.

3. Tony Hurst, *Farewell to Steam: Four decades of change on New Zealand railways* (Auckland: HarperCollins, 1995), 97; Rob Merrifield, 'Land Transport Deregulation in New Zealand, 1983–1989', *New Zealand Railway Observer* 47:2–3 (no. 202–03), 1990, 68; Ian Duncan and Alan Bollard, *Corporatization and Privatization: Lessons from New Zealand* (Auckland: Oxford University Press, 1992), 67.

4. New Zealand Railways Corporation Restructuring Act 1990 no. 105.

5. *New Zealand Railway Observer* 48:1 (no. 205), 1991, 34; *New Zealand Railway Observer* 48:3 (no. 207), 1991, 120.

6. Kevin Brady, controller and auditor-general, to Jo Brosnahan, Auckland Regional Council chief executive, 'Auckland region passenger rail service report', 4 November 2003, LG03-0002: https://web.archive.org/web/20200218233542/https://www.oag.govt.nz/2003/akld-rail/docs/passenger-rail-service.pdf

7. *New Zealand Railway Observer* 48:1 (no. 205), 1991, 34 and 50:2 (no. 214) 1993, 77.

8. There was a particularly strong push in 1973–74, initiated

by the Putaruru Chamber of Commerce, which secured support from councils and individuals along the route. See J. Haggerty, secretary of the Putaruru Chamber of Commerce, to T.M. McGuigan, Minister of Railways, 5 August 1973, and other letters in ANZ AAJM 12/640 part 11 (Rotorua Branch: timetable).

9. Intercity Rail memo to all staff (signature cut off), 11 November 1991, ANZ AAJM 12/640 part 11.

10. *New Zealand Herald*, 8 February 1978; Francis Small, group general manager, to Ian Ambler, general manager Railfreight Systems, and Terry Atkinson, general manager Railnet Services, 17 July 1990; both in ANZ AAJM 12/640 part 11; *New Zealand Railway Observer* 46:2 (no. 198, winter 1989), 78.

11. *Rails* 25:4 (1995), 87.

12. Matt Lowrie, 'How rail was saved in Auckland', Transportblog.co.nz (now Greater Auckland), 22 April 2014: www.greaterauckland. org.nz/2014/04/22/how-rail-was-saved-in-auckland/ and reprinted as 'Electric trains to make Auckland's history books', *New Zealand Herald*, 26 April 2014: www.nzherald. co.nz/nz/news/article.cfm?c_id=1&objectid=11244299

13. For a detailed account see Graham Bush, *From Survival to Revival: Auckland's public transport since 1860* (Wellington: Grantham House, 2014), 249–56, 291–94.

14. Philip G. Laird, 'Government Rail Asset Sales, and Return to the Public Sector, in New Zealand and Tasmania', *Research in Transportation Business and Management* 6 (2013), 116–22.

15. Transport Accident Investigation Commission report RO-1993-112.

16. Transport Accident Investigation Commission revised report RO-1994-117R; Katie Kenny, 'A graduation day unlike any other', *Press*, 20 April 2013: www.stuff.co.nz/the-press/news/8574703/A-graduation-day-unlike-any-other; Kim Newth, 'Train-accident survivor Morgan Jones' life of independence', *Stuff*, 27 April 2018: www.stuff.co.nz/life-style/life/103151520/trainaccident-survivor-morgan-jones-life-of-independence

17. Ministerial Inquiry into Tranz Rail Occupational Safety and Health, Report to the Ministers of Labour and Transport (Wellington: Occupational Safety and Health Division, Department of Labour, August 2000).

18. *Southland Times*, 19 July 1997, 10.

19. Brian Gaynor, 'Looking Back: Alex van Heeren, Tranz Rail and legal humiliation', *Business Desk*, 27 June 2021, https://web.archive.org/web/20210629004016/https://businessdesk.co.nz/article/the-life/looking-back-alex-van-heeren-tranz-rail-and-legal-humiliation

20. Paul Little, *Air New Zealand: Celebrating 75 years* (Auckland: Bauer Media Group, 2014), 178–84.

21. Murray Horton, 'Tranz Rail shunted into Hall of Shame', 11 June 2003: http://web.archive.org/web/20190310232520/http://canterbury.cyberplace.co.nz/community/CAFCA/publications/Roger/shunted.html; the 2016 Roger Award was the last and no other company joined Tranz Rail in the Hall of Shame.

22. *Waikato Times*, 6 June 2000, 3.

23. Roeland van den Bergh, 'Tranz Rail may raise rates after losses', *Dominion*, 2 February 2001, 13.

24. James Weir, '3400 jobs affected in rail shakeup', *Dominion*, 11 October 2000, 1–2.

25. Hank Schouten, 'Tenders close for trains', *Evening Post*, 8 March 2001, 15.

26. Andrew Moffat, 'Tranz Rail plans to close, sell services', *Press*, 27 June 2001, 1.

27. Mary Ann Gill and Tania Hall, 'Only a dozen on train service', *Waikato Times*, 27 June 2001, 1.

28. *Timaru Herald*, 27 June 2001, 1.

29. Tina Nash, 'Reynolds rallies for rail', *Manawatu Standard*, 29 June 2001, 1.

30. Bernard Carpinter, 'Planning to keep the Bay Express on track', *Dominion*, 2 July 2001, 7.

31. Murray Bond, letter to the editor, *Dominion*, 13 July 2001, 8; Bernard Carpinter, 'Luxury wine-route plan to save train', *Dominion*, 23 July 2001, 3; *Evening Post*, 24 July 2001, 4.

32. Bernard Carpinter, 'Bay Express survival chances look better', *Dominion*, 10 July 2001, 7.

33. Bernard Carpinter, 'Higher subsidy threatens service', *Dominion*, 4 August 2001, 10.

34. Bernard Carpinter, 'Tranz Rail blamed as hopes fade', *Dominion*, 7 August 2001, 8.

35. Bernard Carpinter, 'Wheels come off train rescue bid', *Dominion*, 18 August 2001, 8; *Evening Post*, 25 August 2001, 4.

36. *Manawatu Standard*, 4 October 2001, 3.

37. *Evening Post*, 30 July 2001, 13.

38. Daniel Adams, 'Waikato train services appear to be doomed', *Waikato Times*, 31 August 2001, 2.

39. *Waikato Times*, 1 September 2001, 3.

40. Bernard Carpinter, 'Last ticket to ride', *Dominion*, 8 October 2001, 1.

41. *Evening Post*, 7 July 2001, 17; Louise van Uden, 'Southerner talks continue', *Timaru Herald*, 1 September 2001, 3.

42. Kirsty Macnicol, 'Govt lifeline for Southerner', *Southland Times*, 21 September 2001, 1.

43. *Dominion*, 17 October 2001, 3; Market Economics Ltd and Gravitas Research and Strategy Ltd, 'Southerner Rail Passenger Service Viability Study' (November 2001): https://web.archive.org/web/20040221133741/http://www.med.govt.nz/irdev/reg_dev/southerner/southerner.pdf

44. Karen Potter, 'End of the line for Southerner', *Southland Times*, 7 December 2001, 3.

45. *Southland Times*, 2 February 2002, 2.

46. 'Greens angered by loss of Southerner rail service', *New Zealand Herald*, 10 February 2002: www.nzherald.co.nz/nz/news/article.cfm?c_id=1&objectid=889464; 'Southerner farewelled', *Southland Times*, 10 February 2002: www.stuff.co.nz/southland-times/news/150-stories-in-150-days/8191124/Southerner-farewelled

47. General information in this section sourced from Tony Hurst, *The Otago Central Railway: A tribute*, 5th edn (Wellington: Transpress, 1990 [2008]) and communication from Grant Craig, James Eunson and Toby Mann, with thanks also to Katjo Buissink and Aaron Hawkins for their assistance. The Wayback Machine can be used to browse historical websites with route information and timetables, e.g. The Seasider, 'About', 23 May 2010: https://web.archive.org/web/20100523120038/http://seasider.co.nz/about.php

48. John Lewis, 'New look for railway operation', *Otago Daily Times*, 23 October 2014: https://web.archive.org/web/20200218115454/https://www.odt.co.nz/news/dunedin/new-look-railway-operation

49. Rebecca Ryan, 'Silver Fern to run regular services', *Otago Daily Times*, 7 May 2015: https://web.archive.org/web/20190309125952/https://www.odt.co.nz/news/dunedin/silver-fern-run-regular-services; Tim Brown, 'Middlemarch to fight tourist train route closure', RNZ News, 5 December 2019: https://web.archive.org/web/20191205112914/https://www.rnz.co.nz/news/national/404939/middlemarch-to-fight-tourist-train-route-closure

50. Hamish McNeilly, 'Dunedin council's support for tourist train back on track as sell-off plan derailed', *Stuff*, 13 April 2021: https://web.archive.org/web/20210413024050/https://www.stuff.co.nz/travel/experiences/train-journeys/300275584/dunedin-councils-support-for-tourist-train-back-on-track-as-selloff-plan-derailed

51. *Evening Post*, 2 July 2002, 4.

52. *Evening Post*, 1 December 2001, 17.

53. 'Tranz Scenic moots passenger service for Rotorua', *New Zealand Herald*, 11 June 2003: https://web.archive.org/web/20210121042406/https://www.nzherald.co.nz/nz/tranz-scenic-moots-passenger-service-for-rotorua/7WLB63GLB7HLQR7PGWFJXYC5FI/

54. Neill Atkinson, *Trainland: How railways made New Zealand* (Auckland: Random House, 2007), 180–83.

55. The survivors from the second carriage at Tangiwai were Ted Brett (the author's grandfather) and Anne Lennox. Ted travelled with Douglas and John Cockburn and Anne with Thomas Moir,

all of whom were killed. Ted later married Patricia Cockburn, sister of Douglas and John. For more, see André Brett, 'Tangiwai survivor's story shared after death', *Dominion Post*, 24 December 2013, A2 (also online: www.stuff.co.nz/southland-times/news/9551530/Tangiwai-survivors-story-shared-after-death), and André Brett, 'Lahar meets locomotive: New Zealand's Tangiwai railway disaster of Christmas Eve 1953', *Arcadia: Explorations in environmental history* (Autumn, 2018), 31: www.environmentandsociety.org/node/8476

56. Shayne Carter, *Dead People I Have Known* (Wellington: Victoria University Press, 2019), 178–79.

57. Hank Schouten, 'End of the line for Northerner', *Dominion Post*, 30 October 2004, A1.

58. *Dominion Post*, 15 November 2004, A5.

59. Adam Ray, 'Cullen turned down plea for Overlander', *Dominion Post*, 27 July 2006, A3.

60. Esther Harward, 'Overlander campaigning gathering steam', *Waikato Times*, 22 August 2006, 3.

61. Colin Espiner, 'Door not closed to train-service rescue', *Press*, 23 August 2006, A5.

62. *Dominion Post*, 15 September 2006, A2; Esther Harward, 'Rail petition signatures ruled invalid', *Waikato Times*, 15 September 2006, 3; *Waikato Times*, 23 September 2006, A8.

63. Ruth Laugesen, 'Overlander hopes high for train service stay of execution', *Sunday Star-Times*, 24 September 2006, A3; Adam Ray, 'Government rejects Overlander rescue bid', *Dominion Post*, 26 September 2006, A1.

64. Adam Ray, 'Train gets last-minute reprieve', *Dominion Post*, 29 September 2006, A3.

65. *Daily Telegraph* (Sydney), 29 September 2006, 34.

66. Matthew Dearnaley, 'Once-endangered Overlander thrives', *New Zealand Herald*, 12 June 2009: https://web.archive.org/web/20190304015603/https://www.nzherald.co.nz/auckland-region/news/article.cfm?l_id=117&objectid=10578154; Katie Chapman, 'Rail on a roll with the Overlander picking up steam', *Dominion Post*, 1 September 2010, A3.

67. Quoted in Katie Chapman, 'Rail on a roll with the Overlander picking up steam', *Dominion Post*, 1 September 2010, A3.

68. Emma Horsley, 'Explorer arrives late for first day on job', *Manawatu Standard*, 26 June 2012, 3; Jimmy Ellingham, 'Numbers down on rail service', *Manawatu Standard*, 6 September 2012, 3.

69. KiwiRail, *Annual Integrated Report* 2018.

70. Rob Merrifield, *The Kaikoura Job: Rebuilding KiwiRail's Main North Line* (Wellington: New Zealand Railway and Locomotive Society, 2018), 5 and 16.

71. Bush, *Survival to Revival*, Chapters 10–11.

72. Auckland Regional Transport Authority, Half-year Report July–December 2009, 6.

73. Lowrie, 'How rail was saved in Auckland'; Bush, *Survival to Revival*, 297–300.

74. *Sunday Star-Times*, 1 November 1998, C8.

75. Matthew Dearnaley, 'Electioneering claims fly over rail passenger service', *New Zealand Herald*, 28 June 2007, A5; Matthew Dearnaley, 'West's rail campaign building up steam', *New Zealand Herald*, 15 August 2007, A8.

76. Matthew Dearnaley, 'Costs balloon for western railway trial', *New Zealand Herald*, 24 June 2008, A7.

77. Matthew Dearnaley, 'Passenger boom sparks rise in rail services', *New Zealand Herald*, 18 June 2009, A7.

78. Auckland Regional Transport Authority, 'Helensville rail trial service ends', press release, 10 November 2009: https://web.archive.org/web/20190304015516/http://www.scoop.co.nz/stories/AK0911/S00191.htm

79. Matthew Dearnaley, 'Extra night trains for Christmas shoppers', *New Zealand Herald*, 21 December 2009, A7.

80. Kim Ace, 'Calls for rail to ease congestion in Auckland's north-west', *Nor-West News*, 27 September 2016: https://web.archive.org/web/20190304015434/https://www.stuff.co.nz/auckland/local-news/

nor-west-news/84700776/calls-for-rail-to-ease-congestion-in-aucklands-northwest

81. Danielle Clent, 'Campaign launched to increase pressure for trains to Huapai', *Nor-West News*, 12 July 2017: https://web.archive.org/web/20190304015216/https://www.stuff.co.nz/auckland/local-news/nor-west-news/94567264/campaign-launched-to-increase-pressure-for-trains-to-huapai; campaign website is http://www.trainstohuapai.org/ (archived version: https://web.archive.org/web/20190304015310/http://www.trainstohuapai.org/)

82. Mike Lee to Cameron Pitches, 7 June 2002, reproduced in Mike Lee, 'After 8-year battle – Onehunga line and station opens in grand style' (speech at Onehunga reopening), 18 September 2010: https://web.archive.org/web/20190115125253/http://www.mikelee.co.nz/2010/09/after-8-year-battle-onehunga-line-and-station-opens-in-grand-style/

83. Matthew Dearnaley, 'Hundreds pack on phantom train from West Auckland', *New Zealand Herald*, 12 April 2004.

84. Paul Mees and Jago Dodson, 'Backtracking Auckland: Bureaucratic rationality and public preferences in transport planning', *Urban Research Program Issues Paper 5* (2006), 8–9.

85. Matthew Dearnaley, 'Delight at govt's decision to reopen Onehunga line', *New Zealand Herald*, 14 March 2007, A7; Lee, 'After 8-year battle'; Campaign for Better Transport, 'Reopen Onehunga rail', 22 November 2006: https://web.archive.org/web/20190115125421/http://www.bettertransport.org.nz/2006/11/reopen-onehunga-rail/

86. Matthew Dearnaley, 'Train plans on track, Onehunga told', *New Zealand Herald*, 5 May 2009, A7.

87. Matthew Dearnaley, 'ARC chief unhappy at delay to new service', *New Zealand Herald*, 12 May 2010, A7.

88. *Dominion Post*, 12 July 2010, B4; Matthew Dearnaley, 'ARC boss furious new rail platform too short for trains', *New Zealand Herald*, 8 July 2010, A1.

89. *New Zealand Herald*, 27 August 2010, A5.

90. Matthew Dearnaley, 'Stuck in traffic', *New Zealand Herald*, 4 June 2011, A9.

91. Romy Udanga, 'New $50m rail route gets under way', *Manukau Courier*, 10 July 2009: https://web.archive.org/web/20190304015126/http://www.stuff.co.nz/auckland/2549415/New-50m-rail-route-gets-under-way; Matthew Dearnaley, 'Work starts on $90m rail link', *New Zealand Herald*, 18 September 2009, A8.

92. Matthew Dearnaley, 'Excavations done for $98m Manukau rail link', *New Zealand Herald*, 12 July 2010, A7.

93. Matthew Dearnaley, 'Agencies "too busy" to open rail link on time', *New Zealand Herald*, 10 May 2011, A8 (at this stage, the opening was pushed back only to February 2012, later blowing out further to April); Matthew Dearnaley, 'First rail line in 82 years declared open', *New Zealand Herald*, 5 April 2012, A6.

94. Matthew Dearnaley, '$81m rail line yet to catch on with commuters', *New Zealand Herald*, 29 May 2012, A7.

95. Ibid.; Auckland Transport, *Statistics Report June 2012*: https://web.archive.org/web/20190304014720/https://at.govt.nz/media/imported/3790/AT-PT-statistics-report-June2012.pdf

96. Auckland Transport, 'Buses to replace future Waitakere to Swanson rail services', press release, 30 May 2013: https://web.archive.org/web/20190304014525/https://at.govt.nz/about-us/news-events/buses-to-replace-future-waitakere-to-swanson-rail-services

97. Matthew Dearnaley, 'Big day as rail goes electric', *New Zealand Herald*, 20 July 2015, A8.

98. Matthew Dearnaley, 'Swanson to lose passenger trains', *New Zealand Herald*, 4 June 2013, A9 (the headline's incorrect reference to Swanson is not replicated in the body of the article).

99. Rose Rees-Owen, 'Waitakere trains' passing marked with mock funeral', *Western Leader*, 8 June 2015:

https://web.archive.org/
web/20190304035707/
https://www.stuff.co.nz/
auckland/local-news/
western-leader/69180564/null;
Matthew Dearnaley, '"Funeral"
train trip to protest at railway
cut', *New Zealand Herald*, 2
June 2015, A9.

100. Matt Lowrie, 'End of
the line for Waitakere',
Transportblog.co.nz (now
Greater Auckland), 30 May
2013: https://web.archive.
org/web/20190304031129/
https://www.greaterauckland.
org.nz/2013/05/30/
end-of-the-line-for-waitakere/

101. Clent, 'Campaign launched';
Trains to Huapai, 'Myth
busters': https://web.archive.
org/web/20181020215644/
http://www.trainstohuapai.org/
myth-busters

102. Bernard Orsman, 'Goff happy
as $3b works approved', *New
Zealand Herald*, 31 January
2020, A17; New Zealand
Transport Agency, 'Auckland
Light Rail': https://web.archive.
org/web/20200221072030/
https://www.nzta.govt.
nz/roads-and-rail/rapid-
transit/auckland-light-
rail/; Greater Auckland,
'Congestion free network
2': https://web.archive.org/
web/20200221072351/https://
www.greaterauckland.org.nz/
congestion-free-network-2/

103. Swanson–Waitākere passenger
trains are not mentioned
in any Auckland Transport
annual reports between
that for the year ended 30
June 2013, during which the

decision was taken to cease
operations beyond Swanson,
and the year ended 30 June
2016, during which the service
ceased.

CHAPTER 9
WHITHER PASSENGER RAIL IN NEW ZEALAND?

1. Ross Garnaut, 'Projecting
Australian climate change',
The Garnaut Climate
Change Review (Canberra:
Commonwealth of Australia,
2008): https://webarchive.nla.
gov.au/awa/20190509072839/
http://www.garnautreview.org.
au/chp5.htm

2. Lily D'Ambrosio, 'Victoria's
largest solar farm up
and running', Victorian
government press release, 19
July 2019: https://web.archive.
org/web/20191012094248/
https://www.premier.vic.gov.
au/victorias-largest-solar-
farm-up-and-running/

3. Simon Calder, 'Virgin Trains
triples Anglo-Scottish
passengers in a decade',
Independent, 11 November
2019: https://web.archive.
org/web/20191111123434/
https://www.independent.
co.uk/travel/news-and-advice/
virgin-trains-london-glasgow-
anglo-scottish-passengers-air-
rail-record-a9197041.html

4. G.T. Bloomfield, *New Zealand:
A handbook of historical
statistics* (Boston: G.K. Hall,
1984), 240.

5. Andre Chumko, 'Coronavirus:
KiwiRail cuts rail routes

and Interislander services,
DOC cancels hut bookings',
Stuff, 22 March 2020:
https://web.archive.org/
web/20200322102755/
https://www.stuff.
co.nz/national/health/
coronavirus/120483079/
coronavirus-kiwirail-
suspends-tourist-rail-routes-
cuts-interislander-services

6. 'Taieri Gorge track
mothballed, 51 jobs likely to
go', *Otago Daily Times*, 20 April
2020: https://web.archive.
org/web/20200420110455/
https://www.odt.co.nz/news/
dunedin/taieri-gorge-track-be-
mothballed-51-jobs-likely-go

7. David Loughrey, 'Luxury
carriages take shape at
Hillside Workshops', *Otago
Daily Times*, 8 August 2018:
https://web.archive.org/
web/20200410060432/https://
www.odt.co.nz/news/dunedin/
luxury-carriages-take-shape-
hillside-workshops; Daisy
Hudson, 'Budget 2021:
Millions for Hillside to build
wagons', *Otago Daily Times*, 20
May 2021: https://web.archive.
org/web/20210520225635/
https://www.odt.co.nz/
business/budget-2021-
millions-hillside-build-wagons

8. 'Hamilton–Auckland
commuter train tipped to start
in November', *Stuff*, 19 May
2020: https://web.archive.
org/web/20200816020445/
https://www.stuff.co.nz/
national/121558113/
hamiltonauckland-commuter-
train-tipped-to-start-in-
november

9. New Zealand Government, 'The New Zealand Rail Plan' (Wellington: Ministry of Transport Te Manatū Waka, April 2021).

10. Shamubeel Eaqub, *Growing Apart: Regional prosperity in New Zealand* (Wellington: Bridget Williams Books, 2014).

11. Margaret Brown, Bill Kaye-Blake and Penny Payne (eds), *Heartland Strong: How rural New Zealand can change and thrive* (Auckland: Massey University Press, 2019). This paragraph cites Brown, Kaye-Blake and Payne, 'Introduction', 10–14; Payne, 'Talking to communities: How other small towns view their resilience', 50; and Bruce Small, 'How will technology affect the fabric of rural communities?', 148–63.

12. Philip Laird, 'New Zealand transport – the years to come', *Logistics and Transport NZ* 9:1 (2010), 16.

13. Janeane Joyce, 'Bay of Plenty Region Passenger and Freight Rail: Phase 1 Investigation' (Bay of Plenty Regional Council, 30 May 2019), 8.

14. Vincent Verbavatz and Marc Barthelemy, 'Critical factors for mitigating car traffic in cities', *PLOS One* 14:7 (2019): https://doi.org/10.1371/journal.pone.0219559

15. Roar Stenersen, 'Development of Norwegian railways, 1854–2002', *Japan Railway and Transport Review* 31 (2002), 39–41.

16. David Briginshaw, 'Norway to replace diesel traction with battery trains', *International Railway Journal*, 3 January 2020: https://web.archive.org/web/20200416051831/http://web.archive.org/screenshot/https://www.railjournal.com/technology/norway-to-replace-diesel-traction-with-battery-trains/

17. Paul Mees and Jago Dodson, 'Backtracking Auckland: Bureaucratic rationality and public preferences in transport planning', *Urban Research Program Issues Paper 5* (2006), 12.

18. Nick Lovett, 'Transport funding – taxes, fees and fairness', 15 June 2020: https://medium.com/@NickLovettNZ/transport-funding-taxes-fees-and-fairness-18543d73324f

19. Roger Boulter and Don Wignall, 'Identifying the value of long-distance rail services: Current issues in transport assessment and evaluation' (Victoria Transport Policy Institute, 2008): https://web.archive.org/web/20180413000513/https://www.vtpi.org/rail_evaluation.pdf

20. Peter Newman, Mark Bachels and Jeffrey Kenworthy, 'How we compare: Patterns and trends in Australian and New Zealand cities', in Philip Laird, Peter Newman, Mark Bachels and Jeffrey Kenworthy, *Back on Track: Rethinking transport policy in Australia and New Zealand* (Sydney: UNSW Press, 2001), 66.

21. Dileepa Fonseka, 'Fixing broken infrastructure promises', *Newsroom*, 21 September 2020: https://web.archive.org/web/20201001010446/https://www.newsroom.co.nz/fixing-broken-infrastructure-promises

22. Philip Laird and Peter Newman, 'How we got here: The role of transport in the development of Australia and New Zealand', in Laird et al., *Back on Track*, 21

23. Harriet Gale, 'Northland rail', *Greater Auckland*, 29 November 2017: https://web.archive.org/web/20200228054746/https://www.greaterauckland.org.nz/2017/11/29/northland-rail-2/; Mike Dinsdale, '$109 million for Northland rail network in latest govt announcement', *Northern Advocate*, 30 January 2020: https://web.archive.org/web/20200228055701/https://www.nzherald.co.nz/nz/news/article.cfm?c_id=1&objectid=12304468&fbclid=IwAR3_UO95bC7_G6qNp3-8n3LBx0seO5TDIw4UysLtyIvSm8atpsTEHMX9E0s; Susan Botting, 'Northland mayors band together to call for more infrastructure spending', RNZ *News*, 2 February 2020: https://web.archive.org/web/20200228054838/https://www.rnz.co.nz/news/national/408671/northland-mayors-band-together-to-call-for-more-infrastructure-spending

24. Gwynn Compton, 'Kāpiti–Horowhenua commuter rail campaign': https://web.archive.org/web/20200302113517/https://www.gwynncompton.co.nz/kapitihorowhenuarail

25. BERL, 'Tūranga ki Wairoa Rail: Feasibility study into reinstatement of rail line' (BERL ref no. 5993, November 2019): https://web.archive.org/web/20200817065333/https://berl.co.nz/sites/default/files/2019-12/T%C5%ABranga%20ki%20Wairoa%20Rail%20-%20Feasibility%20Study%20Into%20Reinstatement%20of%20Rail%20Line.pdf; see also appendix 14.8 by TRC Tourism, 'Tourism opportunities: Using the Gisborne to Wairoa rail line/corridor' (August 2019): https://web.archive.org/web/20200817065502/https://berl.co.nz/sites/default/files/2019-12/14.8%20Tourism%20opportunities.pdf

26. NZR Staff Bulletin 9:2 (1960), 29.

27. Joel MacManus, 'Auckland-to-Wellington sleeper train could happen without KiwiRail', Stuff, 30 July 2020: https://web.archive.org/web/20200817073851/https://www.stuff.co.nz/travel/back-your-backyard/122296375/aucklandtowellington-sleeper-train-could-happen-without-kiwirail

28. KiwiRail, 'Coastal Pacific to start premium service', media release, 23 November 2018: https://web.archive.

org/web/20200229025817/https://www.kiwirail.co.nz/media/coastal-pacific-to-start-premium-service/

29. Janna Sherman, 'Bid to bring train south to Hokitika', Hokitika Guardian, 31 October 2017: https://web.archive.org/web/20200229054921/https://www.odt.co.nz/regions/west-coast/bid-bring-train-south-hokitika

30. Tracy Neal, 'New scenic rail service part of West Coast revitalisation plan', RNZ News, 20 July 2018: https://web.archive.org/web/20200229055946/https://www.rnz.co.nz/news/national/362268/new-scenic-rail-service-part-of-west-coast-revitalisation-plan; Stafford Strategy, 'Hokitika to Westport tourist rail feasibility study stop/go report' (July 2019): https://web.archive.org/web/20200411004352/https://fyi.org.nz/request/12020/response/46800/attach/4/KiwiRail%20Hokitika%20to%20Westport%20Tourist%20Rail%20Feasibility%20Study%20Stop%20Go%20Report%20Final.pdf

31. Len Richardson, People and Place: The West Coast of New Zealand's South Island in history and literature (Canberra: ANU Press, 2020), 11–12.

32. Railway historian David Leitch rode J^A locomotives at 122km/h in the 1960s and considered driver accounts of exceeding 137km/h to be reliable: Railways of New

Zealand (Auckland: Leonard Fullerton, 1972), 179.

33. New Zealand Rail Timetables and Fares, effective 4 July 1993, Hocken Collections Uare Taoka o Hākena E210 Box 1012A (Ephemera – New Zealand Railways – Timetables and Menus).

34. Press, 24 September 1888, 6; Otago Daily Times, 18 August 1938, 6.

35. Waikato Regional Council, 'Waikato Regional Public Transport Plan 2018–2028', 25: https://web.archive.org/web/20200229112347/https://www.waikatoregion.govt.nz/assets/WRC/Council/Policy-and-Plans/Transport/RPTP/RPTP-2018-2028.pdf

36. Future Proof, 'Hei Awarua ki te Oranga: Corridor for Wellbeing' (12 February 2019, AMI18/19010053), 33: https://web.archive.org/web/20200229112200/https://futureproof.org.nz/assets/FutureProof/Corridor-Plan/Hei-Awarua-ki-te-Oranga-H2A-Shared-statement-of-spatial-intent-FINAL.pdf

37. Tom Rowland, 'Commuter train launch delayed but Waikato Metro Rail plans likely to be boosted', New Zealand Herald, 31 March 2020: https://web.archive.org/web/20200401105450/https://www.nzherald.co.nz/north-island/news/article.cfm?c_id=1503932&objectid=12321248; Lawrence Gullery, 'Waipā explores public transport options to keep pace with expanding

population', *Stuff*, 22 July 2020: https://web.archive.org/web/20200817095721/https://www.stuff.co.nz/waikato-times/news/122199210/waip-explores-public-transport-options-to-keep-pace-with-expanding-population; Chloe Blommerde, 'Hamilton–Auckland commuter train on track for trials as committee looks into new train projects', *Stuff*, 30 July 2020: https://web.archive.org/web/20200817091254/https://www.stuff.co.nz/national/122266482/hamiltonauckland-commuter-train-on-track-for-trials-as-committee-looks-into-new-train-projects;

38. 'Bay of Plenty Rail Strategy', Environment Bay of Plenty Transportation Publication 2007/03 (August 2007), 18; Joyce, 'Bay of Plenty Region passenger and freight rail', 6–10.

39. *NZPD* 1972 vol. 380 (31 August 1972), 2323–26; 'Bay of Plenty Rail Strategy', 17; URS New Zealand, 'Review of reports on railway crossings of Tauranga Harbour', prepared for Environment Bay of Plenty, 25 September 2008; Geoffrey B. Churchman and Tony Hurst, *The Railways of New Zealand: A journey through history* (Auckland: HarperCollins, 1991), 113.

40. Georgia May, 'Could a commuter train service to Central Hawke's Bay be on the cards?', *Hawke's Bay Today*, 20 March 2019: https://web.archive.org/web/20200225084001/https://www.nzherald.co.nz/business/news/article.cfm?c_id=3&objectid=12214114

41. Brendon Harre, 'Christchurch's future is a fat banana', 17 November 2018: https://web.archive.org/web/20200301102606/https://medium.com/land-buildings-identity-and-values/greater-christchurchs-future-the-fat-banana-aba0402f16a4

42. James Dann, 'A new plan for Christchurch rail', *Spinoff*, 24 November 2018: https://web.archive.org/web/20190528230315/https://thespinoff.co.nz/society/24-11-2018/a-new-plan-for-christchurch-rail/

43. Aurecon New Zealand, 'Greater Christchurch northern rail – rapid assessment' (17 July 2014), Environment Canterbury report C16C/114767, and MWH, 'North and southwest public transport corridors study: Stage two non technical summary', April 2010, Environment Canterbury report C16C/114760; Environment Canterbury, 'Canterbury regional public transport plan 2018–2028', 25: https://web.archive.org/web/20200229132909/https://www.ecan.govt.nz/your-region/plans-strategies-and-bylaws/canterbury-transport-plans/

44. Chris Morris, 'Commuter train trial mooted', *Otago Daily Times*, 12 December 2018: https://web.archive.org/web/20200225113238/https://www.odt.co.nz/news/dunedin/commuter-train-trial-mooted; Emma Perry, 'DCC votes to reduce bus fares', *Otago Daily Times*, 30 January 2020: https://web.archive.org/web/20200225113635/https://www.odt.co.nz/news/dunedin/dcc/dcc-votes-reduce-bus-fares

45. *Evening Post*, 10 June 1938, 10.

46. H.M. Boot, 'Government and the colonial economies: A reply to Frost', *Australian Economic History Review* 40:1 (2000), 89.

Appendix 1

ROUTES OPEN TO PASSENGERS ON 1 JANUARY 1920

First-named place is always a junction or existing terminus; second-named place is either a new terminus or, in the case of lines that connect with another route, a second junction.

- Kaihu Valley Railway (Dargaville–Whatoro)
- North Auckland Line, northern section (Whangārei–Ōpua) and branches:
    » Ōtiria-Kaikohe
    » Whangārei–Ōnerahi
- North Auckland Line, southern section (Newmarket–Ranganui)
- North Island Main Trunk (Auckland–Wellington) and branches:
    » Penrose–Onehunga
    » Huntly–Pukemiro
    » Ngāruawāhia–Glen Massey (private, Waipā Collieries)
    » Ohakune–Raetihi
    » Longburn–Foxton
- East Coast Main Trunk (Frankton–Waihī) and branches:
    » Ruakura–Cambridge
    » Morrinsville–Rotorua
    » Paeroa–Thames
- Mount Maunganui–Matatā (PWD)
- Stratford–Ōkahukura Line, western end (Stratford–Kōhuratahi by NZR, Kōhuratahi–Tahora by PWD)
- Marton–New Plymouth Line and branches:
    » Lepperton–Waitara
    » Aramoho–Whanganui
    » Whanganui–Castlecliff (private, Castlecliff Railway Co.)
- Palmerston North–Napier Line
- Gisborne–Moutohorā and branch:
    » Makaraka–Ngātapa (PWD)
- Wairarapa Line (Wellington–Woodville) and branch:
    » Woodside–Greytown
- Nelson Section (Nelson–Glenhope)
- Westport Section (Westport–Mōkihinui Mine) and branch:
    » Westport–Tauranga Bay (Cape Foulwind Branch, by the Westport Harbour Board)
- Stillwater–Westport Line, southern section (Stillwater–Īnangahua) and branch:
    » Ngāhere–Blackball
- Midland Line, western section (Greymouth–Ōtira) and branches:
    » Greymouth–Rewanui
    » Greymouth–Ross
- Midland Line, eastern section (Rolleston–Arthur's Pass):
    » Darfield–Whitecliffs
    » Sheffield–Oxford West (where it met branch from Rangiora)

- Main North Line, northern section (Picton–Wharanui)
- Main North Line, southern section (Christchurch–Parnassus) and branches:
    » Waipara-Waiau
    » Rangiora–Oxford West (where it met branch from Sheffield)
    » Kaiapoi–Bennetts (known as Eyreton Branch, met Oxford Branch)
- Main South Line (Lyttelton–Invercargill) and branches:
    » Hornby–Southbridge, and branch:
        • Lincoln–Little River
    » Rakaia–Methven
    » Tinwald–Springburn
    » Washdyke–Fairlie
    » Studholme–Waimate and branch:
        • Waimate–Waihao Downs (this appears as a direct line on the maps but they were operated as separate branches and a locomotive running Studholme–Waihao Downs had to change ends of the train in Waimate)
    » Pukeuri–Hakataramea (known as Kurow Branch)
    » Waiareka Junction–Ngātapa and branch:
        • Windsor Junction–Tokarahi
    » Palmerston–Dunback
    » Sawyers Bay–Port Chalmers
    » Mosgiel–Outram
    » Milton–Beaumont
    » Stirling–Kaitangata (private, Kaitangata Coal Co.)
    » Balclutha–Tahakopa (known as Catlins River Branch)
    » Waipahi–Edievale (known as Tapanui Branch)
    » McNab–Waikākā
    » Edendale–Glenham
    » Invercargill–Bluff
    » Invercargill–Tokanui (known as Seaward Bush Branch)
- Otago Central Railway (Wingatui–Clyde by NZR, Clyde–Cromwell by PWD)
- Waimea Plains Railway (Gore–Lumsden) and branch:
    » Riversdale–Waikaia
- Kingston Branch (Invercargill–Kingston) and branches:
    » Lumsden–Mossburn
    » Winton–Hedgehope
    » Makarewa–Tūātapere and branch:
        • Thornbury–Wairio

Appendix 2

TIMELINE 1920–2020

The colour-coding pertains only to the operator; in some instances, the physical infrastructure had a different owner.
Green: service commenced by NZR and its successors
Green in italics: service commenced by PWD
Orange: service commenced by Dunedin Railways
Blue: service commenced by another operator
Purple: change of passenger train operator
Red: service cancelled by NZR/successors
Red in italics: service cancelled by PWD

Orange in italics: service cancelled by Dunedin Railways
Blue in italics: service cancelled by another operator
(Black, in brackets): The overall line to which the segment belonged
  Routes are ordered by calendar year, then alphabetically (not chronologically) within the year.
  In all instances this refers to the very first or last regular passenger service. It does not include, for example, the extension of electrified commuter trains further up the North Island Main Trunk where long-distance trains were already operating.

YEAR	COMMENCED	CANCELLED
1920	Kioreroa Junction–Portland (North Auckland Line) Ranganui–Huarau (North Auckland Line)	
1921	Clyde–Cromwell, PWD to NZR (Otago Central Railway) *Portland–Waikiekie* (North Auckland Line) Westport–Omau, Westport Harbour Board to NZR (Cape Foulwind Railway)	Oxford West–Sheffield (Oxford Branch) Kurow–Hakataramea (Kurow Branch; first cessation) *Omau–Tauranga Bay* (Cape Foulwind Branch)
1922	*Huarau–Waikiekie* (North Auckland Line) *Ōkahukura–Mātīere* (Stratford–Ōkahukura Line) Paerātā–Waiuku (Waiuku Branch)	

1923	Arthur's Pass–Ōtira (Midland Line)
	Kaikohe–Ōkaihau (North Auckland Line, later
	  re-designated Ōkaihau Branch)
	Matatā–Awakeri (East Coast Main Trunk)
	Napier–Eskdale (Palmerston North–Gisborne Line)
	Whatoro–Donnellys Crossing (Kaihu Valley Railway, later
	  re-designated Donnellys Crossing Branch)	

1924	Kōhuratahi–Tahora, PWD to NZR (Stratford–Ōkahukura Line) Kurow–Hakataramea (Kurow Branch; trial resumption) Makaraka–Ngātapa, PWD to NZR (Palmerston North– Gisborne Line, later re-designated Ngātapa Branch) *Mātīere–Toi Toi* (Stratford–Ōkahukura Line) Pukemiro–Glen Afton (Glen Afton Branch) *Tauranga–Te Maunga* (East Coast Main Trunk) Wairio–Ōhai (Ōhai Railway Board line)	Kurow–Hakataramea (Kurow Branch; second cessation)
1925	*Awakeri–Tāneatua* (East Coast Main Trunk) Beaumont–Millers Flat (Roxburgh Branch) Huarau–Portland, PWD to NZR (North Auckland Line) Tūātapere–Ōrawia (Ōrawia Branch)	
1926	Glenhope–Kawatiri (Nelson Section) *Tahora–Tāngarākau* (Stratford–Ōkahukura Line) Te Roti–Ōpunake (Ōpunake Branch) *Toi Toi–Ōhura* (Stratford–Ōkahukura Line)	Waiareka Junction–Ngāpara (Ngāpara Branch) Windsor Junction–Tokarahi (Tokarahi Branch)
1927	Petone–Waterloo (Waterloo Branch, later part of Hutt Valley Line) Waihī–Tahawai (East Coast Main Trunk)	Kioreroa Junction–Ōnerahi (Ōnerahi Branch)

YEAR	COMMENCED	CANCELLED
1928	Millers Flat–Roxburgh (Roxburgh Branch) Tahawai–Tauranga (East Coast Main Trunk) Tauranga–Tāneatua, PWD to NZR (East Coast Main Trunk) Waiōtira–Kirikōpuni (Dargaville Branch)	Darfield–Whitecliffs (Whitecliffs Branch) *Te Maunga–Mount Maunganui* (Mount Maunganui Branch) Wyndham–Glenham (Glenham Branch)
1929	*Kurow–Waitaki Dam* (Waitaki Dam construction line) Woburn–Hutt Workshops (Gracefield Branch)	
1930	Auckland–Westfield (Westfield Deviation, North Island Main Trunk) Eskdale–Pūtōrino (Palmerston North–Gisborne Line) *Kirikōpuni–Tangowahine* (Dargaville Branch) Ngāruawāhia–Glen Massey, Waipā Collieries to Wilton Collieries (Glen Massey Line)	Makaraka–Ngātapa (Ngātapa Branch) Palmerston–Dunback (Dunback Branch) Tūātapere–Ōrawia (Ōrawia Branch) Westport–Omau (Cape Foulwind Branch)
1931		Edendale–Wyndham (Wyndham, formerly Glenham, Branch) Glenhope–Kawatiri (Nelson Section) Kaiapoi–Bennetts (Eyreton Branch) McNab–Waikākā (Waikākā Branch) Napier–Pūtōrino (Palmerston North–Gisborne Line) Rangiora–Oxford (Oxford Branch) Riversdale–Waikaia (Waikaia Branch) Studholme–Waimate (Waimate Branch) Waimate–Waihao Downs (Waihao Downs Branch) Winton–Hedgehope (Hedgehope Branch)
1932	*Ōhura–Heao* (Stratford–Ōkahukura Line)	Longburn–Foxton (Foxton Branch) Seddonville–Mōkihinui Mine (Westport Section; later re-designated Seddonville Branch) *Whanganui–Castlecliff* (Castlecliff Railway)
1933	*Tāngarākau–Heao* (Stratford–Ōkahukura Line) Tahora–Ōkahukura, PWD to NZR (Stratford– Ōkahukura Line)	Tinwald–Springburn (Springburn Branch) Waipahi–Edievale (Tapanui Branch)
1935	Ngāruawāhia–Glen Massey, Wilton Collieries to NZR (Glen Massey Line)	
1936		*Kurow–Waitaki Dam* (Waitaki Dam construction line) Milton–Roxburgh (Roxburgh Branch)
1937	Wellington–Tawa Flat (Tawa Flat Deviation, North Island Main Trunk)	Johnsonville–Tawa Flat (North Island Main Trunk) Lumsden–Kingston (exc. holiday seasons) (Kingston Branch) Lumsden–Mossburn (Mossburn Branch) *Stirling–Kaitangata* (Kaitangata Line)
1939	Napier–Wairoa (Palmerston North–Gisborne Line) Parnassus–Hundalee (Main North Line)	Waikari–Waiau (Waiau Branch)
1940		Ngāhere–Blackball (Blackball Branch) Waipara–Waikari (Waiau Branch)
1941	Tangowahine–Dargaville (Dargaville Branch) Kirikōpuni–Tangowahine, PWD to NZR (Dargaville Branch)	
1942	Īnangahua–Westport (Stillwater–Westport Line) Wairoa–Gisborne (Palmerston North–Gisborne Line) Wharanui–Clarence (Main North Line)	
1943	Hundalee–Ōaro (Main North Line)	
1944	Clarence–Kaikōura (Main North Line)	

CAN'T GET THERE FROM HERE

YEAR	COMMENCED	CANCELLED
1945	Ōaro–Kaikōura (Main North Line)	Gisborne–Moutohorā (Moutohorā Branch) Gore–Lumsden (exc. holiday seasons) (Waimea Plains Railway) Rakaia–Methven (Methven Branch; first cessation)
1946	Waterloo–Naenae (Hutt Valley Railway)	Lepperton–Waitara (Waitara Branch) Ruakura–Cambridge (Cambridge Branch) Westport–Seddonville (Seddonville Branch)
1947	Naenae–Taitā (Hutt Valley Railway)	Pukeuri–Kurow (Kurow Branch)
1948	Rakaia–Methven (Methven Branch; resumption)	Paerātā–Waiuku (Waiuku Branch)
1950		Mosgiel–Outram (Outram Branch)
1951		Hornby–Southbridge (Southbridge Branch) Lincoln–Little River (Little River Branch) Ohakune–Raetihi (Raetihi Branch) Paeroa–Thames (Thames Branch) Thornbury–Wairio (Wairio Branch; first cessation)
1952	Thornbury–Wairio (Wairio Branch; resumption)	
1953		Washdyke–Fairlie (Fairlie Branch) Woodside–Greytown (Greytown Branch)
1954	Taitā–Manor Park (Hutt Valley Railway)	Makarewa–Tūātapere (Tūātapere Branch) Melling–Manor Park (Western Hutt Line) Nelson–Glenhope (Nelson Section) Thornbury–Wairio (Wairio Branch; second cessation)
1955	Upper Hutt–Featherston via Remutaka Tunnel (Wairarapa Line)	Eltham–Ōpunake (Ōpunake Branch) Upper Hutt–Featherston via Remutaka Incline (Wairarapa Line)
1956		Invercargill–Lumsden (Kingston Branch)
1957		Gore–Lumsden–Kingston (seasonal trains) (Waimea Plains Railway and Kingston Branch)
1958		Alexandra–Cromwell (Otago Central Railway) Balclutha–Tahakopa (Catlins River Branch) Ngāruawāhia–Glen Massey (Glen Massey Line) Rakaia–Methven (Methven Branch; second cessation)
1959		Aramoho–Whanganui (Whanganui Branch) Dargaville–Donnellys Crossing (Donnellys Crossing Branch) Te Puke–Tāneatua (East Coast Main Trunk)
1960		Invercargill–Tokanui (Seaward Bush Branch)
1961		Mussel Bay–Port Chalmers (Port Chalmers Branch)
1966		Invercargill–Bluff (Bluff Branch)
1967		Maungatūroto–Wellsford (North Auckland Line) Morrinsville–Te Puke (East Coast Main Trunk) Stillwater–Westport (Stillwater–Westport Line) Waiōtira–Dargaville (Dargaville Branch)
1968	Putāruru–Rotorua (Rotorua Branch; resumption)	Frankton–Morrinsville–Rotorua (East Coast Main Trunk and Rotorua Branch; first cessation for Putāruru–Rotorua)
1971		Putāruru-Rotorua (Rotorua Branch; second cessation)
1972		Greymouth–Ross (Ross Branch) Huntly–Glen Afton (Glen Afton Branch)
1973		Penrose–Onehunga (Onehunga Branch)
1974		Ōtiria–Ōkaihau (Ōkaihau Branch)
1975		Helensville–Wellsford (North Auckland Line) Maungatūroto–Whangārei (North Auckland Line) *Wairio–Ōhai* (Ōhai Railway Board line)

Timeline 1920–2020

YEAR	COMMENCED	CANCELLED
1976		Christchurch–Lyttelton (Main South Line) Napier–Gisborne (Palmerston North–Gisborne Line; first cessation) Whangārei–Ōpua (North Auckland Line) Wingatui–Alexandra (Otago Central Railway)
1977		Marton–Stratford (Marton–New Plymouth Line)
1978	Napier–Gisborne (Palmerston North–Gisborne Line; resumption)	
1979		Sawyers Bay (formerly called Mussel Bay)–Port Chalmers (Port Chalmers Branch)
1980		Waitākere–Helensville (North Auckland Line; first cessation)
1982		Woburn–Hutt Workshops (Gracefield Branch)
1983		New Plymouth–Stratford–Ōkahukura (Marton–New Plymouth Line and Stratford–Ōkahukura Line)
1984		Greymouth–Rewanui (Rewanui Branch)
1987	Wingatui–Middlemarch (Otago Central Railway; resumption)	
1988		Masterton–Woodville (Wairarapa Line) Napier–Gisborne (Palmerston North–Gisborne Line; second cessation)
1991	Frankton–Tauranga (East Coast Main Trunk) Waharoa–Rotorua (Rotorua Branch)	
2001		Frankton–Tauranga (East Coast Main Trunk) Palmerston North–Napier (Palmerston North–Gisborne Line) Waharoa–Rotorua (Rotorua Branch)
2002		Rolleston–Invercargill (exc. Dunedin–Wingatui) (Main South Line)
2003	Quay Park Junction–Britomart (North Island Main Trunk)	
2004	Dunedin–Palmerston (Main South Line; resumption)	
2008	Waitākere–Helensville (North Auckland Line; resumption)	
2009		Waitākere–Helensville (North Auckland Line; second cessation)
2010	Penrose–Onehunga (Onehunga Branch; resumption)	
2012	Wiri–Manukau (Manukau Branch)	
2013		Waitati–Palmerston (Main South Line; second cessation)
2015		Swanson–Waitākere (North Auckland Line)
2019		Pukerangi–Middlemarch (Otago Central Railway; second cessation)
2024 TBC	Britomart–Mount Eden (City Rail Link)	

Notes:

- On four lines, NZR operated passenger trains with PWD approval before the formal handover of responsibility for the physical infrastructure. These are listed above as NZR. The lines are: Arthur's Pass–Ōtira (1923, handover in 1924); Tangowahine–Dargaville (1941, handover in 1943); Īnangahua–Westport (1942, handover in 1943); and Hundalee–Ōaro (1943, handover in 1945). When NZR began carrying passengers from Waiōtira to Dargaville to 1941, it replaced a previous NZR service Waiōtira–Kirikōpuni and a PWD service Kirikōpuni–Tangowahine, but Kirikōpuni–Tangowahine–Dargaville remained in PWD hands until 1943.
- The PWD began operating goods trains Wairoa–Waikōkopu in 1925.

Initially intended as a branch of the Palmerston North–Gisborne Line, it ultimately became part of the main route. Passenger excursions ran on this line while under PWD control, but it does not appear that a regular timetable existed prior to NZR taking ownership.

- Passenger trains Lumsden–Kingston (from 1937) and Gore–Lumsden (from 1945) were timetabled as 'runs as required', normally during holiday seasons, and last ran in 1957.
- The table does not show lines where passenger services were suspended for a lengthy period, e.g. on account of earthquake damage or the Covid-19 pandemic. At the time of writing, it is too early to confirm if the Dunedin Railways network has contracted since Covid-19.

Appendix 3

LINES WITH A TIMETABLED PASSENGER SERVICE AT 1 JANUARY 2020

PHYSICAL LINES OPEN TO PASSENGERS

- North Auckland Line (Westfield Junction–Swanson) and branches
    - » Newmarket–Quay Park Junction (joining North Island Main Trunk)
    - » Penrose–Onehunga
- North Island Main Trunk (Britomart–Wellington) and branches:
    - » Wiri–Manukau
    - » Wellington–Johnsonville
- Wairarapa Line (Wellington–Masterton) and branch:
    - » Petone–Melling
- Main North Line (Christchurch–Picton)
- Main South Line (Christchurch–Rolleston and Waitati–Wingatui)
- Midland Line (Rolleston–Greymouth)
- Otago Central Railway (Wingatui–Pukerangi)

OPERATORS AND ROUTES OPERATED

- Great Journeys of New Zealand
    - » *Northern Explorer* (Auckland Strand–Wellington)
    - » *Capital Connection* (Palmerston North–Wellington)
    - » *Coastal Pacific* (Christchurch–Picton)
    - » *TranzAlpine* (Christchurch–Greymouth)
- Auckland Transport
    - » Eastern Line (Britomart–Manukau via Westfield Deviation)
    - » Onehunga Line (Britomart–Onehunga)
    - » Southern Line (Britomart–Pukekohe via Newmarket)
    - » Western Line (Britomart–Swanson)
- Greater Wellington Regional Council
    - » Hutt Valley Line (Wellington–Upper Hutt)
    - » Johnsonville Line (Wellington–Johnsonville)
    - » Kāpiti Line (Wellington–Waikanae)
    - » Melling Line (Wellington–Melling)
    - » *Wairarapa Connection* (Wellington–Masterton)
- Dunedin Railways
    - » *The Seasider* (Dunedin–Waitati)
    - » *Taieri Gorge Limited* (Dunedin–Pukerangi)

MAJOR NETWORK CHANGES SINCE 1 JANUARY 2020

- Waikato Regional Council
    - » *Te Huia* (Frankton–Papakura, started April 2021)
- Dunedin Railways
    - » All services cancelled (March 2020) and company mothballed (April 2020)
    - » Sunday services ran from 27 December 2020 to 28 March 2021 for a summer of 'Trains Not Planes':
        - º *The Inlander* (Dunedin–Hindon)
        - º *The Seasider* (Dunedin–Waitati)

Bibliography

Note: NZR's records at Archives New Zealand are held under multiple agency codes, which sometimes splits up a series. Many items held under agency ADQD begin with 18xx or 19xx, referring to the year the first item in the series was opened (not necessarily its oldest holding), while those held under other agencies often drop the 18 or 19. Researchers should be aware that a search by record number will, sometimes, not bring up the full series. For example, a search for 1909/3714/1 will only bring up parts 1–2 held under ADQD, not part 3 in AAEB or part 4 in ABJP, which are numbered 09/3714/1.

PRIMARY SOURCES

ARCHIVES NEW ZEALAND TE RUA MAHARA O TE KĀWANATANGA

AAEB (New Zealand Government Railways Department, General Manager's Office)
03/381/1 part 2 (Waitara Branch passenger services)
03/3964 part 2 (Outram Branch)
04/833/23 part 6 (railcar services Auckland District)
04/833/50 parts 11–12 (railcar service Wellington–New Plymouth)
04/833/32 part 3 (railcars Otago Central)
04/833/60 parts 4–6 (purchase of railcars)
04/3006/1 part 3 (Seaward Bush Branch train services)
04/3962/1 part 4 (Rakaia–Methven service)
06/161 (carriage accommodation Rotorua Line)
09/3714/1 part 3 (proposed Wellington–Paekakariki Deviation)
09/5300/24 part 1 (review and planning of new provincial passenger trains 1973)
11/1511/1 part 2 (carriage accommodation and conditions of same on Auckland northwards line)
16/1544/1 part 8 (train services – Whangarei northwards)

16/1795/1 part 5 (train services Wanganui–New Plymouth–Marton–Palmerston North)
16/1795/10 part 2 (fast passenger trains numbers 524 and 525 ['Flier'] Wanganui–New Plymouth)
16/2134 part 3 (Auckland–Onehunga train services)
16/2222/1 part 4 (Fairlie Branch train services)
16/3642 part 3 (Wairio Branch Line)
16/5002/1 part 3 (Invercargill–Kingston train services)
16/5896/2 (timetable Gisborne–Ngatapa Branch)
16/6018 part 5 (train services Tuatapere Branch)
23/551/1 part 13 (NZ Railway: Endeavour Passenger Service – Wellington–Napier)
25/985 part 1 (NZ Railway: General file – Opunake Branch)
28/800 (rail link – Haywards to Plimmerton)

AAFD (Cabinet Office)
CAB 183/4/2 (railways – equipment – locomotives etc)
CAB 183/6/1 (railways – passenger services)
CAB 183/6/2 (railways – passenger services – termination of services)
CAB 183/7/1 part 1 (railways – termination of services – general)

AAJM (Tranz Rail Limited, Corporate Office)
4/833/23 part 7 (railcar services: Auckland District)
09/5300/24 part 13 (review and planning: new provincial passenger trains)
12/640 part 11 (Rotorua Branch – timetable)
16/913/1 part 12 (Auckland–Whangarei training: Auckland–Whangarei–Opua express trains)
23/551/1 part 19 (rail passenger service: Wellington–Gisborne)
23/551/8 part 2 (rail passenger service: Napier–Gisborne [AC cars])
72/282 (railcars for provincial services)

AAVK (New Zealand Railways Corporation, Head Office)
PUB 1/5 part 2 (construction and history of: North Auckland railways)
PUB 7/3 part 2 (railcars – services and timetables – general)
PUB 7/6, part 1 (railcar services – Auckland southwards)
PUB 13/6 part 2 (suburban train service – Christchurch)
PUB 13/7 (suburban train services – Dunedin district)

ABIN New Zealand Railways Corporation, Lower Hutt Office)
W3337 Box 36 (miscellaneous reports – provincial railcars)
W3337 Boxes 189–93 (working timetable – North Island main line and branches 1951–82)
W3337 Box 209 (New Zealand railways country passenger services)

ABJP (New Zealand Rail Limited, Corporate Support Services Group)
04/3785/1 parts 4–5 (train service Invercargill–Bluff)
04/833/78 part 1 (conversion of railcars to loco-hauled trains)
08/1357/4 part 6 (train service Greymouth–Rewanui)
08/1357/17 part 1 (Rapahoe Branch trains)
15/2130/1 part 8 (train service – Huntly–Rotowaro)
16/1546/1 part 7 (suburban train service – Christchurch–Lyttelton)
16/5896/1 part 5 (passenger timetable – Gisborne–Moutohora)

ABKU (Works Consultancy Services Ltd, Napier Office)
W3748 Box 35 PW 19/13 (Waikokopu Branch railway – railway passenger fares – goods rates)

ADQD (New Zealand Railways)
34/280A parts 8–39 (twinset railcars)
081/100/30 part 2 (Dargaville–Donnellys Crossing)
500/3/11 part 3 (transport co-ordination: World War II and after – coal-saving timetable – 1940 – S.I.)
1900/2881 part 1 (passenger steamer competition – Auckland northwards)
1902/329 part 2 (Cambridge Branch train service)
1902/1559 parts 2–4 (train services Westport Seddonville section)
1903/111/1 parts 1–3 (passengers travelling by goods trains)
1903/1866 part 1 (Eyreton Branch train service)

1903/3964 part 1 (Outram Branch)
1904/833/15 part 1 (Ford rail motor cars)
1904/833/17 parts 3–4 (rail motor statistics)
1904/833/60 parts 1–3 (purchase of railcars)
1904/1613/1, part 2 (Oxford Branch – train services)
1905/3261 part 4 (Thames Branch timetable)
1908/1357/5 part 2 (Greymouth–Blackball train services)
1909/3714/1 part 2 (Wellington–Paekakariki Deviation)
1911/1130/1 parts 3–5 (Waipa Valley and collieries)
1913/3255 part 1 (timetable – Whitecliff Branch)
1914/2419 part 1 (proposed Martinborough railway)
1914/4756/1 part 8 (Little River Branch train service)
1915/2884/3 (timetable Cape Foulwind Line)
1915/4135/8 part 1 (review of branch lines)
1916/913/8 part 1 (timetable – Kirikōpuni Branch)
1916/2333 part 2 (Springfield Branch train service)
1916/2334 part 2 (Shag Point railway line)
1916/2624/1 part 3 (timetable – Nelson Section)
1917/1704 part 2 (Mount Somers Branch Line)
1917/4540/1 (timetable – Waiuku Branch)
1917/4650/1 part 3 (Tapanui Branch Line [Waipahi to Edievale])
1917/4975/2 (train service between Kurow and Hakataramea Point)
1918/1998/1 part 2 (Raetihi Branch timetable)

1920/1685/12 part 2 (road passengers services)

1922/400/5 part 1 (steamer competition – Auckland/Thames Valley)

ADRM (New Zealand Railways District Office – Wellington)

00/700/7/5 (Greytown Branch services)

ARCHIVES NEW ZEALAND – AUCKLAND REGIONAL OFFICE

BAEI (New Zealand Railways Auckland District Civil Engineers Office)

10003/155/a 7985 (extension of North Auckland Railway)

ARCHIVES NEW ZEALAND – CHRISTCHURCH REGIONAL OFFICE

CAAA (Department of Education, Southern Regional Office)

CH45 box 155/a 33/10 part 2 (primary education – school transport Southland – Invercargill schools)

CAHV (New Zealand Railways Corporation, Railfreight Systems, Regional Office Southern)

11/658 part 2 (trolleying passengers on isolated lines)

14/1289 part 1 (passenger traffic general)

25/282/4 (registered file – train services Christchurch–Waiau)

25/282/3 parts 10–11 (Christchurch–Lyttelton train services)

25/282/14 parts 4–5 (train services Christchurch–Greymouth–Ross)

1925/282/17 box 39/d (railcars, Methven Branch)

1925/282/17 box 39/e part 1 (train services, Methven Branch)

25/282/23, part 3 (train services Hokitika–Ross)

25/282/56 part 8 (North Line train services)

25/952/1 part 8 (railcars general)

1925/282/10 part 2 (train service, Christchurch–Little River)

1925/282/13 (train services, Whitecliffs Branch)

1925/282/15 (train service, Whitecliffs Branch)

1929/975/3 (Rapahoe, opening of line between Rapahoe and Rūnanga)

1933/348 (cancellation of rail passenger service on Tapanui Branch)

ARCHIVES NEW ZEALAND – DUNEDIN REGIONAL OFFICE

DABM (NZ Railways Corporation, Area Traffic Manager's Office, Dunedin)

09/336 part 2 (Ohai Railway Board private line)

11/290 (trolleying passengers on isolated lines)

30/446/12 (economy proposals – Dunback Branch trains)

DABO (Mr J A Dangerfield)

D544 box 10/e (contract for erection of new station building Mussel Bay – contract no. 1466)

DAFV (New Zealand Railways Department, District Traffic Manager's Office, Dunedin)

00/540 (Kaitangata Coal Company's private line – passenger service)

13/331 (improvements at Mussel Bay – new station built and named Port Chalmers)

20/358

(Invercargill–Lumsden–Kingston train services)

23/603 part 1 (motor competition – wool traffic, Kurow–Dunedin)

30/446/8 (economy proposals – Kurow Branch train services)

D454 20155 Boxes 9/b, 10/d, 11/e, 12/a, 14/d, 15/d, 15/e (New Zealand Railways – Working Timetable)

ALEXANDER TURNBULL LIBRARY

New Zealand Railways, *Time-table of Train and Road Services* (new series). Turnbull serials collection. Numbered series from 1950; title varies between issues. Some issues consulted at the Hocken Collections Uare Taoka o Hākena

AUCKLAND COUNCIL ARCHIVES

Halcrow–Thomas Report on Auckland's Transport Problems (ACC 275, Box 346, Record 50-299)

HOCKEN COLLECTIONS UARE TAOKA A HĀKENA

Ephemera – New Zealand Railways – Timetables and Menus (E210 Box 1012A)

New Zealand Government Railways, *Appendix to the Working Time-Tables*, effective 1 August 1908 (MS-3070)

——, *Time-table for the New Zealand Government Railways*, Pamphlets collection. Numbered series pre-1950. Some issues consulted at Alexander Turnbull Library

Papers Relating to Kurow Branch Railway and Clayton Railcar (MS-3088/008)

SOUTHLAND DISTRICT COUNCIL ARCHIVES

Ōhai Railway Board, meeting minutes
Ōhai Railway Board, ORB01585 box 53 (1974–75)

OFFICIAL

Appendices to the Journals of the House of Representatives
Census of New Zealand
New Zealand Legal Information Institute. New Zealand Acts as Enacted: http://www.nzlii.org/nz/legis/hist_act/
New Zealand Official Year-Book
New Zealand Parliamentary Debates (aka Hansard)

NEWSPAPERS, NEWS WEBSITES, PERIODICALS AND MAGAZINES

Ashburton Guardian
Auckland Star
Bay of Plenty Beacon
Bay of Plenty Times
Business Desk
Christchurch Star-Sun
Daily Telegraph (Sydney)
Dominion (Wellington)
Dominion Post (Wellington)
Dunstan Times
Evening Post (Wellington)
Evening Star (Dunedin)
Gisborne Herald
Greymouth Evening Star
Grey River Argus
Hawera and Normanby Star
Hawke's Bay Today
Hokitika Guardian
Hutt News
Independent (UK)
International Railway Journal
Lake Wakatip Mail
Levin Daily Chronicle

Manawatu Evening Standard (later Manawatu Standard)
Manukau Courier
Mt Benger Mail
Nelson Evening Mail
New Zealand Herald
New Zealand Railway Observer
New Zealand Railways Magazine
Newsroom
North Canterbury Gazette
Northern Advocate (Whangārei)
Northland Times
Nor-West News (Auckland)
NZ Truth
NZR Staff Bulletin (later NZR Bulletin)
Opotiki News
Opunake Times
Otago Daily Times
Otaki Mail
Otautau Standard
Poverty Bay Herald
Press (Christchurch)
Pukekohe and Waiuku Times
Rails
RNZ News
Southland Times
Southlandian
Spinoff
Stratford Evening Post
Stuff
Sunday Star-Times
Tapanui Courier
Taranaki Herald
Thames Star
Timaru Herald
Waihi Telegraph
Waikato Independent
Waikato Times
Wairarapa Daily Times
Wanganui Chronicle
Wanganui Herald
Western Leader (Auckland)
Westport News

REPORTS

Auckland Regional Transport Authority, yearly and half-yearly reports and press releases
Aurecon New Zealand, 'Greater Christchurch northern rail – rapid assessment', 17 July 2014, Environment Canterbury report C16C/114767
'Bay of Plenty rail strategy', August 2007, Environment Bay of Plenty Transportation Publication 2007/03
BERL, 'Tūranga ki Wairoa Rail: Feasibility study into reinstatement of rail line' (BERL ref no. 5993, November 2019): https://web.archive.org/web/20200817065333/https://berl.co.nz/sites/default/files/2019-12/T%C5%ABranga%20ki%20Wairoa%20Rail%20-%20Feasibility%20Study%20Into%20Reinstatement%20of%20Rail%20Line.pdf
Booz Allen Hamilton, Comprehensive Review of Operations and Strategic Options Evaluation, 8 November 1983, Wellington: New Zealand Railways Corporation
Brabhaharan, Pathmanathan, 'Let's get Wellington moving: Resilience of recommended programme of investment', 5 September 2018, WSP Opus report GER 2018-65 for the New Zealand Transport Agency: https://web.archive.org/web/20200111045339/https://lgwm.nz/assets/Documents/Technical-Documents/Resilience/19-Resilience-of-the-recommended-programme-WSP-Opus.pdf

Brady, Kevin, 'Auckland region passenger rail service report', 4 November 2003, LG03-0002: https://web.archive.org/web/20200218233542/https://www.oag.govt.nz/2003/akld-rail/docs/passenger-rail-service.pdf

Environment Canterbury, 'Canterbury regional public transport plan 2018–2028': https://web.archive.org/web/20200229132909/https://www.ecan.govt.nz/your-region/plans-strategies-and-bylaws/canterbury-transport-plans/

Future Proof, 'Hei Awarua ki te Oranga: Corridor for wellbeing', 12 February 2019, AMI18/19010053: https://web.archive.org/web/20200229112200/https://futureproof.org.nz/assets/FutureProof/Corridor-Plan/Hei-Awarua-ki-te-Oranga-H2A-Shared-statement-of-spatial-intent-FINAL.pdf

Garnaut, Ross, 'Projecting Australian climate change', *The Garnaut Climate Change Review*, Canberra, 2008: https://webarchive.nla.gov.au/awa/20190509072839/http://www.garnautreview.org.au/chp5.htm

Joyce, Janeane, 'Bay of Plenty region passenger and freight rail: Phase 1 investigation', 30 May 2019, Bay of Plenty Regional Council

KiwiRail, Annual reports

Market Economics Ltd and Gravitas Research and Strategy Ltd, 'Southerner rail passenger service viability study', November 2001: https://web.archive.org/web/20040221133741/http://www.med.govt.nz/irdev/reg_dev/southerner/southerner.pdf

MWH, 'North and southwest public transport corridors study: Stage two non-technical summary', April 2010, Environment Canterbury report C16C/114760

New Zealand Government, 'The New Zealand Rail Plan' (Wellington: Ministry of Transport Te Manatū Waka, April 2021).

New Zealand Railways, *Tangiwai Railway Disaster: Report of the board of inquiry*, Wellington: Government Printer, 1954

Pacific Maritime Association, 'The London dock strike October 1954', 22 November 1954, Special research report: https://web.archive.org/web/20200129041807/https://digitalassets.lib.berkeley.edu/irle/ucb/text/lb000219.pdf

Rapid Transit Steering Committee, 'Report of the steering committee set up to investigate the recommendations of the working party which reported 30th May 1969', Auckland: The Committee, 1972

Stafford Strategy, 'Hokitika to Westport tourist rail feasibility study stop/go report', July 2019: https://web.archive.org/web/20200411004352/https://fyi.org.nz/request/12020/response/46800/attach/4/KiwiRail%20Hokitika%20to%20Westport%20Tourist%20Rail%20Feasibility%20Study%20Stop%20Go%20Report%20Final.pdf

Transport Planning Department, 'The future of Auckland suburban rail services: A short-term appraisal', Auckland: Auckland Regional Authority, 1983

Transport Accident Investigation Commission, Report RO-1993-112

———, Revised report RO-1994-117R

TRC Tourism, 'Tourism opportunities: Using the Gisborne to Wairoa rail line/corridor' (August 2019): https://web.archive.org/web/20200817065502/https://berl.co.nz/sites/default/files/2019-12/14.8%20Tourism%20opportunities.pdf

URS New Zealand, 'Review of reports on railway crossings of Tauranga Harbour', prepared for Environment Bay of Plenty, 25 September 2008

Waikato Regional Council, 'Waikato regional public transport plan 2018–2028': https://web.archive.org/web/20200229112347/https://www.waikatoregion.govt.nz/assets/WRC/Council/Policy-and-Plans/Transport/RPTP/RPTP-2018-2028.pdf

Waitangi Tribunal, 'Te Mana Whatu Ahuru: Report on Te Rohe Pōtae claims', Wai 898, 2018

OTHER

Birks, L., 'Economic and scientific developments resulting from the Lake Coleridge hydro-electric power-supply', *New Zealand Journal of Science and Technology* 1:1 (1918), 16–26

Boulter, Roger, and Don Wignall, 'Identifying the value of long-distance rail services: Current issues in transport assessment and evaluation', Victoria Transport Policy Institute, 2008: https://web.archive.org/web/20180413000513/https://www.vtpi.org/rail_evaluation.pdf

Campaign for Better Transport, 'Reopen Onehunga rail', 22 November 2006: https://web.archive.org/web/20190115125421/http://www.bettertransport.org.nz/2006/11/reopen-onehunga-rail/

Carter, Shayne, *Dead People I Have Known*, Wellington: Victoria University Press, 2019

Compton, Gwynn, 'Kāpiti–Horowhenua commuter rail campaign': https://web.archive.org/web/20200302113517/https:/www.gwynncompton.co.nz/kapitihorowhenuarail

D'Ambrosio, Lily, 'Victoria's largest solar farm up and running', Victorian government press release, 19 July 2019: https://web.archive.org/web/20191012094248/https://www.premier.vic.gov.au/victorias-largest-solar-farm-up-and-running/Dunedin Railways: www.dunedinrailways.co.nz/

Farrington, S. Kip, Jr, *Railroading Around the World* (New York: Castle Books), 1955

Brian Gaynor, 'Looking back: Alex van Heeren, Tranz Rail and legal humiliation', *Business Desk*, 27 June 2021: https://web.archive.org/web/20210629004016/https://businessdesk.co.nz/article/the-life/looking-back-alex-van-heeren-tranz-rail-and-legal-humiliation Greater Auckland blog posts: www.greaterauckland.org.nz/

Harre, Brendon, 'Christchurch's future is a fat banana', 17 November 2018: https://web.archive.org/web/20200301102606/https://medium.com/land-buildings-identity-and-values/greater-christchurchs-future-the-fat-banana-aba0402f16a4

Hayward, T.M., *Time for Change* (Wellington: New Zealand Railways), 1979

KiwiRail, 'Coastal Pacific to start premium service', media release, 23 November 2018: https://web.archive.org/web/20200229025817/https://www.kiwirail.co.nz/media/coastal-pacific-to-start-premium-service/

Lee, Mike, 'After 8-year battle – Onehunga Line and station opens in grand style', 18 September 2010: https://web.archive.org/web/20190115125253/http://www.mikelee.co.nz/2010/09/after-8-year-battle-onehunga-line-and-station-opens-in-grand-style/

Lovett, Nick, 'Transport funding – taxes, fees and fairness', 15 June 2020: https://medium.com/@NickLovettNZ/transport-funding-taxes-fees-and-fairness-18543d73324f

New Zealand Mapping Service, series 1 and 17, available from the Geospatial Data Repository, GeoDataHub, University of Auckland Library, https://geodatahub.library.auckland.ac.nz/gdr

New Zealand Maritime Museum, 'The turbo electric vehicle *Rangatira* of 1971', New Zealand Maritime Record: https://web.archive.org/web/20200825075345/http://www.nzmaritime.co.nz/r4.htm

Parry, E., 'The electrification of railways in New Zealand', *New Zealand Journal of Science and Technology* 1:6 (1918), 323–28

Trains to Huapai: www.trainstohuapai.org/

SECONDARY SOURCES

BOOKS

Adams, Jill and Norma Nisbet, *East of the Twinlaws: Centennial history of the Wairio school and district* (Invercargill: Craigs Printing, 1981)

Aimer, Peter, *Wings of the Nation: A history of the New Zealand National Airways Corporation 1947–78* (Takapuna: The Bush Press, 2000)

Atkinson, Neill, *Trainland: How railways made New Zealand* (Auckland: Random House, 2007)

Bassett, Michael, *Coates of Kaipara* (Auckland: Auckland University Press, 1995)

——, *Confrontation '51: The 1951 Waterfront Dispute* (Wellington: Reed, 1972)

Bellamy, A.C., *The Napier–Gisborne Railway: The story of its construction and development* (Napier: New Zealand Railway and Locomotive Society – Hawke's Bay Branch) 1969

——, *New Zealand Railways Road Services* (Dunedin: Southern Press, 1981)

——, *Private Railways in Hawke's Bay*, rev. edn (Wellington: New Zealand Railway and

Locomotive Society, 1984) (1962)

Bloomfield, G.T., *New Zealand: A handbook of historical statistics*, (Boston: G.K. Hall, 1984)

Brett, André, *Acknowledge No Frontier: The creation and demise of New Zealand's provinces, 1853–76* (Dunedin: Otago University Press, 2016)

Bromby, Robin, *New Zealand Railways: Their life and times* (Sydney: Highgate Publishing, 2014)

——, *Rails that Built a Nation: An encyclopedia of New Zealand railways* (Wellington: Grantham House, 2003)

Brown, Margaret, Bill Kaye-Blake and Penny Payne (eds), *Heartland Strong: How rural New Zealand can change and thrive* (Auckland: Massey University Press, 2019)

Bush, Graham, *From Survival to Revival: Auckland's public transport since 1860* (Wellington: Grantham House, 2014)

Cameron, W.N., *A Line of Railway: The railway conquest of the Rimutakas* (Wellington: New Zealand Railway and Locomotive Society, 1976)

Cape, Peter, *An Ordinary Joker: The life and songs of Peter Cape* (Wellington: Steele Roberts, 2001)

Cassells, K.R., *The Sanson Tramway* (Wellington: New Zealand Railway and Locomotive Society, 1962)

Churchman, Geoffrey B. and Tony Hurst, *The Railways of New Zealand: A journey through history* (Auckland: HarperCollins, 1990)

Conly, Geoff and Graham Stewart, *New Zealand Tragedies on the Track: Tangiwai and other railway accidents*, rev. edn (Wellington: Grantham House, 1991) (1986)

Cooper, N.J., *Vulcan Railcars in New Zealand* (Wellington: New Zealand Railway and Locomotive Society, 1981)

Couchman, Jenny, *Okaihau: Our people, our places* (Kerikeri: the author, 2018)

Cowan, W.C., *Rails to Roxburgh: The story of a provincial railway* (Dunedin: Molyneux Press, 2010)

Dalziel, Raewyn, *Julius Vogel: Business politician* (Auckland: Auckland University Press, 1986)

Dangerfield, J.A., *Dunedin's Matchbox Railway: The Dunedin, Peninsula and Ocean Beach Railway Company and other suburban transport ventures* (Wellington: New Zealand Railway and Locomotive Society, 1986)

—— and G.W. Emerson, *Over the Garden Wall: Story of the Otago Central Railway*, 3rd edn (Dunedin: Otago Railway and Locomotive Society, 1995) (1962)

Dew, Leslie, *The Country Commuter: The regional railway network of Christchurch* (Christchurch: Christchurch Transport Board, 1988)

Duncan, Ian and Alan Bollard, *Corporatization and Privatization: Lessons from New Zealand* (Auckland: Oxford University Press, 1992)

Easton, Brian, *Not in Narrow Seas: The economic history of Aotearoa New Zealand* (Wellington: Victoria University Press, 2020)

Eaqub, Shamubeel, *Growing Apart: Regional prosperity in New Zealand* (Wellington: Bridget Williams Books, 2014)

Ebbett, Eve, *When the Boys Were Away: New Zealand women in World War II* (Wellington: Reed, 1984)

Edgar, John, *Urban Legend: Sir Dove-Myer Robinson* (Auckland: Hodder Moa, 2012)

Emerson, G.W., J.A. Dangerfield and A.C. Bellamy, *Coalfields Enterprise: Private railways of the Ohai district, Southland*, 2nd edn (Dunedin: New Zealand Railway and Locomotive Society – Otago Branch, 1975) (1964)

Evans, Laurence, *The Commuter, the Car and Metropolitan Wellington* (Wellington: Victoria University of Wellington, 1972)

Glennie, Alex C., *The Invercargill–Bluff Railway and Bluff School Train* (Invercargill: SBHS Old Boys' Association, 2018)

Hendy, Shaun, *#NoFly: Walking the talk on climate change* (Wellington: Bridget Williams Books, 2019)

Hurst, Tony, *Farewell to Steam: Four decades of change on New Zealand railways* (Auckland: HarperCollins, 1995)

——, *The Otago Central Railway: A tribute*, 5th edn (Wellington: Transpress, 2008) (1990)

Knight, Catherine, *New Zealand's Rivers: An environmental history* (Christchurch: Canterbury University Press, 2016)

Laird, Philip, Peter Newman, Mark Bachels and Jeffrey Kenworthy (eds), *Back on Track: Rethinking* transport policy in Australia and New Zealand (Sydney: UNSW Press, 2001)

Leitch, David, Railways of New Zealand (Auckland: Leonard Fullerton, 1972)

——, Steam, Steel and Splendour (Auckland: HarperCollins, 1994)

—— and Brian Scott, Exploring New Zealand's Ghost Railways, rev. edn (Wellington: Grantham House, 1998) (1995)

—— and Bob Stott, New Zealand Railways: The first 125 years (Auckland: Heinemann Reed, 1988)

Little, Paul, Air New Zealand: Celebrating 75 years (Auckland: Bauer Media Group, 2014)

Mahoney, J.D., Down at the Station: New Zealand railway stations remembered (Palmerston North: Dunmore Press, 1995)

——, Kings of the Iron Road: Steam passenger trains of New Zealand (Palmerston North: Dunmore Press, 1982)

Mahoney, Paul, The Era of the Bush Tram in New Zealand (Wellington: IPL Books, 1998)

Mason, Greg, An Accident in Waiting? The Hyde rail disaster 1943 (Kingston: E.E. Coleman, 2011)

McAloon, Jim, Judgements of All Kinds: Economic policy-making in New Zealand 1945–1984 (Wellington: Victoria University Press, 2013)

McClure, Margaret, The Wonder Country: Making New Zealand tourism (Auckland: Auckland University Press, 2004)

McKinnon, Malcolm, The Broken Decade: Prosperity, depression and recovery in New Zealand,

1928–39 (Dunedin: Otago University Press, 2016)

——, Treasury: The New Zealand Treasury, 1840–2000 (Auckland: Auckland University Press, 2003)

McLean, Gavin, The Southern Octopus: The rise of a shipping empire (Wellington: New Zealand Ship and Maritime Society, 1990)

Merrifield, Rob, Beyond Dashwood: A history of the railway in Marlborough (Wellington: New Zealand Railway and Locomotive Society, 1990)

——, The Kaikoura Job: Rebuilding KiwiRail's Main North Line (Wellington: New Zealand Railway and Locomotive Society, 2018)

Miles, Robert, The End of the New Zealand Passenger Train (Timaru: the author, 1995)

Millar, David P., Once Upon a Village: A history of Lower Hutt, 1819–1965 (Wellington: New Zealand University Press, 1972)

Millar, Sean, The NZR Steam Locomotive (Wellington: New Zealand Railway and Locomotive Society, 2011)

Morrell, W.P., The Provincial System in New Zealand, 1852–76, rev. edn (Christchurch: Whitcombe and Tombs, 1964) (1932)

Natusch, G.G., Waitaki Dammed: And the origins of social security (Dunedin: Otago Heritage Books, 1984)

Noonan, Rosslyn J., By Design: A brief history of the Public Works Department (Wellington: A.R. Shearer, 1975)

Orr, S., New Zealand Railway Corporations: A short history

of previous experiences with New Zealand Railways as a corporation (Wellington: Ministry of Transport Economic Division, 1981)

Pierre, W.A., Canterbury Provincial Railways: Genesis of the N.Z.R. system (Wellington: New Zealand Railway and Locomotive Society, 1964)

Redward, Rodger, Railway Electrification in New Zealand: An illustrated survey (Wellington: Southern Press, 1974)

Richards, Jeffrey and John M. MacKenzie, The Railway Station: A social history (Oxford: Oxford University Press, 1986)

Richardson, Len, People and Place: The West Coast of New Zealand's South Island in history and literature (Canberra: ANU Press, 2020)

Scanlan, A.B., Taranaki's First Railway (New Plymouth: the author, 1977)

Sole, Laraine, Castlecliff: The community on the coast (Whanganui: the author, 2008)

Somerset, H.C.D., Littledene: Patterns of change (Wellington: New Zealand Council for Educational Research, 1974) (1938)

Stewart, Graham, Auckland Before the Harbour Bridge (Wellington: Grantham House, 2002)

——, The End of the Penny Section: When trams ruled the streets of New Zealand, rev. edn (Wellington: Grantham House, 1993) (1973)

Thornton, Geoffrey, Bridging the Gap: Early bridges in New Zealand 1830–1939 (Auckland: Reed, 2001)

Tyrrell, A.R., *Catlins Rail: The story of the Catlins River Branch Railway 1879–1971*, 4th printing (Ōwaka: Catlins Historical Society, 2005) (1996)

Voller, Lois, *Rails to Nowhere: The history of the Nelson Railway* (Nelson: Nikau Press, 1991)

Ward, Gillian, *Tragedy and Heroism at Kopuawhara* (Gisborne: the author, 2019)

Watson, James, *Links: A history of transport and New Zealand society* (Wellington: GP Publications, 1996)

Waugh, Richard, with Peter Layne and Graeme McConnell, *NAC: The illustrated history of the National Airways Corporation 1947–1978* (Invercargill: Kynaston Charitable Trust in conjunction with Craig Printing, 2007)

Welch, David, *Port to Plains: Over and under the Port Hills, the story of the Lyttelton Railway Tunnel* (Invercargill: Craigs Design and Print, 2017)

Wood, Chris, *Steaming to the Sunrise: A history of railways in the Gisborne region* (Wellington: IPL Books, 1996)

Yonge, John, *New Zealand Railway and Tramway Atlas*, 4th edn (Exeter: Quail Map Company, 1993) (1965)

ARTICLES AND BOOK CHAPTERS

Bassett, Michael, 'Ward, Joseph George', *Dictionary of New Zealand Biography*: http://web.archive.org/web/20200306015509/https://teara.govt.nz/en/biographies/2w9/ward-joseph-george

Boot, H.M., 'Government and the colonial economies: A reply to Frost', *Australian Economic History Review* 40:1 (2000), 86–91

Brett, André, 'A sudden fancy for tree-planting? Forest conservation and the demise of New Zealand's provinces', *Environment and History* 23 (2017), 123–45

——, 'Dreaming on a railway track: Public works and the demise of New Zealand's provinces', *Journal of Transport History* 36:1 (2015), 77–96

——, 'Lahar meets locomotive: New Zealand's Tangiwai railway disaster of Christmas Eve 1953', *Arcadia: Explorations in Environmental History* (Autumn 2018) 31: www.environmentandsociety.org/node/8476

——, 'Wooden rails and gold: Southland and the demise of the provinces', in Lloyd Carpenter and Lyndon Fraser (eds), *Rushing for Gold: Life and commerce on the goldfields of New Zealand and Australia* (Dunedin: Otago University Press, 2016), 253–70

Brown, Margaret, Bill Kaye-Blake and Penny Payne, 'Introduction', in Brown, Kaye-Blake and Payne (eds), *Heartland Strong: How rural New Zealand can change and thrive* (Auckland: Massey University Press, 2019), 9–21

Dowie, J.A., 'Business politicians in action: The New Zealand railway boom of the 1870s', *Business Archives and History* 5:1 (1965), 32–56

Dodson, Jago and Paul Mees, 'Realistic sustainability? Urban transport planning in Wellington, New Zealand', *New Zealand Geographer* 59:2 (2003), 27–34

Edgar, John, 'Robinson, Dove-Myer', *Dictionary of New Zealand Biography*: https://web.archive.org/web/20200311050456/https://teara.govt.nz/en/biographies/5r19/robinson-dove-myer

Gunder, Michael, 'Auckland's motorway system: A New Zealand genealogy of imposed automotive progress, 1946–66', *Urban Policy and Research* 20:2 (2002), 129–42

Harris, Christopher E., 'Slow train coming: The New Zealand state changes its mind about Auckland transit, 1949–56', *Urban Policy and Research* 23:1 (2005), 37–55

Imran, Muhammad and Jane Pearce, 'Discursive barriers to sustainable transport in New Zealand cities', *Urban Policy and Research* 33:4 (2015), 392–415

Kranenburg, Alice, 'Down on Main Street: The depopulation of the central North Island', in Paul Spoonley (ed.), *Rebooting the Regions: Why low or zero growth needn't mean the end of prosperity* (Auckland: Massey University Press, 2016)

Laird, Philip G., 'Government rail asset sales, and return to the public sector, in New Zealand and Tasmania', *Research in Transportation Business and Management* 6 (2013), 116–22

——, 'New Zealand transport: The years to come', *Logistics and Transport NZ* 9:1 (2010), 16

Secondary sources

—— and Peter Newman, 'How we got here: The role of transport in the development of Australia and New Zealand', in Philip Laird, Peter Newman, Mark Bachels and Jeffrey Kenworthy, *Back on Track: Rethinking transport policy in Australia and New Zealand* (Sydney: UNSW Press, 2001), 1–21

Malcolm, C.W., 'The railway that never was', *Ohinemuri Regional History Journal* 26 (1982): https://web.archive. org/web/20200111143638/ http://www.ohinemuri.org. nz/journals/54-journal-26- november-1982/1055-the- railway-that-never-was

Mees, Paul and Jago Dodson, 'The American heresy: Half a century of transport planning in Auckland', in Peter Holland, Fiona Stevenson and Alexander Wearing (eds), *2001, Geography –A Spatial Odyssey: Proceedings of the third joint conference of the New Zealand Geographical Society and the Institute of Australian Geographers* (Dunedin: New Zealand Geographical Society, 2002), 279–86

——, 'Backtracking Auckland: Bureaucratic rationality and public preferences in transport planning', *Urban Research Program Issues Paper* 5 (2006)

Merrifield, Rob, 'Land transport deregulation in New Zealand, 1983–1989', *New Zealand Railway Observer* 47:2–3 (nos 202–03), 1990, 59–69

Murray, Anne C., 'Environmental assessment: The evolution of policy and practice in New Zealand', MSc thesis, University of Canterbury, 1990

Newman, Peter, Mark Bachels and Jeffrey Kenworthy, 'How we compare: Patterns and trends in Australian and New Zealand cities', in Laird et al., *Back on Track: Rethinking transport policy in Australia and New Zealand* (Sydney: UNSW Press, 2001), 45–67

Payne, Penny, 'Talking to communities: How other small towns view their resilience', in Brown, Kaye-Blake and Payne (eds), *Heartland Strong: How rural New Zealand can change and thrive* (Auckland: Massey University Press, 2019), 46–59

Pawson, Eric and Tony Hoare, 'Regional isolation, railways and politics: Nelson, New Zealand', *Journal of Transport History* 10:1 (1989), 22–40

Rosanowski, G.J. (John), 'The West Coast railways and New Zealand politics, 1878–1888', *New Zealand Journal of History* 4:1 (1970), 34–53

——, 'Politics and railways: The Midland Line, 1887–1918', in Philip Ross May (ed.), *Miners and Militants: Politics in Westland, 1865–1918* (Christchurch: Whitcoulls, 1975), 80–100

Small, Bruce, 'How will technology affect the fabric of rural communities?', in Brown, Kaye-Blake and Payne (eds), *Heartland Strong: How rural New Zealand can change and thrive* (Auckland: Massey University Press, 2019), 148–63

Stenersen, Roar, 'Development of Norwegian railways, 1854–2002', *Japan Railway and Transport Review* 31 (2002), 39–41

Ville, Simon, 'The coastal trade of New Zealand prior to World War One', *New Zealand Journal of History* 27:1 (1993), 75–89

Verbavatz, Vincent and Marc Barthelemy, 'Critical factors for mitigating car traffic in cities', *PLOS One* 14:7 (2019): https://doi.org/10.1371/journal. pone.0219559

Wynn, Graeme, 'Conservation and society in late nineteenth-century New Zealand', *New Zealand Journal of History* 11:2 (1977), 124–36

——, 'Pioneers, politicians and the conservation of forests in early New Zealand', *Journal of Historical Geography* 5:2 (1979), 171–88

Acknowledgements

This book began in a late-night Twitter chat, of all things. André made a rough timeline of passenger train cancellations and a month later, in an Archives New Zealand reading room, he knew he had a book on his hands. Another participant in the chat, Anthonie Tonnon, introduced André to Sam. We both thank Anthonie for his sustained warm interest.

We have strived to be comprehensive but more details will likely emerge, especially for obscure short-lived trains. We invite any information that has escaped our notice.

*

I would like to thank the staff of Stavanger Universitetssjukehus, the hospital of Stavanger, for saving my life when I became critically ill while visiting Norway. This book came uncomfortably close to not happening: nobody had a copy of my near-complete draft. Let this be a lesson! Tyson Retz is a fine scholar and finer friend who saw me through my initial recovery. I am fortunate to have wonderful parents: my father, Douglas, came all the way from Wellington to Stavanger; my mother, Sharon, helped me return to regular life in Wollongong. Working on this book brought joy while convalescing.

Thank you to Philip Laird, Lewis Holden and Scott Martin for commenting on drafts. The suggestions of two anonymous reviewers enriched the text; Imogen Coxhead at Otago University Press refined it, bringing clarity for readers not immersed in railway culture. Rachel Harris gave valuable research assistance in Wellington; and I am in Lea Doughty's debt for help in Dunedin. Jago Dodson and Chris Harris provided advice and useful sources; Rosi Crane passed on material; Suzie Best aided with the history of the railway through Ōtautau. I visited all four branches of Archives New Zealand and met with friendliness and ready help. Many people gave feedback and encouragement, especially online – I cannot possibly name everyone, but some are recognised in endnotes and Jordan McCluskey and Gwynn Compton deserve special mention.

I cannot prepare acknowledgements without recognising the role music plays in my writing. During the composition of this book the following artists influenced me: Death and the Maiden, Emma Ruth Rundle, Film School, Habitants, The Hundred in the Hands, Infinite Void, The Jezabels, Little May, The Luxembourg Signal, Metric, Midas Fall, Save Ends, Suldusk, Westkust and Wolf Alice. The title affectionately recalls the R.E.M. song 'Cant Get There from Here', although in my punctuation I am more conventional than Michael Stipe. On a research trip to Dunedin I achieved a lifelong goal of seeing The Chills perform a hometown gig. I was also fortunate to see Shayne Carter's bands Dimmer and Straitjacket Fits in Sydney and Wellington; the propulsive rhythm of 'Seed' is a sonic journey that rolls along like an express train.

André Brett

I would like to thank the many supporters of this project whose enthusiasm has been inspiring. I have been sketching, creating, refining, restarting and polishing these maps for almost three years and, like any creative endeavour, motivation recedes and returns without warning.

There are two Twitter communities I would like to recognise: transit map enthusiasts and New Zealand urbanists. I am heartened by the support I received from both. My particular thanks to Luke Christensen, who provided his shapefile of New Zealand's past rail network.

Thank you to everyone who gave feedback on map design and content. Fiona Moffat at Otago University Press helped bring structure to what were a hundred-and-something rather disparate maps; Natasha Murachver and Daniel Blackball provided invaluable commentary and advice on typography, design and layout. My workplace colleagues graciously accommodated absences during the final revisions.

Thank you to my friends and flatmates over the last few years – you all endured exasperated rants as I became stuck in creative ruts. I am especially grateful to my brother Alex for helping me escape these ruts through walks, chats and laughs; and to my parents, Tony and Rachel, for their immeasurable love, encouragement and wisdom.

Finally, thank you to my partner Bonnie for her love and support throughout this lengthy process. I could not have made it through the harder weeks without your guidance and love.

You helped me see the larger scope when I became paralysed by minor decisions and frustrations.

Music plays an important role in my process too. In particular, the following Radio One 91FM, Dunedin, programmes helped inspire and focus me: JB's Dream Land, Alex and Angus' History Bonanza, Kate and Abby's Drama Club, Liam's Wednesday Morning Spectrum, Barney's Starters Tuesday Nooner, Bonnie's Sunday Service, Hannah's Suite As and the R1 News.

Sam van der Weerden

IMAGE CREDITS

Archives Central, Archives New Zealand, Alexander Turnbull Library, Auckland Libraries, Hawke's Bay Museums Trust, Manawatū Heritage, Puke Ariki, Wairarapa Archives and Wellington City Archives gave permission to reproduce material. Simon Mathew and Moritz Krähe kindly provided photographs, and Wilson Lythgoe generously made available not only his own but also those of the late J.M. Creber. Bill Prebble filled gaps with images held by the NZ Railway and Locomotive Society; Lemuel Lyes dug into his personal collection. The late Weston Langford's pictures are licensed under a Creative Commons Attribution-NoDerivatives 4.0 International Licence and can be found by file number within his excellent collection online: https://westonlangford.com/

Index

Bold denotes illustrations

A class steam locomotive **143**
A^B class steam locomotive **98**, **147**, **219**
accidents, railway 136–37, **153**, 156, 250, 329n55
Addington Workshops 208, 221
ADK/ADB diesel multiple units **247**
ADL/ADC diesel multiple units **267**
advertisements **69**, 179, **252**
A^F class car-van **68**
Aickin, Francis 144–45, **144**, **145**, 172, 316n12
Air New Zealand 234, 250, 256
air travel
  climate change 14, 270
  competition from 95, 185, 202, 298, 192, 219, 284, 298
  National Airways Corporation (NAC) 146, 147, 185, 192, 202, 221, 234
  Union Airways 95, 123, 146
AM class electric multiple unit 264
Amalgamated Society of Railway Servants 79, 146, 149
American influences on transport policy 160
Amopiu, T.J. 203
Anderton, Jim 252
Angus, Percy 172
Antipodean Explorer (Auckland–Invercargill luxury service) 273
Aramoho 92–93, 178
Ardern, Jacinda 273, 282, 285
Armstrong, Tim 125
Arthur, Basil 216–17
Ashburton Guardian (newspaper) 97
Ashburton/Hakatere **35**, 108, 173, 182, 218, **219**, 275, 288, 318n58
asset stripping 24, 79, 250, 251, 298
Atkinson, Neill 20, 67
Auckland
  Auckland–Hamilton 144, 208, 251, 273

Auckland Harbour Bridge 160, 189
Auckland One Rail 25
Auckland passenger rail (1973–1980) **226–27**
Auckland passenger rail (2003–2024) **262**
Auckland rail proposals (1946–50) 158–61, **161**
Auckland rapid transit proposal (1972) **225**
Auckland Regional Authority (ARA) 217, 224, 227–29
Auckland Regional Council 25, 245, 258, 260–61
Auckland Regional Transport Authority (ARTA) 260, 261, 263, 264–65
Auckland station (Beach Road/Strand) 14, 84, 145, 159, 226, 260
Auckland–New Plymouth service 98–99, 178–79
Auckland–Te Puke 190–91
Auckland Transport 25, 160, 260, 265–267
Auckland–Whangārei passenger service 53, 189–90
Avondale–Southdown Line 159, 160
Britomart station 226, 247, 260, **261**, 264, 266, 273, 274
car-dependency 160, 161
City Rail Link 160, 273
Eastern Line 266
electrification 261, 273
Morningside Deviation **145**, 158–59, 160–61, 260, 273
North Auckland Line **41**, 52, 63, 86, 263, **268**, 282
North Shore 160, 282
Onehunga Branch/Onehunga Line 85, 217, 221, 264–67, **264**, 273

Regional Rapid Rail plan 281, 289
Southern Line 217, 223, 224, 261
suburban services 25, 150, 158–59, 160, 189, 217, 223–27, **225**, **226–27**, 227, 246–47, 260–67, 274
Te Huia service 11, 14, 273, **274**
Western Line 223, 263, 264, 266, 281
Westfield Deviation 84–85, **85**
Auckland Star (newspaper) 55, 97, 125
Australia 78
  Air New Zealand 250
  bush fires 270
  climate change 270
  electrification 108, 246–47
  high-speed trains 277
  line gauges 224, 277
  Melbourne 108, 270
  Perth 246–47
  Queensland 277
  royal commission 51
  suburban services 277
  tilting technology 277
  Toll Holdings 24, 256, 258–59
  West Coast Railway 251–52, 253, 256
  World War II 137
Avondale–Southdown Line 159, 160
Awakeri **40**
Awanui 52

Bailey, Ron 212
Baker, E.B. 180
Barthelemy, Marc 277
Bay Express 230, 235, 252, 253, 284, 294
Bay of Plenty
  Bay of Plenty Regional Council 277, 292
  eastern Bay of Plenty 36, **40**, 55, 85, 113, 140, 179, 292

operation of rail services 18, 38
railcar service 179
see also East Coast Main Trunk;
Tauranga; *individual towns*
B^B class steam locomotive **19, 183**
Beard, Michael 251
Belgrove 92, 155
Bell, Bob 213
Belmont Viaduct 111
bimodal trains 277, 282, 283, 284
biracial tensions 55–56, 140
Birks, Lawrence 144
Black, Bob 176, 177, 179, 203,
317n26
Black, George 86
Blackball/Blackball Branch **40**, 121
Blenheim–Picton railway 37, 118,
173
Blue Streak railcars 208, **209**, 212,
215, 216, **271**, 272
Bluff/Bluff Branch 36, **41**, **141**, 173,
179–82, **181**, 185
Bolger, Jim 244, 256
Boot, Mac 298
Booz Allen Hamilton 229–30
Brabender, Alan 252
branding 24–25, **108**, **214**, 215, 280
Brett, Ted (Richard Edward) 257
bridges 118
Auckland Harbour Bridge 160,
189
Esk River bridge 116
Tauranga harbour 55, 292
Whangaehu River 153, 257
see also tunnels; viaducts
Britomart station 226, 247, 260, **261**,
264, 266, 273, 274
Bromby, Robin 20, 184, 300n10
Brown, Margaret 276
Buller Gorge/Buller line 37, 58, 125,
140, 285, 306n99
Burke, Kerry 231
Bush, Graham 159, 247, 260

Cambridge/Cambridge Branch
139–40, **289**, 290
Campaign for Better Transport 264
Canterbury *see* Christchurch;
Coastal Pacific; Main North Line;
Main South Line; *TranzAlpine*
Cape Foulwind 63–64, 81–82
Cape, Peter 206, 257

Capital Connection 245, 251, 260, 282
carbon emissions 14, 227, 270, 282
Carter, Shayne 257
car-vans **68**, 142, **143**, 151, 179, 182,
193, 203, 221, 318n58
see also guard's vans
Castlecliff Railway Company 37,
92–93, 179, 308n55
Catlins River Branch 108, **184–85**
Cayford, Joel 261, 263
Christchurch
Christchurch–Hokitika 190, 192
earthquake 260, 294
growth 293
passenger rail (1950–1976) **218**
passenger rail proposal 294–95,
294
Southerner express service
(Christchurch–Invercargill)
209–10, 212, 213, 223, 232,
250, 253, 254, 256, 288, 295
suburban rail services 217–21,
218
see also Main North Line;
TranzAlpine
Christchurch–Picton *see* Main
North Line
Churchman, Geoffrey 20
Cityline/CityRail 24, 229, 245, 246
City Rail Link (Auckland) 160, 273
Clark, Helen 24, 250, 251, 256
Clent, George **154**
climate change 14, 15, 270, 279
closure/cancellation of services
16–17, **83**, 336–39
buses replacing passenger
services 16, 50, 66, 67–69,
79–81, 82, 90, 118, 120, 122,
136, 138–42, 151–53, 185, 192,
205, 212–13, 217, 221, 223,
271, 307n48
coal-mine train services 121,
203–6, 231
freight-only services **40**
mixed trains 59, 82, 84, 90–91,
96–97, 141–43, 148, 151, 152,
178, 182, 183–84, 207, 219
passenger services 37, 63–64,
66–69, 81, 82–84, 91, 94–96,
118–19, 139, 147–48, 152, 155,
172, 178, 183–85, 189, 230,
232–34, 251–57

protests/petitions against closures
65–66, 84, 85, 111–13, 116–17,
148, 149, 151, 155–56, 180,
189, 211, 213, 215–16, 230, 258,
264–65
railcar services 210–11, 213, 215,
216
road transport, competition from
25, 38–39, 50, 60, 63, 64, 66, 78,
79–81, 97, 118, 119–20, 121–22,
149, 160, 202
royal commission
recommendations 85–92,
88–89, 93
rural services 50, 51, 66–69, 81,
82–84, 85–90, 91, 118, 121–22,
142–43, 148, 178, 183, 185, 190,
203
services closed or freight only by
1920 **41**
suburban services 92–93, 185,
217, 219–23, 226, 266
suspension of railway projects 51,
53, 86, **87**, 94, 114–15, 124, 148
with-car goods trains 68, 120,
142, 179, 185, 203, 206–8
coal industry
closure of mine train services
203–6, 231
coal-saving timetable 65, 92, 137,
139, 146–47, **147**, 148, 151, 152
coal shortages 137, 138, 144, 146,
148, 151, 156, 178
Glen Afton **19**, 60, 146, 203, **204**,
205
Huntly **19**, 60, 146, 203, **204**
Kaitangata Coal Company 37,
122
Liverpool Mine 230
Mōkihinui Mine 95
Ōhai Railway Board (ORB) 9,
60–61, 122, 149, 203, 204, 205–6
Rewanui 203–4
State Mines Department 38, 40,
122, 182, 205
Wilton Collieries 122
coal to oil conversion 137, 146,
314n67
Coastal Pacific 14, 86, 230, 250, 251,
260, 273, 285
Coates, Gordon 50–51, 53, 58–59, 62,
63, 66, 67, 78, 112, 171–72

Collingwood, R.G. 22

commissioners 18, 39, 60, 66, 81, 85, 90, 95, 145, 152, 155, 156, 173–76

commissions *see* Fay–Raven report; royal commissions

commuter services
  Capital Connection 14, 245, 251, 260, 282
  Cityline/CityRail 24, 229, 245, 246
  Port Chalmers 185, 222, 223, 256, 295–96
  proposals for future 277, 281, 284, 290, 291, 293, 295–96, 297
  Te Huia service 11, 14, 273, **274**
  Wairarapa Connection 14, 245, 251, 253, 282, **283**
  Whanganui 92
  see also suburban rail services

competition to rail 25, 38–39, 50, 60, 63, 64, 66, 78, 79–81, 97, 118, 119–20, 121–22, 149, 160, 202

Compton, Gwynn 282

concessionary travel 149–51

construction of railway lines
  early railway lines 34–35
  East Coast Main Trunk 53–55, **54**
  Eastern North Island **54**
  Great Public Works Policy 34
  Nelson–West Coast 58
  Northland 52–53, **52**
  Ōtira Tunnel 36, **57**
  post-World War I 50
  Public Works Department (PWD) 18, 38, 52–53, 54–55, **55**, 58, 63, 116, 156
  Remutaka Tunnel 150, 171–72, **173**
  Stratford–Ōkahukura Line 58, 98–99
  Tawa Flat Deviation 97–98, 99, 110, **111**, 112–13
  topographical challenges 36, 38, **41**, 53, 55, 98, 112, 118, 210, 284, 297
  viaducts 111, 115–16, **115**, 310n26

Covid-19 232, 256, 273, 274, 285, 290, 295, 299

Cromwell 36, 38, 56, 178

Cromwell Gorge 56, **178**

Cross Creek 172

Cullen, Michael 258, 265

Cumberland, Kenneth 160

Cyclone Bola 234

D^A class diesel locomotive **207**

Daily Telegraph (newspaper) 259

Dann, James 294

Darfield 67–69

Dargaville/Dargaville Branch 36, 52, 53, 61, 86, 113, 122, 123–24, **123**, 147, 176, 182, 189

Davies, Sonja 155–56

D^B class diesel locomotive **204**

DBR class diesel locomotive **263**

deregulation 229, 244

Derrett, Rod 299

developmental railways 34, 35, 51, 58, 59, 60, 64, 78, 95, 229–34, 298, 302n18

Dick, Alan 252, 293–94

diesel locomotives
  bimodal trains 277, 282, 283
  Britomart 274
  diesel-electric multiple units 177, 227, 324n85
  dieselisation 145, 172, 209, 210, 220, 227
  diesel maintenance 188
  diesel multiple units 246–47, **267**, 317n26
  diesel vs electric 145, 266, 277
  Ōtira Tunnel **57**
  see also individual locomotive classes and railcar types

dining cars 16, 209–10

D^J class diesel locomotive **255**

D^M/D class electric multiple units **109**, 156, **275**

Dodson, Jago 160

Donald, Rod 253–56

Donnellys Crossing 61, 123, 124, 147, 182
  see also Kaihu Valley Railway

Drewry Car Company 170, 172–73, 176

D^S class diesel locomotive **20**

Dunback Branch **40**

Dunedin
  Abbotsford 10, **40**
  car-vans **68**
  Dunedin City Council 79, 232, 256

Dunedin–Mosgiel 79–81, 222–23, 295

Dunedin–Port Chalmers 34

Dunedin Railways 14, 19, 223, 232, 253, 255–56, 260, 272, 273, 288, 295

Dunedin Railways network (2019–2020) **254**

Green Island 10, **40**

Hillside Workshops **41**, 273

Ocean Beach Railway **41**, 92

passenger rail proposal 295–96, **296**

railway station **121**, 295, **297**

Seasider (Dunedin–Palmerston sightseeing service) 254, 255, 256, 273, 288

Southerner express service 209–10, 212, 213, 223, 232, 250, 253, 254, 256, 288, 295

suburban rail services 92, 185, 221–23, **222**

Taieri Gorge Limited 14, 232, 254, 255–56, 255

Eaqub, Shamubeel 275

early/first railway lines, New Zealand's 34–35
  Dunedin to Port Chalmers 34
  East Coast Main Trunk 36
  Hurunui–Bluff network 36–37
  Kaiapoi and Rangiora 35
  Main South Line 36
  Nelson/Marlborough 37, 56
  North Island 36
  Otago Central Railway 35–36
  Public Works Department (PWD) 38
  Southland 35
  steam railway, first **41**
  West Coast 37

earthquakes 93–94, **94**, 115, 260, 295

East Coast Main Trunk 9, 113, 304n58
  Bay of Plenty 54–55, 113
  construction 53–55, **54**
  forestry 150
  freight-only services **40**
  Napier/Napier–Gisborne 36, 53–54, 63, 113, 118, 213, 216, 232–34
  proposals for future 290, 291

plans for 36, 38, 53–54
  Tauranga 36, 53, 54–56, 114, 148
Eastern Line (Auckland) 266
E^C class electric locomotives **108**, 219
economic viability of rail services 22,
  39, 64, 78–79, 81, 82, 84, 90, 94, 119,
  121, 138, 147, 148, 180, 181, 188,
  191, 192, 222, 223, 229, 247, 251,
  273, 298
Ede, A.J. 173
Edenius, R. 144, **145**
Edgecumbe 150
Education Department 67, 180–82
EF class electric locomotives **258**
El 18 class electric locomotives
  (Norway) **278**
electrification/electric trains 144–45
  AM class electric multiple units
    264
  Auckland 261, 273
  D^M/D class electric multiple units
    109, 156, **275**
  E^C 9 **108**
  EF class electric locomotives **258**
  El 18 class electric locomotives
    (Norway) **278**
  electrification systems 277, 283
  EM/ET electric multiple units
    223, 227, 235, 260, 275
  E^O class locomotives **57**
  FP/FT class Matangi electric
    multiple units **12–13**, **112–13**,
    260, **275**, 277
  Main South Line 295
  North Island Main Trunk 145,
    227, 229
  Ōtira Tunnel **57**, 108
  Palmerston North to Waikanae
    (future) 283
  recommendations for 108,
    144–45, 281, 283, 284, 288, 295,
    309n2
  removal of electrification **57**, 219
  Wellington suburban network
    108, **109**, 144, 156, 158
  Wellington to Paekākāriki 112
  see also Lyttelton Line
Elsey, Wayne 257
EM/ET electric multiple units 223,
  227, 235, 260, **275**
End of the Penny Section, The
  (Stewart) 18

Endeavour (Wellington–Napier
  service) 212, 213, 230, 232–34, 272
English Electric (company) **109**, 156,
  172, 260, **275**
Environment Canterbury 295
E^O class locomotives **57**
Era of the Bush Tram in New Zealand,
  The (Mahoney) 18
Eskdale 54, 292
Eskdale–Pūtōrino line 85, 116
Evening Post (newspaper) 156
Exploring New Zealand's Ghost
  Railways (Leitch and Scott) 20
Eyreton Branch **65**, 82, 84, 90, 97

Fairlie/Fairlie Branch 152, 155
'Fairlie Flyer' 152
fares, passenger train 69, 97, 121,
  140, 149, 151, 180, 210, 221, 229,
  259, 280, 285
farmers 65, 79, 82, 111–13, 139
Farrington, Kip 144
Fay–Raven report 51, 60, 66, 85, 90,
  271
Fay, Sam 51, 60, 66
feasibility studies 253, 284, 285–88
Featherston 62, 172
Fell mountain railway systems **171**,
  230, **233**
Fell, John Barraclough 171
Fiat railcars **15**, **20**, **170**, **173**, 172–
  79, 187–88, 191, 192, 208, 215, 299
Fiordland 120, 297
Fitch, A.N. 215
floods 98, 115, 116, 124–25, 184
Forbes, George 78, 86, 93, 95, 97–98,
  99, 113
Foxton 38, 95–96
Foxton–Palmerston North 95–96
Frankton Junction 108, 144–45, **274**
Fraser, Peter 123, 137, 144, 146, 156
Frater, John & Mary **137**
freight services
  'Golden Triangle' 290
  goods-only trains/lines **40**, 65,
    69, 79, 81, 139, 141, 142, 149,
    152, 203, 282
  livestock transportation 66,
    111–13
  services closed or freight only by
    1920 **41**
  Tranz Rail 247, 251

with-car goods **20**, 22, 58, 68,
  120, 142, **143**, 151, 155, 179,
  182–83, **183**, 185, 189, 193,
  203, 206–7, **207**, 213, 223, 232
  see also coal industry
Furkert, Frederick 62, 112
Future Proof (partnership) 289–90,
  291
future proposals/solutions (suggested
  by authors)
  bimodal units 277, 282, 283, 284
  Christchurch–Hokitika 192
  Christchurch passenger rail
    294–95, **294**
  community engagement 281
  design standardisation 279
  Dunedin passenger rail 295–96,
    296
  electrification 281, 283, 284,
    288, 295
  fares, affordable 280, 285
  frequency increase 283, 291
  Hamilton passenger rail 289–91,
    289
  infrastructure upgrades 284,
    285–88, 290, 296
  integrated transport 275
  investment/funding 279
  long-distance services 283–84,
    286–87
  lower North Island 282–84
  modal integration 279
  multimodal transport 279, 281,
    295
  Napier–Hastings passenger rail
    292–94, **293**
  national ticketing system 279–80
  North Island Main Trunk
    284–85
  overnight trains 285
  political collaboration 280–81
  South Island 285–88
  Tauranga passenger rail proposal
    291–92, **291**
  tilting technology 277, 285
  tourism 284, 285–86, 292–93,
    297
  train speed 284, 288
  tram-trains **280**, 290–91, 292,
    295
  upper North Island 281–82

Gale, Harriet 282
Gandell, Alan 176, 180
Ganz-Mávag *see* EM/ET class electric multiple units
Garnaut, Ross 270
gauges, track 224, 276–77, 280
general managers, New Zealand Railways (NZR) 18, 51
   Aickin, Francis 144–45, **144**, **145**, 172, 316n12
   Gandell, Alan 176, 180
   Hayward, Trevor 215, 223–26
   Hiley, Ernest Haviland 112
   Lusty, Horace 145, 172, 176, 177
   Mackley, Garnet Hercules 110, 116, 117
   McVilly, Richard 39, 62, 81
   Roussell, Philip 93, 110, 302n21
   Sawers, James 127, 140, 141
   Small, Tom 213, 216
   Sterling, Herbert Harry 78–80, 81, 84, 93, 95–96, 111, 112
   Thomas, Ivan 182, 188–89, 190, 208, 227
Germany **280**
Geyserland Express 245–46, 251, 253
Gibson, Don 251–52
Gillsepie, O.N. 116
Gisborne
   buses replace trains **138–39**, 213
   freight-only/closed lines 41
   Gisborne Chamber of Commerce 116–17
   isolated railway sections 36
   Napier–Gisborne Line 63, 113, 213, 216, 232–34
   passenger numbers 39
   plans, railway network 36, 38, 53
Gisborne Herald (newspaper) 234
Glen Afton Branch **19**, 60, 146, 203, **204**, 205
Glenbrook **40**
Glenham/Glenham Branch 67, 81, 85
Glenhope **23**, 37, 58, 91–92, 155
Glen Massey 37, 122, 182, **183**
Goff, Phil 267–68
goods trains *see* freight services; mixed trains
goods-only trains/lines **40**, 65, 69, 79, 81, 139, 141, 142, 149, 152, 203, 282
   see also freight services; mixed trains

Goods with car *see* with-car goods trains/services
Goodwin, Len 257
Goosman, Stan (William Stanley) 147, 155, 160, 161, 172
Gordon, Peter (John Bowie) 188–89, 190, 192, 210
Gore 35, 90, 120, 139
Gosche, Mark 265
governments, New Zealand
   Labour Government (1935–1949) 86, 110, **119**, 123, 137, 144, 146, 156, 288
   Labour Government (1957–1960) 177
   Labour Government (1972–1975) 210, 211, 212, 221, 224, 272
   Labour Government (1984–1990) 229, 230, 234, 244
   Labour Government (1999–2008) 24, 250, 251, 252, 256, 258, 265
   Labour Government (2017–present) 273, 274, 282
   National Government (1949–1957) 114, 144, 146, 152, 155, 160, 191
   National Government (1960–1972) 187–88, 210
   National Government (1975–1984) 24, 216, 234
   National Government (1990–1999) 244, 256
   National Government (2008–2017) 265, 295
   Reform Government (1912–1928) 50–51, 62, 78
   United Government (1928–1931) 78
   United–Reform Coalition Government (1931–1935) 95, 97–98
Gracefield workshops/industrial line 59, **80**, 157, 227
grassgrubs (refurbished Fiat railcars) 215, 216, **217**, 230
Great Britain *see* United Kingdom
Great Depression 16, 63, 78, 86, 93, 95, 97–98, 99, 113, 124, 141, 148, 183, 271
Great Journeys of New Zealand 19, 259

see also long-distance train services; KiwiRail
Great Public Works Policy 34
Greater Wellington rail network (1935) **158**
Greater Wellington Regional Council 25, 251, 260, 285
Green Island 10, **40**
Green Party 258, 259, 281
Greymouth
   Greymouth–Blackball 121
   Greymouth–Hokitika 120, 190, 211, 285–86
   Greymouth–Ross 190, 211
   Greymouth–Westport 125–26, 190, **191**
   Ōtira–Greymouth **20**
   TranzAlpine 14, 202, 230, 232, 235, 245, 250, 251, 273, 285
Greytown/Greytown Branch 62, 82, 85, 147
guards 60, 122, **154**, 232
guard's vans 17, 22–23, **23**, **40**, 68, 92, 96, 171, 207, 212
   see also car-vans

Hakataramea 64–66, 81, 85
Hakatere *see* Ashburton/Hakatere
Halcrow–Thomas Report 158–59, 160
Halcrow, William 158, 159–60
Hamilton
   Auckland–Hamilton 144, 208, 251, 273
   Cambridge–Hamilton 139
   express services, possible 281–82, 285
   Frankton Junction (Hamilton station) 108, 144–45, **274**
   Hamilton Central station (underground) 274, 290
   Hamilton passenger rail proposal 289–91, **289**
   Hauraki Plains link 114
   Northerner service 251
   Overlander service 258
   Palmerston North–Hamilton 145, 229, 277
   Te Huia service 11, 14, 273, **274**
Harre, Brendon 294
Hastings 50, 116, 292–94, **293**
Hauraki Plains, link across 113, 114–15, **114**

Hāwea 56

Hāwera 179, 182, 183, 215, 284

Hawkens Junction **40**

Hawke's Bay *see* East Coast Main Trunk; Hastings; Napier; *individual Hawke's Bay towns*

Hawke's Bay Regional Council 252, 293–94

Hayward, Trevor 215, 223–26

health and safety 153, 250
see also accidents

Heartland Strong: How rural New Zealand can change and thrive (Brown, Kaye-Blake and Payne) 276

'Hei Awarua ki te Oranga: Corridor of Wellbeing' (Waka Kotahi NZTA) 289–90

Helensville 41, 189, 190, 206, 207, 223, 226, 261, 263

Helensville–Waitākere 263

Hendy, Shaun 14, 15, 235

Herd, Joyce 213

heritage railways 19, 120, 184, 202, 282, 297

Hiley, Ernest Haviland 112

Hillside Workshops **41**, 273

Hokianga Harbour 52, 53, 86

Hokitika 120, 192, 211, 285–86

holiday-season travel 92, 120–21, 139, 178–79, 184, 190, 230–31, 246, 250, 254, 256

Holland, Sidney 114, 127, 144, 146, 152, 155

Holyoake, Keith 191, 210, 224

Houltham, Garth 264, 265

Huapai 263–64, 266, 281

Huarau 52, 53

Hunter, James 95

Huntly **19**, 60, 146, 203, **204**, **289**, 290

Hurst, Tony 20

Hurunui–Bluff network 36

Hutt Valley 59, **111**, 138, 156–57, **157, 172**

Hutt Workshops *see* Gracefield workshops/industrial line

Hyde rail disaster 136–37, **137**

hydroelectric power **65**, 80, 122, 144, 145, 278, 288

Īnangahua 37, **57**, 58, 86, 113, 123, 155

industrial action *see* strikes; waterfront dispute

industrial railways/lines 18, 22, **40**, **41**, 80, 157, 217, 227
see also coal industry

InterCity 24, 229, 245

Interislander (ferry service) 229

interisland ferries 24, 25, 64, 86, 95, 173, 192, 208, 213, 219, 221, 229

Invercargill
Antipodean Explorer (Auckland–Invercargill luxury service) 273
Bluff services 180
buses replace trains 120, 149, 253
express services 95, 120, 209, 212, 219, 253, 273
Main South Line 36
mixed trains 139, 183, 185
Ōrawia to Invercargill 61
rail passenger services proposal 179–80, **181**, 182
school trains 180, 182
Seaward Bush Branch 16, **184**–**85**
Southerner express service (Christchurch–Invercargill) 209–10, 212, 213, 223, 232, 250, 253, 254, 256, 288, 295
suburban services 93, 202
timetables 149–51, 184, 185

isolated sections of railway 17, 34, 36–37, 52, 53, 56, 61, 63, 118, 123, 124

J class steam locomotive **19**, 314n67

J^A class steam locomotive **220**, 314n67

Japan 203, 209

Jennings, William 58–59

jiggers 17–18, **147**, 300n5

Jones, Morgan 250

Joyce, Steven 265

junction stations **36**, 60

Kaihū Valley 36, 61, **147**, 182

Kaihū Valley Railway 52, 124
see also Donnellys Crossing

Kaikohe 52, 53, 206, 303n14

Kaikōura 118, 126, 127

Kaikōura earthquake 260

Kaimai Express 245–46, **246**, 251, 253

Kaimai Tunnel 115, 245

Kaipara **41**, 123

Kaitaia 52, 53, 86

Kaitangata Coal Company 37, 122

Kāpiti Coast 112, 227, 245, 260, 282, 284
Kāpiti Line 9, 158
Paekākāriki **109**, 112–13, 156, 158, 227, 284
Paraparaumu **15**, 158, 227, 260, 285
Pukerua Bay **12**–**13**, **112**–**13**, 284
Waikanae 9, **12**–**13**, 260, 283, 284

Kāpuni 61

Karlsruhe model **280**

Kawakawa 52, 282

Kawatiri 58, 86, 91–92

Kawerau 9, **40**, 56, 150, 292

Kedgley, Sue 259

Kent, R.S. 67–69

Key, John 265, 295

Khandallah **109**

King, Annette 265

Kingston 19, 120–21, 139, 183–84

Kingston Flyer 19, 120, 184, 202

Kinzett, Amanda 265

Kirikōpuni 53, 86, 122, 124

Kirk, Norman 210

KiwiRail 18, 19, 270, 279, 298
Auckland suburban rail network 265, 274
Avondale–Southdown Line 160
freight capacity 281
Great Journeys of New Zealand 25, 285
Kaikōura earthquake 260
Main South Line 296
Manukau Branch 265
mothballed lines 230, 282
Onehunga service 265
re-nationalisation 24
Scenic Journeys 24, 259
tourism, fixation on 273
TranzAlpine 285
Wellington suburban trains 260
see also New Zealand Railways (NZR)

Kōhuratahi 38, 58, 59

Kopaki **271**

Kōpuawhara 117, 124
Koutu 246, **252**
Kranenburg, Alice 16
Kumeū 41, 159, 267
Kurow/Kurow Branch 64, **65**, 66, 80, 122, 141–42, **141**, 313n42

Labour governments
    1935–1949 86, 110, **119**, 123, 137, 144, 146, 156, 288
    1957–1960 177
    1972–1975 210, 211, 212, 221, 224, 272
    1984–1990 229, 230, 234, 244
    1999–2008 24, 250, 251, 252, 256, 258, 265
    2017–present 273, 274, 282
Laird, Philip 247, 276
Lake Waitaki 141
    see also Waitaki Dam
Lake Wakatipu 120–21, 184
Lambton station (Wellington) **41**, 92, 111
Lange, David 229, 230, 234, 244, 246
Latter, Edward 208, 213
Lawrence 61, 121–22
Lee, Mike 261, 263, 264, 265
legislation 14, 64, 94–95, 112, 119, 146, 298
Leitch, David 20, 34, 35, 151, 184, 215, 333n32
Levin Daily Chronicle (newspaper) 96
light rail 224, 229, 267, 275, 285, 289, 290–91, 295
    see also trams/tramways; tram-trains
Links (Watson) 20
literature, railway 19–20, 21
Little River Branch 90, 110, **147**, 148, 149, **218**
Liverpool Mine 230
locomotive/rollingstock classes 9
    A class steam locomotive **143**
    A^B class steam locomotive **98**, **147**, **219**
    ADL/ADC diesel multiple units **267**
    ADK/ADB diesel multiple units **247**
    A^F class car-van **68**
    AM class electric multiple units **264**

B^B class steam locomotive **19**, **183**
Blue Streak railcars 208, **209**, 212, 215, 216, **271**, 272
Clayton railcar 141
D^A class diesel locomotive **207**
D^B class diesel locomotive **204**
DBR class diesel locomotive **263**
D^J class diesel locomotive **255**
D^M/D electric multiple units **109**, 156, **275**
D^S class diesel locomotive **20**
E^C class electric locomotive **108**, 219
EF class electric locomotive **258**
El 18 class electric locomotive (Norway) **278**
EM/ET class electric multiple units 223, 227, 235, 260, **275**
E^O class electric locomotive **57**
Fiat railcars **15**, **20**, 172–79, **170**, 187–88, 191, 192, 208, 215, 299
FP/FT class Matangi electric multiple units **12–13**, **112–13**, 260, **275**, 277
J class steam locomotive **19**, 314n67
J^A class steam locomotive **220**, 314n67
J^B class steam locomotive 314n67
K class steam locomotive 314n67
K^A class steam locomotive 314n67
Midland class railcars 116
Model T Ford railcars **91**, 110
SA/SD class carriages **261**
Silver Fern railcars 203, **209**, **210**, 211, 212, 230, 234, 245, **246**, 253, 255, 272
SX class carriages 260, **263**
U^B class steam locomotives **149**
Vulcan railcars 120, 124, 125–26, 141–42, 178, 180, 187, 188, **191**, 212
Wairarapa railcars **115**, 116, 171, 173, 177, 316n12
W^F class steam locomotive **23**
W^W class steam locomotive **233**
see also railcars; steam engine conversion from coal to oil
long-distance train services
    Bay Express 230, 235, 252, 253, 284, 294

Booz Allen Hamilton analysis 229–230
Coastal Pacific 14, 86, 230, 250, 251, 260, 273, 285
Geyserland Express 245–46, 251, 253
Kaimai Express 245–46, **246**, 251, 253
Northerner 229, 251, 256–58
Northern Explorer 14, **258–59**, 273, **274**, 284, 285
Overlander 245, 251, 256, 257, 258–60, **258**, **274**
Silver Star 15, 203, 209, 229, 230, 245, 257
Southerner express service 209–10, 212, 213, 223, 232, 250, 253, 254, 256, 288, 295
South Island Limited (express train) 95, 209
TranzAlpine 14, 202, 230, 232, 235, 245, 250, 251, 273, 285
Lovett, Nick 279
Lower Hutt 59, 156, 157, 297
    see also Hutt Valley
Lowrie, Matt 267
Lumsden 120, 139, 183–84
Lusty, Horace 145, 172, 176, 177
luxury trains 16, 203, 209–10, 230, 259, 273
Lyttelton/Lyttelton Line **41**, 86, 95, **108**, 110, 144, 208, 217–18, 219, 220–21, 295

Mackay, F.K. 121, 141, 143
Mackley, Garnet Hercules 110, 116, 117
Macpherson, Dave 290
Mahoney, Paul 18
Main Highways Act 119
Main North Line **126–27**
    Christchurch–Picton 14, 61, 127, 136, 192, 207–8, 215, 216, 230
    Hundalee to Wharanui 126
    interisland ferries, connection with 208, 213
    Kaikōura earthquake 260
    NZR express good train 207–8
    route options 117–18, **118**
Main South Line 9
    Ashburton station **35**
    branch connections 90, 148

electrification 295
freight-only services 254, 256
infrastructure upgrades, proposed
    288, 296
opening of last portion 36
private railways 37
proposal for future (suggested by
    authors) 288, 295
road transport competition 50
train speed 288
    see also Christchurch; Dunedin;
    Invercargill and other
    individual entries for towns
Makaraka 38, 304n58
Mākareao **40**
Makarewa 179
Mallard, Trevor 258
Mamaku **252**
Manaia 61, 62
Manapōuri Power Station 288
Manawatū 34, 96, 215, 234, 252, 283
Manawatū County Council 19, 38, 96
Mangamuka 53, 86
Māngere 267
Manukau 158, 264, 265
Manukau Branch 265–66, 273
Manukau Harbour 61, 142
Māori 51, 55–56, 140, 171, 193, 206,
    244, 281
maps, national network
    1920–1928 **42–49**
    1929–1934 **70–77**
    1935–1945 **100–107**
    1945–1954 **128–35**
    1955–1968 **162–69**
    1970–1989 **194–201**
    1990–2020 **236–243**
    January 1920, as of **26–33**
    long-distance services (1991–
        2002) **248–49**
    long-distance services (proposed
        by author) **286–87**
    network cuts (1930) **83**
    proposed railcar routes (1950–
        1951) **174–75**
    royal commission
        recommendations (1930) **88–89**
    suspended projects (1929–1931)
        87
maps, regional/local
    Auckland passenger rail (1973–
        1980) **226–27**

Auckland passenger rail (2003–
    2024) **262**
Auckland rail proposals (1946–
    1950) **161**
Auckland rapid transit proposal
    (1972) **225**
Christchurch passenger rail
    (1950–1976) **218**
Christchurch passenger rail
    proposal **294**
Dunedin passenger rail proposal
    296
Dunedin Railways network
    (2019–2020) **254**
Eastern North Island (1920) **54**
Hamilton passenger rail proposal
    289–91, **289**
Hutt Valley changes (1946–1955)
    157
Invercargill passenger rail
    (1950–1966) **181**
Kurow Branch and Waitaki Dam
    Branch **65**
Main North Line route options
    118
Main North Line (Waipara–
    Picton) **126–27**
Napier–Hastings passenger rail
    proposal **293**
Northland rail services (1967)
    190
Oxford Branch and Eyreton
    Branch **65**
Palmerston North railways
    (1960) **186**
Seaward Bush Branch and
    Catlins River Branch **184–85**
Sockburn–Styx Deviation **150**
Tapanui Branch **96**
Tauranga passenger rail proposal
    291
Upper South Island **57**
Waiau Branch **126–27**
Wellington (1937) **111**
Wellington passenger rail
    (1973–83) **228**
Western Taranaki **62**
Marlborough *see* Blenheim; *Coastal
Pacific*; interisland ferries; Main
    North Line; Picton
Marshall, Jack 210
Martin, J. 96

Marton–New Plymouth Line **40, 41**
Massey, William 50, 51, 61, 112
Masterton–Wellington 14, 234, 245,
    251, 253, 282, **283**
    see also Wairarapa Line
Matamata **246**
Matangi electric multiple units **12–
    13, 112–13**, 260, **275**, 277
Matapihi 55
Matatā 38, 54, 55
Mātiēre 58–59, **231**
Maungatūroto 124, 189, 207
Maungatūroto–Whangārei 207
McAlpine, John 114–15, 187, 188
McGlashan, Isobel 121
McKinnon, Malcolm 78
McLachlan, Colin 210–11, 212–13,
    215–16, 221, 223
McLellan, William 108, 144, 309n2
McQueen, Euan 222, 257
McVilly, Richard 39, 62, 81
Mees, Paul 160
Melbourne 108, 270
Merrifield, Rob 260
Merz, Charles 108, 144, 309n2
Methven/Methven Branch **36**, 141,
    142, **143**, 182, 318n58
Metlink 25, 260
Middlemarch 178, 232, 254–56, **255**,
    273
Midland railcars 116
Midland Line 64, 67–69, 86
Midland Railway Company 56, **57**
Midland Red (livery) **108**, 215, **275**
Mills, Stephen 216
Milson Deviation 186–87, **186**
ministers of public works 18, 50, 59,
    86, 110
    see also Coates, Gordon; Semple,
    Bob; Williams, Kenneth
ministers of railways 18, 24
    Bailey, Ron 212
    Forbes, George 78, 86, 93, 95,
        97–98, **99**, 113
    Goosman, Stan 147, 155, 160,
        161, 172
    Gordon, Peter (John Bowie)
        188–89, 190, 192, 210
    McAlpine, John 114–15, 187, 188
    McLachlan, Colin 210–11,
        212–13, 215–16, 221, 223
    Moohan, Mick 177, 179

Prebble, Richard 234
Taverner, William 78, 79
Veitch, Bill 78, 79, 81, 82, 84, 112
Ministry of Works (MoW) 18, 113, 150, 157–58
see also Public Works Department (PWD)
mixed trains 23, **98**, 108, **220**
closure/cancellation 59, 82, 84, 90–91, 96–97, 141–43, 148, 151, 152, 178, 182, 183–84, 207, 219
coal-mine trains 121
connections to other services/ timetabling 136, 138–39, 148
definition 22
Fay–Raven report 271
livestock, transport of 66
passenger numbers 140–41, 149
profitability 138–39
PWD-operated mixed trains 38
replacement by buses 66, 67–69, 79–81, 138–39, 142, 152–53, 271, 307n48
rural services 38, 58, 60, 65, 66, 84, 108, 123–24, 139, 178, 180, 182, 183, 207
schoolchildren, transporting 139
timekeeping 148
see also freight services: with-car goods trains/services
modal shift 14, 15, 296, 299
Mōhaka Viaduct 115–16, **115**, 310n26
Mōkihinui Mine 95
Moohan, Mick 177, 179
Morningside Deviation **145**, 158–59, 160–61, 260, 273
Morrish, Arthur 159
Moses, R. 190
Mosgiel–Outram line 79–81, 90, 143–46
mothballing of lines 14, **40**, 230, 256, 282, 284, 295
motorways 10, 39, 119, 160, 161, 224, 227, 235, 294, 295, 298
Mount Maunganui/Mount Maunganui Branch 38, 53–54, 56, 150, 245, 291, 292
Moutohorā/Moutohorā Branch 36, 38, 39, 53, 113, 136, 138–39
Mt Ruapehu **153**

Mulcare, James 121
Muldoon, Robert 24, 145, 211, 212–13, 216–17, 221, 224, 229, 234, 244, 272
multimodal transport 244, 275, 279, 281, 295
multiple units 22, **12–13**, **112–13**, 156, 260, **275**, 277
Murupara **40**, 150, 203
myths, passenger rail 276–78

Napier
Bay Express 230, 235, 252, 253, 284, 294
bus services 50
earthquake (1931) 93–94, **94**
East Coast Main Trunk 36, 53–54, 63, 113, 118, 213, 216, 232–34
Endeavour (Wellington–Napier service) 212, 213, 230, 232–34, 272
freight-only services **41**
Napier–Gisborne 63, 113, 213, 216, 232–34
Napier–Hastings 50
Napier–Hastings passenger rail proposal 292–94, **293**
Napier–Pūtōrino 85, 94–95, 115
Napier–Wairoa 115–17
Wellington–Napier 212, 213, 230, 232–34, 272, 284
Nash, Thomas 285
Nash, Walter 177
National Airways Corporation (NAC) 146, 147, 185, 192, 202, 221, 234
National governments
1949–1957 114, 144, 146, 152, 155, 160, 191
1960–1972 187–88, 210
1975–1984 24, 216, 234
1990–1999 244, 256
2008–2017 265, 295
National Union of Railwaymen 208, 221
natural disasters 113
cyclone 234
earthquakes 93–94, **94**, 115, 260, 295
floods 98, 115, 116, 124–25, 184
lahar 153
Nelson Provincial Progress League 155

Nelson region railways 56, 58, 86, 91, 155–56
Nelson station **154**
neoliberalism 244, 298
New Lynn 264
Newmans bus service 208
Newmarket 84, 226
New Plymouth
Auckland to New Plymouth service 98–99, 178–79
Marton–New Plymouth Line **40**, 41
New Plymouth Express **207**, 215
New Plymouth–Waitara 140
Taumarunui–New Plymouth 211
Wellington–New Plymouth service 209, 284
Whanganui–Taranaki 178
see also Stratford–Ōkahukura Line
New Zealand First (political party) 115
New Zealand Herald (newspaper) 79, 82, 99, 161, 179
New Zealand Railways (NZR)
buses replace trains 16, 50, 69, 79–81, 82, 90, 118, 120, 121, 138–42, 151–52, 185, 192, 205, 217, 221, 271
construction of railway lines 38
deregulation 229, 244
employee numbers 244
Fay–Raven report 51, 60, 66, 85, 90, 271
Gracefield workshops/industrial line 59, **80**, 157, 227
interisland ferries, connecting with 208
Interislander (ferry service) 229
legislation 119
ministerial control of 110, 156
Northland services 52, 189
NZR Road Services 50, 67, 81, 90, 119–20, 121, 138, 143–46, 151, 152–53, **178**, 202, 271, 298
operation of networks 18, 52, 54, 55, 57–58, 80, 98–99, 116–17
Passenger Business Group 24, 229, 244, 245, 246
passenger services, cancellation of 63–64, 66–69, 84, 91, 94–96, 118–19, 139, 147–48, 152, 155,

172, 178, 183–85, 189, 230, 232–34, 251–57
Petone workshops 59, 91
privatisation 10–11 24, 244–45
railcars 170, 172–73, 176, 177, 187–89, 192, 208–17
Railway Board (1925–28) 51, 67, 78; *see also* commissioners, general managers
Railways Board (1931–36) 93, 110; *see also* commissioners, general managers
road/air competition 25, 38–39, 60, 66, 97, 119–20, 121–22, 160
schoolchildren, transporting 66–67, 180–82, 189, 204–5, 220
staff morale 202
timetable publications 23–24
timetable reductions 64, 65
tourism 202, 230–31, **231**
Transport Licensing Act 95
TranzAlpine 14, 202, 230, 232, 235, 245, 250, 251, 273, 285
see also KiwiRail; royal commissions; Tranz Rail
New Zealand Rail Ltd (NZR Ltd) 24, 244–45
New Zealand Railway and Tramway Atlas (Yonge) 20
New Zealand Railways Corporation 24, 229, 244
New Zealand Transport Agency *see* Waka Kotahi New Zealand Transport Agency (NZTA)
Ngahere 121
Ngāpara 16, 50, 51, 66, 69
Ngāruawāhia 37, 122, 182
Ngātapa/Ngātapa Branch 38, 53–54, **54**, 81, 82, 304n58
Nightcaps **205**, 206
#NoFly: Walking the talk on climate change (Hendy) 14
North Auckland Line **41**, 52, 63, 86, 263, **268**, 282
North Canterbury Gazette (newspaper) 118
North Island Main Trunk 9, 37, **112**, **204**, **210**, 257–61, **271**
  electrification 144–45, 227, 229
  passenger numbers 212, 259–60, 261
  Silver Fern railcars 212

Stratford–Ōkahukura Line 58
Tawa Flat Deviation 97–98, 99, 110, **111**, 112–13
upgrades 158
Wellington–Johnsonville section 110
Westfield Deviation 84–85, **85**
see also long-distance services; Wellington–Auckland service
Northern Advocate (newspaper) 63
Northerner 229, 251, 256–58
Northern Explorer 14, **258–59**, 273, **274**, 284, 285
see also Overlander
Northland
  closing of services 189–90, 223
  early rail services 51–52, **52**
  isolated railways 36, 61
  maps, rail network **52**
  proposals for future (suggested by authors) 282
  rail services (1967) **190**
  with-car good trains 206–7
  see also Dargaville; Whangārei; *individual Northland towns*
Norway **278**
NZ Truth (newspaper) 180, 182

Ōamaru 34, 50, 65, 66, 69, 80, 108, 141, 142, 255–56, 288, 313n42
Ōaro 126–27
Ocean Beach Railway **41**, 92
Ōhai 203, **205**, 206
Ōhai Railway Board (ŌRB) 9, 60–61, 122, 149, 204, 205–6
Ohakune 152
Ōhura 59, 98, 309n85
Ōkahukura 38, **209**
Ōkaihau 53, 86, 176, 189, 206, **207**, 303n14
O'Malley, Jim 295
Omau 64, 304n70
Onehunga/Onehunga Branch/ Onehunga Line 85, 217, 221, 264–67, **264**, 273
Onehunga Business Association 264, 265
Ōnerahi 52, 67
Ontrack 24, 263, 264–65
opening of lines/services
  Bay Express 230
  Capital Connection 245

Coastal Pacific 230
Cromwell–Dunedin railcars 178
Dargaville Branch 53, 123–24
Geyserland Express 245
Kaimai Express 245
Main North Line 126–27
Main South Line 36
Manukau Branch 265–66
Napier–Wairoa–Gisborne **115**, 115–16, 124–2
Ngāpara Branch 50
non-passenger services **40**
Northland 51–53, **52**
Onehunga Branch 264, 265
Ōpunake Branch 62
opening ceremonies 58–59, **99**, 116, 125, 126–27, 178, 265
Overlander 245
Seasider 254
Stillwater–Westport Line 125–26
Stratford–Ōkahukara Line 58–59, 98–99, **99**
Tawa Flat Deviation 111
Tokarahi Branch 50
TranzAlpine 230
Waikaia Branch 35
Waikākā Branch 35
Wairarapa Connection 245
Westfield Deviation 84–85, **85**
see also construction of railway lines
Ōpōtiki 36, 55, 85, 113, 123, 179
Ōpua 176, 189, 206–7, 282
Ōpunake/Ōpunake Branch 62, 182–83, 319n64
Ōrawia 61, 81, 84, 91
Otago Central Railway 35–36, 56, 173, 178, 232
Otago Daily Times (newspaper) 34, 50
Ōtāhuhu **247**
Ōtaki 112, 113, 283
Ōtautau 149
Ōtira **20**, 36, 57, 190
Ōtira Tunnel 36, **57**, 108, 125, 144, 172, 192
Ōtiria 189, 206, 282
Ōtiria–Ōkaihau 206
Outram/Outram Branch 79–81, 90, 143–46

Overlander 245, 251, 256, 257, 258–60, **258**, **274**
  see also Northern Explorer
overnight train services 153, 207, 285
  Northerner 229, 251, 256–58
  Silver Star 15, 203, 209, 229, 230, 245, 257
Ōwaka 185
Owens, Bob 224
Oxford/Oxford Branch 35, 60, 64–65, **65**, 84, 90, 307n48
Oxford West–Sheffield line 66, 81

Paekākāriki **109**, 112–13, 156, 158, 227, 284
Paerātā **40**, 143
Paeroa 108
Paeroa–Pōkeno line 113, 114–15, **114**, 123
Page, Ruth 155–56
Pahīatua 234, 235
Pahīatua Railcar Society 253
Pākehā settlement 34, 51, 58, 60
Palmerston North
  Palmerston North–Foxton 95–96
  Palmerston North–Hamilton 145, 229, 277
  Palmerston North–Masterton 234
  Palmerston North railways (1960) **186**
  Palmerston North station **173**, **186**, **187**, **258**, 283
  Palmerston North–Wellington 14, 245, 251, 260, 282
Palmerston North–Gisborne Line *see* Gisborne, Mōhaka Viaduct, Napier, Whakarongo Deviation
Papakura 189, 223, 224, 261, 266, **267**, 274
Papatoetoe 160
Paraparaumu **15**, 158, 227, 260, 285
Parker, Charlie 153
Parnassus–Wharanui line 86, 113, 117–18
Parnell **267**
Parr, James 95
Parry, Evan 144
Passenger Business Group 229
  Cityline/CityRail 24, 229, 245, 246
  InterCity 24, 229, 245

Railfreight 229
  Speedlink 229, 244
passenger numbers
  declining 37, 39, 66, 67–69, 78–79, 82, 96, 111, 118, 120, 122, 136, 143, 148, 152, 203, 211–12, 221, 223, 246, 250, 251
  increasing 111, 136, 176, 202, 208, 212, 231, 247, 253, 255, 259, 260–61, 263, 266, 270, 272, 276, 299
passenger routes (open as of 1920) 335
Patumāhoe 61
Pāuatahanui 157, 158
Payne, P.L. 64
Peet, William 265
Petone workshops 59, 91
petrol railcars 60, **91**, 110
Picton 14, 37, 61, 86, 127, 173, 192, 207, 208, 215, 216, 219, 230
  see also Interislander ferries; Main North Line
Picton–Blenheim railway 37, 118, 173
Picton–Christchurch *see* Main North Line
Pitches, Cameron 264, 265
Plimmerton 112, 150, 158, 284
Pōkeno 113
population demographics 34, 35, 50, 90, 92, 125, 136, 202, 211, 261, 277–78, 281, 288, 289, 291–92
Porirua 113, 150, 157, 158
Port Chalmers 34, 185, 222–23, 254, 256, 295–96
Portland 52–53, 302n10
postcards **35**, **187**
Potton, Fred 155
Prebble, Richard 234
Press (newspaper) **69**, 84
private railways 18, 34, 37, **41**, 69, 92, 122, 308n55
privatisation 24, 244–45, 256, 258–59
profitability 22, 39, 64, 78–79, 81, 82, 84, 90, 94, 119, 121, 138, 147, 148, 180, 181, 188, 191, 192, 222, 223, 229, 247, 251, 273, 298
proposals for the future *see* future proposals/solutions (suggested by authors)

protests/petitions against closures 65–66, 84, 85, 111–13, 116–17, 148, 149, 151, 155–56, 180, 189, 211, 213, 215–16, 230, 258, 264–65
Public Transport Users Association 263, 264, 266
Public Works Department (PWD)
  construction of railway lines 18, 38, 50, 52–53, 54–55, **55**, 58, 63, 116, 156, 186
  early train services 38
  electrification 144
  engineer-in-chief 62, 112
  Ministry of Works (MoW) 18, 113, 150, 157–58
  operating services 52–53, 53–54, 56, 80, 86, 98, 123–24
  Southerner express service 288
Puhinui 265
Pukekohe 108, 114, 253, 261, 266
Pukemiro 60, **204**
Pukerua Bay **12–13**, **112–13**, 284
Puketutu **271**
Pūtāruru **40**, 150, 193, 203, 282, 327n8
Pūtōrino 85, 94, 115, 116

Queenstown 36, 56, 120, 184, 254, 297

racial tensions 55–56, 140
Raetihi 90, 152
Raetihi/Raetihi Branch 90, 152
railcars 108–10, 141–42
  Blue Streak railcar 208, **209**, 212, 215, 216, **271**, 272
  classification as RM 170
  Clayton railcar **141**
  definition 22
  Edison battery-electric railcars 110, 148
  Fiat railcars **15**, **20**, 172–79, **170**, 187–88, 191, 192, 208, 215, 299
  Midland railcars 116
  Model T Ford railcars **91**, 110
  petrol railcars 60, **91**, 110
  proposed railcar routes (1950–1951) 173–76, **174–75**
  refurbishment of Fiat railcars 208, 213–15, **214**
  Silver Fern railcars 203, **209**, **210**, 211, 212, 230, 234, 245, **246**, 253, 255, 272

Standard railcars **21**, 116, **117**, 124, 126, 178, 188, 215
steam railcars **141**
Vulcan railcars 120, 124, 125–26, 141–42, 178, 180, 187, 188, **191**, 212
Wairarapa railcars **115**, 116, 171, **173**, 177, 316n12
RailCruising **252**
Railfreight 229
Rails that Built a Nation (Bromby) 20
Railway Board (1925–28) 51, 67, 78
    see also commissioners, general managers
Railways Board (1931–36) 93, 110
    see also commissioners, general managers
Railways Authorization Act 112
Railways Commission *see* commissioners; Railway Board (1925–28), Railways Board (1931–36); royal commissions
Railways Magazine 230
Railways of New Zealand (Leitch) 20
Railways of New Zealand, The (Churchman & Hurst) 20
Railway Tradesmen's Association 146
Rakaia **36**, 141, 142, **143**, 182, 318n58
Ranganui 52
Rangatira, TEV (ferry) 221
Rangiahua 53, 86, 307n41
Rangiora 35, 90, 173, 189, 218–19, 221, 294, 307n48
Rangitīkei River 96, **210**
Ransom, Alfred 86
Rapahoe **40**, 61
rapid transit **225**, 277, 295
Raven, Vincent 51, 66
    see also Fay–Raven report
Redman, Lance 153
Reefton 58, 125, 126, 190
Reform Government (1912–1928) 50–51, 62, 78
refreshment rooms 108, **109**, 209, 257
Regional Rapid Rail plan (Greater Auckland) 281, 289
Reidy, Peter 260
Remutaka Incline 116, 150, 171–72, **171**

Remutaka Tunnel 150, 171–72, **173**, 176, 234, 253, 316n12
restoration *see* heritage railways
Rewanui/Rewanui Branch 171, 190, 203–4, 206, 207, 230, 232, **233**, 300n5
Richardson, Len 288
Riverton 149, 151
RM class *see* railcars
Road Services, NZR 50, 67, 81, 90, 119–20, 121, 138, 143–46, 151, 152–53, **178**, 202, 271, 298
road transport
    buses replacing passenger services 16, 50, 66, 67–69, 79–81, 82, 90, 118, 120, 122, 136, 138–42, 151–53, 185, 192, 205, 212–13, 217, 221, 223, 271, 307n48
    capital investment 90, 202, 235
    car-dependency 160, 161, 292, 299
    competition to rail 25, 38–39, 50, 60, 63, 64, 66, 78, 79–81, 97, 118, 119–20, 121–22, 149, 160, 202
    motorways 10, 39, 160, 161, 224, 227, 235, 294, 295, 298
    private car ownership 38, 39, 78, 121, 202, 292
'Robbie's Rapid Rail' 224, **225**
Robinson, Dove-Myer 224, **225**
Rodie, Daniel 67–69
Roger Award 250–51
rollingstock *see* car-vans; guard's vans; locomotive/rollingstock classes; railcars
Rose, Christine 263
Rotorua
    buses replace trains 192, **193**
    cancellation of services 192–93, 203, 212
    express trains 179
    Geyserland Express 245–46, 251, 253
    Koutu station 246, **252**
    National Airways Corporation (NAC) 146
    Rotorua Branch **40**, 193, 282
    Rotorua Limited (express train) 14
    Rotorua Railway Station **193**, 246, **252**
    Rotorua–Taupō 86, 113, 150

Rotowaro 204, 205
Roussell, Philip 93, 110, 302n21
routes, passenger (open as of 1920) 335
Rowling, Bill 210, 212, 217
Roxburgh/Roxburgh Branch 61, 121–22
royal commissions
    1880 61, 64
    1912 61
    1924 (Australia) 51
    1930 81, 84, 85–90, **88–89**, 92, 93, 95–96, 97, 142–43, 182–83
    1952 145, 152, 155, 173–76, 177, 186
    see also Fay–Raven report
Ruakura 290
Rūnanga **40**
Russell-Bethune, Mary 258

SA/SD class carriages **261**
Sanson Tramway 18–19, **37**, 38, 96
Savage, Michael Joseph 86, 110, **119**, 146, 172, 288, 298
'Save Rail' campaign 230
Sawers, James 127, 140, 141
schoolchildren, transporting 17, **19**, 52–53, 61, 66–67, 180–82, 189, 204–5, 220
Scott, Brian 20, 34, 35, 184
SeaRail *see* Interislander (ferry service)
Seasider (Dunedin–Palmerston sightseeing service) 254, 255, 256, 273, 288
Seaward Bush Branch 16, **184–85**
Seddonville/Seddonville Branch 37, **40**, 95, 125, 140, 141, 312n33
Semple, Bob 110, 113, 114, 116, **119**, 123, 124, 125–27, 138, 140, 141, 142, 172
Shadbolt, Tim 253
Shag Point **40**
Sheffield 64, 65, 66, 81
shortages 51
    coal 137, 138, 144, 146, 148, 151, 156, 178
    housing 59, 156
    labour 51, 62, 112, 114
    petrol and rubber 123, 125, 126, 138
Siddalls, Raymond 246, 247

Silver Fern railcars 203, **209, 210,** 211, 212, 230, 234, 245, **246,** 253, 255, 272

Silver Star 15, 203, 209, 229, 230, 245, 257

Small, Tom 213, 216

Smith, Bruce 285

Sockburn **147**

Sockburn–Styx Deviation **150,** 295

Somerset, Crawford 60

Southbridge 147, 148–49, **149, 218**

Southern Line (Auckland) 217, 223, 224, 261

Southerner express service 209–10, 212, 213, 223, 232, 250, 253, 254, 256, 288, 295

South Island Limited (express train) 95, 209

South Island Main Trunk 9, 86
    see also Main North Line; Main South Line

Southland *see* Invercargill; Main South Line; Ōhai Railway Board (ŌRB); *Southerner* express service; *individual Southland towns*

Speedlink 229, 244

speeds, train 113, 263, 276–77, 280, 284, 288, 333n32

Springburn Branch 82, 84, 97

Springfield 67, 219, **220**

Standard railcars **21,** 116, **117,** 124, 126, 178, 188, 215

State Mines Department 38, 40, 122, 182, 205

stationmasters 54, 68, 96, 142, 184, 185, 298, 306n99

stations, railway
    Ashburton **35**
    Auckland (Beach Road/Strand) 14, 84, **145,** 159, 226, 260
    Britomart station 226, 247, 260, **261,** 264, 266, 273, 274
    Christchurch 218, 221, 295
    Dargaville 124
    Dunedin **121,** 295, **297**
    Frankton Junction (Hamilton) 108, 144–45, **274**
    Green Island 10
    Hamilton Central (underground) 274, 290
    Hokitika 285
    Invercargill 182

junction stations **36,** 60

Kaikōura 127

Kawatiri 91

Koutu 246, **252**

Lambton (Wellington) **41,** 92, 111

Manukau 266

Nelson **154**

Onehunga 265

Pahīatua 234

Palmerston North **187,** 283

Parnell **267**

Port Chalmers 185, 222

purpose/importance 38

Rakaia **36**

Rapahoe **40**

Rotorua **193,** 246, **252**

Tāneatua 55

Taumarunui 257

Taupō Quay (Whanganui) 92, 178, 179

Tauranga 56

Te Awamutu **290**

Thorndon 111

Waiōtira **268**

Wairoa 116

Waitākere 226

Wellington 92, 111, 217

steam engine conversion from coal to oil 146, 314n67

steam engines/railcars 19, **20,** 41, 64, 110, 112, 120, **141,** 145, 156, 170, 173, 184, **187,** 202, **233**

Steamer Express (Union Steam Ship Company) 95, 208, 219

steamships/coastal shipping 38–39, 54, 67, 146
    see also interisland ferries

Sterling, Herbert Harry 78–80, 81, 84, 93, 95–96, 111, 112

Stewart, Graham 18, 161

Stillwater **20,** 125–26

Stott, Bob 151, 224

Stratford–Ōkahukara Line **58–59,** 98–99, **99,** 124, 230, **231**

strikes 65, 146, 173
    see also waterfront dispute

subsidies, government 67, 82, 140, 205, 221, 229, 234, 251–52, 253, 258

suburban rail services 17, 25–26
    Auckland 25, 150, 158–59, 160,

189, 217, 223–27, **225, 226–27,** 227, 246–47, 260–67, 274
    branding 25–26
    Christchurch 217–21, **218**
    closures 92–93, 185, 217, 219–23, 226, 266
    Dunedin 92, 185, 221–23, **222**
    Invercargill 179–80
    Kāpiti Coast 158, 260
    Wellington 25, 92, 108, **109,** 144, 156, 158, 217, 227–29, **228,** 260
    Whanganui 37, 92–93, **93,** 179, 308n55

Sullivan, Bill 136

Sullivan, Dan 110, **115,** 118, **119,** 120

suspension of railway projects 51, 53, 86, **87,** 94, 114–15, 124, 148

Svensson, Hakan 258

Swanson 266, 267, 273, 331n103

SX class carriages 260, **263**

Tahawai 55

Tahora 38, 58, 59, 98, 309n85

Taieri Gorge Limited 14, 232, 254, 255–56, **255**

Taieri Gorge Railway 178, 232, **254,** 255–56, **255,** 273

Tāita 157

Tāneatua 9, 38, **40,** 55, 56, 113, 123, 150, 177, 179

Tāngarākau 59, 98, 211

Tangiwai rail disaster **153,** 156, 257, 329n55

Tangowahine 86, 122, 123, 124

Taonui 34, **40, 41**

Tapanui Branch 82, 96–97, **96**

Tapanui Carrier (newspaper) 97

Taranaki rail network 61–62, **62, 99**
    see also New Plymouth; *individual Taranaki towns*

Tarukenga **252**

Taumarere 282

Taumarunui 38, 98, 99, 108, 206, 211, 216, 229, 257, 266, 276, 309n85

Taumarunui–New Plymouth 211

'Taumarunui on the Main Trunk Line' (Cape) 257

Taupō 34, 86, 113, 150, 296

Taupō Quay station (Whanganui) 92, 178, 179

Taupō Tōtara Timber Company 40, 150

Tauranga
    biracial relations 55–56
    bridge, harbour 55, 292
    commuter rail, potential for
      291–92, **291**
    East Coast Main Trunk 36, 53,
      54–56, 114, 148
    Golden Triangle 281, 290
    Hauraki Plains, link across
      114–15, **114**
    Kaimai Express 245, **246**
    operation of services 38, 56
    passenger rail proposal 291–92,
      291
    passenger services, lack of 251,
      275
    population 291
    port 115
    tourism 245
    see also Bay of Plenty; Mount
      Maunganui
Tauranga Bay (Buller) 64
Taverner, William 78, 79
Tawa Flat Deviation 97–98, 99, 110,
  111, 112–13
Te Awamutu **2**, **4**, **289**, **290**
Te Huia service 11, 14, 273, **274**
Te Kūiti **271**
Te Puke 38, 54, 67, 179, 190–91, 192,
  291
Te Tiriti o Waitangi/Treaty of
  Waitangi 244, 281
Thames/Thames Branch 114, 147,
  148
Thelander, Thorsten 144, **145**
'Think Big' programme 145, 229
Thomas, Ivan 182, 188–89, 190, 208,
  227
Thomas, J.P. 158, 159, 160
Thomson, David 216
Thornbury 149, 151
Thorndon station 111
ticketing 79, 218, 279–80
tilting technology 277, 285, 288
Timaru 152–54, 288
timber industry 40, **41**, 56, 150
timeline, New Zealand railways
  (1920–2020) 336–39
timetables
    coal-saving timetable 65, 92,
      137, 139, 146–47, **147**, 148,
      151, 152

    nationwide 65, 120
    public 23–24, 40
    research tools, as 11
    Sanson Tramway **37**
    Te Awamutu **2**, **4**
    working 24
    see also closure/cancellation of
      services; *individual lines and
      services*
Tokanui 16, 182, 184, 185
Tokarahi 16, 50, 51, 66, 69, 81
Tokoroa 150, 282
Toll Holdings 24, 256, 258–59
topographical challenges to railway
  construction 36, 38, **41**, 53, 55, 98,
  112, 118, 210, 284, 297
tourism 18, 19
    Bay of Islands Vintage Railway
      282
    Coastal Pacific 14, 86, 230, 250,
      251, 260, 273, 285
    Covid-19 256
    Forgotten World Adventures
      230, **231**
    Geyserland Express 245–46, 251,
      253
    Kaimai Express 245–46, **246**,
      251, 253
    Northern Explorer 14, **259**, 273,
      274, 284, 285
    Overlander 245, 251, 256, 257,
      258–60, **258**, **274**
    proposals for future (suggested
      by authors) 284, 285–86,
      292–93, 297
    Queenstown 56, 184, 120
    RailCruising **252**
    Seasider (Dunedin–Palmerston
      sightseeing service) 254, 255,
      256, 273, 288
    Southland 120
    Taieri Gorge Railway 178, 232,
      254, 255–56, **255**, 273
    TranzAlpine 14, 202, 230, 232,
      235, 245, 250, 251, 273, 285
trade unions 69, 85, 146, 151, 204,
  205, 208, 256
Trainland (Atkinson) 20, 67
trams/tramways 18–19, **37**, 38,
  92–93, **93**, **94**, 96, 150, 158, 160,
  202, 270, 285
    see also light rail

tram-trains **280**, 290–91, 292, 295
Transdev 25, 260, 285
Transit New Zealand 244
    see also Waka Kotahi New
      Zealand Transport Agency
      (NZTA)
Transport Licensing Act 39, 95
Transport Licensing Amendment
  Act 119
TranzAlpine 14, 202, 230, 232, 235,
  245, 250, 251, 273, 285
Tranz Metro 24–25, 251, 260
Tranz Rail 10–11, 24, **40**, 57, 245,
  247, 250–51, 252–53, 256
Tranz Scenic 24–25, 250, 251, 256,
  257, 259, 298
Treasury, New Zealand 137, 138,
  188–89, 212–15, 223, 234, 272
Troup, George **297**
Tūātapere 61, 151, 302n18
tunnels
    Kaimai Tunnel 115, 245
    Ōtira Tunnel 36, **57**, 108, 125,
      144, 172, 192
    Purewa Tunnel 84–85
    Remutaka Tunnel 150, 171–72,
      173, 176, 234, 253, 316n12

U^B class steam locomotive **149**
Union Airways 95, 123, 146
Union Steam Ship Company 95, 173,
  208, 219, 221, 308n67
United Government (1928–1931) 78
United Kingdom 137, 270
United–Reform Coalition
  Government (1931–1935) 95,
  97–98
Upper Hutt 157, 172
    see also Hutt Valley

Veitch, Bill 78, 79, 81, 82, 84, 112
Verbavatz, Vincent 277
viaducts 111, 115–16, **115**, 310n26
Ville, Simon 38
vocabulary, railway 22
Vogel, Julius 34–35, 56, 299
Voller, Lois 155
Vulcan railcars 120, 124, 125–26,
  141–42, 178, 180, 187, 188, **191**,
  212

Wahine, TEV (ferry) 221
Waiau/Waiau Branch 117, 118, 304
Waihī 36, 53, 114
Waikaia 35, 91
Waikākā 35, 90
Waikanae 9, **12–13**, 260, 283, 284
Waikari 118
Waikato Connection 251, 253, 274
Waikato Regional Council 289–90
Waikiekie 52, 302n10
Waikōkopu **54**, 63, 86, 110, 116, 117, 123, 124, 213
Waimangaroa/Waimangaroa Junction **40**, 68, 312n33
Waimate 90
Waimauku 263–64
Waiōtira 52, 53, 62, 123, 124, **268**, 304n58
Waiōuru 153, **259**
Waipōua Forest 61
Waipū 52, 62–63
Waipuku **40**
Waipukurau 108, 293
Wairarapa class railcars **115**, 116, **173**
Wairarapa Line **41**, 59–60, 62, 171–72
Wairio/Wairio Branch 60–61, 147, 149, 151, 203, **205**
    see also Ōhai Railway Board (ŌRB)
Wairoa 115–17, **117**, **217**
Waitākere 189, 223, 226, 261, 263, 266, 267, 273, 330n96, 331n103
Waitaki 64, **65**, 80, 122, 141
Waitaki Dam **65**, 80, 122
Waitara 39, 140, 297
Waiuku **40**, 61, 142, 143, 297, 304n58
Waka Kotahi New Zealand Transport Agency (NZTA) 244, 279, 289–90
Walker, Alex 293
Wallbank, Allan 234
Wānaka 36, 56, 178
Ward, Joseph 78, 86, 93, 113, 117
waterfront dispute 137, 146–51, 183
Waterloo Branch 59, 150, 156–57
Watson, James 119
Webb, Paddy 125, 126, 141

Wellington
    Gisborne–Wellington 136
    Greater Wellington rail network (1935) **158**
    Greater Wellington Regional Council 25, 251, 260, 285
    Lambton station **41**, 92, 111
    passenger rail (1973–83) **228**
    rail services (1937) **111**
    suburban rail services 25, 92, 108, **109**, 144, 156, 158, 217, 227–29, **228**, 260
    Tawa Flat Deviation 97–98, 99, 110, **111**, 112–13
    Thorndon station 111
    Wellington–Johnsonville 110
    Wellington–Masterton 14, 234, 245, 251, 253, 282, **283**
    Wellington–Napier 212, 213, 230, 232–34, 272, 284
    Wellington–New Plymouth 209 284
    Wellington–Paekākāriki 112
    Wellington–Palmerston North 14, 245, 251, 260, 282
    Wellington Station 110–11, **170**, **275**
Wellington and Manawatū Railway Company 111, 112, 277, 308n55
Wellington–Auckland service 16, 150, 203
    Blue Streak railcars 208, **209**, **271**, 272
    Northern Explorer 14, **258–59**, 273, **274**, 284, 285
    Northerner 229, 251, 256–58
    Overlander 245, 251, 256, 257, 258–60, **258**, **274**
    Silver Fern railcars 203, **209**, **210**, 211, 212, 230, 234, 245, **246**, 253, 255, 272
    Tangiwai rail disaster **153**, 156, 257, 329n55
Wellsford 189–90
Wellsford–Helensville 190, 206, 207
West Coast Railway (Australia) 251–52, 253, 256
Western Line (Auckland) 223, 263, 264, 266, 281

Westfield Deviation (Auckland) 84–85, **85**
West, H.P. 66
Westport 64, 125–26, 140–41, 285
    Westport–Greymouth 125–26, 190, **191**
    Westport Harbour Board 38, 64, 304n70
    Westport–Īnangahua **57**, 86, 113, 123
    Westport–Seddonville 140, 141
Westport News (newspaper) 141
W^F class steam locomotive **23**
Whakarongo Deviation **186**
Whakatāne **40**, 55, 140, 292
Whangaehu River **153**, 257
Whangamōmona 39, **98**, 99, 309n85
Whanganui
    suburban rail services 37, 92–93, **93**, 179, 308n55
    Taupō Quay station 92, 178, 179
    Whanganui–Taranaki 178
Whangārei
    Auckland–Whangārei passenger service 53, 189–90
    construction of railway 52
    passenger service from Auckland 53, 189–90
    Whangārei–Maungatūroto 207
    Whangārei–Ōpua 206–7
Wharanui 37, 86, 113, 118, 123, 126
Whitecliffs/Whitecliffs Branch 67–69
Wilton Collieries 122
wine industry 252, 284, 293
with-car goods trains/services **20**, 22, 58, 68, 120, 142, **143**, 151, 155, 179, 182–83, **183**, 185, 189, 193, 203, 206–8, **207**, 213, 223, 231–32, 311n56
    see also freight services; mixed trains
Woburn **21**, 80, 227
women passengers 22–23
Wood, Chris 63, 94
Wood, Michael 274
World War I 16, 50, 62
World War II 16, 18, 86, 113, 114, 123, 136, 137–38, 146, 178, 276, 288
W^W class steam locomotive **233**
Wyndham 67, 81, 85, 91

Published by Otago University Press
Te Whare Tā o Te Wānanga o Ōtākou
533 Castle Street
Dunedin, New Zealand
university.press@otago.ac.nz
www.otago.ac.nz/press

First published 2021

Text copyright © André Brett
Maps copyright © Sam van der Weerden
The maps on pages 85, 111, 123, 150, 157, 158, 159, 161, 186, 225, 254, and 262 contain data sourced from the LINZ Data Service licensed for reuse under CC BY 4.0, and data sourced from Luke Christensen licensed for reuse under CC BY-SA 4.0.

The moral rights of the authors have been asserted.

ISBN 978-1-99-004809-8

Editor: Imogen Coxhead
Design and layout: Fiona Moffat
Index: Lee Slater

Printed in China through Asia Pacific Offset